THE AMERICAN HISTORICAL SOCIETY INC.
P9-DIA-290

*The Story of Georgia*

GENERAL JAMES EDWARD OGLETHORPE

**Statesman, Soldier and Founder of Georgia, Whose Great Victory Over the Spanish Army at Bloody Marsh Saved American Colonies from Domination by Spain.**

# THE STORY OF GEORGIA

*By*

WALTER G. COOPER

VOLUME I

THE AMERICAN HISTORICAL SOCIETY, INC.
NEW YORK
1938

# *Foreword*

HE Georgia Legislature in 1929 adopted a resolution stating that, although the bicentennial would be celebrated in 1933, there was no complete history of the State, and called on the judges of Superior Courts to lay the matter before the Grand Jury of each county and urge it to select a competent person to write the history of the county and file a copy in the State Archives in order that existing historical material might not be lost.

Acting on that recommendation, presented to it by Judge John D. Humphries, the Grand Jury of Fulton County selected Walter G. Cooper, of Atlanta, as the official historian of the county.

His history of Fulton County, which includes the capital of the State, necessarily dealt with much Georgia history. It was a large octavo volume, with numerous illustrations, and was the result of several years' careful research. It was received by the press and public with so much favor that when The American Historical Society, Inc., of New York, projected a comprehensive history of Georgia and sought a competent person to write it, Mr. Cooper was suggested for the task, and at the request of the publishers undertook the work. In that he had the coöperation of an advisory committee composed of leading men and women from every part of the State. He submitted the manuscript of parts of the narrative to several members of the committee well versed in Georgia history, and profited by their criticism in matters concerning which there might be a difference of opinion.

After two years of careful research Mr. Cooper has written a history which I think will stand the test of time.

It is remarkable that, as the Legislature said, there is up to the present, no complete history of Georgia, the Empire State of the South, which had a leading part in the life and progress of the country from the earliest times. The histories of Colonel Charles C. Jones, Bishop William Bacon Stevens and Hugh McCall were excellent for their times, but only carried the narrative to about the year 1800. Since then there have been notable books on features of Georgia history, by able and distinguished authors, but there was, until the appearance of this *Story of Georgia* by Mr. Cooper, none that covered the whole period from prehistoric times through Indian civilization, the Spanish period and the Colonial and Revolutionary periods up to the present time.

The publishers, with years of experience and ample resources, have done their part well, and the typography, illustrations and binding are in keeping with the character of the work.

Few even of educated people realize the great and heroic service to posterity, given in many cases at the cost of their lives, by our forebears in the American Revolution. Their heroism is only equaled by that of Georgians in the War Between the States, when one-fifth of the entire white population fought for the State in the Confederate armies.

We would fail in our duty if we did not give to the rising generation and those who follow a clear account of Georgia's great past and the great deeds and heroic lives of those who made the State the great Commonwealth it is. It is a moving tale that stirs the blood and moves men and women to high endeavor.

IVAN ALLEN,
*Chairman Advisory Committee.*

---

## *Advisory Committee*

Hon. Walter F. George
Hon. S. Price Gilbert
Hon. W. F. Jenkins
Hon. John D. Humphries
Hon. S. H. Sibley
Hon. M. D. Collins
Dr. S. V. Sanford
Dr. Harvey W. Cox
Dr. M. L. Brittain
Dr. J. R. McCain
Miss Ruth Blair
Miss Ella May Thornton
Milton Fleetwood

ATLANTA

Ivan Allen
Samuel N. Evins
Robert J. Guinn
Dr. Louie D. Newton
T. Guy Woolford
Jack J. Spalding
Dr. W. S. Elkin
Dr. David Marx
Haynes McFadden
Robert C. Alston
J. Walter Mason
Dr. Willis A. Sutton
Henry C. Peeples
Mell R. Wilkinson
J. J. Haverty

AUGUSTA

Thomas J. Hamilton
James M. Hull, Jr.
Fielding Wallace

THROUGHOUT THE STATE

Orville A. Park, Macon
Claude Christopher, Barnesville
Millard Reese, Brunswick
Rhodes Browne, Columbus
John S. Thomas, Dalton
Raymond Stapleton, Elberton
Judge W. E. H. Searcy, Griffin
Victor Davidson, Irwinton
Bishop W. N. Ainsworth, Macon
Warren Grice, Macon
Dr. Guy H. Wells, Milledgeville
Mrs. J. L. Beeson, Milledgeville
W. C. Vereen, Moultrie
Miss Martha Berry, Rome
Rabbi George Solomon, Savannah
Hon. J. Randolph Anderson, Savannah
Howard Coffin, St. Simons Island
Dr. Geo. H. King, Tifton
Jack Williams, Waycross
Thomas J. Lance, Young Harris

# *Author's Preface*

S a native of the State who can remember some of the gruelling experiences of the Reconstruction era, I have a natural interest in the history of Georgia, and this was increased by the revelations of more recent years, which opened a new vista into the far past. Dr. Herbert Bolton, of the University of California, and his able assistant, Miss Mary Ross, of Brunswick, Georgia, by their investigations in Spain, brought into view a new world of Georgia history in the Spanish period that preceded the coming of Oglethorpe. Their epoch-marking book, *The Debatable Land,* dealt with the Spanish Missions on the Georgia Coast and the age-long contest between Spain and England for the soil of Georgia.

Spanish adventurers explored the Atlantic Coast from southern Florida to the Chesapeake Bay and claimed the country for their Sovereign. Realizing the danger to her American Colonies, Great Britain established the Colony of Georgia as a bulwark to protect them against Spain's advance. The coming of a great Spanish fleet to take Georgia in 1742 showed that England made no mistake when she sent Oglethorpe, one of her greatest men and ablest soldiers, to take charge of the Colony, and backed him with men and money as she backed no other American Colony. The victory of Bloody Marsh ended the long contest between Spain and England for American soil and made it certain that this would be an English-speaking country, with Anglo-Saxon institutions. That gave the history of Georgia a paramount interest for all Americans.

The philanthropic motive was also connected with the founding of Georgia, but the great moving cause which enlisted England's strong support was the need to protect her American Colonies.

The history of Georgia, from the coming of Oglethorpe through the Revolution, has great and tragic interest. Colonel Charles C. Jones and Bishop William Bacon Stevens did a fine service in giving the world a clear picture of the great deeds and heroic lives of Georgians in the Revolutionary War. The Spartan endurance and death-defying courage of those heroes in times that tried the souls of men and women have been an inspiration to those who came after them.

It is a matter of regret that the histories of Jones and Stevens ended with the eighteenth century, although they lived in times that followed and were eminently qualified to carry forward the work so well begun, but it has fallen to the lot of others to bring the record up to the present. A number have undertaken that task, in part or in whole, but did not have material that has come to light in recent years. This work is an attempt to present the whole story from the earliest times to the present. I must admit, what the reader will see, that the work is by no means perfect. The most careful research does not escape error, but I think the effort is worth while to body forth a great past, which should guide the present and the future.

Acknowledgment is due to many for their aid and encouragement, but I can only mention a few. Honorable J. Randolph Anderson of Savannah, Honorable Warren Grice of Macon and James Walter Mason of Atlanta read parts of the manuscript and gave me constructive criticism. Honorable Ivan Allen of Atlanta has been a wise counselor. I have had the kind coöperation of Miss Ella May Thornton, State Librarian, Miss Ruth Blair, for years State Historian, and the highly efficient ladies in the Reference Department of the Carnegie Library. Senator Walter F. George, Congressman Robert Ramspeck and John M. Slaton, Jr., secured valuable information for me from the War Department, and Mrs. Samuel M. Inman furnished a list of the war dead from Georgia in the World War, which she and other patriotic women in Georgia counties prepared with great care and tireless work. To these and others I make grateful acknowledgment.

WALTER G. COOPER.

# *Contents*

VOLUME I


| | PAGE |
|---|---|
| Introductory | 1 |
| A Bird's-Eye View of Georgia | 9 |
| Chapter I—Prehistoric Georgia | 19 |
| Chapter II—Indian Civilization | 35 |
| Chapter III—Spain in Georgia | 58 |
| Chapter IV—DeSoto's March Through Georgia | 65 |
| Chapter V—De Luna's, Villafane's, Pardo's, and Boyano's Explorations | 76 |
| Chapter VI—A Pen Picture of Georgia in 1562 | 81 |
| Chapter VII—French Attempts to Colonize by Ribault and Laudonnière | 82 |
| Chapter VIII—Spanish Missions | 86 |
| Chapter IX—Bloody Contest for Western Georgia | 98 |
| Chapter X—Spain's Claim to Georgia and the Atlantic Coast | 102 |
| Chapter XI—Early Grants of Georgia Land | 107 |
| Chapter XII—Georgia Under the Trustees | 112 |
| Chapter XIII—The First Shipload of Colonists—Early Years | 123 |
| Chapter XIV—The Second Shipload—Savannah Laid Out | 135 |
| Chapter XV—Progress of the Colony | 146 |
| Chapter XVI—Indian Chiefs in England | 151 |
| Chapter XVII—A Period of Difficulty and Discontent | 162 |
| Chapter XVIII—Savannah in 1736 | 177 |
| Chapter XIX—Fortifying Cumberland | 188 |
| Chapter XX—Difficulties in Savannah | 205 |
| Chapter XXI—General Oglethorpe's Trip to Coweta to Meet the Indians | 224 |
| Chapter XXII—War with Spain | 228 |
| Chapter XXIII—The Battle of Bloody Marsh | 243 |
| Chapter XXIV—General Oglethorpe's Departure | 256 |
| Chapter XXV—The Courts, Education and Land Tenures | 260 |
| Chapter XXVI—Religious Development | 267 |
| Chapter XXVII—William Stephens in Charge—The Colony as Oglethorpe Left It | 281 |
| Chapter XXVIII—The Plot of Christian Priber and the Bosomworth Conspiracy | 287 |
| Chapter XXIX—Discontent and Depression—Repeal of Laws Against Rum and Slavery | 304 |
| Chapter XXX—Return of Prosperity | 316 |
| Chapter XXXI—Royal Government | 329 |
| Chapter XXXII—Administration of Governor Reynolds | 335 |

PAGE

Chapter XXXIII—The Midway Settlement........................ 348
Chapter XXXIV—Reynolds Recalled and Ellis Comes.............. 361
Chapter XXXV—An Era of Good Will Under Governor Ellis....... 368
Chapter XXXVI—Governor James Wright's Administration......... 390
Chapter XXXVII—Georgia's Territory Extended Southward—Indian Treaties ........................................... 396
Chapter XXXVIII—South Carolina Grants Georgia Land........... 402
Chapter XXXIX—New Parishes Created—Chief Justice Removed.... 409
Chapter XL—The Stamp Act Starts the Movement for Independence.. 415
Chapter XLI—Repeal of Stamp Act—Governor Wright's Clash With Assembly ........................................... 427
Chapter XLII—Governor Wright Dissolves the Assembly—He Leaves Georgia ............................................ 438
Chapter XLIII—Habersham Dissolves the House—Indians Cede Two Million Acres—Settlements Checked by Indian Outbreaks.. 448
Chapter XLIV—British Tyranny Rouses Resistance of Colonies—The Provincial Congress ................................ 460
Chapter XLV—Houses of Legislature Differ—South Carolina's Attitude to Georgia.................................... 470
Chapter XLVI—Lexington and Concord Battles Unite the Colonies—Seizure of Powder Magazine—Powder Ship Captured..... 477
Chapter XLVII—Georgia Joins Other Colonies.................. 484
Chapter XLVIII—Georgia Articles of Association—State's Government Reorganized—Preparing for War—Arrest of Governor Wright ...................................... 493
Chapter XLIX—Georgia's First Constitution.................... 507
Chapter L—Georgia's First Battle With the British Forces—Bombardment of Fort Moultrie.............................. 514
Chapter LI—Declaration of Independence—Georgia as a State........ 529
Chapter LII—Gwinnett's Rise to Power—His Fatal Duel With McIntosh ........................................... 547
Chapter LIII—McIntosh Leaves Georgia—John Houstoun Governor.. 563
Chapter LIV—Expedition to Florida Fails...................... 572
Chapter LV—War Centers in the South—Savannah Captured........ 581
Chapter LVI—The Fight to Recover Georgia—Brilliant Victory at Kettle Creek—Campbell Evacuates Augusta................ 593
Chapter LVII—Georgia Plundered by British—Heroic Resistance—Two Governors Elected.......................... 608

## VOLUME II

Chapter LVIII—Return of Sir James Wright—Americans Outlawed—Siege of Savannah.................................... 1
Chapter LIX—Dark Days in Georgia—Heroic Resistance Led by Elijah Clarke ............................................ 19

Chapter LX—The Coming of General Greene Gives Hope to Georgians—Augusta Retaken ..... 45
Chapter LXI—Colonel Jackson's Activity on the Coast ..... 64
Chapter LXII—Surrender of Cornwallis—Savannah Evacuated by British ..... 69
Chapter LXIII—The Aftermath of War—Georgia Rises from Desolation to Progress ..... 81
Chapter LXIV—Administrations of Telfair and Matthews—Boundary Dispute With South Carolina Settled ..... 92
Chapter LXV—Georgia Adopts a New Constitution—Seven New Counties—Washington's Visit ..... 103
Chapter LXVI—Trouble With the Indians—Alexander McGillivray, the Creek Statesman ..... 110
Chapter LXVII—The Oconee War—Clarke and Genet—Clarke's Independent State—He Yields at Last ..... 129
Chapter LXVIII—The Constitution of 1798 ..... 140
Chapter LXIX—The Yazoo Fraud—The Darkest Chapter in Georgia History ..... 145
Chapter LXX—The Yazoo Act Rescinded and the Records Publicly Burned ..... 171
Chapter LXXI—Yazoo Money Refunded by the State—Washington's Message—Supported by Congress—Sale of Georgia's Western Land to the United States ..... 189
Chapter LXXII—The Act of Cession and Agreement of 1802 ..... 197
Chapter LXXIII—The Pine Barren Speculation ..... 203
Chapter LXXIV—The Invention of the Cotton Gin and Its Far-reaching Effect ..... 210
Chapter LXXV—Georgia's Governors for Forty-one Years ..... 225
Chapter LXXVI—Effect of Agreement of 1802—Politics Embittered for Years ..... 231
Chapter LXXVII—Removal of the Creek Indians ..... 258
Chapter LXXVIII—The Seminole War ..... 286
Chapter LXXIX—Removal of the Cherokee Indians from Georgia ..... 293
Chapter LXXX—Internal Improvements ..... 332
Chapter LXXXI—Political Parties in Georgia ..... 346
Chapter LXXXII—Georgia in the Panic of 1837 ..... 359
Chapter LXXXIII—Early Religious Denominations ..... 362
Chapter LXXXIV—Georgians Fought for Freedom of Texas ..... 379
Chapter LXXXV—Early Education in Georgia ..... 388
Chapter LXXXVI—The University of Georgia, First State University in the United States ..... 397
Chapter LXXXVII—Denominational Schools and Universities ..... 417
Chapter LXXXVIII—Mercer Institute ..... 421
Chapter LXXXIX—Mercer University ..... 423
Chapter XC—Oglethorpe University ..... 433

PAGE
Chapter XCI—Emory University .................................. 438
Chapter XCII—Wesleyan Female College.......................... 450
Chapter XCIII—The Southern Female College..................... 454
Chapter XCIV—Agnes Scott and Shorter Colleges With Other Institutions ........................................ 456
Chapter XCV—Berry School ...................................... 465
Chapter XCVI—Organization of the Supreme Court................ 468
Chapter XCVII—Dr. Long's Discovery of Anesthesia.............. 471
Chapter XCVIII—Cherokee Georgia Made Ten Counties—Governors McDonald, Crawford and Towns....................... 483
Chapter XCIX—The Issue of Slavery............................. 487
Chapter C—Southern Statesmen Add New Territory................ 500
Chapter CI—Georgia on the Eve of War.......................... 506
Chapter CII—The Secession Convention and Ordinance............ 520
Chapter CIII—Preparing for War................................ 527
Chapter CIV—Georgia in the Confederacy........................ 544
Chapter CV—The Great American Tragedy That Took a Million Lives 552
Chapter CVI—The Western Campaign.............................. 570
Chapter CVII—Governor Brown Differs With President Davis...... 573
Chapter CVIII—Events of 1862.................................. 590
Chapter CIX—The Andrews' Raid................................. 596
Chapter CX—Atlanta a War Center............................... 604
Chapter CXI—Georgia in 1862................................... 608
Chapter CXII—The Battle of Chickamauga........................ 615
Chapter CXIII—Maryland and Kentucky Campaigns, 1862, and Battle of Fredericksburg ................................ 621
Chapter CXIV—The War in 1863—Chancellorsville and Gettysburg—Morgan's Raid in Kentucky and Ohio.................. 625
Chapter CXV—The Georgia Campaign of 1864....................... 634

VOLUME III

Chapter CXVI—The Virginia Campaign in 1864..................... 1
Chapter CXVII—The Atlanta Campaign Begins...................... 10
Chapter CXVIII—President Davis' Error Cost the Confederacy's Life 19
Chapter CXIX—The Evacuation ................................... 41
Chapter CXX—Hood's Tennessee Campaign—Sherman's March to the Sea ................................................ 49
Chapter CXXI—Citizens Return to Atlanta—Georgia Legislature in Session ............................................ 54
Chapter CXXII—Wheeler Defeats Kilpatrick at Augusta............ 60
Chapter CXXIII—The Hampton Roads Conference.................... 65
Chapter CXXIV—Sherman in Carolina.............................. 67
Chapter CXXV—Last Battles in Georgia........................... 72

PAGE

Chapter CXXVI—Flight and Capture of President Davis............ 76
Chapter CXXVII—Georgia Under Federal Officers................. 86
Chapter CXXVIII—The Reconstruction Era...................... 90
Chapter CXXIX—The Constitutional Convention of 1865........... 98
Chapter CXXX—Georgia Under the Iron Heel—Military Rule With Best Men Disfranchised—Political Obstacles............. 105
Chapter CXXXI—Governor Jenkins' Appeal to the Supreme Court—Senator Hill's Davis Hall Speech...................... 116
Chapter CXXXII—Governor Jenkins Deposed by Military Order—Bayonets at the Polls............................... 123
Chapter CXXXIII—The Ashburn Murder Case................... 134
Chapter CXXXIV—Bullock and Republican Legislature in Power.... 138
Chapter CXXXV—The Great Bush Arbor Meeting................ 145
Chapter CXXXVI—Legislature Reorganized by a Non-Resident—Condemned by Congress as Illegal........................ 160
Chapter CXXXVII—The Era of Public Plunder.................. 163
Chapter CXXXVIII—Bullock's Attempt at New Reconstruction Denounced by Democrats.............................. 176
Chapter CXXXIX—Black Record of Republican Legislature......... 187
Chapter CXL—A Ghastly Revolution........................... 201
Chapter CXLI—The Dawn of a New Time....................... 203
Chapter CXLII—Georgians Rule Again.......................... 209
Chapter CXLIII—New Issues ................................... 219
Chapter CXLIV—Governor Colquitt's Administration.............. 235
Chapter CXLV—The Constitution of 1877........................ 252
Chapter CXLVI—The Cotton Exposition of 1881.................. 264
Chapter CXLVII—Large Gifts to Education...................... 283
Chapter CXLVIII—A Progressive Era........................... 290
Chapter CXLIX—Gordon's Second Administration................. 314
Chapter CL—Rise and Rule of the Farmers' Alliance.............. 328
Chapter CLI—Northen Governor and Crisp Speaker of the House.... 336
Chapter CLII—The Cotton States and International Exposition...... 350
Chapter CLIII—Administrations of Candler and Terrell............ 370
Chapter CLIV—Watson and the Populist Party.................... 388
Chapter CLV—Hoke Smith's Administration as Governor........... 396
Chapter CLVI—Joseph M. Brown Elected Governor................ 406
Chapter CLVII—John M. Slaton, Governor....................... 426
Chapter CLVIII—Georgia in Last Years of World Peace............ 436
Chapter CLIX—End of Governor Slaton's Administration........... 442
Chapter CLX—Georgia in the World War........................ 461
Chapter CLXI—World War Dead from Georgia Who Were Killed in Battle, Died of Wounds or from Other Causes........... 485
Chapter CLXII—Administrations from Dorsey to Rivers............ 501

PAGE

Chapter CLXIII—Georgia's Bicentennial ........ 513
Chapter CLXIV—State Officers—1917 to 1936........ 519
Chapter CLXV—Radical Changes Made in the Government of Georgia at the Beginning of 1937........ 526
Chapter CLXVI—A Great Educational Revival—Eighteen Large Buildings Added to Georgia University Plant and Seventy-two for Schools ........ 529
Chapter CLXVII—Georgia State Parks........ 535
Chapter CLXVIII—Georgia Currency and Finance........ 543
Chapter CLXIX—The Development of the Georgia Court System........ 548
Chapter CLXX—Over Four Hundred Millions Spent in Georgia by the Federal Government ........ 557
Chapter CLXXI—More of Present Interests........ 561
Chapter CLXXII—Art, Music and Literature in Georgia........ 574

# *Illustrations*

VOLUME I — PAGE

Stone Mountain, near Atlanta........ 10
A View of Explorations........ 20
Detail of House Site Exploration at Lamar Swamp Village........ 22
1. John Ross, Cherokee Chief. 2. Wm. McIntosh, Creek Chief. 3. Sequoia, Who Invented Cherokee Alphabet. 4. The Cherokee Alphabet........ 38
Indian Villages in Fulton........ 42
Enota Mountain, North Georgia, Height 4764 Feet Above Sea........ 45
Key to Indian Relics........ 52
Map of Indian Cessions of Georgia Land........Facing 56
Hernando DeSoto........ 66
Celtic Cross, Augusta........ 77
Victory Drive, Savannah........ 93
Oglethorpe Monument........ 114
Monument to the Signers, Augusta........ 132
Richmond Academy, Augusta, Now Used as a Library........ 165
Bethesda Orphanage, Savannah........ 197
Liberty Hall, Home of A. H. Stephens, Crawfordville........ 230
Wesley Oak, Christ Churchyard, Frederica........ 244
Confederate Powder Works Chimney........ 261
The Burns Cottage, Atlanta........ 276
Meadow Garden, Augusta, Home of George Walton, One of the Signers 313
Cotton Wharf in Savannah Harbor........ 331
Henry Grady Monument, Atlanta........ 359
Naval Stores Wharf, Savannah Harbor........ 364
Monument to A. H. Stephens........ 397
Aerial View, Macon........ 430
Aerial View of Atlanta........ 453
Noble Wimberly Jones........ 494
Old Executive Mansion, Milledgeville........ 503
Boyhood Home of Woodrow Wilson, Augusta........ 526
Bulloch Hall, with Mittie Bulloch as a Bride, Mother of Theodore Roosevelt, and Her Husband, Theodore Roosevelt, Sr........ 568

VOLUME II

Nancy Hart Holding British Soldiers at Bay........ 35
Wormsloe Library, Savannah........ 79
Christ Church, Savannah........ 131

Savannah Hospital .................................................. 191
Wesleyan Conservatory—Originally Wesleyan Female College, Macon. 243
Georgia State Woman's College, Valdosta; front view: Converse and Ashley Halls .................................................. 246
Bishop Benjamin J. Kelley .................................................. 296
Bishop Warren A. Candler .................................................. 366
Bishop John W. Beckwith .................................................. 369
Salem Camp Meeting in 1936 .................................................. 377
Old College, University of Georgia .................................................. 398
Greater Wesleyan Female College Near Macon .................................................. 451
Colonel George W. Scott .................................................. 457
Shorter College, Rome .................................................. 460
Martha Berry, Founder of Berry Schools .................................................. 467
Governor Joseph E. Brown .................................................. 507
Robert Toombs .................................................. 518
Alexander H. Stephens .................................................. 524
Confederate Line—Federal Fort, No. 12—Federal Fort, No. 10....... 553
Confederate Picket Post—Confederate Fort—Confederate Line....... 567
Brigadier-General Henry Lewis Banning ..................Facing 585
Confederate Fort—Confederate Fortifications—Interesting Confederate Fort .................................................. 601
Confederate Lines (3) .................................................. 606
Soldiers on Guard—Confederate Line—Confederate Fortifications.... 637

VOLUME III

Federal Fort, No. 8—Federal Fort, No. 7—Federal Fort, No. 9....... 4
Battlefield West of Atlanta—Confederate Line—Confederate Battery.. 15
View of Cyclorama, Atlanta ..................................................
Potter House—Rolling Mill—Ruins of War .................................................. 37
Federal Fort, No. 11 (2 views)—Federal Fort, No. 12 .................................................. 45
Federal Fort, No. 19 (2 views)—Spot Where General McPherson Was Killed .................................................. 61
Atlanta Terminal Station .................................................. 87
Peachtree Street, Atlanta .................................................. 103
City Post Office, Forsyth Street, Atlanta—Atlanta's New Post Office Building .................................................. 124
Rufus B. Bullock, Republican Governor of Georgia .................................................. 139
Benjamin Harvey Hill .................................................. 150
The Fulton County Court House .................................................. 173
Three Governors from Fulton County, Colquitt, Slaton, and Dorsey.... 237
Nathaniel J. Hammond .................................................. 258
First Home of Lummus Products at Juniper, Georgia, 1877-98........ 265
Governor and Senator Joseph E. Brown .................................................. 268
City Hall, Atlanta .................................................. 284

PAGE

Main Building, Georgia State Sanitarium, Milledgeville .............. 307
Henry Woodin Grady .............. 323
Atlanta's Greatest Enterprise, the Cotton States and International Exposition .............. 352
Three Governors Who Became Senators, Gordon, Smith, Terrell .............. 371
Samuel Spencer, Organizer of the Southern Railway .............. 398
Savannah Sugar Refinery Plant .............. 413
Piedmont Driving Club, Atlanta .............. 432
Some Atlanta Schools .............. 455
Mrs. Rebecca Latimer Felton, First Woman United States Senator .............. 470
East Lake Country Club, Atlanta .............. 503
Richard B. Russell, Jr., Governor and U. S. Senator .............. 507
Savannah Public Library .............. 531
First National Bank Building, Atlanta .............. 546
Aerial View of Candler Field, Atlanta .............. 566
Federal Reserve Bank of Southeast, Atlanta .............. 570
Capital City Country Club, Brookhaven, Atlanta .............. 581

# *Introductory*

GEORGIA was strategic ground in the contest between European powers for possession of the Western Hemisphere, and in the result of the conflict between Spain and England for the land of this State the future of our country and the character of its institutions were involved. Spain, France, and England engaged in a long contest for American land with an area twenty-four times their own and resources incalculably great and rich.

In that contest they won for a time the prize they fought for, but in the end lost nearly all they had won. Spain and France lost all they had taken, and England lost all but Canada, Newfoundland, Nova Scotia and a little in South America and the West Indies, but they opened a new world of civilization and peopled it with their sons, half of whom speak English, the others Spanish, Portuguese, Italian and French.

The Crusades opened the eyes of Europe to the wealth of Asia, and by the Thirteenth Century, Venice and Genoa had become rich on overland trade with the Orient. Marco Polo's account of the wealth of China created a great sensation in Europe and led to the discovery of America.

Europe was awakened from its long sleep by the renaissance, the invention of printing, which spread the new learning, and a great movement among the people for religious liberty. There was a revival of architecture, painting, and sculpture, and great advances were made in natural science by Roger Bacon, and in astronomy by Copernicus and Galileo, whose revelations of the movement of planets and the rotundity of the earth caused men to think of sailing around it.

Christopher Columbus realized the importance of China as a market for Europe. Knowing the rotundity of the earth, he conceived the idea of sailing West to reach the East and sailed West to the vicinity of America, discovered San Salvador, other islands of the West Indies, and later the coast of South America, all the time believing that he was in the vicinity of Asia.

Spain was mistress of the West Indies, Cuba, Porto Rico, Santo Domingo, Jamaica, Mexico, Peru, and Florida. Ponce de Leon had claimed Florida in the name of Spain and it was hers, with some intermission, until John Forsyth, of Georgia, as Minister to Spain, negotiated the treaty by which that country ceded Florida to the United States.

Leaders in the Spanish advance into America, after Columbus, were Velasquez, who conquered Cuba; Ponce de Leon, who discovered Florida; Cortes, who conquered Mexico; Pizarro, who conquered Peru, and Hernando DeSoto, a lieutenant of Pizarro in Peru, who was the first white man to march through Georgia.

The character, customs, religion, and government of the Indians when white men came to America, their kindness to the new-comers, the baneful influence of white adventurers upon them, and their eventual expulsion from the State is a sad and tragic story, the darkest page in the history of Georgia.

In 1521 Lucas Vasquez de Ayllon sent a Spanish expedition from Santo Domingo, and it landed on the coast of North Carolina, near the site of Wilmington, but did not remain. Several years later he sent two ships under Pedro de Quexos, who explored the Atlantic Coast for some distance, but made no settlement. On the third voyage de Ayllon went with the ships and tried to make a settlement on the Pedee River, in South Carolina, but starvation killed the colony.

**Hernando DeSoto**—The Emperor Charles the Fifth of Spain and Germany appointed DeSoto Governor of Cuba and Adelantado or President of Florida, then regarded in Spain as another Peru. He sailed from Spain for America in 1538, stopped a year in Cuba and landed at Espiritu Santo Bay, on the coast of Florida, June 1, 1539, with six hundred soldiers, the flower of Spain's young men, a number of priests, and equipment for refining gold.

Passing through Florida into Georgia, he marched northward and camped on the Savannah River, at Silver Bluff, not far from the site of Augusta, where he was kindly received by an Indian princess, who hung a necklace of pearls around his neck. DeSoto took from his finger a gold ring, set with ruby, and placed it on the finger of the princess. Leaving Silver Bluff, DeSoto went north, taking the princess with him as a prisoner, but she escaped in the vicinity of Nacoochee Valley.

DeSoto continued across North Georgia and the remains of a fort on a mountain in Murray County seem to mark the presence of Spaniards there, but probably later. Turning south, he came to an Indian village at the junction of two rivers, supposed to have been the Oostanaula and Etowah, where the city of Rome stands, though some locate it farther north. Some claim it was in Carolina or Tennessee. There he remained a month, then continued into Alabama, and finally reached the Mississippi River, sickened with fever in the malarial country near that stream, died, and was buried in its waters in 1542.

Spain made the first settlement on the Georgia coast, consisting of missions in which Jesuit or Franciscan priests sought to convert Indians to Christianity, and soldiers were sent with them to protect the ecclesiastics. These missions were supported by the Spanish Governor at St. Augustine, and other missions were established on the Chattahoochee River, supported by the Spanish commander at Tallahassee.

Spain claimed the soil of Georgia by right of discovery and prior settlement, while England held that Sebastian Cabot, under a commission from England's Sovereign, had discovered Georgia when he sailed down the Atlantic Coast as far as Florida in 1497, long before any Spaniards saw that land. England also claimed the only permanent settlements.

By the year 1600, Spain held a large part of the Western Hemisphere, including the West Indies, Mexico, and Peru, had a strong hold on Florida, and had explored and claimed as hers the Atlantic Coast of this country as far north as Chesapeake Bay.

Although Spain was less powerful after the defeat of the Spanish armada, which threatened England in 1588, she was still strong enough to give trouble, and her presence and aggressive attitude on this continent seriously threatened the American colonies, the first of which was planted at Jamestown in 1607, and danger to English colonies continued until Oglethorpe defeated the Spaniards at the Battle of Bloody Marsh, in July, 1742.

The active conflict between England and Spain for Georgia soil began soon after the establishment of an English colony at Charleston in 1670. English traders went across Georgia to trade with the Creek Indians, and the Spaniards, regarding this as an encroachment on their territory, sent soldiers to meet them. They halted the expedition of Dr. Henry Woodward, but he secured the friendship of a great Creek chief and continued trading with the Indians.

The Spaniards strengthened their missions on the Chattahoochee and encouraged negro slaves in South Carolina to rebel by giving them a place of refuge at St. Augustine. A bloody insurrection of negro slaves in Carolina, supposed to have been incited by Spanish emissaries, cost the lives of a number of white people before it was subdued.

Governor Moore of the Charleston colony made two expeditions against the Spaniards, one down the coast, destroying the Spanish missions and attacking St. Augustine, another in 1703 across Georgia to the Chattahoochee Valley, where he took a Spanish fort, destroyed most of the Apalache Indian towns and carried away 1,400 prisoners. That destroyed Spain's hold on Western Georgia, but she threatened the coast region until checked by Oglethorpe's victory on St. Simons Island.

France had failed to establish settlements in Georgia and Spain had only a few missions and forts. It remained for England to colonize and people the State.

**Georgia as an English Province**—The coming of General James Edward Oglethorpe in 1733 was the beginning of a new era in Georgia, for within ten years he built up a substantial settlement at Savannah and others lower on the coast, anticipated a Spanish attack on Georgia by his own attack on St. Augustine, and finally ended the conflict with Spain by his victory at Bloody Marsh.

The movement to establish an English colony in Georgia, or a province, as it was first known, under trustees appointed by the King of England, owed its inception partly to a great philanthropic movement, headed by General Oglethorpe, for the relief of poor debtors in English jails, partly for the purpose of developing in Georgia industries whose products coming to England would be the basis of a profitable trade by which it was hoped many thousands of people would be employed, and largely as a military measure for the protection of England's American colonies against encroachment by Spain and unfriendly Indians supporting the Spaniards.

After military service in Europe under Prince Eugene of Savoy, Oglethorpe returned to England, and in 1722 was elected to Parliament, where he held a seat for thirty-two years.

In 1729 he led the movement for an investigation of British jails, and headed the investigating committee which included several members of Parliament who were subsequently Georgia Trustees. Their report led to action by Parliament which improved a very bad condition. There were thousands of poor people and 4,000 persons a year were imprisoned for debt in the city of London. Many of them were honest but unfortunate men who had been thrown into jail where it was impossible for them to earn anything to meet obligations. One of them, an architect, a friend of Oglethorpe, was thrown into a jail ward where smallpox was raging. He took the disease and died, accusing the warden of murder, and that tragedy aroused Oglethorpe to action.

The suggestion of a colony in America where poor but honest debtors might make a new start in life and produce something which should return to England as a basis of valuable trade was approved by public opinion and a petition signed by Oglethorpe and others, asking the creation of a body of trustees and a grant of land for them in America, was referred to the Board of Trade, received its favorable report and resulted in the grant of Georgia land to the trustees and their incorporation as agents of the Crown to administer the government and make laws for the new province subject to the approval of the King.

Oglethorpe led the first party of men and women who sailed from England for Georgia late in 1732, arrived at Charleston, where they were cordially received, and went on to Savannah, where they arrived in February, 1733. These and other immigrants were carefully selected, and none but honest, industrious, and sober persons were allowed to come.

General Oglethorpe had a far-reaching vision of the future of Georgia, realized the danger threatening it from the south, and prepared to ward it off. Washington was the great leader in defending the thirteen colonies from their mother country when she sought to crush them, but Washington would not have had thirteen colonies to defend but for the great service of Oglethorpe in building up in the southeast a bulwark between the southeastern colonies and the aggressive Spaniards, who had a strong hold on Florida and were powerfully supported from Cuba. England, realizing the danger of losing some of her American colonies by Spain's aggression, strongly supported General Oglethorpe and spent more on Georgia than she spent on any other of the thirteen colonies.

Oglethorpe left Georgia in 1743 on his final return to England, and there lived quietly until he was eighty-nine years old. It has been said of him that he was the only man who founded a colony and lived to see it become a great independent state.

The events of the Revolutionary War, in which Georgia had an important part and suffered greatly, cannot be told in brief prospectus, but as usual in such periods a great crisis developed great men and their deeds shine in the history of Georgia.

Georgia statesmen had part in the Declaration of Independence and in the convention which made the Federal Constitution. The State Constitution of 1777, during the Revolutionary War, was remarkable, and contained a provision for public schools supported by taxation.

The attempt of General Elijah Clarke to found an independent state in Western Georgia on land claimed by Spain was supported by the French Ambassador Genet, and for a time threatened serious results, but General Washington promptly sent Genet back to France and General Clarke's Fort Advance was destroyed by militia under Generals Irwin and Twiggs by order of Governor Mathews. That caused Clarke to abandon his enterprise.

After the Revolution, Georgia offered great inducements to settlers from Virginia and the Carolinas. The white people then occupied only a belt of counties along the coast and on the Savannah River. The rest of the State was occupied by Indians, and the guerilla warfare they kept up on white people was cruel and bloody. To end this nightmare, Georgia statesmen took measures to secure the title to all Indian lands in the State, with the aid of the United States Government, and to fill up that territory with good white people from states to the north. They offered free land to Revolutionary veterans, and thousands of good people were attracted to Georgia from Virginia and the Carolinas, and settled in Eastern and Middle Georgia, notably in the counties of Franklin, Wilkes, Washington, Hancock, Putnam, and Greene.

The development of agriculture and industry in Georgia was affected by unusual factors. The plan of the trustees for silk culture proved a failure, but in its stead came the great cotton industry, which grew from a small beginning to one of world-wide proportions, furnishing an occupation for millions of southern people and more in New England, Old England, and other parts of Europe. The export of cotton for many years gave the United States an immense balance of trade, which with the manufacturing industries of this and other sections made the country rich.

The invention of the cotton gin by Eli Whitney, a son of New England then living in Georgia, made the cotton industry possible, and also made possible the vast increase of negro slavery in the South, for without cotton, in growing which the negroes were largely employed, there would have been little need for slave labor. It seemed likely that the use of slaves would be entirely abandoned in the South, until the great demand for their labor arose with the rapid extension of cotton culture.

The consequences of this change were far-reaching. The profitable use of slave labor on plantations in which the wealth of the South was then largely invested did not encourage the development of manufacturing industries except in North Georgia and the cotton factories, which were a part of the cotton industry.

The great planters were men of wealth and culture and looked down upon the tradesmen of the towns and cities, who were largely of the middle class. The exceptions were bankers and cotton factors upon whom the planters largely depended in moving the cotton crop to market. Thus, indirectly, slavery built up a social class at the top of society while it labored at the bottom. This condition was reversed by the war of the 'sixties. It left the plantations desolate. Many of their owners were ruined by war and emancipated negroes left work and went to town, where they were decimated by disease and want. Wealth and social leadership left the country and went to the cities. Negroes gradually returned to farms and agriculture slowly improved.

The threatened extension of slavery into the new land of the West started the long conflict between the South and the North, which ended in the War between the States. That conflict came near destroying the National Government. At the first Battle of Manassas, where thousands of Georgians fought, the Federal Army was routed by the Confederates and fled back to Washington in disorder. If President Davis had held a strong reserve of cavalry ready, as he had been advised to do, they would have taken Washington, but they were not there and Washington was spared. In that battle the 8th Georgia Regiment held the bloody angle.

An overruling providence turned the scale at Manassas, for had the Confederates taken Washington this country would have been divided, and Mason and Dixon's Line would have been a line of forts across the country. War would have been repeated, blood would have flowed and the progress of the country would have been seriously retarded.

The progress of this country from 1865 up to the World War cannot be told in figures, and hardly in words. In this, Georgia had a large part. With less than a million people in 1860, she has three millions. Instead of slave labor she has educated labor, and in her society the middle class are the backbone of the Commonwealth. The aristocracy of wealth is seriously questioned and cannot make good its claim unless its wealth is used fairly and wisely in ways that will give employment and encourage progress.

The industrial progress of Georgia before the War Between the States is not generally known. On the farms cotton was not the only crop. Planters raised food for man and beast. Wheat growing in North Georgia was extensive, and in Bartow County there was a five-story flour mill built of stone, with a capacity of three hundred barrels a day. Cotton mills were numerous, and in Bartow County there were fourteen iron furnaces and a rolling mill.

Good progress was made in education. Georgia had the first State university and the first woman's college chartered by a State. The Baptist, Methodist, and Presbyterian churches established colleges which have grown to be universities from which thousands of graduates have gone out. In science, medicine, law, art, and letters, Georgians have made a record worth while, and in trade, industry, and finance, the State leads the Southeast. In 1836 the State chartered and later built the Western and Atlantic Railroad, the only great railroad owned by a State in this country, operated it profitably for years and still owns it. The traffic on that road is the heaviest in the Southeast.

It took years for Georgia to recover from the waste of war, but she reached that point in 1888 and has since gone far beyond it. She has passed through the brick and mortar stage into one of greater culture and refinement, in which the arts, occupations, and institutions of a high civilization have their place.

# *A Bird's-Eye View of Georgia*

THE history of Georgia will be clearer, more realistic and more interesting if we begin by taking a bird's-eye view of the State as it spreads out before us with its mountains, valleys, hill country, and plains; its forests, mines, and farms; its rivers, harbors, coast line, railroads, highways, and air lines; with a glimpse of its people, at work and at home, in schools and in churches, with their industry, wealth, and the forms of government under which they live.

No drama is good without a stage, and the drama of our history is inseparable from the great theatre on which it was enacted. That theatre we see in a bird's-eye view of Georgia.

Georgia is the largest State east of the Mississippi River, with an area of 59,265 square miles, almost as much as all New England, and more than England and Wales.

The break-up of the Blue Ridge makes a Switzerland in North Georgia, with mountains nearly a mile high, and the varied topography of the State, from seacoast to mountains, gives its five degrees of latitude, the climate of ten degrees, without extremes of heat or cold.

With abundant rainfall and great rivers flowing from the highlands to the Atlantic Ocean or the Gulf of Mexico, Georgia is in the path of recurring rain movements coming up from the Caribbean Sea through the Gulf of Mexico to warm and fructify the land.

Georgia is in the same belt of latitude as Morocco, Algiers, Tunis, Tripoli, Northern Egypt, Palestine, Arabia, Persia, parts of India, China and Southern Japan. Atlanta, its capital city, is on the same parallel that passes through Jerusalem.

The greatest length of the State is three hundred and twenty miles from north to south, and its greatest width from east to west is two hundred and sixty miles. Diagonally the distance from the Tennessee line at the northwest corner of the State to the Florida line at the St. Mary's River is four hundred miles.

Georgia has some of the finest harbors on the South Atlantic Coast, and a great coastwise and international commerce flows through the ports of Savannah and Brunswick.

The boundary line between Georgia and South Carolina is the eastern bank of the Savannah River from its mouth to its junction with Tugaloo

STONE MOUNTAIN, NEAR ATLANTA

River, and thence along the latter river to its junction with Tallulah River, from which point it follows Chattooga River to the North Carolina line.

The northern boundary line of the State was intended to be at thirty-five degrees of north latitude. It is in that position only at its eastern end, and elsewhere is nearly one mile south of the latitude line.

The western boundary line begins at a cornerstone on the Tennessee State line marked on its south side, "Geo. lat. 35 degrees north; J. Camak." This stone stands near the top of Nickajack Mountain, one mile and twenty-eight rods from the south bank of Tennessee River, and near the center of the old Indian town, Nickajack. From the Nickajack corner, the State line between Georgia and Alabama runs south approximately one hundred and forty-six miles to West Point, on the Chattahoochee River. Thence down the west bank of the Chattahoochee approximately one hundred and fifty miles to its junction with Flint River, in latitude thirty degrees, forty-two minutes, forty-two seconds, and longitude eighty degrees, fifty-three minutes, fifteen seconds.

The southern boundary line, beginning at the junction of the Chattahoochee and Flint rivers, runs one hundred fifty-eight and thirty-five one-hundredth miles to a point thirty-seven links north of Ellicott's Mound. Thence it follows the meanderings of St. Mary's River to the Atlantic Ocean.

**Topography**—The topography of Georgia naturally falls into five divisions, the coastal plain, the central uplands (usually spoken of as the Piedmont Plateau), the valley region of Northwest Georgia, the highlands of the Blue Ridge in Northeast Georgia, and the Lookout Plateau in the extreme northwestern corner of the State.

The coastal plain, which includes three-fifths of the State, extends from the southern boundary to the southern fall line, corresponding to a line drawn from Augusta on the east through Milledgeville and Macon to Columbus on the west. Water courses running from the higher land of the central uplands onto the coastal plain, because of the softer earth there, cut their way deeply, and this causes a series of falls along the southern boundary of the central uplands. That gave rise to the expression, "Southern Fall Line," applied to the line where the harder strata of the uplands and the softer strata of the coastal plain begin.

The central uplands extend northward from the southern fall line to a point between Marietta and Rome, where they are succeeded by the valley region, including Rome, Dalton, and Cartersville. This valley area is interspersed with hills and high ridges running southwest and northeast into Alabama and Tennessee.

East of this valley region, between Dalton and Tallulah Falls, are the Blue Ridge Highlands, in which the highest mountains of Georgia are located. The highest of these, Bald Mountain, called Enota in the United States Geodetic Survey, is in Towns County, rising from the valley of the Hiawassee

River, a few miles south of the North Carolina line, to a height of 4,768 feet above sea.

**How the Mountains Were Made**—In an article prepared for college classes, Richard W. Smith, State Geologist, shows the mineral wealth of Georgia and explains the vast operation of natural forces which raised up the mountains, spread out the valleys and cut away from the mountains, by the slow erosion of water, thousands of feet of earth and weathered rocks, carrying to the coastal plain below immense quantities of sand, clay and limestone.

The process of raising mountains and cutting them down by erosion was not continuous, but in cycles, says Mr. Smith. "Elevation was followed by a rapid cutting of V-shaped valleys by the streams, a more gradual widening of these valleys, sometimes progressing long enough to reduce the land to a low plain over which the streams sluggishly meandered, and then another elevation and repetition of the cycle.

"As some rocks were not as hard as the crystalline rocks of the Piedmont and mountain sections, some were worn away faster than others by erosion, and the result of such erosion was the formation of the Appalachian Valley, which extends from Alabama to New Jersey."

Of the tremendous changes in the surface of Georgia by erosion, he says:

"The once mighty range of the Appalachian Mountains has been worn down to a rolling plateau, broken only by a few isolated mountains caused by areas of harder rock, and by our present mountains at the head of the drainage. The depth of material that has been eroded from the Piedmont Plateau can be estimated by remembering that Stone Mountain is composed of granite that was formed by the very slow cooling of molten rock deep under the surface of the earth. At least three to five thousand feet of rock was once overlying what is now the top of Stone Mountain. It has been removed by the slow agencies of erosion and transportation, working through eons of time."

**Great Mineral Wealth**—By the vast operations of nature through millions of years the Great Architect has made Georgia a storehouse of immense mineral wealth.

The valuable minerals found in the State include: Marble, granite, corundum, copper, graphite, clay products, Portland cement materials, bleaching clays, limestone, barite, pyrite, manganese, ocher, iron ore, bauxite, and gold.

The quarries of Pickens County have furnished marble for the State capitols of Minnesota and Utah, the Corcoran Art Gallery, the Lincoln Memorial, the Atlanta Post Office, and public buildings in many states.

Gold is found in four belts running through twenty-four counties. Before the gold rush to the West, the Federal Government maintained a mint for gold at Dahlonega. High-grade iron ore is found in four counties, and red ore in two. Iron pyrite is the basis of an important fertilizer industry, for which it furnishes the sulphuric acid. Coal occurs in two of the northern counties.

**Forests**—The forest land is about three-fourths of the area of the State, and nearly two-thirds of it is in the pine region of the coastal plain. Most of the twenty-eight million acres of forest has been cut over and less than a million acres of virgin timber remain, but there is second growth timber on 20,000,000 acres, and from that a valuable lumber product comes annually. One-fourth of that vast area is protected by the State Forestry Department, with the coöperation of owners, 6,000 of whom have signed contracts to coöperate with the State department in protecting forests from fires.

Reforesting forest land has begun and 10,000 acres have been successfully replanted. The State Forestry Department aids this with two tree nurseries, one at Albany for slash pine, long-leaf pine, and loblolly pine, and one at Blairsville for black locust, black walnut, and white pine. Young trees from these nurseries are furnished land owners at cost. Many millions of such seedlings have been taken and planted by owners of forest land.

The Forest Department has vocational courses in practical forestry in one hundred and ninety-two high schools in different parts of the State, and 6,000 boys receive instruction in those courses. The brightest of them are encouraged to take regular forestry courses at the State College of Agriculture. To stimulate this work, the Georgia Forestry Association, composed of leading men, awards prizes to the students and teachers doing the best work in the high school forestry courses.

Dr. C. H. Herty, who perfected a process for making paper out of second-growth pines, has found that such trees will in four to seven years be large enough for making paper. Other uses of this timber are developing. A great deal of the framing lumber used in Georgia buildings is of second-growth pine.

The close relation between forests, rivers, and climate was well expressed some years ago by the French Ambassador to this country, Monsieur Jusserand, who, in a talk to the Rivers and Harbors Congress, made this significant remark:

"You call the Mississippi River the 'Father of Waters,' but I tell you that the forests are the mother of the Mississippi."

He said that forests had been cut away from mountains in France in the region tributary to the River Seine, and, as a result, the erosion of the land on those mountains had been so great that the Seine had been largely filled with silt, which caused the river, in flood seasons, to overflow into part of the city of Paris.

This experience of France has been duplicated to a large extent during the last sixty years in the watersheds of Georgia rivers, like the Etowah and the Oostanula, which caused destructive floods at Rome, and the Chattahoochee, which gave trouble at West Point. Federal engineers have recommended high dams on North Georgia rivers to impound flood water, stop erosion, and regulate water power. France cured erosion by reforesting the mountains.

The development of reforestation on a large scale in Georgia, which is well begun, means many millions added to the wealth of the State by saving farm lands from erosion, restoring waste land to productive condition, and the production of a valuable crop of second-growth timber, with the incidental result of building up a great paper industry.

**Water Supply and Power**—The abundant rainfall of Georgia, averaging about fifty inches a year, and well distributed through the seasons, gives an ample supply of water for general use and develops great potential water power. Dr. McCallie, then State Geologist, in Bulletin 42, gave a statement of the potential water power of seven rivers in Georgia, followed by a report of the hydroelectric power developed in this State in 1923. It showed 2,381,800 potential horse power in the seven watersheds, and 601,869,490 kilowatt hours of hydroelectric power developed in the State that year.

The rivers of the central highlands run southeast through the coastal plain to the Atlantic Ocean and southwest through the Flint and the Chattahoochee into the Gulf of Mexico. Steamboats ply on the Chattahoochee below Columbus, the Flint, St. Mary's, Satilla, Altamaha, Ocmulgee, Oconee, Savannah, and Coosa rivers.

**The Coast Line**—The coast line of Georgia by direct distance from Savannah to St. Mary's is one hundred and twenty-five miles, but measured by its windings, is nearly five hundred miles. If to this is added the seven hundred miles of coast line of the islands that skirt the coast, Georgia has a total coast line of 1,200 miles.

The harbors are the ports of Savannah, Darien, Brunswick, and St. Mary's. The Brunswick Harbor is one of the best on the South Atlantic Coast, and Savannah is a great cotton port and the chief port of the naval stores industry, which is one of large proportions in the fine forests of the coastal plain.

**Railways and Highways**—There were 11,500 miles of railways in Georgia in 1936, about the same as in 1932. In the four years from 1932 to 1936 the operating revenue of Georgia's railways increased from $45,585,480 to $60,400,000. That increase of thirty-two and one-half per cent. is a fair measure of Georgia's recovery from the depression in those four years.

The great development of good roads in Georgia has been since the Highway Department was created in 1919. Since then the State has spent $162,057,417 on roads without issuing bonds for the purpose, and of 9,272 miles of road, the State has 4,600 miles of hard surface highways.

Most of the money spent on road construction came from tax on gasoline, which yields about two-thirds of the revenue of the department. The rest came from license fees and the Federal allotment to Georgia for road building.

The increased use of automobiles and the improvement of roads have come together and stimulated each other. The great growth of motor traffic on the highways of Georgia was shown by a traffic survey made by the Public Service Commission in October, 1932, when the cars passing twenty-five strategic points in twenty-four hours were counted and listed according to classes of vehicles. It showed 61,423 motor cars passing in a day.

While this survey covered vehicles passing the most important points, it did not include all. In that year (1932) the Public Service Commission licensed three hundred and seventy-four busses and 1,100 motor trucks. The total length of bus routes in Georgia that year was 8,309 miles.

**Effect of Automobile Competition**—The competition of automobiles and busses has seriously affected the passenger business of the railroads, and railroad passenger fare has been reduced to two cents and in some cases one and one-half cents a mile. By these reductions the railways have recaptured much of the passenger business which had been taken by automobiles. Motor trucks carry a great deal of freight and this has been felt by the freight departments of the rail lines.

In spite of this competition, the railroads still carry the bulk of the traffic, as indicated by their receipts.

**Aviation**—Airplanes serve directly one-fifth of Georgia's population, with forty-six airports and landing fields.

In 1934 airplanes in this State flew 843,240 miles and carried 15,175 passengers. The mail planes carried, north, south, east and west, to and from Atlanta, thirty-two tons of mail a month.

Candler field, a great municipal airport, built by the city of Atlanta, is one of the best equipped and is the third aviation center in the country.

Georgia has eight hundred and six miles of air routes, all lighted except between Atlanta and Augusta, and plans are made to light that.

The State is served by these four air mail routes:

Route 5—From Newark to New Orleans *via* Atlanta.
Route 6—From Newark to Miami *via* Savannah.
Route 10—From Chicago to Jacksonville *via* Atlanta.
Route 24—From Charleston to Dallas *via* Atlanta.

Train connections carry air mail and passengers to all parts of Georgia. On three routes large Douglas Air Line planes, the finest in the world, are used. The air lines connect Atlanta with New York, Chicago, Philadelphia, Washington City, and New Orleans. For South and Central America, Atlanta has good connections *via* Miami and Brownsville, Texas.

**Telegraphs, Telephones, and Radio**—Through telegraphs, telephones, and radios, Georgia's voice reaches many millions every day.

Atlanta is the third telegraph center of the world, surpassed only by New York and Chicago, and is the telephone center of the South, having direct connection with one hundred and seventy-four Georgia towns and with all the great cities of the country.

There are in Georgia eleven radio stations, three in Atlanta, and one each in Macon, Augusta, Columbus, Savannah, Rome, Athens, Americus, and Thomasville.

The great station, WSB, owned and operated by the Atlanta *Journal,* with 50,000 watts of power, is heard in every State of the Union, and in Canada, Mexico, South America, Alaska, Australia, New Zealand, England, Germany, and many other countries. The voice of Georgia is heard all over the world.

**The Population**—The population of Georgia by the census of 1930 is 2,908,506, or forty-nine per square mile, which is above the average density of the country. They are ninety-nine and one-half per cent. native-born, sixty-three per cent. white, thirty-seven per cent. negroes; and of the whole number, sixty-nine per cent. are in rural districts and thirty-one per cent. in towns and cities.

**School and Church Enrollment**—One million and ninety-three thousand are of school age, and two-thirds of the school population are in educational institutions. Fifty-two per cent. of the school ages are in Sunday schools.

The church membership of Georgia is forty-six per cent. of the people, and they worship in 9,283 churches valued at $52,607,000.

The illiteracy of native whites is three and four-tenths per cent.; of foreign whites, four per cent., and of negroes, nineteen and nine-tenths per cent.

In 1930, sixty-one per cent. of the men and fifty-nine per cent. of the women of those over fifteen years old were married.

**Work, Wealth, and Product**—The gainful workers of Georgia are forty per cent. of the population, and the wealth of the people, by the census estimate, is about $4,000,000,000, or $1,300 per capita. The bonded debt of the State, $4,680,202, is only one-fourth the value of the State's railroad, the Western and Atlantic, estimated at $20,000,000, and leased for $540,000 a year to the Nashville, Chattanooga and St. Louis Railway.

Two-thirds of Georgia's land is in farms, and the farm population is nearly half the people.

The farm and factory product reported in 1929 and 1931 was $712,000,000 a year, and the wholesale trade $1,000,000,000.

The State Government is a representative democracy, with one hundred and fifty-nine counties and fifty-one senatorial districts represented in the Legislature. There are thirty-four judicial circuits, presided over by Superior Court judges and appeals from their decisions go to the Court of Appeals or the Supreme Court. Below the Superior courts are City courts, Juvenile courts, Municipal courts, justices of the peace, and city recorders, with judges, and in the higher courts, prosecuting officers.

The Executive Department of the State consists of the Governor and the usual department officers, commissions, and bureaus.

## CHAPTER I.

# *Prehistoric Georgia*

We can almost see the Indians who lived in Georgia more than a thousand years ago. Those ancient people are bodied forth by things they left in the ruins of their habitations in the Ocmulgee Old Fields, on both sides of the river, at and below Macon. There, near a large factory and close to a Bibb County public school, excavation has revealed their dwellings, pottery, implements, cornfields, council house, burial places, and a mile of prehistoric fortifications which protected their community from attack.

All this has been brought to light by the work of the last three years, inaugurated by leading men and officials of Macon and Bibb County, with the coöperation of the Macon Junior Chamber of Commerce, Congressman Vinson, the Smithsonian Institution, and the Federal Emergency Relief organization.

Although Georgia historians have known of Old Ocmulgee Fields for more than two hundred years, no attempt was made to develop the site into a park or have proper explorations made until 1933. The movement started in the summer of 1933 as an outcome of the organization of the Society for Georgia Archæology, under the leadership of J. M. Mallory, of Savannah, and General Walter A. Harris, of Macon. This society was organized early in October of that year, and Dr. Charles C. Harrold was elected president; General Harris, chairman of the board of directors, and Linton M. Solomon, secretary. Very soon after this, General Harris persuaded the Macon Junior Chamber of Commerce to undertake raising money to purchase key sites in Old Ocmulgee Fields for a city park. The key sites were bought with funds advanced by friends, and the Macon Junior Chamber of Commerce raised the money for the final payment.

Through the coöperation of Mayor H. I. Smart, a Federal Emergency Relief Administration project was requested to build roads and clear up the sites. The immediate coöperation of the local relief engineer, Robert Watkins, made the State Relief Administrator, Miss Gay Shepperson, familiar with all plans, and from the beginning the entire work had the whole-hearted support of the entire State relief forces. Without this support less could have been done.

It developed that the Smithsonian Institution, which had known of the Old Ocmulgee Fields for many years, was contemplating work on this site at the same time, having secured a Civil Works Administration grant for this work without having asked the permission of the property owners to do any excavations. The Chief of the Bureau of Ethnology, Dr. M. W. Stirling, had visited the site six years ago at the request of General Walter A. Harris, the president of the Macon Historical Society, and had been invited to return for excavations when funds were available. Dr. Stirling knew nothing of the plans for the city park, but as soon as he heard of them he suggested that

**A view of explorations in progress to uncover the ceremonial earth lodge on the Macon Plateau. The entrance passage, circular clay walls, floor, clay-moulded seats, and central hearth or altar can be seen in the picture.**

forces be combined. This was done and active work commenced in December, 1933.

Dr. A. R. Kelly was put in charge of the excavations, and has been in charge since the beginning of the work. The Smithsonian Institution had nothing official to do with the work after the first eight weeks, but has kept up an active interest in it. Many visits have been made by the officers of that institution and the National Museum and they have kept in contact with the work.

It was seen early that State-wide interest in the excavations was being aroused, and General Harris requested Congressman Carl Vinson, of the Sixth Georgia District, to introduce a bill in Congress creating a National Park within the confines of Old Ocmulgee Fields. This was done, and the bill passed Congress and was signed by President Franklin D. Roosevelt. The land, however, had to be purchased and donated to the United States Government. In this work, the aid of the Macon Junior Chamber of Commerce, as the original sponsors, was very important. Later, the coöperation of Mayor H. I. Smart and County Commissioner Leon S. Dure, more than any two individuals in Macon, made the park possible.

The site was described by Adair in 1760. It was visited by Colonel James Moore, of Charleston, in 1703, and it was here that the 1,000 fighting Creek warriors were assembled in December of that year. In January, 1704, they exterminated the Spanish Apalache Indians, and made the settlement of Georgia by the English a possibility.

Here in these Old Ocmulgee Fields, two hundred and thirty years later, the largest archæological project ever undertaken in America has been studying the ancient remains of these historic and prehistoric people. Under the leadership of Dr. A. R. Kelly, hundreds of white Federal Emergency Relief Administration, Civil Works Administration, Public Works Administration, and Works Progress Administration men have secured wholesome and interesting work during the greatest financial depression America has ever known. As work progressed, interest has grown. Many students believe this work has been one of the outstanding relief projects in the United States. The wholesome effect upon hundreds of workers has been of inestimable value to their morale and their worth to themselves and their families, the community, and the State. At the same time their work has made possible the interpretation of the life of the prehistoric people of Old Ocmulgee Fields a thousand and more years ago.

There are indications that these mounds were the center of an immense Indian population, extending along the Ocmulgee River for many miles, and the excavations of the last three years have revealed the remains of several periods of Indian life and culture, imposed on each other successively through a period of 1,500 years.

Dr. Kelly, who was a professor of anthropology in American colleges before he came to this work, was requested by the author of this history to furnish a statement outlining the results of excavations in the Old Ocmulgee Fields, and did so in the following article:

**Excavations in Other Parts of Georgia**—Dr. John R. Swanton, of the Smithsonian Institution, who is familiar with excavations of Indian Mounds in other parts of Georgia, particularly the one in Bartow County near Cartersville, has written by request a brief statement of what they show and this is printed here as a supplement to Dr. A. R. Kelly's statement concerning the excavations in the Old Ocmulgee Fields near Macon:

"The Etowah site has been known for a long time, having been described by Cornelius in 1818, by C. C. Jones in 1873 and Whittlesey in the Smithsonian Report for 1881. Since the survey made by the Bureau of American Ethnology and the exploration of some of the smaller mounds in 1885 the site has become almost classic, owing more than anything else perhaps to the discovery of some copper plates with figures stamped upon them bearing some resemblance to Mexican figures. Parts of three or four stone images were also found. More recently work was done here by Dr. Warren K. Moore-

**Detail of house site exploration at Lamar swamp village. Burned roof timbers and sod show on the floor of the house; a flexed burial is exposed on the flank or ramp of the house mound. A heap of broken pottery is to be seen in the right foreground.**

head of Andover, Mass., who found additional copper plates and images. The group consists of one very large mound, exceeded in size by few except Monks Mound at Cahokia, and covering three acres, and several smaller mounds. Not far away are other groups. Somewhat higher is the great mound at Colomokee in Early County; and the Nacoochee Mound, near Clarkesville, explored by the Museum of the American Indian, is also notable. Indian sites of importance occur in Elbert County, around Augusta, along the entire Georgia seacoast and on the Chattahoochee and Upper Flint.

"Speaking roughly the Savannah River marks the eastern boundary of the more highly developed tribes, those which constructed the great domiciliary and burial mounds. Although their culture reached a high level in the State, the center of it seems to have been along the Mississippi, though much of that section had been abandoned when Europeans came into the Gulf region. The work that has been done on Georgia sites up to the present time shows clearly an intrusion of several successive peoples, or else perhaps the spread of several different cultures, but we are as yet not in a position to untangle the different historical threads with which archeology provides us and to weave out of them a coherent pattern.

"Among the interesting remains I should have noted the eagle effigies near Eatonton, Ga., which while suggestive of the effigy mounds of Wisconsin and the effigies of South Dakota outlined in stones, are yet quite distinct from them.

"The most important finds for the archeologist, it should be said, are potsherds since the potsherds of a people are in a measure trade marks by which it may be recognized and its movements traced."

## EXPLORATION OF ARCHÆOLOGICAL SITES AT MACON, 1933-35.

**By Dr. A. R. Kelly.**

In December, 1933, archæological exploration was initiated on large mound and village sites on the Ocmulgee River, near Macon, as a Civil Works Administration project, sponsored by the Smithsonian Institution, with the coöperation of the Society for Georgia Archæology. Work on this project has been in continuous operation. With the establishment of a National monument, still further investigation is contemplated.

The basin of the Ocmulgee River, at Macon, was defined by early ethnographers as an important center of settlement of historic Creek Indian tribes, the location of Old Ocmulgee Town described by the English naturalist and traveler, William Bartram, and the probable seat of still older Muskogean-speaking tribes, the Hitchiti, who would seem to have been the numerically dominant population in the region of Central and Southern Georgia in protohistoric times.

Two years' exploration at Macon make clear a much longer period of cultural development than anyone anticipated. Successive levels of occupation and variations of archæological material indicate a long prehistory extended over 1,500 years. Some flint implements represent culture of a still earlier population on the Macon Plateau.

Historical data relating to the settlement of the larger rivers in Central Georgia are scanty and extremely confusing. Early maps of the area are vague and patently incorrect in sketching the location of important streams. Indian towns and villages are described and located in a manner which makes exact placement difficult, if not impossible, except by extensive archæological reconnaissance and careful checking of all items of material culture to provide historical cross-reference to sites, using characteristic designs on pottery, specialized bone and stone implements, peculiarities of burial customs and residence construction as cultural indices.

The methods of history and archæology must be combined to arrive at satisfactory conclusions. Whether the patterns of material culture belonging to different Indian tribes are sufficiently distinctive to be identified or isolated is a difficult problem. Unhappily American archæologists have been primarily preoccupied with the study of prehistoric sequences.

A program of research calculated to obtain reliable results would assume State-wide, probably regional, scope. Consequently, information gleaned from one site alone, howbeit a major or key site, is inadequate to give any clear picture of the migrations and mingling of diverse linguistic and cultural groups even during the last five hundred years of occupation.

Further complication of the problem comes from the fact that not only the Georgia territory, but the whole southeastern cultural province, 1,200 miles long and six hundred miles broad, as recently defined by Dr. J. R. Swanton, remains relatively unexplored territory so far as the elucidation of its prehistory is concerned.

In consideration of these limiting factors, it is possible to evaluate briefly results of two years of archæological exploration at Macon. Investigations were concentrated upon two main site locations: Lamar mounds and village site about two and one-half miles south of Macon, in the Ocmulgee swamps, and the Macon Plateau village site and related mounds on the flat bluffs overlooking the river to the east of Macon.

**The Lamar Site**—The Lamar site was explored over a three months' period. Considerable material came from trenching of one of the mounds. Mound A, a rectangular flat-topped mound of the temple-pyramid type. The other Lamar mound, Mound B, is a conical truncate with a graded approach or spiral pathway leading up to the summit from the level of the plain, ascending counter-clockwise, a structural peculiarity correlated with the assumed ceremonial use of the area on top of the mound. The details of buildings on mound summits have yet to be worked out, as most of the work at Lamar was confined to the exploration of the rich midden deposits and house sites in the village area.

Three house sites, indicated as small artificial hillocks in the plain, covered with a richer growth of vegetation, were completely excavated. These yielded rectangular house floors of puddled yellow river clay, built on small ramped house mounds, rising three feet high above the plain. The walls were timber uprights, supplemented with a covering of reeds. Sod roofs were evidenced by the roof débris mounded over the clay floors, the sod having fallen over collapsed roof timbers when the house was burned. Smothering of the fire by roof sod had served to preserve many of the supporting timbers in charred form. Reconstructions of these houses from archæological data suggests that they must have been very much like those built in recent times by refugee Creek and Hitchiti (Seminole) Indians in the Everglades of Florida. The plan of the Lamar Swamp village, including the mounds, houses, square grounds, chunky courts, presented striking similarities to the plan of an early Creek village given by William Bartram.

Burials were found in the ramps of the house mounds and in the village ground between houses. Interments were either flexed or extended primary burials.

Considerable collections of pottery show agreement in all important pottery characters as between the mounds and the village. The pottery from the Lamar site is characterized by specific peculiarities in regard to both ware and decorative features. The ware is smooth, hard, with a lustrous finish, apparently attained by rubbing a thin wash of dissolved clay over the surfaces of the pottery before firing. Grit or sand temper predominates. Decorative motifs fall into two large categories: Carved paddle decorations in many patterns and deep; broadly incised designs. Both techniques are carried out in broad, sweeping lines, which present a striking effect of elaboration and ornateness, combined with boldness in execution. Design elements may be applied either on the rim, rim and shoulder, or over the whole body of the pot. Rim decorations show frequent specializations in the form of applique moulds of pottery paste pinched or beaded in various forms, effigy faces, mostly human, occur; notched, serrated, punctate are other variations, while cross-sectioned reed impressions are frequent.

The stone implements and weapons present no specialized features which can as yet be distinguished from assembled materials from other sites. Bone and shell were used as both implements and ornaments. Some of these appear to be more specialized and likely to be useful in identifying the cultural complex to which the Lamar Swamp village belongs.

Very few historic materials in the form of European trade objects were found in the Lamar site; such as were found might have been intrusive in the mounds and upper village midden. The data suggest a chronological position for Lamar village with attenuated European influences, or possibly a settlement abandoned before intimate contact with white colonists was experienced. On the other hand the mass of materials accumulated on the occupation level implies several generations of occupancy and a rather large population inhabiting the Ocmulgee lowlands.

The tentative conclusion is drawn that the Lamar Swamp village is a type town or village of the Indians living on the Ocmulgee at or before the period of abandonment, *circa* 1715, when the hegira to the Chattahoochee took place. The villagers would be Lower Creeks, possibly mingled with some of the older Hitchiti tribal remnants absorbed or adopted after the more recent migrations of Muskogean invaders. The archæological findings fit historical intimations in implying cultural fusion between recently arrived and more aboriginal groups.

The archæological situation found at Lamar is duplicated at numerous other sites either explored or reconnoitered on the Ocmulgee, Oconee, Flint, and Chattahoochee rivers. While the evidence is incomplete and a long period of intensive study of many sites and the archæological material therefrom is needed to permit of specific allocations and identifications, it seems possible to delimit a set of material culture-traits which define a cultural focus present over a large part of Georgia, demonstrably surviving at some points at the time of first European contact which may be denominated as the typical remains of the historic Creek tribes.

**The Macon Plateau**—In contrast to Lamar Swamp is the village occupation explored for nearly two years on the low plateau on the Ocmulgee, nearer Macon. While the vast amount of material taken, and still being catalogued from different levels on this site, has not been systematically analyzed, it is apparent that we have to do with an older, quite prehistoric settlement, possibly several of them, but with no sharp breaks in the continuity of cultural development indicated by the pottery, mound, or building complexes. That the assemblage of features denotes a different focus from that exhibited by Lamar is beyond controversy.

The mounds on the Macon Plateau are pyramidal truncates which appear to have been constructed as artificial elevations on which important public or religious buildings were built. Mound C, west of the plateau and nearer the river, seems to have served a double purpose. Over a hundred burials were brought out in the exploration of less than one-fifth of the whole mound, whereas there were evidences that buildings were erected on the summits of the four or five flat-topped mounds which were built one upon another to constitute this very remarkable composite mound. The mosaic of varie-colored basket-laid sand in the bodies of these superimposed mounds, capped on summit and slope with blue, yellow, red, and orange clay bands, is a thing of unusual beauty. The core mound, first to be built, in particular seems to have been a burial mound, as a number of large burial pits, lined with bark or logs, were sunk beneath a specially prepared clay platform, over which the mound was later built.

Mound A, located on the extreme south end of the Macon Plateau, is one of the largest and most imposing pyramidal mounds in the Southeast. Exploration has only just begun upon this gigantic pile of earth. Enough information is available to show that it, too, was built in several mound stages; each stage serving as a building epoch, with aprons and graded approaches leading up from the plateau.

Fifty years of research show that American tribes are descended from immigrants who came to America by Bering Straits from Northeastern Asia, and that it took the American race fifteen or twenty thousand years to develop from that stock.

Pottery remains the index fossil of the archæologist. The pottery of the Macon Plateau is technologically a poorer grade ware than that of the Lamar Swamp village. Shell and vegetal tempers give a porosity and lack of tensile strength. Even where grit and sand tempered ware occur on the plateau, these are always rough, coarsely finished, in marked contrast to the smoother, more glossy product of the swamp dwellers. Moreover, the plateau pottery is less highly decorated, embellishment of pottery rims in the form of crudely modeled animal heads and highly specialized lugs being the only frequent occurrence. Where design elements are found, these will be either simple cord-marked, crudely incised, or will show impressions of baskets, nets, and

**A study of the massive pyramidal mound dominating the Macon plateau group of satellite mounds. The terraces and projecting apron of earth in front of the pyramid are part of the prehistoric landscaping developed in the construction of this mound.**

other simple weaves of the containers in which the pot was built up. A few stamped sherds occur, but these belong, stylistically and technologically, to a different order than that of the rich carved-paddle decorations characteristic of the Lamar technique.

Two other lines of archæological data help to show differentiation between the Macon and Lamar foci, burial customs and house types, but space does not offer opportunity for a discussion of these. There is more evidence of secondary or bundle burial at Macon Plateau village and at Mound C. At least two, and possibly three, divergent house types have been brought out on the Macon site.

Flint industry also provides a clue to cultural diversity. Flint artifacts at Macon show numerous specialized types of rather simple knives, end and side scrapers, drills, projectiles, not found in the swamp village sites. It is possible that further study may indicate a still more remote archæological horizon for some of the Macon flints.

**Ancient Cornfield and Ceremonial Chamber**—Important archæological discoveries on the Macon Plateau relate to the uncovering of a prehistoric cultivated field brought out under Mound D. The sand mound, plated with red clay, had preserved the furrows of the ancient field for perhaps a thousand years. The ceremonial chamber or earth lodge on the east plateau rim, near Mound D, is unique in many respects, and differs from ceremonial structures hitherto found in the Southeastern area. Extensive dugouts or linked pits, carved out of red clay, encircling the rim of the plateau for more than a mile, are still something of an archæological mystery at the present writing. Evidences now rapidly appearing suggest that the plateau may have been fortified with raised ramparts of earth, log stockades set out in ditches, and a rather remarkable series of terraces cut in the natural terrain of the hill slopes.

The exact implications of these devices are not all clear at present. The developments mentioned are important, and theoretical speculation is not lacking to account for them. It is necessary to note, however, that archæological synthesis and fact-finding are still in process, not yet justifying any hypothetical pronouncements.

## THE ABORIGINES OF GEORGIA.

**By Dr. John R. Swanton, Ethnologist of the Smithsonian Institution.**

*(Written by Request for the Story of Georgia.)*

Before white men appeared, the territory now embraced in Georgia was occupied by the American Indians, a relatively homogeneous race, exhibiting only minor variations and allied to the Mongolian populations of Eastern Asia. At present it is generally held that they did not enter that part of America south of Alaska until toward the end of the glacial period, but the exact time is in debate and subject to serious modification. The earliest Americans of whom we have definite knowledge were the makers of the Folsom arrow points, and flint points of Folsom type have been found in Georgia. These points seem to be ancient, and they and certain crude pot sherds of a later period apparently indicate several thousand years of occupancy by relatively primitive hunting and fishing tribes before agriculture was introduced.

In time, these hunters and fishers learned the use of corn, beans, and pumpkins, which probably reached them from the West, coming from Mexico, and they may have learned the use of tobacco from the same region.

At a later date the ancestors of the tribes actually found in occupancy made their appearance, perhaps coming from the West, after the introduction of agriculture. Many of these people erected mounds for their ceremonial buildings and the dwellings of their chiefs, or as sepulchres for their dead. They were mound-building Indians, but they were Indians none the less. There was no distinct race of "Mound Builders."

The first Western Indians to reach Georgia may have been ancestors of the Catawba, now in South Carolina, or people related to them. They are an important branch of the great Siouan linguistic family which has been named from the famous Sioux or Dakota nation of the Northwest and embraced a great body of Indians in the Piedmont region of Virginia and the Carolinas, and many famous tribes beyond the Mississippi besides the Sioux. Very likely some of these Catawba Siouans were in Georgia, as well as South Carolina, as late as the Sixteenth Century.

Another group of tribes, perhaps, crossed Southern Georgia at about the same time, the greater part of them moving on into Central Florida, while a few remained in Southeastern Georgia, on Cumberland Island and the neighboring mainland. These are usually known as Timucua, after one name of a leading tribe. They were found by the French and Spaniards in the Sixteenth Century in the region indicated and were missionized by the Spanish Franciscans. The mission on Cumberland Island, called Tacatacuru in the native language, was known to the Spaniards as San Pedro, and it was the chief of San Pedro who protected the missionaries when driven from the Georgia coast farther North in the great uprising of 1597 and repelled their pursuers when an attempt was made upon the island itself. Late in the Seventeenth Century these Indians were withdrawn to the neighborhood of St. Augustine, where they and their Florida representatives presently disappeared under attacks of the English and Creeks and by absorption among other Indians.

It is probable that both the Siouan and Timucua Indians were remotely related to those who succeeded them. The successors belong to the Muskhogean family, named from the dominant tribe of the Creek confederation, the Muskogee. In historic times it was the stock most widely spread in the Southeast, embraced three of the great nations of the section which played leading rôles during Colonial times, and, with the addition of the Seminole tribe, which separated from the Creeks in the Eighteenth Century, constituted four of the "five civilized tribes" of Indian Territory, the modern Oklahoma. Georgia prehistory and early Colonial history is intimately bound up with the Creek confederation, which came to occupy fully two-thirds of the present area of the State.

The Indians later incorporated into this nation appear to have entered the country in two distinct waves. First, a group of tribes affiliated with the Choctaw and Chickasaw spread along the Gulf Coast and the immediate hinterland until they reached the southern part of South Carolina. They were represented by the Pensacola and Apalachee Indians, the Yamasee in the forks of the Altamaha, and probably by the Carolina coast tribes. Besides the Yamasee, those in South Georgia included the Hitchiti, Ocmulgee, Oconee, Sawokli, Apalachicola, and Tamathli, all of whom called themselves Atcik-hata, a name said to refer to the ashes of their ceremonial grounds.

At a later date there entered from the Northwest a people who came to be known as Muskogee (probably a Shawnee word), who were either more numerous or more united than their predecessors. Their language was related to that of the first comers, but not so as to be intelligible to them. There is evidence that they had pushed their way down Savannah River to the coast and constituted the dominant element in the so-called province of Guale.

Among the Lower or Georgia Creeks there were two principal Muskogee towns, Coweta and Kasihta, said to have resulted from the fission of one original body. The rest of the confederacy was built around these. It is said that these two tribes resorted to the well-known Southern Indian ball game, to be noted later as a substitute for war.

As tribe after tribe was brought in, two divisions or "sides" grew up and extended throughout the nation, one including Kasihta and its allied towns, being considered the white or peace side; Coweta and its towns the red or war side, and the towns of the peace side were "cities of refuge" for strangers, or those who had taken human life. Nearly all the Atcik-hata belonged to the peace side, the only exception being the Chiaha.

At an early date some other Muskogee towns settled in Georgia as far east as the coast, but most of these last were driven inland by a Spanish expedition sent to avenge the slaughter of the missionaries in 1597. After the Yamasee War in 1715 many of them moved back from the Ocmulgee to the Chattahoochee, and, later, to the Tallapoosa, leaving only the two great tribes above mentioned and a band of Eufaula Indians.

The Uchee, or Yuchi, were a peculiar people with a unique language. From Spanish documents we know that they came into these territories long after the first white contact. In the Sixteenth Century they were in East Tennessee, and may have extended to the Cumberland or the Ohio. There were some near Muscle Shoals, but their principal seats were farther east. Early in the Seventeenth Century, because of pressure of the Cherokee and other Northern tribes, they moved Southward in successive waves toward Florida, much to the annoyance of the Spanish governors. The first wave entered West Florida and later united with the Upper Creeks.

In 1681 the Westo, representing probably a second wave of Yuchi, were driven from Savannah River by the white colonists, with the help of a band of Shawnee, when they moved to the Ocmulgee, and, later, to the Chattahoochee. Another band of Yuchi took their places. In 1716, evidently as a result of the Yamasee War, they passed over the Chattahoochee and from there seem to have gone to the Tallapoosa. They were followed on the Savannah by another branch of the tribe which, when Oglethorpe came with the first Georgia colonists, had established itself between Silver Bluff and Ebenezer Creek. Owing in part to intermarriage with the Kasihta Indians, they presently began to transfer their towns to the Chattahoochee, though they maintained hunting rights in their old territories as late as 1740, and were scrupulously protected therein by General Oglethorpe. Soon after that date this right was abandoned and the Yuchi followed the fortunes of the Creeks among whom they had settled.

The other group mentioned consisted of Shawnee. This tribe belongs to the great Algonquian stock of the North and East. Late in the Seventeenth Century, Shawnee established themselves on Cumberland River and began trading with the Spaniards at St. Augustine. Between 1674 and 1681 a body of them moved to the Savannah River, and, in the latter year, aided South Carolina by driving off the Westo. They remained in the neighborhood of Augusta for a considerable period, giving off to the Chattahoochee in 1716 a band which settled upon the Tallapoosa and continued there until shortly before the Creek War of 1813-14, when they probably rejoined their kindred in the North. Several other bands went from the Savannah to the Potomac and Susquehanna rivers, leaving their name to the river and city of Savannah as a permanent memorial of their residence in this State.

The Cherokee are today the largest tribe of those who formerly lived in the Gulf region, and probably the largest in Colonial days. Important historically, they were late comers into the Southern Appalachian region, and particularly into Georgia. Cherokee tradition was that they had formerly dwelt in Western Virginia and had worked their way Southward along the headwaters of the Tennessee, probably along the great Indian war trail which went up from the Ohio along Kanawha and New rivers and down portions of the Holston and French Broad, near the western skirts of the mountains. It was probably not until the Seventeenth Century that Cherokee began to come into the mountainous regions of the State, where many place names adopted by them, such as Etowah, Euharlee, and Canasauga, appear to be Creek. The last stage in this movement was due to pressure of the Tennessee colonists when the hard-pressed Cherokee acquired from the Creeks the right to settle in the valley of the Coosawatee ("Old Creek Place") and in the neighboring territory. Thus the southernmost boundary claimed by them was that attained last. Among other noted accomplishments, this tribe will always be remembered as having produced Sequoya, the only Indian of any tribe north of Mexico who undertook, without direct missionary promptings, to reduce his language to writing.

Of the former Indian inhabitants of Georgia known or suspected, the Timucua are wholly extinct, a handful of Catawba remain in South Carolina, the Atcik-hata and Muskogee are represented well in Oklahoma and Florida, a small body of Yuchi lives in Oklahoma, and the Georgia Shawnee are represented in the Absentee band of Shawnee in Oklahoma. There are about 2,000 Cherokee in North Carolina and Tennessee, and many thousands in

Oklahoma. Most of these surviving Indians are mixed bloods and their ultimate fate will probably be absorption in the general body of our people.

Aboriginal life was much the same among the Creeks, the Cherokee, and the other tribes above mentioned. They were in that stage of culture called neolithic, the new stone age, in which implements now made of metal were chipped from flint or ground from other varieties of stone. Some, of course, were made of bone, shell, wood, and horn. The Indians were acquainted with copper, but did not know how to harden it, and employed it mainly for ornamental purposes. Their weapons were bows and arrows, spears, and clubs, and they also had shields. Their vessels were of pottery, ornamented in later times mainly with stamped or incised designs, and there was a great variety of baskets, principally woven of cane, of which scarcely any specimens remain. They made mats of the same material, or of rushes, and textiles suitable for clothing out of the inner bark of the mulberry and a kind of native hemp. Cords were of the same material, of linden bark, or of the sinews of deer and other animals. The woven garments were used mainly by women, who, like the men, employed skins, which they knew how to dress very successfully.

The one essential male garment was the breechclout, which, before the Indians had trade goods, consisted of a deerskin passed between the legs and tucked under the belt before and behind. They wore moccasins, especially when traveling, and leggings, brought up high and fastened to the belt, largely to protect their legs from bushes and briars. When it was not too warm, they added shirts, and, in very cold weather, blankets made of skin. At one side they wore a large pouch to contain the pipe, tobacco, medicines, and other possessions. The women wore a short skirt instead of the breechclout, and an upper garment which passed over one shoulder. They also had moccasins, and, sometimes, leggings. The costumes of Southern Indians, shown in works of Catlin, McKenney, and Hall, belong to a much later date, and are much altered from the aboriginal patterns.

Women wore their hair long, divided in the middle, and gathered into braids, which were often clubbed at one or both sides of the head. The men generally shaved their hair off at the sides, leaving a central roach, and, sometimes, a fringe above the forehead. The ends of the remaining hair were wound together and often passed through a hollow reed or bound about with a beaded string, and the hair was rubbed with bear grease and powder from a certain plant and adorned with feathers, but they had nothing resembling the Sioux war bonnet, which has been so industriously foisted upon all Indians by popular writers and illustrators. They wore ornaments of metal or shell in their ears, and about their necks, and, sometimes, in their noses, as also on their fingers, wrists, arms, and legs. Beads were extensively employed in ornamentation, but much less in aboriginal times than after the appearance of white traders. Their faces and parts of their bodies were elaborately tattooed, mainly to indicate war honors, and the use of paint was general, varying in elaboration with the individual and the occasion. Men were more addicted to ornamentation than women, and, it is said, that the women of certain tribes used little or no paint.

Some tribes spent the winter in circular houses made of a framework of poles, interlaced with withes and small branches, and plastered with mud mixed with grass, the whole sometimes covered with bark or mats. There was one narrow, low door, and, sometimes, a smokehole. Around the interior, next the wall, ran a raised bench upon which the inmates sat or slept, and the doorway was protected from drafts by a covered approach. Each town generally had a big house of this kind, often called the "mountain house," made after the same general pattern, but much more elaborately. The summer houses were quadrangular, lighter in construction, and, sometimes, provided with porches, but among the Creeks the winter house was usually made like the summer house, except for more careful plastering. Close to the buildings for habitation stood a granary or storehouse raised on posts.

The town was made up of small groups of buildings, which, in time of peace, were scattered through the forest, sometimes for miles. In time of war the Indians gathered in a stockaded fort with walls like those of the winter house, carefully defended gates, and towers placed at intervals to prevent enemies from approaching near enough to set the structure on fire.

Besides the enclosed, circular town house, built in the same way by Cherokee and Creeks, there were more open buildings about a cleared space where ceremonials were held and business conducted during pleasant weather. One section of the ceremonial ground was provided with a ball post and devoted to the single-post ball game which seems to have had a ceremonial character. In later times the greatest game of the Southeast was the two-stick ball game, similar to our lacrosse, which is itself of Indian origin.

Match games were played between two towns or sets of towns, accompanied with much ceremony, and were extremely rough affairs. Much property was wagered on the result.

Most work about the house was performed by women. They did all of the weaving, skin dressing, basket and pottery making, cooking and sewing, and brought in firewood and game that had been killed near the house. Men attended to the work in stone, made implements for hunting, fishing, fighting, and gaming, and used them for the purposes intended, and they took principal charge of the ceremonials. The small private gardens were worked by women, but the large fields belonging to each town were planted by members of both sexes, and the subsequent cultivation was shared between them, though it bore more heavily on women than on men.

These Indians had begun to pass over from the hunting and fishing stage to the stage of agriculture. They raised corn, beans, squashes, pumpkins, sunflowers, and tobacco, but had no domestic animal except the dog. This made it necessary for them to obtain meat by hunting and fishing, while the women gathered part of the vegetal food from wild roots and fruits. Such dependence on nature made annual removals essential, and the lack of fertilizer tended to force the removal of the town itself from time to time.

Within historic times all of these tribes were divided socially into clans—fictionally extended family groups—ordinarily bearing the name of some animal and perpetuated in the female line, children taking the clan and clan prerogatives of the mother. The Cherokee had only seven clans when they were known to Europeans, but the Creeks had many and were gathered into two great sides or "moieties," which opposed each other in practice games within the town. All of the Creek towns, numbering about fifty, were again divided into sides devoted to war and peace. The government of each town was vested in a civil chief and various assistants, whose positions were determined partly by birth and partly by merit. There were several grades of warriors, headed by another chief, whose places had nearly always been acquired through deeds performed in battle. The warriors acted as an internal police, and certain towns had peculiar influence. Leadership in the Creek and Cherokee nations depended on personal ability rather than inheritance. National councils were made up of men who had risen to the top in several communities.

## CHAPTER II.

# *Indian Civilization*

The Indians of the Southeast, the Cherokees and the Creeks, had a well developed civilization of their own before white men came to America. They lived upon a higher plane morally and were essentially a better people than they were after several centuries of contact with European adventurers, whose baneful influence demoralized them.

They were friendly to white men until despoiled by them, and, as a reward for their friendship, they were taught the vices of civilization, and eventually driven from their homes and hunting grounds to a far country.

### THE GEORGIA INDIANS.

**Their Homes and Manner of Life**—We have much to learn from the Indians. They knew things we have never learned and solved problems that baffle us. There is much to admire in their customs and characteristics when the Europeans came, before they were demoralized by unscrupulous white men, who robbed them, burned their homes, and taught them the vices of civilization.

The Cherokees had their homes and hunting grounds in the beautiful mountain region of North Georgia, with its endless succession of hills and valleys, and running streams.

The Creeks lived in Middle Georgia and in the southern part of the State, largely covered with primeval forests of great pines rising fifty or seventy-five feet, with no underbrush to obstruct the view between their lofty trunks and the ground carpeted with pinestraw.

Both were regions of great natural beauty, which is bodied forth in the lines:

CHEROKEE GEORGIA

Oh, grand is the land
Of the brave Cherokee,
With the sheen of its beautiful water;
With the hills and the vales
And the clouds that you see,
And their shadows following after;

Across the slanting hills they fly,
As fleet as fancy flyeth,
The while above fair castles move
Where fancy never dieth.

THE PINE FOREST

Oh, wonderful sea, that washes no shore,
Thy waves have a voice and it sings evermore,
For a song everlasting ariseth afar
Where the winds and thy billows are ever at war;
No commerce hath darkened,
No blood ever shed
Where the waves never sport
O'er the graves of the dead,
But the sea birds aflit on thy evergreen tide
Make their nests in its crests and there ever abide.

Life in Georgia before the coming of the white man was picturesque, and, in some respects, romantic and beautiful. The Cherokees and Muscogees were superior to most American Indians. The Cherokees, especially, were a noble race, with many fine characteristics, and had a considerable degree of civilization. They wore clothes and shoes, or moccasins, lived in houses, cultivated fields, worshipped the Great Spirit, venerated their dead leaders, and built large mausoleums ornamented with statues, irridescent shells, and strings of pearls. They had arms and implements pointed with copper or flint, and built magazines for them, and granaries for corn. They had domesticated at least one animal, the dog. Colonel Charles C. Jones gives an interesting picture of these people in the first chapter of his *History of Georgia,* and devotes a whole book to the subject in his *Antiquities of the Southern Indians.* Colonel Jones says the Cherokee Indians were dignified, courteous to strangers and brave, but fierce in war. Their women, he says, were beautiful, graceful, and some almost as fair as Europeans. Accounts of the Indians by numerous credible witnesses, who saw them at the time when they first came in contact with Europeans, are in substantial agreement in showing that the Indians of the Southeast were far advanced beyond the condition of wandering, savage nomads. They had local habitations and highly developed systems of agriculture, industry, and ceramic arts. Marriage was regarded as a sacred institution, and was protected by severe penalties for violation of marriage vows. The marriage of blood relatives was forbidden, and the home was the property of the mother of the family.

In government they had made remarkable progress. Their tribal and clan organization was the basis. Families were grouped in clans, and clans were grouped in tribes, similar to the gentes, phratries, and tribes of ancient Europe and Asia. The tribe was ruled by a chief, called Mico or Tustannuggee, aided by a head warrior, and a council of wise men, and the tribes were federated under a king. The Creek confederacy, composed of forty-seven tribes, is said to have been the finest example of federation among American Indians. The Cherokees at first did not show the same capacity for federation, but early in the Nineteenth Century, under their great chief, John Ross, they formed a government modeled on that of the United States.

In religion, these Indians had ideas above those of some races supposed to have been more civilized. They believed in a supreme being, the ruler of the universe, whom they called the Great Spirit, who ruled not only in heaven, but on the earth, directing its affairs, rewarding good, and punishing evil. After death, according to their belief, those who had led worthy lives were translated to happy hunting grounds and everlasting enjoyment in a world of bliss, and those who had led evil lives were sent to a place of everlasting punishment.

This picture of the Indians, which we get from men like James Adair, who lived among them forty years; William Bartram, the naturalist, who traveled among them in 1773 and later, and before that time, from the accounts left by Spanish chroniclers accompanying DeSoto, is radically different from the description written by Governor George Gilmer after he had served as a lieutenant in the latter part of the Creek War and had seen something of Creeks and Cherokees at the Standing Peachtree Village, in Fulton County, when the passions of war were still hot in the breasts of the Indians, He described them as cruel and barbarous savages, with hardly a redeeming trait.

The fact seems to be that the influence of white men had demoralized the red men during the long period between the first arrival of Europeans and the expulsion of the Indians, and a sad retrogression of the red men resulted from their intercourse with unscrupulous adventurers and conscienceless traders who cheated them, sold them fire water, and used them as pawns in the great game of land grabbing, which went on for a long age between England, Spain, and France.

**Their Agriculture and Art**—According to Colonel Charles C. Jones and other writers, there was a well developed system of agriculture among the Georgia Indians when the white men came. He says:

"When the Europeans first visited the territory embraced within and adjacent to the limits of the modern State of Georgia, they found it peopled by Indian tribes, well organized, occupying permanent seats, and largely engaged in the cultivation of maize, beans, pumpkins, melons, and fruits of several sorts . . .

"In the neighborhood of their cornfields were villages, play grounds, tumuli, fish preserves, and defensive works. Encouraged by their improved possessions to forego the uncertainties and privations of a nomadic life, long prior to the dawn of the historic period, these peoples had become provident of the future, obedient to the will of rulers, jealous of the conservation of

**1—John Ross, Cherokee Chief. 2—Wm. McIntosh, Creek Chief. 3—Sequoia, Who Invented the Cherokee Alphabet. 4—The Cherokee Alphabet**

their homes, attached to fixed abodes, and, to a certain degree, tolerant of labor.

"Each year, at the appointed season, under the superintendence of overseers, the inhabitants of the town, as one family, prepared the ground and sowed the seed."

**Indian Handicrafts**—Wonderful skill was developed by the Indians in making weapons, utensils, agricultural implements, and ornaments of copper, stone, and other materials. Their industrial products were works of art, wrought with infinite care, and the materials were often brought long distances, hundreds and even thousands of miles. Evidence of this inter-tribal commerce is seen in the remains of Indian trails, which covered the country.

Their arrow heads and spear points, from a half inch to fourteen inches long, were made of jasper, quartz, crystals, chalcedony, and flint, chipped into shape and ground and polished by patient toil. In the same way they made stone axes, hatchets, and ceremonial axes, weighing from a quarter of a pound to twelve pounds.

**Inter-Tribal Traffic**—The American Indians had an elaborate system of commerce and transportation which moved over a network of trails that covered the country, several of them crossing Georgia.

There was much travel among Indians, sometimes for exchange of articles by barter, sometimes for social or religious visits, and sometimes on warlike expeditions. Long journeys of 1,000 or 2,000 miles to friendly tribes were made, and they were absent from home at times two months or more.

Long trips were necessary to secure materials used in making weapons, household utensils, tools for tillage, implements of the chase, pipes, and ornaments. They got copper from the lake region, steatite from the Appalachians, obsidian from the Rocky Mountain region, catlinite from Minnesota or Wisconsin, abalone and dentalium shells from the Pacific, and conch shells from the Atlantic and Gulf.

**A Democracy Ruled By Its Best**—Somehow the Indians possessed one of the secrets of good government which is almost a lost art with white men. Their leaders were their wisest and strongest men, whose authority was based on merit.

Adair, who lived among them so long, says: "In general their government consists of a federal union of the whole society for mutual safety. Every town is independent of another town. Their friendly compact constitutes the union.

"They are very deliberate in their councils and never give an immediate answer to any message sent them by strangers, but suffer some nights first to elapse. They reason in a very orderly manner, with much coolness and good-natured language, though they may differ widely in their opinions. Through respect to the silent audience, the speaker always addresses them in a standing posture. In this manner they proceed till each of the head men has given his opinion on the point in debate. Then they sit down together and determine upon the affair."

**Religion of the Indians**—The Indians were strong believers in predestination. They held that there is a certain fixed time and place when and where everyone must die. On the death of a chieftain they said, "The days appointed to him are finished."

Adair says that each of the Indian nations had a house or town of refuge, which was a sure asylum to protect a man slayer or an unfortunate captive, if they could enter it before the avenger of blood overtook them. Murderers sometimes sought this refuge, but if they left it they were immediately killed. One such place was near Fort Loudon, in Tennessee, and another was in the upper western part of the Creek territory, at a village called Koosah.

**Marriage, Divorce, and Polygamy**—Swanton says it was usual for the groom or his family to transfer property to the parents or other relatives of his bride, and this was called a "purchase price" by whites. He adds that polygamy was allowed everywhere, but was usually limited to a few of the wealthiest men. In the great number of cases the wives were own sisters, or, at least, clan sisters.

While intermarriage was common between clans, marriage into the clan of the mother was prohibited, and marriage into the clan of the father was frowned upon. Other authorities say that marriage to blood relatives was prohibited. It is said that strong efforts were made to prevent divorces.

According to Adair the Creek law required widows to live chaste, single lives for four years after the death of their husbands. During that period of mourning, they were required to refrain from public company or diversion, and to go with long, flowing hair, which they were not allowed to anoint with oil.

**Indian Pyramids**—Some Indian mounds were so large that they may be called pyramids.

Swanton says: "We may note the existence of truncated pyramids, constructed of earth, rising from ten to seventy-five feet above the level of the valleys and fertile plains upon which they are located. Generally four-sided pyramids, they materially differ in size; some of the largest containing, at the top, a level area of an acre.

"Some of the more prominent of these truncated pyramids and cones may, we think, be recognized as elevations prepared for the erection of temples for sun worship, while others of less altitude were seemingly intended as foundations for the residences of kings, micos, and priests."

This seems to confirm the Muscogee tradition that Mexico was their ancient home, as they seem to have had some customs like the Mayas.

Archæologists think that the Indians, Aztecs, Toltecs, and Mayas came to America from Asia by the northwest passage.

Striking evidence of such migration was discovered a few years ago by Dr. Thomas Gann, an archæologist of the British Museum. After visiting Yucatan and finding there, carved on the wall of a temple, an image of Buddha, sitting on a two-headed lion and holding a lotus flower in his hand, he went to Southeastern Asia and found in a temple of Cambodia an exact duplicate of the image he saw in Yucatan.

Dr. Gann's account of his discovery was given in the following statement, quoted by the *Living Age* for June, 1929:

"On the walls of the temples, carved in stone, were the gods, the mythological animals, the life of the people, fighting, eating, hunting, sleeping, exactly as I found them in the Maya area. I found the five-, seven-, and nine-headed snakes in the temples of Cambodia to be exactly like those in Maya cities. The pillars, the walls, the steps leading up from four sides—all were the same.

"These things were convincing, but the thing that convinced me beyond all doubt was this: In one of the temples of the old Maya city, on the stone wall, is depicted a Buddha sitting upon a two-headed lion, a suppliant, holding in one hand a flower, presumably a lotus, and in the other a pot of incense. During my investigations in Cambodia our elephant train came upon an old Cambodian temple, which is seldom visited. I found, upon entering many similarities, many images and carvings of which those of the Maya area are undoubtedly replicas, but I was suddenly struck dumb when I saw before me on the wall a Buddha sitting upon a double-headed lion. I stood for what must have been fifteen minutes, gazing upon the old stone carving. There was the same extended hand with the lotus and there was the pot of incense. Upon closer inspection I found the image to be the same down to the minutest detail. My investigations were over. I was firmly and finally convinced."

The carving of an image of Buddha on the temple in Yucatan indicates that the migration occurred since the Sixth Century B. C., for that was the time when Buddha appeared in India.

The union of Scotch and Indian blood in Georgia produced men above the average, among them several of extraordinary ability and force of character, like William McIntosh and Alexander McGillivray, the Creek statesmen; John Ross, the principal chief of the Cherokees, and Sequoya, who made the Cherokee alphabet. They made a long and heroic struggle to lead their people upward to a higher plane of life and to protect them against the relentless forces which eventually drove them from Georgia.

It was the irony of fate that the Indians, who aided the struggling colony and probably saved it from destruction in the long and bloody contest between Englishmen and Spaniards for possession of Georgia soil, were later denied citizenship and driven out of their happy hunting grounds by the children of those colonists.

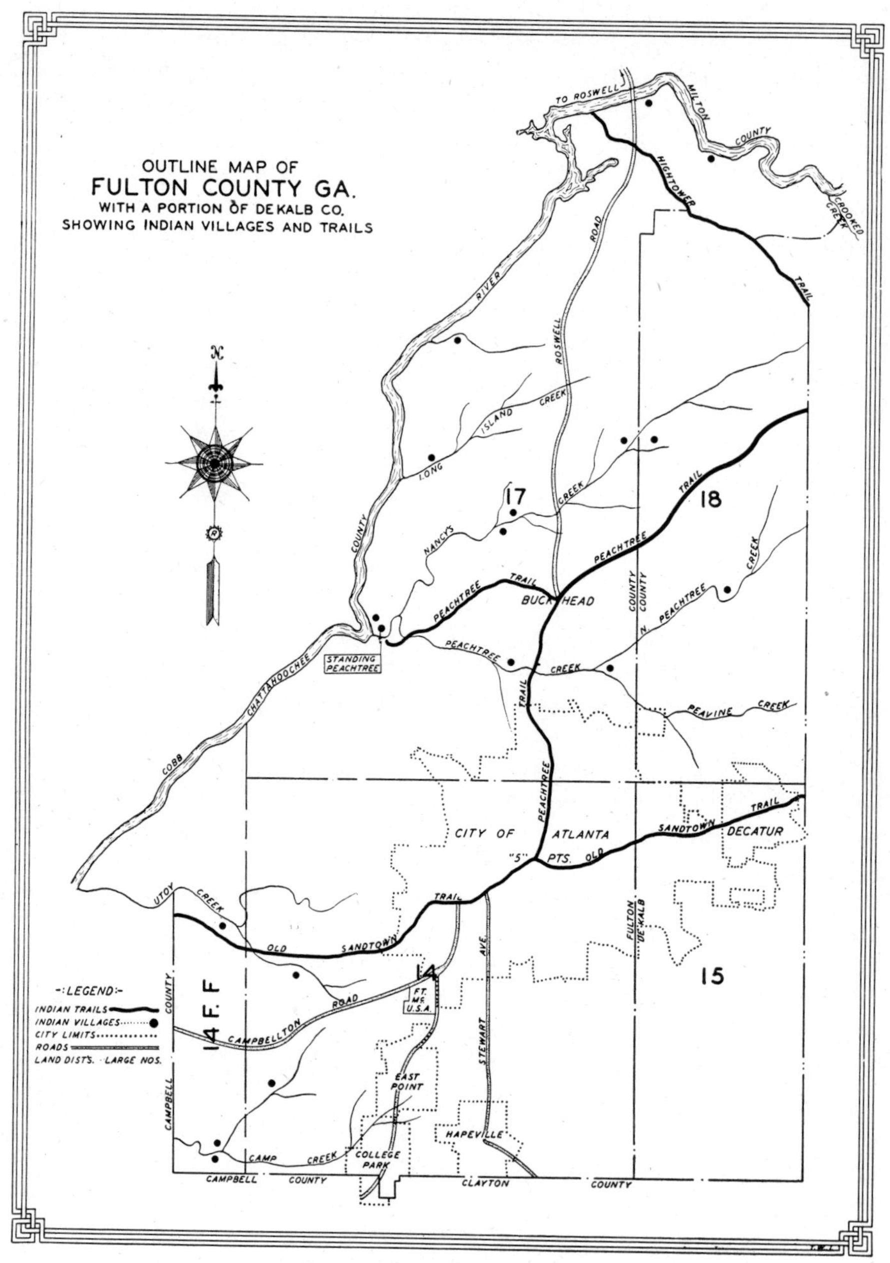


INDIAN VILLAGES IN FULTON

**The Cherokee Indians**—The Cherokee Indians, who occupied the northern part of Georgia above the Chattahoochee River, were originally the largest and most important tribe of Indians east of the Alleghany Mountains, and, perhaps, the highest in culture, according to a statement in the *American Cyclopedia's* article on the subject.

They were of the great Iroquoian group of Indians and occupied the Ohio and Alleghany valleys until driven South by the Delawares and other Iroquois Indians. According to their own tradition they came from the West, which is supposed to have meant the Northwest.

James Mooney, in his sketch of the Cherokees, says they were a third of the Iroquois Indians.

They were divided into two main branches, the Upper Cherokees, located around the headwaters of the Tennessee and Cumberland rivers; and the Lower Cherokees, in Northern Georgia and Western North Carolina, around the headwaters of the Savannah and Chattahoochee rivers.

By the pressure of the early settlement of East Tennessee by Sevier and Shelby, and their followers, the Upper Cherokees were forced south into the region of the Lower Cherokees.

The Cherokees were composed of seven clans, who were forbidden to intermarry. Their principal seat of government in the Seventeenth and Eighteenth centuries was at Old Echota, in East Tennessee, and, in the Nineteenth Century, at New Echota, in the northern part of Gordon County, Georgia.

In the time of Oglethorpe, or just before he came, the Cherokees are said to have had sixty-four towns and 6,000 warriors, but by 1769 their number of warriors had declined to 3,000, and by 1793 to 1,500.

In 1755 they ceded a large tract of land to South Carolina, but in 1758 the killing of some Cherokees for horse stealing started a bloody Indian war in South Carolina. They were overcome and sued for peace in 1761, when fourteen of their villages were burned. In 1773 they made a large cession of land to Georgia.

In the Revolutionary War the Cherokees sided with the British, but they were conquered by General Pickens in 1785, and, by the treaty of Hopewell, they acknowledged the sovereignty of the United States, at which time they ceded most of their lands in Tennessee.

By the treaty of 1835, said to have been obtained without the approval of John Ross, their principal chief, and a majority of their people, the Cherokees ceded their land in Georgia. This was bitterly opposed by Ross and many others of their leaders, but was favored by John Ridge and Elias Boudinot, editor of the *Cherokee Phenix,* who thought removal was inevitable and advocated acceptance of the Government's offer of $5,700,000 and an equal area in the Indian Territory for their lands in Georgia.

They were forcibly removed in 1838 by the United States Army, under General Winfield Scott, and about 20,000 Cherokee men, women, and children left Georgia. It was in November, and some died on the way. Others, about 1,500, escaped and settled in North Carolina, where their descendants still reside.

In the Indian Territory, John Ridge and Elias Boudinot were assassinated for their part in the removal.

John Ross lived in what is now West Rome and his letters to Lewis Cass, the United States Secretary of War, were dated "Head of the Coosa." He was of Scotch and Indian blood and Ross' Landing, now Chattanooga, was his earlier residence and named for him. His letters to Cass showed him to have been a statesman of high character and ability.

Sequoya, who invented the Cherokee alphabet of eighty-five letters, one for each syllable in their tongue, and taught the Cherokees to read in their own language, was a genius, one of the greatest of American Indians.

The forcible removal of the Indians from Georgia by the United States Army was in compliance with the Federal Government's agreement of 1802, by which in consideration of the cession by Georgia of what is now Alabama and Mississippi, the United States Government agreed to acquire for Georgia the title to all the Indian lands in this State. That agreement was in violation of a previous treaty guaranteeing the Indians in perpetuity their title to the land they then occupied in Georgia.

Seizure of those lands could only be justified by a purchase with the consent of the Indians, and that consent, which the United States Government claimed to have secured by the treaty of 1835, was declared by John Ross to have been secured by unfair means and only approved by a small minority of the Cherokees.

**The Creek Indians**—The Creek Indians had a great and tragic part in the contest between Spain and England for Georgia soil. That contest raged for decades before and after the coming of Oglethorpe, not only upon the coast, but in the Chattahoochee Valley, where those Indians supported the Englishmen with deadly effectiveness.

At the Battle of Bloody Marsh, Creek Indians supported a few hundred colonists under Oglethorpe, and did terrible execution upon the Spaniards. In the Revolutionary War and the War of 1812, the Creeks fought on the side of England.

Finally the Creeks were conquered by General Jackson and their warfare on the Georgians ended with the treaty of 1814. Not long before that, in 1813, Governor Gilmer, then a young lieutenant, was sent to build a fort at Standing Peachtree on the Chattahoochee River, where the city of Atlanta gets its water, to protect the Georgia frontier from the Creeks.

Atlanta's historic thoroughfare, Peachtree Street, took its name from that Indian Village, and the name perpetuates the connection of that community with its original inhabitants.

The Creek confederacy developed a system of government that excites wonder and admiration because of its elastic but well-knit federation, its smooth functioning, and its success in choosing the ablest and wisest men for chiefs, kings and head warriors. According to Swanton it had forty-seven tribes composed of families and clans, with a population estimated at 20,000.

ENOTA MOUNTAIN, NORTH GEORGIA, HEIGHT 4764 FEET ABOVE SEA

The Creek Indians regarded the sun as a visible representative of the Great Spirit, ruler of heaven and earth, whom they called "The Great Fire above," and fire, to them an emanation from the sun, was regarded as sacred. The fire was rekindled but once a year with a solemn ceremony, and it was an impious act to put it out in the meantime.

According to Adair, the Indians were no idolators and worshipped neither images, celestial luminaries, evil spirits, nor any created being. He declared, after long residence among them, that they worshipped "The Great, Beneficent, Supreme, Holy Spirit of Fire, who resides, as they think, above the clouds and on earth among unpolluted people." With them, this Great Spirit was the sole author of light, heat, and all animal and vegetable life.

**Sacrifices**—According to John Pope, who visited the Southeast in 1792, the Creeks regularly made a burnt offering of the most delicious parts of every animal killed, about two or three pounds from a buffalo, and less in a regular gradation down to the smallest quadruped, fish or bird.

**Origin of the Creeks**—The Creek Indians had several traditions of their origin, handed down in their tribes for generations. As a rule they are so clearly myths that they cannot be taken seriously.

They all agree in saying that their ancestors came from the West, and one tradition, which is more circumstantial than the others, and apparently more credible, traces the migration of the Muscogees from Mexico, through the Mississippi Valley, to Alabama and Georgia.

**The Creek Confederacy**—*The Handbook of American Indians,* in Bulletin 30, Bureau of Ethnology, has this account of the Creek confederacy:

"A confederacy forming the largest division of the Muskhogean family. They received their name from the English on account of the numerous streams in their country. During early historic times the Creeks occupied the greater portion of Alabama and Georgia, residing chiefly on Coosa and Tallapoosa rivers, the two largest tributaries of the Alabama River, and on Flint and Chattahoochee rivers.

"They claimed the territory on the east from the Savannah to St. Johns rivers, and all the islands, thence to Appalachee Bay, and from this line northward to the mountains. The southern portion of this territory was held by dispossession of the earlier Florida tribes.

"They sold to Great Britain, at an early date, their territory between the Savannah and Ogeechee rivers, all the coast to the St. Johns River, and all the islands up to tidewater, reserving for themselves St. Catherine, Sapelo, and Ossabaw islands, and from Pipemakers Bluff to Savannah (Morse, *North America,* 218, 1776).

"Thus occupying a leading position among the Muskhogean tribes, the Creeks were sufficiently numerous and powerful to resist attacks from the Northern tribes, as the Catawba, Iroquois, Shawnee, and Cherokee, after they had united in a confederacy, which they did at an early day. The dominating tribes at the time of the confederation seem to have been the Abihka (or Kusa), Kasihta, Kawita, Oakfuskee, and some other tribe or tribes at the junction of Coosa and Tallapoosa rivers.

"Nothing certain can be said of their previous condition, or of the time when the confederacy was established, but it appears from the narratives of DeSoto's expedition that leagues among several of these towns existed in 1540, over which head chiefs presided.

"For more than a century before their removal to the West, between 1836 and 1840, the people of the Creek confederacy occupied some fifty towns, in which were spoken six distinct languages, *viz.,* Muscogee, Hitchiti, Koosati, Yuchi, Natchez, and Shawnee.

"Geographically, the towns were grouped as Upper Creek, on Coosa and Tallapoosa rivers, Alabama, and Lower Creek, on middle or lower Chattahoochee River, on the Alabama-Georgia border.

"While the Seminoles were still a small body, confined to the extreme north of Florida, they were frequently spoken of as Lower Creeks.

"The history of the Creeks begins with the appearance of DeSoto's army in their country in 1540. Tristan de Luna came in contact with part of the group in 1559, but the only important fact that can be drawn from the record is the deplorable condition into which the people of the sections penetrated by the Spaniards had been brought by their visit.

"The Creeks came prominently into history as allies of the English in the Apalachee wars of 1703-08, and from that period (except in the Oconee War, 1784-1796, and the Revolution) continue almost uniformly as treaty allies of the South Carolina and Georgia colonies, while hostile to the Spaniards of Florida.

"A serious revolt of the Creeks against the Americans took place in 1813-1814—the well-known Creek War, in which General Jackson took a prominent part. This ended in the complete defeat of the Indians and the submission of Weatherford, their leader, followed by cession of the greater part of their lands to the United States.

"The extended and bloody contest in Florida, which lasted from 1835 to 1843, and known as the Seminole War, secured permanent peace with the Southern tribes. The removal of the larger part of the Creek and Seminole people and their negro slaves to the lands assigned them in Indian Territory took place between 1836 and 1840.

"In the last quarter of the Eighteenth Century, the Creek population may have been about 20,000, occupying from forty to sixty towns. Knox, in 1789 (*American State Papers,* I, 1932), estimated them at 6,000 warriors, or a total of 24,000 inhabitants in one hundred towns, but these evidently included the Seminoles of Florida. Bartram, about 1775, credits the whole confederacy, exclusive of the Seminoles, with 11,000 in fifty-five towns. Hawkins, in

1785, gave them 5,400 men, representing a total of about 19,000. Estimates made after the removal to Indian Territory place the population between 15,000 and 20,000.

"Some of the more important earlier treaties of the United States with the Creek Indians are: Hopewell, South Carolina, November 28, 1785; New York, August 7, 1790; Coleraine, Georgia, June 29, 1796; Fort Jackson, Alabama, August 9, 1814; Creek agency on Flint River, January 22, 1818; Indian Spring, Creek nation, January 8, 1821; Washington, District of Columbia, January 24, 1826, and March 24, 1832; Fort Gibson, Indian Territory, November 23, 1838."

**Adair's Description of the Indians and His Unique View of Their Origin**—James Adair, who lived among the Indians for forty years, wrote a book called *A History of the American Indians,* which was published at London in 1775, and in it he gives interesting descriptions of the red men of the Southeast.

It is a singular fact that his theory of the oriental origin of the American Indians, which was against the view of learned authors of his time, is now more and more the accepted view of modern ethnologists, who think the American natives came from Asia by the Northwest passage many centuries before the discovery of America. Though an Indian trader, Adair seems to have been well versed in the history of races and nations, judging by his citations. His theory was that the Indians were descended from the lost tribes of Israel, and he cites interesting facts from the history of the ancient Jews to sustain his theory. He may have gone astray in making his theory so specific, as the hair and color of the Indians were more like those of the Mongolians than those of the Semitic race. He describes the American Indians as follows:

"That the Indian color is merely accidental or artificial appears pretty evident. Their own traditions record them to have come to their present lands by way of the West, from a far distant country, where there was no varigation of color in human beings; and they are entirely ignorant which was the first primitive color. Besides that, their rites, customs, etc., as we shall presently see, prove them to be Orientals.

"The hotter or colder the climate is, where the Indians have long resided, the greater proportion have they either of the red or white color. I took particular notice of the Shawano Indians, as they were passing from the Northward, within fifty miles of the Chikkafah country to that of the Creeks, and by comparing them with the Indians whom I accompanied to their camp, I observed the Shawano to be much fairer than the Chikkafah, though I am satisfied their endeavors to cultivate the copper color were alike.

"Many incidents and observations lead me to believe that the Indian color is not natural, but that the external difference between them and the whites proceeds entirely from their customs and method of living."

**Adair's Argument for Asiatic Origin**—Adair bases his argument to prove the Indians descended from the Jews mainly on these points of similarity, which he discussed at length in some two hundred pages:

1. Their division into tribes.
2. Their worship of Jehovah.
3. Their notions of theocracy.
4. Their belief in the ministration of angels.
5. Their language and dialects.
6. Their manner of counting time.
7. Their prophets and high priests.
8. Their festivals, fasts, and religious rites.
9. Their daily sacrifice.
10. Their ablutions and anointings.
11. Their laws of uncleanness.
12. Their abstinence from unclean things.
13. Their marriages, divorces, and punishment of adultery.
14. Their several punishments.
15. Their cities of refuge.
16. Their purifications and ceremonies preparatory to war.
17. Their ornaments.
18. Their manner of curing the sick.
19. Their burial of the dead.
20. Their mourning for their dead.
21. Their raising seed to a deceased brother.
22. Their choice of names adapted to their circumstances and the times.
23. Their own traditions, the accounts of our English writers, and the testimonies which the Spanish and other authors have given concerning the primitive inhabitants of Peru and Mexico.

**A Pen Picture of Georgia Indians**—William Bartram, a naturalist of Pennsylvania, who traveled through parts of South Carolina, Georgia, and Florida in 1773, gave this pen picture of the Indians:

"The males of the Cherokees, Muscolgulgees, Seminoles, Chicasaws, Choctaws, and confederate tribes of the Creeks are tall, erect, and moderately robust; their limbs are well shaped, so as generally to form a perfect human figure; their features regular and countenance open, dignified, and placid, yet the forehead and brow so formed as to strike you instantly with heroism and bravery; the eye, though rather small, active, and full of fire; the iris always black, and the nose commonly inclining to the aquiline. Their countenance and actions exhibit an air of magnanimity, superiority, and independence. Their complexion of a reddish-brown or copper color; their hair long and coarse, and black as a raven, and reflecting the like lustre at different exposures to the light. The women of the Cherokees are tall, slender, erect, and of a delicate frame; their features formed with perfect symmetry, their countenance cheerful and friendly; and they move with a becoming grace and dignity.

"The Muscogulgee women, though remarkably short of stature, are well formed; their visage round, features regular and beautiful, the brow high and arched, the eye large, black and languishing, expressive of modesty, diffidence, and bashfulness. These charms are their defensive and offensive weapons, and they know very well how to play them off; and, under cover of these alluring graces, are concealed the most subtle artifices; they are, however, loving and affectionate. They are, I believe, the smallest race of women yet known, seldom above five feet high, and, I believe, the greater number never arrive to that stature; their hands and feet not larger than those of Europeans of nine or ten years of age; yet the men are of gigantic stature, a full size larger than Europeans; many of them above six feet, and few under that, or five feet eight or ten inches. Their complexion much darker than any of the tribes to the north of them that I have seen. This description will, I believe, comprehend the Muscogulgees, their confederates, the Choctaws, and, I believe, the Chicasaws (though I have never seen their women), excepting some bands of the Seminoles, Uches, and Savaunucas, who are rather taller and slenderer, and their complexion brighter. The Cherokees are yet taller and more robust than the Muscogulgees, and by far the largest race of men I have seen; their complexions brighter and somewhat of the olive cast, especially the adults; and some of their young women are nearly as fair and blooming as Europeans.

"The Cherokees, in their dispositions and manners, are grave and steady; dignified and circumspect in their deportment; rather slow and reserved in conversation, yet frank, cheerful, and humane; tenacious of the liberties and natural rights of man; secret, deliberate, and determined in their councils; honest, just, and liberal, and ready always to sacrifice every pleasure and gratification, even their blood and life itself, to defend their territory and maintain their rights.

"The national character of the Muscogulgees, when considered in a political view, exhibits a portraiture of a great or illustrious hero. A proud, haughty, and arrogant race of men, they are brave and valiant in war, ambitious of conquest, restless, and perpetually exercising their arms, yet magnanimous and merciful to a vanquished enemy when he submits and seeks their friendship and protection; always uniting the vanquished tribes in confederacy with them, when they immediately enjoy, unexceptionably, every right of free citizens, and are, from that moment united in one common band of brotherhood. They were never known to exterminate a tribe, except the Yamassee, who never submit on any terms, but fought it out to the last, only about forty or fifty of them escaping at the last decisive battle, who threw themselves under the protection of the Spaniards at St. Augustine. The Muscogulgees are more volatile, sprightly, and talkative than their northern neighbors, the Cherokees."

**Cession of Georgia Land by Indians**—The governments of this country and England recognized the right of the Indians, as original occupants, to hold the lands on which they lived, and, in order to secure title to such land for white men, it was necessary to negotiate treaties with the Indians for the purchase of that territory.

Such treaties were made from the time of Oglethorpe, but after the Revolution the United States Government took up the matter and secured at different times treaties conveying to it the land in Georgia.

By the agreement of 1802, in consideration of the cession to the United States of the territory now in Alabama and Mississippi, the Federal Government undertook to secure for Georgia title to all the Indian lands in the State.

There was difficulty in carrying out that agreement, as the United States Government had by treaty guaranteed to the Indians the right to hold their land in perpetuity. Much negotiation, running through many years, was necessary to secure the land by purchase, and the last treaty by the Cherokees, conveying all the land they then had in Georgia, was not secured until 1835.

That treaty was denounced by John Ross, principal chief of the Cherokees, as invalid, because, he claimed, that it was secured by unfair means and was only approved by a small minority of the Cherokees. Nevertheless, it was enforced by the Federal Government, and General Scott made the Indians move to the Indian Territory. Twenty thousand of them, men, women, and children, went in November, and some died on the way. In Indian Territory, John Ridge and Elias Boudinot were assassinated for advocating removal.

**The Districts Ceded**—The districts ceded by the Georgia Indians at different times, from 1790 to 1835, are shown on the accompanying map. The map and the descriptions of the tracts ceded, as given below, were taken from the eighteenth annual report of the United States Bureau of Ethnology. The descriptions by numbered districts follow and the same numbers on the map show the locations of the different tracts.

### The Cession of Tract 7 by the Creeks.

1790—By the treaty concluded at New York on August 7, 1790, the boundaries of the Creek nation were defined as follows:

Beginning where the old line strikes the Savannah; thence up the said river to a place on the most northern branch of the same, commonly called the Keowee, where a northeast line to be drawn from the top of the Ocunna Mountain shall intersect; thence along the said line in a southwest direction to the Tugalo River; thence to the top of the Currahee Mountain; to the source of the main south branch of the Oconee River, called the Appalachee; thence down the middle of said main south branch and River Oconee to its confluence with the Oakmulgee, which form the Altamaha; and thence down the middle of the Altamaha to the old line on the said river, and thence along the said old line to River St. Mary's. The Creeks cede all claim north and east of the foregoing boundaries.

### The Cession of Tract 44 by the Creeks.

1802—By the treaty of 1802 concluded at Fort Wilkinson, Georgia, on June 16, 1802, the Creeks ceded to the United States the following tract:

All land between the following bounds and lines of the extinguished claims of said nation heretofore ascertained and established by treaty:

Beginning at the upper extremity of the High Shoals of the Appalachee River, the same being a branch of the Oconee River, and on the southern bank of the same, running thence a direct course to a noted ford of the south branch of Little River, called by the Indians, Chattochuccohatchee; thence a direct line to the main branch of Commissioner's Creek, where the same is intersected by the path leading from the Rock Landing to the Ocmulgee Old Towns; thence a direct line to Palmetto Creek, where the same is intersected by the Uchee path leading from the Oconee to the Ocmulgee River; thence down the middle waters of the said creek to Oconee River, and with the western bank of the same to its junction with the Ocmulgee River; thence

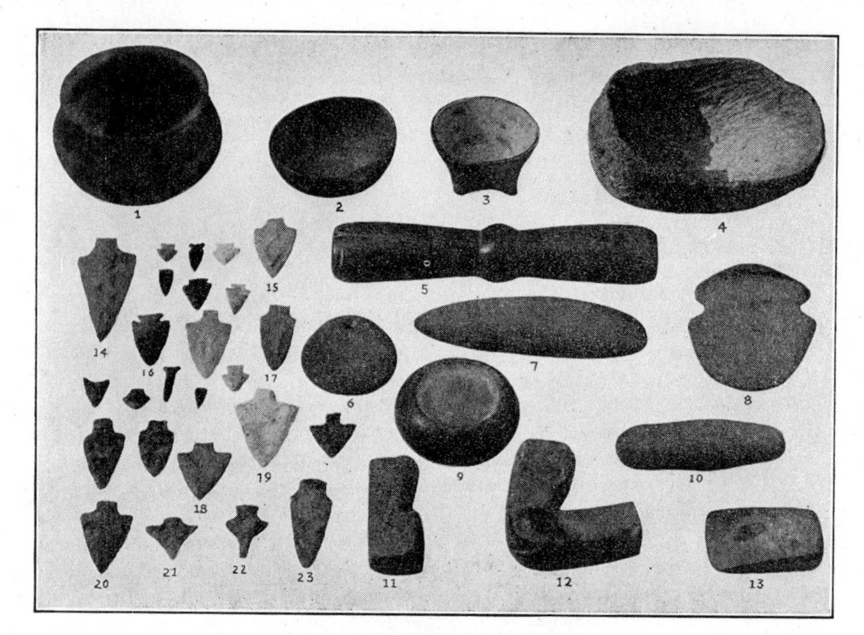


**KEY TO INDIAN RELICS**

**1 and 2—Clay pots from Carter's Quarters, near Chatsworth, Ga. 3—Clay pot, with legs, from Chattahoochee River, near Suwanee, Ga. 4—Stone pot from stream north of Ashford Park Nurseries. 5—Stone medicine or cupping tube from Chattahoochee River, near Suwanee, Ga. 6—Stone pendant or net sinker. 7—Stone hand celt from Chattahoochee River, south of Atlanta. 8—Stone grooved axe. 9—Discoidal stone, used in playing game of Chungke. 10—Stone plummet. 11—Stone pipe from Peachtree Creek, just east of Piedmont Road. 12—Stone pipe. 13—Stone chisel or wedge-shaped axe. 14 to 23—Stone arrowheads and spearheads**

across the Ocmulgee River to the south bank of the Altamaha River, and down the same at low-water mark to the lower bank of Goose Creek, and from thence by a direct line to the Mounts on the margin of the Okefinocan Swamp; raised and established by the Commissioners of the United States and Spain at the head of the St. Mary's River; thence down the middle waters of said river to the point where the old line of demarcation strikes the same; thence with the said old line to the Altamaha River and up the same to Goose Creek.

### Cession of Tract 60 by the Creeks.

1805.—By the treaty concluded at Washington, District of Columbia, November 14, 1805, the Creeks ceded to the United States this territory:

Beginning at the High Shoals of Apalacha, where the line of the treaty of Fort Wilkinson touches the same; thence running in a straight line to the mouth of Ulcofauhatche, it being the first large branch or fork of the Ocmulgee above the Seven Islands, provided, however, that if the said line should strike the Ulcofauhatche at any place above its mouth, that it shall continue round with that stream so as to leave the whole of it on the Indian side; then the boundary to continue from the mouth of the Ulcofauhatche, by the water's edge of the Ocmulgee River, down to its junction with the Oconee; thence up the Oconee to the present boundary at Tauloohatchee Creek; thence up said creek, and following the present boundary line, to the first mentioned bounds, at the High Shoals of Apalacha.

From the foregoing cession the Creeks reserve a tract five miles in length and three in breadth, and bounded as follows: Beginning on the eastern shore of Ocmulgee River, at a point three miles on a straight line above the mouth of a creek called Oakchoncoolgau, which empties into the Ocmulgee, near the lower part of what is called the Old Ocmulgee fields; thence running three miles eastwardly, on a course at right angles with the general course of the river, for five miles below the point of beginning; thence from the end of the three miles to run five miles parallel with the said course of the river; thence westwardly at right angles with the last mentioned line to the river, and by the river to the beginning.

Upon this tract the United States reserve the right to erect a military or trading post.

The Creeks further agree that the United States shall have a right to a horse path through the Creek country, from the Ocmulgee to the Mobile, in such direction as the President shall consider most convenient.

### Cession of Tract 75 by the Creeks.

1814—By the treaty of August 9, 1814, concluded at Fort Jackson, Alabama, at the end of the Creek War:

The United States demand an equivalent for all expenses incurred in prosecuting the war to its termination by a cession of all the territory belonging to the Creek nation, within the limits of the United States, lying west, south and southeasterwardly of a line to be run as follows: Beginning at a point on the eastern bank of Coosa River, where the south boundary line of the Cherokee nation crosses the same; thence down the Coosa River, with its eastern bank, to a point one mile above the mouth of Cedar Creek at Fort Williams; thence east two miles; thence south two miles; thence west to the eastern bank of Coosa River; thence down the eastern bank thereof to a point opposite the upper end of the great falls (called by the natives, Woetumka); thence east from a true meridian line to a point due north of the mouth of Ofucshee; thence south, by a like meridian line, to the mouth of Ofucshee, on the south side of Tallapoosa River; thence up the same to a point where a direct course will cross the same at the distance of ten miles from the mouth thereof; thence a direct line to the mouth of Summochico Creek, which empties into the Chatahouchie River on the east side, below the Eufaulau town; thence east from a true meridian line to a point which shall intersect the line dividing the lands claimed by the Creek nation from those claimed and owned by the State of Georgia. If in running east from the mouth of Summochico Creek it shall happen that the settlement of the Kennards fall within the limits of this cession, then the line shall be run east on a true meridian to Kitchofoonee Creek; thence down the middle of the creek to its junction with Flint River, immediately below the Oakmulgee town; thence up the middle of Flint River to a point due east of that at which the above line struck the Kitchofoonee Creek; thence east to the old line dividing the lands claimed by the Creeks from those claimed and owned by the State of Georgia.

The United States demand the right to establish military posts and trading houses and to open roads within the territory still retained by the Creeks.

Chiefs and warriors of the Creek nation who were friendly to the United States during the Creek War are each entitled to locate a reserve of one square mile, to include their improvements, as near the center as may be of the tract first above ceded.

### Cession of Tract 83 by the Cherokees.

1817—By the treaty concluded at Cherokee Agency, Tennessee, on July 8, 1817, the Cherokees ceded to the United States the following:

Beginning at the High Shoals of the Appalachy River and running thence along the boundary line between the Creek and Cherokee nations westwardly to the Chatahouchy River; thence up the Chatahouchy River to the mouth of Soque Creek; thence continuing with the general course of the river until it reaches the Indian boundary line, and should it strike the Turrurar River; thence with its meanders down said river to its mouth, in part of the proportion of land in the Cherokee nation east of the Mississippi, to which those now on the Arkansas and those about to remove there are justly entitled.

Said nation also cede to the United States all the lands lying north and west of the following boundary lines: Beginning at the Indian boundary line that runs from the north bank of the Tennessee River opposite to the mouth of Hywassee River at a point on the top of Walden's Ridge, where it divides the waters of Tennessee River from those of Sequatchie River; thence along said ridge southwardly to the bank of the Tennessee River at a point near to a place called the Negro Sugar Camp, opposite to the upper end of the first island above Running Water town; thence westwardly a straight line to the mouth of Little Sequatchie River; thence up said river to its main fork; thence up its northernmost fork to its source, and thence due west to the Indian boundary line.

The Cherokee nation also cede to the United States all right to the reservations made to Doublehead and others by the treaty made at Washington City, January 7, 1806.

### Cession of Tracts 92 and 93 by the Creeks.

1818—By the treaty of January 22, 1818, concluded at the Creek Agency on Flint River, the Creeks ceded the United States the following tract of land:

Beginning at the mouth of Goose Creek, on the Alatamahau River; thence along the line leading to the Mounts at the head of St. Mary's River to the point where it is intersected by the line run by the Commissioners of the United States under the treaty of Fort Jackson; thence along the said last mentioned line to a point where a line leaving the same shall run the nearest and a direct course by the head of a creek, called by the Indians, Alcasalekie, to the Ocmulgee River; thence down the said Ocmulgee River to its junction with the Oconee, the two rivers there forming the Alatamahau; thence down the Alatamahau to the first mentioned bounds at the mouth of Goose Creek.

The Creeks also cede to the United States the following tract, *viz.:* Beginning at the High Shoals of the Appalachee River; thence along the line designated by the treaty of November 14, 1815, to the Ulcofouhatchie, it being the first large branch or fork of the Ocmulgee above the Seven Islands; thence up the eastern bank of the Ulcofouhatchie by the water's edge to where the path leading from the High Shoals of the Appalachie to the Shallow Ford on the Chatahochie crosses the same, and from thence along the said path to the Shallow Ford on the Chatahochie River; thence up the Chatahochie River, by the water's edge on the eastern side, to Suwannee Old Town; thence by a direct line to the head of Appalachie; and thence down the same to the first mentioned bounds at the High Shoals of Appalachie.

### Cession of Tract 116 by the Creeks.

(This Tract Includes Atlanta.)

1821—By the treaty of January 8, 1821, concluded at Indian Springs, the Creeks ceded to the United States:

The land east of the following boundaries, *viz.:* Beginning on the east bank of Flint River, where Jackson's line crosses, running thence up the eastern bank of the same along the water's edge to the head of the principal western branch; from thence the nearest and a direct line to the Chatahooche River, up the eastern bank of the said river, along the water's edge, to the Shallow Ford where the present boundary line between the State of Georgia and the Creek nation touches the said river, provided, however, that if the said line should strike the Chatahooche River below the Creek village, Buzzard Roost, there shall be a set-off made, so as to leave the said village one mile within the Creek nation.

From the foregoing cession there is reserved to the Creek nation the following tracts:

> 1—One thousand acres to be laid off in a square, so as to include the Indian spring in the center thereof.
>
> 2—Six hundred and forty acres on the western bank of Oakmulgee River, so as to include the improvements at present in the possession of the Indian chief, General McIntosh.

It is also agreed that the title and possession of the following tracts of land shall continue in the Creek nation so long as the present occupants shall remain in personal possession thereof: One mile square each, to include as near as may be in the center thereof the improvements of Michey Barnard, James Barnard, Buckey Barnard, Cussena Barnard, and Efauemathlaw, on the east side of Flint River, which reservation shall constitute a part of the cession made by the first article so soon as they shall be abandoned by the present occupants.

It is also agreed that so long as the United States continue the Creek Agency at its present situation on Flint River the land included within the following boundary, *viz.:* Beginning on the east bank of Flint River at the mouth of the Boggy Branch and running out at right angles from the river one and one-half miles; thence up and parallel with the river three miles; thence parallel with the first line to the river, and thence down the river to the place of beginning, shall be reserved to the Creek nation for the use of the

United States Agency and shall constitute a part of the cession made by the first article whenever the agency shall be removed.

### Cession of Tract 127 by the Creeks.

1825-26—By the treaty of February 12, 1825, concluded at Indian Springs, the Creeks ceded the land in Tract 127. For signing that treaty the Creek chief, William McIntosh, a cousin of Governor George M. Troup, was assassinated by a band of the Upper Creeks from Alabama.

The Creek nation cede to the United States all lands lying within the boundaries of the State of Georgia, as defined by the compact of April 24, 1802, between the United States and Georgia, now occupied by said nation, or to which said nation claims title.

The Creek nation also cede to the United States all other lands occupied or claimed by them lying north and west of a line to be run from the first principal falls upon the Chatahoochie River, above Cowetau town, to Ockfuskee Old Town upon the Tallapoosa; thence to the falls of the Coosaw River at or near the place called the Hickory Ground.

It is further agreed that the United States will give in exchange for the lands above ceded the like quantity, acre for acre, westward of the Mississippi, on the Arkansas River, commencing at the mouth of the Canadian Fork thereof and running westward between said rivers Arkansas and Canadian Fork for quantity.

The Creeks also relinquish all right to the two reservations at Indian Springs and on the Ocmulgee River, respectively, granted to General William McIntosh by treaty of 1821.

The Federal Government for some reason held this treaty of 1825 invalid and a new treaty was concluded on January 24, 1826, at Washington, District of Columbia.

The treaty concluded at Indian Springs, February 12, 1825, between the Creek nation and the United States and ratified on March 7, 1825, is declared null and void.

The Creek nation cede to the United States:

> 1—All the land belonging to said nation in the State of Georgia and lying on the east side of the middle of Chatahoochie River.
>
> 2—The general boundaries of the foregoing cession also include the tract reserved at Oakchoncoolgau Creek by treaty of 1805.
>
> 3—Also tract reserved at Indian Springs by treaty of 1821.
>
> 4—Also tract reserved at General McIntosh's by treaty of 1821.
>
> 5—Also tract reserved for Creek Agency by treaty of 1821.
>
> 6—The Creeks also cede a tract lying within the State of Georgia and bounded as follows: Beginning at a point on the western bank of Chatahoochie River, near the Buzzard's Roost, measuring the same distance in a direct line and not following the meanders of said river; and from the point of the beginning running in a direct line to a point in the boundary line between the said Creeks and the Cherokees thirty miles west of the said Buzzard's Roost; thence to the Buzzard's Roost, and thence with the middle of said river to the place of beginning.

That portion of the Creek nation known as the friends and followers of the late General William McIntosh having intimated to the United States their desire to remove west of the Mississippi, it is agreed with their assent that a deputation of five persons shall be sent by them to examine the Indian

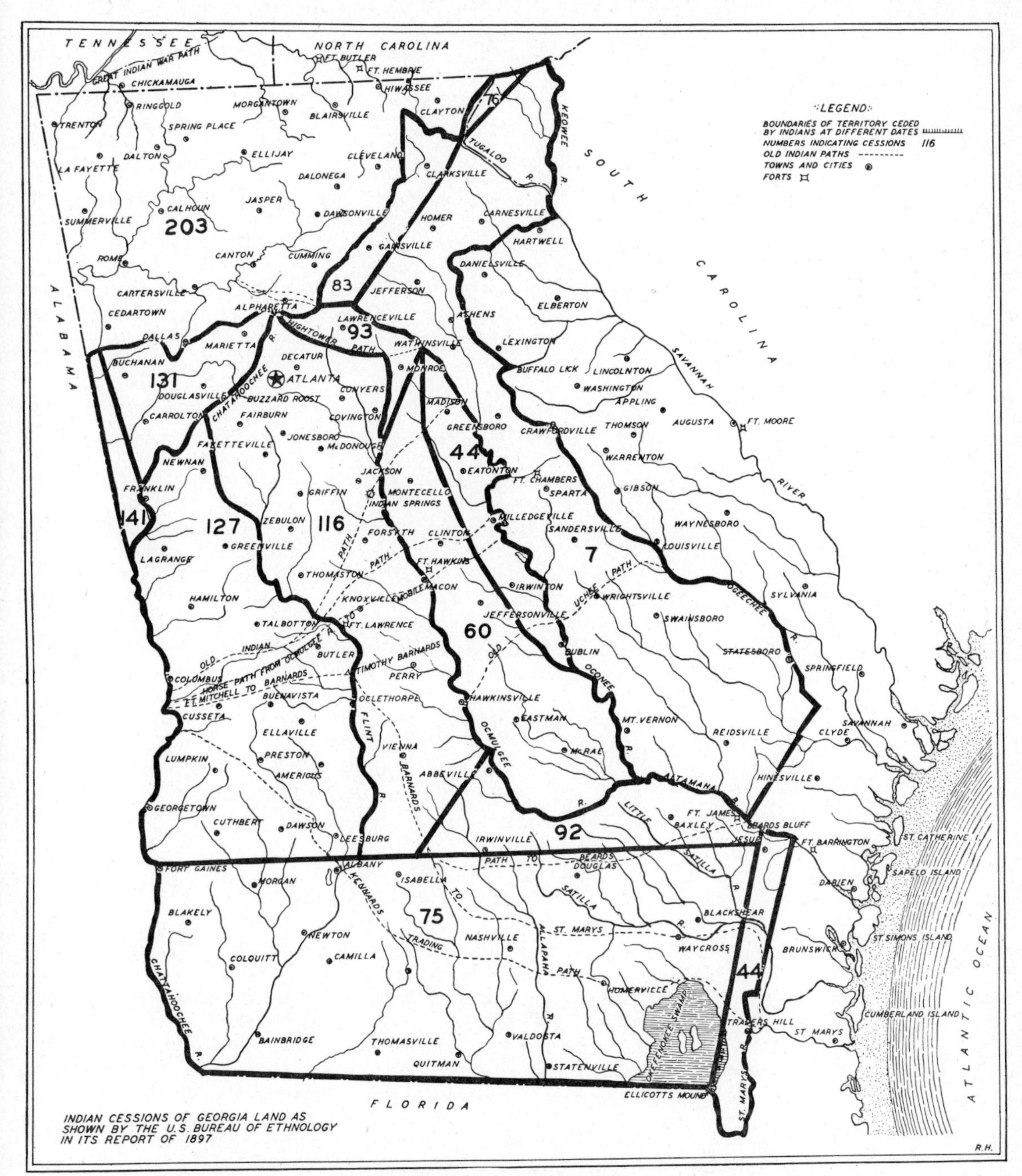


INDIAN CESSIONS OF GEORGIA LAND AS SHOWN BY THE U.S. BUREAU OF ETHNOLOGY IN ITS REPORT OF 1897

## THE DISTRICTS CEDED

**The districts ceded by the Georgia Indians at different times, from 1790 to 1835, are shown on the accompanying map. The map and the descriptions of the tracts ceded were taken from the eighteenth annual report of the United States Bureau of Ethnology. The descriptions by numbered districts follow, and the same numbers on the map show the locations of the different tracts. For convenience the numbers and dates of cessions are given here:**

## CESSIONS BY DATES AND NUMBERS

**1790—Tract 7 by Creek Indians.**
**1802—Tract 44 by Creek Indians.**
**1805—Tract 60 by Creek Indians.**
**1814—Tract 75 by Creek Indians.**
**1817—Tract 83 by Cherokee Indians.**
**1818—Tracts 92 and 93 by Creek Indians.**
**1821—Tract 116 by Creek Indians.**
**1825-26—Tract 131 by Creek Indians.**
**1827—Tract 141 by Creek Indians.**
**1835—Tract 203 by Cherokee Indians.**

country west of the Mississippi not within either of the states or territories and not possessed by the Choctaws or Cherokees. And the United States agree to purchase for them, if the same can be done upon reasonable terms, wherever they may select, a country whose extent shall in the opinion of the President be proportioned to their numbers.

### Cession of Tracts 141 and 131 by the Creeks.

1827—By the treaty concluded at the Creek Agency on November 15, 1827, the Creeks made the final cession of their land in Georgia, including the tract marked 141 on the map. The tract's limits were thus described:

The boundaries of the cession of January 24, 1826, not having comprised, as was expected, all the Creek lands within the limits of Georgia, the Creek nation now therefore cedes to the United States all the remaining land owned or claimed by the Creek nation not previously ceded, which on actual survey may be found to lie within the chartered limits of Georgia.

### Cession of Tract 203 by the Cherokees.

1835—By the treaty of December 29, 1835, at New Echota, Georgia, the Cherokees ceded to the United States the following:

The Cherokee nation cede to the United States all the lands owned, claimed or possessed by them east of the Mississippi River and agree to remove west of that river.

The Cherokees fearing that the land granted to them by the United States as described in the treaties of May 6, 1828, and February 14, 1833, will prove insufficient for the accommodation of their whole nation, the United States therefore agree to convey to the said Indians and their descendants by patent in fee simple, the following additional tract of land situated between the west line of the State of Missouri and the Osage Reservation, beginning at the southeast corner of the same and runs north along the east line of the Osage lands fifty miles to the northeast corner thereof; and thence east to the west line of the State of Missouri; thence with said line south fifty miles; thence west to the place of beginning, estimated to contain 800,000 acres. But it is expressly understood that if any of the lands assigned the Quapaws shall fall within the aforesaid bounds the same shall be reserved and excepted out of the lands above granted and a pro rata reduction shall be made in the price to be allowed to the United States for the same by the Cherokees, which price it is agreed shall be $500,000.

It is agreed that the military reservation at Fort Gibson shall be held by the United States, but should the United States abandon said post and have no further use for the same, it shall revert to the Cherokee nation.

The United States agree to extinguish for the benefit of the Cherokees the titles to the reservations within their country made in the Osage treaty of 1825 to certain half-breeds.

# CHAPTER III.

## *Spain in Georgia*

The Spanish period of Georgia history has not until recent years received the attention it deserved. This was due largely to the fact that Spanish records of the activities of Spanish explorers and missionaries were not accessible to or were unknown to those who wrote our histories. The mission buildings on the Georgia coast and remains of mining activities in the gold region of North Georgia were there to arrest attention and cause research, but little was known of Spanish activities in this State covering more than a century before the coming of Oglethorpe. At last the Spanish records have been studied by historians and a flood of light has been shed upon our early history. It is in order therefore, in a narrative of important events in Georgia history to give some attention to those times before taking up the history of the Colonial period. There is not space to present all the details here, but some account of the most important events is worthwhile.

**The Atlantic Coast Explored by de Ayllon and Gomez Between 1521 and 1526**—The voyages of Lucas Vasquez de Ayllon in 1521, 1525, and 1526, and that of Esteban Gomez in 1525, are important, because they appear to have explored the Atlantic Coast and to have taken possession of it in the name of the King of Spain, although the settlement made by de Ayllon ended in disaster and like DeSoto and DeLuna, a few years later, he suffered great hardship and lost his life in trying to extend Spain's territory in North America.

**Gomez Explores the Atlantic Coast**—The voyage down the Atlantic Coast by Esteban Gomez in 1525 has an important bearing on Spain's claim to primacy in North America.

The works of Herrera and Navarrete, and the map of the coast made in 1529 by Diego Ribero, a Portuguese in the service of Spain as Royal Cosmographer, show that Esteban Gomez, a Portuguese navigator, under orders from the Emperor Charles the Fifth of Spain, sailed from Corunna in the fall of 1524, or early in 1525, crossed the Atlantic Ocean and searched the coast of Labrador for a channel through which ships could reach the Orient by sailing west. Not finding the channel, he explored the coast and its bays and rivers from Cape Race to Florida, bringing with him Indians taken from the coast, and from Florida sailed to Cuba and thence to Spain.

The map of Ribero, copies of which are preserved at Weimar and Rome, records the discoveries of Gomez. From that map, and references to it by contemporaneous writers, it appears that Gomez saw and gave his own names to Massachusetts Bay, Cape Cod, Narragansett Bay, and the Connecticut, Hudson, and Delaware rivers.

It appears, as Justin Winsor says, that this voyage completed the exploration of the American coast from the Rio Grande to the Bay of Fundy. With the exploration of the coast by de Ayllon's ships about the same time, and their taking possession of the land in the name of the Spanish King, Spain seems to have laid the foundation for her claim to a large part of North America.

**De Ayllon's First Voyage**—In 1520 Lucas Vasquez de Ayllon, a native of Toledo, was at Hispaniola (Hayti), where Ovando, with whom he came from Spain, had made him alcalde of several towns and he had become one of the auditors of the island.

According to Herrera, he was well educated, a man of intelligence and virtuous according to the standard of the times, but unskilled in the arts of war. He was considered very rich, having received of Ovando four hundred Indians in payment of his salary, according to the custom of the times.

In 1520 de Ayllon sent a caravel from La Plata, in command of Francisco Gordillo as captain, and Alonzo Fernandez as pilot, with orders to sail northward until they reached the Continent.

Just before that another auditor of Hispaniola, Juan Ortiz de Matienzo, sent a caravel under Pedro de Quexos to hunt Caribs for slaves, a license for such slave-hunting raids having been issued in 1503.

De Quexos, failing to get any slaves, was returning to Hispaniola when he met de Ayllon's vessel. After conference, de Quexos joined Gordillo and sailed for the mainland, expecting to get a cargo of slaves there.

In June, 1521, after being driven about some time by rough weather, the two vessels reached mainland at the mouth of a large river in latitude about thirty-three degrees thirty minutes. That stream, supposed to have been the Cape Fear River, near Wilmington, they named John the Baptist, because they came to it on the feast day of that saint.

Twenty men were put ashore, but alarmed by the sight of ships, which appeared to them as sea monsters, and by the curious dress of the Spaniards, the Indians fled in terror. By hot pursuit, the Spaniards caught a man and woman, clothed them in doublet and hose and sent them after the others. This kind treatment reassured the Indians, whose chief sent men with provisions for the ships.

Taking possession of the country in the name of the King of Spain, the Spaniards explored the surrounding region and were entertained by the Indians with presents of food, skins, and pearls.

The Spaniards invited the Indians on their ships and when a hundred and fifty were aboard, sailed for Santo Domingo with the Indians as prisoners, intending to sell them as slaves.

On that return voyage, one of the vessels was lost and many of the Indians, on reaching land, sickened and died. De Ayllon condemned the seizure of the Indians and a commission, headed by Diego Columbus, ordered them freed and returned to their homes.

**De Ayllon's Second Voyage**—Returning to Spain in 1523, de Ayllon was accompanied by an Indian servant, Francisco Chicora, who had learned to speak Spanish, had a lively imagination, and regaled de Ayllon and the men at the Spanish court with marvelous accounts of giants and white men in his home country and told of nineteen fruitful islands and provinces. Oviedo and Peter Martyr met de Ayllon and Chicora at the court of Spain and gave some account of their wonderful stories of the New World.

The report evidently impressed Charles V, who made de Ayllon adelantado and governor, with the right to explore the Atlantic Coast eight hundred leagues in his own vessels.

He was to start in 1524 and make the exploration within three years, with exclusive rights of fishery, lands, gold, silver, and gems, of which one-tenth was reserved for the Emperor.

De Ayllon was to provide each ship with a chaplain, a doctor, a surgeon, and an apothecary, with the medicines necessary for the health of the crew. With the fleet the Emperor was to send his agent and treasurer, who was to supervise the administration of the province. De Ayllon was to promote agriculture and was authorized to buy prisoners held as slaves by the natives.

**Conversion of the Indians**—A remarkable part of the Emperor's instructions related to the conversion of the Indians to Christianity. It showed how the Spaniards combined religious zeal with thirst for gold. The Emperor said:

"And, whereas, our principal intent in the discovery of new lands is that the inhabitants and natives thereof, who are without the light or knowledge of faith, may be brought to understand the truths of our Holy Catholic faith, that they may come to a knowledge thereof and become Christians and be saved, and this is the chief motive that you are to bear and hold in this affair, and to this end it is proper that religious persons should accompany you, and, by these presents, I empower you to carry to the said land the religious whom you may judge necessary, and the vestments and other things needful for the observance of divine worship; and I command that whatever you shall thus expend in transporting the said religious, as well as in maintaining them and giving them what is needful, and in their support, and for the vestments and other articles required for the divine worship, shall be paid entirely from the rents and profits which in any manner shall belong to us in the said land."

In 1525 de Ayllon sent two caravels to the mainland under Pedro de Quexos, who explored the coast for two hundred and fifty leagues, took possession of the land in the name of the King of Spain, and returned to Santo Domingo in July, the same year.

This statement, taken from Herrera's account, indicates that de Quexos explored almost the whole Atlantic Coast of this country north of Georgia. As the most southerly point mentioned in either of de Ayllon's voyages was the mouth of the Pedee River, in South Carolina, in latitude thirty-three, the exploration of the coast for two hundred and fifty leagues north of that would reach the vicinity of New York.

De Quexos brought back several Indians to be trained as interpreters and also some gold, silver, and pearls, according to Oviedo.

**De Ayllon's Last Voyage**—In July, 1526, de Ayllon sailed from La Plata, on the northern coast of Hispaniola, with six ships and five hundred men and women from the West Indian Islands. De Quexos went with the expedition and it carried eighty-nine horses, a number of slaves, and three Dominican friars, notable among them Antonio Montesino, who had denounced the enslavement of Indians.

De Ayllon landed at the mouth of Cape Fear River, which he named Jordan for the captain of one of his ships. One of the vessels was lost with the provisions aboard, but the crew was saved. To replace the loss, de Ayllon built a boat with a mast and oars.

Some of the leaders of the expedition explored the interior and some followed the coast northward, looking for a strait which they imagined would lead to the Orient. The nineteen wonderful provinces told of by Francisco Chicora were not found, and he, with other Indian interpreters, deserted and went back to their tribes.

Proceeding south forty or forty-five leagues, de Ayllon came to a large river called Gualdape, supposed to have been the Pedee, in latitude thirty-three degrees, and there he founded the settlement of San Miguel de Gualdape. In that neighborhood, the Indians lived in huts or in communal houses fifteen or twenty feet wide and three hundred feet long, each of which sheltered three hundred persons.

On the nearby islands were the Indian mausoleums, built of stone, cemented with lime of sea shells. The bones of children stored there were kept separate from those of adults.

As winter approached, the cold was severe and many of the colonists became sick and died of exposure or starvation. De Ayllon grew sick and died on October 18, 1526, but before he died named his nephew, Johan Romirez for governor of the colony. Romirez being in Porto Rico, the command fell to Francisco Gomez.

A mutiny was started by two soldiers, Gines Doncel and Pedro de Bacan, who gathered the malcontents, arrested Gomez and other officers and ruled the colony roughly.

Some negro slaves set fire to Doncel's house, and, in the confusion, Doncel and Bacan were imprisoned and Gomez liberated. Bacan was executed, and his associates being prisoners, the colony sailed for Santo Domingo. The body of de Ayllon was buried at sea, and a number of the colonists froze to death on the voyage.

Seven years later, Biedma, a historian of the DeSoto expedition, learned at Silver Bluff, on the Savannah River, that little exploration of the interior had been made by members of de Ayllon's expedition who remained on the coast until his death.

**De Vaca Crosses the Continent**—Spain was the first to discover America and for a long time led in its exploration, conquest, and settlement. Taking the West Indies, Mexico, Peru, and Florida, DeSoto and Luna, sent by her, explored Georgia and Alabama; Cabeca de Vaca crossed the continent from Florida to Mexico, and Balboa discovered the Pacific Ocean.

The wonderful journey of Cabeca de Vaca in crossing the continent connected the eastern coast with the west and completed the pattern of Spain's exploration of North America from the Atlantic Coast to California. For that reason it is worth while here to notice briefly Cabeca de Vaca's epoch-making journey from Florida to Mexico.

De Vaca was treasurer and high sheriff of the expedition of Narvaez, directed against Florida and the South Atlantic Coast, which sailed from Spain on June 17, 1527, with six hundred soldiers and colonists, Franciscan friars, negro servants, and the wives of some of the men. Disaster ended that expedition. Narvaez and nearly all the others lost their lives at sea on the Gulf of Mexico, and others, in ships that were wrecked, reached the shore of the Gulf and were killed by the Indians.

De Vaca and a boatload of fifty men were cast upon the shore of an island on the coast of Louisiana or Texas. Others from another boat joined them later, and there were on the island at the end of 1528 some eighty Europeans. During the winter, all but fifteen perished from starvation and exposure. The survivors called the island, Malhado, or Misfortune.

Remaining on the island a year with the survivors, de Vaca was called on to cure sick natives, and the call was so urgent that he did his best. He said of it, in his report:

"Our method was to bless the sick by breathing upon them, reciting a Pater Noster and an Ave Maria, praying with all earnestness to God, our Lord, that he would give health and influence to make us some good return. In His clemency He willed that all those for whom we supplicated should tell the others that they were sound and in good health directly after we had made the sign of the Blessed Cross over them."

Escaping from the island after a year, de Vaca made his way farther west toward the Red River, where he lived some time with another tribe of Indians, and maintained himself by bartering sea shells for skins and other articles. Returning to the island of Malhado, he was joined by Oviedo and started west. After crossing four rivers, they overtook Dorantes and Costello, with a black Egyptian. They had been separated and were captured by Indians, who made slaves of them. De Vaca joined them and the four planned to escape when that tribe of Indians went to South Texas to eat the fig-like fruit of the prickly pear.

Failing to escape then, they were held prisoners by the Indians another year, and were cruelly treated, but on the return of the tribe to South Texas the second year they got away. Oviedo had left them.

When at last they reached South Texas again, Cabeca, Dorantes, and the Egyptian began their journey across Texas and Northern Mexico toward the Pacific Ocean.

The first evening of the journey they found Costello, who was living with another tribe of Indians, and they spent the night at an Indian village, where Costello performed a cure by making the sign of the cross, for which the Indians repaid him with meat and prickly pear fruit. Cold weather coming on, the Spaniards decided to remain there until the pear season returned next year, and, in the meantime, they were called on to perform cures.

Costello refused to do that in dangerous cases, and de Vaca yielded to the entreaty of the Indians and made some cures which gave the party great fame with the natives. The Spaniards remained there eight months, going naked in the daytime and covered with skins at night.

Taken south again when the pear season returned, they resumed their journey west, going from one tribe to another, and secured food by cures of afflicted Indians. Crossing Trinity River, they came to the River Brazos and reached an Indian village where they were received as children of the sun, with power to heal or destroy. At a village on the Colorado River, they were given a buffalo robe.

There they heard of the New Mexican Pueblos from Indians who showed them a copper bell, and said it came from a people dwelling in houses.

Crossing the southern part of the staked plains, the Spaniards finally reached the Rio Grande. Following up its course, they found the natives in permanent dwellings and heard of the Pueblos to the northward as people of great wealth with mantles of cotton.

They crossed Chihuaha, in the northern part of Mexico, and going through a pass of the Sierra Madre Mountains, came to settlements of more civilized people.

Those people lived in houses, had crops of corn, pumpkins, beans and grain, and wore cotton mantles. The women wore long cotton garments, with skirts of dressed deer skin reaching to the ground. The natives wore moccasins and washed their garments with the soapy root of the bayonet plant. For ornaments they wore emeralds and turquoises obtained from a country north of them. They had a sign language by which de Vaca and his companions could make themselves understood.

From the west side of the Sierra Madre Mountains, the Spaniards went through the Sonora Valley, rested awhile at a village, and going thence down the river they saw the buckle of a sword belt on the neck of an Indian, with a horseshoe fastened to it.

Seeing more and more evidences of the presence of white men, they passed through a fertile, beautiful, and well-watered country, where the towns were deserted by their inhabitants. They had fled from Spanish slave hunters, who raided that region, carrying away half the men and all the women and boys.

At last de Vaca's party met a Spanish party, consisting of Diego Alcatraz and twenty men, four of them on horseback, who were out on a slave-hunting raid, and Cabeca and his companions were escorted some distance by the raiders. They were received kindly by the alcalde of San Miguel, and came to Compostella, the capital of New Galicia, where Governor Guzman received them with great consideration and gave them some of his own clothes.

De Vaca's account of it says they were so accustomed to going without clothes that they could not wear any for some time and could not sleep anywhere but on the ground.

Finally, on Sunday, July 24, 1536, the four weary travelers reached the city of Mexico, where they were handsomely received by Antonio Mendoza, the vice-roy.

Sailing from Vera Cruz, Cabeca de Vaca reached the port of Lisbon on August 9, 1537. Reaching Spain, he was summoned to court and appeared before Charles V at Valladolid, where he made his report to the Emperor and presented him with a bison hide and some emeralds.

De Vaca asked for the governorship of Florida, but Charles the Fifth had given that to DeSoto three weeks before de Vaca reached Spain. Although he was the first European to cross the continent of North America and suffered great hardships in the service of Spain, de Vaca received little reward.

Three years after his return to Spain, he was sent to South America to conquer the Pariembos, a tribe of Paraguay Indians. There he spent most of his fortune and showed the energy and courage he had given to his adventure in North America, but enemies made charges against him and he was arrested and sent to Spain, where he was kept in prison for six years and then stripped of his titles and exiled to Africa.

## CHAPTER IV.

# *DeSoto's March Through Georgia*

The accounts we have of DeSoto's march through Georgia came from several sources, differing somewhat in detail, but agreeing in the main. They were written by Garcilaso de la Vega, Rodrigo Ranjel, a Portuguese, and Hernandez Biedma.

Garcilaso de la Vega, born at Cuzco, in 1537, was the son of a Spanish officer in the conquest of Peru, and his mother was the sister of the last Inca, Huayna Capac. As a boy in Peru, before going to Spain, he knew some of the men who later composed DeSoto's party in Georgia, and from one of them, on his return to Spain, received a narrative of the expedition. That narrative was corroborated by the journals of two other soldiers with DeSoto.

Rodrigo Ranjel was DeSoto's secretary and kept a diary of the events as the expedition moved along. Hernandez Biedma was the factor of the expedition. These accounts were corrective of each other where they differed, and on them the narrative which follows is based.

Hernando DeSoto's march through Georgia in the spring and summer of 1540, with six hundred Spanish cavaliers, priests and scribes, attended by servants, was the first exploration of the State by white men throughout its length so far as we have record. Although the expedition failed in its object of finding gold, it led to later expeditions which spent some time mining gold in North Georgia. Evidences of those mining operations were discovered in the early part of the Nineteenth Century, and led to gold mining on a larger scale. The establishment of the United States Mint at Dahlonegha was the result.

DeSoto was at that time in the flower of his age, of a fine presence, being a little above the medium height, and having an agreeable though somewhat swarthy face. He was a skillful horseman, dexterous in all warlike exercises, of strong constitution, fitted to endure hardships, and of ripe experience in the conduct of Indian campaigns. He was surrounded by stewards, ushers, equerries, pages, and all the glitter and pageant of the household of a rich nobleman, displaying the magnificent gifts the Inca Atahualpa had lavished upon him, for his manly and courteous address had endeared him to the royal captive. DeSoto was a companion of Pizarro in the conquest of Peru, and rose to the rank of lieutenant-general. For his services in that campaign, he received a large share of the gold taken from the Incas. His portion was valued at 180,000 gold crowns. Charles the Fifth of Spain and Germany gave him a commission to "Subdue and settle all the region from the River Palmas eastwardly to the Island of Florida."

HERNANDO DE SOTO

"For the purpose," said the King, "you will take from these, our kingdoms, and our said Indies, five hundred men, with the necessary arms, horses, munitions, and military stores; and that you will go hence from these, our kingdoms, to make the said conquest and settlement within a year first following, to be reckoned from the day of the date of these articles of authorization; and when you shall leave the Island of Cuba to go upon that enterprise, you will take the necessary subsistence for all that people during eighteen months, rather over than under that time, entirely at your cost and charges."

In this the King was not entirely unselfish, for he reserved for himself for the first six years one-tenth of all the gold to be taken from mines and one-fifth to be secured by barter or spoil during incursions. He also required half of the gold, silver, precious stones, and other articles of value which might be taken from sepulchres, temples, public places, or private hoards of the natives. To strengthen DeSoto in this enterprise, he was made governor of Cuba.

The success of Cortez in Mexico, and Pizarro in Peru, and the rich finds of gold in Peru had fired the imaginations and excited the cupidity of Spanish adventurers. The reports of wealth in Florida and the fabulous tales of the fountain of youth, which had lured Ponce de Leon to his death, caused a great number of the most ambitious young Spaniards to seek passage with DeSoto when he sailed for America.

From a much larger number, he selected six hundred young men of the best blood of Spain, inured to arms, well equipped and ready for any adventure. With them were twenty priests, several writers to record the events of the expedition, servants, two hundred and ten horses, arms, armor, and equipment for refining gold. Sailing from San Lucar, Spain, in 1538, he landed in Cuba, remaining there a year, and, with nine vessels and additional supplies, including a herd of swine, sailed for Florida, landing at Tampa Bay in May, 1539, in the province of an Indian chief called Ucita. A survivor of the Narvaez expedition, John Ortiz, who had been a captive for twelve years, was found in Ucita's tribe. He had been twice condemned to death and twice saved by the pleading of the chief's daughter, the unsung Pocahontas of the land of flowers. Ortiz had learned the Indian language and became DeSoto's interpreter, without whose aid he would probably have perished of starvation.

**Itinerary of DeSoto's March**—Itinerary of Hernando DeSoto, while marching through the territory of the modern State of Georgia, as contained in the *True Relation,* given by a fidalgo of Elvas:

Mar. 3, 1540—Left Anhaica (Tallahassee, Florida).
Mar. 7, 1540—Crossed a deep river (the Flint).
Mar. 9, 1540—Arrived at Capachiqui.
Mar. 21, 1540—Came to Toalli.
Mar. 24, 1540—Left Toalli.
Mar. 25, 1540—Arrived at Achese.
Apr. 1, 1540—Departed from Achese.
Apr. 4, 1540—Passed through the town of Altamaha.
Apr. 10, 1540—Arrived at Ocute.
Apr. 12, 1540—Left Ocute. Passed through a town whose lord was called Cofaqui, and came to the province of another lord named Patofa.
Apr. 14, 1540—Departed from Patofa.
Apr. 20, 1540—Lost in a pine barren. Six days consumed in fording two rivers and in the effort to find a way of escape.
Apr. 26, 1540—Set out for Aymay. Reached Aymay before nightfall.
Apr. 28, 1540—Departed for Cutifachiqui.

May 3, 1540—Left Cofitachiqui.
May 10, 1540—Arrived at Chelaque.
May 15, 1540—Arrived at Xualla.
May 20, 1540—Arrived at Guaxule.
May 22, 1540—Arrived at Conasauga.
June 5, 1540—Arrived at Chiaha.
July 1, 1540—Departed from Chiaha.

After wintering at the site of Tallahassee, DeSoto began his march through Georgia in March, 1540. Crossing the Ocmulgee River and passing the Indian town of Altamaha, he came to the town of Ocute on April 10th, where, according to the chroniclers of the march, he was met by Indians bearing presents from the Indian chief, consisting of rabbits, partridges, corn bread, turkeys, and dogs.

Having obtained from the chief four hundred burden bearers, he moved northward on the 12th of April. At Patofa he was hospitably entertained by the Indians, and as a reward for this hospitality, DeSoto levied on the chief a contribution of seven hundred burden bearers and four days' supply of corn.

During the next six days he marched northeasterly, coming into a pine barren, where he lost all trace of inhabitants and the Spaniards came near starving. After much hardship they reached a village on April 26th, and found food.

**An Indian Burned to Death**—Four Indians captured by the Spaniards refused to give information about native villages, and to encourage frankness, one of them was burned. The others then said that the province of Cofitachiqui was two days' journey distant and the queen of that province awaited the army in her chief town. One of the Indians was sent with a friendly message from DeSoto to the queen, with the announcement that he would speedily visit her. The town is supposed to have been at Silver Bluff, on the Savannah River, twenty-five miles below Augusta. When the Spaniards reached the river, four canoes came over with Indians, who brought an invitation to DeSoto to cross over and partake of the hospitality of the queen.

**A Beautiful Indian Queen**—A messenger returned with DeSoto's thanks, and very soon the queen came out of the village seated in a chair of state, which was borne by some of the principal men to the water's edge. She entered a canoe, the stern of which was sheltered by an awning, and reclined on cushions which lay in the bottom. The queen was accompanied by her chief men and other subjects in canoes. On landing, she approached DeSoto and spoke to him with courteous words of welcome.

The Spanish historian relates this incident of the Indian beauty:

"Drawing from over her head a string of pearls, she put it over DeSoto's neck in token of amity, and presented him with shawls and dressed skins, which constituted the clothing of the country. Finely formed, with great beauty and much grace and dignity, she made a deep impression on the Spaniards by her queenly conduct. She was the first female ruler DeSoto had met and he was so much moved by her generous welcome that he took from his finger a gold ring set with a ruby and put it on her finger."

Of the Indians, he says:

"The inhabitants, well proportioned and of a good countenance, were more civilized than all other peoples seen in the wide extended territory of Florida. They wore clothing and shoes. The country in the early springtime was beautiful and gave every indication of fertility. The temperature was delightful and the woods most attractive. The Spaniards were particularly gratified with the profusion of walnut and mulberry trees. To all but the governor, it seemed good to form a permanent settlement here."

Nearby were large vacant towns overgrown with grass, and the Spaniards were told that two years before their coming there had been a plague in the land and the inhabitants had moved away from these towns to escape its ravages. They left large stores of clothing, shawls made of thread from the bark of trees, colored feathers, and dressed deer skins. From the sepulchres the Spaniards took three hundred and fifty pounds of pearls, and figures of babies and birds made from irridescent shells.

**The Queen Mother**—Learning that the mother of the queen lived some leagues down the river and was a widow, DeSoto expressed a strong desire to see her. This was no doubt due to the fact that she was said to be the owner of many valuable pearls. The Indian queen sent messengers to her mother, asking her to come and meet DeSoto, but the old woman refused and reproved her daughter for the request. A gallant and handsome young Indian, who had formerly served the queen's mother, was given DeSoto as a guide, and he sent Juan de Anasco and thirty soldiers to find the old woman and bring her to Cofitachiqui.

**An Indian Martyr**—After several days of travel, while the soldiers rested for their noon meal, the young Indian guide, seated by himself on the ground, became very sad and thoughtful. He drew out the arrows from his quiver until he found one with a sharp flint point like a dagger. This he suddenly plunged into his throat and fell dead. The other Indians explained by saying that the young man was unwilling to disobey the queen or to offend the queen's mother, whom he had served, and chose death in preference to disloyalty and disgrace. Without a guide, the expedition failed, and the queen mother was never found.

DeSoto and his chief men visited Talimeco, the former chief town of the province, where there was a mausoleum containing many dead and a large store of pearls, of which the Spaniards took three hundred and fifty pounds.

**An Indian Temple**—The temple was one hundred steps long and forty broad, with walls high in proportion. The roof was ornamented with shells of different hues connected by strings of pearls. The doors were guarded by twelve gigantic statues made of wood and bearing clubs, maces, and axes, pointed with copper and flint. The inside walls were ornamented with statues under festoons of shells and pearls. On the benches at the foot of the walls were the coffins of the lords of the province and their families. Above them on the walls were statues of individuals entombed there. Intervening spaces on the walls were decorated with shields made of reeds woven together and ornamented with pearls. Around the temple was a magazine of eight halls filled with arms, pikes, maces, hammers, bows and arrows, oars, and shields, decorated with pearls and pointed with copper or flint. Pearls seem to have been valued as sacred to the memory of the dead and their removal by the Spaniards was a serious offense.

The Indian queen was so much incensed at the outrages perpetrated by the Spaniards on her people that she refused to furnish guides or burden bearers to DeSoto, and he placed her under guard and compelled her to accompany him on foot with her female attendants. In seven days they reached an Indian village where they got seven hundred turkeys. After two days' rest they went to Xualla and halted by a swift stream near the foot of a mountain. After two days' rest they pushed on through a rough mountainous country to Guasuli. From Guasuli they went to Chiaha, an Indian town supposed to have been on the site of Rome at the junction of the Etowah and Oostanaula rivers.

There they were entertained by the Indians from the 5th of June to the 1st of July, when they left for Alabama.

While at Chiaha, the Spaniards saw many pearls, and seeing their interest in these ornaments, the chief sent forty canoes down the river to fish for mussels. Fishing all night, they returned in the morning and placed mussel shells on the fire. The shells opened and the Indians ate the oysters and took out many pearls, which were discolored by the fire.

DeSoto asked the chief for thirty women for slaves, but by night the Indians fled with their women. DeSoto pursued, laying waste their fields, and found they had taken refuge on an island. Relenting, he sent them word that if they would return he would not molest their women. They did so and DeSoto left them on good terms, after the chief had presented him with a few slaves.

This ended DeSoto's march through Georgia. The disaster and death that awaited him on the Mississippi are known. Only a few survivors made their way to Mexico.

Survivors of DeSoto's expedition carried home stories of wealth and gold in Georgia and in 1560 a party of three hundred Spaniards, under DeLuna, went from Pensacola up into Georgia looking for gold. Either that or some other expedition of Spaniards started the gold mining in Nacoochee Valley and built the fort on the Cohutta Mountain, in Murray County.

Remains of the mining operation in Nacoochee Valley were discovered in 1834. The mountain and fort in Murray County were given the State by Hon. Ivan Allen and are a State park.

**DeSoto's Route Traced by Jones, Irving, Swanton and Others**—There has been some difference of opinion concerning the route of DeSoto in his march through Georgia. Colonel Charles C. Jones, in his history, said DeSoto went from Cofitachiqui, at Silver Bluff on the Savannah River, into Franklin County, and thence to the Nacoochee Valley, in White County. Resting there a short time, near Yonah Mountain, DeSoto proceeded west to the Conasauga River, in Murray County, Georgia, and thence down that stream and the Oostanaula to the Indian town of Chiaha, on the site of Rome, between the Etowah and Oostanaula rivers, where they join to form the Coosa. After resting there a month, DeSoto resumed his march, following the Coosa River into Alabama.

Theodore Irving, in his *Conquest of Florida by DeSoto,* published in 1851, after he had studied Spanish documents on the subject at Madrid, takes the same view, and the Spanish historians of DeSoto's expedition agree that in leaving Xualla, which Jones locates in Nacoochee Valley, DeSoto went westward sixty miles across a mountain region to the Conasauga River.

As the Conasauga River joins the Oostanaula below Murray County, and the Oostanaula leads to Rome, there seems strong reason to agree with Jones and Irving as to DeSoto's route through Georgia.

Theodore Irving was the son of Washington Irving, who spent much time in Spain, wrote the *Conquest of Grenada* and the *Life of Columbus,* and was later United States Minister to Spain.

Theodore says in his preface that he was greatly aided by his father in preparing his history of DeSoto's expedition.

That view of Jones and Irving was generally accepted for many years, and a suburb of Rome west of the Oostanaula was called DeSoto until it became a ward of the city of Rome.

In recent years some ethnologists have taken a different view, and a leader among them, Dr. John R. Swanton, of the United States Bureau of Ethnology, has made a special study of the subject, going over the ground carefully. By request, Dr. Swanton gave the following statement about DeSoto's route:

**Dr. Swanton's View of DeSoto's Route**—"It is generally conceded that DeSoto passed his first winter in America, the winter of 1539-40, near the present Tallahassee, Florida, *i. e.,* in the country of the Apalachee Indians. Although the chroniclers represent his course after breaking camp in the spring to have been northeast, I think that he first went slightly toward the northwest, crossing the Flint at or near Bainbridge. The Flint appears to be the only river corresponding to the one they had so much difficulty in passing.

I believe that he then went about north, but a trifle west through Decatur and Miller counties and then swung northeast, through Pine Island, in Dougherty County, recrossed the Flint somewhere between the present Lee and Worth or Lee and Crisp counties, and reached the Ocmulgee, in the then province of Altamaha, near Abbeville. He and his army were sent across that river by the chief of Altamaha, and, I believe, continued north along the east side of the Ocmulgee to Hawkinsville, or, possibly, as far as Westlake. Then I take them northeast, across the Oconee, at Carr Shoals, about six miles above Dublin, in Laurens County, the only place on the river below Milledgeville where the topography corresponds at all closely with the description of Rodrigo Ranjel, DeSoto's secretary, whose narrative is considered the most reliable. The trail which crossed here was later known as the Lower Uchee Path, and on the highlands just east of the ford there was an Indian settlement.

"On Saturday, April 17, 1540, according to Ranjel:

"They crossed a very large river, divided into two branches, wider than a long shot from an arquebuse. And the fords were very bad, with many flat stones, and the water came up to the stirrups, and, in places, to the saddle-pads. The current was very strong and none of the horsemen dared to take a foot soldier on the croup. The foot soldiers crossed the river further up, where it was deeper in this way. They made a line of thirty or forty men tied together, and so they crossed over supporting each other; and, although some were in much danger, it pleased God that none was drowned, for the horsemen helped them with their horses and gave them the butt of the lance or the tail of the horse, and in that way they all got out and passed the night on a hill. That day they lost many pigs of those which they had brought tame from Cuba, as they were carried down by the current. *(Narrative of DeSoto,* Bourne edition, volume 2, page 93.)

"Although the channel has been altered by Government engineers and most of the water has been deflected from the west side to the east, there were always two channels at Carr Shoals, there are stones in the river, and the strength of the current is particularly noteworthy at this spot. Finally, a high hill, suitable for camping, is within sight of the river on its eastern side (figure 73).

"I think Cofitachiqui was on the Savannah River at or near Silver Bluff From that noted town I believe they marched northwest on the watershed between the Savannah and Saluda rivers, and I feel that I have identified Towns Hill in the northwestern part of Oconee County, South Carolina, as the most probable site of Xualla, where Indian remains are constantly being unearthed (figure 74). Thence an Indian trail led across Burrell's Ford, and up through Horse Cove and Highlands and down to Franklin. There was another Indian trail from Franklin over Black Gap to the head of Shooting Creek and down the latter to the present Murphy. This is the trail I believe they followed, and I place Guasili at the Old Hiwassee site, at the mouth of Peachtree Creek, above Murphy. From this point I think they kept on along the north bank of Hiwassee to the mouth of Conasauga Creek, where they entered upon a well-known Indian trail running on southwest to the present site of Chattanooga and the towns on the Tennessee below.

"I can give you only roughly my reasons for laying out the route as above indicated. I have mentioned already the fact that Flint River is the only water course corresponding in volume to the one the Spaniards encountered three days out of their Apalachee headquarters. The Rio Grande, which they crossed later on, must have been again the Flint, as that was the only one that would justify the name. And what is equally important, perhaps even more important, is the fact that the next river, encountered in the province of Altamaha, was flowing east. That is conspicuously the case, as you know, with the Ocmulgee. I bring him up along the east side of the Ocmulgee instead of carrying him across to the Oconee at once, as some do, for two main reasons, or rather I should say for three: (1) It was a populous country, more populous than the remains along the Oconee would indicate; (2) they met a tribe called Ocute, which I have in Bulletin 73 identified with the Hitchiti, who lived upon the Ocmulgee when the whites found them again in the Seventeenth Century, and (3) if Cofitachiqui was on the Savannah River, as is almost universally believed, the distances check reasonably well only if we suppose they started eastward across country from the Ocmulgee. Cofitachiqui must be placed not far below the fall line of the Savannah, because a later explorer, Juan Pardo, states that on reaching it from the coast, deep marshes were encountered until they came to that point, shallow marshes there, and no marshes at all beyond."

Up to this point, Dr. Swanton seems correct, but the rest of his route is not so clear. He says:

"The rest of the route is established largely by arguing back from the Tennessee River. That this river, and not the Coosa, was the large river with many islands on which were towns is shown by the size of the river itself and relative absence of islands of sufficient size in the Coosa, by the fact that some tribes found by DeSoto on this river were on the Tennessee in 1700, and by the fact that a map drawn shortly after the return of DeSoto's men to Mexico, intended to show the results of his explorations, indicates clearly that the big river with the islands was distinct from the Coosa. Working back along the Tennessee we seem able to identify the place where 'they crossed by Canasoga' as the point where the great north-south war trail crossed the Hiwassee at the mouth of Conasauga Creek. And working back from that, we come to Old Hiwassee Town, at the mouth of Peachtree. There is every reason to think that Guasili is a corruption of Hiwassee (Ayuthwasi), plus the locative ending—li."

**The Contrary View**—The following statements, which Theodore Irving takes from the narratives of Garcilaso de la Vega and *The Gentleman* *of Elvas,* make it difficult to reconcile with the authentic narratives the route from Cofitachiqui through South Carolina and North Carolina into Tennessee as suggested by Dr. Swanton.

Theodore Irving says that when DeSoto left Cofitachequi on May 3, 1540, his route lay towards the north northwest, in the direction of the province of Coosa, which was said to be at the distance of twelve days' journey. He passed through the province of Achalague (Chelaque or Cherokee), which the Portuguese historian called the most wretched in Florida, inhabited by feeble, peaceful Indians almost naked and living on roots, herbs, and wild fowl. Passing through that region DeSoto came to Xualla, supposed to be in the Nacoochee Valley of White County, near Yonah Mountain.

*The Gentleman of Elvas* says that on leaving Xualla DeSoto went a day's march through a country covered with fields of corn and that he "had inclined his route to the westward, in search of the province of Quexale," where the territory of the princess of Cofitachiqui ended.

"During the next five days," says he, "they traversed a chain of easy mountains covered with oak and mulberry trees, with intervening valleys and irrigated by clear and rapid streams. These mountains were twenty leagues across and quite uninhabited."

At that point in the narrative, Theodore Irving has this footnote:

"Probably the termination of the Apalachian or Allegany range running through the northern part of Georgia. Martin, in his *History of Louisiana,* makes the Spaniards traverse the State of Tennessee, and even penetrate the State of Kentucky as far north as the thirty-seventh degree of north latitude. This supposition is evidently erroneous, as both the Portuguese and Spanish chroniclers state that from the province of Xualla, DeSoto struck in a westerly direction, and we find him in a few days on the banks of the River Conasauga.

"Belknap, volume I, page 189, suggests that the Spaniards crossed the mountains within the thirty-fifth degree of latitude.

"(The thirty-fifth degree is the northern boundary of Georgia.)"

After passing through these mountains, DeSoto reached the province of Gauxule, where he was met by an Indian chief with five hundred warriors, who received him cordially. The town of three hundred houses "stood in a pleasant spot bordered by small streams that took their rise on the adjacent mountains," and he rested there four days.

"The many streams that traverse this province soon mingled their waters and formed a grand powerful river."

In a footnote, Irving says: "Mr. McCulloch suggests that this river was the Etowah, which falls into the Coosa."

On the second day from Gauxule they reached the Conasauga River, and five days later the town of Chiaha, as the Portuguese historian called it.

The distance from the Indian town in Murray County on the Conasauga River through the watersheds of the Conasauga and Oostanaula to Rome is about sixty miles, which they traveled in five days, about the time it must have taken hundreds of men, most of them on foot, to march that far through a rough country with no roads but Indian trails.

The Indian town of Chiaha seems to have been on the site of Rome, between the Etowah and Oostanaula rivers. The island referred to in the narrative may have been the tongue of land between the rivers, or the island in the Etowah, about opposite the center of Rome.

## CHAPTER V.

# *De Luna's, Villafane's, Pardo's, and Boyano's Explorations*

**Expedition of Tristan De Luna**—The failure of DeSoto to find gold in Georgia, and the hardships and disaster attending his march, from which only a few survivors finally made their way to Mexico, did not discourage other attempts of the same kind, although, in the meantime, several parties of Spaniards suffered shipwreck and nearly all survivors were slain by the Indians when they reached the shore of the Gulf of Mexico.

In 1545 a vessel carrying several hundred persons was wrecked, and, of those reaching the shore, two hundred were slain by the natives, and others enslaved.

In 1553 a Spanish fleet, bound for Spain, laden with treasure and carrying 1,000 soldiers, merchants, women, children, and five Dominican monks, was wrecked on the Gulf Coast. Three hundred of them reached the shore, but most of them were slain by Indians or died of hardship. One wounded monk, Fray Marcos, was buried in the sand on the river bank, supposed to be near death from wounds received from the savages. Later, recovering consciousness, he arose and followed his comrades, but found them all dead, where they had been killed by the Indians. He was finally rescued by two friendly Indians, who carried him back to Tampico.

The next year a fleet of fifteen Spanish vessels was wrecked on the Atlantic Coast.

Philip the Second of Spain in 1558 decided on two expeditions, one to colonize Florida, and the other to reach Santa Elena, on the South Carolina coast. This was entrusted to de Velasco, viceroy of Mexico, who sent Guido de las Bazares with three vessels and sixty soldiers to reconnoiter the country. Bazares, sailing on September 3, 1558, from San Juan de Ulloa, landed on the Texas shore. Thence going southeastward, he passed the Alacranes Islands, north of Yucatan, and sailed for Florida, but was driven to the Mississippi coast by adverse winds and went thence to Mobile Bay. After some time in that vicinity, he returned to San Juan de Ulloa on the 14th of December.

CELTIC CROSS, AUGUSTA

**Erected by Colonial Dames Marking Site of Fort Augusta Between St. Paul's Church and Savannah River. One of Oglethorpe's Cannon Shown**

In the meantime, flattering reports of the country were received from the survivors of the expeditions of Narvaez and DeSoto, whose accounts of rich country near the Province of Coca (Coosa), in Northeast Alabama, made it easy to get volunteers for a new expedition of thirteen vessels, which sailed from Vera Cruz, where they had been attended by the viceroy, de Valesco, of Mexico. The expedition included fifteen hundred persons, soldiers, women, and children, servants, negro slaves, and a number of Florida Indians, with two hundred and forty horses. There were six companies of infantry and six of cavalry, and many of the officers commanding them were acquainted with the country. This was true also of a number of the soldiers, some of whom were survivors of DeSoto's expedition. Accompanying the party were three Dominican friars, one of whom, Bartalome Mathoes, had been a gunner with Pizarro's expedition in Peru. The captain-general of the fleet and governor of Florida, Tristan De Luna, was in charge of the expedition.

After a favorable voyage, but for a loss of one hundred horses, which died at sea, the expedition landed on the coast of Florida, near the Apalachicola River, on the 17th day of July, 1559.

The members of this expedition suffered great hardships and came near starving to death in their effort to reach Northeast Alabama, according to the account given by Woodbury Lowery, in his book, *The Spanish Settlements in the United States,* but Colonel Charles C. Jones says that in Nacoochee Valley proofs of occupancy by white men, supposed to have been members of De Luna's party in 1560, were found. On this subject, Colonel Jones says, referring to DeSoto's visit to the Nacoochee Valley:

"In this valley physical proofs of primitive occupancy are still extant, and metallic fragments of European manufacture have there been found confirmatory of the fact that many years prior to the settlement of this region by the whites, it had been visited by kindred peoples. We do not now allude to the remains of an ancient village—the cabins of which were made of logs hewn and notched by means of chopping axes—unearthed by Colonels Merriwether and Lumsden in Duke's Creek Valley in 1834, or to the traces of early mining in Valley River Valley and adjacent localities, where deep shafts passing through gneiss rock, their sides scarred by the impression of sharp tools, and windlasses of post oak with cranks and gudgeon holes, were observed; the trees growing above this old settlement and springing from the mouths and sides of these abandoned pits being not less than two hundred years old. These are to be referred to the labors of Tristan De Luna, who, in 1560, at the command of Luis de Velasco, came with three hundred Spanish soldiers into this region and spent the summer in eager and laborious search for gold."

**Spaniards Mining for Gold in Georgia**—There has been much interest in the discovery in 1834 of shafts and mining tools of European manufacture in the Nacoochee Valley of White County, Georgia. As that discovery was soon followed by the discovery of gold near Dahlonega, the rush of people to that part of the State and the establishment of a mint at Dahlonega by the United States Government, the identity of the men who began to mine for gold in North Georgia in the Sixteenth Century has been the subject of curious interest. Colonel Charles C. Jones had this to say about it:

"In recalling the instances of temporary occupancy, by Europeans, of limited portions of the territory at a later period conveyed to the trustees for establishing the colony of Georgia, it is proper that we should allude to mining operations conducted by the Spaniards at an early epoch among the auriferous mountains of Upper Georgia. Influenced by the representations made by the returned soldiers of DeSoto's expedition of the quantity of gold, silver, and pearls existent in the province of Coosa, Luis de Velasco dispatched his general, Tristan De Luna, to open communication with Coosa by the way of Pensacola Bay. Three hundred Spanish soldiers of this expedition, equipped with mining tools, penetrated to the valley of the Coosa and passed the summer of 1560 in Northern Georgia and the adjacent region. Juan Pardo was subsequently sent by Aviles, the first governor of Florida, to establish a fort at the foot of the mountains northwest of St. Augustine, in the province of the Chief Coaba. It would seem, therefore, that the Spaniards at this early period were acquainted with and endeavored to avail themselves of the gold deposits in Cherokee Georgia.

"The German traveler, Johannes Lederer, who visited North Carolina and Virginia in 1669 and 1670, and wrote in Latin an account of his adventures, asserts that the Spaniards were then working gold and silver mines in the Appalachian Mountains. He avers that he saw specimens of the ore in the possession of the natives, and that he brought back samples with him.

"In 1690, while journeying over the 'Apalathean Mountains' for inland discovery and trade with the Indians, James Moore was informed by them that the Spaniards were at work in mines within twenty miles of the place where he then was. The Indians described to him the bellows and furnaces used by them, and offered to convey him to the spot where their operations were being conducted. A difference between himself and his guides prevented his visiting these mines.

"Thus are we advised that the Spaniards, long before the advent of the English colonists, permeated the valleys of the Cherokees in earnest quest for gold. Thus are we enabled to account, with at least some degree of probability, for those traces of ancient mining observed and wondered at by the early settlers of Upper Georgia—operations of no mean significance, conducted by skilled hands and with metallic tools, which cannot properly be referred either to the red race or to the followers of DeSoto."

**Villafane Explores the Atlantic Coast**—Angel Villafane, having left the expedition of Tristan de Luna on the Gulf Coast, sailed to Havana, where a number of his party deserted. From there he went to Santa Elena (Port

Royal), which he reached on May 27, 1561, and took possession in the name of the King of Spain.

Finding no place suitable for a settlement, he sailed up the coast, and, on June 2nd, took possession of a great river. On the 8th, he went up a river, supposed to have been the Pedee. Alonzo Velasquez, the treasurer of the expedition, was sent up the coast and explored it as far as Cape Hatteras. Stormy weather put the ships in great peril, and Villafane sailed for Hispaniola, reaching there July 9th.

**Pardo and Boyano Explore Georgia**—Late in 1566 an expedition from the coast into the interior began. Captain Pardo left Santa Elena in November, going northwest, and is supposed to have followed the Combahee River.

About a hundred miles from Santa Elena, he built a fort and thence going west toward the Savannah River, came to the Indian town of Cofitachiqui, where DeSoto was entertained by an Indian queen in 1540. Continuing northward, he came to Broad River, and finding the mountains covered with snow, he built the fort of San Juan at an Indian village, left Boyano there with a few men and returned to Santa Elena.

A month later Pardo received a letter from Boyano, saying that he had won a victory over a host of Indians at Chisca, a place supposed to have been in North Georgia.

Boyano, who seems to have been a rival of Baron Mun Chausen, wrote that he had attacked an Indian stockade, captured it and killed 1,500 Indians. After that he reported his arrival at Chiaha and there waited for Pardo to join him.

Pardo, in 1567, marched across Georgia, following somewhat DeSoto's routes, reaching Cofitachiqui, on the Savannah River, and the fort of San Juan. Then he crossed mountains in Upper South Carolina and reëntered Georgia, near the head of the Savannah River.

After crossing the mountainous region, he reached Tocox, supposed to have been Toccoa. From there his party went to Chiaha. Leaving thirty men at Chiaha in a blockhouse and twelve men in a fort at Cauchi on the Upper Chattahoochee, Pardo returned to San Felipe.

It is said that the men Pardo left at Cauchi mined for gold in that region. Metal tools of European manufacture have been found in the Nacoochee Valley and deep shafts, with old trees growing from the mouths and sides of abandoned pits, indicate mining there before the English reached that part of Georgia.

**Pedro Menendez Marques Explores the Coast**—After the departure of Menendez de Aviles, in 1573, his nephew, Pedro Menendez Marques, was acting governor of Florida and explored the Atlantic Coast from latitude twenty-five degrees on the Florida coast to the Chesapeake Bay and mapped the rivers, ports, bays, bars, and shoals. He subdued the Indians of those regions and took possession of the territory in the name of the King of Spain.

# CHAPTER VI.

## *A Pen Picture of Georgia in 1562*

When Jean Ribault, with his colony of French Huguenots, visited the Georgia coast in 1562, he was so impressed with the beauty and fertility of the country that he gave the Georgia rivers flowing into the Atlantic the names of well known rivers in his own country. He gave his impression of the country in an account entitled *The True and Last Discovery of Florida by Captain Jean Ribault in the Year 1562.* The following extract in the quaint spelling of that time gives a pleasant picture of the Georgia coast as he saw it:

"It was a fayre coast, stretchyng of a great length, couered with an infinite number of high and fayre trees. The waters were boyling and roaring through the multitude of all kind of fish. The inhabitants were all naked and of a goodly stature, mightie, and as well shapen and proportioned of body as any people in ye world; very gentle, courteous, and of a good nature."

Entertained by the natives, in the delightful springtime, the Frenchmen were charmed with all they beheld. As they entered and viewed the country, they pronounced it "the fairest, fruitfullest, and pleasantest of all the world, abounding in hony, venison, wilde foule, forests, woods of all sorts, Palm trees, Cypresse, and Cedars, Bayes ye highest and greatest, with also the fayrest vines in all the world, with grapes according, which, without natural art and without man's helpe or trimming, will grow to toppes of Okes and other trees that be of a wonderful greatnesse, and height. And the sight of the faire medowes is a pleasure not able to be expressed with tongue: full of Hernes, Curlues, Bitters, Mallards, Egrepths, Wood-cocks, and all other kinds of small birds: with Harts, Hindes, Buckes, wilde Swine, and all other kindes of wilde beastes, as we perceiued well, both by their footing there, and also afterwardes in other places by their crie and roaring in the night.

"Also there be Conies and Hares: Silke Wormes in merueilous number, a great deale fairer and better than be our silk wormes. To be short, it is a thing vnspeakable to consider the things that bee seene there, and shal be founde more and more in this incomperable lande, which, neuer yet broken with plough yrons, bringeth forth al things according to his first nature wherewith the eternall God indued it."

# CHAPTER VII.

## *French Attempts to Colonize by Ribault and Laudonnière*

The activity of Spanish explorers aroused the adventurous spirits of other nations to action. Before the Edict of Nantes, some of the Huguenots sought to leave France in order to escape persecution, and Admiral Coligny, who was their friend, undertook to find a new home for them in America. He sent Jean Ribault to South Carolina in 1562 to establish a colony of Huguenots there, but that attempt at Port Royal failed.

Ribault left France with a party of Huguenots on February 18, 1562, and sailing across the Atlantic reached Florida at a point thirty degrees north latitude. Following the coast northward, they came to the River St. Johns, and called it May, for the month in which they saw it.

Sailing up the Georgia coast, Ribault gave French names to the rivers he passed, calling them the Seine, Loire, Charente, Garonne, Gironde, Belle, and Grande.

Coming to a broad river, and impressed with the width of the stream at its mouth, he called it Port Royal, which is still the name of that harbor. At Port Royal he built a fort, left a colony of twenty-eight men and left Albert Pierria in charge.

When Ribault had sailed up the coast some distance, he left for France, and the colony at Port Royal completed their fort and began to explore the country. They made friends with the Indians by bartering them iron articles and other merchandise for food.

Starting auspiciously, their enterprise came to grief when fire destroyed the house in which their provisions were kept. Dissension among them caused more trouble. Disappointed in their attempt to find gold in the interior, suffering from famine and resenting the harshness of Albert Pierria, they killed him and chose Nicolas Barre to succeed him in command.

Determined to return to France, they built a rough kind of vessel and embarked in it. Tossed by violent winds, the vessel drifted. Weakened by thirst and famine, some of them died, and, it is said by Parkman, that the survivors cast lots for a human sacrifice. Having eaten the victim, they lived to reach land and were rescued by an English vessel, by which some were carried to England and the rest to France.

**Laudonnière Builds Fort Caroline**—Two years later a French squadron of three ships sailed from France for America, in command of Rene de Laudonnière, a nobleman connected with the House of Chatillon, of which Admiral Coligny was the head.

On June 22, 1564, they reached Florida, and, on June 25th, anchored at the mouth of the River St. John's, which Ribault had named May. It seemed to Laudonnière a good place to establish a colony, as there was an abundance of food in the neighboring Indian towns. Exploring the coast farther, they returned to the place where they had anchored, and, going ashore, passed through a pine forest into a beautiful meadow through which a brook flowed.

There they rested on beds of boughs and leaves, in the shade of trees near the meadow and spent the night in sleep.

Rising at dawn, after singing a psalm, they began to build a fort near St. John's Bluff, overlooking the river. It was in the form of a triangle, with palisades of timber on the side next to the river. On the other sides the ramparts were protected by a ditch. At each angle there was a bastion, and in one of them a magazine. The enclosure was large enough for a parade ground inside, with buildings for storage and lodging. On the side toward the river, there was a house for Laudonnière and the officers.

In honor of Charles the Ninth, the reigning King of France, they named the fortification Fort Caroline. Not finding the great wealth they had heard of, but hard labor in a fort under a hot sun, with famine in prospect, the men were disappointed and discontented and rebelled against Laudonnière, whose life was in danger. The worst of the malcontents planned a piratical expedition in the West Indies, and by some kind of pressure got a commission from Laudonnière for a cruise. Forcing a pilot to go with them, they took two of the ships that brought them from France and sailed away on December 8, 1564. Starving and disconsolate, they returned in March, 1565, and sought pardon.

They were tried by court-martial, found guilty and four of the ringleaders were shot. That restored order at the fort.

There the Frenchmen remained for three years on the border of starvation, and the men were mere skin and bones.

In this condition, Laudonnière saw on the 3rd of August a great ship entering the mouth of the river, followed by three smaller ones. They proved to be the ships of Sir John Hawkins, the English privateer, who had taken a cargo of slaves from the coast of Guinea and had sold them to the Spaniards of Hispaniola.

Landing, Hawkins was received by Laudonnière and kindly sold him a ship to take his party to France, taking in payment the cannon of the fort and Laudonnière's note.

A short time later French ships came and with them Ribault, who brought a letter from Admiral Coligny, calling for Laudonnière's resignation and his return to France to answer charges made by discontented colonists against him. Ribault saw the falsity of the charges and urged Laudonnière to remain, but he declined to do so.

Before the French men could get away, another vessel came in sight. It was a great ship with cannon, and bore the flag of Spain.

The coming of Laudonnière and his establishment of Fort Caroline on the St. John's River, near the site of Jacksonville, had roused Spain to action, and Philip the Second sent Menendez de Aviles to eject the French intruders from Florida. Menendez came in September, 1565, and founded St. Augustine. He not only had a colony but soldiers, and by a quick, forced march surprised the Frenchmen at Fort Caroline, took the fort and put most of the occupants to death. Leaving a strong force of Spaniards to guard the fort, he began his advance into Georgia.

**The Massacre of Fort Caroline Avenged**—Dominique de Gourges, a soldier of noble birth, fighting in the war against Spain, was taken prisoner and put in chains by the Spaniards, who made him a galley slave. The galley was captured by the Turks, who kept him in the galley, but was later captured by Knights of Malta, who liberated de Gourges.

Bitter with resentment against Spain and resolved to avenge the insult of putting him in chains as a galley slave, he sold his property, borrowed money from a relative and equipped three ships for America, assembling on them one hundred soldiers, many of them, like himself, of noble birth, and eighty sailors who could be depended on to fight in case of need.

Sailing from France on August 21, 1567, and passing the African coast, the ships reached the West Indies and stopped on the coasts of Hispaniola and Cuba. Sailing for the mainland, they passed the Spanish fort of San Mateo, in the place where Fort Caroline had been. They were saluted by a Spanish vessel and de Gourges replied with the guns from his ship. He then passed on to the St. Mary's River, leaving the Spaniards ignorant of the fact that he was an enemy.

At St. Marys, de Gourges' ship anchored and as they did so the shore was alive with Indians, armed for war, as they hated the Spaniards, who had oppressed them, and thought the new arrivals were some of their enemies.

There was on one of the French ships a soldier who had been in Florida before and knew the Indians. When he made himself known to them and told them the new-comers were Frenchmen, the natives were delighted and friendly intercourse was at once established between de Gourges and the Indians. By his burning eloquence, de Gourges had set his own men on fire for a fight with the Spaniards and the Indians were ready to join in the attack on Fort San Mateo, where Menendez had slain Laudonnière's men a few years before. The Indian chief, Saturina, who had aided Laudonnière, sent runners out into the country to call more Indians, and by morning the woods were full of them.

De Gourges, having landed with his men, sat beside the Indian chief, with the red warriors ranged around them, in war paint and ready for the fray.

The Indians welcomed the opportunity for revenge on the Spaniards who had driven them from home, stolen their corn, killed their children, and abused their wives. Saturina spoke to them, fiercely denouncing the Spaniards.

The fort was taken by surprise in a fierce attack by the Frenchmen under de Gourges and the Indians under their leaders. The shock of the attack frightened many of the Spaniards and sixty of them tried to escape, but were caught between Indians and Frenchmen and every one of them killed. Other Spaniards in the fort fired on the attacking party with cannon and the Frenchmen replied with captured guns. A great host of Indians reënforced the attack of the Frenchmen, coming on with yells and war whoops, and the Spaniards remaining in the fort were terrified and tried to escape, but were caught between the Frenchmen and Indians and nearly all killed.

A few remaining as captives were hanged by de Gourges. When Menendez hanged the Frenchmen he took captive, he put over their bodies the inscription, "Not as Frenchmen, but as Lutherans."

De Gourges put over the bodies of the Spaniards he hanged the inscription, "Not as Spaniards, but as traitors, robbers and murderers."

# CHAPTER VIII.

## *Spanish Missions*

After Columbus, the brightest page in the history of Spain's adventures in America is that which tells of the heroic lives of her missionaries.

When Spain sent its best navigators and boldest spirits to the New World for exploration, conquest and settlement, it sent with them devoted missionaries to preach the gospel to the inhabitants and convert them to Christianity.

With every commission granted by the kings of Spain there was a command to the navigator to take with him pious men of God to preach to the Indians and convert them to the faith of the Catholic Church.

When the pope, Alexander Borgia, solemnly divided the world between Spain and Portugal, giving the Western Hemisphere to Spain, he laid this solemn duty upon Ferdinand and Isabella:

"Furthermore, I command you, in the virtue of holy obedience, to send to said lands honest, virtuous, and learned men, such as fear God, and are able to instruct the inhabitants in the Catholic faith and good manners, applying all their possible diligence in the premises."

The agreement made with the pope by Ferdinand and Isabella was carried out in good faith by them and their successors.

With this command, the pope gave the Spanish sovereigns power to select missionaries and bishops, and to reprove or recall them if necessary.

Later popes confirmed this grant of authority and the Spanish sovereigns exercised the power thus given them by sending, with the navigators and soldiers who went to America, missionaries of the different Catholic orders, mainly the Dominicans and Franciscans, who, by their vows, were relieved of the thirst for gold and devoted themselves earnestly and heroically to the work of converting the Indians and teaching them better ways of living.

To meet the expense of the missions, the pope authorized the kings of Spain to use the tithes of the new lands which would have been the property of the church. It is said that a few years later most of the revenue from this source was returned to the church in salaries, endowments, and other forms.

To carry out the purpose of such missions, sees of the Catholic Church were created for Cuba, Porto Rico, and Santo Domingo. In 1511 and in

1522, the see of Santiago de Cuba was created, with Florida and Georgia as parts of it. The see of Mexico, created in 1530, included Arizona and New Mexico. The see of Guadalajara, created in 1545, included the territory now in Texas, which no one but Cabeca de Vaca had visited.

**Spain's Missions in Georgia**—In the Sixteenth Century the Georgia coast was known to the Spaniards as the district of Guale, and part of the province of Florida.

Most Spanish settlements on the Georgia coast were on the islands, because the coast was low and marshy, but in the Seventeenth Century a line of missions extended across the southern part of Georgia from Cumberland Island to the Apalatchicolas River, and a mission was established on the Chattahoochee, at the village of Sabacola. Below the falls of the Chattahoochee, near Columbus, a Spanish fort was built in the territory of the Apalatchicolas or Lower Creeks. These Spanish missions were established by men sent out from Spanish headquarters at San Luis, on the site of Tallahassee, and the missionaries were protected by soldiers.

In establishing missions with Jesuit or Franciscan priests, protected by soldiers, Spain had two objects, the conversion of the Indians to Christianity, and the establishment of her title to Georgia soil by occupancy.

In 1564, Hernando Manrique de Rojas was sent from Cuba to remove what was left of the French colony placed at Santa Elena by Ribault, and while in that vicinity stopped at an Indian town called Guale, which is supposed to have been the same that Menendez visited two years later.

**Spanish Outposts in Guale**—In April, 1566, Pedro Menendez de Aviles, governor of Florida, went to Saint Catherine's Island and made a friend of its chief, Guale, for whom the Spaniards called Georgia the district of Guale. The adelantado left his nephew and another Spaniard with Guale as hostages and went north to Port Royal, where the mission of Santa Elena and the fort of San Felipe were established. He left one hundred and ten men with six cannon to guard the fort.

Returning later he planted a garrison of thirty soldiers on Saint Catherine's Island. That was the first of Spain's chain of settlements on the Georgia coast, and for a hundred years the Spaniards maintained those settlements, in spite of cruel Indian attacks in which some of the mission priests were killed and missions were destroyed.

Soon afterward Menendez built the fort of San Pedro on Cumberland Island and left one hundred soldiers with four cannon to protect it. A mission soon followed.

In 1569 and 1570, when Menendez de Aviles was in Spain, the Spanish settlements in Georgia, South Carolina, and Florida suffered severely. Supplies sent from Spain were not sufficient to maintain the population. They were threatened with starvation and tortured by the stings of mosquitoes.

The soldiers, suffering long without pay, rebelled and a number of them, led by Alas, the commander of Santa Elena and Guale, took possession of a ship and sailed to Spain. The garrison on Cumberland Island was reduced to fifty men, San Felipe was reduced, and Saint Catherine's Island was deserted. A fleet having come from Spain with supplies, Menendez sent relief to San Mateo and Santa Elena, and reënforced St. Augustine, San Mateo, and San Felipe with seven hundred and fifty soldiers, of whom one hundred and ninety-three went to San Felipe under Captain Pardo.

**Menendez de Aviles**—Menendez has been called a soldier of God, as well as a soldier of the King. His report to the Spanish King of the massacre of French prisoners at Fort Caroline is a strange mixture of fanatical zeal, with stony-hearted cruelty. In that letter he expressed great satisfaction, because he had put so many heretics to death. The men he called heretics were worshippers of the same God, but called themselves Lutherans.

He brought to America a number of Jesuit and Franciscan missionaries to teach the Indians Christianity, and many of them gave their lives in that work as victims of the Indians whom they were trying to convert. Among them were Domingo Augustin and Pedro Ruiz, who came to Guale in 1568, followed by Brother Domingo, a linguist who translated the catechism and wrote a grammar in the Yamassee language, which is said to have been the first grammar ever written in this country. Domingo died within a year of an epidemic.

The missionaries had to leave their missions in Guale and South Carolina during an Indian uprising in 1570, and several of them, led by Father Segura, went to Virginia, where they were killed by hostile Indians. The Jesuits having left Georgia, their places were taken by the Franciscans, whose work lasted for a century.

Menendez, after seven years in Florida, left America in 1572 for Spain, and did not return. There were then only two Spanish settlements on the Georgia coast on Cumberland, and Saint Catherine's islands. His nephew, Pedro Menendez Marques, took his place and had to deal with the Indian uprising in Santa Elena and Guale. An Indian chief of Guale, who had professed Christianity, was killed and the Spanish commander at Santa Elena went down to Guale and hanged the offenders. To avenge that, the Guale Indians killed nine Spaniards at Espogache, a village on the Altamaha. Among the victims was Pedro Menendez, the cross-eyed, another nephew of Menendez the First. It is said that these Indian uprisings were encouraged by French pirates, who raided the coast. Some of these lost their lives, notably Estrozi, head of a pirate band who was taken to St. Augustine and executed with twenty-two of his men. Captain Gil, another leader of French piracy, was killed in a battle on the St. John's River.

After this there was less trouble with Indians and French pirates, and a number of Franciscan missionaries came to Georgia, Santa Elena, and St.

Augustine. Some of them were slain, but the work did not stop and churches were built in the principal towns of Guale, at Tolomato, Tupique, on the island of Saint Catherine, and on Cumberland Island. Cumberland was a missionary center, where Franciscan missionaries did a great work. Baltasar Lopez and Alonso Reynoso were there. Reynoso is described as devout, gentle, zealous, tireless, and a hero in the service of the church.

**Spain's Rise and Decline**—Up to this time Spain was a formidable rival of England on the sea, and England was far behind her in the exploration and conquest of America. The crisis came when the Spanish armada threatened London in 1588. The failure of that daring stroke at England was the beginning of Spain's decline as a sea power, but for a long time she was ahead of England in America.

**Raids by Drake and Hawkins**—In the meantime, the Spanish settlements in the West Indies and Florida were harried by the raids of Sir Francis Drake and Sir John Hawkins, great sea rovers, called by some pirates, but encouraged by Queen Elizabeth.

Drake raided the Spanish settlements of the West Indies and took much booty. His attack and capture of St. Augustine resulted in the removal of the Spanish garrison from Santa Elena to St. Augustine in 1587, to fortify that place against further attack.

In 1595, Governor Avendano sent five more missionaries to Guale, and in seven towns on the Georgia coast old churches were repaired and new ones were built. The active leaders in the missionary work then were Fathers Chozas and Pareza, on Cumberland Island; Davila on Jekyll; Velascola, on St. Simons; Corpa, on the mainland at Tolomato, opposite Sapelo Island; Rodriguez, at Tupique, and Aunon and Badagoz, at Santa Catalina.

It is said that Father Chozas and Father Velascola made a trip of eight days on horseback to the Indian towns of Tama and Ocute, on the upper watershed of the Altamaha, and brought back enthusiastic reports from that region.

**Missionaries Massacred by Indians**—An Indian uprising led by Juan, a young chief of Tolomato, came suddenly in 1597, and a number of missionaries were slain. Father Corpa was killed and beheaded, and Fathers Rodriguez, Aunon, Badagoz and Velascola were put to death. Father Davila was wounded and held in captivity for a year.

Cumberland Island escaped the massacre. Its appeal for help, sent to St. Augustine, roused Governor Canzo, who arose from a sick bed and went to the relief of the missions with one hundred and fifty soldiers. The Indians fled before him and he destroyed their towns and cornfields. The Indians then submitted and Father Davila was released from captivity. A young man named Lucas, who confessed a part in the uprising, was hanged at St. Augustine. This vigorous action cowed the Indians, who were granted pardon and again supported the work at St. Augustine and the missions on the Georgia coast.

**Restoration of the Missions**—The missions on the Georgia coast were restored and Governor Canzo undertook to establish a colony in the interior of Georgia, at Tama. His successor visited the Guale town, and after another year, seven more missionaries came to Florida and Georgia. Father Juan de Capillas went to Cumberland; Pedro Delgado to the towns of Talaje and Espogache, and Pedro Ruiz to Santa Catalina. They worked to such good purpose that the bishop of Cuba, who visited Georgia that year, 1606, reported that he confirmed 1,070 Indians at four Georgia missions.

**Georgia a Bulwark to Florida**—The work of the Spanish missionaries not only made Christians of thousands of Indians, but built up in this State a wonderful support for the Spanish authorities at St. Augustine. Governor Canzo wrote to the King of Spain in 1602 concerning Guale:

"This province is of vast importance, for everything which may be undertaken regarding expansion and the conquest of the interior country. It is of great assistance to this presidio, because, besides supplying everything needed by way of food and sustenance, every time that I have sent to it for a number of Indians, either to work on the fortification or to cultivate and plant the fields, they have sent me or brought me all that I have requested. I pay them adequately for their labor, so that they are well content and grateful. And thus a great area of land is planted and a large quantity of maize and vegetables are harvested. If that province is not kept quiet and peaceful, this presidio will find itself in dire straits and necessity."

In 1612, Georgia was included in a new missionary province called Santa Elena, and a Georgia missionary, Juan de Capillas, went to Havana as head of the province. The same year twenty-four more missionaries came and others followed for one hundred years, coming thirty, forty, or fifty at a time.

**Missions on the Georgia Coast**—In 1655 there were these Spanish missions on the coast of Georgia:

Tolomato on the mainland;
San Pedro, on Cumberland Island;
San Buenaventura, on St. Simon's Island;
Santo Domingo, at Talaje, on the mainland;
San Jose, on Sapelo Island;
Santa Catalina, on Saint Catherine's Island;
Santa Maria, near St. Mary's River—a mission on St. Simon's Island.

The work of the missionaries was industrial, medical, and educational, as well as religious. They supervised the building of churches and houses and the clearing of fields; the instruction of children, solemnizing marriages, baptizing babies, giving medical aid to the sick and performing the last rites for the dying. Records had to be kept of all these activities and full reports were made to their superiors. To the Spanish governor at St. Augustine they had to report trouble among the Indians, or expected incursions from the French or English. They were community builders, as well as spiritual teachers, and served both church and state with great zeal and fidelity, not hesitating to risk their lives in doing so.

The establishment of an English colony at Jamestown, Virginia, in 1607, caused some apprehension in Georgia, as the Englishmen, led by John Smith, had followed the James River into the interior. Some Englishmen are said to have approached the Spanish border and the Indians of Guale reported strange men on horseback.

Spanish expeditions were sent out to investigate. In 1624, Governor Salinas, of Florida, sent soldiers and Indians into the interior of Georgia and South Carolina for one hundred and fifty leagues, but found no white men. It is said that another party of ten soldiers and sixty Guale Indians traveled into the interior of Georgia and Carolina four months and went two hundred leagues in 1628, but found no Englishmen. Rumors of white men continuing to come, a Spanish expedition as late as 1661 went across Georgia to the region of Apalachicola.

**Spanish Activities in Southern Georgia**—In the meantime, the Spaniards and their missionaries were active in Southern Georgia. Their missions to the Indians went as far as the present site of Valdosta, and a movement toward Apalachee was strengthened by the establishment of San Luis (on the site of Tallahassee) as new headquarters for the Spaniards.

It appears that the Apalachee Indians had asked for missionaries sometime before, but this request could not be answered until about 1633, when a leading missionary of St. Augustine went to them. Within twenty years there were nine missions in the Apalachee region within a few leagues of San Luis, and Indians went to them from Southwest Georgia.

**Commercial Activities**—Missionary activities in the Southwest were accompanied by commercial activities, supported by a garrison at San Luis. In 1639 the Apalachee region was a center of trade. Three or four thousand bushels of corn and beans were shipped to St. Augustine yearly, and a royal plantation was opened at Aucilla. With pirates in the Gulf, and English traders to the north, the military post of San Luis was made stronger and became a base for the advance up the Chattahoochee.

**Apalachee Missions in 1655**—The ten missions in the Apalachee region, with their distances in leagues from St. Augustine, are given as follows by Dr. John R. Swanton:

San Lorenzo de Apalache ..... 75
San Francisco de Apalache .... 77
La Concepcion de Apalache .... 77
San Josef de Apalache ....... 84
San Juan de Apalache ........ 86
San Pedro y San Pablo de Kpal (Kpal evidently for Apal) ... 87
San Cosme y San Damian ..... 90
San Luis de Apalache ........ 88
San Martin de Apalache ...... 87

In the list of 1680, one was added, *viz.:*

Coaba, en la cordillera de Apalache.

**Bishop Altamirano Visits Georgia in 1606**—The first visit of a Catholic bishop to the missions in Georgia occurred in 1606, when Bishop Juan de las Cabezas Altamirano came, inspected a number of missions and confirmed a large number of Indians.

There was some delay for the bishop in leaving Havana, as there was danger that he might be captured by pirates and held for a large ransom on his trip from Cuba to the mainland. He had that experience once before, and hearing that there were pirates in the West Indies, delayed his departure until he thought it was safe. Captain Mexia had instructions to convey the bishop from Santiago to St. Augustine, but the captain's ship was driven out of the harbor by a storm. Not to be deterred by this misfortune, Bishop Altamirano bought a captured English pirate ship, raised the Spanish flag upon it and sailed from Santiago in December, 1605, but, being delayed by bad weather, did not reach St. Augustine until the middle of March, 1606. The arrival of the Spanish bishop in a pirate's ship, flying the flag of Spain, was something unusual, but that did not deter the bishop from his intended course. With four soldiers and interpreters, Bishop Altamirano reached Cumberland Island on April 11, 1606, and they were met by Father Juan Baptista de Capilla and Dona Maria, the chieftainess of the island, her son, and five other chiefs. The bishop confirmed three hundred and eight persons, including these Indians. With them were Juan Quevedo, chief of San Juan; Don Antonio Gaspar, chief of Santo Domingo; Pedro Lopez, chief of Cotocoya, and Andres Lopez, chief of Puturibato.

Resting at Cumberland until April 18, the Bishop reached Talaje, on the Altamaha, and the Santo Domingo mission, where he was welcomed by Father Diego Delgado. Among those present were: Don Diego, head chief; his brother, Don Mateo, and the chiefs of the southern towns of Guale, Assao, Fasque, Alaje, Ofulo, Cascangue, and Tuque. These Indians entertained the bishop with the delicacies of an Indian dinner. Here two hundred and sixty-two Indians were confirmed.

Leaving there on April 24th, the bishop went to Tolomato, where he was received by the chiefs of Fasquiche, Zapala, Espogue, and Tuguepi. There he confirmed two hundred and eight Indians and baptized Chief Tuguepi, head of a warlike tribe which is said to have had part in the massacre of missionaries nine years before.

On April 30th, the bishop reached Saint Catherine's Island, where he was received by the natives with great enthusiasm, in which the head chief of Guale, Don Diego, and the chiefs of Oluste, Otafe, Oculeya, Unalcapa, Culopola, Talapo, and Chatufo participated. There the bishop confirmed two hundred and eighty-six natives.

VICTORY DRIVE, SAVANNAH

On May 9th, the bishop returned to Cumberland Island and was met by a large gathering of natives before whom he celebrated a thanksgiving mass. He was shocked at the poverty of the natives, as the children and some of the men were naked and the women were scantily clothed. The bishop had his assistants to search among his effects and improvise clothing for the congregation, and four hundred and eighty-two were confirmed.

On May 12, 1606, the bishop returned to St. Augustine. In Florida he confirmed many Indians, including their chiefs, and again he had to furnish clothing for some of the Indians.

Altogether on that trip of visitation, Bishop Altamirano had confirmed three hundred and seventy whites and 2,074 Indians. Of these, 1,652 were in what is now the State of Georgia, besides four hundred and eighty-two others, mostly from Nassau County, Florida. Altogether in Florida he confirmed nine hundred and eighty-one.

**Effect of the Mission Work**—The effect of more than a century of mission work in Georgia was very great, and though the Indians were not entirely educated away from their savage ideas, and repeatedly were guilty of bloody attacks on the Spaniards, the English or other Indians, thousands of them were converted to Christianity. A statement, based on Spanish records by Lowery and restated by Dr. John R. Swanton, in his *Early History of the Creek Indians,* gives this information:

"Governor Canzo estimated about 1,200 Christians in the four vistas of San Pedro, San Antonio, San Juan, and Nombre de Dios. Pedro Ruiz seems to have been the missionary at San Pedro in 1604. In 1606 these various missions, along with those in the province of Guale, were visited by the bishop of Cuba, who confirmed 2,075 Indians and three hundred and seventy Spaniards. Letters of Alonso de Panaranda and Francisco Pareja, of November 20, 1607, complain of attacks made by wild Indians on those who had been Christianized. They state that between November, 1606, and October, 1607, 1,000 Indians had been Christianized, and that in all there were over 6,000 Indians. In 1608, Governor Ibarra claims that 4,000 Indians had been converted in a year and a half and that 1,000 more were under instruction by the missionaries. He says that the church in San Pedro was as big as that in St. Augustine; that it had cost the Indians more than three hundred ducats, and had they not worked on it themselves, it would have cost them more than 2,000 ducats. In 1609, the chief of Timucua (Utina), with his heir and leading men of his tribe, were baptized in St. Augustine; and later we are told that twenty-eight Timucua and Apalachee chiefs begged for baptism. A letter from the missionaries, dated January 17, 1617, informs us, however, that in the preceding four years more than half of the Indians had died of pestilence. Yet they claim 8,000 Christianized Indians still living. It is stated that many missionaries died of the pest in 1649 and 1650; yet, in the latter year, there were seventy in Florida."

After the establishment of the Spanish military post at San Luis (on the site of Tallahassee), mission work in that region increased, but a few years later the Apalachee Indians were almost exterminated by the bloody contest between the Englishmen and Spaniards in the Chattahoochee region, with Creek Indians fighting with the English and the Apalachees fighting with the Spaniards.

**Ruins of Spanish Missions on the Georgia Coast**—Dr. John T. Lanning, of Duke University, who has made a very careful study of the Spanish records of missions on the Georgia coast and also the ruins of those missions, says, in his recent book on *Spanish Missions in Georgia,* that almost a score of the mission type ruins have been located from Port Royal to St. Marys, but only half a dozen have been authenticated by Spanish records. The ruins are there to speak for themselves, and the weight of authority seems to be that they are ruins of Spanish missions, although recently the idea has been suggested that they are not mission ruins, but the remains of sugar mills.

That idea is not convincing, because the sugar product of the Georgia coast at that early period was far too small to have justified the expenditure in erecting costly buildings and groups of buildings. That they were costly can be seen from the fact that the tabby structures, composed of sand and the lime obtained from burnt shells, practically amounted to cement.

Dr. Lanning says that only nine of the twenty missions represented by known ruins were ever in active service at the same time. This is explained by the fact that practically all of the missions were destroyed by the Indians in the uprising of 1597 and some at other times.

**Authenticated Ruins of Missions**—THE TOLOMATO MISSION: Founded by Fray Pedro in 1595 and rebuilt by Fray Diego Delgado in 1605, with additions between 1605 and 1680. The ruins are on the Mansfield place or "The Thicket," property of Lewis Crum, five miles northeast of Darien, on Pease Creek, in McIntosh County.

This mission is said to have once included seven buildings, *viz.:* A chapel and central mission building; a small fortress for defense; a circular well and monastery buildings, used at different periods as cells, dungeons, and barracks, as there was once a garrison just across Doboy Sound, on Sapelo Island. A wire fence now surrounds the chapel.

This mission was destroyed in the Indian insurrection of 1597, but was rebuilt in 1605 at the village of Espogache. Twenty Indian chiefs, including those of Espogache and Tupique, attended the rededication of the mission church. Their presence caused the Tolomato mission to be confused with that of Tupique. About the middle of the Seventeenth Century, the Tolomato mission became the mission center from St. Simon's to Saint Catherine's Island.

THE TUPIQUE MISSION was located in the northeastern part of McIntosh County. It was destroyed by the Indians in 1597, and the chief of Tupique then went to the Tolomato mission to worship. That caused the confusion of the Tolomato and Tupique missions.

THE ESPOGACHE MISSION overlooked Doboy Sound and commanded a view of the ocean between Sapelo and Wolf islands.

THE SANTO DOMINGO MISSION: Ruins of the mission of Santo Domingo de Talaje are fifteen miles north of Brunswick, on the south bank of the Altamaha River. This mission was built just before the visit of Governor Ibarra in 1604, and was dedicated by Father Pedro Ruiz on November 1. When Governor Ibarra's ship entered the mouth of the "Talaxe" River, the chief, Don Domingo, met him and attended mass the next day.

Santo Domingo was the center of the missions of St. Simons and Sapelo Islands, and the Tolomato mission.

The ruins of the Santo Domingo mission remain on the bank of the Altamaha River, on the property of Cator Woolford, of Atlanta, who recently conveyed the land to the State of Georgia upon the State's agreement to preserve the ruins, which include an octagonal structure supposed to have been a presidio or fort for the defense of the mission, besides a chapel and monastic buildings.

THE MISSION OF SAN JOSE DE ZAPALA: On Sapelo Island are the ruins of the mission of San Jose de Zapala, built as a "visita" by Fray Diego Delgado about 1605. From this mission he drew converts for confirmation by Bishop Altamirano in 1606. Among them was the chief of Zapala. In 1655 this mission was raised from the status of a "visita" to that of a "doctrina."

Howard E. Coffin, who owns Sapelo Island, has built a house over the ruins of the Zapala mission, but has preserved the original walls.

With these ruins are the remains of an octagonal building for a presidio, said to have been built by Governor Cabrera's order in 1680, to protect Captain Francisco Feuntes and his men when they retired to Sapelo from Saint Catherine's.

SANTA MARIA MISSION: The Santa Maria mission, on Amelia Island, was the center of religious work among the Timucua Indians, whose headquarters are said to have been at the village of Tlathlothaguphta, on the bank of the St. Mary's River.

Governor Menendez de Aviles is said to have built a chapel here in 1566, and Fathers Francisco Pareja, Pedro Fernandez Chozas, and Baltazar Lopez are said to have been interested in the work there. Like other missions, it was destroyed in the Indian uprising of 1597, but was rebuilt later. Governor Cabrera is said to have sent a priest there in 1606, but the permanent tabby structure was not begun until 1615 or 1616.

CUMBERLAND ISLAND MISSION: The San Pedro mission on Cumberland Island was an important one until the Spaniards withdrew from that island in 1597, at the time of the Indian insurrection. The church there was ruined, but Governor Canzo had a wooden church built there, and Father Juan Baptista Capilla was assigned to that work.

St. Marys a Central Mission: Professor John T. Lanning says:

"The best preserved mission-type ruins in Georgia, the square detached columns, and the perfectly preserved two-story wall—seventy-five by one hundred and fifty feet—with thirty-four small windows intact, now stand at their full height in Camden County, near St. Marys, Georgia, the hunting preserve of James C. Wilson, of Louisville and New York.

"Growing up around these beautiful ruins, so gaunt and redolent of a rich history, are many healthy trees—a virgin forest of rich tropical vegetation—primordial testimony of the antiquity of the ruins.

"Here more than anywhere else nature has conspired to impress upon us the scale, extensiveness, and age of the coastal missions; but the relative security of the South—far from the Yamassees and the English—permitted the Spaniards to place special stress upon this mission and to keep it in a good state of repair, although the marks of the English and Indian attacks long remained upon it. The physical evidence, as well as many other facts, point to this as a central mission of no mean proportions during the last fifty years of Georgia's mission history."

Santa Catalina and Other Missions: The mission of Santa Catalina de Guale, on Saint Catherine's Island, one of the first established, was burned by Indians in 1597, and rebuilt in 1604.

There were other missions on Saint Catherine's and Ossabaw islands, which apparently were offshoots of the original Saint Catherine's mission. Santa Catalina was not only the first of the Georgia missions, but the most important in Guale when the English came.

Saint Catherine's Island is owned by Mrs. C. M. Keyes, of New York, and Ossabaw is the property of Dr. H. M. Torrey, of Detroit.

It is believed that on St. Simon's Island the ruins of the missions of Assao and Ocotonico may be found; Assao near the ruins of Fort Frederica, and Ocotonico between the lighthouse and Frederica River. Another may be between Frederica River and Hampton River, near Butler's Point.

# CHAPTER IX.

## *Bloody Contest for Western Georgia*

There are three accounts, from English, French, and Spanish sources, of the bloody war in 1702 and 1703 and 1704, between the English colonists and Creek Indians on one side and the Spaniards and Apalachee Indians on the other. These bloody conflicts decided the long contests between England and Spain for possession of Western Georgia, then known as Apalachia. The following extracts are from Dr. Swanton's *Early History of the Creek Indians:*

"The first encounter on a large scale between the English and the allies on the one hand and the Apalachee and Spaniards took place in the following manner, as related by an English chronicler:

"In 1702, before Queen Anne's declaration of war was known in these parts, the Spaniards formed another design to fall upon our settlements by land, at the head of nine hundred Apalachee Indians from thence. The Creek Indians, in friendship with this province, coming at a knowledge of it, sensible of the dangers approaching, acquainted our traders, then in the nation with it, when this army was actually on their march coming down that way. The traders, having thereupon encouraged the Creeks to get together an army of five hundred men, headed the same, and went out to meet the other. Both armies met in an evening on the side of Flint River, a branch of the Chatahoochee (Chattahoochee). In the morning, just before break of day (when Indians are accustomed to make their attacks), the Creeks stirring up their fires drew back at a little distance, leaving their blankets by the fires in the very same order as they had slept. Immediately after the Spaniards and Apalachees (as was expected) coming on to attack them, fired and run in upon the blankets. Thereupon the Creeks rushing forth fell on them, killed and took the greatest part, and entirely routed them. To this stratagem was owing the defeat of the then intended design."

Shortly after this affair, in the winter of 1703-04, occurred the great Apalachee disaster, the invasion of Apalachia by Colonel Moore with a body of fifty volunteers from South Carolina and 1,000 Creek auxiliaries, and the almost complete breaking up of the Apalachee nation.

A graphic account of that great tragedy is given in Colonel Moore's letter to the governor of South Carolina. The letter follows:

"To the Governor of Carolina:—May it please your honour to accept of this short narrative of what I, with the army under my command, have been doing since my departure from the Ockomulgee, on the 19th (there is evidently a mistake in this, which should be the 9th instead of 19th) of December (1703).

"On the 14th of December we came to a town, and strong and almost regular fort, about sun rising, called Ayaville. At our first approach the Indians in it fired and shot arrows at us briskly; from which we sheltered ourselves under the side of a great mud-walled house till we could take a view of the fort, and consider the best way of assaulting it; which we concluded to be, by breaking the church door, which made a part of the fort, with axes. I no sooner proposed this, but my men readily undertook it; ran up to it briskly (the enemy at the same time shooting at them), they were beaten off without effecting it, and fourteen white men wounded. Two hours after that we thought fit to attempt the burning of the church, which we did, three or four Indians assisting us. The Indians obstinately defending themselves, killed us two men, *viz.*, Francis Plowden and Thomas Dale. After we were in their fort, a fryar, the only white in it, came forth and begged mercy. In this we took about twenty-six men alive, and fifty-eight women and children. The Indians took about as many more of each sort. The fryar told us we killed, in the storms of the fort, twenty-five men.

"The next morning the captain of St. Lewis Fort, with twenty-three men and four hundred Indians, came to fight us, which we did; beat him, took him and eight of his men prisoners; and, as the Indians, which say it, told us, killed five or six whites. We have a particular account from our Indians of one hundred and sixty-eight Indian men killed and taken in the fight; but the Apalatchia Indians say they lost two hundred, which we have reason to believe to be the least. Captain John Bellinger, fighting bravely at the head of our men, was killed at my foot. Captain Fox dyed of a wound given him at the first storming of the fort. Two days after, I sent to the cassique of the Ibitachka, who, with one hundred and thirty men, was in his strong and well-made fort, to come and make his peace with me, the which he did, and compounded for it with his church's plate, and ten horses laden with provisions. After this, I marched through five towns, which had all strong forts, and defences against small arms.

"They all submitted and surrendered their forts to me without condition. I have now in my company all the whole people of three towns, and the great part of four more. We have totally destroyed all the people of four towns; so that we have left of the Apalatchia but that one town which compounded with one part of St. Lewis; and the people of one town which ran away altogether; their town, church, and fort, we burnt. The people of St. Lewis come to me every night. I expect and have advice that the town which compounded with me are coming after me. The waiting for these people makes my marches slow; for I am willing to bring away with me, free, as many of the Indians as I can, this being the address of the commons to your honour to order it so. This will make my men's part of plunder (which otherwise might have been one hundred pounds to a man) but small. But I hope with your honour's assistance to find a way to gratifie them for their loss of blood. I never see or hear of a stouter or braver thing done, than the storming of the fort. It hath regained the reputation we seemed to have lost under the conduct of Robert Macken, the Indians now having a mighty value for the whites. Apalachia is now reduced to so feeble and low a condition that it can neither support St. Augustine with provisions, nor distrust, endamage or frighten us; our Indians living between the Apalachia and the French. In short, we have made Carolina as safe as the conquest of Apalachia can make it.

"If I had not so many men wounded in our first attempt I had assaulted St. Lewis Fort, in which is about twenty-eight or thirty men, and twenty of these came thither from Pensacola to buy provisions the first night after I took the first fort.

"On Sabbath, the 23rd instant, I came out of Apalachia, and am now about thirty miles on my way home; but do not expect to reach it before the middle of March, notwithstanding my horses will not be able to carry me to the Cherraque's Mountain. I have had a tedious duty, and uneasy journey; and though I have no reason to fear any harm from the enemy, through the difference between the whites, and between Indians and Indians, bad way and false alarms, I do labour under hourly uneasiness. The number of free Apalachia Indians that are now under my protection, and bound with me to Carolina, are 1,300, and one hundred slaves. The Indians under my command killed and took prisoners on the plantations, whilst we stormed the fort, as many Indians as we and they took and killed in the fort.

"Dated in the wood, fifty miles north and east of Apalachia."

**A Spanish Account**—"An account of this from the Spanish side is contained in a letter to the King, written by Governor Don Jose de Juniga, March 30, 1704, though there is a discrepancy in the dates, which difference in calendar does not seem fully to account for. The mention of Guale is evidently a mistake; probably Ayaville is intended. He says:

"After the late siege of St. Augustine the enemy invaded San Jose and San Francisco, destroying everything in their path, killing many Indians and carrying with them over five hundred prisoners.

"They returned afterward, accompanied by the English, who laid siege to this fort and invaded the province of Apalachee, destroying all the lands. They then assaulted Ayaville, on the 25th of January of the present year, which was vigorously defended by the Indians and the clergyman, Fray Angel de Miranda, who bravely defended the position, fighting from early in the morning until two o'clock in the afternoon, when their ammunition was exhausted. The enemy then advanced through the passage adjoining the church, which they set on fire, gaining possession of the passage.

"On the 26th I sent my lieutenant, Juan Ruiz, with thirty Spanish soldiers mounted and four hundred Indians. They attacked the enemy, inflicting a loss upon them of seven Englishmen and about one hundred Indians killed, besides others that were killed by Fray Miranda and his Indians. But our men, having run out of ammunition, they were in their turn finally defeated. My lieutenant was wounded by a shot that knocked him down from the horse, and the clergyman, Fray Juan de Parga, together with two soldiers were killed. The rest of the force withdrew, leaving in the hands of the enemy, my lieutenant, eight soldiers, and a few Indians as prisoners, whom the infidels treated in the most cruel and barbarous manner. After having bound the unfortunate Indian prisoners by the hands and feet to a stake, they set fire to them, when they were burned up alive. This horrible sight was witnessed by my lieutenant and soldiers, who naked, were tied up in the stocks. Only Fray Angel de Miranda was free.

"The affliction of the clergymen is great, and they have written to me and to their prelate urging that they be moved away from the danger that threatens them.

"The enemy released the clergyman, the lieutenant, and four soldiers, but with the understanding that each one was to pay a ransom of four hundred dollars, five cows and five horses. But the captain whom my lieutenant had left in his place, in charge of the defence of the strong house at San Luis, sent word to the English governor that he would not send him anything. Finally, sir, the governor withdrew with his forces without attacking the strong house, but not before he had succeeded in destroying five settlements, carrying with him the Indians of two of them, together with all the cattle, horses, and everything else that they could carry. The Indians that abandoned their settlements and went away with the enemy numbered about six hundred.

"The enemy carried away the arms, shotguns, pistols, and horses, and with flags of peace marched upon the strong house at old San Luis in order to ill treat the captain that was stationed there."

Dr. Swanton adds:

"The only satisfactory French account is contained in a letter written by Bienville to his government. This also contains the best statements relative to the settlement of a part of the Apalachee refugees near Mobile. I venture to translate it as follows:

"The Apalachee have been entirely destroyed by the English and the savages. They made prisoners thirty-two Spaniards, who formed a garrison there, besides which they had seventeen burned, including three Franciscan fathers (Peres Cordelliers), and have killed and made prisoners six or seven thousand Apalachee, the tribe which inhabited this country, and have killed more than 6,000 head of cattle and other domestic animals, such as horses and sheep. The Spaniards have burned the little fortress which they had there and have all retired to St. Augustine. Of all the Apalachee savages there have escaped only four hundred persons who have taken refuge in our river and have asked my permission to sow there and establish a village."

# CHAPTER X.

## *Spain's Claim to Georgia and the Atlantic Coast*

Antonio de Arredondo, the Spanish captain of engineers who had built the fortifications at St. Augustine and was chief of staff of the great Spanish fleet which sailed from Havana in the summer of 1742 and attacked St. Simons Island, wrote at Havana before that expedition started a statement of Spain's claim to the land of Georgia. It is an elaborate argument, which covers many pages, and is interesting because of its statement of facts or alleged facts concerning Spanish exploration of the Atlantic Coast of America as far as the Chesapeake Bay and the settlements in the form of Spanish missions protected by soldiers which were established on the Georgia coast and in the Chattahoochee Valley in the Sixteenth Century.

In his argument Arredondo makes these points:

America was discovered in 1492 by Columbus, under the auspices and at the expense of Ferdinand and Isabella.

Voyages of Englishmen, Swedes, Norwegians, Danes, Hollanders, and Bretons were made after the discovery by Columbus.

(Here he ignores the voyages of the Norsemen in the Eleventh Century.)

Sebastian Cabot, sailing under a commission from the King of England, reached Labrador four years after Columbus discovered the West Indies.

England's claim that Cabot sailed south as far as Florida before the mainland of America was discovered is denied by Arredondo, who says Cabot never set foot on the land.

Ponce de Leon discovered Florida in 1512 and took possession in the name of the King of Spain. Florida included the whole Atlantic Coast.

De Ayllon explored the coast, including Chicora and Orista, named that region Santa Elena and reported to Spain that he had examined the country from Santa Elena north to thirty-seven degrees north latitude (which was about the location of Chesapeake Bay), but he was attacked by Indians, lost some of his men and retired to Hispaniola, where he died in 1524.

Ribault's attempt to establish a Huguenot colony at Port Royal in 1562 was unsuccessful. The name Carolina, which he gave to that region in honor of his King, Charles the Ninth of France, could not apply to all the territory between the twenty-ninth and thirty-ninth degrees of latitude as claimed, because it was impossible for the twenty-six Frenchmen left there to take in all that territory.

The building of Fort Caroline on the St. John's River by Laudonnière, with the establishment of a French colony there, soon ended in disaster. Menendez, sailing from Spain in 1565 with 2,646 Spaniards, reached Florida on August 28th, founded St. Augustine on September 7th, and, in a few days, surprised the Frenchmen at Fort Caroline, captured the fort and put most of its occupants to death. Leaving three hundred men there, he established the Fort San Mateo.

While Menendez was in Spain, de Gourgues came, captured the fort of San Mateo, killed most of the Spaniards and hanged the prisoners.

Returning from Spain, Menendez retook the fort, rebuilt it and killed most of the Frenchmen.

By the year 1574 the Spaniards were in possession of the country from Cape Florida at twenty-five degrees north latitude to Santa Elena (Port Royal) in thirty-two degrees, thirty minutes, with settlements, forts, and missions; and were also proprietors in possession of the coast as far north as Cape Henry, in latitude thirty-six degrees, thirty minutes, which was about the southern line of Virginia.

The English had no settlement in this country until Sir Walter Raleigh came in 1584. His settlement at Roanoke, North Carolina, failed.

The English settlement of Virginia was extended southward, dividing it into seigniories, counties, and baronies, until it reached as far as the Spanish settlement of Santa Elena.

In 1586, Queen Elizabeth of England sent Francis Drake with twenty-one ships and 2,300 men to the West Indies. They burnt and sacked Santo Domingo, Cartagena, and Santiago de Cuba. On his return to Europe, he destroyed San Juan de Pinos on the Florida coast and captured St. Augustine, destroying the town and the fortress in the absence of its defenders, who had retreated to San Mateo.

A storm prevented Drake from attacking Santa Elena and he retired to Virginia.

The Spanish governor returned from San Mateo with his soldiers and their families and completely rebuilt the fort at St. Augustine. Drake did not hold the place.

The English made no further attempt until Jamestown was settled in 1606.

James the First of England, in giving to Gosnold and his company the American coast between the thirty-fourth and forty-first degrees of north latitude, granted territory that did not belong to him.

In the meantime, Spanish settlements spread southward from Santa Elena, or Port Royal, as far as Apalachee, Apalachicola, Cassita, Caueta.

Mission work in that territory was so fruitful among the Indians that in 1612 the Franciscan order created the province of Florida and named it Santa Elena. The convent of Havana was the head of this province.

The English settlement established in North Carolina during the reign of Charles the First was attacked and subdued in 1651 and 1652 by a fleet with 2,000 men sent over by Cromwell, and the royal governor was removed.

That British province attracted many British subjects, was extended southward to the thirty-third degree latitude, and was divided into North and South Carolina in 1665.

Although de Ayllon and Pedro Menendez had explored the coast as far as Cape Henry in 1573, and Menendez had written an itinerary of it, no other nation reached it until Walter Raleigh settled it under the name of Virginia.

The Spanish were before the English and entitled to the country from the southern line of Virginia (thirty-six degrees, thirty minutes) to Santa Elena (Port Royal), but that territory was usurped by the English.

In the year 1670 a treaty of peace was made between Charles the Second, King of Great Britain and Charles the Second, King of Spain, by which both of them recognized the right of each to the American territory then in their actual possession.

The Spanish King then had possession of the country between Santa Elena in latitude thirty-two degrees, thirty minutes, and the southern end of Florida, in latitude twenty-five.

The Spanish then had settlements and missions on nearly all the islands and mainlands of the coast and in the interior in the provinces of Guale, Coava, Orista, Timucua, Santa Fe, San Martin, San Pedro, Azile, Vitachuco, Apalache, Caueta, Apalachicola, Talapuses, and others, while the English were undoubtedly owners from the cape and bay of Santa Maria as far as South Carolina, or South Charleston.

Thus, by solemn treaty, the right of England to all territory on the Atlantic Coast of America, north of Port Royal, and the right of the Spaniards to all south of that place was fully agreed upon.

In 1680, Indians from the Santa Elena region and the coast of Georgia attacked Santa Elena and murdered Spanish officials on their way there to pay the troops. The Yamassee Indians declared war on the Indians of Timucua, in Southern Georgia, and burnt the town and mission of Santa Catarina, robbed the churches and killed many people. Others they carried to Carolina as slaves.

Because of these Indian attacks on Santa Elena, Governor Cabrera of Florida abandoned the settlement at Santa Elena and withdrew his soldiers from Santa Catarina and Sapelo, uniting them with those on St. Simons Island. That combined force attacked the English and Yamassee Indians at Santa Elena, burned the houses there and brought away thirty-seven Christian Indians who had been enslaved.

The Indian, Niquesalla, who sold the territory of Santa Elena to the English was a bandit chief and not even a native of the country.

After 1693 the English continued possession of Santa Elena and the Spaniards held St. Simons, Santa Maria, and Santa Cruz, in Georgia, until 1701. Then, war having been declared, Vice-Admiral Benbow came to the Indies with twenty ships of troops and reënforced Virginia, Carolina, San Cristoval, and other islands.

The King of Spain sent to America a fleet of ships with 2,000 Galicians, and some went to Havana and some to St. Augustine.

With this force, Governor Zuniga of Florida met the attack on St. Augustine by the English, under Governor Moore of Charleston.

Because of Moore's attack, Spaniards and Indians in Guale and Timucua retired to St. Augustine to unite with others in defending that place against the English. In that way the Spanish missions and forts on the Georgia coast were abandoned.

In 1721 an Englishman stopped at St. Augustine with a carload of flour and informed the captain-general that the English were building a fort on St. Simon's Island. The captain-general sent a protest to the English governor of Charleston, who replied that he had orders from his sovereign to provide for the safety of his dominions with fortifications and settlements.

Following this there were diplomatic negotiations between Spain and England, Spain demanding that the fort be abandoned.

The Duke of Newcastle agreed for England that the governors of Florida and South Carolina should meet and decide the limits of each territory, and that if the fort was in Spanish territory it should be demolished unless a satisfactory equivalent could be arranged for.

By the treaty of Utrecht, July 13, 1713, which ended the war of the Spanish Succession, the British Queen agreed that she would aid in restoring to Spain the former boundaries of regions in America belonging to her in the time of Charles the Second.

Spain, in the time of Charles the Second, held the territory as far north as Santa Elena, and this was confirmed by the treaty of 1713.

In reply to that the Duke of Newcastle, in 1724, wrote the Spanish minister in London that the fort was erected at the mouth of the Altamaha River, which Charles the Second had ceded to the English King.

Arredondo denies that Charles the Second made such a cession, but on the contrary, in 1688, approved Cabrera's expedition against the English at Santa Elena and ordered the next Spanish governor of Florida to continue until the English were completely dislodged, holding that it was territory belonging to Spain.

Spain's abandonment of her settlements in Georgia, in 1702, did not extinguish her right to that territory and the long controversy between Spain and England for Georgia land did not change matters, although England held her ground.

Arredondo continues his argument for many pages and states that Governor Horcasitas of Cuba, in 1732, sent an official (Arredondo) to confer with Oglethorpe "concerning the wrongful possession of thirty-eight leagues of territory from north to south which he had occupied," and a demand was made in the name of the Spanish King "that the English retire from, evacuate and quit all that they had wrongfully settled, with such notorious breach of faith, from the island of Santa Elena as far as the San Juan River."

Arredondo says Oglethorpe alleged that the country had been discovered by Sebastian Cabot in 1497, under patents from Henry the Seventh of England, and the title had subsequently been sustained by Francis Drake, who, by order of Queen Elizabeth, had taken and destroyed the fort of San Augustin, and that all the lands as far south as twenty-nine degrees north latitude had been granted to the lords proprietors by King James the First, Charles the First, and Charles the Second.

Arredondo argues against that claim at great length, denying that Sebastian Cabot sailed as far south as the Georgia coast and asserting that Drake's conquest of the Spanish fort at San Augustin gave his sovereign no title to that land.

## CHAPTER XI.

# *Early Grants of Georgia Land*

The grant of Georgia land for colonial purposes was first made by King Charles the First of England, in 1605, to Sir Robert Heath, then attorney-general of the realm. It conveyed territory called then Carolina Florida, which extended from the River Matheo, in the thirtieth degree of north latitude, to the River Passa Magna, in the thirty-sixth degree of north latitude. The thirtieth degree of north latitude runs a little south of the Georgia line, between the St. Mary's and St. John's rivers, and the thirty-sixth degree runs through Albemarle Sound, in North Carolina. The effort to colonize that land failed and the grant expired.

Charles the Second of England in 1647 granted to the lords proprietors of Carolina all that part of the New World lying between the thirty-sixth and twenty-ninth degrees of north latitude. The twenty-ninth parallel crosses Florida about ninety miles south of Jacksonville.

As Menendez founded St. Augustine in 1566, and soon established Spanish missions and forts at Port Royal, South Carolina, and on the Georgia coast on Saint Catherine, Ossapaw, Sapelo, St. Simon's and Cumberland islands, it appears that the grant of Charles the Second to the lords proprietors was in conflict with the claims of Spain to the Georgia and South Carolina coast. Thus began the age-long conflict between Spain and England for Georgia soil.

Under the grant to the lords proprietors of Carolina they undertook to establish a proprietary government there, but that enterprise was beset with so many difficulties that they eventually returned their proprietary rights to the crown.

**The Margravate of Azilia**—In June, 1717, the lords proprietors of Carolina granted to Sir Robert Montgomery all the land between the Altamaha and Savannah rivers, with permission to make settlement south of the Altamaha. This land was to be a separate province independent of South Carolina, and was granted to Sir Robert Montgomery, his heirs and assigns forever under the name of Margravate of Azilia. For this land he was to pay yearly a quit-rent of a penny an acre for all land "occupied, taken up or run out," but that payment was not to begin until three years after the first ships conveying colonists had arrived. In addition to that Sir Robert agreed to give the lords proprietors a fourth of all the gold, silver and royal minerals found within the ceded land. Courts of justice were to be organized and laws made by the freemen of the Margravate for the general good and not in conflict with the laws and customs of England. Navigation of the rivers was to be free to the inhabitants of North and South Carolina. A duty was to be laid on skins and the revenue from it was to be given to maintain the clergy. Sir Robert agreed to transport at his own expense to this land a number of families and all things necessary to form a new settlement. If such settlement was not made within three years the grant was to be void.

Sir Robert issued enthusiastic propaganda on the enterprise under the heading "Discourse concerning the Designed Establishment of a New Colony to the South of Carolina in the most delightful Country of the Universe," which was printed in London in 1717. He declared that the land granted to him was the most amiable country of the universe and that "Nature had not blessed the world with any tract which can be preferable to it; that paradise, with all her virgin beauty, may be modestly supposed at most but equal to its native excellencies. It lies in the same latitude with Palestine herself, that promised Canaan which was pointed out by God's own choice to bless the labors of a favorite people." He had an elaborate plan for the settlement, enclosed by military lines, impregnable to the attacks of savages, and laid out elaborate plans for the development of the colony. His plan provided for one hundred and sixteen squares, each a mile square. Estates were to be given gratis to honest and qualified gentlemen of Great Britain or elsewhere, with numerous and well-educated families, but no fortunes except their industry. There were to be four great parks or forests, each four miles square, and there the cattle were to be kept.

Subscription books were opened in London at the Carolina Coffee House, near the Royal Exchange, but the enterprise proved a failure, and at the end of three years, as there were no colonists, Sir Robert's grant expired.

**Sir Alexander Cuming's Treaty with the Indians**—A treaty of peace between England, France, and Spain, signed at Seville in 1729, though intended to settle the existing difficulties between those nations, did not effect that. The efforts of Spaniards on the south and French on the west to monopolize Indian trade continued and they sought alliances with the Cherokees, which would have been a serious thing for the English colonists.

To meet this situation, with its attending danger for the settlers, the British government sent Sir Alexander Cuming, of Aberdeenshire, Scotland, on a secret mission to win over the Cherokees to the support of England.

He left Charleston, South Carolina, on March 13, 1730, and went to the heart of the Cherokee nation at Keowee, where he found a number of leading Indians in their council house. Learning that the Cherokees were hostile toward the English, and that the Lower Creeks, who supported the French, were trying to induce the Cherokees to join them, with the probable result that the Cherokees would soon announce their hatred of the English, Sir Alexander Cuming met this grave danger by a bold stroke. At night, without previous notice, and attended by only a few men, he entered the Indian council house, where three hundred Indians were present, and demanded that they acknowledge the sovereignty of the King of England over them and their country. Surprised by his boldness, the Indians at once submitted, and, upon warning from Sir Alexander, that if they violated their promise their nation would be destroyed, they pledged solemnly upon their knees allegiance to the British crown. Messengers were sent for three head men of the Indians to meet Sir Alexander at Nequassee on the 3rd of April, with full power to make the settlement permanent. The Indian traders present, with Joseph Cooper, the interpreter, who were eye witnesses of the interview with the Indians, said they would not have believed it possible, if they had not witnessed it, and, if they had known what was Sir Alexander's purpose, they would not have entered the council house with him. Taken by surprise, and amazed at the bravery of Sir Alexander Cuming, the Indians quickly yielded to the demand. Standing up in their midst, he delivered his address through an interpreter, and, although armed with pistols, gun, and sword, he kept them concealed under his overcoat and made no attempt to intimidate the Indians by show of weapons.

During the next two weeks, Sir Alexander went through the Cherokee country, visiting its towns and made friends with their chiefs, head warriors and medicine men. The Cherokees were then governed by these mother towns: Tanassie, Kettooah, Ustenary, Telliquo, Estootowie, Keeowee, and Noyohee, each having a king and a head warrior. At Nequessee, on April 3, 1730, a great number of Indians from all parts of the Cherokee country met Sir Alexander Cuming in a solemn concourse, and he received from all the Indians present, on bended knees, their submission to the King of England, with the presentation of eagles' tails, scalps, and other emblems to Sir Alexander in token of their submission. It was a day of rejoicing among the Indians, with singing, dancing, speeches, and the creation of Moytoy as emperor.

On the 20th of April, Sir Alexander Cuming returned to Charleston, accompanied by seven leading Cherokees and their emperor, Moytoy, who was prevented from going to England by the sickness of his wife. After resting two weeks at Charleston, Sir Alexander returned to England, accompanied by the seven Cherokee leaders, who arrived in England and were treated with great consideration. Their portraits were painted as they stood in English garments among the tall trees of a park in London.

On one of the engravings the Cherokees' entertainment was thus described:

"The above Indian kings or chiefs were brought over from Carolina by Sir Alexander Coming, Bart. (being the chiefs of the Cherokee Indians), to enter into Articles of Friendship and Commerce with his Majesty. As soon as they arriv'd they were conducted to Windsor & were present at the Installation of Prince William and the Lord Chesterfield. The Pomp and Splendor of the Court and ye Grandeur not only of the ceremony as well of the Place was what struck them with infinite Surprise and Wonder. They were handsomely entertaine'd at his Majesty's Charge, and Cloathed with these Habits out of ye Royal Wardrobe. When the Court left Windsor they were brought to Town and proper Lodgings & Attendance provided for them near Covent-Garden. They were entertain'd at all ye publick Diversions of the Town, and carried to all Places of Note & Curiosity. They were remarkably strict in their Probity and Morality. Their Behaviour easy & Courteous; and their Gratitude to his Majesty was often express'd, in a publick Manner, for ye Many Favours they receiv'd. On Monday, Sept. 7, 1730, Articles of Friendship and Commerce were accordingly propos'd to them by ye L. Commissioners for Trade and Plantations and were agreed on Two Days after, *viz.:* on ye 9th at Whitehall and Sign'd on ye Part of their Lordships by Alured Popple, Esq.; upon which Ketagustah, after a short Speech in Complement to his Majesty, concluded by laying down his Feathers upon ye Table & said: This is our Way of Talking which is ye same Thing to us as ye Letters in ye Book are to you; and to you, Beloved Men, we deliver these Feathers in Confirmation of all that we have said."

After being generously entertained in England for four months, the Indians returned to Charleston, and thence to their homes in North Georgia, impressed with the power and wealth of England and remembering with gratitude the kind reception they received. This gave rise to their determination to support England permanently.

This great feat by Alexander Cuming had the same effect on the Cherokees which a similar procedure by General Oglethorpe had on the Creeks a few years later, when he journeyed several hundred miles almost alone to meet them in council and took thirty Indian chiefs to England.

**Events in Carolina**—The progress of the South Carolina colony under the lords proprietors was not satisfactory. Indian wars and the protection of the coast against pirates were a heavy burden on the colonists, in which they were not well supported by the lords proprietors. The Carolina Legislature sent a memorial to the lords proprietors, setting forth their enfeebled condition, the dangers by which they were confronted, threatening their destruction, and asked assistance and protection. The agent of Carolina was instructed to seek aid from the British crown, if it was not furnished by the lords proprietors.

The Carolina agent who went before the lords proprietors, in 1715, emphasized the danger to the colonists by telling them that the Yamassee Indians, instigated by Spanish emissaries, claimed South Carolina land by ancient occupancy, and supported by other Indian nations threatened the colony with attack.

Receiving no satisfaction from the lords proprietors, the Carolina agent petitioned the House of Commons for relief for the colony and the Commons asked the King to assist the Carolinians. The Commissioners of Trade and Plantations to whom the matter was referred by the King, said that if the English nation was to be at the expense of protecting the colony its government should be vested in the crown.

As the result, a bill was introduced in the House of Commons to regulate the charters and proprietary governments of England in America. The object was to replace proprietary governments with royal governments. In the meantime, matters grew worse in Carolina and there were disputes between the colonists and the lords proprietors.

Under these circumstances seven of the eight proprietors surrendered their rights to King George the Second, for the sum of 22,500 pounds sterling. Only Lord Carteret retained his interest. He held it for some years, and then transferred it to the crown, on the 28th of February, 1732.

Consequently, King George, in granting the charter to the Georgia trustees and conveying the Georgia land to them, only conveyed seven-eighths of it. The remaining one-eighth interest, held by Lord Carteret, was conveyed to the trustees by deed on February 28, 1732.

It is clear from the procedure of the South Carolina Legislature, in asking the British government for aid, from the recommendation of the Commissioners of Trade and Plantations from the action of the King in taking over the government of Carolina, and from the subsequent action of Parliament and the crown in spending more money on the colony of Georgia than spent on any other American colony, largely expended for fortification and military measures to protect Georgia against anticipated attacks by the Spaniards, then strongly established at St. Augustine and in Cuba, that one of the leading objects of the English government was to build up on the soil of Georgia a buffer state and a bulwark which would protect the American colonists from Spanish aggression.

# CHAPTER XII.

## *Georgia Under the Trustees*

Georgia was the last of the thirteen English colonies established in this country and was essentially different from the others. They were either royal provinces, under governors appointed by the crown, with legislative assemblies of their own choosing, or proprietary provinces, under lords proprietors, to whom the monarch had granted land and the power to govern.

The lords proprietors differed from the Georgia trustees, in that they owned the land over which they held sway, while the Georgia trustees, as individuals, could not own a foot of land in the colony and received no compensation for their services. In the first instance, these trustees, or the original incorporators among them, seemed to have been moved mainly by the appeal made by Oglethorpe and others for the establishment of a colony in America as a place where poor but worthy people in England could find free land and the means of subsistence.

With this was combined a commercial motive in the plan for the development of the silk industry, which they thought likely to be profitable, and that it would furnish, by the shipment of silks to England, the basis of a large trade for the mother country, in which thousands of poor but deserving people would find employment.

The idea of building in this colony a bulwark against Spanish aggression, which would protect the older colonies to the north of Georgia, seems to have been the dominant idea which induced the English government to spend an immense sum on the upbuilding and defense of the colony.

**Oglethorpe's Early Life**—James Edward Oglethorpe, generally credited with originating the plan for the colony of Georgia, was born June 1, 1689, of an ancient family known before the Norman conquest. Thorsby, in his *History of Leeds,* says: "Tradition saith that one of the family of Oglethorpe was Reeve (Sheriff) of the county at the time of the Norman advent, and condemned by the Conqueror for opposing his designs. The ancient seat of Oglethorpe continued in the family till the civil wars, when it was lost for their loyalty, and it is said that several of the name died in the bed of honor, being slain in a battle near Oxford, of the King's party.

"Because of his loyalty, Sutton of Oglethorpe was mulcted by Parliament of 20,000 pounds and his estate eventually fell to the lot of Fairfax."

Sutton was the grandfather of James Edward Oglethorpe. His youngest son, Theophilus, entered the army, was a lieutenant-colonel at the Battle of Sedgemoor, was knighted for his service there and was a major-general in command of the army opposing the Prince of Orange.

After the Revolution, Theophilus bought the Manor of Westbrook and married Eleanor Wall, daughter of Richard Wall and Katharine de la Roche, of the Roche family of Ireland, which was connected by marriage with the Scottish house of Argyle. Theophilus served some time in Parliament, died in his fiftieth year, and was buried in Westminster Abbey.

Lady Eleanor, the mother of James Edward Oglethorpe, was influential at the Court of Queen Anne. She had seven children, three of them sons. The two eldest, Lewis and Theophilus, had a good record in military service and in Parliament. The remaining son was the founder of Georgia.

**Oglethorpe's Relation to Georgia**—James Edward Oglethorpe matriculated at Corpus Christi College, Oxford, but remained there only a short while before he became an ensign in the British Army in 1710, in the War of the Spanish Succession, where he first came in contact with the Spaniards, and he continued in that service until the war ended in 1713. Soon afterward he entered the service of Prince Eugene of Savoy, in the War of Austria with the Turks. In that war he distinguished himself, especially in the capture of Belgrade.

An incident during that service showed Oglethorpe's spirit and ready resourcefulness. Sitting at table where Prince Eugene presided at dinner, a German prince of the House of Württemberg, who was somewhat overbearing, thought to humiliate the young English officer and took up a glass of wine from which by a filip he made some of it fly into Oglethorpe's face. The young officer could not challenge a superior officer, but he could not afford to let the insult go unnoticed. Keeping his eye fixed on the prince, and smiling as if he took what had been done in jest, Oglethorpe exclaimed: "That's a good joke, but we do it much better in England!" With that he threw a whole glass full of wine in the prince's face. Seeing this, an old general said, "It is well done, my prince; you commenced it." And thus the affair ended in good humor.

Oglethorpe returned to England in 1718, when peace was concluded between Austria and Turkey, and for some years lived the life of a country gentleman at Westbrook on the family estate, then valued at nearly a million dollars. Subsequently he inherited that estate and it was there that he entertained Tommochichi and thirty Indian chiefs when he brought them to England some years later.

OGLETHORPE MONUMENT

In 1722, Oglethorpe was elected to a seat in Parliament as a representative of the town of Haslemere, formerly represented by his father and elder brothers. He retained that seat in Parliament until 1754—thirty-two years.

In 1729 a friend of Oglethorpe's, who was an architect of distinction, involved in debt, was thrown into a debtor's prison and the warden put him in a ward where smallpox was raging. Contracting the disease, the unfortunate man died, accusing the warden of murder. Aroused to action by this outrage, Oglethorpe moved in Parliament for a committee to investigate the British jails. He was made chairman of the committee and personally visited the jails of London, where, under the law of imprisonment for debt, 4,000 poor debtors were annually imprisoned with no chance to earn anything by which to discharge their debts. Oglethorpe's activity in this matter brought him into national prominence and his interest in the subject seemed to have led him to propose a colony in America where worthy but unfortunate debtors might make a new start in life.

**Georgia as an English Province**—On June 9, 1732, the charter creating a corporation "For Establishing the Colony of Georgia in America" was granted upon the petition of lords and gentlemen, designated as follows:

"His majesty willed, ordained, constituted, declared, and granted, that our right trusty, and well beloved John, Lord Viscount Percival of our Kingdom of Ireland, our trusty and well beloved Edward Digby, George Carpenter, James Oglethorpe, George Heathcote, Thomas Tower, Robert Moor, Robert Hucks, Roger Holland, William Sloper, Francis Eyles, John Laroche, James Vernon, William Beletha, Esqrs., A. M., John Burton, B. D., Richard Bundy, A. M., Arthur Beaford, A. M., Samuel Smith, A. M., Adam Anderson, and Thomas Coram, gentlemen, and such other persons as shall be elected in the manner hereinafter mentioned, and their successors to be elected in the manner hereinafter directed, shall be one body politic and corporate in deed and in name, 'The Trustees for Establishing the Colony of Georgia in America'."

**Terms of the Grant of Georgia Land**—The conditions of the grant to the Georgia trustees are thus set forth in the charter given them:

"And whereas the said corporation intend to settle a colony and to make a habitation and plantation in that part of our province of South Carolina, in America, hereinafter described: Know ye that we, greatly desiring the happy success of the said corporation, for their further encouragement in accomplishing so excellent a work have, of our aforesaid grace, certain knowledge, and mere motion, given and granted, and by these presents, for us, our heirs and successors, do give and grant to the said corporation and their successors under the reservation, limitation, and declaration hereafter expressed, seven undivided parts, the whole in eight equal parts to be divided, of all those lands, countries, and territories situate, lying, and being in that part of South Carolina, in America, which lies from the most northern part of a stream or river there commonly called the Savannah, all along the sea coast to the southward, unto the most southern stream of a certain other great water or river called the Altamaha, and westerly from the heads of the said rivers respectively in direct lines to the South Seas; and all that share, circuit, and precinct of land within the said boundaries, with the islands on the sea lying opposite to the eastern coast of the said lands, within twenty leagues of the same, which are not inhabited already or settled by any authority derived from the Crown of Great Britain, together with all the soils, grounds, havens, ports, gulfs, and bays, mines, as well royal mines of gold and silver as other minerals, precious stones, quarries, woods, rivers, waters, fishings, as well royal fishings of whale and sturgeon, as other fishings, pearls, commodities, jurisdictions, royalties, franchises, privileges, and preëminences within the said frontiers and precincts thereof, and thereunto in any sort belonging or appertaining, and which we by our letters patent may or can grant; and in as ample manner and sort as we may, or any our royal progenitors have hitherto granted to any company, body politic or corporate, or to any adventurer or adventurers, undertaker or undertakers of any discoveries, plantations, or traffic of, in, or unto any foreign parts whatsoever, and in as legal and ample manner as if the same were herein particularly mentioned and expressed: To have, hold, possess and enjoy the said seven undivided parts, the whole into eight equal parts to be divided as aforesaid, of all and singular the lands, countries, and territories, with all and singular other the premises hereinbefore by these presents granted or mentioned, or intended to be granted, to them the said corporation and their successors forever, for the better support of the said Colony; to be holden of us, our heirs and successors, as of our honour of Hampton Court, in our County of Middlesex, in free and common socage, and not in capite; yielding and paying therefor to us, our heirs and successors, yearly forever, the sum of four shillings for every hundred acres of the said lands which the said corporation shall grant, demise, plant, or settle; the said payment not to commence or to be made until ten years after such grant, demise, planting, or settling, and to be answered and paid to us, our heirs and successors, in such manner, and in such species of money or notes as shall be current in payment by proclamation from time to time in our said province of South Carolina; all which lands, countries, territories, and premises hereby granted, or mentioned, and intended to be granted, we do by these presents make, erect, and create one independent and separate province by the name of GEORGIA, by which name we will that the same shall henceforth be called; and that all and every person or persons who shall at any time hereafter inhabit or reside within our said province shall be, and they hereby are declared to be free, and shall not be subject to, or be bound to obey any laws, orders, statutes, or constitutions which have been heretofore made, ordered, and enacted, or which hereafter shall be made, ordered, or enacted by, for, or as the laws, orders, statutes, or constitutions of our said province of South Carolina (save and except only the command in chief of the militia of our said province of Georgia to our governor, for the time being, of South Carolina, in manner hereafter declared), but shall be subject to and bound to obey such laws, orders, statutes and constitutions as shall from time to time be made, ordered, and enacted for the better government of the said province of Georgia in the manner hereinafter declared. And we do hereby, for us, our heirs and successors, ordain, will, and establish that for and during the term of twenty-one years, to commence from the date of these our letters patent, the said corporation assembled for that purpose shall and may form and prepare laws, statutes, and ordinances fit and necessary for and concerning the government of the said colony, and not repugnant to the laws and statutes of England, and the same shall and may present, under their common seal, to us, our heirs and successors, in our or their Privy Council for our or their approbation or disallowance; and the said laws, statutes, and ordinances being approved of by us, our heirs and successors, in our or their Privy Council, shall from henceforth be in full force and virtue within our said province of Georgia."

The trustees, through their corporation so constituted, were a self-perpetuating body with power to purchase and use lands which they might acquire and all personal property needed to settle and maintain the colony. They had power to grant, lease, and convey property, but the form of tenure by which property was conveyed to individuals was limited and not by fee simple. They had the right to sue and be sued, use a common seal, appoint a common council, and hold meetings where and when convenient to transact the business of the corporation. The annual meeting on the third Thursday in March of each year was fixed as the time for the election of members of the corporation and filling any vacancies which might occur. Members of the council, appointed by the trustees, were required to take an oath for the faithful performance of their duties, and the president of the trustees was to administer the oath.

Of the trustees mentioned in the charter as incorporators, five were ministers of the Church of England, ten were members of the House of Commons, and two were members of the House of Lords. One was a commissioner of excise, another a philanthropist, one a clerk in a South Sea house, and one a country gentleman. None of them were political leaders or men of great wealth. Their motives seemed to be mainly philanthropic.

Of seventeen trustees chosen the next year, twelve had been liberal contributors to the colony fund, one was a member of the House of Lords and three members of the Commons. In 1734, four more members of the House of Commons and one of the House of Lords were elected, with the addition of a clergyman and an eminent lawyer. Between 1738 and 1743, thirteen more members of Parliament were elected trustees. During the last ten years of the trusteeship, six more members of Parliament, a clergyman, and the lord mayor of London were elected.

With twenty-six trustees holding seats in Parliament, a good foundation was laid for securing favorable action by that body in great emergencies, and it was no doubt largely due to this fact that the trustees were able to secure appropriations amounting to more than 100,000 pounds sterling for the support of the colony, in spite of apparent indifference by the lord chancellor and supposed antagonism by the Board of Trade.

In addition to this the British government eventually took on the burden of defending the colony against Spanish aggression.

No other American colony of Great Britain in this country received such financial and military support from England, and this was largely due to the fact that Georgia was regarded to be, and was, in fact, a strong bulwark between the other colonies and the aggressive Spaniards.

Lord John Viscount Percival was made the first president of the trustees, and required within thirty days from the grant of the charter to convene the incorporators and effect organization, after which they were to proceed to business.

The charter provided that the common council should consist of fifteen members, and nine of them were named by the charter as follows:

John, Lord Viscount Percival, Edward Digby, George Carpenter, James Oglethorpe, George Heathcote, John Laroche, James Vernon, William Belitha, Esqs., and Stephen Hales, Master of Arts, were appointed and constituted the common council of the corporation, to continue in office during good behavior.

During the twenty years of its existence the trust included seventy-one trustees, appointed at different times, forty-seven during the first three years, fourteen during the next nine, and ten during the remainder of the trusteeship, which ended by a deed of reconveyance to the King on June 23, 1752.

The main objects of the British government in chartering these trustees to establish the colony of Georgia were stated by the charter as follows:

*First*—The relief of poor subjects made poor by misfortune or want of employment.

*Second*—The establishment in Georgia of industries such as silk culture and indigo, which would produce articles of commerce that would form the basis of valuable trade in England and give employment to thousands of people who were sadly in need of work.

*Third*—The establishment of a barrier or bulwark which would defend the colony of South Carolina and provinces further north against the ravages of Indians.

The charter does not specifically mention the defense of those provinces against Spanish aggression from the south. This omission was probably made for prudential reasons to avoid giving offense to Spain, with which England was then at peace, although it was recognized that as the Spaniards sometime before had explored the Atlantic Coast as far north as Chesapeake Bay, claimed it as Spanish territory and had actually established missions on the Georgia coast and a line of mission settlements from ocean to ocean between South Carolina and San Diego, California, there was good reason to apprehend further aggression from the Spaniards, directed from their strongholds at St. Augustine and in Cuba. That the British government had such apprehensions is clear from the strong military and financial support it gave the colony.

The trustees, as a corporation, were granted land, but as individuals, received no compensation for their services and were not permitted to acquire or own land in Georgia. The expenses of the colony were defrayed by appropriations by Parliament and private subscriptions. These subscriptions amounted to 36,000 pounds sterling.

The trustees were empowered to make laws for the colony and appoint the necessary officers, including a governor, but they never appointed the governor because the selection had to be approved by the Board of Trade, which was antagonistic to the trustees.

Although Oglethorpe accompanied several shiploads of immigrants to the colony, spent ten years in building it up and won the Battle of Bloody Marsh, which ended the Spanish threat of aggression, he was never made governor by the trustees and had very little authority except in a military capacity. The trustees made the serious mistake of trying to direct the administration of affairs in Georgia from their London office 3,000 miles from the colony without the full detailed information and knowledge of its affairs necessary to deal wisely with every situation.

By force of circumstances, General Oglethorpe, in order to meet serious emergencies as they arose, was obliged to assume and exercise a great deal of authority, which had never been formally given to him by the trustees.

It is not surprising that under these circumstances General Oglethorpe, having devoted ten years to this arduous service without compensation, and paying his own expenses, returned to England for the last time, in 1743, after the colony was well established and the victory of Bloody Marsh had made it safe from Spanish aggression.

The trustees also wearied of the difficult task of governing a colony 3,000 miles away through agents to whom they had not given power to act and to whom they undertook to give specific instructions in particular cases.

They were much troubled by the attitude of Sir Robert Walpole, the powerful chancellor of the exchequer, through whom they had to secure the King's consent to the grant of money by Parliament for the expense of the colony.

Walpole was apprehensive that the large expenditure of money on the colony and its defense on the coast south of Savannah would antagonize the Spanish government and make difficult the securing of a treaty which he was negotiating with Spain. In spite of these difficulties, Parliament voted the colony 10,000 pounds the first year, and 56,000 pounds during the next three years, because the trustees were able to convince Parliament that the Spanish were threatening Georgia and South Carolina. The financial assistance given the colony was largely for defense, and finally the government took entire charge of the defense of Georgia and relieved the trustees of responsibility, for that and everything but the civil affairs of the colony.

After that it was hard for the trustees to secure more money from Parliament, but they did get 8,000 pounds, and, in 1739, another 8,000 pounds.

In the meantime, the affairs of the colony needed more money, and the trustees asked for 20,000 more in 1739. In making their appeal to Parliament for this appropriation, the trustees sought the support of both the minority against Walpole and majority supporting him. By so doing, they apparently lost strength on both sides of the house. In the meantime, Walpole was losing strength in Parliament, and as a number of trustees were members of that body, he sought their support, and so passed his measure by a vote of two hundred and sixty to two hundred and thirty-two. In return for the support of the trustees in Parliament, he secured for them the 20,000 pounds they had asked for.

**The Leading and Most Active Trustees**—As usual with large bodies, most of the work was done by a few members. Of 1,162 reports for committee duty, more than half were made by seven men. A large part of the business of the trustees was in hearing and approving the work of committees.

The organization consisted of trustees and the common council, which included in all forty-eight members selected from the whole number of trustees. As two never accepted the office, forty-six actually composed the council. The council was an executive body within the whole corporation.

The actual working of this plan of service is made clear by the record of service by ten of the most active trustees, all of whom were also members of council. The record follows:

Number of Meetings Attended by Leading Trustees from 1732 to 1752.

| *Name.* | *Corporation Meetings.* | *Council Meetings.* | *Committees.* |
|---|---|---|---|
| Vernon | 394 | 176 | 142 |
| Egmont | 343 | 161 | 110 |
| L'Apostre | 294 | 138 | 94 |
| Smith | 352 | 75 | 43 |
| T. Towers | 193 | 125 | 100 |
| Laroche | 161 | 110 | 62 |
| Hucks | 187 | 82 | 60 |
| Hales | 152 | 95 | 53 |
| Oglethorpe | 147 | 70 | 50 |
| Shaftesbury | 138 | 80 | 48 |

**The Georgia Trustees**—A full list of the trustees, with the dates of their appointment follows:

| *Name.* | *Chosen.* |
|---|---|
| John, Lord Viscount Percival (Later Earl of Egmont) | 1732 |
| Hon. Edward Digby, Esq. | 1732 |
| George Carpenter, Esq. (Later Lord Carpenter) | 1732 |
| James Oglethorpe, Esq. | 1732 |

| *Name.* | *Chosen.* |
|---|---|
| George Heathcote, Esq. | 1732 |
| Thomas Towers, Esq. | 1732 |
| Robert More, Esq. | 1732 |
| Robert Hucks, Esq. | 1732 |
| Rogers Holland, Esq. | 1732 |
| William Sloper, Esq. | 1732 |
| Francis Eyles, Esq. | 1732 |
| John Laroche, Esq. | 1732 |
| Hon. James Vernon, Esq. | 1732 |
| William Belitha, Esq. | 1732 |
| Rev. Stephen Hales, D. D. | 1732 |
| Rev. John Burton | 1732 |
| Rev. Richard Bundy, D. D. | 1732 |
| Rev. Arthur Bedford | 1732 |
| Rev. Samuel Smith | 1732 |
| Mr. Adam Anderson | 1732 |
| Mr. Thomas Coram | 1732 |
| James Earl of Derby | 1733 |
| Anthony Ashley Cooper, Earl of Shaftesbury | 1733 |
| John, Lord Viscount Tyrconnel | 1733 |
| James, Lord Viscount Limerick | 1733 |
| James, Lord D'Arcy | 1733 |
| Hon. Richard Chandler, Esq. | 1733 |
| Thomas Frederick, Esq. | 1733 |
| Henry L'Apostre, Esq. | 1733 |
| William Heathcote, Esq. | 1733 |
| (Later Sir Wm. Heathcote, Bart.) | |
| Robert Kendall, Esq. | 1733 |
| (Later Sir Robert Cater) | |
| John Page, Esq. | 1733 |
| William Hanbury, Esq. | 1733 |
| Erasmus Phillips, Esq. | 1733 |
| (Later Sir E. Phillips, Bart.) | |
| Christopher Towers, Esq. | 1733 |
| Sir John Gonson, Knight | 1733 |
| George Tyrer, Esq. | 1733 |
| John White, Esq. | 1733 |
| Rev. Thomas Rundle, D. D. | 1734 |
| (Later Lord Bishop of Londonderry) | |
| Hon. William Talbot, Esq. | 1734 |
| (Later Lord Talbot) | |
| Richard Coope, Esq. | 1734 |
| William Wollaston, Esq. | 1734 |
| Hon. Robert Eyre, Esq. | 1734 |
| Thomas Archer, Esq. | —— |
| (Later Lord Archer) | |
| Henry Archer, Esq. | 1734 |
| Robert Tracy, Esq. | 1734 |
| Francis Wollaston, Esq. | 1734 |
| Sir Jacob Des Bouverie, Bart. | 1737 |
| (Later Lord Viscount Folkstone) | |
| Sir Harry Gough, Bart. | 1738 |
| Sir Roger Burgoyne, Bart. | 1738 |
| Lord Sidney Beauclerk | 1739 |
| Hon. Henry Bathurst, Esq. | 1741 |
| Hon. Philip Percival, Esq. | 1741 |
| John Frederick, Esq. | 1741 |
| Hon. Alexander Hume Campbell, Esq. | 1742 |
| Sir John Barrington, Bart. | 1742 |
| Samuel Tuffnell, Esq. | 1742 |
| Henry Calthrope, Esq. | 1742 |
| (Later Sir Henry Calthrope) | |
| John Phillips, Esq. | 1743 |
| (Later Sir John Phillips, Bart.) | |
| Velters Cornewall, Esq. | 1743 |
| John Wright, Esq. | 1743 |
| Rev. Thomas Wilson, D. D. | 1745 |
| Francis Cokayne, Esq. | 1747 |
| Samuel Lloyd, Esq. | 1747 |
| Hon. John Earl of Egmont | 1749 |
| Anthony Ewer, Esq. | 1749 |
| Edward Hooper, Esq. | 1749 |
| Sir John Cust, Bart. | 1749 |
| Slingsby Bethel, Esq. | 1749 |
| Stephen Theodore Jansen, Esq. | 1749 |
| Richard Cavendish | ? |

In addition to the regular members listed above, there were chosen, on March 19, 1747, two corresponding members of the trust for the service of Salzburghers and other Germans who might be inclined to go to Georgia. These were Mr. Cretien Von Munch and Rev. Samuel Urlsperger, of Augsburgh. They never attended any meetings of the trust, but frequently gave information and advice through letters to the trustees.

**Religious Affiliations of Trustees**—Difference on religious matters caused some feeling among the trustees. Most of them were members of the Church of England and they wished it to prevail in Georgia, but there was a minority composed of Presbyterians and other sects who resented the domination of the home church. It has been said that this difference caused some coolness between members of the trust.

**Unselfish Leaders**—Of seventy-one trustees, thirty-six contributed money for the expense of the colony, the total of which was about nine hundred pounds or $4,500 in American money. Besides this, one of the trustees,

Bouverie, gave 1,000 pounds from a fund given him for charity. As the trustees were not wealthy men, these contributions were not unimportant for those times.

The most important contribution was in the unselfish service of men like Oglethorpe, Vernon, Egmont, L'Apostre, Smith, Hales and Shaftesbury.

Colonel Charles C. Jones says of the trustees as a body in his *History of Georgia:* "At every stage of progress and in every act, whether trivial or important, these trustees capable and worthy, evinced a clear conception of duty, a patience of labor, a singleness of purpose, an unselfish dedication of time and energy, an integrity, and a rigid adherence to all that was pure, elevated and humanizing, which become quite conspicuous when their proceedings are minutely and intelligently scanned."

The unselfish service of the trustees is clear, from the fact that although they were a self-perpetuating body with power to elect trustees and fill vacancies among them, they were forbidden by the charter to receive any salary or profit from their connection with the colony. This was very different from the conditions in other American colonies, some of which appear to have been sources of profit to their owners. As the Georgia trustees had no possibility of profit, their service was entirely disinterested and largely philanthropic. When it appeared to them that Georgia was likely to be a buffer State between the English colonies and the Spaniards, they asked the British government to become responsible for the defense of the colony, in order that they might concentrate upon its civic matters and its general upbuilding.

Not only were the trustees working without salary or profit, but they were forbidden to hold office or employment created by their body. They could make laws for the colony, create offices from a governor down, and appoint officers, but they could not serve in such capacities.

**Appointment of Officers**—Before Oglethorpe landed with the first shipload of immigrants, the common council of the trustees appointed for the colony three bailiffs, a recorder, two constables, two tithing men, and eight conservators of the peace.

For these offices on November 8, 1732, they chose as bailiffs, Peter Gordon, William Waterland, and Thomas Causton. For recorder, they chose Thomas Christie; for constables, Joseph Fitzwalter and Samuel Parker; for tithing men, John West and John Penrose. In addition to these, they appointed a storekeeper, who held a very important position.

The salaries were small. For the storekeeper, forty pounds or two hundred dollars a year. For the second and third bailiffs, the recorder, and two constables, ten pounds a year each.

## CHAPTER XIII.

# *The First Shipload of Colonists—Early Years*

Very soon after the charter was accepted by the trustees, they began actively to prepare for the first expedition of colonists to Georgia. Having received by contribution sufficient money to begin operation, they gave public notice that they would receive applications from worthy persons who wished to emigrate to Georgia. There were numerous responses and a committee of trustees was appointed to examine the applicants. They also visited prisons and examined applicants who were confined there. If they proved worthy, the trustees arranged compromises with the creditors of applicants and secured consent for the release of those prisoners in order that they might come to Georgia.

Great care was taken in the selection of applicants, and it has been said that no such thorough examination was made before the admission of immigrants to other American colonies.

The idea of the trustees was that the colonists should be both soldiers and planters, able-bodied and reliable and that they should be instructed in the use of arms by sergeants of the Royal Guard.

By the third of October, 1732, one hundred and fourteen men, women and children had been accepted for embarkation, and all of them agreed to accept the terms of the trustees.

The ship *Anne* was comfortably fitted to carry the emigrants and supplied with provisions and other things necessary for the voyage; also with arms, agricultural implements, tools, stores and munition for the use of the colonists after their arrival in Georgia.

Although the admission of rum into the colony was prohibited by the trustees, they supplied the emigrant ship with ten tons of Parson's best beer, and several tons of wine.

By the time of embarkation, November 16, 1732, there were one hundred and thirty emigrants ready to sail. On the last Sunday in England, they attended divine service in a body at a parish church.

General Oglethorpe, as one of the trustees and the originator of the colony, was selected to go with the emigrants on the first ship that took them over.

He volunteered to pay his own expenses and give his time and best efforts to the enterprise. The following tributes to General Oglethorpe by two leading historians of early Georgia give a pen picture of the general.

Colonel C. C. Jones said of him:

"Most fortunate were the trustees in having such a representative. To no one could the power to exercise the functions of a colonial governor have been more appropriately confided. Attentive to the voice of suffering, and ready to lend a helping hand wherever the weak and the oppressed required the aid of the more powerful and the noble-minded for the redress of wrongs and the alleviation of present ills; 'in the prime of life, very handsome, tall, manly, dignified, but not austere, the beau ideal of an English gentleman, and blessed with ample means for the gratification of every reasonable desire;' possessing a liberal education, a fearless soul, a determined will, a tireless energy, a practical knowledge of military affairs and of the management of expeditions, and an experience of men and climes and matters which only years of careful observation, intelligent travel, and thoughtful study could supply, there was that about his person, character, attainments, and abilities which inspired confidence and rendered Mr. Oglethorpe, beyond all dispute, the man of his age and people best qualified to inaugurate and conduct to a successful issue an enterprise so entirely in unison with his own philanthropic sentiments and so important to the interests of both England and America."

William Bacon Stevens paid this tribute to Oglethorpe:

"To see a gentleman of his rank and fortune visiting a distant and uncultivated land, with no other society but the miserable whom he goes to assist, exposing himself freely to the same hardships to which they are subjected, in the prime of life, instead of pursuing his pleasures or ambition, intent on an improved and well-concerted plan from which his country must reap the profits, at his own expense and without a view or even a possibility of receiving any private advantage from it; this, too, after having done and expended for it what many generous men would think sufficient to have done,—to see this, I say, must give every one who has approved and contributed to the undertaking the highest satisfaction, must convince the world of the disinterested zeal with which the settlement is to be made, and entitle him to the truest honour he can gain,—the perpetual love and applause of mankind."

Several other trustees came to Gravesend to see the colonists and encourage them with words of cheer.

The ship *Anne,* of two hundred tons capacity, was commanded by Captain Thomas. With Mr. Oglethorpe, Rev. Dr. Henry Herbert, a minister of the Church of England, went as chaplain, and a Mr. Amatis, from the Piedmont section of Italy, went along to instruct the colonists in breeding silk worms and winding silk.

There were thirty-five families on the ship, and among them were carpenters, bricklayers, farmers, and mechanics.

General Oglethorpe furnished his own cabin, and at his own expense put on board enough provisions for himself, his servants, and his fellow-passengers.

The ship sailed from England, touched at the Island of Madeira, taking there five tons of wine, and thence sailed for Charleston, where she arrived on January 13, 1733. The voyage was pleasant as a whole, but was saddened by the death of two delicate children.

On the night of their arrival at Charleston, the colonists assembled and gave thanks to God for the favorable voyage. Oglethorpe went into the city and waited upon Governor Robert Johnson, of South Carolina, who with his council welcomed the general warmly. Oglethorpe had been preceded by a letter from the Duke of New Castle, head of the office of colonial affairs at London, to the governors of the American colonies, commending Oglethorpe to their courtesy and favor, and similar letters went from the admiralty to naval commanders on the Virginia and Carolina coasts.

The governor and leading men of Charleston were very cordial in their reception of Oglethorpe, not only because of the letters received from the English government, but because they believed that the colony of Georgia would be a protection to all the American colonies, especially to Carolina, against encroachments of the Spaniards.

Governor Johnson, of South Carolina, ordered Mr. Middleton, the King's pilot, to attend General Oglethorpe, and conduct the ship *Anne* to Port Royal at the same time other craft were ordered to convey the colonists to the Savannah River.

The next day Oglethorpe sailed with the ship *Anne* to Port Royal. Thence he went to Beaufort, reaching there on the 19th of January, and, on his arrival, was saluted by the artillery, and the new barracks, built for the soldiers, were used to house the colonists temporarily. Leaving the colonists there, Oglethorpe went with Colonel William Bull to the Savannah River and went up the river to Yamacraw Bluff, which he selected as the site for the town he proposed to build, and he called the place Savannah from the river of that name. The bluff rose forty feet above the river and extended nearly a mile along it. South of the bluff was a plain shadowed by pine trees, among which were live oaks and magnolias. On the east and west were creeks and swamps which drained the territory. The river up to that point was deep enough to admit ships of ordinary size close enough to the shore to load and unload cargoes without difficulty. To the northward was a dense growth of cypress, gum, and other trees, with the yellow jasmine perfuming the air, which was made vocal by the songs of birds.

Nearby was an Indian village of the Yamacraws, of which the aged Tomochichi was chief. Convenient to that Indian village a Carolina trader, named Musgrove, who had married a half-breed Indian, named Mary, established a post.

Oglethorpe's first act on arriving at this place was to make friends with the Indians, and he called at the village to talk with Tomochichi. Mary Musgrove could speak both English and the Indian language. She was favorable to the white men, because of her marriage to Musgrove, and not only acted as an interpreter for Oglethorpe, but used her influence with the Indians in his behalf.

At first the Indians were uneasy and threatened to use force to keep the white men from making a settlement there, but being assured of the friendly intentions of the English and the benefit which would result from association with them, they withdrew their opposition and entered into an informal agreement by which the land desired by Oglethorpe was ceded and promises were given that the colonists would be kindly received.

Having thus made the way safe for the colonists, Oglethorpe returned to Beaufort and found the immigrants greatly refreshed by their rest on the land. They had been kindly treated and the next Sunday was observed as a day of thanksgiving. Rev. Lewis Jones, of Beaufort, preached to the colonists, and their chaplain, Dr. Herbert, preached in Mr. Jones' pulpit, at Beaufort. Gentlemen of the neighborhood were present with the colonists, and after the services, General Oglethorpe gave them a bountiful dinner, which is said to have included four fat hogs, eight turkeys, other fowls, English beef, a hogshead of punch, a hogshead of beer, and liberal servings of wine. In spite of the liberal allowance of wine and beer, it is said that everything was conducted in good order and the occasion was a happy one.

On January 30th, the colonists sailed for Savannah, but were forced by a storm to stop and spend the night at Point Lookout. The next night they spent at a place called Johns, where eight men sent in advance by Oglethorpe had prepared huts for them. They had a bountiful evening meal, with a good supply of venison, and rested one night. The next morning they reëmbarked, and by afternoon reached Yamacraw Bluff. Early in the morning of February 2 (old style), 1733, Oglethorpe called the people together to thank God for His safe conduct of the colonists and to ask His blessings upon the settlement. He reminded them of their duties as founders of Georgia and warned them that the future would be good or bad, according to their conduct at that time. He especially warned them against intemperance and idleness, and cautioned them to be careful and just in dealing with the Indians.

The colonists then went to work with a good will. Some built a crane to unload the ship, others cut down trees to make temporary shelter, and others proceeded to unload the vessel and build a stockade around the town with a fort on the bluff. With characteristic energy, Oglethorpe led his people, planning, supervising, and keeping them in good spirits.

In those early days, Oglethorpe and the colonists had great help from Carolina. Colonel William Bull, of Charleston, assisted General Oglethorpe in laying out streets, squares and lots, and lent the colonists four of his servants, who were expert sawyers, to aid in preparing lumber for the houses. General Oglethorpe contented himself with a tent, and lived there for nearly a year.

**Oglethorpe's Letter to the Trustees**—On the 10th of February, 1733, Oglethorpe wrote from Savannah to the trustees the following letter:

GENTLEMEN:—I gave you an Account in my last of our Arrival at Charles-Town. The Governor and Assembly have given us all possible Encouragement. Our People arrived at Beaufort on the 20th of January, where I lodged them in some new Barracks built for the Soldiers, while I went myself to view the Savannah River. I fix'd upon a healthy situation about ten miles from the sea. The River here forms a Half-Moon, along the Southern Side of which the Banks are about forty Foot high, and on the Top a Flat which they call a Bluff. The plain high Ground extends into the Country five or six miles, and along the Riverside about a Mile. Ships that draw twelve Foot Water can ride within ten Yards of the Bank. Upon the Riverside, in the Centre of this Plain, I have laid out the Town. Opposite to it is an Island of very rich Pasturage, which I think should be kept for the Trustees' Cattle. The River is pretty wide, the water fresh, and from the Key of the Town you see its whole Course to the Sea, with the Island of Tybe, which forms the Mouth of the River; and the other way you see the River for about six Miles up into the Country. The Landskip is very agreeable, the Stream being wide, and border'd with high Woods on both sides. The whole People arrived Here on the first of February. At Night their Tents were got up. Till the seventh we were taken up in unloading and making a Crane which I then could not get finish'd, so took off the Hands, and set some to the Fortification and began to fell the woods. I Mark'd out the Town and Common. Half of the former is already cleared, and the first House was begun Yesterday in the Afternoon. Not being able to get Negroes, I have taken ten of the Independent Company to work for us, for which I make them an allowance. I send you a copy of the Resolutions of the Assembly and the Governor and Council's Letter to me. Mr. Whitaker has given us one hundred Head of Cattle. Colonel Bull, Mr. Barlow, Mr. St. Julian, and Mr. Woodward are come up to assist us with some of their own Servants. I am so taken up in looking after a hundred necessary Things, that I write now short, but shall give you a more particular Account hereafter. A little Indian Nation, the only one within fifty Miles, is not only at Amity, but desirous to be Subjects of his Majesty King George, to have Lands given them among us, and to breed their Children at our Schools. Their Chief, and his Beloved Man, who is the Second Man in the Nation, desire to be instructed in the Christian Religion. I am Gentlemen,

Your Most Obedient, Humble Servant,

JAMES OGLETHORPE.

**Letters of South Carolina Officials to Oglethorpe**—The letter of the governor and council of South Carolina, and the resolutions of the assembly alluded to, were:

SIR:—We cant omit the first opportunity of congratulating you on your safe Arrival in this Province, wishing you all imaginable Success in your charitable and generous Undertaking in which we beg Leave to assure you any Assistance we can give shall not be wanting in promoting the same. The

General Assembly having come to the Resolutions inclosed, we hope you will accept it as an instance of our sincere Intentions to forward so good a Work, and of our Attachment to a Person who has at all times so generously used his Endeavours to relive the Poor and deliver them out of their Distress, in which you have been hitherto so successful that we are persuaded this Undertaking cant fail under your prudent conduct, which we most heartily wish for. The Rangers and Scout-Boats are order'd to attend you as soon as possible. Col: Bull, a Gentleman of this Board, and whom we esteem most capable to assist you in the Settling your new Colony, is desired to deliver you this, and to accompany you and render you the best Services he is capable of, and is one whose Integrity you may very much depend on.

We are with the greatest Regard and Esteem, Sir:

Your most obedient Humble Servants,

Council Chamber
26th of Jan: 1732.

| | | |
|---|---|---|
| JOHN PENWICKE, | ROBERT JOHNSON, | THOMAS BROUGHTON, |
| THOMAS WARING, | AL: MIDDLETON, | A. SKEENE, |
| J. HAMMERTON, | FRA: YONGE, | JAMES KINLOCK. |

**Resolutions of the Carolina Assembly**—"The Committee of his Majesty's Honourable Council, appointed to confer with a Committee of the Lower House on his Excellency's Message relating to the Arrival of the Honourable James Oglethorpe Esqr:

"Report: That agreeable to his Majesty's Instructions to his Excellency, sent down together with the said Message, we are unanimously of Opinion that all due Countenance and Encouragement ought to be given to the Settling of the Colony of Georgia.

"And for that End your Committee apprehend it necessary that his Excellency be desired to give Orders and Directions that Captain MacPherson, together with fifteen of the Rangers do forthwith repair to the new Settlement of Georgia to cover and protect Mr. Oglethorpe, and those under his care, from any Insults that may be offered them by the Indians, and that they continue and abide there till the new Settlers have enforted themselves, and for such further time as his Excellency may think necessary.

"That the Lieutenant and four Men of the Apalachucola Garrison be ordered to march to the Fort on Combahee to Join those of the Rangers that remain; that the Commissary be ordered to find them with Provisions as usual. That his Excellency will please to give directions that the Scout Boat at Port Royal do attend the new Settlers as often as his Excellency shall see Occasion. That a Present be given to Mr. Oglethorpe for the new Settlement of Georgia forthwith of an hundred Head of breeding Cattle, and five Bulls, as also twenty breeding Sows, and four Boars, with twenty Barrels of good and merchantable Rice; the whole to be delivered at the Charge of the Publick at such Place in Georgia as Mr. Oglethorpe shall appoint.

"That Parriaguas be provided at the Charge of the Publick to attend Mr. Oglethorpe at Port Royal in order to carry the new settlers, arrived in the ship *Anne* to Georgia with their Effects and the Artillery and Ammunition now on Board.

"That Col. Bull be desired to go to Georgia with the Hon: James Oglethorpe Esq: to aid him with his best Advice and Assistance in the Settling of that Place."

Colonel Bull, with four of his servants, went to Savannah and spent a month there, rendering valuable services. Mr. Whitaker and his friends sent one hundred head of cattle as a gift to the colony. Mr. St. Julian helped for several weeks in erecting houses and advancing the settlement. A present of a silver boat and silver spoon were made and given by Mr. Hume for the first child born in the Georgia colony. For two months Joseph Bryan gave personal attention and the labor of his servants who were sawyers. Mrs. Anne Drayton lent four sawyers, and Colonel Bull and Mr. Bryan together furnished Oglethorpe twenty servants to use as he thought best. Governor Johnson presented seven horses.*

The generous help of the governor and leading citizens of South Carolina shows clearly that they thought the establishment of the colony of Georgia, south of them, would be a great protection for the Carolinas and other colonies against the attacks of Indians and Spaniards. Already fugitive slaves from South Carolina had found refuge in Florida and there was serious danger of Indian warfare, inspired by the Spaniards.

In the meantime, General Oglethorpe was making rapid progress in laying the foundation for the colony of Georgia and providing comfortable dwelling places for the colonists he had brought over. His activity and foresight are clearly shown by his letters to the trustees, from which the following extracts are quoted:

**Oglethorpe's Letters to the Trustees**—On February 20, 1733, Oglethorpe wrote the trustees as follows from Savannah:

"Our People are all in perfect Health. I chose the situation for the Town upon an high Ground forty Foot perpendicular above High-Water Mark: The Soil dry and sandy, the Water of the River fresh, Springs coming out from the Sides of the Hills. I pitch'd on this Place not only for the Pleasantness of its Situation, but because from the above-mention'd and other Signs I thought it Healthy, for it is shelter'd from the Western and Southern Winds (the worst in this Country) by vast Woods of Pine-trees many of which are an hundred, and few under seventy Foot high. There is no Moss on the Trees, tho' in most Parts of Carolina they are cover'd with it, and it hangs down two or three Foot from them; The last and fullest Conviction of the Healthfulness of the Place was that an Indian Nation, who knowing the Nature of this Country, chose it for their Habitation."

On March 12, 1733, Oglethorpe wrote the trustees as follows:

"This Province is much larger than we thought, being one hundred and twenty miles from this river to the Altamaha. The Savannah has a very

*Steven's *History of Georgia,* Vol. I, p. 92.

long course, and a great trade is carried on by the Indians, there having about twelve trading boats passed since I have been here. There are in Georgia, on this side the mountains, three considerable nations of Indians; one called the Lower Creeks, consisting of nine towns, or rather cantons, making about a thousand men able to bear arms. One of these is within a short distance of us and has concluded a peace with us, giving us the right of all this part of the Country; and I have marked out the lands which they have reserved to themselves. Their King comes constantly to Church, is desirous to be instructed in the Christian religion, and has given me his nephew, a boy who is his next heir, to educate. The two other Nations are the Uchees and the Upper Creeks; the first consisting of two hundred, the latter of 1,100 men. We agree so well with the Indians that the Creeks and the Uchees have referred to me a difference to determine which otherwise would have occasioned a war.

"Our people still lie in tents, there being only two clap-board houses built and three sawed houses framed. Our crane, our battery cannon, and magazine are finished. This is all that we have been able to do by reason of the smallness of our number, of which many have been sick and others unused to labour; though I thank God they are now pretty well, and we have not lost one since our arrival here."

**A Newspaper Account of the Colony**—The South Carolina *Gazette* of March 22, 1733, contained this interesting account of the Georgia colony from a correspondent:

"On Tuesday, the 13th Instant, I went on board a Canoe, in company with Mr. George Ducat and Mr. John Ballantine, with four Negroes; and about 10 O'clock we set off from Mr. Lloyd's Bridge for Georgia and, passing by Port Royal on Wednesday Night we arrived on Friday Morning an Hour before Day at Yammacraw,—a place so called by the Indians, but now Savannah in the Colony of Georgia. Some time before we came to the Landing the Centinel challenged us, and understanding who we were, admitted us ashore. This is a very high Bluff,—Forty Feet perpendicular from High-water Mark. It lies, according to Captain Gascoigné's Observations, in the Latitude 31:58, which he took off Tybee, an island that lies at the Mouth of the Savannah River. It is distant from Charles-Town S. W. according to the Course and Windings of the Rivers and Creeks about 140 Miles out; but, by a direct Course, 77, allowing Sullivants Island to be in the Latitude 32:47 from Augustine N. E. and by E. about 140 miles, and by the Course of the Rivers is distant from Fort Moore 300 miles; but upon a direct Line but 115 Miles N. W. and by W. This Bluff is distant 10 Miles from the Mouth of the Rivers on the South Side; and Purrysburgh is 24 Miles above it on the North, and is so situated that you have a beautiful Prospect both up and down the River. It is very sandy and barren, and consequently a wholesome Place for a Town or City. There are on it 130 odd souls; and from the Time they embarqued at London to the Time I left the Place there died but two sucking Children, and they at Sea. When they arrived, there was standing on it a great Quantity of the best Sorts of Pine, most of which is already cut down on the Spot where the Town is laid out to be built. The Land is barren about a Mile back, when you come into very rich Ground; and on both sides within a Quarter of a Mile of the Town is choice, good Planting Land. Colonel Bull told me that he had been Seven Miles back, and found it extraordinary good.

"Mr. Oglethorpe is indefatigable, takes a vast deal of Pains; his fare is but indifferent, having little else at present but salt Provisions. He is extremely well beloved by all his People the general Title they give him is FATHER. If any of them is sick he immediately visits them and takes a great deal of Care of them. If any difference arises, he is the Person that decides it. Two happened while I was there, and in my Presence; and all the Parties went away, to outward Appearance, satisfied and contented with his Determination. He keeps a strict Discipline; I neither saw one of his People drunk or heard one swear all the Time I was there; He does not allow them Rum, but in lieu gives them English Beer. It is surprising to see how cheerfully the Men go to work, considering they have not been bred to it; There are no Idlers there; even the Boys and Girls do their Parts. There are Four Houses already up but none finished; and he hopes when he has got more Sawyers, which I suppose he will have in a short time, to finish two Houses a Week. He has ploughed up some Land, part of which he sowed with Wheat, which is come up and looks promising. He has two or three Gardens which he has sowed with divers Sorts of Seeds, and planted Thyme, with other Sorts of Pot-herbs, Sage, Leeks, Skellions, Celeri, Liquorice, &c. and several Sorts of Fruit trees. He was palisading the Town round, including some Part of the Common, which I do suppose may be finish'd in a Fortnight's time. In short he has done a vast deal of Work for the time, and I think his Name Justly deserves to be immortalized.

"Mr. Oglethorpe has with him Sir Walter Raleigh's written Journal, and, by the Latitude of the Place, the Marks and Tradition of the Indians, it is the very first Place where he went ashore and talked with the Indians, and was the first Englishman that ever they saw. And about half a Mile from Savannah is a high Mount of Earth under which lies their chief King; and the Indians informed Mr. Oglethorpe, that the King desired, before he died, that he might be buried on the Spot where he talked with that great good Man.

"The River Water is very good, and Mr. Oglethorpe has proved it several Ways and thinks it as good as the River of Thames. On Monday the 19th we took our Leave of Mr. Oglethorpe at Nine o'clock in the Morning and embarked for Charles Town; and when we set off he was pleased to honour us with a Volley of small Arms, and the Discharge of Five Cannon: And coming down the Rivers, we found the Water perfectly fresh Six Miles below

MONUMENT TO THE SIGNERS, AUGUSTA

the Town, and saw Six or Seven large Sturgeon in which Fish that River abounds, as also with Trout, Perch, Cat, and Rock Fish &c, and in the Winter Season there is a Variety of Wild Fowl, especially Turkeys, some of them weighing Thirty Pounds, and abundance of Deer."

**Oglethorpe's Address to Carolinians**—Going to Charleston to thank the governor, council, and people for their kindness to the Georgia colony, Oglethorpe received an additional contribution from the council. Returning to Charleston on June 9, 1733, he delivered this address to the governor and council:

"I should think myself," said he, "very much wanting in Justice and gratitude if I should neglect thanking your Excellency, you Gentlemen of the Council, and you Gentlemen of the Assembly, for the assistance which you have given to the Colony of Georgia. I have long wished for an opportunity of expressing my sense of the universal zeal which the inhabitants of this Province have shown for assisting that Colony, and could not think of any better opportunity than now when the whole Province is virtually present in its General Assembly. I am therefore gentlemen, to thank you for the handsome assistance given by private persons as well as by the public. I am to thank you not only in the name of the Trustees and the little Colony now in Georgia, but in behalf of all the distressed people of Britain and persecuted Protestants of Europe to whom a place of refuge will be secured by this first attempt.

"Your charitable and generous proceeding, besides that self satisfaction which always attends such actions, will be of the greatest advantage to this Province. You, Gentlemen, are the best Judges of this since most of you have been personal witnesses of the dangerous blows which this country has escaped from French, Spanish and Indian Arms. Many of you know this by experience, having signalized yourselves personally either when this Province by its own strength, and unassisted by anything but the courage of its inhabitants and the Providence of God, repulsed the formidable invasions of the French, or when it defeated the whole body of the Southern Indians who were armed against it and was invaded by the Spaniards who assisted them. You Gentlemen, know that there was a time when every day brought fresh advices of murders, ravages, and burnings; when no profession or calling was exemptd from arms; when every inhabitant of the Province was obliged to leave wife, family, and useful occupations and undergo the fatigues of war for the necessary defence of the Country; and all their endeavors scarcely sufficient to guard the western and southern frontiers against the Indians.

"It would be needless for me to tell you who are much better judges, how the increasing settlement of a new Colony upon the southern frontiers will prevent the like danger for the future. Nor need I tell you how every plantation will increase in value by the safety of the Province being increased; since the lands to the southward already sell for above double what they did before the new Colony arrived. Nor need I mention the great lessening of the burden of the people by increasing the income of the tax upon the many thousand acres of land either taken or taking up on the prospect of future security.

"The assistance which the Assembly have given, though not quite equal to the occasion, is very large with respect to the present circumstances of the Province; and as such, shows you to be kind benefactors to your new come countrymen whose settlements you support, and dutiful subjects to his Majesty whose revenues and dominions you by this means increase and strengthen.

"As I shall soon return to Europe I must recommend the infant Colony to your further protection; being assured, both from your generosity and wisdom that you will, in case of any danger or necessity, give it the utmost support and assistance."

Encouragement to the Georgia colony came in colonies farther north than the Carolina.

Thomas Penn, proprietor of the colony of Pennsylvania, personally contributed a hundred pounds to aid the Georgia colony, and wrote an encouraging letter to the trustees.

Governor Belcher, of Massachusetts, wrote to Oglethorpe, on May 3, 1733, as follows:

"It is with great pleasure that I congratulate you upon your safe arrival in America; and I have a still greater interest in the advantages which these parts of his Majesty's dominions will reap from your noble and generous pursuits of good to mankind in the settlement of Georgia. May God Almighty attend you with his blessing, and crown your toils with success."

## CHAPTER XIV.

# *The Second Shipload—Savannah Laid Out*

On the 14th of May, 1733, the ship *James,* of one hundred and ten tons burden, with six guns, arrived at Savannah with a number of passengers and stores for the Georgia colony. On board were some Italians skilled in the propagation of silk worms and the manufacture of raw silk, who had been engaged by the trustees to teach the colonists in the cultivation of mulberry trees, the breeding of silk worms, and the reeling of silk thread from cocoons.

Unlike the first vessel, the *Anne,* which stopped at Charleston, and Port Royal, the ship *James* came up the Savannah River and landed her passengers and cargo at Yamacraw, where Oglethorpe and the first shipload of colonists were busy laying the foundations of Savannah.

Captain Yoakley, of the *James,* received from the trustees for bringing the first vessel of sea-going size up the Savannah River a handsome prize.

General Oglethorpe began early to protect the colony by military measures against possible attacks by Indians or others. Captain McPherson, with his company of South Carolina rangers, was stationed on the Savannah River at a point called "Horse-Quarter." As the work at Savannah proceeded, the battery of cannon had been placed and a stockade had been built around the town, some of the rangers were sent to a point on the Ogeechee River, where Indians hostile to South Carolina had been accustomed to cross on their way to attack that colony. There Oglethorpe built a fort and called it Fort Argyle, in honor of his friend, the Duke of Argyle. Ten families were sent with the rangers to build dwellings there and cultivate land in the neighborhood.

About the same time villages were established at the following places:

The village of High Gate, with twelve families, mostly French, five miles south of Savannah.

The village of Hampstead, one mile east of High Gate, with twelve German families.

At Thunderbolt, a small fort, with several families.

On the northeast end of Skidoway Island, ten families, with a fort to protect them.

Joseph-Town on the Savannah River, opposite Argyle Island, with Scotch colonists.

Fifteen miles above Savannah on a creek tributary to the Savannah River, the village of Abercorn.

Between there and Savannah the plantations of Sir Francis Bathurst, Walter Augustin, Captain Williams, Mrs. Matthew's place, the Indian School House Irene, the Horse Quarter, and the land reserved for the Indians.

These settlements did not last long, because the settlers suffered from malarial fever.

A fort was built to defend the Skidoway Narrows and garrisoned by some of Captain Noble Jones' marines, quartered near his residence of Wormsloe, on the Isle of Hope.

A lighthouse to be ninety feet high was started and a guard was posted near the north end of Tybee Island.

As more immigrants came, there were plantations on Augustine Creek, Wilmington Island, the Isle of Hope, at Bewlie on the Little Ogeechee, and as far as the Great Ogeechee.

**Oglethorpe's Address to the Colonists**—On July 7, 1733, when substantial progress had been made by planting a battery of cannon, putting a palisade around the town, making a commodious garden and laying out the general outlines of Savannah, General Oglethorpe called the colonists together, and explained to them the plan of the town, with the names and locations of the wards, tithings, town lots, gardens and farms.

The business of the meeting began with prayer, and the plan of the town was then revealed to the colonists as follows:

**Savannah Laid Out**—General Oglethorpe laid out the town of Savannah in this form:

Four wards, each containing four tithings:

PERCIVAL WARD, named in honor of John, Lord Percival, the first Earl of Egmont, and president of the trustees for establishing the colony of Georgia, in America;

HEATHCOTE WARD, named in honor of George Heathcote, M. P., an alderman of London, and one of the most active and influential members of the board of trustees;

DERBY WARD, so called in compliment to the Earl of Derby, who was one of the most generous patrons of the colonization;

DECKER WARD, so named in honor of Sir Matthew Decker, whose benefactions had been conspicuous.

Percival Ward was composed of the following tithings: Moore, Hucks, Holland, and Sloper, in honor of Robert Moore, Robert Hucks, Roger Holland, and William Sloper, members of Parliament and influential trustees. Heathcote Ward was composed of Eyles, Laroche, Vernon, and Belitha tithings, so named for Sir Francis Eyles, Bart., one of the commissioners of the navy and a member of Parliament; John Laroche, also a member of Parliament; James Vernon, Esq., and William Belitha, all members of the trust. The four tithings constituting Derby Ward were Wilmington, Jekyll, Tyrconnel, and Frederick. These were named for the Earl of Wilmington; Sir Joseph Jekyll, Master of the Rolls, who, with his lady, had contributed six hundred pounds; Lord John Tyrconnel, and Thomas Frederick, M. P., both members of the board of trustees. The tithings into which Decker Ward was divided were named Digby, Carpenter, Towers, and Heathcote, in honor of Edward Digby; George, Lord Carpenter; Thomas Towers, M. P., and George Heathcote, M. P., trustees.

The public square, to serve as a model for others, was called Johnson Square, named to compliment Robert Johnson, governor of South Carolina.

The streets laid out were Abercorn, Drayton, Bull, and Whitaker, running north and south, and Bay, Bryan, and St. Julian streets, interesecting them at right angles. In naming these streets, Oglethorpe sought, in an enduring manner, to express the gratitude of the colony and its founder. The principal street bore the name of Colonel William Bull, who accompanied Oglethorpe when he selected Yamacraw Bluff as a suitable site for Savannah, and on various occasions rendered the plantation valuable services. The liberality of Mr. Whitaker, of South Carolina, and of the Earl of Abercorn was in this manner publicly acknowledged. In the middle of Johnson Square a large sun-dial was erected for the convenience of the inhabitants.

Christ Church occupies the trust lot then designated as a site for a house of worship, and the general plan of the lots, streets, and squares, established at this time, served for a guide in subsequent years. The dwellings were placed on the lots and the gardens and farms were situated on the outskirts of the town. Each male inhabitant of full age participating in the allotment, became possessed of a town lot containing sixty feet in front and ninety feet in depth, a garden lot embracing five acres, and a farm containing forty-four acres and one hundred and forty-one poles. The grant, therefore, aggregated fifty acres, thus conforming to the instruction of the trustees and supplying support of the colonists who came at the charge of the trust and brought no servants with him.

**First Grantees of Land**—The allotment of land to the Georgia colonists at Savannah was made in July, 1733, but the formal deed giving effect to the allotment was not executed until December 21, 1733. As it gives the name of the first settlers and the land they had, it is here given:

"To all to whom these Presents shall come: We, Thomas Christie and William Calvert, send greeting. Whereas by Indentures of Lease and Release made between the Trustees for establishing the Colony of Georgia in America on the one part; and us the said Thomas Christie and William Calvert and Joseph Hughes, deceased, on the other part, bearing the date the twenty-fifth day of October Anno Domini One thousand seven hundred thirty and two, under the common seal of the said Trustees, they and said Trustees did for the considerations therein mentioned Grant and convey unto us the said Thomas Christie and William Calvert and the said Joseph Hughes, deceased, and to the Survivors of us and our Assigns, Five Thousand Acres of Land lying and being in the Province of Georgia in America, being part and parcel of the Land which his Majesty graciously granted to the said Trustees by his Letters Patent bearing date the Ninth day of June Anno Domini One Thousand Seven Hundred thirty and two, to be set out in such parts of the said Province as should be thought convenient and proper by such Person as should be appointed by the Common Council for that purpose, under such limitations and in trust for such uses and purposes as are therein mentioned, as in and by the said Indentures, relation being to them had, may more fully appear; And Whereas the said Common Council did by deed, under the Common Seal of the said Trustees, bearing Date the Twenty Sixth day of October Anno Domini One thousand seven hundred thirty and two authorize and appoint James Oglethorpe Esquire, of Westbrook Place in the County of Surry, to set out and limit the said Five Thousand Acres in such part of the said Province as he should think most convenient; and Whereas the said James Oglethorpe hath set out and limited the said Five thousand Acres in such a regular manner as is most convenient for the support of a Town and the Inhabitants thereof, and hath set out part of the said Five Thousand Acres for a Town called Savannah, with Lotts for Houses, and left a Common round the Town for convenience of Air; And, adjoining to the Common, hath set out Garden Lotts of Five Acres each, and beyond such Garden Lotts hath set out Farms of Forty four acres and One hundred forty and one Pole each, and hath drawn a Plan of the Town, and Plot of the Garden Lotts and Farms respectively with proper Numbers, References, and Explanations for the more easy understanding thereof, which Plan and Plot are hereunto annexed and set forth in Folio One and Folio Nine of this Book:

"Now Know Ye, that we, the said Thomas Christie and William Calvert, pursuant to the said Deed, and in performance of the said Trust, do Grant and Enfeoff unto John Goddard one House Lot in Wilmington Tything in Derby Ward, expressed in the said Plan by Number One, containing Sixty feet in front and Ninety feet in depth, and one Garden Lot containing Five Acres, expressed on the said Plot by Number Eleven, lying South East from the Center of said Town, and Farm expressed in the said Plot by Number Five and Letter A in the said ward and Tything, containing Forty Four Acres and One Hundred Forty and One Pole, making together Fifty Acres of Land: To Have and To Hold the said Fifty Acres of Land unto him the said John Goddard during the term of his natural life, and after his decease then to the Heirs Male of his Body forever, Upon the Conditions and under the express Limitations hereinafter mentioned."

Upon similar conditions, town lots in the various tithings and wards in Savannah, garden lots, and farms were conveyed in and by this deed to Walter Fox, John Grady, James Carwall, Richard Cannon; Frances Cox, relict of William Cox; William Cox, Jr.; George Sims, Joseph Fitzwalter; Mary Samms, relict of John Samms; Elizabeth Warren, relict of John Warren; William Warren, son of the said John Warren; Mary Overend, relict of Joshua Overend; Francis Mugridge, Robert Johnson, William Horn, John Penrose; Elizabeth Hughes, relict of Joseph Hughes; Mary Hodges, relict of Richard Hodges; Mary Hodges, Elizabeth Hodges, and Sarah Hodges, daughters of the said Richard Hodges; James Muir, Thomas Pratt, Thomas Christie, Joseph Cooper, John West, James Wilson, William Waterland; Elizabeth Bowling, relict of Timothy Bowling; Mary Bowling, daughter of the said Timothy Bowling; Elizabeth Millidge, relict of Thomas Millidge, heirs male of the said Thomas Millidge; William Little; Jane Parker, relict of Samuel Parker; Thomas Parker, son of the said Samuel Parker; Mary Magdalene Tibbeau, relict of Daniel Tibbeau, heirs male of the said Daniel Tibbeau; Hannah Close, relict of Henry Close; Ann Close, daughter of the said Henry Close; Joseph Stanley, Robert Clark, Peter Gordon, Thomas Causton, John Vanderplank, Thomas Young, Joseph Coles, Thomas Tebbit, John Dearn, John Wright, Noble Jones; Ann Hows, relict of Robert Hows; John Clark, William Gough, William McKay, Thomas Ellis, Edward Johnson, Isaac Nunez Henriquez, William Mears, Moses le Desma, Paul Cheeswright, Samuel Nunez Ribiero, John Musgrove, Noble Wimberly Jones, Daniel Ribiero, Charles Philip Rogers, Moses Nunez Ribiero, Robert Gilbert; Edward Jenkins, Sr.; Jacob Lopez d'Olivera, William Savory; Edward Jenkins, Jr.; Isaac de Val, David Cohen del Monte, Benjamin Shaftell, Bearsley Gough, Robert Hows, Abraham Nunez Monte Santo, John Millidge, Jacob Yowel; Samuel Parker, Jr.; Abraham Minis, Jacob Lopez de Crasto, and David de Pas; the said grantees "Yielding and paying for such Town Lott, Garden Lott, and Farm, containing together Fifty Acres as aforesaid, to the said Trustees for establishing the Colony of Georgia in America, and to their Successors, yearly and every year, the Rent or Sum of two Shillings of lawful Money of Great Britain, the same to be paid to such person or persons and at such place in the said Town of Savannah in the said Province of Georgia as by the Common Council (for the time being) of the said Trustees shall be appointed. The first payment to be made on the first Day of the Eleventh year to be computed from the Day of the date of these Presents; provided always, and these Presents are upon these conditions, that if it shall happen that the said yearly Rent of Two Shillings or any part thereof be unpaid by the space of Twelve Kalendar Months next after the day of Payment, on which the same ought to be paid as aforesaid, And if the said several persons or their respective Heirs above mentioned shall not within the space of Eighteen Kalendar Months from the date hereof erect one House of Brick, or framed, square timber work, on their respective Town Lotts, containing at the least Twenty four feet in length, upon Sixteen in breadth, and eight feet in height, and abide, settle, and continue in the said Province for and during the full term of three years to be computed from the date hereof, and if the said several Persons and each of them respectively shall not, within the space of ten years, to be likewise computed from the date hereof, clear and cultivate Ten Acres of the said Land herein before to them respectively granted; And if the said several Persons aforesaid shall not plant or cause to be planted, One Hundred plants of the White Mulberry Tree which are to be delivered unto them respectively by the said Trustees, so soon as the same or sufficient part thereof be cleared, and sufficiently fence and preserve the same from the bite of Cattle, and in stead of such Trees as shall happen to die or be destroyed shall not set other Trees of the same sort, And if any or either of the said several persons above mentioned who shall by virtue of these Presents, or of the Grant and Enfeoffment hereby made or intended to be made, now or at any time or times hereafter become possessed of the said Fifty Acres of Land or any part or parcel thereof respectively, at any time or times alien, transfer, or convey the same or any part thereof for any term of years, or any estate or interest in the same, to any Person or Persons whatsoever without special leave and licence of the said Common Council (for the time being), or of such Officer as the said Common Council shall from time to time authorize to Grant such licence; And if the said Person or Persons or any other Person who shall by virtue of these Presents and of the Grant in Tail Male hereby made from time to time become possessed of the said Fifty Acres of Land shall do or commit any Treason, Misprison of Treason, Insurrection, Rebellion, Counterfeiting the Money of Great Britain, or shall commit Murder, Felony, Homicide, Killing, Burglary, Rape of women, unlawful Conspiracy or Confederacy, and shall be thereof lawfully convicted; and if any of the said Person or Persons hereinbefore mentioned or any other Person or Persons who shall by virtue of these Presents and of the Grant hereby made, from time to time become possessed of any of the said Fifty Acres of Land shall at any time hire, keep lodge, board, or employ within the limits of the said Province of Georgia any person or persons being Black or Blacks, Negroe or Negroes, or any other Person or Persons being a Slave or Slaves, on any account whatsoever without the special leave and licence of the said Common Council (for the time being) of the said Trustees, that then and from henceforth in any or either of the aforesaid cases it shall be lawful to and for the said Trustees for establishing the Colony of Georgia in America and their Successors into and upon the said Fifty Acres of Land hereby granted of such person so offending, and upon any and every part thereof in the name of the whole to reënter and the same to have again, retain repossess and enjoy as if this present grant had never been made; And all and every such Person or Persons so neglecting, or misbehaving him or themselves in any or either of the cases aforesaid, and all other the occupyers and possessors of the said Fifty Acres of Land (to such person so misbehaving as aforesaid belonging) or any part of parcel thereof, thereout and from thence utterly to expel, put out, and amove; And also upon the Entry in any of the cases before mentioned of such Officer or Officers who shall by the said Common Council (for the time being) be for that purpose authorized and appointed, the Grant hereby made of the said Fifty Acres of Land unto such Person so misbehaving as aforesaid shall cease, determine, and become void.

"In Witness Whereof the said Thomas Christie, and William Calvert have hereunto set their Hands and Seals this twenty-first day of December in the year of Our Lord One Thousand Seven Hundred Thirty and Three.

"THOS. CHRISTIE [L. S.],
"WM. CALVERT [L. S.]."

Grants for more than fifty acres, when approved, were made by the common council. After the royal government took charge of the colony, large grants were made by the crown; the grantee agreed to pay, after three years, two shillings a year per hundred acres, and cultivate three acres in every fifty; also to keep stock on grazing land.

**Coming of the Salzburgers**—The motto of the fathers of this country that America should be an asylum for the oppressed of all nations was well illustrated in the early history of the colony of Georgia. It was from the first intended by the trustees that they would aid worthy Protestants seeking homes in the New World in order to escape persecution in their native lands. At first there was lack of money to do this, but in 1733, on motion of Sir Charles Turner, the English House of Commons voted an appropriation of 10,000 pounds, equal to about $50,000 in American money, to defray the expense of carrying over and settling foreign and other Protestants in the Georgia colony.

Persecution of the Salzburgers had aroused the sympathy of Protestants in England and other European countries. During the years 1729 to 1732, inclusive, more than 30,000 Salzburgers, to escape religious persecution, left their homes in Salza Valley and sought refuge in Prussia, Holland, and England, where their suffering enlisted profound sympathy. Oglethorpe and his trustees shared this sympathy, and so did the Society for the Propagation of Christian Knowledge. The result was that the trustees and the society coöperated in bringing the Salzburgers to Georgia.

On December 15, 1733, the common council of the trustees adopted these resolutions:

"Resolved, That the Trustees for establishing a Colony in Georgia, in America, do greatly approve the proposal of the Society for promoting Christian knowledge for defraying the expense of settling certain of the poor Saltzburghers in Georgia in America, and will readily join and concur in sending and settling so many of them as by the contributions which the said Society shall transmit to the Trustees, and what other money the Trustees shall for that purpose receive, shall be enabled to send and settle in the said Colony.

"Resolved, That the said Society be desired to inquire, by their Correspondents in Germany, in the name of the said Trustees, whether any of the said Saltzburghers will be willing to become British subjects and to settle in the said Colony of Georgia on the terms to be offered by the said Trustees.

"Resolved, That the said Society be desired to publish such further Accounts of the deplorable state of the poor Saltzburghers as they shall think proper, and at the same time to make publick the design of the said Society jointly with the said Trustees to apply such contributions as shall be received for the relief of the said poor Saltzburghers to the settling as many of them as they shall be able as British Subjects in Georgia in America.

"Agreed to the following Articles for the poor Saltzburghers to go to Georgia, *viz:*—

"1st. The Trustees will defray, as far as their contributions will enable them, the charges of passage and provisions for the voyage to Georgia in America of such Emigrants, Girnberghers, or Exiles from Bertoldsgoden as are persecuted for the Protestant Religion.

"2nd. To all those who want it, some allowance will be made for tools.

"3rd. On their arrival in Georgia each family will have provisions given them, gratis, till they can take in their harvest, and the seed will be there given them sufficient to sow the lands they shall in the first year make ready for sowing.

"4th. Every man shall be entitled to three lots, *viz:* a Lot for a house and yard within the town, a Lot for Garden plots near the Town, and a Lot for tillage at a small distance from the Town sufficient in the whole to give a comfortable subsistence to themselves and families; and that they shall have the said lands freehold to themselves and their heirs male forever.

"5th. That they shall obey such orders and regulations for the maintenance of property, peace, and good government, as the Trustees shall think necessary from time to time to establish; and on their arrival shall assist each other in clearing their Lands, building houses, and such other works as shall be necessary for their mutual safety in common with his Majesty's other subjects there.

"6th. That they, upon their settling in Georgia, shall become Denizens, and have all the rights and privileges of Englishmen.

"7th. That they shall be protected in the free exercise of their Religion and in the full enjoyment of all the civil and religious rights of the free subjects of Great Britain."

Rev. Samuel Urlsberger, the venerable elder of the Salzburgers, accepted the offer to bring his people to Georgia, with the expenses and transportation paid and the Society for the Propagation of Christian Knowledge undertook to transport them from Rotterdam to Dover, where they would be received by the trustees and sent to Georgia.

Forty-two men and their families, altogether seventy-eight persons, walked from their town of Bechtolsgaden and vicinity to Augsberg, where they were kindly received and furnished with three carts to carry the women and children, the infirm, and their baggage. Under the guidance of Baron Philip George Von Reck, they made their way slowly to Frankfort, and thence sailed down the River Main and the Rhine, and reached Rotterdam on the 27th of November, 1733. There they were joined by their ministers, Martin Bolzius and his Christian Gronau. Crossing the English Channel in rough weather, they reached Dover on the 21st of December, and were met by the Georgia trustees, who supplied them with many comforts and administered to them the oath of loyalty to the British crown.

On January 8, 1734 (old style), they sailed on the ship *Purishburg* for Savannah. After a long and stormy voyage, they reached Charleston on March 7, 1734, and were there met by Oglethorpe, who, for their comfort and refreshment, sent on board the ship fresh beef, two butts of wine, two tuns of spring water, cabbage, turnips, radishes, fruit and so forth, which were greatly enjoyed by the Salzburgers.

Three days later the ship *Purisburg* reached Savannah on a Sunday. They were welcomed by the songs of birds in the delightful atmosphere of Georgia springtime, and Mr. Bolzius, who led the Salzburgers, spoke of their entrance (on shipboard) in coming to rest at Savannah by saying: "Lying in fine calm weather, under the shore of our Beloved Georgia, where we heard the birds sing melodiously. Everybody in the ship was joyful."

The people of Savannah gathered at the landing to meet them and the new-comers were welcomed by huzzahs and the firing of cannon. The Salzburgers were brought on shore and taken into the garden belonging to the trustees, where they were treated with great kindness by the people.

**Ebenezer Located**—Leaving his people in good hands and well cared for by the Georgia colonists, Baron Von Reck went out on horseback with Oglethorpe to view the country and select a place where the Salzburgers could make their settlement. The location they selected on the 17th of March, 1734, was four miles below the present site of Springfield, in Effingham County. Compared with other more fertile land, it was unattractive, but to the Salzburgers, tired of the sea and weary of persecution, it was a haven of refuge and a place of promise. Von Reck thus described it in his journal:

"The Lands are inclosed between two Rivers which fall into the Savannah. The Saltzburg Town is to be built near the largest, which is called Ebenezer, in Remembrance that God has brought us hither; and is navigable, being twelve Foot deep. A little Rivulet, whose Water is as clear as Crystal, glides by the Town; another runs through it, and both fall into the Ebenezer. The Woods here are not so thick as in other Places. The sweet Zephyrs preserve a delicious coolness notwithstanding the scorching Beams of the Sun. There are very fine Meadows, in which a great Quantity of Hay might be made with very little Pains; there are also Hillocks, very fit for Vines. The Cedar, Walnut, Pine, Cypress and Oak make the greatest part of the Woods. There is found in them a great Quantity of Myrtle Trees out of which they extract, by boiling the Berries, a green wax, very proper to make Candles with. There is much Sassafras, and a great Quantity of those herbs of which Indigo is made, and Abundance of China Roots. The Earth is so fertile that it will bring forth anything that can be sown or planted in it; whether Fruits, Herbs, or Trees. There are wild Vines, which run up to the Tops of the tallest Trees; and the Country is so good that one may ride full gallop 20 or 30 miles an end. As to Game, here are Eagles, Wild-Turkies, Roe-Bucks, Wild-Goats, Stags, Wild-Cows, Horses, Hares, Partridges, and Buffaloes."

The location of Ebenezer having been selected, the Salzburgers began work at once. Nine able-bodied men of their party went to Ebenezer and began to cut down trees and build houses for the Salzburgers to live in.

On May 1, 1734, lots were laid out and assigned to the men, so that houses could be built at once.

Mr. Oglethorpe sent them, as a present from the magistrates of Savannah, ten cows and calves and ten casks of seed. The Indians gave them venison, and their English neighbors taught them how to brew beer from molasses, sassafras, and pine tops. The water disagreed with them until they found a spring, which furnished clear, good water. The 13th of May, 1734, they observed as a day of thanksgiving for their new home and freedom from religious persecution.

The Salzburgers were very poor, depending largely on the trustees at the start for supplies, and with few mechanics among their number, but they worked hard and kept at it cheerfully until they were firmly established. Then they kept on working and showed their gratitude to the authorities of the colony by furnishing lumber for a church building in Savannah.

Early in 1735 more Salzburgers came in the ship *Prince of Wales*. Among the number were mechanics, who did fine service in hewing timber, splitting shingles, sawing boards, and building houses. A large wooden structure was built for church purposes, and there their ministers, Bolzius and Gronau, dwelt.

**Von Reck's Impression of Savannah**—In his journal, Baron Von Reck left a pen picture of Savannah as he saw it in 1734:

"I went to view this rising Town, Savannah, seated upon the banks of a River of the same Name. The Town is regularly laid out, divided into four wards, in each of which is left a spacious Square for holding of Markets and other publick Uses. The Streets are all straight, and the Houses are all the same Model and Dimensions, and well contrived for Conveniency. For the Time it has been built it is very populous, and its Inhabitants are all White People. And indeed the Blessing of God seems to have gone along with this Undertaking; for here we see Industry honored and Justice strictly executed, and Luxury and Idleness banished from this happy Place where Plenty and Brotherly Love seem to make their Abode, and there the good Order of a Nightly Watch restrains the Disorderly and makes the Inhabitants sleep secure in the midst of a Wilderness. There is laid out near the Town, by Order of the Trustees, a Garden for making Experiments for the Improving Botany and Agriculture; it contains 10 Acres and lies upon the River; and it is cleared and brought into such Order that there is already a fine Nursery of Oranges, Olives, white Mulberries, Figs, Peaches, and many curious Herbs: besides which there are Cabbages, Peas, and other European Pulse and Plants which all thrive. Within the Garden there is an artificial Hill, said by the Indians to be raised over the Body of one of their ancient Emperors. I had like to have forgot one of the best Regulations made by the Trustees for the Government of the Town of Savannah. I mean the utter Prohibition of the Use of Rum, that flattering but deceitful Liquor which has been found equally pernicious to the Natives and new Comers, which seldom fails by Sickness or Death to draw after it its own Punishment."

# CHAPTER XV.

## *Progress of the Colony*

**The Jewish Colonists Received at Savannah**—When contributions for the purpose of defraying the expense of worthy people sent to Georgia as colonists were solicited in England, the trustees granted commissions in favor of Alvaro Lopez Suasso, Francis Salvador, Jr., and Anthony Da Costa, authorizing them to ask and receive contributions to aid the colonization of Georgia. It was the understanding of the trustees that the money so raised by those three men was to be turned over to the trustees and used by them for the objects specified in the charter. It appears that Suasso, Salvador, and Da Costa raised a considerable sum of money for the purpose indicated, but instead of turning it over to the trustees or depositing it in the bank of England to their credit, they collected forty Hebrew colonists, and without permission from the common council of the trustees, they used the money they had raised in chartering a vessel and paying the expense of sending the Jewish colonists to Savannah.

Hearing this, the trustees on January 31, 1733, instructed their secretary, Mr. Martyn, to demand from Suasso, Salvador, and Da Costa the surrender of their commissions. At first the demand was refused, and the three men persisted in using funds they had raised for expense of the Jewish colonists.

When the ship containing the Jewish colonists arrived at Savannah, Oglethorpe had no information as to the action of the trustees who had forbidden the bringing of the Jews to Georgia. As the charter of the trustees guaranteed religious freedom to all except Papists, Oglethorpe received the Jewish immigrants and notified the trustees of his action.

The trustees disapproved Oglethorpe's action and appointed a committee to prepare and publish a statement about the matter, assuring the public that they did not intend to make a Jewish colony of Georgia. To Oglethorpe they wrote that they heard with apprehension of the arrival of the Jews in Georgia and hoped they would receive no encouragement there. They urged him to see that the Jews were allowed no kind of settlement with any of the grantees.

The official action of the trustees on the subject was as follows:

"PALACE COURT. Saturday, December 22, 1733.

"At a meeting of Trustees, assembled by summons, Ordered That the Secretary do wait on Messrs. Alvaro Lopez Suasso, Francis Salvador, Junior, and Anthony Da Costa with the following message in writing:

"Whereas a message, dated Jan. 31, 1732-3, was sent for the redelivery of their Commissions with which they did not think proper to comply, and which on the said Refusal were vacated by the Trustees: and Whereas the Trustees are informed that by monies raised by virtue of their commissions (which monies ought to have been transmitted to the Trustees) certain Jews have been sent to Georgia contrary to the intentions of the Trustees, and which may be of ill consequence to the Colony: The Trustees do hereby require the said Messrs. Alvaro Lopez Suasso, Francis Salvador, Junior, and Anthony Da Costa immediately to redeliver to Mr. Martyn, their Secretary, the said Commissions and to render an account in writing to the Trustees of what monics have been raised by virtue thereof; and if they refuse to comply with this demand that then the Trustees will think themselves obliged not only to advertize the world of the demand and refusal of the said Commissions and Account, and of the misapplication before mentioned, in order to prevent any further impositions on his Majesty's Subjects under pretence of an authority granted by those vacated Commissions; but likewise to recover those commissions and demand an account of the monies collected in such manner as their Counsel shall advise."

"PALACE COURT. Saturday, Jan. 5th, 1733-4.

"Ordered. That the Secretary do wait on Messrs. Alvaro Lopez Suasso, Francis Salvador, Junior, and Anthony Da Costa with the following Message in writing:

"The Trustees for establishing the Colony of Georgia in America having received a letter from Messrs. Alvaro Lopez Suasso, Francis Salvador, Junior, and Anthony Da Costa, in answer to a message sent for their Commissions, which letter does not appear satisfactory to the said Trustees, they think themselves obliged not only to insist on the redelivery of their Commissions, but as they conceive the settling of Jews in Georgia will be prejudicial to the Colony, and as some have been sent without the knowledge of the Trustees, the Trustees do likewise require that the said Messrs. Alvaro Lopez Suasso, Francis Salvador, Jr., and Anthony Da Costa, or whoever else may have been concerned in sending them over, do use their endeavours that the said Jews be removed from the Colony of Georgia, as the best and only satisfaction they can give to the Trustees for such an indignity offered to Gentlemen acting under his Majesty's Charter."

"PALACE COURT. Saturday, Jan. 19th, 1733-4.

"The Secretary acquainted the Board that pursuant to their order of Jan. 5th instant he had waited on Messrs. Alvaro Lopez Suasso, Francis Salvador,

Junior, and Anthony Da Costa, and left with them the message of the trustees in writing, and that he had received the Commissions formerly given to them; and then he delivered the said Commissions to the Board.

"Resolved that the said Commissions be laid by, and the further consideration of this affair be postponed till Mr. Oglethorpe comes home."

Oglethorpe furnished accommodation and encouragement for these Hebrew colonists, who by their peaceable behavior, orderly conduct, and industry commended themselves to the favorable consideration of Oglethorpe. He wrote the trustees that the Jews had not proved a detriment to the colony and called the attention of the trustees to the good offices of Dr. Nunis. Acknowledging his kindness, the trustees asked Oglethorpe to offer him a gratuity for his medical services, but to insist that all grants of land in the province should be withheld from these Jews. With these instructions, Oglethorpe did not comply. In the general conveyance of town lots, gardens, and farms, executed on the 21st of December, 1733, some of these Hebrews are mentioned as grantees.

As the action of Suasso, Salvador, and Da Costa was without authority, and in defiance of the trustees, that body can hardly be blamed for its action, but Oglethorpe was wise in receiving the Jewish colonists, for they proved to be good citizens and some of their descendants are now respected residents of Savannah.

**Oglethorpe Explores the Georgia Coast**—Oglethorpe, within the first year, laid out the town of Savannah and established the outlying villages and plantations. He was then in position to explore the coast to the south of Savannah. Accordingly, on January 23, 1734, he set out, accompanied by Captain Ferguson with sixteen men, including two Indian guides. They proceeded in a large rowboat, followed by a boatload of provisions and ammunition, and went down the coast between the mainland and the islands. On January 27th they reached St. Simon's Island and spent the night there. From St. Simon's they went to another island close by, which Oglethorpe named Jekyll, in honor of his friend, Sir Joseph Jekyll.

After careful inspection of the mouth of the Altamaha River, he decided to establish a fort near it to protect the entrance of the river from attack by sea. That fort was to be located on St. Simon's Island. On the same occasion, he selected sites on which Frederica and New Inverness were built. Returning thence northward, he examined Fort Argyle, which he had previously established on the Ogeechee, and was gratified by the energy and progress made by Captain McPherson. The fort had been well built and several guns were in position. This fort commanded the crossing of the river at the point where Indians had been in the habit of going over into South Carolina. That Indian trail crossed the Savannah River, near the Indian village, Palachocolas.

**Progress of the Colony**—The progress of the colony during the first year is shown by the report of the trustees to the lord chancellor in June, 1734. It shows that by June, 1733, one hundred and fifty-two persons had already been sent to Georgia by the trustees. Of these, one hundred and forty-one were from England, and eleven were foreign Protestants. Five thousand acres had been set apart for colonists who went over at the expense of the trustees, and, in addition, 4,460 acres had been granted to parties going over at their own expense. The money received by contributions by individuals amounted to 3,723 pounds, and of this, 2,254 pounds had been spent on the colony.

During the year ending June 9, 1734, the number of persons sent to Georgia at the expense of the trustees was three hundred and forty-one, of whom two hundred and thirty-seven were British subjects, and one hundred and four were foreign Protestants. By that time 8,100 acres had been granted to colonists in small tracts, and 5,725 acres to parties who came at their own expense. Including the appropriation by Parliament and contributions by individuals, the trustees had received for the purposes of the colony 11,503 pounds, of which 6,863 pounds had been spent. Colonel Charles C. Jones, in his *History of Georgia,* makes this comment on the management of the Georgia colony:

"With the progress of the colonization, the trustees certainly had good cause to be pleased. Never was a trust more honestly administered. Among all the English plantations, we search in vain for a colony the scheme of whose settlement was conceived and executed upon like exalted, disinterested, and charitable principles, whose colonists were selected with like care, whose affairs were conducted with equal regularity, and whose supervisors and agents could be matched in respectability, culture, and benevolence. By judicious treatment, the red men had been won over to peace and amity. By treaty stipulations, these sons of the forest had surrendered to the Europeans their title to wide domains. The pine-covered bluff at Yamacraw was transmuted into a town, well ordered, regularly laid out, and possessing forty completed houses, and many others in process of construction. A battery of cannon and a palisade proclaimed its power for self-protection. An organized town court was open for the enforcement of rights and the redress of wrongs. From a tall flagstaff floated the royal colors, and a substantial crane on the bluff facilitated the unburthening of vessels in the river below. A public garden and private farms evidenced the thrift of the community, and gave promise of a liberal harvest. An ample storehouse sheltered supplies against a season of want. This little mother town—miniature metropolis of the province—had already sent out her sons; some of them to dwell along the line of the Savannah, others to watch by the Ogeechee, others to build homes upon the islands and guard the approaches from the sea, others to warn the mariner as he entered the mouth of the Savannah, and others still to convert the neighboring forests into pleasant fields. Planters, too, at their own charge, and bringing articled servants with them, were already seeking out and subduing fertile tracts. Thus the colony enlarged its domains and multiplied its settlements."

After an absence of fifteen months, Oglethorpe decided to visit England. The conduct of the colony's affairs was entrusted to Thomas Causton, the storekeeper and a bailiff. In cases of doubt and difficulty, he was to take counsel of James St. Julian, of South Carolina, and of Francis Scott, of Georgia. As Oglethorpe bade adieu to his people, who attended him to the boat which was to convey him to Charlestown, they were all so concerned that, in the language of Von Reck, "they could not refrain their tears when they saw Him go who was their Benefactor and their Father; who had carefully watched over them as a good Shepherd does over his Flock, and who had had so tender a Care of them both by Day and by Night."

# CHAPTER XVI.

## *Indian Chiefs in England*

Realizing that the continued friendship of the Indians was vital to the success of the Georgia colony, Oglethorpe conceived the idea that by taking Tomochichi and a number of Indian chiefs with him to London, where they would be kindly received and well entertained, they would be impressed with the power and greatness of Great Britain. Accordingly, he invited Tomochichi and leading members of his tribe to accompany him on his return to England. The old chief accepted the invitation and took with him his wife, Scenawki, and Toonahowi, his adopted son, and nephew, Hillispilli, the war chief of the Lower Creeks, four other chiefs of that nation, Apakowtski, Stimalchi, Sintouchi, and Hinguithi, and Umphichi, a Uchee chief from Palachocolas, with their attendants and an interpreter.

They left Savannah and reached Charleston on the 27th of March, 1734, remaining there until April 7th, when they sailed for England on the ship *Aldborough*. After a long voyage of ten weeks, they arrived at St. Helens, on the Isle of Wight.

Writing from there to Sir John Phillip, Baronet, Oglethorpe said:

"An aged chief named Tomochichi, the mico or king of Yamacraw, a man of an excellent understanding, is so desirous of having the young people taught the English language and religion, that, notwithstanding his advanced age, he has come over with me to obtain means and assistant teachers. He has brought with him a young man whom he calls his nephew and next heir, and who has already learned the Lord's prayer in the English and Indian language. I shall leave the Indians at my estate till I go to the city, where I shall have the happiness to wait upon you, and to relate all things to you more fully; over which you will rejoice and wonder."

On the evening of the 21st of June, an entertainment was given in honor of Oglethorpe, who gave the trustees a report of progress and a statement of the status of the colony of Georgia.

His reception was cordial and every mark of consideration was bestowed on him. The trustees, at a special meeting convened for that purpose, by unanimous vote, thanked him for the ability, zeal, activity, and perseverance with which he had conducted the affairs of the province. They assured him that they would hold his services in lively and grateful remembrance. His return was heralded throughout the kingdom. His virtues were glowingly recounted in prose and verse. The visit of Tomochichi was also commemorated in an elaborate ode composed for the occasion, the first stanza of which follows:

> What stranger this? and from what Region far?
> This wond'rous Form, majestic to behold?
> Uncloath'd, but arm'd offensive for the War,
> In hoary Age and wise Experience old?
> His Limbs, inur'd to Hardiness and Toil,
> His strong large Limbs what mighty Sinews brace!
> Whilst Truth sincere and artless Virtue smile
> In the expressive Features of his Face.
> His bold free Aspect speaks the inward Mind,
> Aw'd by no slavish Fear, from no vile Passion blind.

The following account of the reception of the Indians by the King is from the *Gentleman's Magazine:*

"Thursday, August 1, 1734.

"Thomohachi, the king, Senauki his wife, with Tooanakowki their son, Hillispilli the war-captain, and the other Cherokee Indians brought over by Mr. Oglethorpe from Georgia, were introduced to his Majesty at Kensington, who received them seated on his throne; when Tomochachi, micho, or king, made the following speech, at the same time presenting several eagle's feathers which are trophies of their country:

"'This day I see the majesty of your face, the greatness of your house, and the number of your people. I am come for the good of the whole nation called the Creeks, to renew the peace which was long ago had with the English. I am come over in my old days, although I cannot live to see any advantage to myself. I am come for the good of the children of all the nations of the Upper and the Lower Creeks, that they may be instructed in the knowledge of English.

"'These are the feathers of the eagle which is the swiftest of birds, and who flieth all round our nations. These feathers are a sign of peace in our land, and have been carried from town to town there; and we have brought them over to leave with you, O great king! as a sign of everlasting peace.

"'O Great king whatsoever words you shall say to me I will tell them faithfully to all the kings of the Creek nations.'

"To which his Majesty graciously answered, 'I am glad of this opportunity of assuring you of my regard for the people from whom you come, and am extremely well pleased with the assurances you have brought me from them, and accept very gratefully this present as an indication of their good disposition to me and my people. I shall always be ready to cultivate a good correspondence between them and my own subjects, and shall be glad of any occasion to show you a mark of my particular friendship and esteem.'

"Tomochachi afterwards made the following speech to her Majesty. 'I am glad to see this day, and to have the opportunity of seeing the mother of this great people. As our people are joined with your Majesty's, we do humbly hope to find you the common mother and protectress of us and all our children.'

"And her Majesty returned a most gracious answer. The war-captain and other attendants of Tomochachi are very importunate to appear at court in the manner they go in their own country,—which is only with a proper covering round their waist, the rest of their body being naked,—but were dissuaded from it by Mr. Oglethorpe. But their faces were variously painted after their country manner, some half black, others triangular, and others with bearded arrows instead of whiskers.

"Tomochachi and Senauki, his wife, were dressed in scarlet trimmed with gold."

**Death of an Indian Chief**—Three days after the Indians were received at court, an Indian chief, who had been ill for some days, died of smallpox, although medical aid and kind attention had been given him. This sad event greatly depressed the other Indians and after the dead chief had been buried with the customary Indian rites, Oglethorpe took the whole party of Indians out to his country estate, where they remained for two weeks, mourning for their lost associate.

On the 7th of August, Tomochichi and the other Indians were entertained by Lady Putney, and the next day they called on the Archbishop of Canterbury, who received them with great kindness and expressed his desire for their education and their instruction in Christianity.

On the visit of the Indians to Eton, where they were received by Dr. George Berriam and the faculty, Tomochichi asked that the boys be given a holiday, which was granted and received with enthusiasm.

Tomochichi was greatly impressed with the wealth and power of the British Empire. The solidity of London buildings drew from him an expression of surprise that short-lived men should erect such long-lived buildings. He was a close observer and seemed oppressed by the contrast between the poverty of his own people, their ignorance and helplessness, and the great power and intelligence, as well as the wealth, of the Englishmen, as he saw it in London. This far-sighted old man realized and said that without the friendship of the English people the Indian tribes would be doomed to extinction.

**The Result**—During their four months' stay in England, the Indians were provided for at public expense and received gifts worth something like four hundred pounds, or $2,000. All this greatly affected the Indians, who received constant attention, especially from the nobility, as well as the masses of people. On their return to Georgia, all the Indians in the party used their influence among the Indian tribes of Georgia in behalf of England, and Tomochichi to his dying day urged his people to be everlastingly faithful to England. They were true to England and even fought against the colonists in the Revolutionary War and the War of 1812.

**The Indians Return to Georgia**—On their departure from England, the Indians received the same attention as when they came, being conveyed to Gravesend in the King's coaches. The *Gentleman's Magazine* for October, 1734, described the scene as follows:

"The Indian King, queen and prince, etc., set out from the Georgia office in the king's coaches for Gravesend, to embark on their return home. During their stay in England, which has been about four months, his majesty allowed them twenty pounds a week for their subsistence, and they have been entertained in the most agreeable manner possible. Whatever is curious and worthy of observation in and about the cities of London and Westminster, has been carefully shown them; and nothing has been wanting among all degrees of men to contribute to their diversion and amusement, and to give them a just idea of English politeness and our respect for them. In return they expressed themselves heartily attached to the British nation. They had about the value of four hundred pounds in presents. Prince William presented the young mico, John Towanohowi, with a gold watch, with an admonition to call upon Jesus Christ every morning when he looked on it; which he promised. They appeared particularly delighted with seeing his highness perform his exercise of riding the managed horse,—the Horse Guards pass in review, and the agreeable appearance of barges, etc., on the Thames on Lord Mayor's day.

"In the same ship embark several relations of the English already in Georgia, who were allowed the preference of going; also Sir Francis Parkhurst, his son, three daughters, and servants, together with fifty-six Saltzburghers newly arrived from Rotterdam. These people were at the German church in Trinity Lane, where forty-seven pounds were collected for them."

The vessel in which Tomochichi returned was the *Prince of Wales,* George Dunbar, captain, arriving at Savannah on the 27th of December, 1734.

Captain Dunbar wrote of the voyage: "We arrived here (Savannah) all cheerful and in good health. The Indians behaved with their accustomed modesty, as did also the Saltzburgers, who are a sober and pious people, and gave much less trouble than I expected; nor do I think any of them were dissatisfied while on board." He adds in conclusion: "Tomochichi, Toonahowi, Hillispilli, and Umpechi were so kind as to come on board on the morning of our intended departure, to see me. They have a very grateful remembrance of the many civilities which they received in England, and desire me to inform your honors that Santechi has gone to the Upper and Middle

Creeks, who are at present extremely well disposed to the British interest, and their deputies are expected down in two months."

**The Indian's Letter of Thanks**—On the return of the Indians to Georgia one of them, a chief, wrote a letter to the trustees. It was drawn in red and black figures, on the dressed skin of a young buffalo, and the ideas it expressed were conveyed in picture writing, a translation of which was furnished by an Indian interpreter, who delivered the original and the interpretation at Savannah in the presence of fifty Indian chiefs and a number of prominent citizens. This strange letter, prepared according to the custom of the Indians, expressed their gratitude for their kind reception in England, their admiration for the British court and kingdom, and their strong friendship for Oglethorpe.

When this hieroglyphic painting was received by the trustees, it was framed and hung up in the Georgia office in London.

The news of the reception accorded the Indian chiefs in London was spread abroad among the Indian nations of Georgia, and produced lasting effects in good will of the Indians for the colony.

**Oglethorpe's Treaty with the Indians**—In its weak state at the outset, the Georgia colony would not have survived the hostility of the Indians by whom it was surrounded. General Oglethorpe was wise and fortunate in securing at the outset the friendship and good will of Tomochichi, and through his influence, the leading men of other tribes within the territory of Georgia came to Savannah on the 18th of May, 1733, to confer with the head of the new colony.

It is well here to take a look at this great Indian, for he was from the first a firm friend of Oglethorpe, and without his good will and active influence among the Indians in behalf of the colony, it might not have survived.

From all accounts, Tomochichi was an unusual man. Colonel Jones says of him:

"Although at this time far advanced in years he was a man of commanding presence, grave demeanor, marked character, established influence, of a philosophical turn of mind and in full possession of all his faculties."

For some unknown reason, Tomochichi and other Indians had been banished by the Lower Creeks, but there seems to have been no ill will against him, for the chief of the Oconas claimed kin with him and called him a good man and a distinguished warrior. After wandering for some time, Tomochichi settled near Savannah before Oglethorpe came, and there he was joined by the Yamacraws, disaffected Indians from the Lower Creeks, and some of the Yamassees, who made him their chief. His character is expressed in the portrait made of him in London by the painter, Verelst, when Tomochichi and a number of other Indian chiefs were taken there by General Oglethorpe as his guests.

**Oglethorpe's Meeting with the Indians**—Oglethorpe's meeting with the Indians is thus described in the publication entitled *Political State of Great Britain,* volume 47:

"On the 14th of May, Mr. Oglethorpe set out from Charlestown on his return to Savannah, which is the name of the town now begun to be built in Georgia. That night he lay at Col. Bull's house on Ashley River, where he dined the next day. The Rev. Mr. Guy, rector of the parish of St. John's, waited upon him there, and acquainted him that his parishioners had raised a very handsome contribution for the assistance of the colony of Georgia. Mr. Oglethorpe went from thence to Capt. Bull's, where he lay on the 15th. On the 16th, in the morning, he embarqued at Daho, and rested at Mr. Cochran's island. On the 17th he dined at Lieut. Watts' at Beaufort, and landed at Savannah on the 18th, at ten in the morning, where he found that Mr. Wiggan, the interpreter, with the chief men of all the Lower Creek nation, had come down to treat of an alliance with the new colony.

"The Lower Creeks are a nation of Indians who formerly consisted of ten, but now are reduced to eight tribes or towns, who have each their different government, but are allied together and speak the same language. They claim from the Savannah River as far as St. Augustin, and up to the Flint river, which falls into the bay of Mexico. All the Indians inhabiting this tract speak their language. Tomochichi, mico, and the Indians of Yamacraw are of their nation and language.

"Mr. Oglethorpe received the Indians in one of the new houses that afternoon. They were as follows:

"From the tribe of Coweeta—Yahou-Lakee, their king or mico. Essoboa, their warrior,—the son of old Breen, lately dead, whom the Spaniards called emperor of the Creeks,—with eight men and two women attendants.

"From the tribe of the Cussetas—Cusseta, the mico, Tatchiquatchi, the head warrior, and four attendants.

"From the tribe of the Owseecheys—Ogeese, the mico, or war king, Neathlouthko and Ougachi, two chief men, with three attendants.

"From the tribe of Cheehaws—Outhleteboa, the mico, Thlauthothlukee, Figeer, Soota-Milla, war-captains, and three attendants.

"From the tribe of Echetas—Chutabeeche and Robin, two war-captains (the latter was bred among the English), with four attendants.

"From the tribe of Pallachucolas—Gillatee, the head warrior, and five attendants.

"From the tribe of Oconas—Oueekachumpa, called by the English 'Long King,' Coowoo, a warrior.

"From the tribe of Eufaule—Tomaumi, the head warrior, and three attendants.

"The Indians being all seated, Oueekachumpa, a very tall old man, stood up, and with a graceful action and a good voice, made a long speech, which was interpreted by Mr. Wiggan and John Musgrove, and was to the following purpose. He first claimed all the land to the southward of the river Savannah, as belonging to the Creek Indians. Next he said that although they were poor and ignorant, He who had given the English breath had given them breath also; that He who had made both, had given more wisdom to the white men; that they were firmly persuaded that the Great Power which dwelt in heaven and all around (and then he spread out his hands and lengthened the sound of his words), and which had given breath to all men, had sent the English thither for the instruction of them, their wives and children; that therefore they gave them up freely their right to all the land which they did not use themselves, and that this was not only his opinion, but the opinion of the eight towns of the Creeks, each of whom having consulted together, had sent some of their chief men with skins, which is their wealth. He then stopped, and the chief men of each town brought up a bundle of buckskins, and laid eight bundles from the eight towns at Mr. Oglethorpe's feet. He then said those were the best things they had, and therefore they gave them with a good heart. He then thanked him for his kindness to Tomochichi, mico, and his Indians, to whom he said he was related; and said, that though Tomochichi was banished from his nation, he was a good man, and had been a great warrior, and it was for his wisdom and courage that the banished men chose him king. Lastly, he said, they had heard in the nation that the Cherokees had killed some Englishmen, and that if he should command them, they would enter with their whole force into the Cherokee country, destroy their harvest, kill their people and revenge the English. He then sat down. Mr. Oglethorpe promised to acquaint the trustees with their desire of being instructed, and informed them that although there had been a report of the Cherokees having killed some Englishmen, it was groundless. He thanked them in the most cordial manner for their affection, and told them that he would acquaint the trustees with it.

"Tomochichi, mico, then came in, with the Indians of Yamacraw, to Mr. Oglethorpe, and, bowing very low, said: 'I was a banished man; I came here poor and helpless to look for good land near the tombs of my ancestors, and the trustees sent people here; I feared you would drive us away, for we were weak and wanted corn; but you confirmed our land to us, gave us food and instructed our children. We have already thanked you in the strongest words we could find, but words are no return for such favors; for good words may be spoken by the deceitful, as well as by the upright heart. The chief men of all our nation are here to thank you for us; and before them I declare your goodness, and that here I design to die; for we all love your people so well that with them we will live and die. We do not know good from evil, but desire to be instructed and guided by you, that we may do well with, and be numbered amongst the children of the trustees.' He sat down, and Yahou-Lakee, mico of Coweeta, stood up and said: 'We are come twenty-five days' journey to see you. I have often been advised to go down to Charles-Town, but would not go down because I thought I might die in the way; but when I heard that you were come, and that you were good men, I knew you were sent by Him who lives in Heaven, to teach us Indians wisdom; I therefore came down that I might hear good things, for I knew that if I died in the way I should die in doing good, and what was said would be carried back to the nation, and our children would reap the benefit of it. I rejoice that I have lived to see this day, and to see our friends that have long been gone from amongst us. Our nation was once strong, and had ten towns; but we are now weak, and have but eight towns. You have comforted the banished, and have gathered them that were scattered like little birds before the eagle. We desire therefore to be reconciled to our brethren who are here amongst you, and we give leave to Tomochichi, Stimoiche, and Illispelle, to call the kindred that love them out of each of the Creek towns, that they may come together and make one town. We must pray you to recall the Yamassees that they may be buried in peace amongst their ancestors, and that they may see their graves before they die; and their own nation shall be restored again to its ten towns.' After which he spoke concerning the abatement of the prices of goods, and agreed upon articles of a treaty which were ordered to be engrossed."

**Reply of the Trustees**—The Georgia trustees ratified the treaty with this communication on October 18, 1733:

"The Trustees for establishing the colony of Georgia in America to the chief men of the nation of the Lower Creeks, SEND GREETING:

"WHEREAS, The great King, George the Second, king of Great Britain, did by his letters patent under the great seal of Great Britain, bearing date of the 9th of June, in the 5th year of his reign, constitute and appoint a body politic and corporate by the name of the Trustees for establishing the colony of Georgia in America:

"And, Whereas, The said Trustees have received from their beloved Mr. James Oglethorpe, of West Brook Place, in the county of Surry, Esquire, one of the common council of the said Trustees, a copy of certain articles of friendship and commerce between the said Trustees, and the said chief men, which is in the words following (that is to say), Articles of friendship and commerce between the Trustees for establishing the colony of Georgia in America, and the chief men of the nation of the Lower Creeks.

"First. The Trustees, bearing in their hearts great love and friendship to you the said head-men of the Lower Creek nation, do engage to let their people carry up into your towns all kinds of goods fitting to trade in the said towns, at the rates and prices settled and agreed upon before you the said head-men, and annexed to this treaty of trade and friendship.

"Secondly. The Trustees do by these articles promise to see restitution done to any of the people of your towns by the people they shall send among you; proof being made to the beloved man they shall at any time send among you, that they who have either committed murder, robbery, or have beat or wounded any of your people, or any wise injured them in their crops, by their horses; or any other ways whatever; and upon such proof the said people shall be tried and punished according to the English law.

"Thirdly. The Trustees when they find the hearts of you the said head-men and your people are not good to the people they shall send among you, or that you or your people do not mind this paper, they will withdraw the English trade from the town so offending. And that you and your people may have this chain of friendship in your minds and fixed to your hearts, they have made fast their seal to this treaty.

"Fourthly. We, the head-men of the Coweta and Cuseta towns, in behalf of all the Lower Creek nation, being firmly persuaded that He who lives in Heaven and is the occasion of all good things, has moved the hearts of the Trustees to send their beloved men among us, for the good of our wives and children, and to instruct us and them in what is straight, do therefore declare that we are glad that their people are come here; and though this land belong to us (The Lower Creeks), yet we, that we may be instructed by them do consent and agree that they shall make use of and possess all those lands which our nation hath not occasion to use; and we make over unto them their successors and assigns all such lands and territories as we shall have occasion to use; provided always, that they, upon settling every new town, shall set out for the use of ourselves and the people of our nation such lands as shall be agreed upon between their beloved men and the head-men of our nation, and that those lands shall remain to us forever.

"Fifthly. We, the head-men, do promise for ourselves and the people of our towns that the traders for the English which shall settle among us, shall not be robbed or molested in their trade in our nation; and that if it shall so happen any of our people should be mad, and either kill, wound, beat or rob any of the English traders or their people, then we the said head-men of the towns aforesaid do engage to have justice done to the English, and for that purpose to deliver up any of our people who shall be guilty of the crimes aforesaid, to be tried by the English laws, or by the laws of our nation, as the beloved man of the Trustees shall think fit. And we further promise not to suffer any of the people of our said towns to come into the limits of the English settlements without leave from the English beloved man, and that we will not molest any of the English traders passing to or from any nation in friendship with the English.

"Sixthly. We, the head-men, for ourselves and people do promise to apprehend and secure any negro or other slave which shall run away from any of the English settlements to our nation, and to carry them either to this town, or Savannah, or Palachuckola garrison, and there to deliver him up to the commander of such garrison, and to be paid by him four blankets or two guns, or the value thereof in other goods; provided such runaway negro, or other slave, shall be taken by us or any of our people on the farther side of Oconee River; and in case such negro or runaway slave shall be taken on the hither side of the said river, and delivered to the commanders aforesaid, then we understand the pay to be one gun, or the value thereof; and in case we or our people should kill any such slave for resistance or running away from us in apprehending him, then we are to be paid, one blanket for his head, by any trader, for carrying such slave's head unto him.

"Lastly. We promise with stout hearts, and love to our brothers the English, to give no encouragement to any other white people, but themselves, to settle amongst us, and that we will not have any correspondence with the Spaniards or French; and to show that we both for the good of ourselves our wives and children do firmly promise to keep the talk in our hearts as long as the sun shall shine or the waters run in the rivers, we have each of us set the marks of our families."

SCHEDULE OF THE PRICES OF GOODS AGREED ON, ANNEXED.

| | |
|---|---|
| Two yards of stroud | Five buck-skins |
| One yard of plains | One ditto |
| White blanket | One ditto |
| Blue ditto | Five ditto |
| A gun | Ten ditto |
| A pistol | Five ditto |
| A gun-lock | Four ditto |
| Two measures of powder | One ditto |
| Sixty bullets | Ditto ditto |
| One white shirt | Two ditto |
| One knife | One doe-skin |
| Eighteen flints | One buck-skin |
| Three yards of cadiz | One doe-skin |
| Ditto ditto of gartering | Ditto ditto |
| One hoe | Two buck-skins |
| One axe | Ditto ditto |
| One large hatchet | Three doe-skins |
| One small ditto | One buck-skin |
| Brass kettles per lb. | Ditto ditto |

Doe-skins were estimated at half the value of the bucks.

"And, Whereas, the said Trustees are greatly desirous to maintain and preserve an inviolable peace, friendship and commerce between the said headmen of the Lower nation of Creeks, and the people the said Trustees have sent and shall send to inhabit and settle in the province of Georgia aforesaid, to endure to the world's end;

"Now know ye that we the said Trustees for establishing the Colony of Georgia in America do by these presents ratify and confirm the said articles of friendship and commerce between the Trustees for establishing the colony of Georgia in America, and the chief-men of the Lower-Creeks, and all and every of the articles and agreements therein contained, and also the rates and prices of goods above mentioned, settled and agreed upon before the said head-men, and annexed to the said treaty of trade and friendship.

"In witness whereof the Common Council of the said Trustees for establishing the Colony of Georgia in America have to these presents made fast the common seal of the corporation of the said Trustees, the eighteenth day of October, in the seventh year of the reign of our sovereign lord George the Second, by the grace of God of Great Britain, France and Ireland king, defender of the faith, etc., and in the year of our Lord one thousand seven hundred and thirty-three.

"By order of the said Common Council.

"BENJAMIN MARTYN, Secretary."

This treaty, concluded between General Oglethorpe and the head men of the Lower Creek Nation on May 21, 1733, pacified the Lower Creek Indians, the Uchees, Yamacraws, and other tribes subject to them. The treaty was also recognized and agreed to later by the Upper Creeks and the Cherokees.

For many years these agreements were kept in good faith and the Colony of Georgia extended its settlements up the Savannah River and along the coast without opposition or interference. The colonists received continued evidence of the good will of these Indians and that was due to the far-seeing wisdom of Oglethorpe in enlisting at the outset the friendship and influence of Tomochichi.

# CHAPTER XVII.

## *A Period of Difficulty and Discontent*

**Communities Without Government**—The remoteness of the trustees from the colonies resulted in strange conditions.

While they created a county government for Savannah, under a president and assistants, who were bailiffs or other minor officials, and, later, a similar one for Frederica, the communities established for the Salzburgers, the Scotch and others were without any form of government at the start.

Seeing the need of some one in the colony to direct its affairs, the trustees hit upon the expedient of dividing the whole territory into two counties, one in Savannah and one south of Savannah, with headquarters in Frederica, including the rest of the province.

For each of these counties they appointed a president and assistants.

Later, to unify the colony, they joined both these counties under one government at Savannah, presided over by a president and assistants.

**No Laws Passed for Two Years**—Another strange result of the remoteness of the trustees from the colonies, was the fact that although a shipload of immigrants landed at Savannah in February, 1733, the trustees made no laws for their government until 1735. Then upon recommendation of General Oglethorpe, they enacted three laws of great importance. These laws were to regulate the trade with Indians and perserve peace with them, to prevent the importation of rum into Georgia and to prohibit the importation of negro slaves into the colony.

Although these laws had the firm support of Oglethorpe and most of the trustees, being intended to operate for the best interest of the colony, they were in the course of years the cause of much dissatisfaction within the colony and serious offense to the people of South Carolina, who had formerly crossed Georgia to trade with the Indians, but, under the law controlling Indian trade, were prevented doing so.

Prohibition against importation of slaves caused dissatisfaction in the colony, because some of the colonists saw that the South Carolina planters profited by the use of negro labor and felt that they were at a disadvantage as compared with the citizens of that colony.

The dissatisfaction so caused by these laws and the activities of selfish interests against them ultimately caused their repeal.

Dissatisfaction was also caused by the system of land tenure, which is discussed more fully in another place.

**Indian Trade**—The act to preserve the peace with the Indians and regulate their trade with the natives of Georgia provided a fine of one hundred pounds, with forfeiture of goods, on any one trading or trying to trade with Indians without a license from the agents of the trustees. To secure such licenses the trader had to appear before a commissioner at Savannah and pay an annual fee not less than five pounds, besides giving security in the sum of one hundred pounds that he would be friendly with the Indians and obey the rules of the trustees. Licenses had to be taken out annually by the traders in person appearing before the commissioner. They were forbidden to give much credit to Indians and could only carry on their business in the territory named in the licenses. This law was approved by the Indians and seemed wise and reasonable, but created much ill will in South Carolina, because traders in that State had before then the monopoly of English trade with the Indians in the south, and much of their trade had been in Georgia. They could not continue this trade without securing the licenses at Savannah.

South Carolina sympathized with the traders, protested against the Georgia law, and sought to nullify it. So it came to pass that the people of South Carolina, who had been cordial and friendly to Georgia, were estranged by the act to regulate commerce with the Indians, and the loss of Carolina's support was a serious disadvantage to Georgia.

**The Law Against Rum**—The law against rum enacted a former regulation of the trustees, who made it because rum caused trouble at Savannah, and Indian chiefs reported that the use of liquor caused great disorder among their people. So the act was regarded as necessary to protect the people of Georgia. Under it no rum, brandy, spirits or strong waters of any kind could be brought into the province. Any person attempting to sell rum to Indians or white people was fined five pounds for the first offense, and for the second offense, he was fined fifty pounds and disfranchised. Half the penalty was to go to the informer and half to the colony. To prevent profanity, debauchery, etc., in public houses, any retailer of wine, beer or ale, violating the rum act, should be fined twenty pounds for the first offense, and his license to keep a public house might be recalled. Over all this the council of the trustees had supervision.

**The Prohibition on Slaves**—The act forbidding the use of negro slaves within Georgia stated that it was passed because experience had shown that slaves in the colonies had prevented the increase of white people and such colonies were weak in suppressing local tumult or carrying on war outside.

To prevent this, the Georgia act of 1735 provided that no negroes should be brought into the colony or sold or bought therein. The offenders were fined fifty pounds, of which half went to the colony and half to the informer. Any negro found within Georgia must be seized, declared the property of the trustees and disposed of for the benefit of the province. If a negro ran away from South Carolina into Georgia and was claimed by his owner within three months, the court at Savannah would confirm the owner's right to the slave, provided he paid the cost of apprehending him; keeping him until claimed, and any damage the negro might have committed. The common council of the trustees had power to mitigate the fines under this act if it saw fit to do so.

**Laws Against Rum and Slaves**—While in England, Oglethorpe resumed his seat in Parliament long enough to secure the passage of important acts prohibiting the importation and sale of rum, brandy, and other distilled liquors in Georgia, and an act prohibiting the introduction of slavery into the colony. It appears that rum had been brought into the colony from South Carolina and the West Indies, and it had caused the death of several colonists and some disorder had resulted from its use.

Although hard liquor was prohibited, beer and wine were not, and they were sold in the colony's store at Savannah.

**Georgia's Silk**—The production of raw silk in Georgia at first appeared to be a success, and, in 1735, the trustees exhibited a specimen to the Queen of England, who had a dress made of the silk and wore it in court on her birthday.

**Fortifying Georgia**—While in England, Oglethorpe had in mind the fortification of the southern coast of Georgia. The danger of aggression from that quarter was made clear by a memorial addressed to the King of Great Britain by the governor and Legislature of South Carolina, on April 9, 1734, in which, after thanking the King for his favor and protection, especially for establishing a province south of them, which would be a protection to South Carolina, they spoke of the effort of the French to enlarge their possessions in America and to win over the Indians from their friendship to English settlements. Speaking of the threatening attitude of the Spaniards in Florida, the governor and Legislature of South Carolina called the attention of the King to the necessity for guarding the harbors and ports of Carolina and Georgia, and for establishing military posts on the southern coasts to defend the territory near the Spaniards and protect the British trade with the Gulf.

Moved by the Carolina petition and the earnest request of the Georgia trustees, Parliament granted 26,000 pounds to settle, fortify, and defend the colony.

**Coming of Scotch Highlanders**—To carry out the purpose of this appropriation, the trustees commissioned Lieutenant Hugh MacKay to recruit

RICHMOND ACADEMY, AUGUSTA, NOW USED AS A LIBRARY

Scotch Highlanders for Georgia colonists. He succeeded in inducing one hundred and thirty Highlanders, with fifty women and children, to come to Georgia, and they were enrolled at Inverness. These Highlanders, who went at the expense of the trustees and several grantees of larger means, sailed from Inverness on October 18, 1735, on the ship *Prince of Wales,* commanded by Captain George Dunbar. They reached Savannah in January, 1736, and proved a strong addition to the colony. They were not adventurers or men exiled by debt and want, but were men of good character, carefully selected for their military qualities. They were picked men, many of them from the Glen of Stralbdean, and their officers were highly connected in the Highlands.

The town council of Inverness, appreciating Oglethorpe's kindness to the Highlanders, conferred on him the title of a burgess of the city.

With these Highlanders there were others like the Mackays, Dunbars, Baileys, and Cuthberts, who secured large tracts of land in Georgia and occupied it with their own servants.

These Highlanders were accompanied by their own minister, Rev. John McLeod, of the Isle of Skye.

Soon after their arrival in Savannah, the Highlanders were transferred southward to the Altamaha River, and landed at a point on the left bank sixteen miles above St. Simon's Island, where they formed a settlement and named it New Inverness (now Darien). There they built a fort with four cannon, a guard house, a store, and a chapel, with huts for residences, until they could build more permanent dwellings.

These Highlanders did heroic service in defending Georgia from the Spaniards in the Battle of Bloody Marsh, and they and their descendants have furnished great names to Georgia in the American Revolution, like John Moore McIntosh, Captain Hugh MacKay, Ensign Charles MacKay, Colonel John McIntosh, and General Lachlan McIntosh.

The settlement of New Inverness grew in wealth and influence and the men were valued in military service in time of danger.

Very soon after the founding of New Inverness, a road was built from there to Savannah, and Indian guides for the survey of that road were furnished by Tomochichi.

**Oglethorpe's Return to Georgia**—After spending some time in England, Oglethorpe sailed from Gravesend the latter part 1735 for America, accompanied by John and Charles Wesley, Rev. Mr. Ingham, and Charles Delamotte, the son of a London merchant and a friend of the Wesleys. Two vessels of two hundred and twenty tons each, the *Symond,* commanded by Captain Joseph Cornish, and the *London Merchant,* commanded by Captain John Thomas, had been chartered by the trustees to convey colonists to Georgia and these ships were accompanied by the sloop-of-war, *Hawk,* commanded by Captain Gascoigne, as a protection to them. On the two ships there were two hundred persons, coming to Georgia at the expense of the trustees. Some of them were English people and a number were German Lutherans, led by Baron Von Reck and Captain Hermsdorf. Twenty-five were Moravians, with their bishop, Rev. David Nitschman. With them came Sir Francis Bathurst, at his own expense, with his son, three daughters, servants, and some relatives of planters already in Georgia. Fine quarters had been fitted up for Oglethorpe on the *Hawk,* but he denied himself that comfort and took a cabin on the *Symond,* where he could take care of the immigrants. It was a long and stormy voyage. The beginning was delayed by contrary winds and the ship did not sail until the 10th of December. The sea was so rough and tempestuous that the ships were in danger of destruction. In the face of this peril the foreign Protestants remained calm. The Wesleys and the other ministers were guests of Oglethorpe and ate at his table. They read prayers twice a day, taught the scriptures, taught the children the catechism, and on the Sabbath administered the sacrament.

Oglethorpe distributed delicate food from his own store among the sick and feeble on the ship, and contented himself with plain fare.

John Wesley was much impressed with the conduct and religious character of the Lutherans and Moravians, and studied German, in order that he might learn more of their views and rules of conduct.

To prevent scurvy, Oglethorpe distributed among the passengers turnips, carrots, potatoes, and onions, to be eaten with the salt provisions. The ships were divided into cabins for families and single men were located in different places. Strict discipline was preserved and the men were taught the use of arms by Oglethorpe in order that they might be able to do their part in defending the colony in case of need after their arrival in Georgia. The women were required to keep busy in making stockings, caps, etc., or mending clothes for their families.

Oglethorpe treated the ministers with great respect and sternly rebuked gentlemen dining with him who took some offensive liberty with the missionaries.

The sloop-of-war, *Hawk,* was separated from the other ships by a storm, but the *Symond* and the *London Merchant,* after a stormy voyage, came in sight of Tybee Island on February 4, 1736, and the next morning anchored in Tybee Roads.

**Erecting a Lighthouse**—Before sailing for England, Oglethorpe had made arrangements for the erection of a lighthouse on the upper end of Tybee Island for the guidance of vessels entering the Savannah River. Returning in February, 1736, he went ashore to inspect the work and was surprised to find little done and that the serious delay had been caused by the idleness, intoxication, and disobedience of the workmen.

Rum was cheap in South Carolina and the workmen had no difficulty in getting enough to keep them drunk a good part of the time. Oglethorpe was in a quandary, for not withstanding the scandalous neglect of the man, Blythman, who had been left in charge of the work, there was no one else capable of finishing it. To prosecute him meant to leave the work undone and lose the material which had been brought there to build the lighthouse. On reflection, Oglethorpe decided to forgive Blythman, and agreed with him to complete the work by a certain time at a specified price. To make sure that the agreement was carried out, Oglethorpe appointed Mr. Vanderplank to see that the work was done according to agreement and that Blythman was paid only for what was actually done.

The lighthouse was twenty-five feet square at the base, ninety feet high, and ten feet square at the top. It was built of pine, resting upon cedar piles, with brick work around the bottom, and was a great advantage to ships bound for Georgia or Carolina ports.

On February 6th, Oglethorpe went to Savannah, after the colonists had been put ashore on Peeper Island, where they dug a well and refreshed themselves.

Arriving at Savannah, Oglethorpe was met by the freeholders of the town under arms and saluted with twenty-one guns from the battery. The colonists were overjoyed by his return and gladly welcomed the ministers who were with him.

For the newly-arrived colonists the people of Savannah supplied fresh meat and vegetables, with beef, pork, venison, wild turkeys, soft bread, strong beer, small beer, turnips, and garden greens in great abundance.

It was Oglethorpe's intention to locate the newly-arrived immigrants at Frederica, on St. Simon's Island, but at the earnest request of the Moravians, they were allowed to settle with their countrymen near the Irene school house, where they were heartily welcomed. Some of the Lutherans were allowed to join their brethren at Ebenezer, but the other Lutherans, under Captain Hermsdorf, remained with General Oglethorpe and went with him to found a new town and fort at the mouth of the Altamaha River.

**Discontent at Ebenezer**—With these and former accessions, Ebenezer had become a town of two hundred people, but it was not prosperous. The soil was poor, much sickness resulted from malarial conditions, and the people were discontented. The town was six miles from the Savannah River, on a creek whose winding course in reaching the river was twenty-five miles.

The Salzburger ministers, Bolzius and Gronau, called on Oglethorpe at Savannah, told him of the conditions at Ebenezer and asked for a change of location. On February 9, 1736, Oglethorpe went with them to Ebenezer and tried to dissuade the Salzburgers from moving their town and abandoning the improvements which had been made with so much labor. He said, however, that if they were determined to move he would not forbid it and would help them in doing so.

The Salzburgers felt that the move was necessary and chose for the new site a high ridge, called Red Bluff, near the Savannah River, and named it

New Ebenezer. There within two years they were thoroughly established, and there was nothing left at the old site but a cow pen, where Joseph Barker had care of the trustees' cattle. So the old Ebenezer became one of the dead towns of Georgia.

The new site was a commanding one, with a view of the Savannah River on the east, Little Creek to the south, old Ebenezer in a distance to the north, and a surrounding country undulating and covered with forest trees, brightened with jessamine, woodbine, and azaleas. The only bad feature was the swamps not far away, giving rise to malarial conditions.

The new town was laid out by Oglethorpe on a plan similar to that he had made for Savannah, with lots and streets of the same dimensions.

The new Ebenezer grew and prospered. Dwellings more comfortable than those at old Ebenezer were erected. Gardens and farms were cleared and cultivated. The land was fertile and the people soon began to enjoy the fruits of their industry. An orphan house was built with funds received from Germany, and it was also used as a church.

**Description of New Ebenezer**—Benjamin Martyn, secretary of the trustees, thus described the condition of New Ebenezer in 1738 and 1739:

"Fifteen miles from Purysburg, on the Georgia side, is Ebenezer, where the Saltsburghers are situated; their houses are neat, and regularly set out in Streets, and the whole Economy of their town, under the Influence of their Ministers, Mess. Bolzius and Gronau, is very exemplary. For the Benefit of their Milch Cattle, a Herdsman is appointed to attend them in the Woods all the Day, and bring them Home in the Evening. Their Stock of outlying Cattle is also under the Care of two other Herdsmen, who attend them in their Feeding in the Day, and drive them into Cow-Pens at night. This secures the Owners from any Loss, and the Herdsmen are paid by a small Contribution among the people. These are very industrious, and subsist comfortably by their Labour. Though there is no regular Court of Justice, as they live in Sobriety, they maintain great Order and Decency. In case of any Differences, the Minister calls three or four of the most prudent Elders together, who in a summary Way hear and determine as they think just, and the Parties always acquiesce with Content in their Judgment. They are very regular in their public Worship, which is on Week-Days in the Evening after their Work; and in the Forenoon and Evening on Sundays. They have built a large and convenient House for the Reception of Orphans, and other poor children, who are maintained by Benefactions among the People, are well taken Care of and taught to work according as their Age and Ability will permit. The Number computed by Mr. Bolzius in June, 1738, whereof his Congregation consisted, was one hundred Forty-six, and some more have since been settled among them. They are all in general so well pleased with their condition, that not one of their people has abandoned the Settlement."

**Salzburgers Grow Cotton and Rice**—In a letter to General Oglethorpe from Ebenezer, on March 13, 1739, signed by forty-nine Salzburgers, with the approval of their ministers, they said that they were well settled in their location, liked the climate and conditions around them, and, although the season was hotter than in Germany, they were accustomed to it and it was their habit to work outdoors from early morning until ten o'clock, attend to matters inside their houses until three, and then work outdoors until sunset.

They ridiculed the idea that rice could only be grown by negroes and reported a good harvest of rice gathered by some of their number, with plenty of corn, peas, potatoes, pumpkins, and cabbage, enough to feed themselves and their cows, calves, and hogs. They closed the letter with a request that negroes be excluded from their town and neighborhood lest they rob the houses and gardens and because they "endangered the lives of white people."

The earliest experiment in cotton-growing in Georgia seems to have been made by the Salzburgers at Ebenezer in 1738, and they were encouraged by a good yield and excellent quality of the cotton, but it is stated that the trustees, having their hope fixed upon the culture of silk and the production of wine, did not encourage the growing of cotton.

In 1741, Benjamin Martyn, secretary of trustees, estimated that up to that year 1,200 German Protestants had come to the colony of Georgia, settling at New Ebenezer, Bethany, Savannah, Frederica, Goshen, and along the road from Savannah to Ebenezer. They were reported as industrious, sober and thrifty.

**Weeding Out the Faint-Hearted; the Trustees Take Steps to Raise the Morale of the Colonists**—Although great care had been taken by the trustees in selecting colonists to be sent over at the public expense, and a number of sober, industrious and worthy people came to Georgia, it was true there as in most any body of people, that some proved to be a disappointment to those who had done so much for them. Having had their way to Georgia paid by the trustees, and having been furnished provisions for some time after their arrival, they did not realize the necessity for the hard work and self-denial which was necessary to success in founding a colony in a strange country, where the forest had to be cleared, the new land tilled, homes built, and military training undergone to make the community safe from attack by Indians or Spaniards.

To meet this condition, the trustees examined with increased care applicants for transmission to the colony and warned them that they would have to work hard and undergo self-denial, living on plain fare and enduring the heat of a warm climate.

This plain talk caused the faint-hearted to withdraw their applications, but their places were taken by men of sterner character and more courage.

In order to make conditions perfectly clear, the trustees published the following rules for the colony in 1735:

**Rules of the Trustees for 1735**—"The Trustees intend this year to lay out a County and build a new Town in Georgia.

"They will give to such Persons as they send upon the Charity; *viz* to every Man a Watch-coat, a Musquet and Bayonet; to those who have them not of their own, an Hatchet, an Hammer, an Handsaw, a shod Shovel or Spade, a broad Hoe, a narrow Hoe, a Gimlet, a drawing Knife, and there will be a publick Grindstone to each Ward or Village. He will also have an Iron Pot, and a Pair of Pot hooks, and a Frying-pan.

"And for his Maintenance in the Colony for one Year he will have, to be delivered in such Proportions and at such Times as the Trust shall think proper, 300 pounds of Beef or Pork, 114 pounds of Rice, 114 Pounds of Pease, 114 Pounds of Flour, 44 Gallons of Strong Beer, 64 Quarts of Molasses for brewing of Beer, 18 Pounds of Cheese, 9 Pounds of Butter, 9 Ounces of Spice, 9 Pounds of Sugar, 5 Gallons of Vinegar, 30 Pounds of Salt, 12 Quarts of Lamp Oil, and a Pound of Spun Cotton, and 12 Pounds of Soap.

"And to the Mothers, Wives, Sisters, or Children of Such Men, Provision will be given in the Colony for one year in the following Manner, *viz:* to be delivered as above, 300 pounds of Beef, or Pork, 114 Pounds of Rice, 114 pounds of Pease, 114 Pounds of Flour, 64 Quarts of Molasses for Brewing of Beer, 18 Pounds of Cheese, 9 pounds of Butter, 9 Ounces of Spice, 9 Pounds of Sugar, 5 Gallons of Vinegar, 30 Pounds of Salt, 6 Quarts of Lamp Oil, and half a Pound of Spun Cotton, and 12 Pounds of Soap.

"And for every Person above the Age of Seven, and under the Age of Twelve, half the said Allowance;—being esteemed half an Head.

"And for every Person above the age of Two and under the age of Seven, one third of the said Allowance;—being esteemed one third of an Head.

"The Trustees pay their Passage from England to Georgia and in the Voyage they will have the following Provisions, *viz,* in every Week four Beef Days, two Pork Days, and one Fish Day; and their Allowance served out daily as follows; that is to say:

"On the four Beef Days four Pounds of Beef for every Mess of five heads, and two Pounds and a half of Flour, and half a Pound of Suet or Plums.

"On the two Pork Days, five Pounds of Pork and two Pints and a half of Peas for every five heads.

"And on the Fish Day two Pounds and a half of Fish and Half a Pound of Butter for every five Heads.

"The whole at sixteen Ounces to the Pound.

"And allow each Head seven Pounds of Bread of fourteen Ounces to the Pound, by the Week.

"And three Pints of Beer and two Quarts of Water (Whereof one of the quarts for drinking and the other for boiling Victuals) each Head by the Day after during their being on their Passage.

"The Heads to be accounted in this Manner: Every Person above the Age of Twelve Years to be accounted a whole Head; all Persons of the age of Seven Years and under the Age of Twelve Years, to be accounted Two for one; all Persons above the Age of Two Years and under the Age of Seven Years, to be accounted Three for One; and any Person under the age of Two Years is not to be accounted.

"And the said Persons are to enter into the following Covenants before their Embarkation: *viz:*—

"That they will repair on Board such Ship as shall be provided for carrying them to the Province of Georgia; and during the Voyage, will quietly, soberly, and obediently demean themselves; and go to such Place in the said Province of Georgia, and there obey all such orders as shall be given for the better settling, establishing, and governing the said Colony.

"And that for the first Twelve Months from landing in the said Province of Georgia they will work and labour in clearing their Lands, making Habitations, and necessary Defences, and in all other Works for the common Good and publick Weal of the said Colony, at such Times, in such Manner, and according to such Plan and Directions as shall be given.

"And that they, from and after the Expiration of the said last mentioned Twelve Months will, during the two next succeeding Years, abide, settle, and inhabit in the said Province of Georgia, and cultivate the Lands which shall be to them and their Heirs Male severally allotted and given, by all such Ways and Means as, according to their several Abilities and Skills they shall be best able and capable.

"And such Persons are to be settled in the said Colony either in new Towns or New Villages.

"Those in the Towns will have each of them a Lot sixty Feet in front and ninety feet in depth whereon they are to build an House; and as much land in the country as in the whole shall make up fifty Acres.

"Those in the Villages will each of them have a Lot of Fifty Acres which is to lie all together, and they are to build their House upon it.

"All Lots are granted in Tail Male and descend to the Heirs Male of their Bodies forever; and in case of Failure of Heirs Maile, revert to the Trust to be granted again to such Persons as the Common Council of the Trustees shall think most for the Advantage of the Colony. And they will have a special Regard to the Daughters of Freeholders who have made Improvements on their Lots, not already provided for by having married, or marrying Persons in Possession, or intitled to Lands in the Province of Georgia in Possession or Remainder.

"All Lots are to be preserved separate and undivided, and cannot be united, in order to keep up a Number of Men equal to the Number of Lots for the better Defence and Support of the Colony.

"No person can lease out his House or Lot to another without License for that Purpose, that the Colony may not be ruined by Absentees receiving and spending their Rents elsewhere. Therefore each Man must cultivate the same by himself or Servants.

"And no person can alienate his land or any part, or any term, Estate, or Interest therein, to any other Person or Persons, without special Licence for that Purpose, to prevent the uniting or dividing the Lots.

"If any of the Land so granted shall not be cultivated, planted, cleared, improved, or fenced with a worm fence or Pales six feet high during the Space of Ten Years from the Date of the Grant, then every Part thereof not cultivated, planted, cleared, improved, or fenced as aforesaid, shall belong to the Trust; and the Grant, as to such Parts, shall be void.

"There is reserved, for the Support of the Colony, a Rent charge forever of Two Shillings Sterling Money for each Fifty Acres, the Payment of which is not to commence until Ten Years after the Grant.

"And the Reversion or Remainder expectant on the Demise of such Persons without issue Male shall remain to the Trust.

"But the Wives of the Freeholders, in case they should survive their Husbands, are, during their Lives, intitled to the Mansion-house and one half of the Lands improved by their Husbands; that is to say, inclosed with a Fence of Six feet high.

"All Forfeitures for Non-residence, High-Treason, Felonies, etc., are to the Trustees for the Use and Benefit of the Colony.

"Negroes and Rum are prohibited to be used in the said Colony; and Trade with the Indians, unless licensed.

"None are to have the Benefit of being sent upon the Charity in the manner above mentioned but

"1st. Such as are in decayed Circumstances and thereby disabled from following any Business in England; and who, if in Debt, must have Leave from their Creditors to go.

"2nd. Such as have numerous Families of Children, if assisted by their respective Parishes, and recommended by the Minister, Church-Wardens, and Overseers thereof.

"The Trustees do expect to have a good Character of the said Persons given, because no Drunkards or other notoriously vicious Persons will be taken.

"And for the better to enable the said Persons to build the new Town, and clear their Lands, the Trustees will give Leave to every Freeholder to take over with him One Male Servant, or Apprentice, of the Age of Eighteen Years, and upwards, to be bound for not less than Four Years; and will, by way of Loan to such Freeholder, advance the charges of Passage for such Servant or Apprentice, and of furnishing him with Cloathing and Provisions hereafter mentioned, to be delivered in such Proportions, and at such Times as the Trust shall think proper; *viz:* With a Pallias and Bolster and Blanket for Bedding: A Frock and Trowsers of Lintsey Wolsey, a Shirt, and Frock, and Trowsers of Osnabrigs, a Pair of Shoes from England, and two Pair of Country Shoes for Cloathing; and 200 Pounds of Meat and 342 Pounds of Rice, Pease, or Indian Corn for Food for a Year.

"The Expense of which Passage, Cloathing and Provisions is to be repaid the Trustees by the Master within the Third Year from their Embarkation from England.

"And to each Man servant and the Heirs Male of his Body forever, after the expiration of his Service, upon a Certificate from his Master of his having served well, will be granted Twenty Acres of Land under such Rents and Agreements as shall have been then last granted to any others, Men Servants, in like circumstances.

"Sign'd by Order of the Common Council of the Trustees for Establishing the Colony of Georgia in America, this Second Day of July, 1735.

"BENJ. MARTYN, Secretary."

"To such Persons who can carry Ten Men Servants, and settle with them in Georgia at their own Expence, and whose Characters the Trustees, upon inquiry, shall approve of, will be granted Five Hundred Acres of Land in Tail Male, and descend to the Heirs Male of their Bodies forever, under the Yearly Rent of Twenty Shillings Sterling Money for every Hundred Acres, for the Support of the Colony; the payment of which is not to commence until Ten Years after the Grant.

"And the Land is so granted upon the following Conditions and Covenants.

"That such Persons do pay the Rent reserved as the same shall become due; and no part to be unpaid for Six months after due.

"That they, within a Month from the Grant, shall register the same, or a Memorial thereof, with the Auditor of the Plantations.

"That they, within Twelve Months from the Grant, shall go to and arrive in Georgia with ten able bodied Men Servants, being each of the age of Twenty Years and upwards.

"That they shall abide in Georgia with such Men Servants Three Years from the Registering the Grant there, building their Houses, and cultivating their Lands.

"That they shall clear and cultivate within Ten Years from the Grant, Two hundred Acres of Land, Part of the said Five Hundred Acres, and plant Two thousand White Mulberry-trees or Plants thereon; and on every Hundred of the other Three Hundred Acres One thousand White Mulberry-trees or Plants, when cleared, and preserve the same Quantity from time to time thereupon, the Trustees obliging themselves to furnish the plants.

"That they do not alienate the said Five Hundred Acres of Land or any Part for any Terms of Years, or any Estate or Interest in the same to any Person or Persons without special Leave.

"That they do not make Pot-ash in Partnership without Leave; but may make it themselves not in Partnership.

"On the determination of the Estate in Tail Male the Land to revert to the Trust.

"That they shall not depart the said Province without License.

"All forfeitures for Non-Residence, High Treason, Felonies, etc., are to the Trustees for the Use and Benefit of the Colony.

"If any Part of the said Five Hundred Acres of Land shall not be cultivated, planted, cleared, and fenced round with a Worm fence, or Pales Six feet high, within Eighteen Years from the grant, all and every such Part shall revert to the Trust; and the Grant as to such Part, to be void.

"And the Common Council of the Trust, at the Expirations of the Terms such Men Servants shall be severally bound for (being not less than Four Years), when requested by the Grantee will grant to each of such Men Servants Twenty Acres of Land in Tail Male, under such Rents, Conditions, Limitations, and Agreements as shall have been then last granted to any others, Men Servants, in like Circumstances.

"When the Land reverts to the Trust on the Determination of the Estate in Tail Male it is to be granted again to such Persons as the Common Council of the Trust shall think most for the Advantage of the Colony. And the Trust will have a Special Regard to the Daughters of those who have made Improvements on their Lots, not already provided for, by having married, or marrying Persons in Possession, or intitled to Lands in the Province of Georgia in Possession or Remainder.

"And the Wives of such Persons, in case they should survive their Husbands, are, during their Lives, intitled to the Mansion-house, and one half of the Lands improved by their Husbands; that is to say, inclosed with a Fence Six feet high.

"Negroes and Rum are prohibited to be used in the said Province, and Trade with the Indians, unless licensed."

**Trespasses on Indian Territory Stopped**—General Oglethorpe was careful to prevent any trespass upon Indian Territory by white men, and when informed by Tomochichi that the Uchees complained that South Carolina planters, with their negroes had formed settlements in the Uchee territory, contrary to the terms of their treaty with Oglethorpe, he promptly issued orders to stop the trespassing, directing Captain Eneas McIntosh to notify the trespassers that they must withdraw their cattle and negroes from Uchee territory within three days. If they were not sent away within that time they were to be arrested, brought to Savannah and delivered to the magistrates, who would institute proceedings for their punishment.

At the same time, Oglethorpe sent to Savannah for a copy of an act by the trustees approved by King George the Second on April 3, 1735, entitled

"An Act to maintain peace with Indians in the Province of Georgia," and the authorities there were instructed to tell every Indian trader the provisions of the act and command strict compliance with its requirements.

By this action, Oglethorpe showed his promptness in meeting emergencies and the care with which he guarded the rights of the Indians and maintained good faith with them.

It was at this time that Tomochichi sent runners to the Upper and Lower Creeks, informing them of Oglethorpe's return to Georgia.

Tomochichi also informed Oglethorpe that a number of his warriors were at Darien helping the Highlanders to build their town.

**Founding of Augusta**—Having already begun the fortification of the southern coast of Georgia at Darien, Frederica, and New Inverness, Oglethorpe turned his attention northward, and in 1735 laid out the town of Augusta. In 1736 a garrison was put there to defend the place, warehouses were built and were furnished with goods suitable for the Indian trade. Boats between Augusta and Savannah or Charleston, carrying 10,000 pounds of freight each were soon navigating the Savannah River, and Augusta became a resort for Indian traders in the spring of the year. There they bought from the Indians 2,000 pack-horse loads of skins in a year, with other articles offered by the natives. The population grew rapidly and including pack-horsemen, boatmen, and servants, it soon amounted to six hundred white persons engaged in commerce with the Indians.

The Indians went there for trade in great numbers, and in trade with the Indians, Augusta exceeded any other point in Georgia or South Carolina. A man named O'Bryan had begun the settlement of the town of Augusta at his own expense, and built a good storehouse. For his energy and public service, Oglethorpe, in March, 1739, asked the trustees to grant him five hundred acres of land. Roger DeLacey, a noted Indian trader, was one of the earliest settlers, and a garrison kept at Augusta by the trustees was commanded by Captain Kent.

# CHAPTER XVIII.

## *Savannah in 1736*

In spite of the many difficulties encountered in building a town in a new country with a varied population, composed of many elements, some of them discordant, Savannah made wonderful progress in the first three years, as will be seen from this pen picture of the young metropolis by Francis Moore, who came over from England with Oglethorpe in 1736, having been appointed keeper of the stores by the trustees at Oglethorpe's request. He was a valuable assistant to the general and a close observer, as this description shows:

"Savannah is about a mile and a quarter in Circumference; it stands upon the flat of a Hill; the Bank of the River (which they in barbarous English call a Bluff) is steep, and about 45 Foot perpendicular, so that all heavy Goods are brought up by a Crane, an Inconvenience designed to be remedied by a bridged Wharf, and an easy Ascent, which in laying out the Town, care was taken to allow room for, there being a very wide Strand between the first Row of Houses and the River. From this Strand there is a very pleasant Prospect; you see the River wash the Foot of the Hill which is a hard, clean, sandy beach a mile in Length; the Water is fresh, and the River 1,000 Foot wide. Eastward you see the River increased by the Northern Branch which runs round Hutchinson's Island, and the Carolina Shore beyond it, and the Woody Islands at the Sea, which close the Prospect at 10 or 12 Miles Distance. Over against it is Hutchinson's Island, great part of which is open Ground, where they mow Hay for the Trust's Horses and Cattle. The rest is Woods, in which there are many Bay-trees 80 foot high. Westward you see the River winding between the Woods, with little Islands in it for many Miles, and Tomachichi's Indian Town standing upon the Southern Banks, between 3 and 4 Miles distant.

"The town of Savannah is built of Wood; all the Houses of the first 40 Freeholders are of the same Size with that Mr. Oglethorpe lives in, but there are great Numbers built since, I believe 100 or 150. Many of these are much larger, some of 2 or 3 Stories high, the Boards plained and painted. The Houses stand on large Lotts, 60 Foot in Front, by 90 Foot in Depth; each Lott has a fore and back Street to it; the Lotts are fenced in with split

Pales; some few People have Pallisades of turned Wood before their Doors, but the Generality have been wise enough not to throw away their Money which, in this Country, laid out in Husbandry, is capable of great Improvements, though there are several People of good Substance in the Town who came at their own Expence, and also, several of those who came over on the Charity, are in a very thriving way; but this is observed that the most substantial People are the most frugal, and make the least shew, and live at the least Expence. There are some also who have made but little or bad Use of the Benefits they received, idling away their Times, whilst they had their Provisions from the Publick Store, or else working for Hire, earning from 2 Shillings the Price of a Labourer, to 4 or 5 Shillings, the Price of a Carpenter, per diem, and spending that Money in Rum and good Living, thereby neglecting to improve their Lands, so that when their Time of receiving their Provisions from the Publick ceased, they were in no Forwardness to maintain themselves out of their own Lands.

"As they chose to be Hirelings when they might have improved for themselves, the Consequence of that Folly forces them now to work for their daily Bread. These are generally discontented with the Country; and if they have run themselves in Debt, their Creditors will not let them go away till they have paid. Considering the Number of People there are but very few of these. The Industrious ones have throve beyond Expectation; most of them that have been there three Years and many others, have Houses in the Town, which those that Let have, for the worst, 10 pounds per annum, and the best let for 30 pounds.

**Profit in Gardening**—"Those who have cleared their 5 Acre Lotts have made a very great Profit out of them by Greens, Roots, and Corn. Several have improved the Cattle they had at first, and have now 5 or 6 tame Cows; others, who to save the Trouble of Feeding them, let them go into the Woods, can rarely find them, and when they are brought up, one of them will not give half the Quantity of Milk which another Cow fed near Home will give.

**Houses Far Apart**—"Their Houses are built at a pretty large Distance from one another for fear of Fire; the Streets are very wide, and there are great Squares left at Proper Distances for Markets and other Conveniences. Near the Riverside there is a Guard-house inclosed with Palisades a Foot thick, where there are 19 or 20 cannons mounted, and a continual Guard kept by the Free-holders. This Town is governed by 3 Bailiffs, and has a Recorder, Register, and a Town Court which is holden every six weeks, where all Matters Civil and Criminal are decided by grand and petty juries as in England; but there are no Lawyers allowed to plead for Hire, nor no Attornies to take Money, but (as in old times in England) every man pleads his own Cause. In case it should be an Orphan, or one that cannot speak for themselves, there are Persons of the best Substance in the Town, appointed by the Trustees to take care of the Orphans, and to defend the Helpless, and that without Fee or Reward, it being a Service that each that is capable must perform in his turn.

**Georgia Laws and Customs**—"They have some Laws and Customs peculiar to Georgia; one is that all Brandies and distilled Liquors are prohibited under severe Penalties, another is that no Slavery is allowed, nor Negroes, a Third, that all Persons who go among the Indians must give Security for their good Behaviour; because the Indians, if any Injury is done to them, and they cannot kill the man who does it, expect Satisfaction from the Government, which, if not procured, they break out into War by killing the first white man they conveniently can.

"No Victualler or Ale-house Keeper can give any Credit, so consequently cannot recover any debt.

**Against Land Monopoly**—"The Free-holds are all entailed which has been very fortunate for the Place. If Peoples could have sold, the greatest part, before they knew the Value of their Lotts, would have parted with them for a trifling Condition, and there were not wanting rich Men who employed Agents to Monopolize the whole Town: And if they had got Numbers of Lotts into their own Hands, the other Free-holders would have had no benefit by letting their Houses, and hardly of Trade, since the Rich, by means of a large Capital, would underlet and undersell, and the Town must have been almost without Inhabitants as Port Royal in Carolina is, by the best Lotts being got into a few Hands.

"The mentioning the Laws and Customs leads me to take notice that Georgia is founded upon Maxims different from those on which other Colonies have been begun. The intention of that Colony was an Asylum to receive the distressed. This was the charitable Design, and the governmental View besides that was with Numbers of free white People, well settled, to strengthen the southern Part of the English Settlements on the Continent of America, of which this is a Frontier. It is necessary therefore not to permit Slaves in such a country, for Slaves starve the poor Labourer. For, if the Gentleman can have his Work done by a Slave who is a Carpenter or a Bricklayer, the Carpenters, or Bricklayers of that country must starve for want of Employment, and so of other trades.

**Land in Small Parcels**—"In order to maintain many People it was proper that the Land should be divided into small Portions, and to prevent the uniting them by Marriage or Purchase. For every Time that two Lotts are united, the Town loses a Family, and the Inconvenience of this shews itself at Savannah, notwithstanding the Care of the Trustees to prevent it. They suffered the Moiety of the Lotts to descend to the Widows during their Lives: Those who remarried to Men had Lotts of their own, by uniting two

Lotts made one to be neglected; for the strength of Hands who could take care of one, was not sufficient to look to and improve two. These uncleared Lotts are a Nusance to their neighbors. The Trees which grow upon them shade the Lotts, the Beasts take shelter in them, and for want of clearing the Brooks which pass thro' them, the Lands above are often prejudiced by floods. To prevent all these Inconveniences the first Regulation of the Trustees was a strict Agrarian Law, by which all the Lands near Towns should be divided, 50 Acres to each Free-holder. The Quantity of Land by Experience seems rather too much, since it is impossible that one poor Family can tend so much Land. If this Alottment is too much, how much more inconvenient would the uniting of two be? To prevent it, the Trustees grant the Lands in Tail Male, that on the expiring of a Male-Line they may regrant it to such Man, having no other Lott, as shall be married to the next Female Heir of the Deceased, as is of good character. This manner of Dividing prevents also the Sale of Lands, and the Rich thereby monopolizing the Country.

**Plan of the Town**—"The Town is laid out for two hundred and forty Freeholds; the Quantity of Lands necessary for that Number is 24 Square Miles; 40 Houses in Town make a Ward to which 4 Square Miles in the Country belong; each Ward has a Constable, and under him 4 Tything Men.

"Where the Town-Lands end, the Villages begin, four Villages make a Ward without, which depends upon one of the Wards within the Town. The Use of this is, in case a War should happen that the Villages without may have Places in the Town, to bring their Cattle and Families into for Refuge, and to that Purpose there is a Square left in every Ward big enough for the Out-Wards to Encamp in. There is Ground also kept round about the Town ungranted, in order for the Fortifications whenever Occasion shall require. Beyond the Villages commence Lotts of 500 Acres; these are granted upon Terms of keeping 10 Servants, etc. Several Gentlemen who have settled on such Grants have succeeded very well, and have been of great Service to the Colony.

"Above the Town is a Parcel of Land called Indian Lands; these are those reserved by King Tomachichi for his people.

**The Trustees Garden**—"There is near the Town to the East, a garden belonging to the Trustees, consisting of 10 Acres, the situation is delightful, one half of it is upon the Top of a Hill, the Foot of which the River Savannah washes, and from it you see the Woody Islands in the sea. The Remainder of the Garden is the Side and some plain low Ground at the Foot of the Hill, where several fine Springs break out. In the Garden is a variety of Soils; the Top is sandy and dry, the sides of the Hill are Clay, and the Bottom is a black rich Garden Mould, well watered. On the North-part of the Garden is left standing a Grove of Part of the old Wood as it was before the arrival of the Colony there. The trees in the Grove are mostly Bay,

Sassafras, Evergreen, Oak, Pellitory, Hickary, American Ash, and the Laurel Tulip. This last is looked upon as one of the most beautiful Trees in the World; it grows straight-bodied to 40 or 50 Foot high, the Bark smooth and whitish, the Top spreads regular like an Orange-tree in English Gardens, only larger; the Leaf is like that of a common Laurel, but bigger, and the under-side of a greenish Brown: It blooms about the Month of June; the flowers are white, fragrant like the Orange, and perfume all the Air around it; the Flower is round, 8 or 10 Inches diameter, thick like the Orange-Flower, and a little yellow near the Heart; As the Flowers drop, the Fruit, which is a Cone with red Berries, succeeds them. There are also some Bay-trees that have Flowers like the Laurel, only less.

**Mulberry Trees**—"The Garden is laid out with Cross-Walks planted with Orange-trees, but the last Winter a good deal of Snow having fallen, had killed those upon the Top of the Hill down to their Roots, but they being cut down, sprouted again, as I saw when I returned to Savannah. In the Squares between the Walks were vast Quantities of Mulberry-trees, this being a Nursery for all the Province, and every Planter that desires it, has young Trees given him gratis from this Nursery. These white Mulberry-trees were planted in order to raise Silk, for which purpose several Italians were brought, at the Trustees' Expence, from Piedmont by Mr. Amatis; they have fed Worms and wound Silk to as great Perfection as any that ever came out of Italy; but the Italians falling out, one of them stole away the Machines for winding, broke the Coppers, and spoiled all the Eggs which he could not steal and fled to South Carolina. The others, who continued faithful, had saved but a few Eggs, when Mr. Oglethorpe arrived, therefore he forbade any Silk should be wound, but that all the Worms should be suffered to eat through their Balls in order to have more Eggs against next Year. The Italian Women are obliged to take English Girls Apprentices, whom they teach to wind and feed; and the Men have taught our English Gardeners to tend the Mulberry-trees, and our Joyners have learned how to make the Machines for winding. As the Mulberry-trees increase, there will be a great Quantity of Silk made here.

**Trees and Plants Flourish**—"Besides the Mulberry-trees there are in some of the Quarters in the coldest part of the Garden, all kinds of Fruit Trees usual in England, such as Apples, Pears, &c. In another Quarter are Olives, Figs, Vines, Pomegranates and such Fruits as are natural to the warm est Parts of Europe. At the bottom of the Hill, well-sheltered from the North-wind, and in the warmest part of the Garden, there was a Collection of West-India Plants and Trees, some Coffee, some Cocoa-Nuts, Cotton, Palma-Christi, and several West Indian physical Plants, some sent up by Mr. Eveleigh a publick spirited Merchant at Charles-Town, and some by Dr. Houstoun from the Spanish West Indies, where he was sent at the expence of a Collection raised by that curious Physician, Sir Hans Sloan, for to collect and send them to Georgia where the Climate was capable of making a garden which might contain all kinds of Plants; to which Design his Grace the Duke of Richmond, the Earl of Darby, the Lord Peters, and the Apothecary's Company, contributed very generously, as did Sir Hans himself. The Quarrels among the Italians proved fatal to most of these Plants and they were labouring to repair that loss when I was there, Mr. Miller being employed in the room of Dr. Houstoun who died in Jamaica. We heard he had wrote an Account of his having obtained the Plant from whence the true Balsamum Capivi is drawn; and that he was in hopes of getting that from whence the Jesuit's Bark is taken, he designing for that Purpose to send to the Spanish West Indies.

"There were no publick Buildings in the Town, besides a Storehouse, for the Courts were held in a Hut 36 Foot long and 12 Foot wide, made of split Boards, and erected on Mr. Oglethorpe's first Arrival in the Colony. In this Hut also Divine Service was performed; but upon his Arrival this time, Mr. Oglethorpe order'd a House to be erected in the Upper Square, which might serve for a Court House and for Divine Service till a Church could be built, and a Work-house over against it; for as yet there was no Prison here."

**Fortifying Frederica**—Having located the Scotch Highlanders on the Altamaha, where they were building the town of Darien, which they called New Inverness, and having sent Captain McPherson with a number of rangers to help the Highlanders, Oglethorpe turned his attention to fortifying the Island of St. Simon's, at Frederica on the north end, and at the lower point of the island.

As the captains of the ships, *Symond* and *London Merchant,* who still had their cargoes on board and remained at anchor in Tybee Roads, where Francis Moore had charge of their contents, were unwilling to enter Jekyll Sound, without some knowledge of its entrance, Oglethorpe bought the cargo of the sloop *Midnight,* which had just arrived, and sent it to Frederica, there to be unloaded. In the meantime, he had an understanding with Captain Cornish and Captain Thomas that they would go to Frederica on the sloop *Midnight* and inform themselves concerning the coast and the entrance to Jekyll Sound, after which they would return to their ships and bring them to Frederica.

With this understanding, Oglethorpe sent Mr. Horton and Mr. Tanner, with thirty men, cannon, arms, ammunition and intrenching tools, to Frederica on the sloop *Midnight.* At the same time, he ordered workmen from Savannah and Tomochichi's Indians to be at convenient points from which they could be transported to St. Simon's Island.

The *Midnight* sailed for St. Simon's Island on the morning of February 16, 1736, and Oglethorpe started the same afternoon in a scout boat to meet the *Midnight* in Jekyll Sound. He was accompanied by Captain Hermsdorf, two colonists, and some Indians. Captain Dunbar followed in another boat.

The scout boat used by Oglethorpe was a strongly built, swift vessel, with ten oars and three swivel guns. Several of these boats were kept for visiting the islands and preventing the attacks of enemies or runaways. The crews were men raised in the colony, bold and hearty, who could lie out in the woods or in a boat upon the water without house or covering and were good hunters and fishermen. Without carrying provisions, they provided themselves with food by killing deer and other game, and, in case of need, could live on oysters and shell fish.

In this way, Oglethorpe and his party passed through the inland channels between the islands and the mainland. They stopped between Wilmington Island and the mainland to inspect the plantations of Mr. Lacy and five other gentlemen, who had built houses on five hundred acre grants. They built their houses near together, surrounded them with palisades and defended them with cannon. The plantation owners and their servants formed a garrison, keeping a guard every night. They had already cleared a hundred acres of land near the fort and had plenty of milk, cattle, hogs, garden stuff, and poultry. This fort commanded the waterway between the islands and Savannah. The resourcefulness of these planters is shown by the fact that Mr. Lacey was sawing timber for the Sugar Islands and splitting staves for Madeira.

The party again stopped at the north end of Skidoway Island and inspected the village, guard house, and the battery of cannon located there. The freeholders on that island did guard duty at the battery and thirty acres of land in the vicinity had been cleared and was under cultivation.

Leaving Skidoway Island, Oglethorpe and his party passed the mouths of the Vernon and Ogeechee rivers, and, conducted by Captain Ferguson through water passages whose many channels were almost like a labyrinth, the boats pressed on towards St. Simon's.

As General Oglethorpe wished to reach his destination as soon as possible, the oarsmen rowed night and day with only a little occasional rest when the wind was favorable. Oglethorpe cheered them and relieved their fatigue by giving them refreshments, and the Indians, seeing the men overworked, offered to take the oars. This they did and rowed as well as the white men, using a somewhat different stroke, called the Yamassee stroke, which was a long stroke and a short stroke alternately.

The party reached St. Simon's Island on the morning of February 18th and found that the sloop *Midnight* had arrived ahead of them. Oglethorpe immediately put every man to work at Frederica. First, the tall grass on the bluff was burnt off, and a booth was made to hold the store of provisions. They dug into the ground three feet and threw up the earth on each side to make a bank. A roof was raised, resting upon uprights with a ridge pole and rafters, with cross pieces consisting of small poles nailed across the top. The roof was thatched with palmetto leaves, which afforded protection from the sun and rain.

Oglethorpe then laid out several booths, thirty or forty feet long and twenty feet wide, covered with palmetto leaves, to lodge the families of the colonists. Having made fine progress the first day, the party rested that evening and made merry, feasting on game brought in by Indians.

On the second day, February 19th, Oglethorpe began to build at Frederica a fort with four bastions, and taught the men how to dig a ditch and form around it a rampart covered with turf. On that day and the next the houses were finished and work on the fort went on.

Frederica was named by General Oglethorpe, and the trustees in honor of Frederick, Prince of Wales. In that town, Oglethorpe built the only home he ever had in Georgia.

Several days later a periagua from Savannah arrived at Frederica with workmen, provisions, and cannon for the new town. Captain Cornish and Captain Thomas returned to their ships in Tybee Road on the 26th of February, after inspecting the coast and Jekyll Sound, where there was ample water for their vessels, but still refused to take their ships southward. Oglethorpe was therefore compelled, much against his will, to have the cargoes of the ships, *Symond* and *London Merchant,* unloaded into the vessels, *Peter* and *James,* each of only one hundred tons capacity, and these vessels, with sloops, carrying some surplus cargo to Savannah. The *Peter* and *James,* with the aid of some periaguas, which were long flat-bottomed boats, carrying from twenty to thirty-five tons each, transferred most of the cargo of the *Symond* and *London Merchant* to Frederica.

Stopping at Darien to see the Highlanders, Oglethorpe was saluted by them with all their men under arms. They were very glad to learn that the town of Frederica was to be so near them and that a road from Darien to Savannah, on the mainland, would soon be completed. Greatly pleased with what he saw at Darien, or New Inverness, Oglethorpe congratulated the Scotchmen on their industry and soldierly appearance.

On the 2nd of March the colonists who had come over with Oglethorpe from England went in a fleet of periaguas to Frederica, accompanied by General Oglethorpe and his scout boat. An amusing incident of the trip down was that as the colonists were in open boats, exposed to the raw weather of February, Oglethorpe encouraged them by putting his supply of strong beer on a fast boat which was leading the fleet. The oarsmen on the other boats worked hard to keep up, for if they were not present at the place of rendezvous at night they lost their share of the beer. Proceeding this way, the party in boats, led by Oglethorpe and a scout boat, reached Frederica on the 8th of March, having been six days on the way from Savannah.

The work at Frederica had made fine progress, and by March 23rd a battery of cannon commanding the river had been mounted and the fort was nearly completed. A storehouse sixty feet wide at the front and intended to be two stories high had a cellar and first story done. The main street, twenty-five yards wide, went from the front into the country. Each land owner had a lot sixty feet wide and ninety feet deep upon the high street for his house and garden, but those on the river front only had lots thirty feet wide and sixty feet deep. Each family had a bower of palmetto leaves on the back of their lot and their house was located in front. There were three large tents on the parade ground near the river, two for Mr. Oglethorpe and one for Mr. Horton.

Oglethorpe's executive ability was shown by the fact he divided the colonists into working parties. One party was cutting the forks, poles and laths for the bowers. Others set them up. Others gathered the palmetto leaves, and a fourth group, superintended by a Jewish workman bred in Brazil and skilled in that work, thatched the roof. Men who understood farming in that region taught the colonists how to cultivate the soil. Potatoes, Indian corn, flax, hemp seed, barley, turnips, lucern grass, pumpkins, and watermelons were planted.

All this labor was done in common for the entire community. Some of the men who would have little share in the result were paid wages for work on the fortifications and public buildings.

**Location of Frederica**—Frederica was located in what had been an Indian field of thirty or forty acres on cleared land. The grass was good and furnished the turf used in sodding the parapet of the fort.

The fort stood on a bluff, dry and sandy, about ten feet above the high-water mark, and a level expanse of land from the bluff extended for a mile into the island.

From its dominating position, the fort commanded the river above and below. The harbor was land-locked with water twenty-two feet deep at the bar and gave safe anchorage for a number of large ships.

The town was surrounded by beautiful forests of live oak, water oak, laurel, bay, cedar, sweet gum, sassafras, and pine, festooned with vines, including the fox grape and the muscadine. These woods were full of deer, rabbits, raccoons, squirrels, wild turkeys, turtle doves, red birds, mocking birds, and rice birds. The neighboring marshes were frequented by geese, ducks, herons, curlews, cranes, plovers, and marsh hens. The water abounded in fish, crabs, shrimps, and oysters. The warm climate of the summer was tempered by delightful breezes from the ocean. With all these pleasant surroundings the colonists were charmed with their new home.

Frederica came into existence as a military post. Oglethorpe made it his headquarters and the town grew rapidly under his supervision. The soil was fertile and the health good. Lieutenant George Dunbar, on January 20, 1739, when Frederica was only ten months old, testified under oath, before Francis Moore, recorder of the town, that since his arrival with the first part of Colonel Oglethorpe's regiment the previous June, all the carpenters and many of the soldiers had been busy building huts, carrying lumber and brick, unloading vessels, often in water up to their necks, clearing the parade ground, burning wood and rubbish continually, their hours of work being from daylight until eleven or twelve in the forenoon, and from two or three in the afternoon until dark. He said that in spite of exposure and hard work, the men kept so healthy that no man in the camp had the least ailment and there was no death in the community except one man who was sick on the ship and never worked at all. In conclusion, he said: "Nor did I hear that any of the men ever made the heat a pretense of not working."

Commenting on this, Colonel Charles C. Jones says that Frederica was the healthiest of all the early settlements in Georgia and St. Simon's Island had always enjoyed a reputation for salubrity. It had a mean temperature of about fifty degrees in winter and eighty-two degrees in summer. Until marred by the desolations of the War between the States, St. Simon's Island was a famous summer resort, and on it were the homes of planters, surrounded by beautiful grounds, with every evidence of comfort and refinement. Their gardens were adorned with flowers and their orchards enriched with plums, peaches, nectarines, figs, melons, pomegranates, dates, oranges, and limes. In the forest, among the oaks and pines, was the beautiful magnolia, with the perfume of the bay, the cedar, and the myrtle, and the air vocal with the songs of birds.

There were serpents in this Eden, notably the rattle snake, and no doubt also the moccasin, but the reptile which seemed to have been most dreaded was the alligator, who was thus described by Francis Moore:

"They are terrible to look at, stretching open an horrible large Mouth, big enough to swallow a Man, with Rows of dreadful large sharp Teeth, and Feet like Draggons armed with great Claws, and a long Tail which they throw about with great Strength, and which seems their best Weapon, for their Claws are feebly set on, and the Stiffness of their Necks hinders them from turning nimbly to bite." In order that the public mind might be disabused of the terror which pervaded it with respect to these reptiles, Mr. Oglethorpe, having wounded and caught one, had it brought to Savannah, and "made the boys bait it with sticks and finally pelt and beat it to death."

Leaving the work at Frederica well begun and thoroughly planned, Oglethorpe left that place on the 18th of March, 1736, to look after the protection of the coast further south.

**A War Dance by the Indians**—A few days later, when Oglethorpe returned to Frederica from Cumberland Island, the Indians gave a war dance in his honor which was described as follows by Francis Moore:

"They made a Ring, in the middle of which four sat down, having little Drums made of Kettles covered with Deer-skins, upon which they beat and sung: Round them the others danced, being naked to their Waists, and round their Middles many Trinkets tied with Skins, and some with the Tails of Beasts hanging down behind them. They painted their Faces and Bodies, and their Hair was stuck with Feathers: In one Hand they had a Rattle, in the other Hand the Feathers of an Eagle, made up like the Caduceus of Mercury: They shook these Wings and the Rattle, and danced round the Ring with high Bounds and antick Postures, looking much like the Figures of the Satyrs.

"They shew'd great Activity, and kept just Time in their Motions; and at certain times answer'd, by way of Chorus to those that sat in the Middle of the Ring. They stopt, and then stood out one of the chief Warriors, who sung what Wars he had been in, and described (by Actions as well as by Words) which way he had vanquish'd the Enemies of his Country. When he had done, all the rest gave a Shout of Approbation, as knowing what he said to be true. The next Day Mr. Oglethorpe gave Presents to Tomochichi and his Indians, and dismiss'd them with Thanks for their Fidelity to the King."

A battery called Fort St. Simon was built at the south end of St. Simon's Island, and its guns commanded the entrance to Jekyll Sound. Near it a camp was established with barracks and huts for the soldiers.

# CHAPTER XIX.

## *Fortifying Cumberland*

Leaving Frederica on the 18th of March, 1736, Oglethorpe, accompanied by Tomochichi with about forty Indians, chosen warriors and hunters, in two scout boats, and Captain Hugh MacKay, with thirty Highlanders and ten men of an independent company, in a periagua, with entrenching tools and provisions, proceeded southward towards the Spanish border.

Stopping at the north end of Cumberland Island, Oglethorpe made plans for Fort St. Andrew and left Captain MacKay with his men to build it, and some Indians to bring in game for their food. Going further, Oglethorpe stopped at the next large island southward, which he called Amelia, the same island which the Spaniards called Santa Maria. It was a beautiful island, covered with myrtle, peach trees, orange trees, vines, and forest trees. Thence Tomochichi guided Oglethorpe to the mouth of the St. John's River and pointed out the dividing line, where there was a Spanish guard and advance post of Florida.

At this point it was hard for Oglethorpe to restrain Tomochichi and his followers from making a night attack on the Spaniards to avenge their people for killing some of the Indians while Tomochichi was in England.

Returning thence Oglethorpe stopped at Fort St. Andrew and was surprised to find how much work had been done there by the Highlanders, who had dug a ditch, raised a parapet of wood and earth on the landside, and had cleared the wood from the ground for fifty yards around the fort.

To support the fort on sandy ground, Captain MacKay had used the same method that Caesar used in Gaul, by laying down trees and earth alternately, so that the trees prevented the earth from falling and the sand protected the wood from fire.

Later the southern end of Cumberland Island was fortified by the construction of Fort William, whose guns commanded Amelia Sound and the inland passage to St. Augustine.

South of that, near the entrance of the St. John's River, Oglethorpe found on San Juan Island the ruins of an old fort. He sent there Captain Hermsdorf and a detachment of Highlanders, with orders to repair the fort and occupy it. Having learned that this island was included in the cession of land made by the Indians to King George, Oglethorpe named the fortification Fort St. George. This was the most southern defense of the colony of Georgia, and was important in holding the Spaniards in check and giving early information of any hostile move by them.

The building of this fort in plain view of the Spanish outpost shows the daring of Oglethorpe, as well as his confidence in the garrisons, which he placed in advanced positions to hold them against the Spaniards.

Returning to Frederica, he converted a marsh below the fort into a water battery, whose guns at the water level would give effective fire against enemy vessels passing on the river.

Apprehending an attack from the Spaniards, Oglethorpe made every effort to put the southern frontier in condition for effective defense. His energy was accompanied by great watchfulness. Scout boats patrolled the water as far as the mouth of the St. John's River and Indian runners watched the walls of St. Augustine, reporting every move of the Spaniards. Lookouts were kept at points of vantage to give warning of danger, and Mr. Bryan and Mr. Barnwell promised that if Frederica or the southern coast were attacked they would bring a strong body of volunteers from South Carolina to reënforce the Georgians. In the meantime, the chiefs of the Cheehaws and the Creeks offered their aid. Volunteers from Georgia and Carolina came in such numbers that Oglethorpe had to issue orders that all who had plantations should remain at home and cultivate them until called to arms. On May 10th, Ensign Delagel, with thirty men of his company, by rowing night and day, reached Frederica and offered their services to Oglethorpe. He put on board their boats provisions and strong beer, with a present of wine for Delagel, and conducting the party in a scout boat, led them to the east point of St. Simon's Island, where it bordered Jekyll Sound. There he posted the company, locating a spot for the fort and ordering a well to be dug. By the 16th of May, Delagel had made a considerable entrenchment and mounted several cannon there. On the 8th of June, Lieutenant Delagel brought the rest of his company and thirteen pieces of cannon to this fort, which was known as Delagel's Fort at the Sea-Point.

In the meantime, workmen at Frederica built a powder magazine under one of the bastions of the fort. It was made of heavy timber, covered with several feet of earth. A large storehouse, a smith's forge, a wheelwright shop, and a corn house were also built.

The colonists were in a state of alarm, and everything possible was done for the defense of the colony. As one man the colonists showed willingness, if necessary, to give their lives in defense of their homes. They were inspired by the boldness, vigilance, fearlessness, and activity of Oglethorpe, who visited the fortifications, inspected men and munitions, and reconnoitered the coast almost to the enemy's line.

**Conference With the Spaniards**—Oglethorpe, in fortifying the coast of Georgia to within sight of the Spanish lines, realized the effect it would have on the Spaniards, for Spain claimed the whole of Georgia. England and Spain were then at peace, and in the face of repeated protests from Spain, through its ambassador at London, the British government showed much concern about a condition which might result in war between the two countries.

Under these conditions, Charles Dempsey was commissioned by the British government to go to St. Augustine and there arrange terms of an agreement between the governors of Georgia and Florida for the settlement of disputes concerning the boundary between those provinces, and Mr. Dempsey had come from England to Georgia with Oglethorpe in the ship *Symond.*

To carry out the purpose of Mr. Dempsey's mission, Oglethorpe, on his arrival in Georgia, instructed Major Richards, of Purrysburgh, to take a suitable boat and convey Mr. Dempsey to St. Augustine. On February 19, 1736, those gentlemen started for St. Augustine, and Mr. Dempsey, in addition to his dispatches from the British government, carried a conciliatory letter from Oglethorpe to the governor of Florida.

When Oglethorpe left Frederica on March 18th to inspect the southern coast, he had heard nothing from Mr. Dempsey. For this reason he hastened his departure for the South to learn something of Mr. Dempsey and also to restrain the Indians whose animosity against the Spaniards might lead them to attack the outpost of Florida and so precipitate hostilities with the Spaniards. He also wished to learn from the Indians the location of the boundary line which they said separated Georgia from Florida.

Reaching the St. John's River, he landed there to make inquiry of the Spanish guard concerning Mr. Dempsey and Major Richards. The guard was not there, but the next morning he met Major Richards returning from St. Augustine in a boat and the delay was explained as follows: Before reaching St. Augustine the yawl carrying the two men capsized and those on board had to wade through breakers to the shore, dragging the boat behind them. After they had walked several leagues on the sand, they were met by Don Pedro Lamberto, a captain of horse, who conveyed them to the Spanish governor, by whom they were courteously received. Mr. Dempsey's return was delayed by necessary repairs on the boat.

Major Richards brought to Oglethorpe letters from Don Francisco del Moral Sanchez, captain-general of Florida and governor of St. Augustine, in which, after the usual compliments and thanks for letters received, he complained that the Creek Indians had attacked some of the Spaniards and defeated them and that he feared further hostilities from Indians, which he asked Mr. Oglethorpe to prevent.

Major Richards said the Spanish authorities at Havana had been informed of what was done on the coast of Georgia and that he had promised the governor of Florida to return within three weeks with Oglethorpe's reply to his communication.

From other sources, Oglethorpe learned that in spite of the profession of friendship by the Spaniards the governor of St. Augustine had sent to Charleston to buy arms which he intended to place in hands of Florida Indians with whose aid and that of the Yamassees he planned an early attack on the colonists at Frederica, expecting to kill them or expel them from the Island of St. Simon's. Oglethorpe also learned that the alleged hostility of the Creeks was only a pretext to cover a secret movement and shift the burden of it from the Spaniards to the English. He further learned that the garrison of St. Augustine consisted of five companies of infantry, with sixty men each, and a company of horse with forty men; also that reënforcements had been asked from Havana and were daily expected.

Under these circumstances, Oglethorpe sent a periagua with twenty oarsmen and four swivel guns, accompanied by a well-armed scout boat, to the mouth of the St. John's River, with orders to patrol it and prevent any Indians from crossing it, so as to cut off any attack on the Spaniards by the Indians.

The fort on the St. George's Island passage was rushed to completion, so its guns might assist the periagua in preventing the passage of hostile boats through the island channels.

Two ships were stationed in the river near Frederica to prevent the entrance of Spanish vessels from the sea, if it should be attempted, and the fortifications on St. Simon's Island was strengthened in every possible way with additional troops called for their defense.

In the meantime, with the aid of Tomochichi, Indians were sent out with instructions to meet the Creek hunters and dissuade them from attacking Spanish outposts until a general conference could be held.

Other Indians were stationed in the woods on the coast opposite Frederica, with orders to prevent any Spanish cavalry from advancing across the country upon the settlement of the Highlanders at Darien, and they were to hold themselves ready to cross over to St. Simon's and unite with the colonists in defense of Frederica, if that place were threatened.

On April 13th, Oglethorpe sent Major Richards and Mr. Horton with his reply to the captain-general of Florida. They went in a marine boat, accompanied by a periagua with three months' supply of provisions. In his letter, Oglethorpe wrote the governor that in order to remove uneasiness and prevent lawless persons from creating a disturbance between the subjects of the two countries, he had sent armed boats to patrol the water separating the British and Spanish territories. He concluded by thanking the governor for his courtesy and commending Major Richards and his companions to favorable consideration.

On reaching Fort St. George, Major Richards sent over to the Spanish side of the river to announce his arrival, but no men or horses were there to conduct him to St. Augustine, as had been promised. Mr. Horton set out on foot, with two servants, to call on the governor at St. Augustine and inform him that Major Richards had arrived at the border with letters from Oglethorpe. A few days later two smokes, the signal agreed upon, were seen at the Spanish lookout. Major Richards sent over a boat, which returned with the information that a guard and horses were ready to conduct Major Richards to St. Augustine, but the Spaniards behaved more like enemies than friends. The officers and men with Major Richards advised him not to go unless the Spaniards left one of their number as security for his safety, but the major went and set out on a journey for Augustine with the Spaniards.

Some days later another smoke appeared at the Spanish post, a boat went over and the officer in charge was handed a dirty paper with a message written in German upon it. The Spaniards said it had been written by Major Richards and addressed to Captain Hermsdorf. It simply said that Major Richards had safely reached the quarters of the Spanish captain of horse. As the Spaniards appeared in greater numbers, Mr. Horton had not returned, and as Major Richards sent such a short dispatch, Captain Hermsdorf thought he was held a prisoner. While Hermsdorf was at anchor at the south end of Cumberland, Oglethorpe came up in Captain Gascoigne's six-oared boat, attended by a scout boat, and ordered him to follow. Leaving Hermsdorf, the periagua and a marine boat at St. George, Oglethorpe went on with a yawl and the scout boat, bearing a flag of truce, to the Spanish side of the St. John's River, in order to learn what had become of Major Richards, Mr. Horton, and their companions. The guard post was deserted, but after some time, when Oglethorpe was about to return, a young man of his party named Frazier came in driving before him a tall man with a musket on his shoulder, two pistols in his girdle and a long and short sword at his side.

"Here, sir, I have caught a Spaniard for you," said the boy. Having treated the captive kindly and given him wine and food, Oglethorpe inquired concerning Major Richards and Mr. Horton. Thereupon the Spaniard pulled out a letter which he said was from Mr. Horton, whom with Major Richards, the governor of St. Augustine had put under arrest. Oglethorpe rewarded the prisoner and said he would return an answer by the next day noon.

Expecting an attack from the Spaniards, Oglethorpe withdrew to St. George, prepared the place for defense and had fires kindled at various points to light up the water and show the enemy if he attempted to pass. Returning to the Spanish lookout the next day at noon, he found the Spaniard had not kept his engagement. Some horsemen were seen concealing themselves behind the sand hills and a launch filled with men was seen lying under the shelter of a sand bank near the mouth of the St. John's River. When Oglethorpe's boat was rowed near this launch, her crew started up and pulled out to sea.

Finally, Oglethorpe found a horseman well mounted, in blue uniform, and gave him the letters for the governor which the Spaniard he met the day before was to carry. The horseman promised to deliver the letters and return the replies, but having no response, after waiting two days, Oglethorpe left the other boats at Fort St. George and returned to Frederica in a yawl.

Expecting an attack on Frederica by the Spaniards, Oglethorpe made every preparation for its defense and garrisons at the various forts were warned and put in good condition for action.

There seems to be little doubt that the Spaniards intended to attack Frederica, but by the time they were ready they had such reports of the strength of fortifications held by the colonists and the probable loss in attacking them that they delayed the expedition.

Oglethorpe and the colonists were greatly relieved by the arrival of Mr. Horton at Frederica on June 14th. To Mr. Francis Moore he gave this account of his adventures:

After departing, with two servants, from the Spanish lookout, he walked along the seashore until he reached the river flowing near the castle of St. Augustine. Arriving there at four o'clock, he fired a gun as a signal, and after some delay, a boat came for him, and he was conducted to the governor, who received him courteously. Then he went to Don Carlos Dempsey's house, and the next day the detachment which had been sent to escort Major Richards to St. Augustine arrived. He and Mr. Horton were welcomed by the people, who thought they brought good news to the effect that English boats patrolling the river would keep out the barbarous Indians.

While they were waiting for the governor's answer to Oglethorpe, Horton and Richards were invited to a dance at the residence of the governor's interpreter, remaining there until one o'clock in the morning, when they returned to Dempsey's house. While they were still in bed, the town major, with a file of soldiers, called on Mr. Dempsey and informed him that Richards and Horton and their servants were charged in making a plan of the town and the castle that morning, and the governor had ordered that they be arrested.

At ten o'clock the same morning, the governor came to Dempsey's lodging with officers and a secretary and began a formal information and examination of Major Richards.

The governor asked him what brought him there; he answered that he was come pursuant to his promise to his excellency of returning to him with letters from Mr. Oglethorpe. He then asked where Mr. Oglethorpe was? He answered he could not tell where he was then, but he had left him at Frederica. Upon which he asked what fortifications and number of men were at Frederica? To which the major replied he did not know. He then asked what fortifications and number of men were at Jekyll Sound, Cumberland Island, Amelia Island, and St. John's, to which the major answered the same as before. Whereupon the governor retired; and some time after sent for the major to his house. He then examined Mr. Horton as to the strength of Georgia; but he refused to give them any answer. Upon which they threatened to send him to the mines. To which he answered that he was a subject of Great Britain, and his sovereign was powerful enough to do him justice.

The next day, at Dempsey's request, the guards were removed on his promise that Richards and Horton would not walk about the town or leave it without the governor's permission.

The Spaniards sent out the lieutenant-colonel of the garrison in a launch with soldiers to inspect the coast of Georgia, and in five days he returned with a report that the islands were all fortified and full of men and armed boats.

After this, Dempsey conferred with the governor, the bishop, and other officers. A council of war was called and they decided to return Major Richards, Mr. Horton, and their companions to Georgia with friendly letters to Mr. Oglethorpe, accompanied by Dempsey, the captain of horse and the adjutant of the garrison, and to desire friendship. Horton was released, and returning with his servants in a boat, he met Oglethorpe and told him of the approach of the Spanish authorities with Mr. Dempsey.

Oglethorpe instructed Horton to go quickly and prepare a suitable reception for the Spanish officers on board Captain Gascoigne's vessel, where they would receive no information as to the strength of Frederica and adjacent forts.

Returning to Frederica in a boat, Oglethorpe passed near Captain Gascoigne's ship, where the commissioners were entertained, but he was not observed by them. At Frederica, he ordered Ensign MacKay to bring from Darien some of the best Highlanders, that they might be present at the conference.

Two handsome tents, with marquises and walls of canvas, were pitched on Jekyll Island, and Oglethorpe sent gentlemen with refreshments to the commissioners to inform them that he would wait upon them the next day.

On the 18th, Oglethorpe appeared on the sea point of St. Simon's, with seven mounted men, and a number of cannons were fired, which could be heard on Jekyll Island. When he arrived at the point, the independent company was drawn up under arms, the men at double distances apart, making their number appear very great to the Spaniards, who were on Jekyll Island. The men saluted Oglethorpe with cannon, reloading and firing them several times, giving the impression that there were many more guns than were there.

Captain Gascoigne came with two scout boats and conveyed Oglethorpe to Jekyll Island, where he was welcomed by the Spanish officers. Captain Gascoigne's invitation to Oglethorpe and the Spanish commissioners to dine the next day on the *Hawk* was accepted and there the general received the commissioners formally. The next day, Ensign MacKay came on board with the Highlanders, who, with their broad swords, targets, plaids, etc., were drawn up on one side of the ship while a detachment of the independent company in uniform lined the other side. The sailors manned the shrouds and kept watch with drawn cutlasses at the cabin door. The Spanish commissioners were handsomely entertained, and at the end of the dinner presented their messages in writing. They drank the health of the King of Great Britain and the royal family, and Oglethorpe drank the health of the King and Queen of Spain. The next day they were entertained in the same way, and had a long conference with the general. On the 21st, he gave them their answer, and they exchanged presents. While they were there a supply of sheep, hogs, and poultry, and garden stuff sufficient for all their men were furnished, with butter, cheese, wine, beer, and other refreshments.

Tomochichi, Hillispilli, and thirty of the leading Indians came on board, painted and dressed as for war, and Hillispilli demanded of the Spaniards justice for killing the Indians and other outrages. The Spanish commissioner, Don Pedro, knew some of the facts, but doubted the rest. The Indians proved that a party of forty Spaniards and Indians had fallen upon the Creeks, who suspected no violence because of the general peace between the Spaniards, the English, and the Indians. Several of the Creeks were killed and taken captives, and the boys captured were murdered by having their brains dashed out. The wounded were slain. Don Pedro, horrified at this report, asked how they knew these facts, and a young Indian who had been wounded in that fight came forward, showed a scar and told how he had escaped by concealing himself among the bushes. He said he had followed the Indians from Florida two days, hiding in thickets and seeing all that passed. It was proved that an Indian who was one of the attacking party boasted of what they had done to the Creeks and said the party had been sent out from St. Augustine.

Oglethorpe asked Don Pedro to report these facts to the governor of St. Augustine and tell him he should expect satisfaction for the Indians, as they were subjects of the King of England.

Hillispilli said, "When this happened I was gone with you to England. Had I not been with you this would not have happened, for had I been with my men they would not have been so surprised. You will go with me and you shall see how I will punish them, but if you will not help me I have friends enough who will go with me to revenge the murder."

At this all the Indians gave a shout.

Don Pedro said there was a party of Indians who went from the neighborhood of St. Augustine, but they were not Spaniards; that he then was in Mexico on business for the government; that such cruelty must be abhorred by every Christian and the people who had committed this outrage should be punished. Pohoia, king of the Floridas, was named as the one who commanded the expedition, and he said that if he ever came into St. Augustine so they could secure him, the governor and council of war would punish him as he deserved, and if he came not within their power they would banish him.

To this Hillispilli replied: "We hear what you say. When we see it done, we will believe you."

Tomochichi persuaded Hillispilli to be content, and he restrained the passions of the Indians to prevent them from insulting the Spaniards and doing them violence.

The conference resulted in an apparent restoration of good feeling, with a pacification between Georgia and Florida, which was not interrupted by violence for two years. The Spaniards left on June 22nd, pleased with their reception and professing a friendly feeling toward the colony of Georgia and Oglethorpe.

In a letter to the trustees, Oglethorpe gave this account of his interview with Spanish officials:

"After dinner we drank the king of Britain's and the king of Spain's health under a discharge of cannon from the ship; which was answered with fifteen pieces of cannon from Delegal's fort at the Sea-point. That again was followed by the cannon from the fort of St. Andrew's, and that by those of Frederica and Darien, as I had before ordered. The Spaniards seemed extremely surprised that there should be so many forts, and all within hearing of one another. Don Pedro smiled and said, "No wonder Don Ignatio made more haste home than out." After the healths were done, a great number of Indians came on board, naked, painted, and their heads dressed with feathers. They demanded of me justice against the Spaniards for killing some of their men in time of peace.

"Don Pedro having asked several questions, acknowledged himself fully satisfied of the fact, excusing it by saying that he was then in Mexico, and that the Governor being newly come from Spain, and not knowing the customs of the country, had sent out Indians under the command of Pohoia, king of the Floridas, who had exceeded his orders which were not to molest the Creeks. But the Indians not being content with that answer, he undertook that, at his return to Augustine, he would have the Pohoia king put to death, if he could be taken, and if he could not, that the Spaniards would supply his people with neither powder, arms, nor anything else, but leave them to the Creeks. The Indians answered that he spake well, and if the Spaniards did what he said, all should be white between them; but if not, they would take revenge, from which, at my desire, they would abstain till a final answer came.

"The Indian matters being thus settled, we had a conference with the Spanish Commissioners. They thanked me first for my restraining the Indians who were in my power and hoped I would extend that care to the upper Indians. They then, after having produced their credentials, presented a paper the contents whereof were to know by what title I settled upon St. Simon's, being lands belonging to the king of Spain. I took the paper, promising an answer next day. The substance was, that the lands belonged to the

BETHESDA ORPHANAGE—SAVANNAH
Founded by George Whitefield

king of England by undoubted right: that I had proceeded with the utmost caution, having taken with me Indians, the natives and possessors of those lands; that I had examined every place to see if there were any Spaniards in possession, and went forward till I found an outguard of theirs, over against which I settled the English without committing any hostilities or dislodging any. Therefore I did not extend the King's dominions, but only settled with regular garrisons that part of them which was before a shelter for Indians, pirates, and such sort of disorderly men.

"The rest of the evening we spent in conversation, which chiefly turned upon the convenience it would be, both to the Spaniards and English, to have regular garrisons in sight of each other. Don Pedro smiled and said he readily agreed to that, and should like very well to have their Spanish guard upon the south side of Helena river, which is within five miles of Charlestown and where the Spaniards had a garrison in King Charles the First's time. I replied I thought it was better as it was; for there were a great many people living between who could never be persuaded to come in to his sentiments. At last Don Pedro acquainted us that he thought the Spaniards would refer the settling of the limits to the Courts of Europe, for which purpose he should write to their Court, and in the meantime desired no hostilities might be committed, and that I would send up a commissary to sign with the government an agreement to this purpose. I thereupon appointed Mr. Dempsey to be my Commissary and to return with them. Don Pedro is the ruling man in Augustine and has more interest with the Council of War than the Governor. As he passed by St. George's point he sent a whole ox as a present to the garrison. He gave me some sweet meats and chocolate. I gave him a gold watch, a gun, and fresh provisions. To Don Manuel I gave a silver watch and sent back a boat to escort them. If the Spaniards had committed any hostilities, I could, by the help of the Indians, have destroyed Augustine with great facility. But, God be praised, by His blessing, the diligence of Dempsey, and the prudence of Don Pedro, all bloodshed was avoided."

**Further Trouble with the Spaniards**—Returning to Frederica in September, 1736, Oglethorpe authorized Mr. Dempsey to agree with the governor of Florida for the adjustment of any misunderstanding which there might be between the two provinces, and Mr. Dempsey arranged a treaty of conciliatory character with the governor of Florida.

This apparent security did not last long. A message was soon received from the Spanish governor of Florida to the effect that a Spanish minister had come from Cuba with a communication which he desired to deliver in person. This resulted in a conference, at which the Spanish minister repudiated the concession made in the treaty between Mr. Dempsey and the Spanish governor, and in the name of the Spanish crown demanded that the English colonists immediately evacuate all the territory south of St. Helena's Sound. In other words, that they should evacuate the whole of Georgia. The minister further said that the King of Spain was determined to enforce his right to that territory and withdrew from the conference.

In view of the threat of a hostile attack by the Spaniards, it was necessary that Oglethorpe go to England, where the trustees asked his aid in presenting to Parliament their petition for the men and money necessary to protect the colony from the Spaniards. Accordingly, Oglethorpe sailed for England on November 29, 1736. Before sailing, however, it was necessary for him to adjust serious difficulties with the South Carolinians and to bring about a peaceful settlement between the Uchee Indians and the Salzburgers and South Carolina planters who had encroached on the Indian territory.

**Trouble with South Carolina Adjusted**—The difficulty with South Carolina is stated by Dr. Harris in his *Biographical Memorials of General Oglethorpe.* The Savannah River, which separated Georgia from South Carolina, also separated the Georgia Indians from that State, and it was essential to the security of Georgia that the good will of the Indians be retained. In order to do this, it was necessary to protect the Indian territory from invasion. Under the regulations of the trustees, no one was allowed to trade with the Indians without a license, and under the regulations of fair trade adopted by the trustees. The licenses for such trading in Georgia territory must be secured from the Georgia commissary.

The Carolina traders were not disposed to apply for such permits, and not being willing to comply with the rules and restrictions imposed by the Georgia commissary, who was stationed among the Creeks, they complained of his action to the provincial assembly of South Carolina. That body appointed a committee to confer with Oglethorpe, and a conference was held at Savannah on the 2nd of August, 1736. The committee reported their grievance as follows:

"The Cherokee, Creek, Chickasaw, and Catawba Indians, at the time of the discovery of this part of America, were the inhabitants of the lands which they now possess, and have ever since been deemed and esteemed the friends and allies of his Majesty's Subjects in this part of the Continent. They have been treated with as allies, but not as subjects of the Crown of Great Britain; they have maintained their own possessions and preserved their independency; nor does it appear that they have by conquest lost, nor by cession, compact, or otherwise, yielded up or parted with those rights to which, by the laws of nature and nations, they were and are entitled.

"The Committee cannot conceive that a charter from the Crown of Great Britain can give the grantees a right or power over a people who, to our knowledge, have never owed any allegiance, or acknowledged the sovereignty of the Crown of Great Britain or any Prince in Europe, but have indiscriminately visited and traded with the French, Spaniards, and English as they judged it most for their advantage; and it is as difficult to understand how the laws of Great Britain or of any Colony in America can take place, or be put in execution in a country where the people never accepted of, nor submitted to such laws; but have always maintained their freedom, and have adhered to their own customs and manners without variation or change."

The committee, having this view, insisted that the regulations adopted by the trustees were not binding on the Indians and could not establish any exclusive traffic with them.

Replying to this, Oglethorpe admitted that the Indians were independent, but said that they had become parties to a treaty of alliance with the colony of Georgia, and had themselves indicated terms and conditions of trade which were adopted and enforced by the trustees; and that this was done to make clear to the Indians what was required of those who might go among them for the purpose of trade.

In reply to the complaint that Carolina traders had been excluded from dealing with the Indians, he said that in granting licenses to trade with the Indians living within the limits of Georgia, he had not refused the application of anyone who agreed to conform to the provisions of the act of the trustees.

He said he had given and would continue to give the same instructions to the Georgia traders as Carolina had given to her traders, and if Carolina issued new instructions to her traders and would communicate them to him, if they appeared to be of equal benefit to both provinces, he would add them to the instructions given Georgia traders and would direct all his officers and traders among the Indians to make no distinction between the two provinces, but to speak in the name and behalf of his majesty's subjects.

This was not satisfactory to the commissioners, who still objected to giving permits, especially because they must come through the hands of the governor of Georgia.

**Carolina Rum in Georgia**—Augusta being a center of trade with the Indians, some Carolina traders opened stores there and as transportation by land was tedious and expensive, goods from Charleston were shipped to Augusta over the Savannah River.

As boats from Charleston were passing Savannah, the Savannah magistrates, suspecting that the boats contained distilled liquor, in violation of the law of Parliament, which prohibited the introduction of distilled liquor in Georgia, had the boats searched. A considerable quantity of rum was found on board and the casks containing the rum were staved and the persons in charge of the boats were arrested and imprisoned.

The Carolinians were very indignant at this procedure and demanded of the Georgia magistrates by what authority they seized and destroyed the effects of their traders and compelled them to submit to their laws.

Fearing that they had transcended their power, the Savannah authorities set the prisoners at liberty and returned in kind as far as they could the goods destroyed. The Carolinians thereupon agreed to smuggle no more strong liquor within the limits of Georgia.

The matter was finally settled by the British Board of Trade. After learning the facts and hearing arguments, the commissioners decided that while the Savannah River was open to navigation by the people of both colonies, and Georgians should render the Carolinians any friendly assistance within their power, it was not lawful for Carolina traders to introduce ardent spirits among the people of Georgia.

**Oglethorpe Stops Encroachment on Indian Land**—The good relations of Georgia colonists with Indians were seriously endangered by the encroachment upon the lands of the Uchees by Salzburgers and South Carolinians.

The Salzburgers had cleared and planted four acres of land beyond the boundary of Ebenezer, within the territory of the Uchees, and other Salzburgers had allowed their cattle to stray into Indian lands, where they ate up the corn planted by the Indians twenty miles from Ebenezer.

The Indians were very indignant, because some people from Carolina swam a great herd of cattle across the Savannah River and bringing negroes with them, established a plantation near the Uchee town. Seeing this and the irritation of the Indians, a certain Captain Green, evidently an enemy of the colonists, urged the Indians to attack the Salzburgers and declare war on the English.

Hearing of this, Oglethorpe immediately forced the Carolinians to go back across the Savannah River with their negroes and cattle, and ordered the Salzburgers to keep within their own territory and keep their cattle within it.

Oglethorpe's prompt action made a good impression on the Indians, and the Uchees sent their king and twenty warriors to thank him for redressing their wrongs before they had even asked him to do so. They said this made them love him and instead of entering on a war against England, they were ready to help the English against the Spanish and offered Oglethorpe the aid of a hundred warriors for a year, if he should need them.

**Oglethorpe's Return to England**—Having put affairs in Georgia to rights, and having prepared the best defense of the colony he could, with the means at his command, Oglethorpe sailed for England on November 29, 1736, and reached London early in January, 1737. On January 19th, he attended a special meeting of the Georgia trustees, to whom he reported the progress of the colony and the amicable relations with the Indians. He gave a full statement of negotiations with Spanish authorities at St. Augustine and made known his anticipation that the treaty with them would be disregarded by the Spaniards. Informing them of what he had done for the defense of the southern boundary of Georgia, he urged the necessity for sending promptly troops to occupy those exposed stations. The trustees unanimously voted him thanks for his services and decided to petition Parliament at once for men, munitions, and money to protect Georgia against the threatened invasion of Spaniards.

Oglethorpe's report and the determination of the trustees to ask Parliament for strong military support of the colony were made public by an article in the London *Post,* which recited the fact, paid a great tribute to General Oglethorpe, and said it was clear that the Spaniards dreaded Oglethorpe's ability and that was strong testimony of his merit and a certificate of his patriotism which should endear him to every honest Briton.

The Spanish ambassador at London made a formal protest against sending troops from England to Georgia and remonstrated against the return of Oglethorpe to the colony.

About that time information came that the authorities at St. Augustine had ordered the English merchants doing business there to depart, that barracks were being constructed there for 2,500 soldiers, who were soon to be sent from Havana in three men-of-war and eight transports, and that provisions in large quantity were being accumulated.

Under these circumstances, the trustees petitioned the crown to raise at once strong forces and send them to Georgia for the defense of the colony. The petition was allowed, Oglethorpe was made colonel of the regiment to be enlisted, and was made general and commander-in-chief of his majesty's forces in Carolina and Georgia, with authority to use the entire military power of both provinces in their defense. The regiment recruited in England consisted of six companies of one hundred men each, not counting officers, and later a company of grenadiers was added.

Without waiting until the Oglethorpe regiment had been recruited, the British government at once sent a detachment of troops from Gibraltar, and they reached Savannah on the 7th of May, 1738. A curious coincidence appears in the fact that on the same ship bearing these soldiers, Rev. George Whitefield, an eloquent ambassador of peace and good will, came to Georgia. About the same time several companies of Oglethorpe's regiment, under Lieutenant-Colonel James Cochrane, arrived at Charleston, and were marched into Georgia.

Oglethorpe secured as officers for his regiment only men of character and good families. He also engaged twenty young men of good character to serve as cadets, with the intention to promote them when vacancies occurred, as their conduct justified. The general also furnished money from his own private fortune to buy uniforms and clothing and pay other expenses of the men.

Hoping that the men who came in this regiment would become permanent citizens of the colony, they were allowed to take their wives with them and were allowed additional pay and rations for their wives. Carefully recruited and officered, Oglethorpe's regiment was one of the best in the service of the King.

Sailing from Portsmouth with the rest of his command, including, with the women and children, between six and seven hundred persons in five transports, convoyed by the men-of-war, *Blanford* and *Hector,* General Oglethorpe reached Jekyll Sound, and the next day the soldiers landed at the soldiers' fort at the southern end of St. Simon's Island. They were welcomed by an artillery salute from the battery and shouts from the garrison.

General Oglethorpe visited Frederica on July 21st and was saluted with fifteen guns from the fort. The people and their magistrates came to him in a body and gave him their congratulations on his return. Several Indians were present and assured him that the Upper and Lower Creeks were ready to come and see him as soon as they were notified of his presence.

Writing to Sir Joseph Jekyll, on September 10th, General Oglethorpe mentioned the fact that the Spaniards, with 1,500 men at St. Augustine, while there was nothing but militia in Georgia, had delayed their attack on the colony until the arrival of regular troops. Commenting on this, he said that God had just given the greatest marks of his protection of the colony. He wrote Sir Joseph that the voyage over had been fine, though one soldier died on the way, and that the inhabitants of the colony who had been harassed by Spanish threats were now cheerful, believing that the worst was over, and being relieved of constant guard duty which they had to perform in his absence, sometimes two days out of five, to the neglect of their crops and other work. They could now go to work for themselves and make comfortable provision for the future.

**Opening the Causeway on St. Simon's Island**—To open a road or causeway between the forts at Frederica and the south end of St. Simon's Island, General Oglethorpe put every available man to work on the 25th of July, and they worked with such energy and effect that they opened the road nearly six miles, much of the way through thick woods, in three days.

As this causeway had much to do with General Oglethorpe's success in defeating the Spaniards at the Battle of Bloody Marsh, it is worth while here to give the following description of it contributed to the first volume of the Georgia Historical Society's collection by Hon. Thomas Spalding in 1840:

"This road, after passing out of the town of Frederica in a southeast direction, entered a beautiful prairie of a mile over, when it penetrated a dense, close oak wood; keeping the same course for two miles, it passed to the eastern marsh that bounded St. Simon's seaward. Along this marsh, being dry and hard, no road was necessary, and none was made. This natural highway was bounded on the east by rivers and creeks and impracticable marshes; it was bounded on the west (the island side), by a thick wood covered with palmetto and vines of every character so as to be impracticable for any body of men, and could only be traveled singly and alone. This winding way along the marsh was continued for two miles, when it again passed up to the high land which had become open and clear, and from thence it proceeded in a direct line to the fort, at the sea entrance, around which, for two hundred acres, five acre allotments of land for the soldiers had been laid out, cleared, and improved. I have again been thus particular in my description, because it was to the manner in which this road was laid out and executed that General Oglethorpe owed the preservation of the fort and town of Frederica. . . . His fort and batteries at Frederica were so situated as to command water approaches, and so covered by a wood, that no number of ships could injure them. And he now planned his land route in such a manner that again the dense wood of our eastern islands became a rampart mighty to save."

# CHAPTER XX.

## *Difficulties in Savannah*

**The Colony Short of Money**—On his return to Georgia, General Oglethorpe found that the affairs of the colony were in bad shape because of the lack of money due to the extravagance of Thomas Causton, who had been left in charge, an account of whose conduct appears later. Under these circumstances, with a new regiment of soldiers to provide for, General Oglethorpe met the emergency by using his own money and pledging his own credit to sustain the constructive work and the operations necessary to make the southern frontier secure. Nevertheless, he met the situation cheerfully and with his accustomed energy. Writing to Alderman Heathcote, he said:

"I am here [at Frederica] in one of the most delightful situations as any man could wish to be. A great number of Debts, empty magazines, no money to supply them, numbers of people to be fed, mutinous soldiers to command, a Spanish Claim, and a large body of their Troops not far from us. But as we are of the same kind of spirit these difficulties have the same effect upon me as those you met with in the City had upon you. They rather animate than daunt me."

Notwithstanding the strong reënforcement which had come over from England, General Oglethorpe maintained a strict discipline, not only with the soldiers, but with the colonists, every able-bodied man of whom was required to keep fit for military service in case of need. The work was divided and systematized with military method. Some of the men were required to range the woods, others were kept in readiness, armed and equipped to respond quickly in any emergency. Vessels were kept ready to patrol the seacoast and secure early information of any hostile movement.

In the face of what was believed to be impending danger of hostile attacks upon the colony, Oglethorpe had the complete confidence of his sovereign. On May 8, 1738, he was instructed by George the Second to learn and report promptly the designs of the Spaniards in Florida and any movement by them. He was further instructed to make such disposition of the forces at his command as would best protect the colony from any surprise attack from the Spaniards and to place all forts in the best condition for offensive and defensive action. In the meantime, he was cautioned to refrain from giving any cause of provocation to the Spaniards and was to assure them of England's desire to maintain friendship with them. He was to permit no encroachment on Spanish territory, and as far as he could, prevent the Indians from committing any hostile acts.

But if the Spaniards should attempt to drive the colonists out of their forts or to invade the territory subject to the English crown, he was instructed with all the forces at his command not only to repel such invasion and preserve the territory of the colonies of Georgia and South Carolina, but to assume the offensive in the way he thought best. If he suspected that the Spaniards intended an attack against either of the provinces, he was authorized to call to his aid all the ships on the coast in the defense of those territories.

**Spies Exposed**—General Oglethorpe was greatly surprised while on the ship *Blandford,* returning from England to Georgia, to find that one of the enlisted soldiers in his regiment was a spy in the service of Spain, and was trying to persuade some of his comrades to desert with him on their arrival in Georgia and to join the Spaniards in Florida. His plan also included the murder of officers at the post to which his company should be assigned and carrying to the enemy such valuables as he could. He was well supplied with money and said he would be rewarded in proportion to the number of men he should induce to go with him to the Spaniards.

When the regiment arrived in Georgia, several other spies were found among the enlisted men and they had tried to persuade comrades to betray a post to the Spaniards.

The men to whom he made this proposition were loyal and revealed it to their commanding officer. A court-martial was held, the spies were found guilty and were whipped and drummed out of the service. One of them, named Shannon, who afterwards committed murder at Fort Argyle, was brought to Savannah and tried, condemned and executed.

In this emergency, the prompt and vigorous action of General Oglethorpe completely wiped out a dangerous element which might have caused trouble if it had not been detected.

**Oglethorpe Received at Savannah**—Having put things in order at Frederica, General Oglethorpe returned to Savannah on October 10, 1738, and was met at the landing by the magistrates and the militia under arms. He was saluted by cannon from the fort and during the day throngs of people met him and his return was celebrated that night with bonfires.

On the next morning, October 11th, Tomochichi, who had been ill, met General Oglethorpe and informed him that the chiefs of several towns of the Creek nation were at his house waiting to call on the general, present their congratulations on his safe arrival and assure him of their loyalty to the King of England.

On October 13th, Tomochichi came down the river with the mico of the Chehaws, the mico of the Oakmulgees, the mico of the Ouchases, and the mico of the Parachacolas, with thirty warriors and fifty-two attendants. As the Indians walked up the bluff at Savannah, they were saluted by a battery of cannon and escorted by militia to the town hall, where General Oglethorpe received them.

On meeting the general, they expressed great joy and told him that the Spaniards, pretending that he was at St. Augustine, had invited them to come down to their fort and meet him there. They went there, but learned that he was not present and returned, although the Spaniards offered them valuable articles and tried to account for his absence by saying that he was very ill on board a ship in the harbor. They said that although the Spaniards urged them to desert the English, they still adhered to the treaty of peace with England and were firm in their attachment to the King. They assured the general that they would help him in repelling the King's enemies and that representatives of the other Indian towns would come down and make similar expressions of good will when they knew of his arrival. They further said that the Creek nation was prepared to send a thousand warriors to any point he might desire and they would be subject to his command.

The Indians took the opportunity to ask that correct brass weights and sealed measures should be deposited with the king of each of their towns, so they might protect themselves against false weights and measures used by traders by whom they were frequently defrauded.

The Indians gave General Oglethorpe a cordial invitation to visit their towns during the next summer and meet their people. He agreed to accept the invitation and that resulted in his remarkable trip to Coweta the next year.

Handsome presents were distributed among the Indians and the interview with General Oglethorpe ended with good feeling. That night they had a dance at which General Oglethorpe was present, and the next day they returned to their homes.

**The Importance of the Intended Conference with Indians**—The conditions which made further conference with the Indians a matter of great importance to the colony were thus set forth in the letter General Oglethorpe wrote the trustees on June 15, 1738. It follows:

"I have received frequent and confirmed advices that the Spaniards are striving to bribe the Indians, and particularly the Creek nation, to differ from us; and the disorder of the traders is such as gives but too much room to render the Indians discontented; great numbers of vagrants being gone up without licences either from Carolina, or us. Chigilly, and Malachee, the son of the great Brim, who was called emperor of the Creeks by the Spaniards, insist upon my coming up to put all things in order, and have acquainted me that all the chiefs of the nation will come down to the Coweta town to meet me and hold the general assembly of the Indian nations, where they will take such measures as will be necessary to hinder the Spaniards from corrupting and raising sedition amongst their people. This journey, though a very fatiguing and dangerous one, is quite necessary to be taken; for if not, the Spaniards, who have sent up great presents to them, will bribe the corrupt part of the nation; and, if the honester part is not supported, will probably overcome them and force the whole nation into a war with England. Tomochichi and all the Indians advise me to go up. The Coweta town, where the meeting is to be, is near five hundred miles from hence; it is in a straight line three hundred miles from the sea. All the towns of the Creeks and of the Cousees and Talapousees, though three hundred miles from the Cowetas, will come down to the meeting. The Choctaws also and the Chickasas will send thither their deputies; so that 7,000 men depend upon the event of this assembly. The Creeks can furnish 1,500 warriors, the Chickasas 500, and the Choctaws 5,000. I am obliged to buy horses and presents to carry up to this meeting."

**Discharge of Thomas Causton**—In the presence of impending danger of hostile attacks by the Spaniards, the difficulty of the situation was greatly increased by the extravagant mismanagement of the colony's affairs by Thomas Causton, the leading magistrate of Savannah, whom the trustees had appointed keeper of public stores. While Oglethorpe had been busy fortifying Frederica and the coast, he was obliged to entrust the management of the colony's business affairs largely to the leading official, Thomas Causton, who was supposed to be capable and worthy of trust.

The extravagant expenditures of Causton had alarmed the trustees. Within a year he had received over 13,000 pounds to meet public expenses, but his use of the money had been so extravagant that on June 2, 1738, Harman Verelst, the trustees' accountant, reported unpaid bills amounting to over 5,000 pounds.

The investigation which followed this disclosure resulted in the dismissal of Causton from office and the appointment of Henry Parker in his stead, but that was not all. The examination of his books and papers, which were seized by order of the common council, showed serious mismanagement by Causton of the trust fund sent for the support of the colony. It further appeared that in administering the affairs of the public stores, he had used the office for his own advancement and acted the part of a petty tyrant, rewarding his favorites and oppressing others.

The prodigal waste of public money and the stores committed to his keeping not only brought the colony to the verge of ruin, but made it impossible for colonists who had deposited their money with the public storekeeper to collect it, and they were threatened with starvation. In the meantime, the scout boatmen, rangers, and others employed in the defense of the colony were unpaid and actually starving.

**The Official Exposure**—The letter of the trustees' accountant to General Oglethorpe follows:

"Georgia Office, Westminster, June 2, 1738.

"SIR:—The Trustees being greatly alarm'd at the great number of certified accounts amounting to 1,401 pounds 13s. 2d. brought for payments since Tuesday last, immediately met to concert the most proper measures to secure their effects in Georgia and Mr. Causton's person to answer for his conduct in receiving three cargoes without any order whatsoever from the Trustees; for these certified accounts unpaid now amount to 5,236 pounds, 0s. 6d. And the sola bills, provisions, and effects receiv'd by Mr. Causton since midsummer last amount to 13,086 pounds 9s. 9d. for the application of which he has given the Trustees no account.

"The situation of the Trustees' affairs is such that they cannot sit still in these circumstances, but must, in their own justification, insist upon an immediate seizure of Mr. Causton, to be detained until he gives sufficient security to answer this surprising conduct of his which may draw the Trustees into the greatest inconvenience and discredit, while at the same time they, on their part, have taken all possible care to prevent such inconvenience happening; and unless he shall produce to you such accounts as you think, when transmitted to the Trustees will prove satisfactory to them, you are desired, forthwith to send him with his books and papers in safe custody to the Trustees that he may make up his accounts with them; but if it should so happen, which the Trustees are afraid cannot be the case, that Mr. Causton should produce such an account as will be in your opinion satisfactory to the Trustees, you are desired forthwith to transmit such his account by the first opportunity, and to continue him upon sufficient security until the Trustees have examined and approved thereof.

"The Common Council will at their next meeting seal an Instrument to remove him from his office of First Bailiff, which is intended as a suspension to wait the making up of those accounts.

"As the Trustees' conduct must stand evidently clear from any imputation of neglect, they strongly recommend it to you (being one of themselves) to use all possible means to preserve that Credit they have hitherto been possessed of, and which they desire to have continued consistent with the characters they bear and which the disinterested manner they have always acted in has justly entitled them to.

"It is almost impossible for the Trustees to express the great resentments which they have entertained at the behaviour of a person to whom they show'd such marks of distinction and favour, who by a conduct for which they cannot as yet find a name, has already disabled them from bearing an expense of an estimate which they had calculated with the utmost frugality and economy for the services of the Colony from Midsummer next.

"I am Sir Your most obedient humble Servant

"HARMAN VERELST, Accountant.

"To the Hon. Gen. Oglethorpe, at Gosport.
"To the care of the Postmaster at Portsmouth."

"Gosport, June 4, 1738.

"HARMAN VERELST ESQR &c &c

"By the accounts you sent me of the state of the Trustees' affairs there has been more expended in Georgia than granted by Parliament, but if it is in store, and forth coming, it will serve for the provision of this year. If I find that the circumstances are such as you apprehend them, I shall not issue any of the 500 pounds sola bills till I have further orders from the Trustees. I do not doubt but I shall set all things to rights. . . . I know there will be a good deal of trouble in it, but I am accustomed to difficulties, so that they never make me despair.

"If there has been any fraud in these certified accounts, and that the persons did not deliver the effects certified to the Trustees' use, but that the certificate was a piece of Roguery, agreed upon between the deliverer and the signer, to be sure such certificates are not binding upon the Trustees, tho' the person signing was employed by them. Therefore, in my poor opinion, the Trustees should delay the payment of those certified accounts till they have the examination from Georgia . . .

"Yours very humble Servant,

"JAMES OGLETHORPE.

"P. S. I have the Trustee's orders for making an immediate seizure on Causton, his books and papers, and shall see them immediately executed. This must be kept with the greatest secrecy, for if he should know the orders before they are executed, the effect will perhaps be prevented. I have not trusted even my Clerk."

**General Oglethorpe's Action Concerning Causton**—The action of the common council on June 7, 1738, in dismissing Causton from office and appointing Henry Parker in his stead was communicated directly to General Oglethorpe. The council, in their letter to Oglethorpe, demanded that Causton be arrested and that his books and papers be secured, but he was to be allowed access to his books and papers in order that he might make up his account from Lady Day, 1734, up to date of his arrest. All the trustees' property was to be taken from him and while he was making out his account he was to be in custody or kept under bond. Thomas Jones was designated and ordered to make a thorough examination of Causton's administration and make full report to the trustees, accompanied by General Oglethorpe's opinion upon it.

When Oglethorpe reached Savannah in October, he was in possession of the accountant's report and the trustees' letter of instructions, and was prepared to act vigorously, but Causton, not knowing what was in store for him, met General Oglethorpe with a bold front at the head of the magistrates of

Savannah to welcome the general on his arrival from Frederica. Causton was accompanied by others whom he had favored who joined in the public salutation to the commander-in-chief, hoping thereby to win his favor.

Causton was soon informed that the grand jury of Savannah had prepared a statement of the grievances, hardships, and necessities of the colonists, in which they complained of the misconduct of Causton, charging that he had spent much larger sums than were authorized by the trustees, that he had brought the colony into debt, had exceeded his powers, was arbitrary and oppressive in official conduct, and was partial in the distribution of public stores. It was suggested by some that as commercial agent of the trustees and keeper of public stores, he had used his position for his own advancement and the benefit of his friends. It was also believed that he had used funds of the trustees for the improvement of his plantation at Ockstead, where he and his family were living in comfort. It appeared that Causton was arrogant and had made the other magistrates subservient to his will, playing the part of a petty tyrant, ruling the people through their necessities, taking advantage of their wants and by such means keeping them in subjection to his pleasure. It also appeared that he had perverted the administration of law and kept from the knowledge of the trustees many just complaints made by the people of Savannah.

After examination, which showed woeful mismanagement by Causton of the funds sent to support the colony, General Oglethorpe, on the 17th of October, called the people together at the town house and explained the situation to them, showing the serious condition resulting from this course of Causton. To meet the situation, he urged the utmost economy, in order that something might remain to support life among the people who were suffering without cause. The next day Causton was dismissed from office and his books, papers, and accounts of public stores were turned over to Thomas Jones. General Oglethorpe demanded bond of Causton. He was unable to make bond, but gave his property at Ockstead as security.

After some time had been spent by Jones in the examination of Causton's account, he reported so much irregularity in the record that no man living could adjust it and he was tired of looking into such confusion, saying he believed that it was by art and cunning made inextricable. He was positive that the balances formerly reported by Causton to the trustees were made at will, and it was impossible to make out such balances from the books.

Causton complained that Jones' report was unfair and objected to being called a villain and a knave. He declared that he had served the trust well and was prepared to defend his character from all attacks.

As it was impossible to adjust these accounts in Savannah, Causton was ordered to London, where he appeared before the common council. Failing there to submit proper vouchers, he was allowed to return to Georgia, where he said he would be able to arrange everything to the satisfaction of the trustees. Sailing for Savannah, he died at sea and was buried in the ocean. The vacancy caused by the removal of Causton and filled temporarily by the appointment of Henry Parker was filled more permanently by the appointment of William Stephens, who was then in Savannah as secretary of the trustees.

**Oglethorpe's Comment**—In a letter written to the trustees on the 19th of October, General Oglethorpe said that Causton had trifled with public money and squandered the resources of the colony. He showed the seriousness of the situation by saying that the scout boatmen, rangers, and others in active service were unpaid and actually starving. He mentioned as the worst result that the industrious poor people who had saved something by economy and lodged their little savings in the store, hoping to receive from it in their necessity, found that the store could not pay them, and they must perish from want. He added that like misery would befall all the trustees' servants and many of the inhabitants whom sickness and misfortune had prevented from making a crop that year. He concluded by saying, "I can see nothing but destruction to the colony unless some assistance be immediately sent us. I support things for a while by some money I have in my hand and the rest I supply with my own money, for I will not incur debts nor draw bills upon you . . .

"If this had not happened the Colony had overcome all its difficulties and had been in a flourishing condition."

He told the trustees that he had already spent a great deal and that as far as the income from his estate and employments for the year would go, he would rather lay it out in support of the colony "than in any other diversion." He estimated that after paying outstanding debts, at least 5,000 pounds would be required to carry on the affairs of the colony.

**Attempt to Assassinate Oglethorpe**—The hard times, resulting from Thomas Causton's extravagance in the expenditure of public money, gave rise to much discontent in the colony, especially in Oglethorpe's regiment, which included some bad characters, and their bad feeling, which centered on the commanding general, was shown by an attempt to assassinate him.

After adjusting matters at Savannah, as well as he could, and putting in effect a method of disbursements from the public stores, which would make the slender resources of the colony go as far as possible, General Oglethorpe set out for Frederica on October 25, 1738, to strengthen the fortifications of the southern coast of Georgia, which the Spaniards evidently intended to attack soon.

He established headquarters at Fort St. Andrew, on Cumberland Island, where he could direct and encourage the building of military defenses. Cumberland was then garrisoned by the companies of soldiers which had been sent from Gilbraltar by the British government. Their pay had at first been supplemented by an extra allowance of provisions, but the condition of the colony was such that these extra rations had to be discontinued. This reduction of rations caused dissatisfaction among the men, and as the general was at the door of his hut talking with Captain MacKay a soldier came up without being called and demanded a renewal of the extra allowance. Oglethorpe told him that the terms of enlistment had been fully complied with and if he wished anything more from the commanding officer his rude and disrespectful behavior would not secure it. The man became very insolent and Captain MacKay drew his sword, but the desperado took it from him, broke it in half, threw the hilt at the captain's head and rushed away to the barracks. There taking up a loaded gun and crying, "One and all," he ran back, followed by five or more of the conspirators and fired at the general. As he was only a few steps away, the ball passed close to Oglethorpe's ear, and the powder scorched his face and singed his clothes. Another soldier raised his gun and attempted to fire, but fortunately it missed fire. A third man drew his hanger and tried to stab the general, but Oglethorpe, having drawn his sword parried the thrust. At this instant, an officer coming up ran his sword through the ruffian's body. At this the mutineers tried to escape, but were caught and put in irons. After trial by court-martial, the ringleaders were found guilty and shot.

General Oglethorpe's narrow escape saved the colony from great danger. for without his guidance Georgia, in its weakened condition, would have been an easy victim of its enemies.

Spanish emissaries from St. Augustine tried to start an insurrection among the negroes of South Carolina by offering them freedom and protection. They not only encouraged desertion by the negroes, but what was worse the massacre of their owners. The governor of Florida had made a regiment of runaway slaves, appointed some of the negroes officers and enlisted them with the same pay and rations allowed to Spanish soldiers.

Encouraged by the course of the Spaniards a band of negro slaves got together at Stono, killed two young men who were in charge of a warehouse there and seized the guns and ammunition stored in the warehouse. They elected one of their number captain and marched toward the southwest with colors flying and drums beating. Entering by force the house of a Mr. Godfrey, they murdered him, his wife and children, took all the arms, set fire to the premises, and went on toward Jacksonborough.

Plundering and burning houses as they went, killing every white person they met, they compelled all negroes on the way to join them.

Governor Bull, returning to Charleston from the South met this armed force and avoiding it, spread the alarm which reached the Presbyterian Church at Wiltown, where the Rev. Archibald Stobo was preaching to a large congregation. As the law required planters attending worship to go armed, the men of the congregation were ready for the emergency. Leaving the women in the church and led by Captain Bee, those men rapidly pursued the negroes, who had already marched twelve miles, spreading desolation where they went. Finding rum, they drank freely of it, and when overtaken by the white men they had stopped in an open field, where they were singing, dancing, and giving forth yells of triumph. Quickly surrounding them, the planters killed some, captured others, and dispersed the rest. The leaders and first insurgents were put to death.

More than twenty persons had been murdered by the negroes, and a number of dwellings had been burned to the ground. But for the prompt action of the armed men worshipping at Wiltown church, the destruction of life and property would have been greater and the uprising would probably have become widespread.

Learning of this bloody insurrection, General Oglethorpe issued a proclamation, ordering the arrest of all negroes found in Georgia, offering a reward for runaways and detailing a company of rangers to patrol the southern frontier and block all routes by which they might escape to Florida.

The seriousness of this servile insurrection is clear from the fact that the negro population of South Carolina was then estimated at 40,000, and that of the whites only 5,000. The condition was almost like a powder magazine which might easily be exploded by the pernicious influence of Spanish emissaries in encouraging insurrection and suggesting a general massacre of the white people in South Carolina and Georgia, with the promise of soldiers' pay and rations to all who should find their way to Florida.

Colonel Jones makes this statement upon information in a publication entitled *Historical Account of the Rise and Progress of the Colonies of South Carolina and Georgia,* Volume II, pp. 72-74, London, 1779. He also refers to McCall's *History of Georgia,* Volume I, pp. 125-26.

He goes on to say that negro sergeants were employed by the Spaniards on recruiting service, with secret locations in Carolina, and that two Spaniards were arrested in Georgia and committed to prison for enticing slaves to leave their Carolina masters.

Colonel Jones closes his statement with this comment: "Thus did Spain grow daily more and more offensive in the development of her plans for the annoyance, disquietude, and destruction of the English colonies adjacent to her possessions in Florida. To the vigilance of Oglethorpe and the services of his scouts was Carolina largely indebted for the retention of her slave property, and for deliverance from the horrors of a general servile insurrection."

**Deplorable Condition of the Colony**—Oglethorpe was so busy with such matters and with military affairs on the southern coast of Georgia that he could not return to Savannah during the rest of 1738, but the financial affairs of the colony were in a deplorable state and the general asked for aid from the British government, in the following letter to Thomas Winnington, paymaster of the forces:

"The Parliament, to defray the charges of the improvements of the Colony of Georgia and the military defence thereof used to grant 20,000 pounds for the year. The King ordered a regiment for the defence of the Colony and thereupon the Trustees were contented to abate 12,000 pounds in their demands, and 8,000 pounds only was granted to them. But as the Regiment did not arrive till near a year afterwards, the Trustees were obliged to support the military charge of the Colony during the whole time, which was very dangerous by reason of the threatened invasion of the Spaniards, of which you received so many accounts. No officer of the Trustees dared abandon a garrison, reduce any men, or dismiss the militia whilst the Spaniards threatened the Province and the King's troops were not arrived to relieve them. A debt of near 12,000 pounds is contracted because by unforeseen accidents the regiment was delayed and the military expence was continued till their arrival, though the Parliamentary grant ceased."

He then entreats Mr. Winnington to aid the trustees in their application to Parliament for a sum sufficient to discharge the debt thus incurred; and for the excellent reason that "if the people who furnished with necessaries a colony then threatened with invasion, and the people who then bore arms for the defence of it (and thereby secured that important frontier till the arrival of the King's troops) should be ruined by not being paid their just demands, it would prevent hereafter any frontier colony from receiving assistance."

The trustees were unable to meet both the ordinary expenses of the colony and the heavy expenses of the military. While cannon and munitions of war were needed many of the inhabitants lacked food. Under these conditions, Parliament appropriated 20,000 pounds, which enabled the common council to meet outstanding obligations and provide for further administration of the colony.

**Dissatisfaction of the Colonists**—The financial difficulties of the province, a scarcity of supplies caused by Causton's defalcation, the unsatisfactory returns from farming, the effect of the warmer climate, and the laws forbidding the ownership of slaves and limiting the title to land granted the colonists, caused so much dissatisfaction and so discouraged some of the people that, despairing of accumulating wealth, they left Georgia, crossed the Savannah River and sought better fortune in South Carolina, where lands were granted in fee simple and the ownership of slaves was permitted by law.

Under these conditions the magistrates of Savannah united with a number of freeholders in a petition to the trustees in which they expressed disappointment that the hope of pleasant and profitable homes in Georgia, held out to them in England, had not been realized and that without the help of cheap slave labor they could not compete successfully with their neighbors in South Carolina and the culture of silk and wine could not be made profitable by the use of white labor. They asserted that commerce languished because they did not have fee simple title to their lands and could not offer them as security to merchants in buying goods as the people of other English provinces did.

After referring to the departure of colonists from Georgia and the few that had come there, they outlined their difficulties as follows:

**The Causes of Complaint**—"FIRST. The Want of a free Title or Fee Simple to our Lands, which, if granted, would both occasion great Numbers of new Settlers to come amongst us, and likewise encourage those who remain here chearfully to proceed in making further improvements, as well to retrieve their sunk Fortunes, as to make Provision for their Posterity.

"SECOND. The Want of the Use of Negroes with proper Limitations; which, if granted, would both induce great Numbers of White People to come here, and also render us capable to subsist ourselves by raising provisions upon our lands until we could make some Produce fit for Export, and in some measure to balance our Importation. We are very sensible of the Inconveniences and Mischiefs that have already, and do daily arise from an unlimited Use of Negroes; but we are as sensible that these may be prevented by a due Limitation, such as so many to each White Man, and so many to such a Quantity of Land; or in any other manner which your Honours shall think most proper. By granting us, Gentlemen, these two Particulars, and such other Privileges as his Majesty's most dutiful Subjects in America enjoy, you will not only prevent our impending Ruin, but, we are fully satisfied, also will soon make this the most flourishing Colony possessed by his Majesty in America, and your Memories will be perpetuated to all future Ages, our latest Posterity sounding your Praises as their first Founders, Patrons and Guardians; but if, by denying us those Privileges, we ourselves and Families are not only ruined, but even our Posterity likewise, you will always be mentioned as the Cause and Authors of all their Misfortunes and Calamities; which we hope will never happen."

**Scotchmen Object to Slaves and Change of Title**—When the Scotchmen of Darien (New Inverness) heard of the foregoing petition, they objected to its statement and wrote General Oglethorpe as follows:

"We are informed that our Neighbours of Savannah have petitioned your Excellency for the Liberty of having Slaves. We hope, and earnestly entreat that before such Proposals are hearkened unto your Excellency will consider our situation and of what dangerous and bad Consequence such Liberty would be to us, for many Reasons;

"I. The Nearness of the Spaniards who have proclaimed Freedom to all Slaves who run away from their Masters makes it impossible for us to keep them without more Labour in guarding them than what we would be at to do their work:

II. We are laborious, and know that a White Man may be by the Year more usefully employed than a Negro:

III. We are not rich, and becoming Debtors for Slaves, in case of their running away or dying, would inevitably ruin the poor Master, and he become a greater Slave to the Negro Merchant, than the Slave he bought could be to him:

"IV. It would oblige us to keep a Guard-duty at least as severe as when we expected a daily Invasion; and if that was the Case, how miserable would it be to us and our Wives and Families to have an Enemy without and more dangerous ones in our Bosom!

"V. It is shocking to human Nature that any Race of Mankind, and their Posterity, should be sentenced to perpetual Slavery; nor in Justice can we think otherwise of it than that they are thrown amongst us to be our Scourge one Day or other for our Sins; and as Freedom to them must be as dear as to us, what a Scene of Horror must it bring about! And the longer it is unexecuted, the bloody Scene must be the greater. We, therefore, for our own sakes, our Wives and Children, and our Posterity, beg your Consideration, and intreat that instead of introducing Slaves, you'll put us in the way to get us some of our Countrymen, who with their Labour in time of Peace, and our Vigilance if we are invaded, with the Help of those, will render it a difficult thing to hurt us, or that Part of the Province we possess. We will forever pray for your Excellency, and are with all submission," etc.

**The Salzburgers Object to Slaves and Change of Title**—The Salzburgers also wrote General Oglethorpe objecting to the introduction of slaves and the change in the title:

"We Saltzburghers, and Inhabitants of Ebenezer that have signed this Letter, intreat humbly in our and our Brethren's names, your Excellency would be pleased to shew us the Favour of desiring the honourable Trustees for sending to Georgia another Transport of Saltzburghers to be settled at Ebenezer. We have, with one Accord, wrote a Letter to our Father in God, the Reverend Mr. Senior Urlsperger, at Augspurg, and in that Letter expressly named those Saltzburghers and Austrians whom, as our friends, Relations, and Countrymen, we wish to see settled here. We can indeed attest of them that they fear the Lord truly, love Working, and will conform themselves to our Congregation. We have given them an Account of our being well settled, and being mighty well pleased with the Climate and Condition of this country, having here several Preferences in spiritual and temporal Circumstances for other People in Germany, which your Honour will find in the here inclosed Copy of our Letter to Mr. Senior Urlsperger, if they fare as we do, having been provided in the Beginning with Provisions, a little Stock for Breed, some tools, and good Land by the Care of the honorable Trustees; and if God grants his Blessing to their work, we doubt not but they will gain with us easily their Bread and Subsistence, and lead a quiet and peaceable Life in all Godliness and Honesty.

"Though it is here a hotter Season than our native Country is, yet not so extremely hot, as we were told on the first time of our Arrival; but since we have been now used to the country we find it tolerable, and, for working People, very convenient; setting themselves to work early in the Morning till Ten O'Clock; and in the afternoon from Three to Sun-set; and having Business at Home, we do them in our Huts and Houses in the Middle of the Day till the greatest Heat is over. People in Germany are hindered by Frost and Snow in the Winter from doing any work in the Fields and Vineyards: but we have this Preference to do the most and heaviest Work at such a time, preparing the Ground sufficiently for planting in the Spring. We were told by several People, after our Arrival, that it proves quite impossible and dangerous for White People to plant and manufacture any Rice, being a Work only for Negroes, not for European People; but having Experience of the contrary we laugh at such a Talking, seeing that several People of us have had, in last Harvest, a greater Crop of Rice than they wanted for their own Consumption. If God is pleased to enable us by some money for building such Mills, convenient for cleaning the Rice, as we use in Germany for making several Grains fit for eating, then the Manufacture of Rice will be an easy and profitable thing. For the present we crave your Excellency's Goodness to allow, for the Use of the whole Congregation, some Rice Sieves, of several sorts, from Charles-Town, which cannot be had at Savannah; We will be accountable to the Store for them.

"Of Corn, Pease, Potatoes, Pomkins, Cabbage, &c., we had such a good Quantity that many Bushels are sold, and much was spent in feeding Cows, Calves, and Hogs. If the Surveyor, according to his order and duty, had used Dispatch in laying out our Farms (which we have got not sooner than last Fall), and we had not been disappointed by long Sickness, and planting the yellow Pensilvania Corn; we would have been able, by the Blessing of God to spare a greater Quantity of Grain for getting Meat-Kind and cloathes, of which we are in Want. It is true that Two-Acres of Ground for each Family's Garden are set out some time ago, but there being very few Swamps fit for planting of Rice, and some Part of them wanting a good deal of Dung, we were not able, in the Beginning, to dung it well; therefore we could not make such a good Use of those Acres as we now have Reason to Hope, by the Assistance of God, after our Plantations are laid out. Hence it will be that we plant the good Ground first, and improve the other soil when Occasion will require it, in the best manner we can. In the first Time when the Ground must be cleared from Trees, Bushes, and Roots, and fenced in carefully, we are to undergo some hard Labour, which afterwards will be the easier and more pleasing, when the hardest Trial is over, and our plantations are better regulated. A good deal of time we spent in building Huts, Houses, and other necessary Buildings in Town and upon the Farms; and since we wanted Money for several Expences several Persons of us hired themselves out for some Weeks for building the Orphan-house and its Appurtenances; also, The Reverend Mr. Gronau's House, which happened to be built in the hottest Summer Season; and now some of us are employed to build the Reverend Mr. Bolzius' House; which Buildings have taken away some time from our Work in the Ground; but the fair Opportunity of earning some Money at Home was a great Benefit to us; this now being so, that neither the hot Summer Season nor anything else hinders us from Work in the Ground, and we wish to lead a quiet and peaceable Life at our Place.

"We humbly beseech the honourable Trustees not to allow it that any negro might be brought to our Place or in our Neighborhood, knowing by Experience that Houses and Gardens will be robbed always by them, and White People are in Danger of Life because of them, besides other great Inconveniences. Likewise, we humbly beseech you and the Trustees not to allow to any Person the Liberty of buying up Lands at our Place, by which, if granted, it would happen that by bad and turbulent Neighbours our Congregation would be spoilt and poor, harmless People troubled and oppressed: But we wish and long for such Neighbours to be settled here whose Good name and honest Behaviour is known to us and our Favourers. The Honourable Trustees have been always Favourers and Protectors of poor and distressed People; wherefore we beseech you and them that they would be pleased to take us further under their fatherly Care, that the Remembrance of their Benevolence and Kindness to our Congregation might be conveyed to our late Posterity, and be highly praised. We put up our prayers to God for rewarding your Excellency and the Honourable Trustees manifold for all their good Assistance and Benefits which are bestowed upon us, and beg humbly the Continuance of your and their Favour and Protection, being with the greatest Submission and Respect, your Honour's most obedient dutiful Servants," etc.

**Oglethorpe's Comment**—What appears to be a correct view of the situation was given in General Oglethorpe's letter to the trustees, written from Savannah on the 12th of March, 1739. He said that a Mr. Williams, to whom many of the people were indebted, had induced the poor people to sign the petition which said that white men could not work in the province. He denied that and said that he can disprove it by hundreds of witnesses, to which he added:

"The idle ones are indeed for negroes. If the petition is countenanced, the province is ruined. Mr. Williams and Dr. Tailfeur will buy most of the lands at Savannah with debts due to them and the inhabitants must go off and be succeeded by negroes. Yet the very debtors have been weak enough to sign their desire of leave to sell."

On the 4th of July of the same year he wrote again, protesting against any material change in land tenure, saying:

"Titles are at present upon a very good footing and those who made most noise about their lands were such as had taken no care to make any use of them."

Still later the General wrote the trustees: "There is one Tailfeur, an Apothecary Surgeon who gives Physick, and one Williams, of whom I wrote to you formerly, a Merchant, who quitted planting to sell rum. To these two almost all the Town of Savannah is in debt for Physick and Rum, and they have raised a strong spirit to desire that Lands may be alienable, and then they would take the Lands for the Debts, monopolize the country, and settle it with Negroes. They have a vast deal of Art, and if they think they cannot carry this, they would apply for any other alteration since they hope thereby to bring confusion, and you cannot imagine how much uneasiness I have had here. I hope, therefore, you will make no alterations."

The Robert Williams and Dr. Patrick Tailfeur mentioned by Oglethorpe were active in stirring up trouble in the Colony by criticising the conduct of affairs and maligning Oglethorpe after they left Georgia and went to South Carolina.

(*Collections Georgia Historical Society,* Vol. III, pp. 70-79. *Stephens Journal,* Vol. I, pp. 8-149.)

**Reply of the Trustees**—After due consideration of these petitions and the advice of General Oglethorpe, the trustees made this reply:

"To the Magistrates of the Town of Savannah in the Province of Georgia:

"The Trustees for establishing the Colony of Georgia in America have received by the Hands of Mr. Benjamin Ball of London, Merchant, an attested Copy of A representation signed by you the Magistrates, and many of the Inhabitants of Savannah on the 9th of December last, for altering the Tenure of the Lands, and introducing Negroes into the Province, transmitted from thence by Mr. Robert Williams:

"The Trustees are not surprized to find unwary People drawn in by crafty Men to join in a Design of extorting by Clamour from the Trustees an Alteration in the fundamental Laws framed for the preservation of the People from those very Designs.

"But the Trustees cannot but express their Astonishment that you, the Magistrates, appointed by them to be the Guardians of the People, by putting those Laws in Execution, should so far forget your Duty as to put yourselves at the Head of this Attempt.

"However, they direct you to give the Complainants this Answer from the Trustees; That they should deem themselves very unfit for the Trust reposed in them by his Majesty on their Behalf, if they could be prevailed upon by such an irrational attempt to give up a Constitution, framed with the greatest caution, for the Preservation of Liberty and Property, and of which the Laws against the Use of Slaves, and for the Entail of Lands are the surest Foundations.

"And the Trustees are the more confirmed in their Opinion of the Unreasonableness of this Demand that they have received Petitions from the Darien and other Parts of the Province, representing the Inconvenience and Danger which must arise to the good People of the Province from the Introduction of Negroes: and as the Trustees themselves are fully convinced that besides the Hazard attending of that Introduction, it would destroy all Industry among the White Inhabitants; and that, by giving them a Power to alien their lands, the Colony would soon be too like its neighbours, void of white inhabitants, filled with Blacks, and reduced to be the precarious Property of a Few, equally exposed to domestick Treachery and foreign Invasion: And therefore the Trustees cannot be supposed to be in any Disposition of granting this Request: and if they have not, before this, signified their Dislike of it, their Delay is to be imputed to no other Motives but the Hopes they had conceived that Time and Experience would bring the Complainants to a better Mind. And the Trustees readily join Issue with them in their Appeal to Posterity, who shall judge between them, who were their best Friends, those who endeavoured to preserve for them a Property in their Lands by tying up the Hands of their unthrifty Progenitors; or they who wanted a Power to mortgage or alien them; who were the best Friends to the Colony, those who with great Labour and Cost had endeavoured to form a Colony of his Majesty's Subjects and persecuted Protestants from other Parts of Europe; had placed them on a fruitful soil, and strove to secure them in their Possessions by those Arts which naturally tend to keep the Colony full of useful and industrious People capable both to cultivate and defend it, or those, who to gratify the greedy and ambitious views of a few negro merchants, would put it into their Power to become sole owners of the Province by introducing their baneful Commodity which, it is well known, by sad Experience, has brought our Neighbour Colonies to the Brink of Ruin by driving out their White Inhabitants, who were their Glory and Strength, to make room for Blacks who are now become the Terror of their unadvised Masters.

"Signed by order of the Trustees this Twentieth day of June 1739.

BENJ. MARTYN, Secretary. (L. S.)."

On October 20th of that year, General Oglethorpe wrote the trustees that their reply to the complainants had been received and published and had a good effect on the colonists. In reply to this, the trustees sent orders dismissing from office the Savannah magistrates who had signed the petition, and appointing others in their stead.

Seeing this, the leading malcontents who had done much of idleness, horse racing and lawless conduct to demoralize the community, left the colony.

It appears that in spite of the reply of the trustees, the petitions of the Scotchmen and the Salzburgers, and the letters of General Oglethorpe there was serious dissatisfaction, because there was a feeling that great sickness among white people was caused by the malarial conditions of the swampy lands near Savannah, and it appeared to the colonists that negroes suffered less from the heat and were less likely to be made sick under those conditions than the white people were. There was also dissatisfaction because the title to land was limited and some planters did leave Georgia for South Carolina.

Under these conditions, although, in June, 1739, the trustees had refused to grant the petition of the magistrates and freeholders of Savannah, they did make some modification of their position in regard to titles by passing a set of resolutions which were published in the London *Gazette* of September 8, 1739, and also published in the Charlestown *Gazette* of South Carolina.

These resolutions provided that in order to provide for the widows of grantees, it was agreed and ordained that lands already granted and those afterward granted should on failure of a male issue descend to daughters of the grantees. If there were no issue, male or female, the grantees might devise such land. In the absence of any devise such land would descend to the heirs at law of the original grantees, but the possession of the devisee could not exceed five hundred acres. Widows of grantees were entitled during their lives to hold and enjoy the dwelling house, garden, and one moiety of which their husbands were in possession when they died.

While this modification was considerable, it did not fully comply with the request for fee simple title, and there was still some dissatisfaction.

**Dissension Among Military Officers**—In addition to his many cares, General Oglethorpe was annoyed by dissensions among the officers of his regiment at a time when good discipline and complete accord were urgently needed to protect the colony of Georgia against expected attacks from the Spaniards.

Captain Hugh Mackay was tried by court-martial on charges made against him by Lieutenant-Colonel Cochrane, and was honorably acquitted. Captain Norbury, convicted of using disrespectful language to his commanding officer, was ordered to beg his pardon.

Not long after he had been tried on charges made by Colonel Cochrane, Captain Mackay accused the colonel of engaging in merchandise at the neglect of duty and of selling things to the soldiers at exorbitant prices, causing a spirit of mutiny, and of breaking the treaty with the Spaniards.

On Captain Mackay's return from St. Andrew, he was attacked by Colonel Cochrane and beaten with a big stick. This occurred in the presence of General Oglethorpe, who immediately had both officers arrested, and as there were no officers in the colony of sufficient rank to try them, they were ordered to report to the War Department in England for investigation. That investigation resulted in the withdrawal of Colonel Cochrane from Georgia, and he was succeeded in Oglethorpe's regiment by Lieutenant-Colonel Cook.

**Oglethorpe in South Carolina**—On April 3, 1739, General Oglethorpe appeared before the Legislature of South Carolina and exhibited his commission as commander-in-chief of the English forces in Carolina and Georgia. He thereupon regulated the military establishment of South Carolina and returned to Savannah.

**Condition of the Colony in 1739**—On July 4, 1739, General Oglethorpe wrote the trustees a letter telling them of the general condition of the colony and of his efforts to make it self-sustaining. He was bothered by violations of the law against rum in Savannah, but conditions were better at Frederica, where the magistrates had suppressed the rum traffic.

The general's regiment was comfortably housed and the frontier islands were protected by regular troops, but additional boats were needed. Watchmen were needed to preserve the peace and horsemen were wanted to range the woods for the protection of cattle, the arrest of outlaws, and the arrest of runaway slaves from South Carolina.

The plantation on Amelia Island, under the management of Hugh Mackay, was in a flourishing condition.

Soon after that General Oglethorpe sent Mr. Auspourger to England with twenty pounds of silk. It appears that the yield would have been better but for the death of many of the silk worms. They were bred in a house which had been used as a hospital and Mr. Camuse thought infection caused the sickness and death of the worms.

# CHAPTER XXI.

## *General Oglethorpe's Trip to Coweta to Meet the Indians*

As the French and the Spaniards were trying to cause trouble among the Indians who were friendly to the colonies of Carolina and Georgia, and wean them away from their allegiance to the British crown, General Oglethorpe saw the necessity of meeting the Indian nations in the conference about to assemble at Coweta, an Indian town more than three hundred miles from Savannah. Peace with 7,000 Indian warriors and their support in war with the Spaniards depended on the result of this conference. In a word, the existence of the colony was at stake, and although it was a long, tiresome, and dangerous journey, General Oglethorpe did not hesitate to make it.

On July 17, 1739, he started, accompanied by Lieutenant Dunbar, Ensign Leman, and Cadet Eyre. They went up the Savannah River on a cutter and landed at the Uchee Town, twenty-five miles above Ebenezer, where they were met by Indian traders with saddle horses. There General Oglethorpe began a journey of three hundred miles through a wilderness, going through ravines, tangled thickets, and over dreary swamps, in which the horses mired. Several times they had to build rafts on which to cross the rivers, and smaller streams were crossed by wading or swimming. Wrapped in his cloak, with a portmanteau for a pillow, General Oglethorpe slept on the ground, or, if the night was wet, under a cover of cypress boughs laid upon poles. For two hundred miles they passed no habitation and saw no human being, but as they approached the end of their journey, they found provisions which the Indians had left for them in the woods.

Within forty miles of his destination, General Oglethorpe was met by Indian chiefs, who escorted him the rest of the way to Coweta, the principal town of the Muskogee or Creek Indians, where he was received by the natives with manifestations of joy.

The general won the hearts of the Indians by coming so far to visit them with only a few attendants, relying on their good faith, and their good will was confirmed by his readiness in adjusting himself to their habits, as well as by his natural dignity and courage.

On August 11, 1739, the chiefs of several Indian tribes met and their great council opened with solemn rites. After many talks, the conditions of intercourse and terms for trade between the Indians and the colonists were agreed upon. As one of their beloved men, Oglethorpe partook of their black medicine drink, called foskey,* and smoked with them the pipe of peace.

On the 21st of August a formal treaty was concluded by which the Creeks renewed their fealty to the King of Great Britain and confirmed their previous grants of territory to the colony of Georgia. In behalf of the trustees, General Oglethorpe agreed that the English would not encroach upon the Indian reserves and promised that the traders would deal fairly and honestly with them. As the bad conduct of some traders had inflamed the Indians, the general found it hard to appease their wrath. On that subject he wrote: "If I had not gone up the misunderstanding between them and the Carolina Traders, fomented by neighboring nations, would probably have occasioned a war which I believe might have been the result of this general meeting; but as their complaints were just and reasonable I gave them satisfaction in all of them and everything is settled in peace." The Choctaws were persuaded not to make war on the French and the chiefs of all the tribes assured Oglethorpe that they would come to his assistance whenever he called for them.

The conference was opened by a speech from Oglethorpe, and after due deliberation the Indians agreed unanimously to continue their ancient love for the King of Great Britain and keep their agreement made with the trustees in 1733.

It was also declared that all the land from the Savannah River to the St. John's River, including the islands on the coast, and from the St. John's to Appalache Bay, embracing Appalache Old Fields, and from that bay to the mountains, did by ancient right belong to the Creek nation, that they had maintained that right by force of arms and could show heaps of bones of their enemies who had died in the attempt to take these lands from them. The Indian commissioners agreed that the Creek nation had long enjoyed the protection of England and that the Spaniards had no claim on the land referred to; also that they would permit no one except the Georgia trustees and their colonists to settle on those lands.

The grant already made to the trustees, including lands on the Savannah River and the seacoast as far as the St. John's and as high as the tide flowed, and all the islands, except St. Catherine, Ossabaw and Sapelo, was reaffirmed. They claimed a reservation extending from Pipe Maker's Bluff to Savannah.

For the English, it was agreed that they would take no land but that mentioned as having been ceded by the Creek nations to the trustees. They also agreed to punish any persons trespassing upon the land reserved by the Creeks.

---

(* For foskey, see Adair's *History of American Indians,* p. 108.)

**The Indians Present at the Conference**—At this conference, so important to the future and welfare of the colony of Georgia, those present were General James Edward Oglethorpe, representing King George the Second of England, and the following Indians: Chickeley Nenia, chief king of Coweta Town, Malatche, mico, son of Brim, late emperor of the Creek nation, the chiefs and warriors of Coweta Town; the king of the Cusetas, Schisheligo, second mico of the Cusetas, Iskegio, third chief of the Cusetas, and other chief men and warriors of that nation; Ochaohapko, one of the chief men of the town of Palachuckolas, Killatee, chief war captain, and other chief men and warriors, "deputies with full powers to conclude all things for the said town"; Towmawme, mico of the Ufawles, with several other chief men and warriors commissioned to represent all the towns of that nation; Metalcheko, captain of the Echeestees, with other chief men and warriors of that people; Neathaklo, chief man of the Owichees, with several other chief men and warriors, Occullaviche, chief man of the Chehaws, with other chief men and warriors; Hewanawge Thaleekeo, chief man of the Oakmulgees, with several of the chief men and warriors of that nation; the king of the Oconees, with several chief men and warriors; and Neachackelo, second chief of the Swagles, with several chief men and warriors, all empowered to represent their several nations and to bind them in the convention.

For the successful result of this dangerous journey by Oglethorpe, almost alone through a wilderness, he received the thanks of the trustees. Commenting on that remarkable achievement by General Oglethorpe, Thomas Spalding said of it, in an article written for the Georgia Historical Society:

"When we call into remembrance the then force of these tribes,—for they could have brought into the field twenty thousand fighting men,—when we call to remembrance the influence the French had everywhere else obtained over the Indians,—when we call to remembrance the distance he had to travel through solitary pathways . . . exposed to summer suns, night dews, and to the treachery of any single Indian who knew—and every Indian knew—the rich reward that would have awaited him for the act from the Spaniards in St. Augustine, or the French in Mobile, surely we may proudly ask, what soldier ever gave higher proof of courage? What English governor of an American province ever gave such assurance of deep devotion to public duty."

**Oglethorpe's Illness**—Continued exposure and anxiety had begun to tell on General Oglethorpe, although he seemed to have an iron constitution, and on his return he was prostrated by severe fever at Fort Augusta. While still suffering there, he was visited by chiefs of the Chickasaws and Cherokees, and the Cherokees complained that some of their nation had been poisoned by rum sold them by traders. For this they were very angry and threatened revenge.

Upon investigation, the general learned that some unlicensed traders had carried the smallpox to the Indians, and because they did not know how to treat it, it killed some of them. The general found it hard to make this clear to the Indians, but they were at length satisfied and left with his assurance that they need not fear trouble in dealing with licensed traders, for Georgia never granted permits to persons unworthy of confidence.

## CHAPTER XXII.

# *War With Spain*

While at Augusta, General Oglethorpe learned that the governor of Rhode Island had issued commissions for privateers to prey on Spanish commerce. This was his first knowledge of open war with Spain. Returning to Savannah, he found dispatches announcing hostilities between England and Spain. On the 3rd of October the freeholders were called together under arms and met in the court house at noon, where the magistrates and General Oglethorpe presided. He addressed the people, telling them that they need have no fear about the Indians, who had been brought into closer alliance with the English by the recent conference, and that English frigates would cruise along the coast for its protection; also that additional land forces were expected. He closed by exhorting the people to watchfulness, activity, and bravery.

At the end of the general's address, the cannon at the fort were discharged and the freeholders fired three volleys.

At this time the people of the colony were saddened by the death of their aged friend, Tomochichi, who died after a long illness on the 5th of October, 1739, at his home four miles from Savannah at the age of ninety-seven. He was conscious to the last and when told that his end was near, showed great calmness, exhorted his people never to forget the favor he had received from the King of England, but to persevere in their friendship for the English. He expressed great affection for General Oglethorpe and seemed to have no care about dying except that his life might have been useful against the Spaniards. As a last request, he asked that his body might be buried among the English at Savannah.

General Oglethorpe, the magistrates, and the people of Savannah met the remains of their aged friend at the water's edge, and his body was taken into Percival Square, with General Oglethorpe, Colonel Stephens, Colonel Montaigut, Mr. Carteret, Mr. Lemon, and Mr. Maxwell as pallbearers, followed by the Indians, the magistrates, and the people. Minute guns from the battery were fired during the funeral, with volleys of small arms by the militia. General Oglethorpe ordered a pyramid of stone to be built over Tomochichi's grave, as a testimony of the people's gratitude. A granite boulder now marks the spot.

**Active Operations Against St. Augustine**—Early in October, 1739, General Oglethorpe sent runners to the Indian towns, asking the chiefs of the Cherokees and Creeks to send a thousand warriors to the Southern frontier to aid him against the Spaniards. Before leaving Savannah for Frederica, he inspected the arms, reviewed the militia, distributed ammunition, settled differences between civil officers, and granted letters of marque to Captain Davis, who soon converted his sloop into a privateer with twenty-four guns. On November 5, 1739, General Oglethorpe left Savannah for Frederica.

On November 15, news came to Frederica that a party of Spaniards had landed on Amelia Island in the night, concealing themselves in the woods, and the next morning had shot two unarmed Highlanders who were looking for fuel and had hacked their bodies with their swords. An account later in the *Gentleman's Magazine* said that the Spaniards cut off the heads of the Highlanders and mangled their bodies.

General Oglethorpe tried to catch the Spaniards, but failing to overtake them swept the St. John's River, drove in the outguard and burnt three outposts. Marching on toward St. Augustine, ravaging the country, he remained in the neighborhood three days collecting cattle and trying to provoke a combat with the enemy. Spanish horsemen with some negroes and Indians appeared, but being attacked by Oglethorpe's forces quickly retreated.

On New Year's Day, 1740, with a detachment of his regiment, accompanied by Captains Mackay and Desbrisay, Lieutenant Dunbar, Ensigns Mackay, Mace, Sutherland and Maxwell, Adjutant Hugh Mackay, the rangers, the Chickasaws led by Fanne Mico, Captain Gray, the Uchee king and his warriors, Hewitt, Hillispilli and Santouchy with their Creek gunmen, Mr. Matthews and Mr. Jones, in a periagua, thirteen boats and a privateer sloop, General Oglethorpe entered the St. John's River, where he surprised and burnt Fort Picolata. Soon afterwards he captured Fort St. Francis de Papa. This fort was only twenty-one miles from St. Augustine, in a neighborhood well stocked with cattle and horses and commanded the ferry across the River Picolata. In this action, General Oglethorpe barely escaped death from a cannon shot. He strengthened the defenses of the fort and left a garrison there.

Oglethorpe, writing to the trustees, said his forces were ready to die hard and would not lose an inch of ground without fighting, but they could not do impossibilities and said that cannon, powder, horses, boats, and money to pay the men were sadly needed, as the Spaniards had a number of launches, horses, and a fine train of artillery. Under these circumstances, he thought the best course was to strike first as his strength consisted in men, as the men of the colony, as well as the old soldiers, handled their arms well and wanted action. He said that it was impossible to keep Georgia or Carolina without destroying St. Augustine or keeping enough horse rangers and scout boats to restrain the active Spaniards. He therefore asked that the trustees insist on

LIBERTY HALL, HOME OF A. H. STEPHENS, CRAWFORDVILLE

the government sending four ten-oared boats for the southern coast and one for Savannah, with a train of artillery, some gunners, at least four hundred barrels of cannon powder, and a hundred barrels of musket powder, with bullets in proportion. He said he was fortifying the town of Frederica at his own expense to protect the houses of merchants, their goods, and the lives of men, women, and children.

**The Siege of St. Augustine**—General Oglethorpe's plan of operation was approved by the home authorities, and as he learned that the galleys which had been guarding the St. John's River and the upper coast of Florida had been sent to Havana for reënforcements and supplies, because the garrison at St. Augustine was suffering from lack of provisions, he decided that it was a good time to attack that town.

Admiral Vernon was instructed to demonstrate against Spanish possessions in the West Indies, while Oglethorpe took his forces against St. Augustine.

General Oglethorpe went to Charleston to urge prompt coöperation and the Legislature, after much discussion and some opposition, agreed to contribute a regiment of five hundred men, commanded by Colonel Vanderdussen, and a troop of rangers with three months' provisions, and presents for the Indians. They also furnished a large schooner with ten carriage guns, sixteen swivel guns and fifty men, commanded by Captain Tyrrell. Commodore Vincent Price, with a small fleet, promised help. In a proclamation, General Oglethorpe recognized Alexander Vanderdussen as colonel of the Carolina regiment, with power for four months to hold courts-martial for the trial of offenders. At the end of four months all connected with that regiment were to be allowed to return to their homes. To the naval forces taking part in the expedition, a full share of the plunder was guaranteed. To the wounded and the widows and orphans of those who died in the service, he promised such share of the spoils as might come to the commander-in-chief. Indian enemies, if taken captive, were to be treated as prisoners of war and not as slaves. The forces under Oglethorpe were to meet at the mouth of the St. John's River.

Runners were sent from the Uchee town to the Indian allies, informing them of the intended attack on St. Augustine, with a request that their warriors come to Frederica at the earliest moment.

Oglethorpe led the advance on the 9th of May, with four hundred men of his own regiment, a number of Indians led by Molochi, son of Brim, the late chief of the Creeks; Raven, war chief of the Cherokees, and Toonahawi, nephew of Tomochichi.

Within a week he had again taken possession of Fort Francis de Papa and Fort Diego, within twenty-five miles of St. Augustine. Leaving Lieutenant Dunbar, with sixty men, to hold Fort Francis de Papa, he returned to the mouth of the St. John's, where he was joined on the 19th of May by Captain McIntosh, with a company of Highlanders, and the Carolina troops, under Colonel Vanderdussen.

From prisoners and others, General Oglethorpe learned that the fort at St. Augustine was built of soft stone, with a curtain wall sixty yards long, a parapet nine feet thick and a rampart twenty feet high, casemated underneath for lodgings, arched over and made bomb-proof. It was armed with fifty cannon, sixteen of brass and some of them twenty-four pounders.

The town of St. Augustine was protected by a line of entrenchments with ten salient angles, in each of which field guns were mounted. Oglethorpe's information was that in January, 1740, the Spanish forces in Florida included one troop of horse, one company of artillery, three independent companies, two companies of the Asturias regiment, one company of the Valencia regiment, one company from Catalonia, two companies from Cantabria, two companies from Mercia, armed negroes, one company of militia, and a number of Indians and laborers, altogether about nine hundred and sixty-five men. During the siege seven hundred more Spaniards came from Havana.

It was General Oglethorpe's plan at the end of March to attack St. Augustine by sea and land and the island in its front. These he thought could be taken easily and then he would surprise the castle and call on it to surrender. As the castle would be too small to shelter 2,000 men, women and children of the town, he thought it might surrender, if not, he would shower it with artillery.

Unfortunately for his plan, before the Georgia and Carolina forces had been concentrated for operations against St. Augustine, that place was reënforced by the arrival of six Spanish half-galleys from Havana, with two hundred men and brass nine-pounder guns, accompanied by sloops loaded with provisions. The Spaniards had massed all their detachments within the lines of St. Augustine, collected cattle from adjacent regions and prepared for a strong defense.

Before making the attack by land, General Oglethorpe instructed the naval commanders to come to the bar of the north channel and blockade that and the mantanzas pass to St. Augustine.

Captain Warren, with two hundred sailors, was to land on Anastasia Island and erect batteries to bombard the town from the front. When the land forces were in position for the attack on St. Augustine, Oglethorpe was to notify Sir Yelverton Peyton, commanding the naval forces, and thus St. Augustine would be attacked by sea as well as by land.

Soon after the middle of May, 1740, General Oglethorpe, with an army of 2,000, including regulars, militia, and Indians, approached St. Augustine. Fort Moosa, within two miles of St. Augustine, was deserted by the Spaniards as he approached, and they retired within the lines of St. Augustine. Having burnt the gates of this fort, they made three breaches in its walls. General Oglethorpe on the 5th of June reconnoitered the defenses of St. Augustine and prepared to attack it. Everything being ready, he gave the agreed signal to the naval forces, but to his great surprise there was no response. His men were eager for the attack, and the signal was repeated, but still there was no response. Believing that the town could not be carried without the aid of the naval forces, and not knowing the cause of their silence, General Oglethorpe withdrew his army to a camp at a short distance away, to remain until he could learn the reason for the failure of the navy to coöperate in the plan agreed upon. This failure was due to the fact that inside the bar so far that they could not be reached by the fire of the six British vessels the Spanish galleys and half-galleys were moored, so as to prevent the entrance of barges intended for the attack and to prevent the landing of troops on Anastasia Island. The water was so shallow that men-of-war could not come near enough to dislodge the galleys and under these circumstances, Sir Yelverton Peyton was unable to take the part assigned to him.

Learning this, Oglethorpe determined at once to convert his planned assault into a siege. The ships of war lying off the bar of St. Augustine were ordered to guard every approach by water and maintain a rigid blockade. Colonel Palmer, with ninety-five Highlanders and forty-two Indians, was left at Fort Moosa, with instructions to scout the woods continually on the land side and intercept any cattle or supplies coming from the interior. To prevent surprise and capture, he was cautioned to change his camp every night and keep always on the alert. He was to avoid anything like a general engagement with the enemies. Colonel Vanderdussen, with his South Carolina regiment, was ordered to take possession of a neck of land known as Point Quartel, about a mile from the castle, and there erect a battery. General Oglethorpe, with his regiment and Indians, embarked in boats and landed on Anastasia Island, drove off a party of Spaniards and with the assistance of sailors from the fleet began mounting cannon to bombard the town and the castle.

Having thus made his investment of St. Augustine, Oglethorpe called on the Spanish governor to surrender. Feeling secure, the governor replied that he would be glad to shake hands with General Oglethorpe in his castle.

Oglethorpe then began to shell the town and the castle. The fire was returned by the fort and the half-galleys in the harbor. The cannonade was maintained for nearly three weeks, but the distance was so great that little damage was done.

As it was evident that the castle could not be reduced by the batteries on Anastasia Island, Captain Warren offered to lead a night attack with men from his ship upon the half-galleys in the harbor, which were keeping Oglethorpe's boats out. A council of war was held on the matter, but as those galleys were protected by the guns of the castle and could not be approached by the larger vessels of the fleet, it was decided that there was too much risk in trying to capture them in open boats and the suggestion was abandoned.

Seeing the attacking forces uncertain in their movements and their operations growing less vigorous, the Spanish governor, sorely pressed for provisions, sent three hundred men to attack Colonel Palmer at Fort Moosa, within two miles of the city.

Unfortunately Colonel Palmer, ignoring his instructions and fearing no danger from the enemy, had remained two or three nights in succession at Fort Moosa. The three hundred Spaniards, commanded by Antonio Salgrado, passed quietly out of the gates of the city on the night of June 14th, and after a desperate resistance captured Fort Moosa at daylight the next morning. Colonel Palmer fell early in the action. The Highlanders fought like lions and made havoc among the Spaniards with their broad swords. It cost the Spaniards more than a hundred lives to capture the fort, while Colonel Palmer, one captain, and twenty Highlanders were killed, and twenty-seven captured. Those who escaped made their way to Colonel Vanderdussen, at Point Quartel. This costly victory by the Spaniards relieved St. Augustine of the embargo on that side which had prevented its intercourse with the surrounding country.

Soon after this a ship of war which had been blockading the Mantansas River was withdrawn and some small Spanish vessels from Havana, with provisions and reënforcements, reached St. Augustine by that channel, bringing encouragement and relief for the garrison. The reënforcement was supposed to be seven hundred men and the provisions a considerable supply. This ended the possibility of starving the Spaniards into surrender, and the Carolina troops, whose enlistment had expired, suffering from heat, weakened by sickness and weary of fruitless efforts, marched away in considerable numbers. It is said that there was so much sickness among them that more than fifty were on the surgeon's list at one time.

**Ramsay's Account**—In his *History of South Carolina,* Dr. Ramsay says:

"All prospects of starving the enemy being lost, the army began to despair of forcing the place to surrender. The Carolina troops, enfeebled by the heat—despairing of success—and fatigued by fruitless efforts, marched away in large bodies.

"The navy being short of provisions and the usual season of hurricanes approaching, the commander judged it imprudent to hazard his Majesty's ships by remaining longer on that coast.

"The General was sick of a fever—his regiment exhausted with fatigue and rendered unfit for action by disease. These combined disasters made it necessary to abandon the enterprise. Oglethorpe with extreme regret fell back to Frederica. On the 13th of August the Carolina regiment returned to Charlestown. Though not one of them had been killed by the enemy, their number was reduced fourteen by disease and accidents . . .

"Thus ended the expedition against St. Augustine, to the great disappointment of both Georgia and South Carolina. Many reflections were afterwards thrown out against General Oglethorpe for his conduct during the whole enterprise. He, on the other hand, declared he had no confidence in the provincials for that they refused obedience to his orders and at last abandoned his camp and retreated to South Carolina. The place was so strongly fortified, both by nature and art, that probably the attempt must have failed though it had been conducted by the ablest officer and executed by the best disciplined troops."

The brunt of the siege was upon Oglethorpe's regiment and the Georgia companies. On the 5th of July the artillery and stores were brought off Anastasia and the men came to the mainland. Vanderdussen and his regiment began what Jones calls a disorderly retreat in the direction of St. John's, leaving Oglethorpe and his men within half cannon shot of the castle. In a dispatch to the Secretary of State, written from Camp St. John, in Florida, on July 19, 1740, General Oglethorpe described as follows the end of the siege of St. Augustine:

**Oglethorpe's Report of Ending the Siege**—"The Spaniards made a sally, with about 500 men, on me who lay on the land side. I ordered Ensign Cathcart with twenty men, supported by Major Heron and Captain Desbrisay with upwards of 100 men, to attack them; I followed with the body. We drove them into the works and pursued them to the very barriers of the covered way. After the train and provisions were embarked and safe out of the harbour, I marched with drums beating and colours flying, in the day, from my camp near the town to a camp three miles distant, where I lay that night. The next day I marched nine miles, where I encamped that night. We discovered a party of Spanish horse and Indians whom we charged, took one horseman and killed two Indians; the rest ran to the garrison. I am now encamped on St. John's River, waiting to know what the people of Carolina would desire me further to do for the safety of these provinces, which I think are very much exposed to the half-galleys, with a wide extended frontier hardly to be defended by a few men."

There was great disappointment at the result and Oglethorpe was harshly criticized for it, but the Duke of Argyle, in the British House of Peers, declared: "One man there is, my Lords, whose natural generosity, contempt of danger, and regard for the public prompted him to obviate the designs of the Spaniards and to attack them in their own territories; a man whom by long acquaintance I can confidently affirm to have been equal to his undertaking, and to have learned the art of war by a regular education, who yet miscarried in the design only for want of supplies necessary to a possibility of success."

**Major Hugh McCall's Statement**—Major Hugh McCall, in his *History of Georgia,* published in 1811, speaking of conditions when the naval force ceased to guard Matanzas Inlet and Spanish vessels came in with reënforcements and provisions for St. Augustine, made this statement:

"All prospects of starving the enemy being lost, the army began to despair of forcing the place to surrender. The Carolina troops enfeebled by the heat, dispirited by sickness and fatigued by fruitless efforts, decamped in large bodies. The navy being short of provisions and the usual season of hurricanes approaching, the Commander judged it imprudent to hazard the ships any longer on the coast. Last of all the General himself, sick of a fever and his regiment worn out with fatigue and rendered unfit for action by a flux, with sorrow and regret returned to Frederica the 10th of July, . . . Taking into view that he had only four hundred regular troops; that the remainder were undisciplined militia and Indians; that his enemy was secured by an impenetrable castle, finished in the highest order, well manned and provided; it only appears astonishing that he returned without a defeat and the destruction of his army."

**Dr. Harris' Comment**—Dr. Thaddeus Mason Harris, in his book, *Biographical Memorials of James Oglethorpe,* published in 1841, has this comment on the result of the siege of St. Augustine:

"On the departure of the fleet, the place was no longer blockaded on the sea side; of course the army began to despair of forcing the place to surrender. The provincials, under Colonel Vanderdussen, enfeebled by the heat of the climate, dispirited by fruitless efforts, and visited by sickness, marched away in large bodies. The General himself, laboring under a fever, and finding his men as well as himself worn out by fatigue, and rendered unfit for action, reluctantly abandoned the enterprise. On the fourth of July everything which he had on the island was reëmbarked, the troops transported to the continent, and the whole army began their march for Georgia; the Carolina regiment first, and the General with his troops in the rear."

**South Carolinians Criticized and Defended**—The South Carolina regiment was severely criticized by William Stephens, secretary of the Georgia colony. In his journal, written soon after the siege of St. Augustine, he charged the volunteers of that regiment with desertion and made the same charge against Captain William Bull, a son of Lieutenant-Governor Bull, of South Carolina, who commanded a company in Vanderdussen's regiment. While General Oglethorpe criticized the men of that regiment, he did not use the severe language employed by Secretary Stephens. In fairness, it should be recalled in this connection that there was a great deal of sickness in the South Carolina regiment, with fifty of them on the sick list at one time, and that most of them seem to have been enfeebled by the intense heat, probably with the malaria that gave General Oglethorpe a fever which prostrated him for several months after his return to Frederica.

It seems strange that the South Carolina Legislature discussed General Oglethorpe's request for aid in the siege of St. Augustine for some time, with some opposition before taking action, although the fate of South Carolina, as well as Georgia, was at stake.

This may be accounted for by the fact that South Carolina had a scourge of the smallpox in 1738, and an epidemic of yellow fever in 1739. No doubt their resources were taxed to meet those conditions, and under the circumstances, an appropriation of 120,000 pounds, equal to $600,000 of our money, was a large contribution, and for a colony with only about 5,000 white people and eight times as many negroes, who had already engaged in a bloody insurrection, to contribute a regiment of four hundred men was a serious matter.

The criticism of the South Carolina regiment resulted in an investigation by a committee of the South Carolina Legislature, whose report is thus summarized by Dr. David Duncan Wallace, in his recently published *History of South Carolina:*

"The failure of the expedition, it has been charged, was due to three sins of theirs: (1) Their tardiness in arriving. The fact is they arrived at the rendezvous as early as Oglethorpe's own troops. (2) The charge of turbulence, inefficiency, and desertion has no support except the fact of two men's deserting, one of whom escaped and the other of whom was retaken and executed. (3) Instead of the South Carolinians early abandoning the siege only some volunteers did so. Colonel Vander Dussen protested against abandoning the siege, and quit only on General Oglethorpe's positive command, and his regiment, the last troops to leave, brought off the artillery and supplies that Oglethorpe had left for them to save or destroy. The detailed account of plans and operations from day to day reveals Colonel Vander Dussen as not only the most earnest for energetic action, but as the wisest counsellor in the army or navy."

This report naturally puts the best face on the matter for the regiment and differs from the statements of Dr. Ramsay, in his *History of South Carolina,* and Dr. William Bacon Stevens and Colonel Charles C. Jones, in their *Histories of Georgia.*

In presenting that report, Dr. Wallace severely criticizes General Oglethorpe, saying that the failure of the siege of St. Augustine was due to a series of blunders by the commanding general. This criticism will hardly stand, in view of General Oglethorpe's action in every emergency, and the failure of the men-of-war to maintain the blockade, without which the success of the siege was impossible.

Another answer to that criticism is found in the result of the campaign, in which the losses of the Spaniards, who were strongly fortified and greatly outnumbered General Oglethorpe's forces, were four hundred killed and wounded against a hundred lost by the colonists.

Oglethorpe's military ability cannot be doubted, in view of the fact that in 1742, by remarkable foresight, resourcefulness and great ability to meet every emergency, he defeated the Spaniards, who outnumbered his own men eight to one, and had the support of a powerful and heavily armed fleet. His victory at the Battle of Bloody Marsh was made possible by his rare foresight in building the causeway on St. Simon's Island, which became a death trap for the Spaniards.

**Dr. William Bacon Stevens' Account**—In his *History of Georgia,* published in 1847, Dr. William Bacon Stevens, after telling of the capture of Fort Moosa by the Spaniards, the withdrawal of the blockading warships, and the arrival of reënforcements and provisions for St. Augustine from Havana, gives this account of what followed:

"All hopes of reducing the place by starvation were at an end. To break the walls and pour storming parties into the city and castle was impracticable with their light park of artillery, to remain where they were exposed to the intense heat of the summer sun was a reckless hazard and to attempt to take the town in any way by storm or siege without a fleet to blockade the harbor was an utter impossibility, yet the Naval Council of war informed the General that they could not remain on the coast longer than the 5th of July, when they must retire into harbor at the approach of the hurricane season. They were induced to remain a few days longer, but with ill concealed reluctance. The Indians also became exceedingly uneasy at the slow advances of the siege, a mode of warfare unsuited to their nomadic habits, and it was only by offering high premiums that Oglethorpe induced them to remain a little longer.

"In addition to these untoward events the Carolinians and other troops were becoming quite sickly, over fifty a day being sometimes reported on the surgeon's roll, their effective force being further weakened by frequent desertions of non-commissioned officers and privates. Finding it impossible therefore to continue the siege with soldiers whose term of enlistment was mostly expired, with Indians sulkily retained by bribes, with cannon unequal to the task required, amidst the prostrating heats of an almost tropical sun, and without a blockading fleet, Oglethorpe ordered the siege to be raised on the 20th of July.

"Such of the train, ammunition and provisions as were serviceable were embarked on board the men-of-war for Charleston; and breaking up his camp at Anastasia, he crossed over with his troops to the mainland, and with drums beating and colors flying, marched in the daytime, within gunshot of the castle, to his encampment three miles distant. The next day he marched nine miles and the day following reached the St. John's, having driven back a party of five hundred men who made a sortie on his rear guard. He reached Frederica the last of July from which point the different corps returned to their several homes.

"The formal siege lasted 38 days from the 13th of June to the 20th of July, during which the English lost less than 50 killed, including those at Fort Moosa, and about as many wounded, while the Spaniards, by their own account, lost four forts with their ordnance, Munitions and garrisons and more than 400 killed and taken prisoners. Though Oglethorpe failed to capture St. Augustine the siege was yet very serviceable to the colony by deterring the Spaniards from their meditated invasion of Georgia and restraining negroes within the English borders.

"It is due the General to say that had his original plans been carried out St. Augustine would in all human probability have fallen into his hands; but a series of events occurred over which he could have no control, which frustrated one by one his well-laid schemes, until he was compelled to raise the siege and march back to Frederica.

"His first misfortune was in the tardy arrival of troops. He purposed to attack the city in March when he knew that its defences were imperfect and its supplies small; but the delay incident to raising, equipping and marching the Carolina regiment and the Georgia rangers cost him nearly two months of most precious time in an operation to be conducted in a climate the damps and heats of which presented such formidable obstacles.

"Having at last got the army in motion his next misfortune was the failure of Colonel Vanderdussen to make the appointed junction where he again lost several valuable days of service. This was followed by the surprise and capture of Fort Moosa in consequence of disobedience to his positive orders. But even this error and misfortune might have been retrieved had he possessed the 36 cannon promised by Carolina, instead of which he had but twelve, with a few mortars and cohorns, all of which were illy mounted, badly served and too light for breaching service.

"Nor would even these deficiencies have materially hindered the reduction of the City, straitened as it then was for provisions, had the blockade been vigilantly sustained. . . . The Matanzas inlet was not properly guarded, the garrison had been succored by adequate supplies and there was no hope of reducing the place unless he had a sufficient force to break down the walls. To have continued the siege without the blockading squadron would have ensured his capture and for the whole naval and military force to have remained could only end in a warfare, not so much with the Spaniards as with miasma, sickness and death.

"The plans of Oglethorpe were eminently military and judicious, his valor was unimpeached, his zeal untiring, and his energy unexhausted. It was not therefore the fault of his skill or of his courage that the expedition failed. The causes of his disaster were such as no commanding general could control and for the results of which no one could be made responsible."

**Oglethorpe's Illness**—Not only the soldiers of the South Carolina regiment suffered illness during the siege of St. Augustine, but General Oglethorpe himself was attacked by fever. In spite of the fever, he managed to stay on duty until his return to St. John's, after leaving St. Augustine. On his return to Frederica, he was prostrated by the fever, and, on September 2nd, when Secretary Stephens called on him there, he was still confined to bed and very much weakened by his long attack.

During this period of illness, scurrilous attacks on the general continued, led by Tailfeur and Anderson, who had left Georgia under a cloud some time before. They published a tract at Charleston in 1740, in which they asserted that only fifty lots at Frederica were built upon and the total number of inhabitants was not over one hundred and twenty men, women, and children, some of whom were leaving daily.

Those false statements were corrected by a document published at London in 1742, under the title, "A State of the Province of Georgia attested upon Oath." In that document this language was used:

"There are many good Buildings in the Town, several of which are Brick. There are likewise a Fort and Storehouse belonging to the Trust. The People have a Minister who has a Salary from the Society for propagating the Gospel. In the Neighbourhood of the Town there is a fine Meadow of 320 Acres ditch'd in, on which a number of Cattle are fed, and good Hay is likewise made from it. At some Distance from the Town is the Camp for General Oglethorpe's Regiment. The Country about it is well cultivated, several Parcels of Land not far distant from the Camp having been granted in small Lots to the Soldiers, many of whom are married, and fifty-five Children were born there in the last year. These Soldiers are the most industrious, and willing to plant; the rest are generally desirous of Wives, but there are not Women enough in the Country to supply them. There are some handsome Houses built by the Officers of the Regiment, and besides the Town of Frederica there are other little Villages upon this Island. A sufficient Quantity of Pot-herbs, Pulse, and Fruit is produced there to supply both the Town and Garrison; and the People of Frederica have begun to malt and to brew; and the Soldiers Wives Spin Cotton of the Country, which they Knit into Stockings. At the Town of Frederica is a Town-Court for administering Justice in the Southern Part of the Province, with the same Number of Magistrates as at Savannah."

**Preparing for Another Attack by Spaniards**—As soon as General Oglethorpe had sufficiently recovered from his attack of fever, he began with his usual energy to prepare the colony for defense against an attack by the Spaniards, which came as he expected two years later.

At the village of St. Simon's, at the south point of the island, a watch tower was built, so that the movements of vessels at sea could be seen, and when seen their number was announced by signal guns and dispatches carried by horsemen to headquarters with the full particulars. Lookouts were kept by rangers at important points, and a guard was stationed at Pike's Bluff. A canal was cut through General's Island to give quick communication with Darien, and fortifications were built on Jekyll Island.

Three batteries were made strong on Cumberland Island at Fort St. Andrew, on the northeast point; another battery on the west, overlooking inland navigation, and one at Fort William, made very strong and commanding the entrance to St. Mary's River. Two companies of Oglethorpe's regiment were stationed near Fort St. Andrew. Upon Amelia Island the Highlanders were stationed with their scout boats, and there they had a good plantation on which they raised corn enough for their food and a stud of horses and mules. Commenting on these defenses, Thomas Spalding, in an article written for the Georgia Historical Society, in 1840, said: "St. Simon's was destined soon to become the Thermopylae of the Southern Anglo-American Provinces."

While this work of defense was going on, Oglethorpe had the active aid of a number of Indians, whose business it was to harass the Spaniards in Florida, annoy their posts and closely invest St. Augustine. They did this so efficiently that the people of St. Augustine did not dare to venture any distance outside the walls of the town, and as a result plantations in the neighborhood were uncultivated. In the town, food, fuel and other necessaries of life became so scarce that the Spanish government had to support the population with supplies sent from Havana. In this General Oglethorpe showed great wisdom, for without the aid of Indians his triumph at Bloody Marsh in 1742 might not have occurred. Speaking of this, Mr. Spalding said that the great ability of Oglethorpe was evident in the devotion of the Indian tribes to him and to his memory for fifty years afterwards, for said he: "It is only Master minds that acquire this deep and lasting influence over other men."

The calm before the storm was broken in 1741, when General Oglethorpe on the 12th of May reported to the Duke of New Castle the arrival at St. Augustine of a reënforcement in which there were eight hundred soldiers, and he informed the home government that the Spanish authorities were determined to invade Georgia and South Carolina as soon as the result of Admiral Vernon's expedition against the Spaniards in the West Indies was known.

Under these circumstances the general made an urgent request for men-of-war to guard the coast, and for a train of artillery, arms, and ammunition, with authority to recruit two troops of rangers to sixty men each, and the Highland company to one hundred; also to enlist one hundred boatmen and to buy or build and man two half-galleys.

In submitting this request to the home government, General Oglethorpe said:

"If our men of war will not keep them from coming in by sea and we have no aid, but decrease daily by different accidents, all we can do will be to die bravely in His Majesty's service. I have often desired assistance of the men of war and continue to do so. I go on fortifying this town, making magazines and doing everything I can to defend the province vigorously and I hope my endeavours will be approved by His Majesty, since the whole end of my life is to do the duty of a faithful subject and grateful servant. I have thirty Spanish prisoners in this place and we continue so masters of Florida that the Spaniards have not been able to rebuild anyone of the seven forts which we destroyed in the last expedition."

It appears that the British government did not furnish the men-of-war and the cannon that General Oglethorpe asked for.

As the Spaniards had the avowed object of destroying both Georgia and South Carolina, it seems strange that Lieutenant-Governor Bull, of South Carolina, did not respond to General Oglethorpe's urgent request for assistance.

The Legislature of South Carolina in 1740 voted 120,000 pounds of Carolina money to meet the expense of the siege of St. Augustine, and furnished a regiment of four hundred men, recruited from Virginia, North Carolina, and South Carolina, under Colonel Vanderdussen, to aid Oglethorpe in that enterprise, but when it came to meeting the Spaniards when they attacked Georgia in 1742, Colonel Jones says, in his *History of Georgia,* that "The Carolinians instead of furnishing supplies and munitions of war and marching to the South to meet the invaders where the Battle for the salvation of both colonies was to be fought, remained at home, leaving the Georgians single handed to breast the storm." This statement Colonel Jones bases on a letter of General Oglethorpe, written from Frederica on June 8, 1742, only a month before the Battle of Bloody Marsh.

It appears that the criticism of the South Carolina regiment in 1740 must have had something to do with the tardiness of that colony in replying to General Oglethorpe's request for aid in meeting the invasion of the Spaniards two years later, when the fate of South Carolina, as well as the fate of Georgia, was at stake.

# CHAPTER XXIII.

## *The Battle of Bloody Marsh*

On the 30th of July, 1742, a short time after his great victory, General Oglethorpe made this report of that engagement:

"The Spanish Invasion which has a long time threatened the Colony, Carolina, and all North America has at last fallen upon us and God hath been our deliverance. General Horcasilas, Governour of the Havannah, ordered those Troops who had been employed against General Wentworth to embark with Artillery and everything necessary upon a secret expedition. They sailed with a great fleet: amongst them were two half Galleys carrying 120 men each and an 18 pound Gun. They drew but five feet water which satisfied me they were for this place. By good great Fortune one of the half Galleys was wrecked coming out. The Fleet sailed for St. Augustine in Florida. Captain Homer the latter end of May called here for Intelligence. I acquainted him that the Succours were expected and sent him a Spanish Pilot to shew him where to meet with them. He met with ten sail which had been divided from the Fleet by storm, but having lost 18 men in action against them, instead of coming here for the defence of this Place he stood again for Charles Town to repair, and I having certain advices of the arrival of the Spanish Fleet at Augustine wrote to the Commander of His Majesty's Ships at Charles Town to come to our Assistance.

"I sent Lieutenant Maxwell who arrived there and delivered the letters the 12th of June, and afterwards Lieut. MacKay, who arrived and delivered letters on the 20th of June.

"Lieut. Colonel Cook who was then at Charles Town, and was Engineer, hastened to England, and his son-in-law Ensign Eyre, Sub-Engineer, was also in Charles Town, and did not arrive here till the action was over; so, for want of help, I myself was obliged to do the duty of Engineer.

"The Havannah Fleet, being joined by that of Florida, composed 51 sail, with land men on board, a List of whom is annexed; they were separated, and I received advice from Captain Dunbar (who lay at Fort William with the Guard Schooner of 14 Guns and ninety men) that a Spanish Fleet of 14 sail had attempted to come in there, but being drove out by the Cannon of the Fort and Schooner they came in at Cumberland Sound. I sent over Cap-

WESLEY OAK, CHRIST CHURCHYARD, FREDERICA

tain Horton to land the Indians and Troops on Cumberland. I followed myself and was attacked in the Sound, but with two Boats fought my way through. Lieutenant Tolson, who was to have supported me with the third and strongest boat, quitted me in the fight and run into a River where he hid himself till next day when he returned to St. Simon's with an account that I was lost but soon after found. I was arrived there before him, for with misbehaviour I put him in arrest and ordered him to be tryed. The Enemy in this action suffered so much that the day after they ran out to sea and returned for St. Augustine and did not join their great Fleet till after their Grenadiers were beat by Land.

"I drew the Garrison from St. Andrew, reinforced Fort William, and returned to St. Simon's with the Schooner.

"Another Spanish Fleet appeared the 28th off the Barr: by God's blessing upon several measures taken I delayed their coming in till the 5th of July. I raised another Troop of Rangers, which with the other were of great service.

"I took Captain Thomson's ship into the service for defence of the Harbour. I imbargoe'd all the Vessells, taking their men for the service, and gave large Gifts and promises to the Indians so that every day we increased in numbers. I gave large rewards to men who distinguished themselves upon any service, freed the servants, brought down the Highland Company, and Company of Boatmen, filled up as far as we had guns. All the vessels being thus prepared on the 5th of July with a leading Gale and Spring Tide 36 sail of Spanish vessels run into the Harbour in line of Battle.

"We cannonaded them very hotly from the Shipping and Batterys. They twice attempted to board Capt. Thomson but were repulsed. They also attempted to board the Schooner, but were repulsed by Capt. Dunbar with a Detachment of the Regiment on board.

"I was with the Indians, Rangers, and Batterys, and sometimes on board the ships, and left Major Heron with the Regiment. It being impossible for me to do my duty as General and be constantly with the Regiment, therefore it was absolutely necessary for His Majesty's service to have a Lieut. Colonel present, which I was fully convinced of by this day's experience. I therefore appointed Major Heron to be Lieut. Colonel, and hope that your Grace will move His Majesty to be pleased to approve the same.

"The Spaniards after an obstinate Engagement of four hours, in which they lost abundance of men, passed all our Battery's and Shipping and got out of shot of them towards Frederica. Our Guard Sloop was disabled and sunk: one of our Batterys blown up, and also some of our Men on Board Captain Thomson, upon which I called a Council of War at the head of the Regiment where it was unanimously resolved to march to Frederica to get there before the Enemy and defend that Place; & To destroy all the Provisions, Vessels, Artillery, &c, at St. Simon's, that they might not fall into the Enemy's hands.

"This was accordingly executed, having first drawn all the Men on shoar which before had defended the shipping. I myself staid till the last, and the wind coming fortunately about I got Capt. Thompson's Ship, our Guard Schooner, and our Prize Sloop to sea and sent them to Charles Town. This I did in the face and spite of thirty-six sail of the Enemy: as for the rest of the Vessells, I could not save them, therefore was obliged to destroy them.

"I must recommend to His Majesty the Merchants who are sufferers thereby, since their loss was in great measure the preserving the Province.

"We arrived at Frederica, and the Enemy landed at St. Simon's.

"On the 7th a party of their's marched toward the Town; our Rangers discovered them and brought an account of their march, on which I advanced with a party of Indians, Rangers and the Highland Company, ordering the Regiment to follow, being resolved to engage them in the Defiles of the Woods before they could get out and form in the open Grounds. I charged them at the head of our Indians, Highland Men and Rangers, and God was pleased to give us such success that we entirely routed the first party, took one Captain prisoner, and killed another, and pursued them two miles to an open Meadow or Savannah, upon the edge of which I posted three Platoons of the Regiment and the Company of Highland foot so as to be covered by the woods from the Enemy who were obliged to pass thro' the Meadow under our fire. This disposition was very fortunate. Capt. Antonio Barba and two other Captains with 100 Grenadiers and 200 foot, besides Indians and Negroes, advanced from the Spanish Camp into the Savannah with Huzzah's and fired with great spirit, but not seeing our men by reason of the woods, none of their shot took effect, but ours did.

"Some Platoons of ours in the heat of the fight, the air being darkened with the smoak, and a shower of rain falling, retired in disorder.

"I hearing the firing, rode towards it, and at near two miles from the place of action, met a great many men in disorder who told me that ours were routed and Lieut. Sutherland killed. I ordered them to halt and march back against the Enemy, which order Capt. Demere and Ensign Gibbon obeyed, but another Officer did not, but made the best of his way to Town. As I heard the fire continue I concluded our Men could not be quite beaten, and that my immediate assistance might preserve them: therefore spurred on and arrived just as the fire was done. I found the Spaniards intirely routed by one Platoon of the Regiment, under the Command of Lieut. Sutherland, and the Highland Company under the Command of Lieut. Charles MacKay.

"An Officer whom the Prisoners said was Capt. Don Antonio Barba was taken prisoner, but desperately wounded, and two others were prisoners, and a great many dead upon the spot. Lieut. Sutherland, Lieut. Charles MacKay and Sergt. Stuart having distinguished themselves upon this occasion, I appointed Lieut. Sutherland Brigade Major, and Sergt. Stuart second Ensign.

"Capt. Demere and Ensign Gibbon being arrived with the men they had rallied, Lieut. Cadogan with an advanced party of the Regiment, and soon after the whole Regiment, Indians, and Rangers, I marched down to a causeway over a marsh very near the Spanish Camp over which all were obliged to pass, and thereby stopt those who had been dispersed in the fight in the Savannah from getting to the Spanish Camp. Having passed the night there, the Indian scouts in the morning advanced to the Spanish Camp and discovered they were all retired into the ruins of the Fort and were making Intrenchments under shelter of the cannon of the ships. That they guessed them to be above 4,000 men. I thought it imprudent to attack them defended by Cannon with so small a number but marched back to Frederica to refresh the soldiers, and sent out Partys of Indians and Rangers to harrass the Enemy. I also ordered into arrest the officer who commanded the Platoons that retired.

"I appointed a General Staff: Lieut. Hugh MacKay and Lieut. Maxwell Aids de Camp, and Lieut. Sutherland Brigade Major. On ye 11th of July the Great Galley and two little ones came up the river towards the Town. We fired at them with the few Guns so warmly that they retired, and I followed them with our Boats till they got under the cannon of their ships which lay in the sound.

"Having intelligence from the Spanish Camp that they had lost 4 Captains and upwards of 200 men in the last Action, besides a great many killed in the sea-fight, and several killed in the night by the Indians even within or near the camp, and that they had held a Council of War in which there were great divisions, insomuch that the Forces of Cuba separated from those of Augustine and the Italick Regiment of Dragoons separated from them both at a distance from the rest near the woods, and that there was a general Terror amongst them, upon which I was resolved to beat up their quarters in the night, and marching down with the largest body of men I could make, I halted within a mile and a half of their camp to form, intending to leave the Troops there till I had well reconitred the Enemy's disposition.

"A French Man who without my knowledge was come down amongst the volunteers fired his Gun and deserted. Our Indians in vain pursued and could not take him. Upon this, concluding we were discovered, I divided the Drums in different parts and beat the Grenadiers march for about half an hour, then ceased, and we marched back with silence.

"The next day I prevailed with a Prisoner, and gave him a sum of money to carry a letter privately and deliver it to that French Man who had deserted. This letter was wrote in French as if from a friend of his, telling him he had received the money; that he should strive to make the Spaniards believe the English were weak. That he should undertake to pilot up their Boats and Galleys and then bring them under the Woods where he knew the Hidden Batterys were; that if he could bring that about, he should have double the reward he had already received. That the French Deserters should have all that had been promised to them. The Spanish Prisoner got into their Camp and was immediately carried before their General Don Manuel de Montiano. He was asked how he escaped and whether he had any letters, but denying his having any, was strictly searched and the letter found, and he upon being pardoned, confessed that he had received money to deliver it to the Frenchman, for the letter was not directed. The Frenchman denied his knowing anything of the contents of the letter or having received any Money or Correspondence with me, notwithstanding which, a Council War was held and they deemed the French Man to be a double Spy, but General Montiano would not suffer him to be executed, having been imployed by him: however they imbarqued all their Troops, and halted under Jekyl: they also confined all the French on board and imbarked with such precipitation that they left behind them Cannon, &c., and those dead of their wounds, unburied. The Cuba Squadron stood out to sea to the number of 20 sail; General Montiano with the Augustine Squadron returned to Cumberland Sound, having burnt Captain Horton's houses, &c on Jekyll. I, with our boats, followed him. I discovered a great many sail under Fort St. Andrew, of which eight appeared to me plain, but being too strong for me to attack, I sent the Scout Boats back.

"I went with my own cutter and landed a man on Cumberland who carried a letter from me to Lieut. Stuart at Fort William with orders to defend himself to the last extremity.

"Having discovered our Boats & believing we had landed Indians in the night they set sail with great haste, in so much that not having time to imbarque, they killed 40 horses which they had taken there and burnt the houses. The Galleys and small Craft to the number of fifteen went thro' the inland Water Passages. They attempted to land near Fort William, but were repulsed by the Rangers; they then attacked it with Cannon and small Arms from the water for three Hours, but the place was so bravely defended by Lieut. Alexander Stuart that they were repulsed and ran out to sea where twelve other sail of Spanish vessels had lain at anchor without the Barr during the attack without stirring; but the Galleys being chased out, they hoisted all the sails they could and stood to the Southward. I followed them with the Boats to Fort William, and from thence sent out the Rangers and some Boats who followed them to Saint John's, but they went off rowing and sailing to St. Augustine.

"After the news of their defeat in the Grenadier Savannah arrived at Charles Town, the Men of War and a number of Carolina People raised in a hurry set out and came off this Barr after the Spaniards had been chased quite out of this Colony, where they dismissed the Carolina vessels, and Capt. Hardy promised in his Letters to cruise off St. Augustine.

"We have returned thanks to God for our deliverance, have set all the hands I possibly could to work upon the Fortifications, and have sent to the Northward to raise men ready to form another Battalion against His Majesty's Orders shall arrive for that purpose. I have retained Thompson's ship, have sent for Cannon, Shott, &c., for Provisions and all kinds of stores since I expect the Enemy, who (tho greatly terrified) lost but few men in comparison of their great numbers, as soon as they have recovered their fright will attack us with more caution and better discipline.

"I hope His Majesty will approve the measures I have taken, and I must entreat Your Grace to lay my humble request Before His Majesty that he would be graciously pleased to order Troops, Artillery and other Necessarys sufficient for the defence of this Frontier and the Neighboring Provinces, or give such direction as His Majesty shall think proper, and I do not doubt but with a moderate support not only to be able to defend these provinces, but also to dislodge the Enemy from St. Augustine if I have but the same numbers they had in this expedition."

**Other Accounts of the Battle**—Among the Shaftesbury papers on file in the public record office at London, there are two other accounts of the battle on and around St. Simon's Island. These accounts, written at the time, give some details not included in General Oglethorpe's report.

One of these accounts, written by a John Smith, then on board the *Success* frigate, of which Captain William Thomson was in command, was dated at Charleston on July 14th, only a few days after the Battle of Bloody Marsh. It was addressed to Skinner and Simson, London merchants, and was as follows:

"This serves to inform you of my safe arrival in Georgia after a passage of 10 weeks. We met with no Molestation from the Privateers in our way, nor could make no Prizes, tho' we pursued and brought to several Vessels. Our People were all healthy 'till the last three weeks of our Passage, when a Malignant Fever came amongst them and sweeped away several soldiers, and the best part of our Ship's Company with our Chief Mate, Carpenter, and Boatswain. I was also visited, but got well over it.

"Three days after our arrival in Georgia we were alarmed by several small Vessels being seen off the Harbour which we took to be Spaniards. The General sent his Privateer Schooner to Fort William which lyes to the Southward of our Harbour to help to defend that Place in case of being attacked, and the next day (being the 22nd of June) sent out his own Barge to make discovery if the Enemy had landed. They returned in the afternoon with Account that the Enemy with eleven Galleys were in the Sound called Cumberland, about 20 miles to the Southward of St. Simon's, where we lay. Upon which the General put two Companies of Soldiers in three Boats and went along with them himself to the relief of Fort Williams, so that crossing Cumberland Sound the Galleys, full of men, bore down upon them. He began the Engagement himself with his own Boats' Crew, and exchanged several Volleys with one of the Galleys. In the meantime two Galleys engaged one of the General's Boats wherein was 50 Soldiers commanded by one Toulson, who thinking himself hard set, bore away and left the General with the other two Boats engaged, but they bravely fought their way through with the loss only of one man, and got to Fort William. Toulson got clear and afterwards came to St. Simon's. That night we heard several great Guns fired, and volleys of small arms to the Southward, so that we got all ready for an attack; next day heard nothing of the General, which put everybody under great concern. The Day after saw a Sail off the Bar which proved to be the General's Schooner with himself aboard, and a Company of Soldiers, who brought account of all being well at Fort William, and that they had beat off 9 Galleys which thought to surprize them. The General came ashore and was saluted by us with 31 Guns, and by the Fort. He confined Mr. Toulson for leaving him, and sent for Captain Thomson, advised him to send his Goods to Town, and get all ready for defence, for he thought of being attacked at St. Simon's. And soon after we had an Account that there were 32 Sails hoisting Spanish Colours where they lay in the same place for 5 days without making the least attempt, but sent out their small Vessels to sound the Bar. July the 4th they got under sail and came to in the right way off the Channel so that we expected to be attacked next day. The General came on board of us and made a very handsome Speech encouraging us to stand by our Liberties and Country. For his part he was resolved to stand it out, and would not yield one inch to them tho' they appeared so formidable. He was convinced they were much superior in Numbers, but then he was sure his men were much better, and did not doubt (with the favour of God) but he would get the better. We having but 10 seamen on board, the General sent us 100 Soldiers, and being well provided with warlike Stores, were ready for twice the number of Spaniards. There were several Vessels in the Harbour which we (as Commodore) placed in the following order, *viz:*—

"The *Success,* Captain Thomson, 20 guns, 100 men, with springs upon our cable.

"The General's Schooner, 14 Guns, 80 men, on our starboard bow.

"The St. Philip Sloop, 14 guns, 50 men, on our starboard quarter.

"Eight York Sloops close in Shore with one man on board each in case of being overpowered, to sink or run them on shore.

"July 5th. The Spanish Vessels got all under Sail and stood in. They sent two Quarter Galleys carrying 9 Pounders, and one Half Galley with two 18 Pounders in her bow to begin the Attack which were warmly received by the Fort, which exchanged several Shot with them. The wind and tide both serving, they soon came up with us and fired upon us, which we returned very briskly. They attempted to come up under our stern, upon which I run out two 6 Pounders at the Stern Ports (they being the Guns I commanded) and fired upon her which made them lye upon their Oars, and drive with the Tide. The Admiral came next, and was saluted with our whole broad-side, then by the Schooner and Sloop, which made him sheer off from us. In short we received all their Fire and returned the same very briskly, having fired near 300 Shot out of our Ship, they coming on one by one just gave us time to load, so that I believe there was not one Ship but had some Shot in her. They fired at the York Sloops which had run aground. Afterward, they came to anchor and landed a great many men, of which they had great Plenty.

"The General sent us off Thanks for our brave resistance and ordered his men ashore and us with what other Vessels could go to make the best of their way to Charles Town or anywhere to save the Vessels; upon which, we got ourselves in train for going to sea, and cutting our Cable dropped down with the Tide. The Schooner and Prize Sloop followed us, next morning got over the Bar, and said 4 Galleys standing after us, we got all ready for a second engagement, and having sea-room, would have made a market of them, but they did not care to come over the Bar.

"All that night saw several fires, and a sloop blow up, which proved the General destroying all that might be of service to the Enemy, intending to march all his men to Frederica and there hold it out.

"July 7th. Got all into Charles Town. Captain Thomson petitioned the Assembly for assistance to the General, and to have his own Ship manned to go against the Enemy with the Man of War and what other Merchantmen they can fit out, which they have taken into consideration.

"The *Flamborough*, Man of War, and two Sloops, with a Galley have been gone from this place a fortnight, and been drove to the Northward by a Gale of Wind. They yesterday came abreast of this place and had account how the General's Affairs stood; upon which they made sail for the Southward.

"I wish our Fleet had been ready to have gone with them, and I dare say we would have catcht them all. Every minute appears an age to me till we can assist our Friends to the Southward and till I have Satisfaction for being left naked: they have got my all amongst them: not having one shirt but as I borrow. I hope next opportunity to write you better news.

"On the 28th of June 1742 thirty three Spanish Vessels appeared off the Bar. The General staid at St. Simon's taking all possible measures for the Defence of the Harbour, and opposed them in such a manner that they could not become Masters of the Bar till 5th instant when they entered the Harbour in line of Battle ahead. The General's Disposition of the Land Troops prevented the Spaniards from landing. The General's three vessels, with Captain Dunbar and a Detachment of the Regiment on Board, and Captain Thomson's Ship, fought stoutly. The Officers and Men in the Merchant Service, as well as those of the Regiment behaved with the greatest courage. After three hours' fight by the Land Batteries as well as the Vessels, the Spanish Fleet broke all through and made for Frederica, but in a very Shatter'd condition, which obliged the General immediately to send the Regiment for the defence of that Place, and followed in the rear himself, and before he would leave St. Simon's, had all the Cannon, Magazines, &c burst and destroyed, and sent out such Vessels as were on float to sea, the Harbour having been left open by the Spaniards running up the River. The loss is very considerable, and chiefly owing to the want of Artillery, Engineers, good Gunners, and Ships of Force,—the Officers of the Regiment, Sailors, Indians &c having done all that men could do for their numbers. The General himself was everywhere but chiefly at the Main Battery and Shipping, Major Heron being with the Regiment on Shore, and Col. Cook at Charles Town, by leave of Absence by reason of sickness, on his way to England. The General is preparing to make the best defence he can in this place.

"General Oglethorpe being arrived on the 6th of July by day break, without the loss of a man, having brought up all the wounded on his Horses, he dismounted and marched on foot himself, and gave his own Horse to me. He immediately gave Orders for the Defence of this Place, sending out Scouts on all sides and supplying the broken and lost arms &c. ordered all the Companies to be Paraded on the afternoon of the same day. The Creek Indians brought in five Spanish Prisoners on the 7th day: On which day about the hour of ten, the Rangers who had been on the Scout came chased in by the Spaniards, giving an account that the Enemy was within a mile of this Place where they had killed one Small. The General leaped on the first Horse and immediately marched the Highland Company, who were then under arms a parading, and ordered sixty from the Guard to follow. He himself galloped with the Indians to the Place which was just within the Woods about a Mile from hence, where he found Captain Sebastian Santio, and Captain Mageleeto with 120 Spanish Troops and forty five Spanish Indians. Captain Grey with his Chickesaws, Captain Jones with his Tomehetans, and Toonahowi with his Creeks, and the General with six Highland Men, who outran the rest, immediately charged them. Captain Mageleeto was killed, Captain Sebastian Santio taken, and the Spaniards entirely defeated. The General took two Spaniards with his own Hands. Captain Mageleeto shot Toonahowi in his right arm as he rushed upon him. Toonahowi, drawing his Pistol with his left Hand, shot him through the Head. The General pursued the Chace for near a mile, when halting at an advantageous Piece of Ground stayed till the Guard came up, and then posting the Highlanders on the right and the guard upon the left of the Road,—hid in a Wood with a large Savannah or Meadow in their Front over which the Spaniards must pass to come to Frederica,—the General returned and ordered the Regiment, Rangers and Companies of Boatmen to march. Whilst they were preparing, we heard Platoons firing. The General immediately got on Horseback, and riding towards it met three Platoons on the left coming back in great disorder, who gave him an account they had been broke by the Spaniards who were extremely numerous. Notwithstanding which, he rallied them and he himself rode on, and to his great satisfaction found Lieut. Sutherland and the Platoon of the Regiment under his command, and Lieut. MacKay with the Highlanders had entirely defeated the Spaniards who consisted of two Companies of Grenadiers, making 100 Men and 200 Foot. Don Antonio Barbara, who commanded them, was Prisoner, but was mortally wounded; they also took several other Grenadiers and the Drum. The General ordered all the Troops to march from Frederica to him. As soon as they arrived he pursued the Enemy four Miles. In the two Actions there were one Captain, one Corporal, and sixteen Spaniards taken, and about 150 killed; the rest are dispersed in the Woods, for the General halted all night at a Pass through the Marshes over which they must go in their return to their Camp, and thereby intercepted them. The Indians are out, hunting after them in the woods, and every hour bring in Scalps.

"July 8. Before daybreak the General advanced a Party of Indians to the Spanish Camp at St. Simon's who found they were all retired into the ruins of the Fort, under the Cannon of the Men of War. Upon which the General marched back and arrived here about Noon. About the same time a Party which the General had drawn from Fort William arrived, notwithstanding the Spanish Fleet lyes between us to secure us from that Place.

"July 9. This day was spent in going on with the Works.

"Frederica. July 9th, 1742."

**Forces of the Spaniards and Colonists**—Hugh McCall gives this list of the forces employed in the invasion of Georgia under the command of Don Manuel de Monteano:

| | |
|---|---|
| One Regiment of Dismounted Dragoons | 400 |
| Havana Regiment | 500 |
| Havana Militia | 1,000 |
| Regiment of Artillery | 400 |
| Florida Militia | 400 |
| Batallion of Mulattoes | 300 |
| Black Regiment | 400 |
| Indians | 90 |
| Marines | 600 |
| Seamen | 1,000 |
| | 5,090 |

General Oglethorpe's command consisted of:

| | |
|---|---|
| His Regiment | 472 |
| Company of Rangers | 30 |
| Highlanders | 50 |
| Armed Militia | 40 |
| Indians | 60 |
| | 652 |

**Colonel Charles C. Jones' Comment**—The remarkable, almost miraculous nature of General Oglethorpe's victory is thus strongly stated by Colonel Charles C. Jones, in his *History of Georgia:*

"That a small force of between six and seven hundred men, assisted by a few weak vessels, should have put to flight an army of nearly five thousand Spanish troops, supported by a powerful fleet and amply equipped for the expedition, seems almost incapable of explanation. General Oglethorpe's bravery and dash, the timidity of the invaders, coupled with the dissensions which arose in their ranks, and the apprehensions caused by the French letter, furnish the only plausible explanation of the victory." Whitefield's commentary was: "The deliverance of Georgia from the Spaniards is such as cannot be paralleled but by some instances out of the Old Testament." The defeat of so formidable an expedition by such a handful of men was a matter of astonishment to all. Had Don Manuel de Monteano pushed his forces vigorously forward, the stoutest resistance offered along his short line of march and from the walls of the town would have been ineffectual for the salvation of Frederica. Against the contingency of an evacuation of this stronghold, Oglethorpe had provided, as best he could, by a concentration of boats in which to transport the garrison to Darien by way of the cut previously made through General's Island. This necessity, however, was fortunately never laid upon him. If the naval forces at Charlestown had responded to his requisition, a considerable portion of the Spanish fleet might have been captured. Oglethorpe's success in his military operations may be explained by the fact that he constantly acted on the offensive. He was never content to grant any peace to an enemy who was within striking distance. The temerity and persistency of his attacks inspired his followers, and impressed his antagonist with the belief that the arm delivering the blow was stronger than it really was.

The memory of this defense of St. Simon's Island and the Southern frontier is one of the proudest in the annals of Georgia. Thus was the existence of the colony perpetuated. Thus was hurled back in wrath and mortification a powerful army of invasion whose avowed object was to show no quarter, but to crush out of existence the English colonies. Had success attended the demonstration against Frederica, the enemy would have advanced upon the more northern strongholds. Appreciating this, and deeply sensible of their great obligations to General Oglethorpe for the deliverance vouchsafed at his hands, the governors of New York, New Jersey, Pennsylvania, Maryland, Virginia, and North Carolina addressed special letters to him, "thanking him for the invaluable services he had rendered to the British-American Provinces, congratulating him upon his success and the great renown he had acquired, and expressing their gratitude to the Supreme Governor of Nations for placing the destiny of the southern colonies under the direction of a General so well qualified for the important trust."

It is strange that the governor of South Carolina did not unite in these congratulations and thanks; but the people of Port Royal did.

**After the Battle**—As Oglethorpe anticipated a return of the Spaniards, he gave his first attention after the battle to strengthening the fortifications at Frederica and other points. In a short time the works on St. Simon's, Jekyll, and Cumberland Islands were made stronger than ever.

In addition to this, finding the Spaniards still very strong at St. Augustine, and that they had defeated the Indians sent against them, and a detachment of Spaniards was marching toward the River St. Mattheo, which he thought was a move to provide quarters for reënforcements from Havana, General Oglethorpe took the aggressive, and with some Creek warriors, Highland Rangers, and a party of his own regiment, he landed in Florida by night in March, 1743, and by rapid movement drove the Spaniards within the lines of St. Augustine.

Having placed his main forces in ambush, the general, with a small party, advanced near the town, hoping to draw the garrison out, but the Spaniards did not leave their fortifications. Oglethorpe then returned to Frederica and continued to strengthen the southern coast of Georgia.

On March 22, 1743, the magazine at Frederica was blown up and this gave great alarm to the general and the people, but, although the magazine contained 3,000 bombs, they were so well bedded that little damage was done by the explosion. A vagabond Irishman was supposed to have been the man who exploded the magazine.

Captain John McClelland, who went from Georgia to England in January, 1743, reported the colonists busy in strengthening the fortifications and in preparing for another attack by the Spaniards. He also reported that the men of the colony were full of spirit, determined to make a strong defense, and that General Oglethorpe had been reënforced by two hundred men from Virginia, raised by Major Heron, many of them disciplined soldiers. In addition to these men, thirty horsemen were coming to add their strength to the rangers.

Frederica at this time was a flourishing town and continued to be so as long as Oglethorpe's regiment remained on St. Simon's Island. When the Peace of Aix-la-Chapelle was confirmed, most of the troops were withdrawn from St. Simons Island and the fortifications there, which had been so important during the war with Spain, began to decay.

# CHAPTER XXIV.

## *General Oglethorpe's Departure*

On July 23, 1743, General Oglethorpe left Georgia, never to return. On his departure, William Stephens, who had been secretary of the colony, was made deputy-general, and Major Horton became military commander at Frederica. The major had no connection with civil matters of the province, except where his assistance as commander-in-chief of the military was called for to enforce the measures of the president and council. In such cases, he is said to have acted with such calmness and humanity that he had the respect and esteem of the good people of Georgia.

As Colonel Jones says, Georgia lost its great benefactor guide and defender when Oglethorpe departed. For ten years he had worked without sparing himself for the founding and establishment of the colony, for the promotion of trade, the propagation of the Christian religion, for relief of the poor, and, in doing so, had denied himself the pleasures of London, his chair in Parliament, of which he was a member, and had exposed himself to danger, and the exhausting effect of several attacks of illness. He had defended the colony against the Spaniards without adequate support from the British government, had spent his own money freely in the public service, and bills he had drawn "for his Majesty's service," amounting to 12,000 pounds, had been returned dishonored.

He had long desired rest and relief from the oppressive cares of his position, but never faltered until he felt the colony was safe. Now that it was established upon a sure basis, the natives were friendly with the English, and the Spaniards had ceased from troubling, he thought the time had come to retire and the government gave him a leave of absence because it did not then regard his separation from the colony as permanent.

In London, he demanded an investigation of charges made against him by Lieutenant-Colonel Cooke, of his regiment, and a court-martial took up the matter in June, 1744, when a board of general officers investigated the charges instigated, and, after three days' session, denounced the whole matter as groundless, false, and malicious, with the result that the act of court-martial was approved and Lieutenant-Colonel Cooke was dismissed from the service.

The English government gave official recognition of Oglethorpe's great service to the country and the American colonies by making him a major-general, and afterwards a lieutenant-general, finally a full general of the British army. He retained his seat in Parliament until 1754, and was recognized as governor of the colony of Georgia until the trustees of the province surrendered their charter in 1752.

In his mature and later years in England, General Oglethorpe was the friend and associate of Dr. Samuel Johnson, Oliver Goldsmith, Edmund Burke, Sir Joshua Reynolds, Hannah Moore, Boswell, Horace Walpole, Mrs. Montague, Mrs. Garrett, Mrs. Boscawen, Mrs. Carter. Dr. Johnson wished to write Oglethorpe's life, and Edmund Burke considered him the most extraordinary person he had ever read of, because he founded a province and lived to see it severed from the empire which created it and made an independent State.

A short time before his death, General Oglethorpe called on John Adams, the first Minister Plentipotentiary of the United States of America at the Court of St. James's.

Full of years and honors, after enjoying a green old age, General Oglethorpe died on July 1, 1785. As Colonel Jones says, "The morning of his life had been stormy, the noon tempestuous, but the evening of his days was full of happiness and tranquility."

"His body lies in Cranham Church and a Memorial tablet installed there proclaims his excellence," says Colonel Jones, "but here the Savannah repeats to the Altamaha the story of his virtues and his valor and the Atlantic publishes to the mountains the greatness of his fame, for all Georgia is his living, speaking monument."

At the suggestion of the writer, Hon. Samuel Tate, one of Georgia's great men, named a great mountain in Pickens County, Mount Oglethorpe, and erected on its top an imposing monument of Georgia marble which was unveiled with appropriate ceremonies in October, 1930, in the presence of Governor Hardman and a large committee from the Georgia Legislature, accompanied by many leading citizens of Atlanta and other Georgia cities. The address on that occasion was delivered by Hon. Jefferson Randolph Anderson, of Savannah, and that utterance was one of great historic value, as well as an eloquent tribute to the founder of Georgia.

**An Assembly Created**—In March, 1750, the committee of correspondence suggested to the common council the creation of an assembly for the colony, because Georgia had many scattered settlements and it was hard for the trustees to get information about the colony as a whole. It was thought that an assembly would bind together the different sections of the province. It was also in the mind of trustees that something must be done to permanently preserve the independence of Georgia as a separate province. They feared that after their trusteeship expired the new colony might be annexed to South Carolina. The trustees approved the idea as recommended by their common council, but wished to try this experiment before making it a permanent institution, and so limited it to the year 1751. So the assembly was created, representation in it being based on the number of families in certain territories. For a village of ten families there was one deputy, and communities with thirty families had two deputies. Savannah had four, Augusta and Ebenezer two each, and Frederica two, if it had thirty families when the assembly was called to meet.

On December 15, 1750, writs were issued for holding the elections and deputies so elected were directed to meet in Savannah, January 15, 1751. As a result of this election the following sixteen deputies from eleven districts met in Savannah on the 15th of January of that year: From the Savannah District, Francis Harris, John Millidge, William Francis, and William Russel; from the Augusta District, George Cadogan and David Douglass; from the Ebenezer District, Christian Reidlesperger and Theobald Keiffer; from Abercorn and Goshen districts, William Ewen; from Joseph's Town District, Charles Watson; from Vernonburg District, Patrick Houston; from Acton District, Peter Morell; from Little Ogeechee District, Joseph Sumners; from Skidoway District, John Barnard; from Midway District, Audley Maxwell; from Darien District, John Mackintosh.

The representatives from Savannah, Augusta, and Darien were leading men in the province. Those from Ebenezer were perhaps least known, and one of them had been recently aided by the government as a pauper. Most of the deputies were owners of five hundred acre tracts of land, but a few of them were not even freeholders.

On January 30, the assembly presented to the president of colony the following list of grievances with the request that they be remedied. The list shows the difficulties encountered by the people of the colony:

1st. The want of a proper pilot boat.
2nd. The want of leave to build a wharf at Savannah, such building to be by subscription.
3rd. The need of standard scales and measures.
4th. The need of a survey of the Savannah River.
5th. The want of an order to prevent ballast from being discharged into the river.
6th. The want of a commissioner to regulate pilots and pilotage.
7th. The need of a sworn packer and inspector to look after the produce of the colony.
8th. The want of a clerk of the market.
9th. The need of proper regulations for the guard.
10th. The want of suitable officers to command the militia.
11th. The need of repairs on the court house.

To these complaints the local authorities returned a favorable reply.

The assembly communicated formally with the trustees as follows:

1st. A complaint against Thomas Bosomworth for attempting to purchase Indian lands, and an urgent plea that private persons be forbidden to secure the reserved Indian lands near Savannah and on the coast islands.

2nd. A suggestion that the charter of Georgia be renewed if possible, and a strong protest against the annexation of Georgia to South Carolina, as the assembly understood had been suggested by some.

3rd. A request that the trustees apply for a reduction of the quit rents.

4th. An account of the interest taken by the people of Georgia in the silk industry and the desire that the trustees may continue to encourage it.

5th. An earnest petition that the assembly might have the power to make by-laws for the colony to be of force until the trustees might disapprove of the same.

6th. The request that a court of equity be established in Savannah to which persons who think themselves aggrieved by verdicts of the town court might appeal.

7th. The desire that the negroes who were already in Georgia before slaves were duly licensed and that those who might be brought from South Carolina or other colonies be freed from the duty on slaves proposed in the negro act of the trustees.

8th. A request for a substantial pilot boat to rescue distressed vessels on the coast and also for an engine to extinguish fires in Savannah.

9th. The desire that conservators of the peace and constables be appointed in those districts which had none; and also that a small body of soldiers be provided to protect the beaten paths into Spanish and Indian territories.

10th. A complaint that one company in Augusta had secured a monopoly of the Indian trade and a request that steps be taken to break its power.

The trustees considered these requests favorably with three exceptions. They refused to give the assembly power to make laws, refused to establish or permit equity courts in Savannah and declined to remove the duties laid upon negroes. They liked the assembly as an experiment and continued it, but without much power except the power to make recommendations to the officers and trustees.

**Where the Trustees Failed**—With the power to make laws the trustees made few and refused to let the Georgia Assembly legislate for the Colony. The result was what might have been expected of a body thousands of miles away from the territory it undertook to govern by specific instructions for particular cases instead of by laws of general application. In his book, *Georgia as a Proprietary Province,* Dr. J. R. McCain makes this comment:

"On the whole, the Trustees were not successful in their legislative activities. Most of the acts they proposed failed to gain the approval of the British government. The laws that they did pass were detrimental to the peace and prosperity of the Colony. If they had taken the inhabitants of Georgia into their confidence at the beginning, and if they had established then an assembly like that of 1750, it is probable that the colonists might have aided in the solution of their own problems; but the Trustees waited until it was too late to be of service to them to establish the colonial assembly."

# CHAPTER XXV.

## *The Courts, Education and Land Tenures*

**Judiciary in the Georgia Province**—The charter gave the trustees power to create courts necessary for the Province and the appointment of court officials was made by the Common Council. Though the trustees controlled the administration of justice in Georgia, it was done in the name of the King, and at the end of twenty years the power of the trustees ended and the King had control of the courts.

The first court was created in November, 1732, before any immigrants reached Georgia. It had great power and could try cases for the town of Savannah with all grades of offense including treason and felonies. It also passed on civil cases and its orders were enforced by the bailiffs and tithingmen.

The council appointed to administer justice in the court at Savannah, three bailiffs, a recorder, two constables and two tithingmen. The bailiffs were designated as "first," "second" and "third." The first bailiff usually presided at trials. It was the duty of the bailiffs and the recorder to preserve the peace and administer justice. The constables and tithingmen were to obey the magistrates.

In 1741 when two counties were created, one at Savannah and one at Frederica, a president and assistants were appointed for each place. Three bailiffs served as assistants to the president in each county for executive work, and in the court they served as bailiffs. Thus both executive and judicial functions were performed by these officers.

The president and his assistants acted as a Court of Appeals for cases of 100 pounds or more in the town courts of Savannah and Frederica, but there was an appeal from their decisions to the trustees, who were the Supreme Court.

The Act of 1741 divided Georgia into two counties, but seems not to have been carried out in Southern Georgia, and in 1743 the president and assistants of Savannah were empowered to act for the whole Province. This gave Georgia a single Appellate Court and consolidated the judicial system of the Colony.

Each county had a town court from which appeals could be made to the president and assistants at Savannah, acting for the whole Colony, and in the last resort to the Trustees as a Supreme Court.

CONFEDERATE POWDER WORKS CHIMNEY—AUGUSTA

This arrangement was not long continued. The town court of Frederica was suspended and the appellate jurisdiction of the president and assistants there and at Savannah ended.

In 1751 the Provincial Assembly asked the trustees to establish a court of equity, but the president and assistants opposed it as unnecessary and the trustees agreed with that view, holding that it would be an unnecessary expense and would increase litigation. In 1748 an effort was made to have an admiralty court established, but it failed.

**Lawyers Not Allowed**—A remarkable feature of the judiciary of Georgia was that lawyers were not allowed in the Colony. It has been supposed that they were excluded by order of the trustees, though no record of such an order has been found. The trustees sought to prevent undue litigation, and the presence of lawyers was thought to promote suits and disputes. Whatever the authority for the custom it appears that for some years a rule against the practice of law was vigorously enforced.

In 1740 a man named Williamson, who claimed permission of the trustees to practice law, was warned against it, and although engaged in several cases, he desisted, apparently for prudential reasons.

Later a man named Watson established a law office in the Colony and did a large business among Indian traders, but his practice is said to have been carried on surreptitiously without the approval of authorities in Georgia or in England.

Without attorneys to guide them, the magistrates, without lawbooks or much learning, were puzzled on difficult points, as it took too long to send to England for advice. In such cases they adopted the plan of getting advice from lawyers in Charleston.

In pleading cases the parties were supposed to represent themselves. At first there were no public prosecutors in criminal cases, but later the constables undertook that duty. Defendants in criminal cases were their own attorneys except where friends appeared for them. It was hard to get juries to act strictly on the evidence without being influenced by their prejudices, and this was true of grand as well as petit juries.

There was a strong sentiment in Savannah against the rum act, and it was hard to convict violators of that law, however clear the evidence against them. Grand juries were charged in a general way by one of the bailiffs, who also called their attention to special matters. Because grand juries were not vigorous in punishing some kinds of lawlessness George Whitefield once addressed the Grand Jury on the urgent need of stopping the sale of rum and the practice of adultery in Savannah.

It is said that two-thirds of the business of the courts was done at Savannah, half the remainder at Frederica and the rest at other places. Disputes at Ebenezer among the Salzburgers, at Irene among the Moravians and at Darien among the Scotch were settled by arbitrators, among whom their religious leaders were prominent, and that practice was found satisfactory and tended to keep down disputes

Among the bailiffs in the town courts there were some given to drink, one who could not read and write, and naturally they had little influence on the result. Thomas Causton, a man of more ability and education, was virtual dictator for several years and was overbearing and otherwise objectionable. Finally he was removed by the trustees for improper conduct of affairs.

As storekeeper Causton used his position to advance himself and rose rapidly. He was made second bailiff in 1734 and first bailiff in 1735. He directed affairs at Savannah for several years and was very unpopular. When he got the Colony in debt the trustees suspected him of fraud, ordered his arrest and suspended him from office. His accounts were investigated for some years. Causton went to England to settle them with the trustees, but was not entirely successful. On the return trip he died at sea.

Under the conditions described it seems remarkable that there was not more serious disorder in the Colony. This seems accounted for by the fact that the colonists were carefully picked and great care was taken to keep out criminals. There was little wealth in Georgia. Civil cases did not involve large sums and few criminal prosecutions were for capital offenses. The good order among the Salzburgers, Moravians and Scots without courts makes clear the high character of the colonists.

**Land System of the Trustees**—The system of land holding in the Province of Georgia as adopted by the trustees had its origin in the idea that each male inhabitant was to be both a planter and a soldier. Grants were made in tail male rather than tail general, because it was desired there should be a man on each tract who would be a planter to produce food and trained as a soldier to meet any emergency that might arise from attacks of Indians or Spaniards.

To this end each lot was held as a military fief and the fifty acres granted to each man brought over at the expense of the trustees were supposed to be sufficient to support his family. He was furnished arms for defense and tools to cultivate the land, and was instructed in the use of both.

The grant in tail male was preferred because grants in tail general would result in possession of the land by female heirs who could not be counted on for military service. Another objection was that under grants in tail general intermarriages might result in merging several tracts into one ownership, thereby reducing the number of male defenders. Under those conditions, the number of male owners being less, with fewer men in a township, the duties of watching and fighting off attacks would devolve on fewer men and the burden on them would be greater. Grants of land in fee simple were objected to because the owners, having the right of sale, could mortgage or sell their land to whom they pleased. The trustees considered that dangerous.

The colonists brought over were carefully selected and none but persons of character were allowed to come. Their passage over had been furnished them free and they were given seed, tools and subsistence, until they got a foothold on their land, which they were expected to continue cultivating.

With inexperience and small means they might sell their holdings to undesirable persons.

The trustees were Protestants and did not wish the land to pass into the hands of persons opposed to their religion. As the French on the west and Spaniards on the south were Roman Catholics, the trustees considered it important to prevent the sale of land to them. At this point it is interesting to note that in the next century and ever since Catholics have been an important element in the population of Savannah and in other Georgia communities, though as a rule they are not Spanish or French Catholics. A more practical reason for preventing the sale of land was to keep it from passing into the hands of slave-dealers, unlicensed Indian traders and dealers in rum.

To promote industry, each settler who was given free transportation, fifty acres of land, seeds, tools, arms and temporary subsistence, had to agree that he would clear and cultivate within a specified time a stated portion of the land allotted to him and to plant 100 white mulberry trees on every ten acres he cleared. If these agreements were not carried out the trustees reserved the right of reëntry on so much of the land as remained untilled. When droughts, Spanish incursions or other unforeseen obstacles prevented settlers from cultivating their land as agreed the trustees cancelled the forfeitures.

To persons of good character who brought ten men servants with them and settled in Georgia at their own expense the trustees granted 500 acres in tail male, but required of the grantee a rent of twenty shillings annually for each hundred acres. This rent did not begin until ten years from the date of the grant.

At first the grants of land were made by the Common Council of the trustees, mainly to persons in England who wished to go to the Colony. Later, when a considerable number of settlers came from Virginia and the Carolinas, it was necessary to provide a means of granting land through, or on recommendation of officers in the Colony. As the recommendations of these officers were made with care they were nearly always approved by the Common Council when brought to its attention. In that way the grant of land became practically a local function in the latter part of the trustees' control.

At first the trustees, through the Council, could only grant a seven-eighths interest in Georgia land, because all of it had been previously granted to the eight proprietors of Carolina to whom it was ceded by Charles the Second in 1660. In 1729 the Crown purchased the interests of seven of the proprietors, but Lord Carteret, the eighth proprietor, refused to sell his interest. That was the condition when the trustees were given their charter, but Lord Carteret's interest was sold to the King in 1744, and that ended the complication.

The rents were not due for the first ten years of occupancy. and as there had been many releases from forfeitures because of war and other calamities, there was great difficulty in collection. The trustees saw that the rent was a hardship on the settlers and on surrendering their charter in 1752 they recommended "that the arrears of quit rents due at this time be remitted, since most of the inhabitants have been prevented, by the war and various obstacles that always occur at the first settling of a colony, from cultivating so much of their lands as might be expected they would; and that the quit rents for the future be reduced from four to two shillings for each hundred acres, this last sum being as much as is usually reserved in any of His Majesty's Provinces in America."

It appears that no money was ever collected for quit rents in proprietary Georgia by the trustees, by the King or by Lord Carteret. It was generally considered that the Colony was not prosperous enough for the collection of rents to be fair.

To facilitate settlement and the allotment of land to charity settlers some thousands of acres were deeded in trust to three of the settlers who were to arrange the conveyance of fifty acre lots to individuals. Larger bodies were granted at first by the Common Council, after appearance of the parties in person or by proxy and careful investigation of the character of the applicants. To receive the grant the applicant had to pay a fee of one pound, one shilling.

Surveyors of small tracts were paid by the trustees, but their compensation for surveying large tracts was paid by the grantees. The surveys were generally satisfactory, except that the surveyors were tardy in making reports to the trustees. Noble Jones was a leader among the surveyors.

By 1735 the business of granting land had so increased that it was necessary to create the office of Register of Grants and Leases, who was also to keep an account of the condition of land which had been granted, and make monthly reports to the trustees.

After 1741, when the government of the Colony was reorganized, applications for grants of land were made to the president and assistants of the Province.

**Education in Provincial Georgia**—Early teaching in Georgia was both religious and secular and sometimes combined both features. In October, 1733, Christopher Ortman, a German Protestant, went to Georgia to serve as a schoolmaster and parish clerk for the Salzburgers at Ebenezer. He was expected to teach English to the Germans, but he was not qualified to teach English, which he could not speak well, and was discharged. The president and assistants, thinking he had been harshly treated, appointed him schoolmaster at Vernonburgh and Acton, but the trustees disapproved that and ordered Ortman discharged. The Salzburgers employed other teachers who seem to have given satisfaction and in 1748 they built a second schoolhouse.

At Frederica John Ulrich Driesler was made schoolmaster, and to help his support he was made chaplain of the regiment, which gave him ten pounds a year. He was diligent and taught the children in English or German, but died after one year's service.

The Creek Indians, at their settlement of Irene upon an island in the Savannah River, received religious instruction from the Moravians until they left Georgia for Pennsylvania. Rev. Benjamin Ingham, of England, assisted the Moravians there and began work on a Creek grammar to teach the Indians the Bible in their own language. The Indians were friendly, but went south to fight the Spanish, and that ended Ingham's work.

In 1736 Charles Delamotte, who had come to Georgia with the Wesleys and Ingham, to do missionary work among the Indians, began to teach children at Savannah. He taught thirty or forty reading, writing, and arithmetic, and in the early morning and at evening gave them religious instruction. He was well educated, the son of a baker in London, and an earnest worker without salary. The trustees paid part of his expenses, but he paid most of them. Delamotte was a good teacher and greatly beloved. When he left the Colony the people followed him to the ship to bid him farewell. It is said that he left because of the treatment of John Wesley, who was his personal friend.

Two great characters succeeded Delamotte at Savannah. George Whitefield and James Habersham, who came over with him, had intended before leaving England to establish an orphanage at Savannah later, but on arrival, seeing the urgent need for one, began at once to prepare for its establishment. Habersham took charge of the school started by Delamotte, and Whitefield returned to England to be ordained a minister of the Church of England and to make a preaching tour to raise money for the orphanage. He had secured 300 pounds for that purpose before coming to America, and on this trip, after his ordination, he raised another thousand pounds. He was a great orator. Lord Chesterfield said of him: "He is the greatest Orator I ever heard and I cannot conceive of a greater."

When he returned to America Whitefield toured the Colonies to raise money for the orphanage at Savannah. At Philadelphia Benjamin Franklin sought to induce Whitefield to locate the orphanage there, but when Whitefield refused to change his plan Franklin is said to have made up his mind to give only small coin to the enterprise. When he heard Whitefield the appeal was so powerful and eloquent that Franklin, deeply moved, emptied his pockets in the collection.

The trustees gave Whitefield 500 acres of land for the orphanage at a point ten miles from Savannah, near the plantations of Noble Jones and William Stephens. In March, 1740, Whitefield began to build the orphan house and laid the first brick. He named the institution "Bethesda," meaning "House of Mercy."

On a trip to northern colonies Whitefield was well received and raised 500 pounds, mostly in Pennsylvania. On another trip into New England he raised 700 pounds.

# CHAPTER XXVI.

## *Religious Development*

The trustees of Georgia were greatly concerned with efforts for the development of religion in the Province, and gave their sanction and aid in the promotion of Christianity among the settlers and the Indians. In this they were aided by several organizations, including The Society for Promoting Christian Knowledge, which had been organized in 1698 by Dr. Bray, Lord Guilford, Sir Humphrey Mackworth, Justice Hook, and Colonel Colchester. Archbishop Tennison and Bishop Henry Compton, of London, presented the matter to the government and secured a charter for the Society. The object was distribution of bibles with religious literature, instruction of the poor and missionary work in various colonies.

This Society had an active part in transporting the Salzburgers and paying the salaries of pastors and other workers among them.

In 1701 Dr. Bray organized another corporation called the Society for Propagation of the Gospel in Foreign Parts and in this work the clergy of the English Church were enlisted and Bishops were to find clergymen willing to go to the British Colonies as missionaries. Clergymen sent as missionaries reported to the secretary of the society, who coöperated with the Bishop of London in locating them for work in the Colonies. Most of the ministers who went to Georgia received some support from this society, whose influence induced the trustees to take an interest in the religious development of the Colony. After Dr. Bray's death his associates organized a society to provide libraries for ministers and carry on missionary work among the negroes.

These organizations were independent of church control, but were affiliated with the Church of England. The Society in Scotland for Promoting Christian Knowledge, affiliated with the Presbyterian Church was active in Georgia in supporting a mission among the Scotch settlers at Darien. The Bishop of London, Edmund Gibson, was commissioned by the King to license ministers and schoolmasters for service in America, and appointed commissaries to visit the churches and missionaries, supervise their work and report to the Bishop. A controversy between Bishop Gibson and the trustees concerning his authority in the Province arose and the trustees objected to his claim of authority, feeling that he was hostile to them.

Bishop Gibson did not appoint any commissary to supervise ecclesiastical affairs in Georgia, but his representative in South Carolina, Alexander Garden, had a controversy with George Whitefield, who was then an ordained minister of the Church of England, located in Georgia. Whitefield and Garden had been friendly, but when the former disregarded some of the forms of the Church of England, Garden reproved him and forbade him to preach at Charleston. Whitefield disregarded Garden's action and continued to preach. Garden sought to have him tried at the Commissarial Court of Charleston, but Whitefield denied the authority of the court to try him and refused to answer. He declared that the Bishop of London could not establish in South Carolina competent courts without the consent of the Colonial Legislature. He added that he was a resident of Georgia, and could not be tried by a South Carolina court and asserted that the Georgia trustees, under whose government he lived, doubted whether the Bishop of London had any authority in the colonies.* Garden again summoned Whitefield to appear. Whitefield disregarded the summons and Garden pronounced a sentence against him, suspending him from the ministry of the Church of England. Whitefield, having referred the matter to the trustees, disregarded Garden's sentence and that ended the controversy.

Although the trustees had full power in religious affairs and guarded their authority they did not seriously restrict religious liberties in the Colony, but proclaimed freedom of conscience in worshipping God to all but Roman Catholics, provided they were content with quiet and peaceable enjoyment of their religion without offense to the government. While most of the trustees were members of the Church of England some were dissenters of considerable influence, but the trustees usually acted harmoniously on religious matters. However, after some opposition they decided that it was their duty to furnish the people of the Province with the gospel according to the usages of the Church of England. Accordingly they appointed from time to time ministers for the province beginning with Dr. Henry Herbert, who went with the first shipload of colonists, but he was taken ill and died returning to England. Rev. Samuel Quincy was sent in 1733, but quarreled with Thomas Causton, the chief bailiff, and in 1735 the trustees revoked his license and appointed John Wesley to succeed him.

**John Wesley in Georgia**—The trustees wished the gospel preached to the colonists and the Indians, and John Wesley was selected by them for that work.

He was then quite young, though a fellow of Lincoln College, Oxford, a classical scholar and distinguished for his learning and piety. His life was exemplary and he showed a willingness to endure hardship. He was a curate of the Church of England and was introduced to Oglethorpe by Rev. Dr. Burton who urged him to go to Savannah in the capacity of a religious teacher.

---

* Cross and Tyerman's *Whitefield.*

After reflection Wesley consented to go, and on October 10, 1735, he was appointed with a salary of fifty pounds a year.

He went to Georgia on the ship with Oglethorpe and was accompanied by his brother, Charles Wesley.

Wesley went as a missionary to Georgia without intending to act as a minister for an established congregation. His purpose was to work for the conversion of Indians, and his interview with Tomochichi as reported by Colonel Charles C. Jones in his *History of Georgia,* throws light on the situation.

**Tomochichi's Idea of God**—When Mr. Wesley and Tomochichi dined with Oglethorpe, the clergyman asked the aged mico what he thought he was made for.

"He that is above," replied the Indian, "knows what He made us for. We know nothing. We are in the dark. But white men know much, and yet white men build great houses as if they were to live forever. But white men cannot live forever. In a little time white men will be dust as well as I."

Wesley responded: "If red men will learn the Good Book they may know as much as white men. But neither we nor you can understand that Book unless we are taught by Him that is above; and He will not teach unless you avoid what you already know is not good."

"I believe that," said the chief. "He will not teach us while our hearts are not white and our men do what they know is not good. Therefore, He that is above does not send us the Good Book."

**Wesley's Interview With Indians**—On July 20, 1736, five Chicasaw Indians visited John Wesley at Savannah. They were all warriors, and two of them the Chiefs Paustoobee and Mingo Mattaw. Their interview with Wesley is thus recorded in his Journal:

"Q. Do you believe there is One above who is over all things?

Paustoobee answered: "We believe there are four Beloved Things above; the Clouds; the Sun, the Clear Sky, and He that lives in the Clear Sky.

"Q. Do you believe there is but One that lives in the Clear Sky?

"A. We believe there are two with him—three in all.

"Q. Do you think He made the Sun and the other Beloved Things?

"A. We cannot tell. Who hath seen?

"Q. Do you think He made you?

"A. We think He made all men at first.

"Q. How did He make them at first?

"A. Out of the ground.

"Q. Do you believe He loves you?

"A. I don't know. I cannot see him.

"Q. But has He not often saved your life?

"A. He has. Many bullets have gone on this side and many on that side, but He would not let them hurt me. And many bullets have gone into these young Men, and yet they are alive.

"Q. Then, can't He save you from your enemies now?

"A. Yes; but we know not if He will. We have now so many enemies round about us that I think of nothing but death. And if I am to die, I shall die, and I will die like a man. But if He will have me to live, I shall live. Tho' I had ever so many enemies, He can destroy them all.

"Q. How do you know that?

"A. From what I have seen. When our enemies came against us before, then the Beloved Clouds came for us. And often much rain and sometimes hail has come upon them, and that in a very hot day. And I saw when many French and Choctaws and other nations came against one of our Towns. And the ground made a noise under them, and the Beloved Ones in the air behind them. And they were afraid and went away, and left their meat and drink and their guns. I tell no lie. All these saw it, too.

"Q. Have you heard such noises at other times?

"A. Yes, often; before and after almost every battle.

"Q. What sort of Noises were they?

"A. Like the noise of drums and guns and shouting.

"Q. Have you heard any such lately?

"A. Yes, four days after our last battle with the French.

"Q. Then you heard nothing before it?

"A. The night before I dream'd I heard many drums up there, and many trumpets there, and much stamping of feet and shouting. Till then I thought we should all die. But then I thought the Beloved Ones were come to help us. And the next day I heard above a hundred guns go off before the fight begun. And I said when the Sun is there the Beloved Ones will help us, and we shall conquer our Enemies. And we did so.

"Q. Do you often think and talk of the Beloved Ones?

"A. We think of them always, wherever we are. We talk of them and to them, at home and abroad, in peace, in war, before and after we fight, and indeed whenever and wherever we meet together.

"Q. Where do you think your souls go after death?

"A. We believe the Souls of Red Men walk up and down near the place where they died, or where their bodies lie. For we have often heard cries and noises near the place where any prisoners had been burnt.

"Q. Where do the Souls of White Men go after death?

"A. We can't tell. We have not seen.

"Q. Our belief is that the souls of bad men only walk up and down, but the souls of good men go up.

"A. I believe so too. But I told you the talk of the nation.

"(Mr. Andrews: They said at the burying they knew what you were doing. You were speaking to the Beloved Ones above to take up the soul of the young woman.)

"Q. We have a Book that tells us many things of the Beloved One above. Would you be glad to know them?

"A. We have no time now but to fight. If we should ever be at peace we should be glad to know.

"Q. Do you expect ever to know what the White Men know?

"(Mr. Andrews: They told Mr. O. they believe the time will come when the Red and the White Men will be one.)

"Q. What do the French teach you?

"A. The French Black-Kings never go out. We see you go about. We like that. That is good.

"Q. How came your nation by the knowledge they have?

"A. As soon as ever the Ground was found and fit to stand upon, it came to us, and has been with us ever since. But we are young men. Our old men know more. But all of them do not know. There are but a few whom the Beloved One chuses from a child, and is in them, and takes care of them, and teaches them. They know these things: and our old men practice: therefore they know: But I don't practice. Therefore I know little."

When John Wesley arrived at Savannah in 1736 he told Oglethorpe of his desire to begin work among the Indians at once, but Oglethorpe replied that the time was not ripe for such missionary work, and at his request Wesley took charge of the Savannah Mission which then included about seven hundred persons, few of whom were members of the Church of England. He worked with zeal, made a good impression and was delighted with the prospects, writing in his Journal: "O Blessed Place, Where having but one end in view, dissembling and fraud are not; but each of us can pour out his heart without fear into his Brother's bosom."* His work showed the methodical tendency greatly developed later in the organization of Methodism. He planned a systematic campaign of religious instruction and organized some of his parishioners as a society for reproof, instruction and exhortation. At the same time he conducted evangelistic work.

Some of his people became offended because they thought he was too strict in enforcing literally the rules of the Established Church, without making due allowance for conditions in a frontier settlement. They also resented what they considered his interfering in affairs that did not belong to him and taking sides with malcontents who were said to be trying to nullify the rules of the trustees.

Under these circumstances the unpleasant ending of John Wesley's love affair with Sophia Hopkins, a niece of Thomas Causton, the chief bailiff, brought matters to a crisis which resulted in Wesley's leaving Georgia. He had been a guest at the home of Causton and there became acquainted with Miss Hopkins to whom he became attached and it seems to have been his wish to marry her. It is said that on advice of Delamotte and the Moravians Wesley changed his mind and showed some coolness toward Miss Hopkins. Whether this was the case or not Miss Hopkins soon married William Wil-

---

* *Wesley's Journal,* 29-34-41.

liamson, a clerk in her uncle's store. Wesley seems to have been piqued by her marriage to another, and used his clerical authority to reprove her in some small matters. This resulted in hard feelings on both sides, and matters were made worse soon afterward when he excluded her from taking communion on the technical ground that she had not notified him of her intention to commune.

As a result of Wesley's refusal to allow Sophia to partake of the Lord's Supper, Mr. and Mrs. Williamson sued him for damages to the amount of one thousand pounds. This plunged the whole community into a bitter controversy, and in addition to the suit Thomas Causton, then chief magistrate of the Colony, charged the Grand Jury to investigate complaints against Wesley. Wesley's friends claimed that the jury was packed with his enemies, and the influence of Causton seems evident in the result. The Grand Jury found a true bill against John Wesley on the following ten counts:

1. Speaking and writing to Mrs. Williamson against her husband's wishes.
2. Repelling her from the holy communion.
3. Not declaring his adherence to the Church of England.
4. Dividing the morning service on Sundays.
5. Refusing to baptize Mr. Parker's child, otherwise than by dipping, except the parents would certify it was weak and not able to bear it.
6. Repelling William Gough from the holy communion.
7. Refusing to read the burial service over the body of Nathaniel Polhill.
8. Calling himself Ordinary of Savannah.
9. Refusing to receive William Aglionby as a godfather only because he was not a communicant.
10. Refusing Jacob Matthews for the same reason; and baptizing an Indian trader's child with only two sponsors.

The minority report, made by twelve members, was not presented to the court, but it was forwarded to the trustees as a protest against the injustice that was being done Wesley. It took up the counts in order and expressed the opinion that none of them were sufficient for the prosecution of the accused.

Twelve of the jurors, three of them being constables and six tithingmen, who would have constituted a majority had that body been properly constituted of four constables and eleven tithingmen, signed the following document which was transmitted in due course:

"To the Honorable the Trustees for Georgia.

"Whereas two Presentments have been made, the one of August 23rd, the other of August 31st, by the Grand Jury for the Town and County of Savannah in Georgia, against John Wesley, Clerk:

"We, whose names are underwritten, being Members of the said Grand Jury, do humbly beg leave to signify our dislike of the said Presentments, being by many and divers circumstances thro'ly persuaded in ourselves that the whole charge against Mr. Wesley is an artifice of Mr. Causton's, design'd rather to blacken the character of Mr. Wesley than to free the Colony from Religious Tyranny as he was pleas'd in his charge to us to term it. But as these circumstances will be too tedious to trouble your Honors with, we shall only beg leave to give the Reasons of our Dissent from the particular Bills.

"With regard to the First Bill we do not apprehend that Mr. Wesley acted against any laws by writing or speaking to Mrs. Williamson, since it does not appear to us that the said Mr. Wesley has either spoke in private or wrote to the said Mrs. Williamson since March 12 (the day of her marriage) except one letter of July the 5th, which he wrote at the request of her aunt, as a Pastor, to exhort and reprove her.

"The Second we do not apprehend to be a true Bill because we humbly conceive Mr. Wesley did not assume to himself any authority contrary to Law: for we understand every person intending to communicate should 'signify his name to the Curate at least some time the day before,' which Mrs. Williamson did not do: altho' Mr. Wesley had often, in full congregation, declared he did insist on a compliance with that Rubrick, and had before repell'd divers persons for non-compliance therewith.

"The Third we do not think a True Bill because several of us have been his hearers when he has declared his adherence to the Church of England in a stronger manner than by a formal Declaration; by explaining and defending the Apostles', the Nicene, and the Athanasian Creeds, the Thirty Nine Articles, the whole Book of Common Prayer, and the Homilies of the said Church: and because we think a formal Declaration is not required but from those who have receiv'd Institution and Induction.

"The Fact alleged in the Fourth Bill we cannot apprehend to be contrary to any law in being.

"The Fifth we do not think a true Bill, because we conceive Mr. Wesley is justified by the Rubrick, *viz.:* 'If they (the Parents) certify that the child is weak, it shall suffice to pour water upon it': intimating (as we humbly suppose) it shall not suffice if they do not certify.

"The Sixth cannot be a true Bill because the said William Gough, being one of our members, was surprised to hear himself named without his knowledge or privity, and did publickly declare 'It was no grievance to him, because the said John Wesley had given him reasons with which he was satisfied.'

"The Seventh we do not apprehend to be a true Bill, for Nathaniel Polhill was an Anabaptist, and desir'd in his life-time that he might not be interr'd with the Office of the Church of England. And further, we have good reason to believe that Mr. Wesley was at Frederica, or on his return thence, when Polhill was buried.

"As to the Eighth Bill we are in doubt, as not well knowing the meaning of the word Ordinary. But, for the Ninth and Tenth we think Mr. Wesley is sufficiently justified by the Canons of the Church which forbid any person to be admitted Godfather or Godmother to any child before the said person has received the Holy Communion; whereas William Aglionby and Jacob Matthews had never certified Mr. Wesley that they had received it."

Wesley demanded trial on the first count, but objected to all the others as they were matters concerning religion and the Savannah Court had no authority to try them. He asked for immediate trial on the first count, but the court refused then and postponed trial five or six times. Wesley then thought it time to take the matter to the trustees. His friends advised further effort to get the trial in Savannah. He made two more efforts without success and then his friends agreed with him that the time had come for him to leave the Colony. He gave public notice of his purpose and sent a written notice to the magistrates. They refused to allow him to leave, but made no effort to detain him, and he left by boat for South Carolina on the night of December 2, 1737.*

Wesley appeared before the trustees on February 22, 1738, gave them an account of his troubles in Georgia and presented certificates from his friends in the Colony, substantiating his report. The trustees appeared to sympathize with him, but Causton and Williamson sought to excuse their action. It appears that no formal action was taken by the trustees, but on April 26, 1738, he was allowed to resign the appointment to do work in Georgia.

Charles Wesley, a brother of John Wesley, was only in Georgia a short time. Arriving in February, 1736, he left within a few months. While here he was secretary of Indian Affairs and chaplain at Frederica. This was a hard combination to succeed in and he was made miserable by the talk of some busybodies whose tattling made General Oglethorpe, for a time, suspicious of him. Later he won back the confidence of General Oglethorpe and some others, but as his usefulness appeared to be at an end he left Frederica in May, 1736, for Savannah, and never returned. He wished to resign, but Oglethorpe asked him to continue a while longer. In July, 1736, he went to England to carry dispatches and becoming too ill to return surrendered his commission to work in the Colony.

It appears that the failure of both John and Charles Wesley to make progress in Georgia was due largely to their youth and inexperience. They seemed to have been so intent on religious matters that they did not give enough attention to practical affairs in communities where the struggle for existence was severe, and expected too much of their parishioners, whom they were disposed to censure unnecessarily for small defects. In a word they seemed to lack tact in dealing with human nature under conditions prevalent in the Colony. Their characters were above reproach and their motives sincere. Their later careers of great usefulness seemed to justify the claim

---

* *Wesley's Journal,* 57-58-59-60 and 61.
*Colonial Records,* Vol. IV, 36 and 37.

of their friends that they did not have in Georgia a fair opportunity to show their real worth.

**George Whitefield**—It was John Wesley who had interested George Whitefield in becoming a missionary in Georgia, and in June, 1737, contributions were taken in England to pay Whitefield's expenses on the trip to Georgia. On December 21, 1737, the trustees assigned him to work at Frederica as a deacon of the Church of England. On Wesley's arrival in England, Whitefield wrote the trustees asking advice as to his work in view of Wesley's absence from the Colony, and they authorized him to officiate at both Savannah and Frederica.

Arriving at Savannah on May 7, 1738, he began work vigorously on the orphanage with the aid of James Habersham, and at the same time began active work in the Savannah church. He made a good impression, held four services on Sunday and three during the week, and was received cordially. He served the people of Savannah without pay, but the irregularity of his preaching reduced the attendance on services. He asked for an assistant, but the trustees declined as Whitefield was not regarded as fully orthodox.

His main efforts seem to have been directed to the establishment of the Bethesda Orphanage, in raising money for which he made a tour of the Colonies, and also canvassed England.

Rev. Christopher Orton, a young man of good character, was sent to the Colony on September 14, 1741. He did good work at first, but the Spanish invasion so disturbed the Colony that it was difficult for him to do much good, though he revived the school work. His career was cut short by fever, and he died August 12, 1742.

The appointment of Rev. Thomas Bosomworth as a minister by the board of trustees was unfortunate. He had been a clerk of Secretary Stephens of Georgia, and had served in the army under Oglethorpe. He was appointed for Savannah, but instead went to Frederica, and the trustees ordered him returned to Savannah. He seems to have been a trouble maker and unfriendly to the orphanage, trying to get the trustees to suppress it. He left the Colony in 1745, claiming that he and his Indian wife had not been well treated by the white people and that the Indians, sympathizing with him, threatened trouble. The trustees seem not to have taken this seriously, as they reproved him and revoked his commission.

Bosomworth returned to the Colony, where he gave the authorities a great deal of trouble, stirring up the Creek Indians against the Colonists, while he and his wife made a fraudulent claim to the land asserting that it had been given them by the Indians.

The trustees were more fortunate in the appointment of Rev. Bartholomew Zouberbuhler, a native of Switzerland, reared and educated in South Carolina. He had made a good reputation in South Carolina, and the German inhabitants in Savannah asked for his appointment as their minister. As he

THE BURNS COTTAGE—ATLANTA

could speak both French and German he was ordained a priest of the Established Church, and the trustees appointed him on November 1, 1745. He was a zealous worker and preached regularly in English and German, held frequent services and made pastoral visits within six or eight miles of Savannah. Another Swiss minister, Rev. John Joachim Zubli, began work among the Germans, but the trustees could not pay the expense. They finally allowed him ten pounds a year to be taken from Zouberbuhler's salary. As Zouberbuhler did not like Zubli, he objected and asked to be allowed to leave Georgia and go to South Carolina. The trustees were not willing to lose his services and after several conferences agreed to double his salary, provide him with two servants, repair the parsonage, give him land in a better place and give to him and each of his two brothers five hundred acres of land. With this encouragement Zouberbuhler returned to the work in which he continued faithful to the end of the trusteeship in 1752.

In 1758, when Georgia as a Royal Province was divided into parishes of the Church of England Zouberbuhler was named rector of Christ Church in Savannah, the leading church of the Colony.*

The people of Augusta, not long before the trusteeship ended, asked the trustees to furnish them a minister, but as their tenure of office was near an end, the trustees declined and asked the Society for Propagation of the Gospel in Foreign Parts to attend to the work there. The Augusta people promised to pay twenty pounds a year salary of the minister, to cultivate his land, to build a parsonage for him, and provide a handsome church, then already under construction, if the Society would send a good minister to them. Rev. Jonathan Copp, an American, a graduate of Yale, ordained in England as a deacon, and a priest, was selected for the work and in 1751 arrived at Augusta, where he was cordially received. It is said that in spite of his education Copp proved to be a failure, as he stirred up disputes among the people, and his work was not a success.

**Religious Work of the Presbyterians**—In 1735, on recommendation of the Society in Scotland for Promoting Christian Knowledge, the trustees commissioned Rev. John McLeod, who had been ordained a minister of the Presbyterian church. He settled at Darien and labored among the Scotch for six years, was successful at first and highly regarded by people in all parts of the Colony. He worked hard to secure a house of worship, and was very much disappointed when he did not succeed. This was due largely to the fact that some of his parishioners lost their lives in the Spanish Invasion. In 1741 he took charge of a church in South Carolina. From there he wrote letters to the Scotch Society, severely criticizing affairs in Georgia, and for that reason the Society supported no further work in Georgia.

Rev. Jonathan Barber, who had come from New England to aid Whitefield in the establishment of the Bethesda Orphanage, was a Presbyterian, and preached occasionally in Savannah as well as at the orphanage.

* *Colonial Records,* Vol. I, 492-93; Vol. XVIII, 261.

**The Moravians**—Coming to Georgia in 1735 the Moravians remained in Savannah until they could clear and improve their lands on the Ogeechee River. Their spiritual leaders were Rev. Augustus Gottlieb Spangenburg, Rev. David Nitschman, and Rev. Peter Boehler.

They were an industrious people, cultivating their land better than any others in the Province, and soon repaid the trustees for the passage money which had been advanced them. It is said that they were the only settlers coming to Georgia during the trusteeship who were entirely self-supporting.

Through their leader, Count Zinzendorf, the Moravians asked that the trustees appoint them missionaries to the Indians, but that was declined on the ground that it would appear a reflection on England. The trustees, however, approved any missionary work the Moravians might do on their own account and at their own expense. They were very active in such work among the Creek Indians at Irene on an island in the river about five miles from Savannah. The custom of Moravians of living among the Indians and largely adopting their customs and habits pleased the natives and made them responsive to religious influence. This influence, however, unfortunately ended when the Moravians left Georgia for Pennsylvania. Their religious principles were against bearing arms and warfare, and this made their position difficult in Georgia, where the protection of the Colony from invasion was a vital matter.

When the Spaniards threatened to invade the Colony, the Moravians were called on to furnish their quota of soldiers for defense. This they declined to do and referred the matter to the trustees, who upheld the Colonial authorities. The people of Georgia felt that the Moravians had not shown the proper spirit, and that the trustees were too lenient with them. Under these circumstances the Moravians decided that it would be best for them to leave Georgia. Some of them went to Pennsylvania in 1738, and the remainder in 1739 and 1740.

**The Jewish Colonists**—When funds were being raised in England for the Georgia Colony three Jews, with the approval of the trustees, raised money for that purpose. Instead of turning it over to the trustees they used it in sending forty Jews to the Colony. They arrived at Savannah in the summer of 1733. Oglethorpe found them useful citizens and welcomed them in spite of efforts of some trustees to have them sent away from the Province. They rented a synagogue and conducted services regularly without the assistance of a rabbi.

**The Salzburgers**—The most permanent and successful religious work done in the Colony during the trusteeship was among the Salzburgers. They were Lutheran Protestants, expelled from the Bishopric of Salzburgh in Austria by the Catholic clergy. They were sent to Georgia by Rev. Samuel Urlsperger, Bishop of Augsburgh, and Chretien de Munch, a banker of that place. These men were non-resident trustees of Georgia, made so because of their aid to persecuted Protestants.*

Seventy-eight Salzburgers left Augsburgh on the first expedition to Georgia and were joined by others at Rotterdam. They were led by Baron Von Reck, and their pastors were Rev. John Martin Bolzius, former superintendent of a Latin orphan school at Halle, and Rev. Israel Gronau, a tutor in the same school.

They settled about twenty-five miles from Savannah at a point now in Effingham County, chosen by their leaders and Oglethorpe. The town was called Ebenezer, and in 1735 and 1736 other Salzburgers joined them, increasing their number to two hundred. The land in that vicinity not being good or suited for a permanent home, they moved in 1736 and 1737 to the Savannah River and established there a town called New Ebenezer. After the old town was abandoned the new place was called simply Ebenezer. Ebenezer was a mission station of the English Society for Promoting Christian Knowledge, and the German Evangelical Lutheran Church. All the pastors and people had to subscribe to the Augsburgh Confession, and a code of rules drawn up by Samuel Urlsperger, of Augsburgh, Frederick M. Ziegenhagen, of London, and G. A. Franke, of Halle. Under these rules seven deacons were to assist the pastor in the discipline and financial management of the church. The people were to support the churches and schools if possible, but the salaries of the pastors were to be paid in England. Regular reports of the mission were to be sent to Augsburgh and Halle in Germany, to the society in London, and to the trustees.

Rev. John Martin Bolzius administered to the Ebenezer congregation through the whole period of the trusteeship. An able and versatile man, he led his people in both temporal and spiritual affairs, superintended agriculture, erected a corn mill and sawmill, supervised silk culture and sold the products of those industries. He acted as arbitrator in disputes, cared for the schools and managed the Ebenezer Orphanage.

Rev. Israel Gronau helped Bolzius largely among outlying plantations, was a faithful preacher and greatly beloved, but died in 1745. After the death of Gronau the trustees of Georgia in 1745 appointed Rev. Henry Lembke to assist Bolzius, and he was well liked. The work of Bolzius and Lembke prospered so that two plantation missions were added, and in 1751 more colonists made another station necessary. By 1752 there were so many settlers that a third minister, Rev. Christian Rabenhorst, was sent to help Bolzius and Lembke. He was a good man and soon won the affection of the people.

The Salzburgers at Frederica had the ministry of Rev. John Ulrich Driesler until he died in 1754, but he had no successor. The Salzburgers in Savannah had no regular minister until Zouberbuhler went there. On the

* *Stephens,* Vol. I, 368-69.
*Colonial Records,* Vol. I, 499.

whole the Salzburgers were religious by nature, having suffered much for religious liberty, which meant a great deal to them, and their pastors were remarkable leaders. In addition to this they were of one uniform faith, and were not troubled by contending religious factions.

**Contributions for Religious Work**—During the first nine years of the trusteeship the contributions made for religious work in Georgia were as follows: For building churches, 702 pounds; for Indian missions, 679 pounds; and for general religious purposes, 522 pounds. To this 100 pounds was added by the trustees. In addition to the amounts stated which were contributed by the general public the religious societies contributed to religious work in Georgia during the twenty years of trusteeship between 3,500 and 4,000 pounds for salaries, besides large sums for servants, supplies and other workers in various places. The total expenses for all religious purposes were about 7,500 pounds.*

The usual salary of ministers paid by missionary societies was fifty pounds a year, and the trustees usually furnished the missionary a house, three hundred acres of land and servants to cultivate the land. Because of his exceptional ability and services Zouberbuhler received a double salary.

There were few church buildings during this period. The first one at Savannah, made of rough boards was only twelve feet wide and thirty-six feet long, but when a court house was built there it was also used for public worship. The foundation of a church in Savannah was laid on March 28, 1744, but funds not being sufficient to complete the house the work ended in 1745, with only the roof, floor and framework done.

In 1747 the Salzburgers at their mill furnished lumber to complete the church, and it was ready for dedication on July 7, 1750. That day was the anniversary of the establishment of civil government in the Colony and the repulse of the Spanish on St. Simon's Island in 1742. That was a large and beautiful church with a stone foundation, walls of cement outside, and plastered white inside. The windows were of glass sent from England.

Less expensive churches were erected in other places. A chapel twenty feet wide and sixty feet long was built at Frederica in 1739. Another chapel was built at Augusta.

The Salzburgers built three churches. One at Ebenezer, they called Jerusalem. Another four miles away, convenient to plantations was called Zion, and a third among the plantations was called Bethany. These churches were built of lumber from the sawmill of the Salzburgers, and were painted inside and treated outside with turpentine to prevent decay.

The Moravians, Scotch and Jews built no churches, but worshipped in public buildings and rented rooms. It appears that the religious work of the Salzburgers and Moravians was successful and above reproach.

---

* *Colonial Records,* Vol. III, 87.

## CHAPTER XXVII.

# *William Stephens in Charge—The Colony As Oglethorpe Left It*

In April, 1741, Colonel William Stephens, the faithful secretary of the Colony, was made president of the county of Savannah with four assistants. At that time General Oglethorpe made Frederica his headquarters and it was unnecessary then to appoint a president there.

At Augusta, in November, 1741, Captain Richard Kent was appointed conservator of the peace for that place and vicinity.

As General Oglethorpe's return to England was expected, the trustees extended the jurisdiction of the president and assistants for the county of Savannah so as to cover the whole province of Georgia and the bailiffs at Frederica were made local magistrates with powers subordinate to those of the president and his assistants. The trustees raised the salary of the recorder at Frederica and instructed him to correspond regularly with the president and his assistants at Savannah and report to them the proceedings of the Town Court at Frederica and such transactions and events in the southern part of Georgia as the president and his assistants should know.

Commenting on this arrangement Colonel Charles C. Jones said: "Thus upon the departure of General Oglethorpe he was succeeded in the office of Colonial Governor by the honest minded and venerable Colonel William Stephens whose devotion to the welfare of the colony and fidelity to the instructions of the Trustees had for more than five years been well approved."

Colonel Stephens was directed to hold in Savannah each year four terms of the General Court for the regulation of public affairs and the settlement of differences affecting persons or property.

**Financial Safeguards**—Under the arrangement thus put into effect by the trustees public money could only be paid out on warrants signed and sealed by the president and a majority of his assistants in council assembled. Monthly reports were made to the board of trustees showing the amount of money disbursed and the purposes for which expenditures were made.

For a while General Oglethorpe's regiment was kept for the defense of the Colony, but notwithstanding that the militia of the province was organized and all men able to bear arms were regularly trained under discipline. Major Horton, who was in command of all the Georgia troops, made his headquarters at Frederica.

Bailiffs or magistrates were appointed in remote parts of the province and their duty was to act as conservators of the peace and to hear and decide small cases and commit for trial by the General Court any offenders whose transgressions exceeded their jurisdiction.

**Silk Culture in Georgia**—It appears that the Georgia trustees were so intent upon the cultivation of silk and grapes and the production of wine that they discouraged the culture of rice, cotton and indigo. The English colonists, not accustomed to this kind of work, became discouraged, but the hardy Highlanders of Darien and the thrifty Salzburgers at Ebenezer made progress.

Though saddened by the death of their ministers, Gronau and Bolzius, the Salzburgers kept up their efforts and made progress in the silk industry. In December, 1742, Oglethorpe had sent to Ebenezer 500 mulberry trees and a machine to manufacture raw silk was installed near Mr. Bolzius' home. In 1747, 847 pounds of cocoons were raised in the Colony, about half by the Salzburgers at Ebenezer. Two years later they turned out 50 pounds of spun silk. In 1750 these Germans turned out 1,000 pounds of cocoons and 74 pounds of raw silk, which sold for 110 pounds. In 1755 a statement signed by forty leading manufacturers of silk said that they had examined 300 weight of Georgia raw silk and found it as good as that produced in Piedmont and better than ordinary Italian silk. In 1764, 15,212 pounds of cocoons were delivered to the filature in Savannah, more than half of it by the Salzburgers. The industry reached its high point in 1766 and the filature at Savannah discontinued operations in 1771. In 1774 Governor James Wright in a message to the Commons House of Assembly said that the filature buildings were falling into decay and suggested that they be used for some other purpose.

Colonel Stephens wrote of the industry at Ebenezer: "So popular had the silk business become at Ebenezer that Mr. Habersham, in a letter dated the 30th of March, 1772, says: 'Some persons in almost every family there understand its process from the beginning to the end.' In 1771 the Germans sent four hundred and thirty-eight pounds of raw silk to England, and in 1772 four hundred and eighty-five pounds—all of their own raising. They made their own reels, which were so much esteemed that one was forwarded to England as a model, and another taken to the East Indies by Pickering Robinson."

**DeBrahm on the Salzburgers**—The settlement at Bethany was effected in 1751 by John Gerar William DeBrahm, who there located one hundred and sixty Germans. Eleven months afterwards these colonists were joined by an equal number. Alluding to the location and growth of these plantations, and speaking of the agricultural pursuits of the Salzburgers, Surveyor-

General DeBrahm says: "The German Settlements have since stretched S: Eastwardly about 32 miles N: W-ward from the Sea upon Savannah Stream, from whence they extend up the same Stream through the whole Salt Air Zona. They cultivate European and American Grains to Perfection; as Wheat, Rye, Barley, Oats; also Flax, Hemp, Tobacco and Rice, Indigo, Maize, Pease, Pompions, Melons—they plant Mulberry, Apple, Peach, Nectorins, Plumbs and Quince Trees, besides all manner of European Garden Herbs, but, in particular, they Chose the Culture of Silk their principal Object, in which Culture they made such a Progress, that the Filature, which is erected in the City of Savannah, could afford to send in 1768 to London 1,084 Pounds of raw Silk, equal in Goodness to that manufactured in Piedmont; but the Bounties to encourage that Manufactory being taken off, they discouraged, dropped their hands from that Culture from year to year in a manner, that in 1771 its Product was only 290 Pounds in lieu of 1,464, which must have been that year's Produce, had this Manufactory been encouraged to increase at a 16 years rate. In lieu of Silk they have taken under more Consideration the Culture of Maize, Rice, Indigo, Hemp & Tobacco: But the Vines have not as yet become an Object of their Attention, although in the Country especially over the German Settlements, Nature makes all the Promises, yea gives yearly full Assurances of her Assistance, by her own Endeavours producing Clusture Grapes in Abundance on its uncultivated Vines: yet there is no Person, who will listen to her Addresses, and give her the least Assistance, notwithstanding many of the Inhabitants are refreshed from the Sweetness of her Wild Productions. The Culture of Indigo is brought to the same Perfection here as in South Carolina, and is manufactured through all the Settlements from the Sea Coast, to the Extent of the interior Country."

**Death of Mr. Bolzius**—The death, on November 19, 1765, of Rev. John Martin Bolzius, who for thirty years had been the minister, teacher, magistrate, counselor and friend of the Salzburgers, caused great sorrow and he was buried in the cemetery of Jerusalem Church.

After his death the conduct of affairs at Ebenezer devolved upon Lembke and Rabenhorst, who worked well together in meeting their civic and religious obligations. Jerusalem Church, which had been built during their ministry, was composed of materials furnished by the Salzburgers and the cost of erection was furnished by friends in Germany.

When Mr. Lembke died a young minister, Christopher F. Triebner, was sent from Germany to aid Mr. Rabenhorst, but the young man, though talented, had an unfortunate disposition, soon raised a tumult in the community and Rev. Dr. Muhlenberg was sent to Ebenezer in 1774 to quiet the disturbance. He succeeded and peace was restored. For the better government of the society Dr. Muhlenberg prepared articles of discipline which were signed by one hundred and twenty-four male members on the 16th of January, 1775, at Jerusalem Church.

The great progress of the church is shown by the following inventory of its property made by Dr. Muhlenberg in 1775:

"1. In the hands of Pastor Rabenhorst a capital of 300 pounds 16s. 5d.

"2. In the hands of John Casper Wertsch, for the store, 300 pounds.

"3. In the mill treasury, notes and money, 229 Pounds, 16 s. 2d.

"4. Pastor Triebner has some money in hands, (400 pounds) the application of which has not been determined by our Reverend Fathers.

"5. Belonging to the Church is a Negro Boy at Mr. John Floerls', and a Negro Girl at Mr. David Steiner's.

"6. A town-lot and an out-lot, of which Mr. John Triebner has the grant in his hands.

"7. An inventory of personal goods in the mills belonging to the estate.

"8. And, finally, real estate, with the mills, 925 acres of land."

With the legacies and gifts of individuals in Germany it was estimated that the property of the church was worth about $20,000.

To provide for the future the funds of the church were carefully invested and that practice was kept up for fifty years, so that in the course of time churches were erected and provision was made for clergymen, teachers and orphans. DeBrahm says that in his time Ebenezer had a library in which there were books written in Caldaic, Hebrew, Arabec, Siriac, Coptic, Malabar, Greek, Latin, French, German, Dutch and Spanish, beside the English, *viz.,* in thirteen languages.

**Failure of Grape Culture**—The trustees sought to encourage grape culture and Abraham DeLyon, a Portuguese Jew, brought vines from Portugal and planted them in his garden at Savannah. Much good was expected but the enterprise did not succeed. Colonel William Stephens, in his *Journal of Proceedings,* gives an enthusiastic description of the native grapes and of the vines planted by Mr. Lyon. He planted about twenty vines and by careful management and pruning they bore plentifully of large and beautiful grapes in large bunches. From those vines he got more than a hundred offshoots, which were planted a foot apart, expecting that within a few years he would have five thousand vines and a vineyard covering forty-five acres, but he was unable to meet the expense and employ the necessary labor, so that little progress was made.

**The Georgia Colony as Oglethorpe Left It**—In spite of the great difficulties, in war and peace, which had to be overcome during the first ten years of its existence, the Colony of Georgia had made great progress when General Oglethorpe left it in 1743. Under his wise planning, fostering care and heroic defense it had grown to such proportions that it was already an important factor in the Colonial system of this country and had strongly established itself as a bulwark for the protection of American Colonies. This clearly appears in the letters from Governors of the other colonies to General Oglethorpe, after his victory at the Battle of Bloody Marsh.

It is well here to take a look at the Colony as it was when ten years old and we get a clear view of it in this pen picture by Dr. William Bacon Stevens, the accomplished author of the *History of Georgia* which bears his name:

"Before we take our final leave of Oglethorpe, let us survey the progress of the colony under his civil and military jurisdiction. He departed from Georgia in 1743. What at that time was its condition? Savannah, expanding according to the beautiful plan of its founder, had increased to about three hundred and fifty houses, besides the public edifices. Some of these were elegant dwellings, surrounded by pleasant gardens. The land adjoining the town was mostly well cleared; and there were delightful plantations in the vicinity, particularly Beaulie, belonging to Colonel William Stephens, and Oakstead, the country-seat of Mr. Causton.

"At this period of Georgia's history Frederica presented much the most attractive scene. Entering the town by either of these two gates—the land port or the water port—we behold on the north side the camp of the general's regiment, and the barracks, a large quadrangular building, of tabby-work; on the west, the parade-ground; on the east, the residences of the settlers; and on the south, a small grove, for the convenience of fuel and pasture. The streets were spacious and planted with orange trees. The soldiers' camps were regularly laid out and, neatly kept and fortified as the whole was with bastions and ramparts, redoubts and ravelins, with their frowning cannon and their slow pacing sentinels, their reveilles and guard mounting, their daily markets, and their thronged streets, where met the soldier and the citizen, in their varied attire, the place was made gay and business-like, and bore an aspect the most pleasing and inviting of any town south of Charleston. In its neighbourhood were the beautiful plantations of Captains Dunbar and Demere, Doctor Hawkins, and the quiet village of the Salzburgers. 'In short,' says a visitor at that time, 'the whole town and country adjacent are quite rurally charming; and the improvements everywhere around are footsteps of the greatest skill and industry, considering its late settlement.' Such was Frederica in the days of its glory.

"New Iverness, or Darien, had suffered severely by the invasion of Florida. Its numbers went backwards in consequence of its reverses. It still, however, maintained an independent company of foot, consisting of seventy men; and the almost crushed hopes of the Highlanders were just beginning to revive at the restoration of tranquility upon their borders.

"Ebenezer had been increased by several emigrations, over one hundred being sent over in 1741, and others since; and the 'Evangelical Community,' quietly pursuing their simple duties and labours, were much prospered in the work of their hands.

"Augusta advanced slowly, yet gained something in population, wealth, and trade, each succeeding year. A small garrison was still maintained there. as also at several other points along the frontier.

"The ten years which had elapsed since Oglethorpe landed on the bluff at Yamacraw had changed the entire aspect of the country, there being now twelve or fourteen towns scattered through the territory. The experiment had been tried, and to a great extent had succeeded. That the colony had not progressed more, was owing not so much to the legislation of the Trustees—though that did somewhat to hinder it—as to the wars and rumors of war, which made life and property insecure, harassed trade, did away commerce, and almost palsied the energies of the few who remained. It had survived the savage menaces which threatened its infancy; it had outlived the searching scrutiny of parliamentary investigation; it had borne the brunt of war, and repelled the invading foes; and yet, amidst these depressing trials from within and from without, God had 'lengthened its cords and strengthened its stakes,' and gathered many thousands under the curtain of its habitation."

## CHAPTER XXVIII.

# *The Plot of Christian Priber and the Bosomworth Conspiracy*

The cordial relations between the Indians and the Colony of Georgia, which had been brought about by the wise, just and considerate policy of General Oglethorpe, had been a great protection to the Province and this was demonstrated in a wonderful way during the siege of St. Augustine, in 1740, and the Battle of Bloody Marsh, in 1742, but by a strange conspiracy which began in 1736, when General Oglethorpe was busily engaged in fortifying the Colony against expected attacks, all his good work came near being ruined and the Colony was in danger of being destroyed by the very Indians who had been its best friends.

In 1736 a German claiming to be a Jesuit, Christian Priber, was employed by the French to set the Cherokee Indians against the English colonists. He was a man of learning and rare ability which enabled him to win favor with the Indians. He went to the chief towns of the Cherokees, put on the Indian garb, learned the Cherokee language and became familiar with the customs of the Indians. He made himself useful to them in both peace and war and soon acquired such an ascendency over them and neighboring tribes that he was almost an absolute ruler. Having that prestige he revealed to the Indians his hatred of the English and sought to bring about a rupture between them and the provinces of South Carolina and Georgia. He shrewdly won the favor of Indian leaders by suggesting that the Chief of the Cherokees be crowned King of the Confederated tribes and pompous titles were given to the head men and leading warriors. For himself Christian Priber secured the appointment of Royal Secretary to the King of the Cherokees. Under this title he wrote Indian agents and Colonial authorities in a dictatorial and insulting manner. His letters claimed the natural rights of the Indians and declared their determination to repossess the land they had ceded. His letters were full of love for the French and hatred of the English.

Learning of the effect of Christian Priber's work upon the Cherokees, the South Carolina authorities sent Colonel Fox to demand that he be surrendered. That officer was courteously received by the Indians and escorted to the council house of the tribes. There he was surprised to find that Priber was treated with great respect by the Indians and surrounded by a strong bodyguard. When Fox announced his errand the Indians refused his demand and he was ordered to leave the Cherokee territory. Curiously Priber offered a detail from his bodyguard to escort the English officer safely out of the Cherokee country.

The affair took an unexpected turn in 1743 when Priber, as he journeyed toward Mobile, unarmed and accompanied by only a few warriors, was arrested at Tallapoosa by some traders and sent down with all his papers under a strong Indian guard to Frederica to be examined and dealt with by General Oglethorpe. The General was surprised to find in this man, coarsely attired in deerskins, a gentleman of polished address, great ability and much learning. He knew the Cherokee language, of which he had prepared a vocabulary and spoke fluently Latin, French, German, Spanish and English. He promptly said that he was a member of the Society of Jesus, and claimed that his superior had directed him to bring about a confederation of all the Southern Indians, inspire them with industry, instruct them in useful arts and induce them to throw off their allegiance to the British Crown. His plan was to form at Cusseta a settlement where disaffected English, French and German colonists and negro slaves would find a refuge. Criminals were to be sheltered there and the place was intended to be an asylum for fugitives from justice, and the cattle or property they might bring with them.

All crimes and licentiousnesses were to be tolerated except murder and idleness. Among his papers there was a well digested plan of government for the Indian confederacy, which he intended to establish. He was so firmly convinced of the success of his scheme that he said to his questioners that within that century Europeans would have very little footing on the American Continent. He carried a private journal, containing memoranda about his project, and in the journal he stated that he had in Charleston a secret treasurer and expected great help from the French and from another nation whose name he left blank. He had letters addressed to French and Spanish governors, demanding protection for the bearer, Mr. Priber, and referring to him for further particulars. Among the privileges to be given citizens of his town were a community of women, the right to dissolve marriage at pleasure and freedom to indulge every appetite.

When it was suggested to him that the kind of government he had in mind was lawless, dangerous and difficult and would require years to establish, he said: "Proceeding properly, many of these evils may be avoided; and, as to length of time, we have a succession of agents to take up the work as fast as others leave it. We never lose sight of a favorite point; nor are we bound by strict rules of morality in the employment of means when the end we pursue is laudable. If we err, our general is to blame, and we have a merciful God to pardon us." He intimated that other Jesuits were working among the Indians to accomplish the same result. As Priber was regarded as a dangerous enemy he was confined in the barracks at Frederica. He bore his captivity with stoical indifference, conversed freely, conducted himself with extreme politeness and attracted the attention of some of the citizens from whom he received favors.

While he was a prisoner at the barracks there was a fire in the magazine near his room, and several thousand shells were exploded. There was a general alarm and it was believed that Priber had been killed by some of the exploding shells, but when some persons went to his apartment they found him unhurt and calmly reading a Greek author. Asked why he had not tried to make his escape he said that the safest place was near the exploding shells, as few if any of them would return to the spot from which they had been ejected by the explosion. Therefore he remained quietly where he was and was unharmed.

Fortunately for the peace and safety of the Southern colonists Priber died suddenly while he was a captive at Frederica, and that ended his remarkable enterprise.

**The Breakdown of Early Government**—While General Oglethorpe was in Georgia in active charge of the affairs of the Colony the inherent weakness of its government was not so apparent as it was after his departure. There was a combination of weak organization with incompetence, and in some cases bad administration bordering on corruption. It seems strange that men of experience in governmental affairs like the Georgia trustees should have framed such an unworkable system.

An example of this is the "Town Court," composed of three bailiffs, with the recorder acting as clerk. Freeholders could only be jurymen. That a court so constituted of persons without legal knowledge or experience and some of doubtful character should have been given plenary power without appeal to a higher tribunal is hard to understand, when it is recalled that the trustees who framed that plan and elected the officers were eminent men of affairs, learned in the law and many of them with parliamentary experience.

This form of government was made by the trustees, and bailiffs were appointed to take charge of the court before the first shipload of colonists left England. The appointment of three bailiffs, a recorder, two constables and two tithingmen was made from among the emigrants. The trustees, in establishing the court said that:

"All manner of crimes, offences, pleas, processes, plaints, actions, matter, causes and things whatsoever, arising or happening within the Province of Georgia, or between persons inhabiting or residing there, whether the same be criminal or civil, or whether the said crime be capital or not capital, and whether the said pleas be real, personal or mixed are to be tried according to the laws and customs of the realm of England and of the laws enacted for said Province."

This court, so constituted and empowered, was formally opened by General Oglethorpe on July 7, 1733, when the first case was tried and the first jury was empaneled.

The bailiffs of Savannah and Frederica were magistrates of burghs, and had more power than the English bailiffs. Large power was there given to men with the humble title of bailiff. If they had been men of knowledge, experience and character requisite to the just and wise administration of the judicial functions given them there might have been no serious result, though the majesty of the law and the importance of the Colony required more dignified titles for those who were to administer the law; but unfortunately the men chosen were unlearned in the law, inexperienced in public business and had not the character or wisdom to inspire confidence and respect.

To make matters worse their dissensions, and their opposition to rules framed by the trustees for the good of the Colony made them obstacles to progress. A writer who visited Savannah at that period said:

"Pity it is that a spirit of opposition to the wholesome rules this colony was first established upon; ingratitude to their great and humane benefactor; an ignorance of their true interest, and a cursed spirit of dissension among themselves, has rendered this sweet place so much less flourishing than it was at the beginning of the settlement."

Commenting on this Dr. William Bacon Stevens says:

"In addition to the hindrances mentioned by this traveler the war in which Georgia was especially involved drove many from Savannah, and prevented many more from emigrating thither. But Savannah found no foe to her peace and welfare equal to those she nursed from the trustees' store, and who, supported by their bounty, lived but to thwart and calumniate their plans."

Comparing the Savannah court with the inferior courts of England Dr. Stevens says:

"In England these minor courts communicated with others of larger jurisdiction, and these again with others of still greater power, ascending gradually from the lowest to the supreme courts; the course of justice, as Blackstone happily describes it, 'flowing in large streams from the king as the fountain, to his superior courts of record, and then subdivided into smaller channels, till the whole and every part of the kingdom were plentifully watered and refreshed.' But the town court of record of Savannah had no communication with a higher. It was itself supreme, blending in one tribunal the several powers usually lodged in common pleas, chancery, probate, nisi prius, sheriff's, coroner's, and exchequer, and all committed to men unread in the principles of law, and unversed in the usages of courts. As for some years there was no lawyer in Georgia, every suitor, as in the old Gothic courts, was obliged to appear in person to prosecute or defend his cause."

**Tyranny and Corruption**—General Oglethorpe, not having the official designation of Governor, was in fact the head of affairs, but when the threat of invasion came he spent most of his time at Frederica and on the lower coast of Georgia. Then the evils of the bailiff system of government at Savannah developed. By a peculiarly unfortunate arrangement the trustees, having to supply the impecunious colonists with food, had established a store for that purpose and had put the control of it and the distribution of provisions in the hands of the chief bailiff, Thomas Causton, who used the power thus placed in his hands to oppress and browbeat the people who came to him for supplies. He became an insolent and tyrannical dictator and ruled the people with a rod of iron until his dishonesty was discovered and he was discharged by the trustees. Such a man at the head of a court of plenary power meant the poisoning of the stream of justice at its source. The same thing happened at Frederica when a similar court was established there.

Dr. Stevens says of the bailiffs conducting those courts, basing his statement on Secretary Stephens' Journal:

"Some of the bailiffs appointed could not write, and scarcely one was qualified for the bench. The power was too great for the irresponsible hands that wielded it; for, having never before held the staff of office, they became intoxicated with their elevation, and used their little brief authority like so many autocrats in miniature. They were charged with setting aside the laws of England, making false imprisonments, wrongfully discharging grand juries, threatening petit juries, blasphemy, irreverence, drunkenness, obstructing the course of law, and other equally grave and heinous offences. Indeed, the frequent courts, the arbitrary adjournments, the bickering of the magistrates, the illegal proceedings, the insufficient securities, the want of proper juries, and the supplanting of justice by private piques and personal prejudices, made the whole system of the town courts, both at Savannah and Frederica, a burden to the people, giving them the shadow of English law without its substance, and compelling them to bow to decisions which, under the name of justice, were but mocking insults to that priestess of human rights.

"The picture of these times, which the secretary for Georgia has so fully delineated in his journal, shows the sad condition of the Colony, and the racking feuds and general distrust which reigned throughout the Province."

As their scheme of government for the Colony had so disastrously failed, the trustees appointed a committee to frame a plan for a constitutional government administered by a president and assistants.

The committee was composed of the Earl of Egmont, the Earl of Shaftsbury and Mr. Vernon, all of whom were members of Parliament. By the report of that committee, approved by the Common Council of the trustees, the Province of Georgia was divided into two counties, one called Savannah, including all territory north of Darien, and the other called Frederica, including St. Simon's and the Altamaha settlements. Over each of these was to be a president and four assistants who were to constitute a civil and judicial tribunal for their counties.

The officers for Frederica were not then appointed, but those for Savannah were: William Stephens, president; Henry Parker, Thomas Jones, John Fallowfield and Samuel Mercer, assistants.

The new constitution and those appointments were read in open court, October 7, 1741, and on October 12, the new officers met and undertook the administration of government. Though well meant by the trustees, the new government seems to have proved a disappointment, due to the character of the people at that early period. Dr. Stevens says of it:

"This was an advance on the former plan, and gave an elevation and dignity to the Colony in the eyes of her neighbours; but Georgia herself received little benefit by the change. The reason was that society did not possess those elements of refinement and civilization upon which a good government could lay hold, and by them elevate and dignify the whole people. It lacked unity, morality, industry, and social integrity; and where these are wanting, there will always be degradation and misery, no matter how wise the laws or how just their administration. A virtuous people will flourish under bad government; an immoral society will display its wretchedness under the wisest administration."

While General Oglethorpe was commander-in-chief, with civil and military control of the province, the evil of conflicting jurisdictions was obviated by centralizing power in him, but when his departure was expected the trustees, on April 9, 1743, united the two counties under one president and assistants, and the bailiffs at Frederica became subordinate magistrates under the Savannah court.

**Conspiracy of Thomas Bosomworth and His Wife, Mary**—The conspiracy of Reverend Thomas Bosomworth and his Indian wife Mary, formerly Mary Musgrove, which developed soon after the departure of General Oglethorpe from Georgia came near ruining the Colony. In the early history of the Colony she had been of great service to General Oglethorpe in establishing cordial relations with the Indians, and continued a friendly influence with the Indians in behalf of the Colony so long as General Oglethorpe remained in charge, but after her marriage to Reverend Thomas Bosomworth, in 1744, her attitude towards the Colony changed, and under his influence she claimed as hers all the land which Indians had ceded to the colonists or the British King.

Mary was born about the year 1700 at Coweta town on the Ocmulgee River, which was then the chief town of the Creek nation. Her Indian name was Consaponakeeso, and according to Dr. William Bacon Stevens, "she was by maternal descent one of the chiefs of the Uchees. Old Brim, the Emperor of the nation, as he was usually styled, being her mother's brother, she claimed, and the Indians conceded to her the title of princess. At the age of ten she was taken by her father to Pompon, in South Carolina, and was baptized, educated, and instructed in Christianity. While there the Indian war of 1715 broke out, and a party of Creeks, headed by her uncle Chichilli, advanced as far as Stono River. But the Yamassees, after their attack of the 13th of April, having been repulsed by Governor Craven, the Creeks returned to their lands without participating in the sanguinary contest.

"Mary accompanied the party on their retreat to the nation and laid aside the civilization of the English for the freedom of the Indian.

"Neighboring tribes, though not actually on the defensive, were still unsettled in their feeling towards the whites, and in 1716 Colonel John Musgrove was sent by the Government of South Carolina to form a treaty of alliance with the Creeks and thus secure their neutrality, if he could not obtain their friendship. The treaty lodged with the Indians certain reserved rights, the principal feature of which was that none of His Majesty's subjects should hold any right to lands or kill any cattle south of the Savannah, which was to be the boundary between the Creeks and His Majesty's subjects of Carolina. John Musgrove, Junior, the son of the colonel, accompanied his father on this embassy, and having seen and admired the youthful princess, was soon united to her by marriage. He remained in the nation several years after the birth of their only child, and about 1723 returned to Carolina, where she resided with her husband upwards of seven years. Mr. Musgrove, by his alliance with Consaponakeeso, obtained considerable influence with the Creeks, and was held in such high repute as a trader, that, at the request of the nation, and with the consent of Governor Johnson, he removed to the south side of the Savannah (June, 1732), and there, on a beautiful bluff belonging to a small tribe of Yamacraws, erected an extensive trading house. Success crowned his efforts, and wealth rewarded his industry. Such was the condition of Mary prior to the arrival of the trustees' colony, enjoying the confidence of her tribes, the friendship of the whites, and versed at once in the English and Indian languages."

When General Oglethorpe arrived with the first shipload of colonists, in 1733, Mary Musgrove was there and her knowledge of both the Indian and the English language with her kinship to the great Chief of the Creeks and her natural ability, gave her great influence with the Indians. Her marriage to John Musgrove made her friendly to the English and she used that influence with fine effect in aiding General Oglethorpe to establish cordial relations with Tomochichi and other chiefs of the natives of Georgia. Although the Indians were at first alarmed by the coming of the white men she quieted their fears and gained their consent for a friendly alliance with General Oglethorpe and the King of Great Britain. For ten years she was the valued friend of the Colony, using a powerful influence and maintaining cordial relations with the Indians to such an extent that they not only welcomed General Oglethorpe and his colonists, but gave them powerful aid in resisting the attacks of the Spaniards. She was so useful to the colony that General Oglethorpe gave her a salary of 100 pounds per year. On the death of her husband, John Musgrove, in 1736, General Oglethorpe, who was fortifying the southern coast and islands of Georgia proposed that she establish a trading station on the Altamaha River to draw the Indians away from Savannah, strengthen the southern frontier and locate her residence near Frederica, where she was frequently called by General Oglethorpe for her counsel and coöperation in time of war, and to act as interpreter. She granted his request and established on the south side of the forks of the Altamaha River a trading house which she called Mount Venture. This trading house became a place of much resort and served to strengthen that part of the colony. There she married Jacob Mathews, whom General Oglethorpe appointed to command the garrison of twenty men, whom he had located there to defend the place.

At that time the Colony was exposed to invasion by Spaniards and Indians friendly to them, and the southern frontier was the seat of merciless and savage warfare. Under these circumstances it was only the fidelity of the Creeks and their strong support which made it possible to continue the Colony. Without their aid it must have been abandoned. It was largely through the influence of Mary Mathews that the Creeks were held firm in their loyalty to the English and in the final contest on St. Simon's Island in 1742 the Indians sent down through the efforts of Mary Mathews and Tomochichi had an important part in the victory of Bloody Marsh, where they wreaked terrible vengeance upon the Spaniards for their former cruelty to Creek Indians.

General Oglethorpe's value of her services is shown by a letter which he wrote from Durham, England, on November 13, 1745, in which he said:

"I find there is the utmost endeavor, by the Spanish faction, to destroy her, because she is of consequence and in the King's interest; therefore it is the business of the King's friends to support her, besides which I shall be desirous to serve her out of the friendship she has always shown me as well as to the Colony."

So great was her influence with the Indians that Dr. Stevens, in his history calls her the Pocahontas of Georgia, and adds:

"If a 'talk' was to be held with the Indians at Frederica, Savannah, or any other point, nothing could be done without the important aid of Mary. If warriors were required for the defense of the Colony, it was through Mary's influence that they were obtained. Did disaffection, leaning on French intrigue or Spanish guile, hold aloft the 'bloody stick' and threaten the massacre of the inhabitants, her power became conspicuous in the soothing of exasperated feelings, and in the recall of half-alienated affection. In 1742, her husband, being ill, removed to Savannah, where about June he died; and during her absence the Yamassees fell upon her establishment at Mount Venture and laid it in ruins."

After that in Savannah Mary had some official relations with Thomas Bosomworth, who had succeeded Clarke as Agent for Indian Affairs. He was a man of liberal education, and as a volunteer in the invasion of Florida had commended himself to General Oglethorpe. Having fitted himself for the ministry he went to England to take orders with the church, and the trustees appointed him for religious and ecclesiastical duties in Georgia. Returning to Georgia he married Mary and with her went to live at Frederica, where he served as deputy chaplain, but the trustees disapproved of that and directed him to go to Savannah, as he had been appointed to that station. In that religious work he was in part supported by the Society for the Propagation of Christian Knowledge, and one of the objects of his mission was to convert the Indians. If he had really wished to engage in missionary work among the Indians his marriage to Mary Mathews would have given him a great opportunity, but it appeared that he had other views. He soon became the evil genius of the colony and his influence over his Indian wife, who had served the Colony so long and so well, made a complete transformation in her attitude toward the Colony.

Until her marriage with Bosomworth Mary's life had been one of generous self-denial and continued labor for the good of the Colony, but from 1744 her whole character changed, and as Dr. Stevens says the Colony which her services had kept in peace and security was now through her misdirected influence to feel the dreadful horrors of expected massacre and extermination.

The year after his marriage Bosomworth returned to England and joined Oglethorpe's regiment as he was marching against the rebels, proceeding with it to the seat of war. He then wrote to the trustees that he did not intend to return to Georgia, but in 1746 he did return to Savannah, gave up his ecclesiastical offices and showed his contempt for the trustees by placing six negroes on his place on the Altamaha River.

The trustees resented this affront to their authority, and instructed the president and his assistants to move the slaves out of the Colony. This action provoked Bosomworth to anger and he sought to revenge himself by a conspiracy which if successful would have destroyed the Colony. He began by conciliating the Indians, and laid plans which included not only compensation for his wife for the destruction of her property on the Altamaha River and payment for her services, but added a demand for possession of Ossabaw, St. Catherine and Sapelo islands, and land between Savannah and Pipe Makers Bluff, which the Indians in their treaty with Oglethorpe had reserved for their own use. For the services of his wife he demanded five thousand pounds, and as Dr. Stevens says: "Put on the iron features of the extortioner determined rather to light up through the nation the fires of the war dance than cancel one claim or relinquish one acre."

As a basis for his outrageous claims Bosomworth prepared a long memorial signed by his wife on August 10, 1747, in which she began by claiming descent on her mother's side from the chiefs of the Creek nation, and said that by their laws and the voice of their people she was their natural and rightful princess. Her further claims are summarized as follows:

That her ancestors were a brave and free-born people who never owed allegiance to or acknowledged the sovereignty of any crowned head, but had maintained their own possessions and independence against all opposers by war and the shedding of their own blood.

That they had made several treaties of peace, friendship and commerce with the representatives of the British Crown, had made several concessions of land in behalf of His Majesty, faithfully observed the treaty of friendship and alliance with General Oglethorpe, and had been always ready to fight His Majesty's enemies.

That the French and Spaniards knew how terrible they were in war, how important their friendship was to Great Britain, and were trying to seduce them from that alliance, which would be a very dangerous thing for the English colonists.

That by her influence in behalf of the Colony of Georgia for fourteen years the Creeks had been faithful to the English.

That by the laws of Great Britain she was a subject of that Crown, had given many proofs of her zeal and loyalty and that she had a right to complain of grievances which had become too great for her to bear, and hoped that redress would be given her.

That she at the age of seven years was brought by her father from the Indian nation to Pompon in South Carolina, and there baptized and bred in the principles of Christianity.

That she was in South Carolina in 1715, when as a result of acts of injustice by the traders toward the Indians an Indian war broke out and her mother's brother, Chichilli, at the head of the Creek Indians advanced as far as Stono River.

That in 1716 Colonel John Musgrove, her father-in-law, was sent as an agent of South Carolina and made a treaty of alliance with the Creek nation in behalf of that government, in which it was agreed that none of the English should live on, hold or claim any land or title to any cattle south of the Savannah River, which was to be the boundary between the Creeks and British subjects.

After that she married John Musgrove and remained in South Carolina seven years until June, 1732, when she and her husband at the request of the Creek nation, with the consent of Governor Johnson, of South Carolina, moved all their goods and cattle south of the Savannah River, and established a trading house at Yamacraw, near the site of Savannah, where they received large quantities of deer skins from the Indians, and had large credit and supplies of goods from the merchants in Charleston to carry on that traffic.

That on the arrival of General Oglethorpe with the first colonists the Indians were uneasy and threatened to take up arms against the English, believing that a settlement of white people there was a breach of the treaty they had made with South Carolina, and it was only by her utmost influence that a treaty was secured between Oglethorpe and the Indians who were there. The ratification of that treaty was brought about with difficulty by her influence.

That her husband, John Musgrove, carried much property into Georgia, and as there was no other house there he supplied the first settlers with every necessity that his plantation afforded or that he could purchase from Charleston.

That she and her husband had lost a great deal by giving credit to persons in public service in Georgia, which they did out of compassion, relieving their necessity, and most of those people had left the colony or were not able to pay her.

That in 1733 and 1734 she took from the Indians 1,200 pounds of deer skins each year and that trade would have greatly increased as the Indians were daily coming to trade with her and she would have made a large fortune had she adopted the methods of other traders, but as there was then no defense for this infant Colony and the southern part of Carolina against the incursions of the Spaniards and their Indian allies, but by the alliance of the Creeks with the English, she preferred to protect the lives and property of the colonists to the care of her own interest, and she not only used her influence to keep the Creeks steady in their alliance with the English, but supported at her own expense numbers of her friends and other war Indians who were always ready to go against His Majesty's enemies. As a result of this her trade decreased and almost went to ruin. Indians who were her hunters being engaged in some expedition for the British service were unable to pay their debts to her, which remained unpaid, some of the debtors being dead and others killed in His Majesty's service, including her brother and near relatives at the siege of St. Augustine in 1740.

That in 1736 and 1737 General Oglethorpe wished to strengthen the southern part of the Province by a settlement on St. Simon's Island and the Altamaha River because the Spaniards were preparing to attack the Colony, she was called to Frederica to talk with the Indians who came there, as they were not disposed to talk freely unless she was there. This caused her absence from home several months at a time, and her own affairs, left entirely to servants, went to ruin.

That at the request of General Oglethorpe she established a trading house on the south side of the Altamaha River, sixty miles up in the country in order that the Creek Indians who would constantly come there would be an outguard to prevent any incursion of Indians friendly to the Spaniards, and the Creek Indians would be always ready when His Majesty's service required.

This put a heavy burden upon her, and because of the absence of herself and her husband at their settlement on the Altamaha, all their affairs at Savannah, which were considerable, went to ruin.

That in 1742 her husband, Jacob Mathews, was taken sick, brought from the Altamaha to Savannah and died there; that her affairs were in great confusion because of her long stay on the Altamaha River, that the Indians at her settlement on the Altamaha were uneasy because she did not return, and the Yamassees, taking advantage of that, came in numbers, committed several murders and destroyed her settlement.

That in 1743 when General Oglethorpe returned to England he paid her 180 pounds, which with 20 pounds received before made 200 pounds, which was all she received for her services from 1732 to 1747, notwithstanding the fact that she had undergone great fatigue, frequently traveling several hundred miles by water in open boats exposed to heat and cold with no covering but the heavens; and the losses sustained in her own private affairs by neglect of them when she was in His Majesty's service amounted to 5,714 pounds 17s. and 11 pence.

And that as she had relied in vain on General Oglethorpe's promises to make restitution of losses in Her Majesty's service and ask redress for her grievances and obtain from the home government adequate rewards for them she humbly begged that Lieutenant-Colonel Heron, commander-in-chief of His Majesty's forces in Georgia would make a statement of these things to the Home Government in such a way as would be conducive to the welfare of the Colony and His Majesty's service.

That in the preamble of the Royal Charter, establishing the Board of Trustees, his British Majesty declared that his intention in a settlement of this Colony was partly as a protection to South Carolina, whose southern frontier was exposed to frequent ravages of enemies.

That His Majesty's intention in the settlement of Georgia had so far answered that no out-settlement had been cut off, boats taken, or men killed since that time. She therefore hoped that on a statement of her case to the Governor and Council of South Carolina that government would be induced to make some restitution to her for losses sustained in His Majesty's service, as she was then largely indebted to merchants in Charleston and other persons in South Carolina.

In concluding she said she was injured and distressed because she was insulted, abused and despised by the ungrateful people who were indebted to her for every blessing they enjoyed. That the only return she had for her services and maternal affection had been unjust loads of infamy; being branded as a traitor for claiming rights to which she was entitled by the laws of God and nature. That she had asked in vain a grant from the Crown, and wished to hold her rightful possessions as a subject of Great Britain.

She declared that the Colony of Georgia was settled by her interest with the Creeks, and had been largely supported by it; that she had now the power to command a thousand fighting men to meet His Majesty's enemies and to countermine the designs of French and Spaniards, if she was given sufficient encouragement to prevent the necessity of her flying to her Indian friends for bread, which would greatly exasperate them.

That French emissaries were making every effort to destroy the faith of the Creeks in the English, were loading them with presents, and sought to make the English contemptible because they were not able to give the Indians the usual presents.

That the safety of the Colony required the continued alliance of the Creeks and to that end large presents should be allowed them, and a proper person sent among them in whom they have confidence and who could remove the insinuations of His Majesty's enemies.

That she asked Colonel Heron to lay her memorial before the Duke of New Castle with assurance that if the government should allow a certain sum per annum to be applied among the Indians she would undertake by her interest among them to do every duty that was ever done by rangers in Georgia, which had cost the government many thousand pounds; and with the regiment under his command and her interest with the Creeks she believed that every foot of His Majesty's possessions on that frontier could be maintained against His Majesty's enemies.

This document with letters commending her past services and present influence, including some from General Oglethorpe, Major William Horton, Captain Richard Kent, Colonel William Stephens and Colonel Alexander Heron, with translation of eulogies by Chikilli, king of the warriors of the Creek nation and Malatche, was forwarded to the home government, and Colonel Heron appears to have sympathized with the claim of the Bosomworths for additional compensation. Colonel Stephens, in one of his letters to the trustees, asserted that this officer was to participate largely in the expected remuneration and that his support of the memorial had been thus purchased.

Not content with this Bosomworth undertook to bring pressure to bear on the Colony through the Indians. On December 14, 1747, the Indian King Malatche of the Creek nation, with sixteen companions from various towns in the Creek Confederacy were on a visit to Frederica and Bosomworth, who was friendly to Malatche, was there. He persuaded that Indian to have himself then and there formally acknowledged as the head of the Creek nation with full power to conclude treaties and transact any other business for the kingly administration of the affairs of his people. This suggestion being approved Malatche was proclaimed Supreme Chief of the Muscogulgee Confederacy.

At the suggestion of Bosomworth a proclamation of the same date declaring Malatche their rightful prince was signed by the chiefs of tribes and head men there present, and witnessed by Colonel Heron, Sir Patrick Houstoun and others. Malatche requested that a copy be sent over to the King of England, and that the original be recorded.

Having thus succeeded in giving Malatche supreme power, Bosomworth prevailed on him to execute a deed by which as Emperor of the Upper and Lower Creek nations he conveyed to Thomas and Mary Bosomworth of the Colony of Georgia the islands on the coast, known as Ossabaw, St. Catherine's and Sapelo. The consideration mentioned in the deed for these vast properties was ten piece of stroud, twelve pieces of duffles, two hundred weight of powder, two hundred weight of lead, twenty guns, twelve pairs of pistols and one hundred weight of vermilion. It was an absolute conveyance with warranty to Bosomworth and his wife, their heirs and assigns so long as the sun should shine and the waters run into the rivers.

Bosomworth then proceeded to stock the islands with cattle bought in South Carolina, and so became largely indebted to Carolina planters.

As his stock raising on the islands did not prove profitable Bosomworth concocted a scheme to secure power and fortune by a bold stroke. He encouraged his wife to announce herself as a sister of Malatche descended from an Indian King who held the entire territory of the Creeks. He induced her to claim this territory as her own, asserting that her right to it was superior to that of the trustees and the King of Great Britain. Acting under his suggestion Mary assumed the title of Empress of the Creeks, disavowing allegiance or subjection to the British Crown, and she summoned a general meeting of the Creeks, to whom in a long speech prepared for the occasion by Bosomworth she told of her claim, explained its justice, said that they, her beloved subjects, had received from the English the loss of their territory and a necessity was upon them to regain it by force of arms. Inflamed by her talk the Indians admitted her claims and pledged themselves to defend her royal person and her land.

Putting herself at the head of a large body of warriors she started for Savannah to demand from the president and council an acknowledgment of her assumed rights. A messenger was sent in advance to notify the president of the Colony of her approach and inform him that she had assumed sovereignty over the entire territory of the Upper and Lower Creeks. This notification was accompanied by a demand for the immediate evacuation by the whites of all land south of the Savannah River, and a threat that in case of a refusal every settlement within the territory specified would be destroyed.

Alarmed by this bold message and knowing her influence over the Creeks, President Stephens ordered the militia to hold themselves ready to march to Savannah on short notice and he at once put the town in strong attitude for defense. Its whole force then was only one hundred and seventy men able to bear arms.

A messenger was sent to meet Mary while she was several miles from town to inquire whether she was serious in her intentions and to try to persuade her to dismiss her followers and abandon her intentions, but she was resolute and inflexible.

The Indians were met boldly. The militia were under arms and as the Indians entered the town Captain Noble Jones at the head of a troop of horse stopped them and demanded whether their visit was of a friendly or hostile character. Receiving no reply he ordered them to ground their arms, declaring that he was ordered not to allow an armed Indian to set foot in the town and he would enforce the order at every hazard. The Indians reluctantly submitted.

Thomas Bosomworth, in his canonical robes, with his Queen by his side, followed by the Kings and Chiefs of the Indians according to their rank, marched into Savannah on the 20th of July, 1747, in formidable array, and the citizens were terror stricken.

Advancing to the parade ground the Indians found the militia drawn up under arms to receive them. They were saluted with fifteen cannon and conducted to the President's house. Bosomworth was commanded to withdraw, and the Indian Chiefs were asked in a friendly manner to declare their object in coming in Savannah in so large a body without being convened by any person in authority. Acting on previous instructions they replied that Mary would speak for them and they were to abide by what she said. They also said they had heard she was to be sent as a captive over the great waters, and they were come to know why they were to lose their Queen; and they intended no harm and wished that their arms might be returned to them.

After consulting with Bosomworth and his wife the Indians gave assurance that they would settle all public affairs amicably. With this their guns were restored to them, but they were given no ammunition until the Council could see more clearly into their dark designs.

The next day, after conference with Mary, the Indians marched about the streets with sullen countenances and in a tumultuous manner, apparently determined on mischief. The men of the Colony were obliged to mount guard and the women and children, afraid to remain in their houses by themselves, were terrified, expecting to be murdered and scalped. It was then that a false rumor was circulated to the effect that the Indians had cut off President Stephens' head with a tomahawk. This so inflamed the people that it was hard for the officers to keep the troops from firing on the Indians. Bosomworth was arrested and told that in case of hostilities he would be the first victim. When he was carried into confinement Mary became frantic, threatening vengeance against the magistrates and the entire Colony, and ordered all white people to depart from her territory at once, cursing Oglethorpe and denouncing his treaties as fraudulent. Stamping her foot on the ground she swore by her maker that the whole globe should know the land she stood upon was her own. To prevent the white men from influencing the chiefs and warriors she kept the leading Indians under her eye and would not allow them to utter a sentence on public affairs except in her presence.

Seeing that it was impossible to pacify the Indians while they were under the influence of their pretended Queen, President Stephens privately had her arrested and put in close confinement with her husband.

To bring about reconciliation with the Indians a feast was prepared for all their chiefs and leading warriors and there they were informed that Bosomworth had involved himself in debt which he was unable to pay, that he wanted not only their lands but a large share of the presents which the King had sent over for the chiefs and warriors as a compensation for their useful services and their firm attachment to him during the war with the Spaniards; that Bosomworth wished to obtain these presents at the expense of the Indians to satisfy his creditors in South Carolina; that the land adjoining Savannah had been reserved for the Indians to encamp on when they came to visit their beloved white friends and the three islands on the coast were reserved for them to fish and hunt upon when they came to bathe in the salt water; that neither Mary nor her husband had any right to those lands, as they were the common property of the whole Creek nation, and that the Great King George had ordered the President to defend the right of the Indians to those lands, expecting that all his subjects both white and red would live together like brethren.

Many of the chiefs, convinced that Bosomworth had deceived them, declared that they would no longer be controlled by his advice. Even Malatche, the leader of the Lower Creeks, appeared to be satisfied and was greatly delighted to hear that presents were to be distributed. President Stephens, taking advantage of this favorable change in their sentiment, determined to make an immediate distribution of the Royal bounty to the Indians and dismiss them.

While preparations were being made for this distribution Malatche, whom the Indians compared to the wind because of his fickleness and variable temper, had an interview with Bosomworth and his wife. Rising up among the chiefs and warriors who were there to receive their shares of the King's gifts, he with a frowning countenance, delivered an inflammatory speech with dangerous insinuations and threats, asserting the paramount claims of Mary as Queen of the Creeks to all the lands in question. Declaring that her words were the voice of the nation and three thousand warriors were ready to support with their lives her right to those lands, he drew from his pocket a document which he delivered to President Stephens in confirmation of what he said. This paper, evidently drawn by Bosomworth, was a violent assertion of Mary's claim and design. The Council members were struck with astonishment, and seeing the effect on them by the paper, Malatche became uneasy and asked that it be returned to him that he might return it to the party from whom he received it. President Stephens, seeing how badly the Indians had been duped by the mercenary and designing Bosomworth addressed the chiefs and warriors as follows:

PRESIDENT STEPHENS' ADDRESS TO THE INDIANS.

"FRIENDS AND BROTHERS: When Mr. Oglethorpe and his people first arrived in Georgia they found Mary, then the wife of John Musgrove, living in a small hut at Yamacraw; he had a license from the governor of South Carolina to trade with the Indians. She then appeared to be in a poor, ragged condition, and was neglected and despised by the Creeks; but General Oglethorpe, finding that she could speak both the English and the Creek languages, employed her as an interpreter, richly clothed her, and made her the woman of the consequence she now appears. The people of Georgia always respected her until she married Bosomworth, but from that time she has proved a liar and a deceiver. In fact, she was no relation of Malatche, but the daughter of an Indian woman of no note by a white man. General Oglethorpe did not treat with her for the lands of Georgia, for she had none, but with the old and wise leaders of the Creek nation, who voluntarily surrendered their territories to the King. The Indians at that time having much waste land which was useless to themselves, parted with a share of it to their friends, and were glad that white people had settled among them to supply their wants."

He also told them that discontent had been artfully instilled into the minds of the Creeks by Mary at the instigation of her husband, who demanded a third of the royal bounty in order to rob the naked Indians of their rights; that he had quarreled with the president and Council of Georgia for refusing to grant his exorbitant demand and filled the heads of the Indians with groundless jealousy in order to cause mischief and induce them to break their alliance with their best friends, who alone were able to supply their wants and defend them against their enemies.

At this the Indians said that their eyes were opened and they were ready to smoke the pipe of peace. Pipes and rum were brought and all joining hands drank and smoked in friendship. The distribution of royal presents was made, leaving out ammunition, with which it was not then thought safe to trust them, and even Malatche seemed satisfied with the share he had received.

While amicable relations had been effected and all were rejoicing in the return of friendly intercourse, Mary, drunk with liquor, rushed like a fury into the assembly, telling the president that these were her people and he had no business with them. The president calmly advised her to retire to her lodgings and quit poisoning the minds of the Indians, for if she did not he would again put her in close confinement.

Turning to Malatche in a great rage Mary repeated to him what the president had said. Malatche thereupon sprang from his seat, laid hold of his arms, called on the rest to follow his example and dared any man to touch his queen. In a moment the house was filled with uproar. Every Indian had his tomahawk in his hand and the president and council expected nothing but instant death.

In this emergency Captain Jones, who commanded the guard, interposed with great courage and ordered the Indians to immediately surrender their arms. They did so reluctantly and Mary was conveyed to a private room, where a guard was placed over her and she was denied all further communication with the Indians while they were in Savannah.

The Indians were persuaded to leave the town peaceably and return to their settlements. Mary and her husband were detained until the first of August, when they confessed their error publicly at the courthouse, asked pardon, and were allowed to depart.

Strange as it may seem, in spite of the conduct of Bosomworth and his wife, Mary's claim was still pressed in London. After some years of negotiation the matter was finally settled in 1759 by paying her 450 pounds for expense she claimed to have made in His Majesty's service in 1747 and 1748 and by paying her back salary of 100 pounds per annum for sixteen and one-half years during which she acted as government agent and interpreter, and by confirming to her and her husband the title of St. Catherine's Island because of their claim that they lived there and had planted the land. In the meantime Thomas and Abraham Bosomworth were dismissed in disgrace from the service of the trustees.

## CHAPTER XXIX.

# *Discontent and Depression—Repeal of Laws Against Rum and Slavery—Tenure Improved*

**Causes of Depression Under the Trustees**—In reviewing the conduct of affairs by the trustees during the twenty years when they were in control of the Georgia Colony, Dr. Stevens shows that with the best motives and an earnest desire to benefit the colonists and serve the British government, the trustees, though able and experienced men, made serious mistakes which caused trouble among the colonists and brought the Colony to a state of deep depression.

That, he says, was not unusual with colonies and cites the experience and the errors of wise and good men in charge of other Colonial ventures. On that subject he said in his history of Georgia:

"In the infancy of all colonial schemes we find difficulties, errors, and failings. It is so generally with all experiments, especially in those which have for their object the ordering of masses of men, and the arranging and scheming for their guidance, equity, and welfare.

"Theory has never yet made a good commonwealth. The 'Republic' of Plato was even more visionary than the dreams of his philosophy. The 'Fundamental Constitutions' of John Locke, though he was one of England's greatest metaphysicians, utterly miscarried in their aim, and brought Carolina to the verge of ruin. William Penn's 'Frame of the Government of the Province of Pennsylvania,' was, after one year, taken down to make room for a new one; and the first constitution, given by the Duke of York to the colony which bore his name, was in eight years changed for a wiser and more liberal patent. Stern experience is the only true teacher of governmental rules. She sees the necessities of men, and points out the means of compassing them; she ascertains their wants, and knows how to provide for them; she is the great instructress of nations; and to go contrary to her teachings, is to do violence to that law, 'whose seat is the bosom of God, whose voice the harmony of the world.'

"It is strange, that with so many warning lights hung out from the drifting wrecks of former schemes, the Trustees for the colony of Georgia did not proceed on wiser principles, and more modern legislation. They, too, theorized the colony into the pangs of civil death, nor saw, nor remedied their error, till, wasted of its strength and substance, there scarcely remained vitality enough to give it a nominal existence."

**Indentured Servants Called Slaves**—The lack of efficient labor to till the farms was one of the worst troubles of the Colony. Without labor enough to produce food for the people they had to draw on South Carolina for supplies and many had to get food from the trustees' store.

Indentured white servants were not equal to the task and the conditions under which they worked Dr. Stevens likened to slavery. He said:

"But while the Trustees disallowed negroes, they instituted a system of white slavery, which was fraught with evil to the servants and to the colony. These were white servants, consisting of Welsh, English, or German, males and females—families and individuals who were indented to individuals or the Trustees, for a period of from four to fourteen years; work to a certain amount being required of all over the age of six. On arriving in Georgia, their service was sold for the term of indenture, or apportioned to the inhabitants by the magistrates, as their necessities required. The sum which they brought when thus bid off, varied from 2 pounds to 6 pounds, besides an annual tax of 1 pound, for five years, to defray the expense of their voyage. On the expiration of their indentures, they received, if they had served their masters faithfully, a small portion of land, and were then thrown upon their own resources. The limited number of these, and their early unwillingness to continue in servile condition, left the grants without the means of efficient cultivation, and the evils of the scheme became speedily apparent."

In a publication of 1741, entitled "A True and Historical Narrative of the Colony of Georgia," it was said that the clearing and cultivation of new lands originated fevers and various other diseases, which brought to many cessation both from work and from life.

"And so general were these disorders," said the statement, "that during the hot season, which lasts from March till October, hardly one-half of the servants or working people were even able to do their masters or themselves the least service; and the yearly sickness of each servant, generally speaking, cost his master as much as would have maintained a negro for four years."

On that Dr. Stevens makes this comment:

"The plan for substituting white for black labour, failed through the sparseness of the supply, and the refractoriness of the servants. As a consequence of the inability of the settlers to procure adequate help, the lands granted them remained uncleared, and even those which the temporary industry of the first occupants prepared, remained uncultivated; for the people, leaving their unfurrowed fields, clustered about the town, eking out a beggarly subsistence by such handicraft as they were partially acquainted with, or else living upon the Trustees' stores."

Writing the trustees in August, 1740, David Douglass, William Sterling and Thomas Baillie said: "The Colony is reduced to one-sixth of its former number," and that "the few who remain are in a starving and despicable condition."

In a letter to General Oglethorpe on the difficulty poor people had of making a living without laborers, James Habersham wrote:

"They droop under these difficulties, grow weary of the colony, get into idle and refractory company; from thence naturally to drinking, and which perhaps ends in the total ruin of themselves and families."

To Governor Belcher, of Massachusetts, he wrote, in 1747:

"I must confess that things have had such a dreadful appearance for some time past that, rather than see the colony deserted and brought to desolation, and the inhabitants reduced to want and beggary, I really, with the Trustees, would have consented to the use of negroes, and was sorry to hear that they had written so warmly against them."

These were the conditions which induced the trustees to repeal the law against negro slavery in Georgia.

The logic of events, to which the Trustees finally yielded, is evidence of the correctness of Dr. Stevens' comment, for the reversal of their policy in regard to slavery, rum and land tenures was followed by prosperity. This is indicated by the growth of exports from the Colony, which trebled during the last two years of the trusteeship and continued to grow so rapidly that within four years more they were nearly ten times as large as in 1750. Major Hugh McCall gives these figures in his history of Georgia:

| | | | |
|---|---|---|---|
| Exports in 1750............ | $8,897.76 | Exports in 1753............ | $28,429.32 |
| Exports in 1751............ | 16,816.40 | Exports in 1754............ | 42,211.08 |
| Exports in 1752............ | 21,494.04 | Exports in 1756............ | 74,485.44 |

**How Parliament Came to Repeal the Rum Act**—The thing that seems to have brought about action by the British Parliament in repealing the law against rum was the extreme measures taken by Georgia magistrates to enforce that law. Dr. Stevens says the law was violated by some of the officials, "who with the law in their hands bought, drank and sold rum, but while they violated the law themselves they resolved that it should not be infringed by others.

"In carrying out the Trustees' act Mr. Causton and the bailiffs arrogated to themselves jurisdiction over the waters of the Savannah and undertook to stop and examine boats passing up either branch of the river before the town. In one instance they stopped two boats laden with dry goods and rum, proceeding from Charleston to New Windsor on the Carolina side. The packages were opened and three hogsheads and ten kegs of rum were staved and the men imprisoned.

"This high-handed measure called for redress and at the next meeting of the assembly three gentlemen, John Hamerton, Charles Pinckney and Othiel Beale were appointed a committee to proceed to Georgia and confer with Oglethorpe about the Indian Trade. They were kindly received by the General who told them he would send orders to his agents and officers in the Indian nations not to molest or seize the traders of that province and that navigation on the river should be settled."

The matter was afterward brought into the British Parliament and by vote of the House of Commons the trustees were directed to repeal the rum act, which they did on July 14, 1742.

**Retirement of President Stephens**—President William Stephens, who became Chief Executive of Georgia with the title of president on the departure of General Oglethorpe in 1743, remained in office until 1751 when, because of the infirmities of age he felt himself unequal to the tasks, responsibilities and difficulties which confronted him. He not only had to deal with the dangerous situation developed by the plot of Thomas Bosomworth, but had many problems which grew out of the dissensions among the people, the lack of prosperity and the increasing discontent with the rules of the trustees forbidding the use of negro slaves and the importation of rum. There was also a great deal of dissatisfaction with the restrictions on land tenures.

Colonel Stephens was a man of noble birth. He was the son of Sir William Stephens, Baronet, Lieutenant-Governor of the Isle of Wight, where he was born on January 28, 1671. He graduated from King's College, Cambridge, and entered the Middle Temple at London, but was never called to the bar. At the age of twenty-five he married Mary, the second daughter of Sir Richard Newdigate, Baronet of Harefield and Arbury, a member of Parliament for Warwickshire. Soon after his marriage young Stephens was elected a member of Parliament for Newport and held his seat there for twenty-six years. There he became acquainted with Colonel Horsey, who afterwards became Governor of South Carolina, and General Oglethorpe. This acquaintanceship with General Oglethorpe led to his appointment as secretary of the trustees in 1737. His Journal as secretary of the trustees is one of the fullest and best sources of information concerning the Colony during the long period when he was connected with it and was transmitted to the trustees, which made it an official document, in which he related events in plain and simple language with occasional comments showing his views of the political and religious condition of Georgia.

He was a staunch friend of the trustees, but because of his connection with the Church of England was opposed to John Wesley and Whitefield and sometimes commented on their doings and their preaching with severity. He was sixty-six years old when he became secretary of the trustees, seventy when appointed president of the county of Savannah, and seventy-two when he became president of the whole Colony. He was, therefore, eighty years old when he resigned as president. In 1750 he retired to his beautiful plantation called Bewlie. There he lived quietly, steadily failing in strength until August, 1753, when at the tea table a cup was handed him. Tasting it, he put it down and said calmly: "I have done eating and drinking in this world." He was led to his bed in the adjoining room, where he lay unable to speak until the next day at noon, when he passed away.

**The Trustees Yield to the Colonists Concerning Negroes, Rum and Land Tenures**—During President Stephens' administration the Colony of Georgia did not prosper. The trustees had sent over on their bounty in the first eight years 915 colonists from England and the whole number sent over at their expense up to the time when they gave up their charter in 1752 was 1,200 British and 1,000 foreign Protestants. In the conduct of the Colony during that period they had received from private sources contributions amounting to 17,600 pounds and from Parliamentary grants 136,600 pounds, altogether 154,200 pounds, equal to about $770,000 of American money.

Of those sent over by charity of the trustees, according to a statement by Dr. Stevens in his history, two-thirds left the Colony and only a few proved worthy of the aid they had received.

Many suffered from malarial fever in the swampy country around Savannah and a majority of the people had the idea that only negroes could live and labor under those conditions. Their discontent was increased by the prohibition against rum and the restriction on land tenures. Believing that they could not compete with South Carolina in the growth of rice, which was produced there by slave labor, and seeing that the silk culture had proved a failure, many went to other colonies where there were no such restrictions. Indentured servants or laborers who came over with a few men of means as a rule left the Colony when their terms of indenture expired and it was difficult to get white help to take their places. Immigration had ceased, money was scarce and labor was high. Farms were neglected and the people were depressed. The only commercial house in Savannah of any importance was that of Harris and Habersham and their shipments at this time were mainly confined to deerskins, lumber, cattle, hogs and poultry.

James Habersham prepared a letter in which he carefully reviewed the condition of the Province, commented upon the unpractical plans of the trustees and suggested changes in their policy. When this letter fell into the hands of the common council of the trustees Mr. Habersham thought it would end his influence with that body and that they would find some way to show him their displeasure, but much to his surprise his strong presentation of the case and effective reasoning attracted their attention and caused serious discussion among them. Instead of incurring their wrath he was made an assistant to the president in Savannah to succeed Samuel Marcer, who was not satisfactory to the trustees.

**Slave Holding Permitted**—Although the trustees had firmly refused to allow the introduction of negro slaves into Georgia and as late as 1748 had adopted a resolution saying that they never would permit it, the growing discontent of the colonists, the continual and almost open violation of the law and the strong statement of Mr. Habersham, caused them to reconsider. Captain McCall is authority for the statement that citizens of Savannah openly bought negroes from slave-traders and that while there were a few seizures a majority of the magistrates favored the introduction of slaves into the colonies, legal decisions were suspended and the courts showed a strong disposition to evade the enforcement of the law.

Several negro servants had been bought for the orphan house and Mr. Habersham, who had charge of it, declared that the institution could not be supported without them. The white servants sent over from England by Mr. Whitefield refused after a few months to perform the menial tasks assigned to them. Many ran away and were supported and secreted in Carolina by friendly countrymen until they could escape farther North, where they would be secure against the conditions of their indentures. Those who remained were too old or too young or too much afflicted by disease to render service sufficient to pay for their food and clothing. Those who had fled soon found they could get land in other colonies on easy terms and engage in work less degrading and more to their advantage.

Much to the mortification of President Stephens his son Thomas was sent to England by landholders in Savannah to secure a redress of grievances from the Crown and the repeal of the law against negro slaves. In doing so he attacked the trustees and appealed to Parliament. The House of Commons took the matter seriously, provided for a hearing and discussed the matter in committee of the whole. That committee exonerated the trustees, but recommended the admission of rum into the Colony.

The influence of James Habersham and Reverend George Whitefield in favor of the introduction of negro slaves into the Colony had great weight with the trustees. Mr. Whitefield boldly asserted that the bringing of Africans from barbarism to a Christian land, where they would be humanely treated and share in the common toil, would be a benefit to them and to the Colony and Mr. Habersham said that the Colony could not prosper without slave labor.

On January 10, 1749, the president and assistants with a number of inhabitants sent the trustees a petition under the official seal of Savannah, suggesting certain restrictions and regulations under which they asked that negro slaves be admitted into the Colony.

After considering this petition the trustees decided to ask the King in council to repeal the act which prohibited the importation and use of black slaves in Georgia, and the Earl of Shaftesbury was made chairman of a committee appointed to prepare an act of repeal.

In reply to the petition from Savannah the trustees sent this communication to the president and assistants of Georgia:

"Georgia Office, July 7, 1749.

"Sir and Gentlemen,—I acquainted you in my Letter dated May 19th last that the Trustees had resolved to petition his Majesty that the Act for rendering the Colony of Georgia more defencible by prohibiting the Importation and Use of black Slaves or Negroes into the same might be repeal'd, and to prepare a Law by which Negroes may be admitted under several Restrictions and Regulations. They have this now under their Consideration, and as you took into Consultation with you upon this Affair several of the principal People of the Colony when you propos'd the Regulations which occurr'd to you, you must assemble such again that they may see the Regulations upon which the Trustees think proper to form the Act, which do not differ widely from those which you transmitted, but there are some additional ones which the Trustees look on as absolutely necessary.

"In the first place they can never lose sight of the colony being a Frontier, of the Danger which must attend too great a disproportion of Blacks and White Men, and the Facility with which the Negroes may make their Escape from Georgia to Augustine. They have resolv'd therefore that every Man who shall have four Male Negroes above the age of 14 shall be obliged to have and constantly keep one indented White Male Servant aged between 20 and 55. If he shall have eight Male Negroes he shall constantly keep two indented White Male Servants of the aforesaid age, and for every four Negroes upward he shall keep one additional White Male Servant of the aforesaid age,—his Sons not to be reckon'd among such White Servants. If any Person having such Numbers of Negroes as aforesaid shall refuse or neglect to provide such Male Servants in proportion within twelve Calender Months, he shall forfeit for every Negro above the Number for which he has White Male Servants so aged, the sum of 10 pounds sterling, and the further sum of 5 pounds sterling each Month after, during which he retains such Negro.

"No artificer shall be suffered to take any Negro as an Apprentice, nor shall any Planter lend or let out a Negro or Negroes to another Planter, to be employ'd otherwise than in manuring and cultivating the Plantations in the Country.

"Proprietors of Negroes shall not be permitted to exercise an unlimited Power over them.

"All Negroes imported into or born in the Province of Georgia shall be registered; and no sale of Negroes from one man to another shall be valid unless registered. Inquisitions shall be made once in every year, or oftener if need be, into the Registers by Juries in the several Districts, who shall immediately afterwards make their Report to the Magistrates.

"As other Provinces have greatly suffer'd by permitting Ships with Negroes to send them on shore when ill of contagious Distempers (as particularly South Carolina has often by the Yellow Fever) proper places must be appointed for such Ships as bring Negroes to Georgia to cast anchor at, in order to their being visited, and to perform such Quarentain as shall be order'd by the President and Assistants, and no Ships must be suffer'd to come nearer than those Places before they are visited by proper Officers and a

Certificate of Health is obtain'd. And in case of any contagious distempers on board, proper places must be appointed at a Distance from the Towns for Lazarettos where the whole Crew of the Ship and the Negroes may be lodg'd and supplied with Refreshments and assisted towards their Recovery. You must acquaint the Trustees by the first Opportunity with the Names and Descriptions of the proper Places for the ships to stop at, and likewise where to perform a Quarentain if there are contagious Distempers on board, that those Places may be specified in the Act.

"No Master shall oblige or even suffer his Negro or Negroes to work on the Lord's Day, but he shall permit or oblige them to attend at some time in that Day for Instruction in the Christian Religion, which the Protestant Ministers of the Gospel must be oblig'd to give them. The Minister or Ministers shall on all occasions inculcate in the Negroes the natural Obligations to a married state where there are Female Slaves cohabiting with them, and an absolute Forbearance of Blaspheming the name of God by Profane Cursing or Swearing. No Inter Marriages between White People and Negroes shall be deem'd lawful Marriages and if any White Man shall be convicted of lying with a Female Negro or any white woman of lying with a male negro He or She shall on such Conviction be . . . . and the Negro shall receive a Corporal Punishment.

"As the Culture of Silk is the great object of the Trustees, and they are determin'd to make it, as far as lyes in their Power, the object of all the People in Georgia by never ratifying any Grants in which the Conditions for planting, fencing, and keeping up the proper Number of Mulberry Trees are not inserted, and by insisting on the forfeiture of all Grants where those Conditions are not perform'd, they have resolv'd that every Man who shall have four Male Negroes, shall be oblig'd to have, for every such four, one Female Negro instructed in the art of winding the silk. The Conditions, as mentioned in my other letter are that 1000 Mulberry Trees shall be planted on every hundred Acres, the same propoertion to be observ'd in less Grants; and that for the Preservation of the Trees against Cattle, the Planter shall fence in his Mulberry Trees or plant them in Places already fenc'd.

"As there are several Publick Works which are absolutely necessary, such as maintaining the Light-house, providing for the Pilot and Pilot Boat, the Repairs of the Church, the Wharf, and the Prison, and building Lazarettos, and other publick Services such as the Support of the Ministers when other Supports shall fail, and several officers of Civil Government, as Constables, Tythingmen &c, and as some Funds will be requisite for these, the Trustees think nothing can be more reasonable than a Duty upon Negroes at Importation, and an annual Tax P Head upon the Possession of them, which Tax and Duty must be paid, for the use of the Trust, into the hands of proper persons appointed by the Trustees. It will therefore be requisite for you in your Consultation to consider what Duty and Tax may, in your opinion, be proper for the aforesaid Services, and other necessary public Uses of the

MEADOW GARDEN, AUGUSTA, HOME OF GEORGE WALTON, ONE OF THE SIGNERS

Colony, and transmit your opinion hereon under the Seal as before, by the first opportunity.

"I am, Sir, and Gentlemen

"Your very humble Servant BENJ. MARTYN Secy."

"To Wm. Stephens, Esq, President
and the Assistants.

"By the Charlestown Galley." Capt. Bogg.

**Suggestions of the Trustees Accepted**—On receipt of the foregoing communication from the secretary of the trustees a convention of the colonists was called and Major Horton the military commander of the Colony presided. The suggestions of the trustees were substantially adopted and on October 26, 1749, a communication was signed by twenty-seven leading men of the Province asking that slavery be at once allowed with the limitations proposed by the trustees. This document with a few changes and additions was approved. Among the changes was the penalty of ten pounds to be paid by every master who either forced or permitted his negro slaves to work on the Sabbath or failed to compel his slaves to attend on Sunday some place of instruction in the Christian religion. He should be fined five pounds for each such neglect on conviction.

**Soldiers Cared For**—General Oglethorpe's regiment was disbanded at Frederica on May 29, 1749, but one company was retained for the defense of the Province. Those of the soldiers mustered out of service who wished to remain in Georgia received the land allotted to them according to a promise made by the trustees when they enlisted. Others who preferred to go to England were transported there by way of Charleston at the expense of the general government.

**Rum Admitted**—About the same time the House of Commons repealed the act which prohibited the introduction into Georgia of rum and other distilled liquor. They also repealed sumptuary laws which forbade the use of gold and silver in apparel, furniture and equipage.

**Restrictions on Land Tenure Removed**—In the infancy of the colony, when it was threatened with invasion by the Spaniards and Indians who sympathized with the Spaniards, the trustees thought it necessary to limit the tenure of land, which was granted only by tail male. Their idea was that by this restriction there would be an able bodied man to do military service with every lot of land granted.

The Colony now being at peace and the danger of invasion having passed by, the trustees thought the time had come to remove the restrictions on tenures and make the grant of land in fee simple. Accordingly they made public the following resolution:

"GEORGIA OFFICE, WESTMINSTER,

"May 25th, 1750.

"Whereas the Trustees for establishing the Colony of Georgia in America, thought it necessary to the first establishment of that Colony to restrain the Grants they made of Lots of Land to limited Tenures only, in order thereby to prevent many abuses which at that time might probably have defeated the good ends proposed by that establishment and during the late War it might have been of dangerous consequence to have alter'd the Tenures, but as a general peace and tranquillity happily prevail, the said Trustees are of opinion that the intended enlargement of the Tenures may now be safely made, and have come to the following resolution, viz:

"That the Tenures of all Grants of Land whatsoever already made to any person within the Province of Georgia be enlarged and extended to an absolute Inheritance, and that all the future Grants of Land shall be of an absolute Inheritance to the Grantees, their Heirs and Assigns."

**Discontinuance of Sola Bills**—The development of trade in the Colony and with other colonies or the home country was retarded by the use of sola bills which were the currency of the province. These were bills of exchange issued by the trustees and used by the officials of the Colony in making payment. At first the trustees sent over English coin which was paid to officers of the trust and through them paid out and put in circulation. At one time they ordered a thousand pounds in silver sent over. At another two tons of half pence were shipped to Georgia. To furnish currency of larger amount the trustees issued the sola bills which were simply the agreement of the trustees to pay the amount stated in the face of the bill thirty days after sight. They were issued for five, ten, twenty and forty pounds. The trustees paid them promptly and when at the expiration of their charter 1,149 pounds of sola bills had not been returned for payment the common council deposited that sum in the hands of Mr. Lloyd, a reputable silk merchant of London, who agreed to redeem them when presented, and public notice was given in American papers, requiring that these bills be presented before the first of January, 1756.

Dr. Stevens said in his history that the sola bills did not circulate well in other colonies and for that reason their use was an obstacle to the growth of commerce. When the bills were presented for payment and redeemed they were cancelled in the presence of one member of the common council and two trustees. A careful record was made of all bills issued and redeemed. In this and other financial affairs the trustees showed great care, prudence and economy.

Herewith is a copy of one of those sola bills:

"Georgia Bill of Exchange A. No. 1.
Payable in England. Westminster, 24th July, 1735.

Thirty days after sight, we, the Trustees for Establishing the Colony of Georgia in America, promise to pay this, our Sola Bill of Exchange, to James

Oglethorpe, Esq., or his order, the sum of one pound sterling, at our office at Westminster, to answer the like value received by him in Georgia, on the issue hereof, as testified by indorsement herein signed by himself.

Sealed by order of the Common Council of the said Trustees for establishing the Colony of Georgia in America."

# CHAPTER XXX.

## *Return of Prosperity*

James Habersham, who had come to Savannah in May, 1738, with Reverend George Whitefield and was later in active charge of the Bethesda Orphan House founded by Whitefield, was also a wise man of affairs and successful in business. The house of Harris and Habersham, in which he was an active partner, did much to develop the commerce of Georgia with the American colonies and Great Britain.

At first their business was mostly with New York, Philadelphia and Boston, but in 1747 they began to export Georgia products to London. In a letter to Secretary Martyn of the Board of Trustees they wrote:

"We have ordered our correspondent, Mr. John Nickelson, in Mansfield Street, Goodman's Fields London, to charter us a small ship to be loaded here next winter with what may offer."

According to Dr. William B. Stevens this was the first ship chartered by a mercantile house in Georgia to be laden with products for England, and by this vessel they sent nearly $10,000 worth of products to the Mother Country.

Their main exports then were pitch, tar, rice and deer skins, but they hoped by furnishing an easy and practical medium of communication to encourage the growth of indigo and by adding that to Georgia products to bring to this Colony a large part of a million dollars which England paid yearly to France for that article.

They had to overcome serious difficulties in developing commerce. "Agriculture," says Stevens, "was neglected, rice plantations could not be tilled and the whole product of the colony was not enough for its own consumption and several articles of food had to be supplied from South Carolina. The Indian trade was unsettled and fluctuating. Its principal article was skins and those brought to Savannah had to be shipped to Charleston at a cost of seven shillings sixpence a hundred pounds. There they had to be entered at the Custom House and pay a duty of a shilling per skin, making a total of duty and freight nearly thirty shillings per hogshead."

The object of Harris and Habersham was to establish commercial intercourse with other places and induce the people to give more attention to agriculture so that the products would be increased to exportable quantity. They also sought to draw to Savannah the products and trade of planters in South

Carolina along the Savannah River, and by enlarging the trade of Savannah to ship direct to England, avoiding the burdensome expense for freight and duty on products shipped through Charleston. By furnishing a direct outlet for products through Savannah and inducing ships to call there they would build up the industries of a seaport, employing artisans there and securing a large revenue for the Colony from that source.

This far-reaching and wise policy was rewarded with success and the aggressive operations of this firm were a great aid to the Colony and added to its wealth.

This result is shown by a letter of James Habersham in which he said:

### The Return of Prosperity.

"My present thoughts are that the colony never had a better appearance of thriving than now. There have been more vessels loaded here within these ten months than have been since the colony was settled. Our exportations for a year past are an evident proof, that if proper labouring hands could have been had years before, this colony before now would have demonstrated its utility to the mother country and the West India Islands. Two days ago a large ship arrived here, addressed to my partner and I, which is the fifth sea vessel which has been here to load within a year; more, I may affirm, than has ever been loaded in this colony before, since its first settlement, with its real produce."

**A Provincial Assembly Established**—On July 26, 1750, Henry Parker was commissioned vice-president of Georgia and James Habersham was made secretary. On that day provision was made for an assembly of the people of the Colony to "propose, debate and represent for the Trustees what shall appear to them to be for the benefit not only of each particular settlement, but of the Province in general."

That was the beginning of legislative action in Georgia. By authority of the trustees writs of election were issued for the choice of delegates to a Provincial Assembly to convene in Savannah on January 15, 1751. A list of the sixteen delegates elected and an account of the proceedings of the Assembly appears in another chapter. Of that body Francis Harris was Speaker.

On April 8, 1751, Henry Parker was appointed president to succeed Colonel William Stephens, who had retired on a pension of eighty pounds a year. Noble Jones was made register of the Province and Pickering Robinson and Francis Harris were made assistants to the president.

A strong effort to revive the silk industry was made early in Mr. Parker's administration as the trustees expected large results from that source. Pickering Robinson had been sent to Europe to learn the best method of propagating silk-worms, managing filatures and preparing silk for market and on his return he was given general charge of the industry with a salary of one hundred pounds a year and twenty-five pounds for a clerk. James Habersham was made a commissioner to act with Mr. Pickering. The latter brought a quantity of silk-worm eggs, but a very few could be vitalized. A filature as a school of instruction to teach the people silk culture was established at Savannah in a board building twenty by thirty-six feet with a loft on which green cocoons were spread. It was completed by April 1, 1751, and reeling began in May. To encourage the colonists in this industry the trustees offered to pay one shilling six pence to two shillings four pence per pound for green cocoons and wind them at the expense of the trust.

As that offer was not satisfactory, Robinson and Habersham on the 26th of April raised the offer to two shillings a pound for the best cocoons, and one shilling three pence for those of inferior quality. For raw silk of the best quality they offered twelve shillings a pound and for silk of double cocoons six shillings a pound. These were considered extravagant prices, offered in the hope of building up the industry, but the result was disappointing. After spending 1,500 pounds, or $7,500 of American money, the trustees up to the time when they surrendered their charter, in 1752, had succeeded in producing only a thousand pounds of raw silk. It was a costly experiment, made with persistence and large expenditure because the trustees believed in its success, that England would be saved 500,000 pounds (equal to $2,500,000), and that employment would be given to forty thousand of the English people.

**An Attempt to Subordinate Georgia to South Carolina**—The Georgia Assembly, which met in Savannah in 1751, submitted to the trustees an address concerning the magistracy, Indian affairs, the introduction of negroes, silk culture, the continuance of the charter and other matters. An important feature was "Objections to annexing Georgia to South Carolina." The reason for that utterance was an attempt made two years before to quarter soldiers under an officer at Frederica with no authority from Georgia officials by a man representing that he would report only to the Governor of South Carolina.

In 1749, when General Oglethorpe's regiment was disbanded at Frederica and some of the released soldiers were sent to England by way of Charleston, Captain Daniel Demetree with a detachment of ten or twelve men from South Carolina landed at Causton's Bluff, where he told some of the people that he was on his way to Frederica and would take command at that place. As he did not report to the president or his assistants and did not inform them of his orders or his intentions, they did not understand his conduct and ordered Captain Noble Jones to wait on him and demand an explanation and an apology for his discourtesy. Captain Demetree told Captain Jones that he was acting under instructions from his Grace, the Duke of Bedford, communicated with the consent of the trustees, and that he was to receive orders from and report only to the Governor of South Carolina. He reluctantly appeared before the council in answer to its summons. Governor Stephens wrote the trustees a communication in which he intimated that Governor Glen's influence had been improperly exerted on the Duke of Bedford and that the intention seemed to be either to lower the dignity of Georgia or place that province under the control of South Carolina. Also that the small force Captain Demetree brought with him would be of little use under his control and none at all if subject to the orders of the Governor of South Carolina.

It appears that the expediency of subordinating Georgia to South Carolina had been seriously discussed in some quarters. Some even proposed that Georgia be merged in South Carolina. The trustees protested at the suggestion and claimed their vested rights. That put a quietus on the attempt to subordinate Georgia.

President Stephens directed the troops and the citizens at Frederica to seize the boats which Captain Demetree had in charge, hold them as the property of Oglethorpe's regiment and until further orders to take no notice of the captain in either a civil or a military capacity. A copy of this letter of instructions and a statement of Captain Demetree's conduct were sent to Governor Glen.

When, in 1751, the trustees received from the Georgia Assembly its protest against the proposed annexation to South Carolina they made the following statement, which was filed with the papers of the Earl of Shaftesbury in the Public Record Office at London:

"As the Assembly of the Province of Georgia have set forth in a Representation dated January 15th, 1751, that the annexing of this Province to South Carolina will soon reduce it to the same desolate condition in which the Southern Parts of South Carolina was before the Establishment of Georgia the trustees think it their Duty in behalf of the People to represent the same to your Lordships; and the Assembly having given us one Reason for this, the great Distance they are at from Charles-Town, and consequently the hazards and intolerable Expence and Inconveniences of attending so remote a Seat of Government as Representatives, and Seat of Justice as Jurymen or Clarks, the Trustees think it incumbent on them to state to your Lordships that the nearest Part of Georgia is at least 80 Miles by Land and 100 Miles by Water from Charles-Town, that the Travellers by Land have many Rivers to cross, and the Roads thro' the Southern Parts of Carolina are in the Winter almost impassable: That the Passage by water is over sounds which in winter are very dangerous, and Boats must be hired at a great expence for this Passage, and that many of the Inhabitants of Georgia in the Southern parts are above 170 miles by land and above 200 miles by water from Charles-Town.

"Another objection which the Trustees beg leave to mention to your Lordships is the jealousy which some of the Charles-Town Merchants have of the Town of Savannah, becoming from the superior fitness of its situation the great Mart for the Indian Trade, to prevent which they will distress the present Inhabitants of Georgia, by all the means in their power, and particularly by reviving old claims to large tracts of Land in Georgia which they never did cultivate and which the Indians would never suffer them to cultivate. By getting these they must dispossess great Numbers of the Inhabitants of Lands which they have long been in possession of and have cultivated under his Majesty's Charter, and this will consequently expose the Inhabitants of South Carolina to another Indian War for the same reasons that that Province was involved in one in the Year 1718 when the Indians laid South Carolina in a manner waste with fire and sword.

"The Trustees think it needless to observe to your Lordships that annexing the Colony is absolutely repugnant to his Majesty's Charter which does expressly declare that it shall be a separate and independent Province and that the Inhabitants shall not be subject to the Laws of South Carolina.

"As the Trustees' Power of governing the Colony will expire on the 9th of June, 1753, but their Trust for granting the Lands is to remain in them, and their successors (to be chosen by them) forever; and as these two Powers being unconnected, and independent of each other may be attended with many unforseen difficulties, the Trustees are ready to accommodate the Administration with a surrender of their Trust on such Terms as they think themselves obliged, in behalf of the People, to stipulate for, which Terms they are ready to offer to his Majesty's Council.

"As the Trustees ought not to surrender their Trust but on such Conditions only as will secure to the Inhabitants of Georgia those Rights and Privileges which were promised them at their first going thither, they hope if such surrender is not accepted of, that for the security of their large property in the Lands as Trustees, they shall be allowed the Alternative, viz of recommending to his Majesty the Persons to be employed in the Government of Georgia."

Colonel Charles C. Jones comments on this incident, as follows, in his history:

"This project for the annexation of Georgia to South Carolina originated with the citizens and friends of the latter province. Among Georgians it was regarded with extreme disfavor. So manifestly unjust was it and so thoroughly at variance with the provisions of the charter, the scheme of the colonization, and the vested rights both of the trustees and of the colonists, that so soon as it was seriously considered it was heartily repudiated."

**Another Effort by the Bosomworths**—On the 9th of February, 1751, the day after the Colonial Assembly adjourned, Thomas Bosomworth and his wife Mary came from St. Catherine's Island and addressed to the Vice-President a long letter, renewing her claim for compensation, complaining that an injustice had been done her and endeavoring to justify her conduct in claiming the country. She said that if her rights were not granted by the President and Council she would go to England and submit her statement and her claim to the King. For that purpose she demanded of the President money to pay her expenses.

The Council took no notice of her communication, believing that this course would impress the Indian chiefs with her insignificance.

Bosomworth sold his wife's claim to land and improvements between Savannah and Pipe Maker's Creek and her house and lot in town to raise money for the expense of going to England.

On the way to Charleston, where he was to go on board a ship he had his conveyance from the Indians proved before a justice of peace in Greenville County, South Carolina, and recorded by William Pinkney, Secretary of State. Thus equipped he embarked for England.

In view of this development the trustees directed Patrick Graham, Agent for Indian Affairs, to carefully inquire of the kings and chiefs of the Creek nation whether the islands of Ossabaw, St. Catherine and Sapelo had been, by their knowledge or consent, sold and conveyed to Thomas and Mary Bosomworth, and if such sale had not been made to purchase those islands from the Indians for the trustees. Graham made careful inquiry, satisfied himself that the Indians were entirely ignorant of the alleged sale to the Bosomworths and made the purchase for the trustees as he had been instructed.

Soon after this Adam Bosomworth, a brother of Thomas, went into the Creek nation and prevailed on the Indians to sign another conveyance to his brother, which was also proved and sent over to England.

The opinion of the best counsel of England was taken on the case and the matter was litigated in the courts of Great Britain for twelve years. An Indian council was held at Augusta in December, 1755, for the purpose of investigating this subject.

In the year 1759 the Court of St. James's made a decision granting to Bosomworth and his wife the island of St. Catherine, and instructions were given to sell the other two islands and the tract of country adjoining Savannah at auction and out of the proceeds of the sale, extinguish all claims of Bosomworth and his wife, first obtaining a general release and acquittance, renouncing all further claims, pretention or demand, report the procedure and hold the surplus subject to the order of the Crown.

In conformity with these instructions the lands were advertised for sale on the premises on December 10, 1759. Isaac Levy entered a protest against the sale, claiming that he had purchased most of the land in question from Bosomworth and his wife, and had petitioned the King for justice. The sale was suspended and a new suit was instituted in England by Levy. He died not long after, and McCall says his case was never legally decided. Bosomworth took possession of and resided on St. Catherine's Island, where Mary died sometime afterward, and he married a chambermaid.

**Militia Organized**—Carrying out his promise to the Assembly the government of President Parker on the sixteenth of April, 1751, undertook to organize the militia of the Province. This was important and necessary, because General Oglethorpe's regiment had been disbanded, there were few military organizations in the Province, and the citizens had to rely on themselves for protection of the frontiers against the Indians and for police duty at home.

Under the plan adopted by the President and assistants all adult white male inhabitants who owned three hundred acres or more of land were ordered to appear with horses and well equipped to be organized as cavalry. White male citizens with less property were armed as infantry. The militia so formed was organized in four companies, one of cavalry and three of infantry, numbering in all three hundred men. The first general muster in the lower district was held at Savannah on Tuesday the 13th of June, 1751, with 220 men of infantry and cavalry, armed and equipped. They paraded under the command of Captain Noble Jones and made a fine appearance.

Populous districts which had no established courts were given conservators of the peace. In this way Captain John McIntosh was appointed for Darien, Audley Maxwell for the district of Midway and the great Ogeechee, and James Fraser for Augusta. Each conservator of the peace, with the assistance of three reputable freeholders in his neighborhood was given power to hold what might have been called a justice's court to try small misdemeanors and decide civil suits involving not more than forty shillings. The courts at Savannah and Frederica were held regularly to act upon weightier matters, both civil and criminal.

**Threat of an Indian Invasion**—The fortifications at Augusta were in bad condition and afforded little protection to the inhabitants. In the spring time when the people were busy on their farms they were alarmed by the threat of an Indian uprising. About the middle of May, 1751, a message from Augusta sent by Patrick Graham to Savannah gave the information that James Maxwell and a number of Indian traders who had fled from the Cherokees to save their lives had just reached Augusta. They said two traders had been murdered and they had been robbed of all their goods. It was feared that the Indians would soon be on the warpath. Fleeing from their plantations the people of Augusta and the vicinity sought refuge in a church. Detachments of mounted militia were sent in every direction, but no traces of the enemy could be found.

Suspecting that the whole affair might be a trick of the traders to bring on a war with the Indians and so screen themselves from the payment of their debts, the President and his assistants decided that the wise course was to place the Colony in a position of defense. The magazine was examined and officers were ordered to muster the militia and put it under discipline. Noble Jones was appointed colonel and Noble W. Jones who had been a cadet in Oglethorpe's regiment was given command of a troop of cavalry. Bourquin and Francis were commissioned as captains of infantry. Captain McIntosh, at Darien, and officers at Frederica and on Cumberland Island were warned of the impending danger. The Governor of South Carolina strengthened his outpost in the neighborhood of the Cherokees and supplied Fort Moore with ammunition. It transpired later that some young Cherokees had insulted some traders because they did not bring the Indians a large supply of ammunition. They said the Cherokees were threatened with an attack by the Notteweges, who were in alliance with the French.

It was suspected that the Cherokees had been seduced by the French, and sought a pretext to declare war against Georgia and Carolina. Not long afterward the Cherokees and Notteweges were found to be friends, attacking the Uchees. Bands of Indians wandered near the settlements, coming within a few miles of Savannah, and created much alarm, but the disturbances soon ceased and the Colony escaped the horrors of savage warfare.

**The Trustees Surrender Their Charter**—As the time approached for the trustees to surrender their charter, which under its terms would expire on the 9th of June, 1753, they became convinced that the resources at their command were not sufficient to meet the civil and military expense of the Colony and do all that was necessary for its prosperity. They, therefore, in April, 1751, appointed a committee of twelve with the Earl of Shaftesbury as chairman to adjust with the general government of England proper means for supporting and settling the Colony and take such measures as might be necessary for its well being. This committee was authorized to act for the trustees, use the seal of the corporation, and present to the Privy Council of England such memorial as they thought appropriate to carry out the intentions of the trustees.

Acting under this charge the committee through a sub-committee composed of the Earl of Shaftesbury and Messrs. Hooker, Vernon, Tracy, Frederick and Lloyd prepared the following memorial:

"To the Right Honorable the Lords of His Majesty's most Honorable Privy Council:

"The Trustees for establishing the Colony of Georgia in America, who are ready for the service of the Crown to surrender their Trust for granting the Lands in the said Colony, think it their indispensable duty to offer the following considerations to your Lordships on behalf of the People settled there.

"That the Colony of Georgia be confirmed a separate and independent Province as it is expressly declared in his Majesty's Charter it shall be, in confidence of which the Inhabitants both British and Foreign, have gone thither, and as the Assembly of the Province of Georgia have petitioned for in a representation to the Trustees dated January the 15th, 1750.

"That the Inhabitants of the Colony be confirmed in their titles and possessions which have been granted to them under the Charter.

"That the arrears of Quit Rents, due at this time, be remitted, since most of the Inhabitants have been prevented by the war and the various obstacles that always occur at the first settling of a Colony from cultivating so much of their Lands as it might be expected they would have done, and that the Quit Rents for the future be reduced from four to two shillings for each hundred acres, this last sum being as much as is usually reserved in any of his Majesty's Provinces in America.

"That as there will be occasion for a Secretary or Agent in England to transact the affairs of the Province here, and to carry on the Correspondence with the Government in Georgia, and as the Trustees' Secretary, Mr. Martyn, has served them ably and faithfully in that capacity from the very date of the Charter, and is much better acquainted with the State of the Colony than any other person residing in England, and as the Trustees have the greatest reason to believe it will be very agreeable and encouraging to the People there, they humbly desire your Lordships will be the means of recommending him to his Majesty for the said employment, with such an appointment as may be thought proper."

This having been submitted to the Lords of the Privy Council and they having taken counsel of the Commissioners of the Treasury and the Commissioners of Trade and Plantations replied that they could not advise the King to recommend to Parliament granting any money to the body of the trustees unless they wished to make an absolute surrender of the charter.

Upon this the committee made the following reply in writing:

"We, whose names are here underwritten, being a Committee appointed by the Common Council of the Trustees for establishing the Colony of Georgia in America, and being fully authorized by them, do hereby signify that we are ready and willing to make an absolute surrender of all the powers, rights, and trusts vested in the said Trustees by his Majesty's Royal Charter bearing date the 9th day of June, 1732, without any condition or limitation, humbly recommending the Rights and Privileges of the Inhabitants of the said Colony to his Majesty's most gracious protection.

SHAFTESBURY,
ROBT. TRACY,
JOHN FREDERICK,
SAML. LLOYD,
EDWARD HOOPER."

The Privy Council referred this reply to the Attorney General and Solicitor, who recommended that a deed of conveyance from the trustees to the King be executed for all the property which had been conveyed to them in 1732, and that they also convey to the Crown the one-eighth interest in that territory which had been conveyed to them by Lord Carteret.

On January 8, 1752, the Earl of Shaftesbury reported to the trustees what had been done and the trustees approved it and voted thanks to the committee, especially for asking that the Crown care for the rights and privileges of the colonists. The committee was empowered to complete the transfer.

The last meeting of the trustees was held on the 23rd of June, 1752, when a copy of the conveyance to the Crown of the Territory of Georgia was submitted, approved and sealed with the seal of the trustees to be exchanged for a statement under the Great Seal signifying His Majesty's acceptance of the surrender and grant.

**The Deed of Surrender**—The trustees' deed of surrender is a long and carefully prepared document, giving the history of the creation, nature, and powers of the trust and the acquisition of all lands within the Province. So much of the deed as refers to the cession of the property, rights and franchises held by the trustees is here reproduced:

"Now this Indenture witnesseth that the said Trustees for establishing the Colony of Georgia in America for themselves and their successors have for the considerations and motives aforesaid, and for divers other good considerations them thereunto moving, granted, surrendered, and yielded up, and by these presents do for themselves and their successors grant, surrender, and yield up unto his said most Excellent Majesty, his heirs and successors, the said recited Letters Patent, and their said Corporation, and all right, title, and authority to be or continue a Corporate Body, and all the Powers of government, and all other Powers, Jurisdictions, Franchises, Preheminences and Privileges therein and thereby granted or conveyed to them: and have granted and do hereby grant unto his said Majesty, his heirs and successors, all the said lands, Countrys, Territorys and Premises, as well the said one eighth part thereof granted, meant, or intended to be granted by the said John Lord Carteret, to them as aforesaid, as also the said seven eighths part thereof granted, meant, or intended to be granted as aforesaid, in and by his said Majesty's Letters Patent or Charter above recited, together with all the soils, grounds, havens, ports, gulphs and bays, mines, as well Royall mines of Gold and Silver as other minerals, precious stones, quarries, woods, rivers, waters, fishings, as well Royall Fishings of Whale and Sturgeon, as other fishings, Pearles, Commodities, Jurisdictions, Royalties, Franchises, Privileges and Preheminences, with the said Territories and the Precincts thereof and thereunto in any sort belonging or appertaining, and all other the Premises, and all rents, reversions, remainders, and other profits reserved, due, or payable, or which may happen upon or by virtue of any demise or grant heretofore made of the premises of any part thereof, and all their estates, rights, title, interest, claim or demand whatsoever of or to the said premises and every part thereof: To Have and to Hold all and singular the premises to his said Majesty, his heirs and successors, to the use of his said Majesty his heirs and successors, subject nevertheless, and without prejudice to all such grants, leases, contracts, estates and interests in law or equity as have been heretofore lawfully made or granted by the said Trustees for establishing the Colony of Georgia in America, or by any acting in authority under them in America, and which are now subsisting according to the said Letters Patent, which said surrender and grant his said most excellent Majesty hath accepted, and by these presents for himself, his heirs and successors doth accept. In witness whereof to one part of this Indenture remaining with the Trustees for establishing the Colony of Georgia in America his said most excellent Majesty has caused his Great Seal to be affixed, and to the other part thereof, remaining with his said Majesty, the said Trustees and with the privity and by direction of the Common Council of the Corporation have caused their common seal to be affixed," etc.

This deed of surrender, having been read and considered, was approved of by the trustees, and the seal of the corporation was affixed to it on the 23rd of June, 1752. The seal was thereupon defaced, and the trustees ceased to exist as a body corporate.

**Leaders of the Trustees**—Of the seventy-two trustees a third were noblemen distinguished by birth, official position and zeal for the general welfare. The others were clergymen, members of Parliament, officers of the army, eminent lawyers and large merchants. When the charter was surrendered only these six of the original trustees remained: General Oglethorpe, James Vernon, Rev. Dr. Burton, Rev. Samuel Smith, Mr. Anderson, and Dr. Hales.

Next to Oglethorpe, James Vernon gave most attention to the affairs of the Colony as both a trustee and a member of the common council. Through him most of the negotiations with German and other foreign Protestants were carried on.

Benjamin Martyn, the secretary of the trustees from their first year to the last, conducted their voluminous correspondence and published several valuable works in defence of the trustees under the titles:

"An impartial inquiry into the state and utility of the Province of Georgia."

"Reasons for Establishing The Colony of Georgia."

"An Account showing the Progress of the Colony of Georgia in America from Its Establishment."

He had already a literary reputation as the author of several works before his connection with the trustees and was a member of the Society For the Encouragement of Learning.

The trustees showed their appreciation of his services by the adoption of a resolution testifying of his faithful service and suggesting his appointment to represent the Colony as its agent in London. He was so appointed and served the Colony many years under the Royal Government.

**The Inter-Regnum**—When the trustees had surrendered their charter the Colony of Georgia would have been left without a government if some provision had not been made for a temporary administration to conduct the affairs of the Colony until a permanent form of government could be constituted. To meet that emergency and give time to frame a suitable government the Lords Justices of England, with the advice of the Privy Council, issued a proclamation to the effect that until the King should see fit to establish another form of government for Georgia all civil and military officers of the Colony holding office under the trustees should continue in their respective positions and receive such compensation as they had been receiving.

They were admonished to be diligent and faithful in the performance of their duties and the colonists were instructed to render them obedience and assistance. As recommended by the trustees Benjamin Martyn was appointed agent for the Colony in England.

On the death of Henry Parker, Patrick Graham succeeded him as president of Georgia and James Habersham, Noble Jones, Pickering Robinson and Francis Harris were appointed his assistants.

The Colony was then under the Board of Trade and Plantations and the president and his assistants reported to them in a letter written April 11, 1753, that the population of Georgia by a recent count was 2,381 whites and 1,061 blacks, besides the King's troops and boatmen then in the Colony. It did not include the Midway congregation coming from South Carolina, with 281 whites and 536 negro slaves, located in the Midway Settlement, or Butler's Colony, with 60 slaves.

The president and assistants also reported six vessels at the Savannah wharves loading for London and American ports.

Joseph Ottolenghe, who had learned in Italy to conduct filatures, was to succeed Pickering Robinson as manager of silk culture. For the support of that industry and to buy presents for friendly Indians, the Board of Trade and Plantations was asked for money.

**The Plan for Royal Government**—On March 5, 1754, the Commissioners of Trade and Plantations submitted this plan for a civil government in Georgia:

"That of the different Constitutions now subsisting in his Majesty's Dominions in America that form of Government established by the Crown in such of the Colonies as are more immediately subject to its direction and government appears to us the most proper form of Government for the Province of Georgia.

"We should therefore propose that a Governor should be appointed by Commission under the Great Seal in like manner as the Governors of his Majesty's other Colonies and Plantations are appointed, with powers and directions to call an Assembly to pass laws, to erect Courts of Judicature, to grant lands, and to do all other necessary and proper things in such manner and under such regulations as shall, upon due consideration, appear to be the best adapted to the present circumstances of the Colony, all of which matters as well as every other regulation necessary to be made for the better ordering and government the Colony conformable to the plan proposed, will come under consideration when we shall receive his Majesty's directions to prepare instructions for the Governor, &c.

"We would likewise propose that twelve persons should be appointed by His Majesty to be his Council of the said Colony, with the same powers, authorities, and privileges as are given to or enjoyed by the Council of his Majesty's other Colonies.

"That the Governor be appointed Vice-Admiral of the said Colony, with the same powers and authorities as are usually given to the Governors of other his Majesty's Colonies, and that he, together with such other Officers as shall be thought proper to be appointed, do constitute a Court of Admiralty for the regulation of matters subject to the Admiralty jurisdiction.

"That proper officers be appointed for the better collecting and regulating his Majesty's Customs and Duties, and for other matters, subject to the Jurisdiction of the Lords Commissioners of his Majesty's Treasury and the Commissioners of the Customs.

"That for matters relative to his Majesty's revenue of Quit Rents and Grants of Land, there be appointed a Register and Receiver of Quit Rents, and a Surveyor of Lands.

"That a Secretary be appointed for the transaction of all affairs, usually belonging to the Office of Secretary in the other Colonies, such as registering of Deeds and keeping the Public Records, and who may likewise act as Clerk of the Council.

"It will also be necessary that a Provost Marshal should be appointed to execute the office of Sheriff until the Province is divided into counties. And we would further propose that an Attorney General should be appointed to assist the Governor and Council in matters of Law which may come before them in their Judicial capacity.

"These are all the establishments which appear to us necessary to be immediately made, the charge whereof, including an allowance heretofore usually given by the Trustees to a Minister and two Schoolmasters, the contingent charges of government, and the bounty upon the culture and produce of Silk will, at a moderate computation, amount to about three thousand pounds per annum during the infancy of the Colony and until it shall be in a condition to bear the expence of its own establishment."

This plan was approved and the Commissioners of Trade and Plantations were directed to nominate suitable and qualified men for the offices named. Their nominations were adopted and these gentlemen were appointed by the King on August 6, 1754, for the Government of Georgia.

### First Officers of the Royal Government.

Captain John Reynolds, Governor.
William Clifton, Attorney-General.
James Habersham, Secretary and Register of Records.
Alexander Kellet, Provost Marshal.
William Russell, Naval Officer.
Henry Yonge and William DeBrahm, Surveyors of land in Georgia with salaries of 50 pounds each.
Sir Patrick Houstoun, Baronet, Receiver of quit rents and Register of Grants, with 50 pounds salary.

### The Council.

Members of the Council were appointed as follows:

Patrick Graham
Sir Patrick Houstoun
James Habersham
Alexander Kellet
William Clifton
Noble Jones
Pickering Robinson
Francis Harris
Jonathan Bryan
William Russell

Clement Martin was added later

# CHAPTER XXXI.

## *Royal Government*

Where the trustees had made few laws and delegated little power to those who conducted the affairs of the Colony, the Royal Government gave large powers to the Governor and other officers appointed by the Crown, and the system of government, executive, legislative and judicial was elaborate compared with that under the trustees.

The official title of Governor Reynolds was:

Captain-General and Governor-in-Chief of His Majesty's Province of Georgia and Vice-Admiral of the Same.

He was addressed as "Your Excellency."

"The Governor," says Colonel Jones, "was in the colony the highest representative of the King, enjoying prerogatives which within a limited jurisdiction and in modified degree, savored of royalty." As captain-general he commanded all land and naval forces appertaining to the province and appointed all officers of the militia. As Governor-in-Chief, he was one of the constituent parts of the General Assembly, possessing the sole power of convening, adjourning, proroguing and dissolving that body. It rested with him to approve or veto any bill passed by the council and the assembly.

All officers who did not receive their warrants directly from the Crown were appointed by him; and if vacancies occurred by death or removal in offices usually filled by the immediate nomination of His Majesty, the appointees of the Governor acted until the pleasure of the home government was promulgated. Until superseded they received the profits and emoluments appertaining to the stations they were called upon respectively to fill. He was custodian of the great seal and, as Chancellor, exercised within the province powers of judicature similar to those reposed in the High Chancellor of England. He presided in the Court of Errors composed of himself and the members of council as judges, hearing and determining all appeals from Superior Courts.

As ordinary he collated to all vacant beneficences, granted probate of wills and allowed administration upon the estates of those dying intestate.

By him were writs issued for the election of representatives to sit in the Commons House of Assembly.

As vice-admiral, while he did not sit in the Court of Vice-Admiralty—a judge for that court being usually appointed in England—in time of war he issued warrants to that court empowering it to grant commissions to privateers.

With him reposed a power to pardon all crimes save treason and murder. It was optional with him to select as his residence such locality within the limits of the province as he regarded most convenient for the transaction of the public business, and he might direct the assembling of the General Assembly at that point. He was invested with authority, for just cause, to suspend any member of council, and in a word to "Do all other necessary and proper things, in such manner and under such regulations as should, upon due consideration appear to be best adapted to the circumstances of the Colony."

The King's council consisted of twelve ordinary members and two others appointed by the Crown to hold office during the King's pleasure. When by death or absence the number of councilors was less than seven the Governor was authorized to fill vacancies up to that number until the King's pleasure was known.

In the event of the Governor's death or absence from Georgia, the administration of affairs devolved upon the Lieutenant-Governor who was addressed as "His Honor." While in charge of the government he was to have half the salary and fees paid to the Governor, but when the Governor was present the Lieutenant-Governor had no compensation.

If both the Governor and the Lieutenant-Governor were dead or absent the senior member of the Council administered the government with the same compensation as that given the Lieutenant-Governor, when acting in place of the Governor. The two extraordinary members of Council, who were the Surveyor-General of Customs and the Superintendent-General of Indian Affairs, could not preside in the absence of the Governor or the Lieutenant-Governor.

When sitting with the Legislature the Council was called the Upper House of Assembly. It also acted as Privy Council to the Governor, assisting him with advice in conducting the government. As an Upper House of Assembly, or as a Privy Council, five members made a quorum, if that many were present. In an emergency three could transact business. The Council met when the Governor called them and on such occasions the Governor presided and suggested matters for consideration and advice.

When sitting as an Upper House members of the Council met when the Commons House of Assembly was convened and were presided over by the Lieutenant-Governor if he was a member of Council and present, or in his absence by the senior member present, and the procedure followed the forms used in the British House of Lords with the exception that no member could make a proxy and there could be no adjournment during the session of Legislature for a longer period than from Saturday to Monday.

The qualification of voters was ownership of fifty acres of land in the parish or district where the voter resided and voted. The qualification of a

COTTON WHARF IN SAVANNAH HARBOR

Representative was the ownership of five hundred acres of land in any part of the Province.

Writs of election were issued by order of the Governor in Council under the great seal of the Province, were attested by him and were returnable in forty days.

The Representatives, when convened, were called the Commons House of Assembly. They chose their own Speaker, who was submitted to the Governor for approval, and the body was the immediate representative of the people, conforming in legislative and deliberative conduct to the rules and customs of the English House of Commons. Its session continued until dissolved by the Governor. Its adjournments were from day to day except when Sunday intervened. The Representatives selected their own messenger and doorkeeper, but their clerk was appointed by the Governor. This Commons House of Assembly had the exclusive power to originate money bills.

The Upper and Lower Houses constituted the General Assembly of the Province and legislated in its behalf. Journals were kept by each body. All bills passed by both Houses were submitted to the Governor. If approved by him the seal of the Colony was attached and the acts were filed. Authenticated copies were transmitted to the home government for information and sanction.

**The Courts Established**—Provision was made for a Court of Records, known as the General Court, to be held four times a year with the same jurisdiction in the Province that the courts of King's Bench, Common Pleas, and Exchequer had in England. Letters-patent were issued for a "Court of Session and Oyer and Terminer and General Gaol Delivery," to be held twice a year. The civil business was to be transacted in the General Court and the criminal business in the Court of Oyer and Terminer. Grand juries were returned twice a year.

As the judges of the two courts were the same and as a general jail delivery only twice a year was found insufficient in a warm climate, where the accused suffered much from close confinement, arrangements were subsequently made to abolish the Court of Oyer and Terminer and transfer its business to the General Court and to provide for four grand juries a year. The General Court was located at Savannah, where its sessions were held regularly.

The presiding judge was styled Chief Justice of Georgia. He was a "Barrister at Law," had attended at Westminster, was appointed by warrant under His Majesty's sign manual and signet and received a salary of five hundred pounds provided annually by vote of Parliament. The assistant justices were three in number. They received no salary except on the death or absence of the Chief Justice and were appointed by the Governor.

During the King's government there was a Court of Vice-Admiralty with a justice appointed by the Crown to judge captors at sea and take cognizance of all maritime causes.

Inferior justices' courts were established for the trial of minor causes. Where the debt or damage claimed did not exceed forty shillings there was no appeal. The jurisdiction of courts of conscience was limited to eight pounds.

Attorneys-at-law, who also acted as counsel, were admitted by the General Court.

The provost marshal was appointed by the Crown and his duties were similar to those of the sheriff of a county in England. He was the returning officer for every district and parish in the Province and had power to appoint deputies "pro hac vice," to hold such elections for him.

Before entering office the Governor was allowed to take oaths of allegiance, of supremacy, of objurgation, for the due execution of his office and for the punctual observance of all acts of Parliament. It was also obligatory upon him to make the declaration against transubstantiation.

Chief Justice Stokes, in his book "View of the Constitution of British Colonies in America," had this to say about the condition of Georgia under the Royal Government:

"Georgia continued under the King's government to be one of the most free and happy countries in the world; justice was regularly and impartially administered; oppression was unknown; the taxes levied on the subject were trifling; and every man that had industry became opulent; the people there were more particularly indebted to the Crown than those in any other Colony; immense sums were expended by Government in settling and protecting that country; troops of rangers were kept up by the Crown for several years; the Civil Government was annually provided for by vote of the House of Commons in Great Britain, and most of the inhabitants owed every foot of land they had to the King's free gift; in short, there was scarce a man in the Province that did not lie under particular obligations to the Crown. As a proof of the amazing progress that Georgia made I should observe that when Governor Reynolds went to that province in 1754 the exports did not amount to 30,000 pounds a year; but at the breaking out of the Civil War they could not have been much less than 200,000 pounds sterling."

**Georgia as a Crown Colony**—After twenty years under trustees and an inter-regnum of two years Georgia was a Crown Colony for twenty-two years. Under the Trustees the Colony suffered the pangs of birth, followed by the diseases of infancy, which no amount of paternal care seemed able to ward off. As a Crown Colony, under governors, legislature and judiciary, it passed through a period of adolescence, overcoming the usual perils of the period by growth into the robust manhood which asserted itself when the time came for independence. Then Georgians were heroic actors in that great tragedy, the birth of a nation.

After many years of depression, when prosperity had only begun, the colonists welcomed with joy a change of government and received the first Royal Governor, John Reynolds, with great cordiality and enthusiasm.

Governor Reynolds started well, had a good understanding with the Council and the Commons House of Assembly and worked energetically for the protection and prosperity of the Province, but after a few years he developed a tyrannical spirit and his conduct of affairs was so bad that he was recalled and sent back to the British Navy, where he had made a good record before coming to Georgia.

The second Governor, Henry Ellis, was a wiser man and a better executive. In his conduct of the affairs of the Colony he typified the motto of Georgia, "Wisdom, justice and moderation." He was tactful in dealing with the people, though firm in matters of principle and gave a good example of the Latin saying, "suaviter in modo, fortiter in re."

The third Royal Governor, Sir James Wright, a native of South Carolina, a son of its Chief Justice and for twenty-one years Attorney-General of that State, was a man of parts and experience, incorruptible, with unquestioned courage and conscientious devotion to duty. His loyalty to the British Crown eventually made his position as Governor difficult and finally untenable, but until that time approached he was a wise and acceptable Governor of the Colony.

# CHAPTER XXXII.

## *Administration of Governor Reynolds*

Sailing from England in the man-of-war *Port Mahon,* Governor Reynolds reached Savannah on October 29, 1754, and was received with a great demonstration by the people. Bonfires at night followed the joyous reception during the day.

After a formal introduction to the President of the Colony and his assistants assembled in Council, Governor Reynolds' commission was read and he was conducted to the President's chair, from which he announced the dissolution of the old board and the formation of a Royal Council under authority from the Crown. The members of the Council met the next morning, took the oath of office and effected organization. Other officers appointed by the King took oath to perform their duties. The Governor's commission as Captain-General and Vice-Admiral of the Province was read at the head of the militia under arms before the Council Chamber. It was heard with profound attention and saluted with rounds of musketry and shouts of loyalty. A public dinner given by members of the Council and leading citizens of Savannah in honor of the Governor closed the public exercises and the Province passed from the hands of the Trustees into the direct control of the Crown with every evidence of joy from the people.

Governor Reynolds' first impressions of the condition and needs of the Province were conveyed to the Commissioners of Trade and Plantations in a letter written from Savannah on December 5, 1754. After telling of his arrival and cordial reception by the people he had this to say of Savannah:

"The town of Savannah is well situated and contains about a hundred and fifty houses, all wooden ones, very small and mostly very old. The biggest was used for the meeting of the President and Assistants, wherein I sat in Council for a few days, but one end fell down whilst we were all there, and obliged us to move to a kind of shed behind the Court-house, which being quite unfit, I have given orders, with the advice of the Council, to fit up the shell of a house which was lately built for laying up the silk, but was never made use of, being very ill-calculated for that purpose as Mr. Ottolenghe informs me, wherefore he says he has no further use for it, but it will make a tolerable good house for the Council and Assembly to meet in, and for a few offices besides."

As the prison was a small wooden structure and unsafe the Governor ordered it strengthened with bolts and bars.

With the advice of the Council a proclamation was issued continuing all officers in their positions until further notice and writs were issued for an election to choose Representatives in the General Assembly which was called to convene in Savannah on January 7, 1755. The establishment of courts of justice, according to the instructions of the Crown, was taken up.

Some Indians who had come down to salute the new Governor said that as soon as the hunting season was over a number of their people would appear to receive the presents which were to be distributed among them.

The Governor urged upon the home government the need for additional troops to guard the southern frontier of the Province and prevent the desertion of negro slaves to the Spaniards in St. Augustine, who were encouraging them to run away from their masters. He also asked that liberal presents be supplied for the Chickasaws, Creeks, Uchees, Choctaws and Cherokees, whom, according to McGillivray and other Indian traders, the French at Mobile were trying to excite to hostility against South Carolina and Georgia. In view of these reports the Governor asked for the protection of the Colony one hundred and fifty infantry soldiers and made requisition for cannon, small arms and ammunition.

The Governor sent the Commissioners of Trade and Plantations with his letter of December 5, 1754, two memorials on the condition and affairs of the Colony. In one of them he asked for an increase of his salary of 600 pounds a year on the ground that the cost of living in the Colony was high and he could not live on it in a manner due his position.

**The Southern Coast Inspected**—A few months after his arrival Governor Reynolds inspected the southern part of the Province, and on his return to Savannah gave a gloomy account of what he saw. In his letter to the Commissioners of Trade and Plantations he said that Frederica on St. Simon's Island, which had been the best fortified town in the Colony, was in ruins, the houses dilapidated, the forts out of repair, and the twenty cannon left there ruined by neglect. Other guns which had been transferred to Savannah were lying in the sand. He regarded Frederica as the best location for a garrison to protect the Province from invasion by sea, but did not think it the best site for a capital.

**Hardwicke Suggested For a Capital**—The new Governor was much impressed with the natural advantages of the Great Ogeechee River, and suggested for the capital of the Province a bluff on its right bank, fourteen miles above its mouth, where a little town had been laid out in February, 1755. That town he had named Hardwicke in honor of his relative, the Lord High Chancellor of England. Of that place he said "Hardwicke has a charming situation, the winding of the river making it a peninsula, and is the only fit place for the capital."

As a result of the Governor's suggestion and his request for money to erect public buildings at Hardwicke twenty-seven lots were sold there very soon, and 21,000 acres of land in the vicinity was granted to parties who favored the choice of capital. The home government did not furnish the money the Governor asked for, the idea of making it the capital of Georgia was abandoned, and the town became simply a little trading village.

**The Courts Organized**—The Attorney-General arrived at Savannah on the 12th of December, 1754, and submitted his report, suggesting the best way to give effect to the King's plan for the establishment of courts in the Colony. The Council then proceeded at once to organize those courts. The General Court, of which Noble Jones and Jonathan Bryan were justices, was organized in Savannah and located there permanently. Four regular terms were held each year on the second Tuesdays of January, April, July and October. It took action upon all cases involving real, personal and mixed property, where the amount involved exceeded forty shillings, and also dealt with criminal matters, its authority being similar to that of the King's Bench, the Common Pleas, and the Court of Exchequer in England. If the amount involved exceeded three hundred pounds, there could be an appeal to the Governor and Council, and if the judgment was for more than five hundred pounds there could be a further appeal to the King in Council, provided the appellant gave proper security to press his appeal and respond to the final judgment. Notice of such appeal was to be given within fourteen days after judgment was rendered.

A Court of Chancery for hearing equity cases was organized, and in it the Governor sat as Chancellor. Its other officers were a master, a register, and an examiner. Its doors were to be opened after each session of the General Court, if its business required. As criminal business was transferred to the General Court, the Court of Oyer and Terminer was discontinued.

To punish violations of the acts of trade and adjudicate claims concerning salvage, the wages of sailors and other maritime affairs, a Court of Admiralty was established. Over this court the Governor presided as Vice-Admiral, and the other officers were James Edward Powell, Judge-Advocate; William Clifton, Advocate-General; Alexander Kellet, Marshal; and William Spencer, Register. An appeal from this court lay to the High Court of Admiralty in England.

Justices were appointed for the various districts in the Colony, and they were authorized to hear and determine cases in which the amount involved did not exceed forty shillings.

For punishing slaves committing capital crimes a commission of Oyer and Terminer might, upon an emergency, be issued to the justice of the district in which the offense was committed, to try the accused without a jury, and if he was found guilty and sentenced to death the justice might award execution and set upon the slave a value which was afterwards to be paid to the owner by the General Assembly, "as an encouragement to the people to discover the villianies of their slaves."

**Governor Reynolds' Inaugural**—In response to the call of the Governor the representatives elected to the Assembly met in Savannah on January 7, 1755, and perfected organization by the election of David Douglass as Speaker. The Council, or Upper House of Assembly, was also present, and Governor Reynolds submitted the following inaugural address:

GOVERNOR REYNOLDS' ADDRESS TO THE ASSEMBLY.

*"Gentlemen of the Council and of the Assembly:*

"I congratulate you upon the regard his Majesty has been graciously pleased to shew this Province in fixing here a regular Form of Government immediately under his royal Authority, the great Advantages of which are too obvious to require mention; and as his Majesty has done me the Honour to appoint me your Governor, I take this first Opportunity to assure you that it shall be my Study, during the Course of my Administration, to promote the Prosperity of the Colony that you and your Posterity may reap the Benefit that will attend its flourishing State; the only Advantage I propose to myself is my Share of the Honour that will arise from the Success of our mutual Endeavours in this Undertaking. I expect therefore that you will all chearfully and loyally contribute your Assistance to this laudable End; and as the most effectual Means to attain it are Unanimity, Method, and close Application, let me recommend it to you and advise that the more weighty and important Affairs of the Colony be taken into your immediate Consideration at your first Meeting, and afterwards Things of lesser Moment.

"I think it proper for the public Service that you first of all frame some Provincial Laws for the well regulating the Militia, for the making public roads, and establishing a Provision for defraying the Expences of holding the two Courts of Oyer and Terminer which his Majesty has directed to be held on the second Tuesday in December and the second Tuesday in June, and I likewise recommend to your Consideration the making a Provision for the Ordinary Contingencies of Government as far as the Circumstances of the People will conveniently admit of the same.

"Gentlemen, as you are called together for no other Purpose but to consult about the best Methods of promoting your own Welfare, I doubt not but you'l take care to suffer nothing to disunite you or drawn off your attention from the public Good. I, for my Part, shall be ready to concur with you in every Thing that can be conducive to your true and lasting Interest."

**Response of the Council and Assembly**—To this courteous, conciliatory and wise address by the new Governor, the Royal Council and the Commons House of Assembly made cordial reply, promising him loyal and cordial coöperation and that they would work with him as he suggested with unanimity, method and application to transact the business of the Colony and would suffer nothing to withdraw their attention from the public good. They also expressed their appreciation of the fatherly care of the King in providing a form of government suited to the condition of the Colony. They thanked the Governor for his hearty desire to promote the good of the Colony and join them in everything proposed for that end.

For these replies the Governor thanked them and assured them that his best endeavor would never be wanting to be worthy of a continuance of their good opinion.

**First Acts of General Assembly**—Cordial relations having been established at the outset with the Governor, the General Assembly began at once to consider and take action on matters of importance and remained in session during the administration of Governor Reynolds with the exception of three vacations which occurred from March 7, 1755, to February 2, 1756; from February 19th to November 1, 1756, and from December 15, 1756 to January 10, 1757. One of the first acts of the Assembly provided for the organization of a militia, including all white male inhabitants, between the ages of sixteen and sixty into companies, troops, battalions and regiments. They were to be armed and drilled at stated intervals and the officers of companies were instructed to inspect the arms and accoutrements of all the men in these commands six times each year.

No persons were exempt from military duty except members of the Council and their officers, members of the Assembly and their officers, the Chief Justice and Justices of the Court of Common Pleas, the Attorney-General, attorneys of the court, the clerk of the Crown and Pleas, the Provost-Marshal, the Master and Register of the High Court of Chancery, the Judge of the Vice Admiralty Court, the officers of His Majesty's Customs, the Surveyor General, the clergy, the Catechist of Savannah, the Public Treasurer, the Powder-Receiver, the Commissary, the Comptrollers, waiters, and all duly qualified and acting Justices of the Peace. During the seasons of rebellion, insurrection, or actual invasion, these exemptions ceased except in the case of members of Council and of the Assembly and their officers, pilots and ferrymen.

It was obligatory on the masters of male indented servants to see that they were armed and were present at all musters and trained.

Except when charged with treason, felony, or breach of the peace, every militia man, while going to, attending on, or departing from a muster was exempt from arrest and from the service of any process. Penalties were specified for disobedience to the orders of a superior officer. Provision was made to concentrate all the manhood of the province when there was general danger, and the method of giving alarms was pointed out. The manner of organizing patrols, of impressing boats, animals, provisions and ammunition in time of peril, the constitution of court martial, the temporary enlistment of slaves, compensations of the owner if his slave was wounded or killed in service, and encouragement to slaves to behave manfully in the presence of the enemy were all specified in detail.

### Other Acts of the Assembly.

(a) An act for imprinting, emitting, and making current the sum of seven thousand pounds sterling, in paper bills of credit, to be let out at interest, on good security, at six per cent. per annum. The object of this act to supply a currency for the province. These bills are declared a legal tender in liquidation of all debts and dues, and ample provision was made for securing their effectual payment by the parties to whom they were issued.

(b) An act levying a specific tax upon negroes, lands, moneys at interest or invested in trade, and upon town-lots, in order to realize a sum sufficient to defray the expenses of the courts of oyer and terminer and some other "contingencies of government."

(c) An act rendering it obligatory upon each planter to protect his fields or other inclosures with a fence at least five feet and a half high.

(d) An act levying an impost upon all ships, scows, brigs, polacres, sactias, sloops, schooners, and crafts, trading with the province, in order to raise an amount large enough to keep the light-house on Tybee Island in repair, and to build a dwelling there for the use of the pilot.

(e) An act to prevent fraudulent deeds and conveyances, and to compel the registration, within specified periods, of all mortgages and alienations of lands and negroes.

(f) An act for establishing a market in the town of Savannah, and to prevent forestalling, engrossing, and unjust exactions therein.

(g) An act fixing the legal rate of interest in the province at ten per cent. per annum.

(h) An act empowering surveyors to lay out public roads in Georgia to facilitate speedy communication between the inhabitants residing in distant parts of the province, and providing for the establishment of ferries. By this act the plantation was divided into districts, surveyors were appointed for each, and the citizens required to perform specified labor in keeping the highways and bridges in repair.

(i) An act entitled "An Act for the better ordering and governing Negroes and other Slaves in the Province."

(j) An additional act for defraying the expenses of the courts of oyer and terminer and other governmental charges.

(k) An act establishing the method of drawing and summoning jurors within the province.

(l) An act authorizing the attachment of the personal estate of absent debtors in order to facilitate the collection of indebtednesses existing on their part. This act is the parent of the attachment and garnishment laws existent to this day in the State of Georgia.

(m) An additional act providing for the laying out and maintenance of public roads in the province, the preservation of the town and common of Savannah in good order, the repair of the wharves, and the regulation of important ferries.

(n) An act empowering justices of the peace to bind out all Acadians in the province, who refused to labor, to such persons as were willing, in consideration of the personal service to be rendered by them, to supply them with sufficient provisions, clothing and lodging.

(o) An act imposing penalties upon all persons who should declare that the acts of the General Assembly of the Province of Georgia were not of force and authority.

(p) An act proclaiming it high treason to counterfeit his majesty's broad seal of this province.

(q) An act requiring the master of every ship or vessel entering any port of Georgia to deliver to the clerk of the naval office, for the use of the colony, four ounces of good, clean, and serviceable gunpowder for every ton which his vessel registered; and in default of such powder, to pay to the officer designated sixpence sterling for every ton expressed in the register of his ship or vessel. The object of this regulation was to accumulate a public store of gunpowder for the defense of the province.

(r) And lastly, an act for confirming sales of lands in Georgia made by attorneys and agents of absent parties and prescribing the proper method of authenticating documents executed beyond the limits of the province and intended to be used and recorded therein.

**Provisions of the Act Concerning Slaves**—The provisions of the act concerning negroes and other slaves were severe and severe penalties were provided for cruelty to slaves. It is hard to understand the necessity for such legislation unless we have in mind the fact, as stated by Colonel Charles C. Jones, that many of the slaves were fresh from Africa, uncivilized, unrestrained by the influence of Christian civilization, and inclined to violent passions. In South Carolina, where at one time there were forty thousand negro slaves and only five thousand white people, there was constant dread of insurrection, which was increased by the encouragement given the slaves to run away to St. Augustine, where the Spaniards gave them a place of refuge and organized a regiment of negroes with negro officers. There was a bloody insurrection of slaves in South Carolina, and before it could be stopped a number of white people were killed. Under those conditions we can understand the reasons which led to the enactment of such a law. Among its provisions the following may be mentioned:

The offspring of slaves were doomed to perpetual slavery.

Slaves could not be absent from residences or plantations of their owners without a written permit.

A slave unaccompanied by a white person without a ticket from his owner could be arrested and punished. If resisting arrest he could be killed.

Assemblages of slaves were forbidden and their houses could be searched without warrant for arms and ammunition.

Persons wounded in arresting runaway slaves were compensated by the Assembly.

Slaves charged with capital crime could be tried by two Justices of the Peace and three to five freeholders of their district.

An extremely severe section of the law provided the death penalty for a slave who destroyed or burnt rice, corn or other grain grown there, or set fire to a tar-kiln, barrel of pitch, tar, turpentine or a residence, or stole another slave, or poisoned anyone.

The death penalty was also provided for a slave who killed a white person, except by accident or in defense of his master; it was also provided for a slave who tried to raise an insurrection or induce one of his fellow-servants to run away from the province.

A white person stealing a slave was fined fifty pounds and the theft of a slave was a felony without benefit of clergy.

Slaves to be executed were appraised by Justices and two freeholders for not exceeding fifty pounds, and half of the appraisement was paid by the public treasurer to the owner of the slave and the other half to the injured party.

On the trial of a slave anyone knowing the facts concerning the offense charged was compelled to appear and testify.

If the owner of a slave charged with capital crime should conceal him or carry him away he was fined fifty pounds.

Compelling a slave to labor on the Lord's Day except in case of necessity was punished by a fine of ten shillings.

No slave could carry or use firearms or other weapons except in the presence of a white person unless he had written permission from his owner, and never on Sunday.

A slave who struck a white person was punished by sentence of the Justice Court for the first and second offense. For the third offense his penalty was death.

Grievously wounding or maiming a white person by a slave unless by command of his owner in defense of the owner's person or property was punished by death.

A fugitive slave was to be arrested and at once returned to the owner.

Free negroes, free persons and slaves who harbored runaway slaves were punished.

No slave without a permit could sell fish, garden products or wares or be employed as a carter, fisherman, or porter.

Any person who sold a slave beer or spiritous liquor without the consent of his owner was fined twenty shillings for the first offense and forty for the second.

No owner of a slave could permit him to work outside the house or family without a ticket in writing, and the penalty was ten shillings for each offense.

No slave could keep a boat or breed a horse or cattle or own them.

Persons living outside of Savannah could authorize their slaves to sell provisions and goods in the town.

Slaves found without tickets outside their master's plantation could be whipped. For carrying arms they received the same punishment, even with a ticket.

**Cruelty to Slaves Prohibited**—If any person willfully killed his own slave or the slave of another, he was on conviction by the sworn testimony of two witnesses to be punished for felony for the first offense and pay the owner for the slave. For the second offense he was punished for murder according to the laws of England and enough of his goods to pay the owner for the loss of the slave so killed were taken for that purpose.

Any person who killed a slave in a sudden heat of passion or by undue correction was fined fifty pounds.

Any person who willfully cut the tongue, put out the eye, castrated or cruelly scalded or burned a slave or destroyed any of his limbs or members or gave him cruel punishment was fined ten pounds for each offense.

For failing to give a slave enough food and clothing the owner had to pay a fine of three pounds for each offense.

If a slave was cruelly treated and no white person was present to testify about it the owner was held guilty unless he proved his innocence.

Slaves could not be made to labor more than sixteen hours a day, and any person making them work beyond that was fined three pounds for each offense.

It was unlawful to teach slaves to write or employ them as scribes.

No one could have slaves at work on a plantation or settlement without keeping a white person there. For every twenty slaves the owner had to keep a white servant able to bear arms. With fifty slaves the owner must have at least two white servants and an additional white servant for every additional twenty-five slaves.

**Edmund Grey's Sedition**—Early in a session of the Legislature the harmony of the body was disturbed by the seditious attempt of Edmund Grey to upset the government. He was said to have been a fugitive from justice from Virginia who had formed a settlement at Brandon above Augusta. Governor Reynolds described the incident and suppression of the sedition, as follows, in a letter to the board of trade written on February 28, 1755:

"There was an appearance of Sedition about a fortnight ago by the instigation of one Edmund Grey, a pretended Quaker, who fled from Justice in Virginia and is a person of no property here, but has an artful way of instilling Jealousy of their liberties into the peoples' minds, and without the least scruple supports his assertion with any falsehoods that may serve his purpose. This man, by getting a qualification made over to him for that purpose, was elected a Representative for Augusta, for he has persuaded many people that he has great interest in England by shewing a letter he pretends to have received from a person of a noble family there with whom he pretends to have formed a scheme for monopolizing the Indian Trade and introducing such sort of Government here as would suit best with that and some other schemes he has the impudence to say he was consulted upon. He tells the People that this Government will soon be at an end, and then he has promised by his interest to give places of profit to many people, and has actually influenced five Representatives with himself to withdraw from the House in order to break the Assembly and prevent business being done; but his design was so ill concerted that he and his Associates have been expelled from the House by a majority of the whole number of Representatives, not only for withdrawing themselves, but for signing a letter which was voted to be a seditious one by both Houses."

Failing in his nefarious scheme Edmund Grey left the Province and located on what was then neutral ground between the Altamaha and the St. John's rivers. Criminals, outlaws and debtors seeking escape from their creditors flocked there and Grey and his gang became, as Colonel Jones says, a pest and a nuisance to the entire region.

**Land Titles Freed of Conditions**—On January 1, 1755, Governor Reynolds issued a proclamation saying that all persons holding land in Georgia under grants from the Trustees or their agents, or by allotment made by the President of the Colony and his assistants, for not over five hundred acres to an individual, were to be relieved of all conditions in such grants or deeds and from payment of the arrears of quit rents, provided that on or before the seventh day of April following they appeared in person or by attorney before the Governor in Council and surrendering the form of title they then held, received new grants in the name of the King under the broad seal of the Colony. These new grants, in the name of the King, were made "of his special grace, certain knowledge, and mere motion" and reconveyed the lands in free and common socage, on the following conditions, *viz.:* that the grantees or their assigns would pay to the Crown on the 25th of March every year two shillings for every hundred acres conveyed, the first payment to be made at the end of two years from the date of the new grant. They were also required to clear and cultivate annually at least five acres in every hundred granted and the grants should be duly registered within six months from that date.

The General Assembly remonstrated to the King against the condition which required the clearing and cultivation each year of five acres in every hundred, saying it was onerous and likely to retard agricultural operations and hinder the colonization of the Province. This memorial was approved by the Governor, forwarded to England, and as a result the objectionable condition was repealed.

**Georgia Unable to Furnish Two Regiments**—Sir Thomas Robinson, one of the British Secretaries of State, having suggested that Georgia help in raising men and supplies for two regiments to be recruited for the defense of America, the General Assembly, on the third of February, 1755, replied that they were anxious to aid any measure for the general security and welfare of North America, but this Colony was unable to assist in the matter proposed as it was itself in great need of assistance.

A little later a memorial stating the defenseless condition of the colonists and asking for troops, artillery, fortifications, arms and ammunition was prepared and sent to the King.

A communication from Whitehall, written March 13, 1756, announced that the Earl of Loudoun had been appointed commander-in-chief of His Majesty's forces in America and was about to start with two regiments of infantry, a train of artillery, and warlike stores. The aid of the Georgia colonists was asked and on the ninth of November of that year the General Assembly replied that while Georgia had no funds and could not raise any for military purposes, she would show her zeal for His Majesty's service and if the King's forces came within the Colony would supply them with forage and provisions as far as they were able.

On November 17 of that year the Governor laid before the General Assembly a communication from the Earl of Loudoun, dated Albany, August 20, 1756, announcing the fall of Oswego, the destruction of the English naval power on the lakes and cautioning Governor Reynolds to place Georgia in the strongest condition of defense as he was not able to do more than check the advance of the French in his neighborhood. The Earl then called on Georgia to aid him with money and recruits.

News of the disaster to British arms and the threatening attitude of the French and the Indians caused grave apprehension in Georgia and the Assembly, on the twenty-second of November, replying to the Governor on the Earl of Loudoun's communication, admitted the weak and impecunious condition of the Province, which made it impossible to give others the protection and assistance which it earnestly desired for itself.

The feeble American provinces were unable to give Lord Loudoun's command the strength he hoped for and realizing that he was not strong enough to take the offensive he camped at Albany and remained on the defensive. In the meantime the French extended their power among the Indian nations. Carolina and Georgia were threatened with an invasion of French and Cherokees and the colonists were greatly alarmed.

**The Assembly Asked Right to Fix Fees**—Under the law shaping the Crown government in Georgia, the Governor and Council had the right to fix the fees of public offices. The Commons House of Assembly, as the direct representatives of the taxpayers, thought they had a right to a voice in the matter and petitioned the Crown to give them that right. Their petition was unheeded and the Governor and Council in making a schedule of fees took as their guide the schedule in South Carolina.

**Qualifications of Electors Changed**—On February 21, 1755, the General Assembly adopted a memorial showing that the qualifications of electors and representatives in Legislature as specified in the instructions of the Crown to the Governor of Georgia worked a hardship on the people and the Representatives and asked that the Assembly should be allowed to prescribe the qualifications of its own members. Under the law at that time a voter had to be the owner of fifty acres of land and a Representative in Assembly must own five hundred acres. Under this law residents of towns owning buildings and improvements of greater value than five hundred acres in the country were excluded from sitting in the Assembly and the owners of town lots worth more than fifty acres of country land could not vote for Representatives. The home government recognized the justice of this complaint and promptly removed the qualifications complained of.

**Arrival of the Acadians**—While Governor Reynolds was in Augusta to superintend distribution of presents among the Indians and use that incident to confirm good relations between the colonists and the natives, he was called to Savannah by a matter demanding his immediate attention. He, therefore, left the presents and the addresses he had prepared for the Indians with William Little, then a Commissioner or Agent for Indian Affairs, who read the addresses to the Indians, distributed presents among three hundred chiefs and head warriors and succeeded in making the occasion peaceful and satisfactory. Well pleased with the royal gifts the Indians renewed their pledges of friendship.

The matter which caused the speedy return of the Governor to Savannah was the unexpected arrival of two transports bringing four hundred French Catholics. They had been sent to Georgia by Lieutenant-Governor Lawrence, of Nova Scotia, who in a letter informed Governor Reynolds that for the security of Nova Scotia and in pursuance of a resolution of his Council he had sent these people to Georgia, believing that they would be received and cared for.

The prohibition against Papists in Georgia had not been repealed and the Colony was not in condition to support such a large number of needy people. The Governor was sorely perplexed but his humane action was thus announced to the Commissioners of Trade and Plantations: "The season of the year would not admit of their going back again, and therefore I was obliged to receive them, and their provisions being all expended and the poor wretches ready to perish, I was obliged to order them to be supplied immediately: which, with the hire of some boats to distribute them about the Province, has occasioned an expence of near 80 pounds."

The expulsion of the Acadians from Nova Scotia was one of the most cruel events in history and can only be compared with the expulsion of Moors from Spain and the Indians from Georgia. They were of French descent and of Roman Catholic faith, leading pastoral lives, busy with agricultural pursuits and the rearing of flocks and herds. When Nova Scotia was ceded to the British Crown by France these people lost the support of France and were subjected to the power of a nation differing from them in race, language, and religion. They were required to swear allegiance to the British Crown or leave their homes. They were willing to take the oath of allegiance with the proviso that they would not be required to bear arms against France or their old Indian allies. This condition was approved by the British Governor of the Province and for some time they were allowed to remain in possession of their homes and property. Then they received an order from the Crown requiring that they take an unconditional oath or depart immediately. As the Acadians refused to comply with that demand it was decided to remove them from Nova Scotia and scatter them among the English colonies of North America, "where they could not unite in any offensive measures, and might be naturalized to the Government and country."

Lieutenant-Colonel Winslow, commanding the Massachusetts forces, was required to enforce the cruel decree of the British Government. By a proclamation all male Acadians were required to be present on September 5, 1755, at Grand Pré, where Colonel Winslow was in command. They assembled in a village church and going into the midst of them Colonel Winslow announced the startling resolution of Lieutenant-Governor Lawrence and his Council, which said: "Your lands and tenements, cattle of all kinds, and live stock of all sorts are forfeited to the Crown, with all your other effects, saving your money and household goods, and you yourselves are to be moved from this province."

Thus they were consigned to poverty, expatriation and desolation. The decree was quickly confirmed by the burning of their dwellings, barns, mills, schoolhouses and churches. An author quoted by Colonel Jones says: "For several successive evenings the cattle assembled around the smouldering ruins as if in anxious expectation of the return of their masters, while all night long the faithful watch dogs of the neutrals howled over the scene of desolation and mourned alike the hands that had fed and the houses that had sheltered them."

Forced out of their homes at the point of the bayonet, crowded into vessels at the rate of two persons for every ton, and carrying little baggage, these Acadians were torn from their homes and distributed by their English masters among the British colonies from Massachusetts to Georgia. Says Colonel Jones: "It was a brutal outrage, the like of which can scarcely be found in history." Said one of the sufferers, "it was the hardest case which happened since our Saviour was on earth." Four hundred of them were allotted to Georgia and, distributed through the Province, were sustained at public expense. In the spring many of them, building rude boats, left for Carolina, hoping to find their way back to the homes from which they had been expelled. For the control of those who remained in Georgia the General Assembly passed a special act approved on the eighth of February, 1757. After stating that most of the Acadians in Georgia were living near or in Savannah and were illegally cutting and using much valuable timber belonging to the people, this act authorized justices of the peace to bind them out to such persons as would be willing to supply them and their families with sufficient food, clothing and shelter. They were practically treated as servants and prohibited from having or using any firearms or offensive weapons except on plantations under the supervision of their masters.

After a short sojourn nearly all of them went to South Carolina, some to France and others to Nova Scotia. Those who remained were the least enterprising and soon lapsed into obscurity.

In contrast to this experience of the Acadians, Colonel Jones places the experience of the colony of Germans which DeBrahm had planted at Bethany. Their original settlement of 160 persons in 1751 increased rapidly and within a year numbered 1,500.

## CHAPTER XXXIII.

# *The Midway Settlement*

In the same year when the Trustees surrendered their charter to the Crown of England there was a notable addition to the population of the Colony by the coming from Dorchester, South Carolina, of Protestants, who founded the famous Midway Settlement of Liberty County, Georgia. They were the descendants of people who left England in the time of Charles the First to escape persecution and find religious liberty in America. First settling at Dorchester, Massachusetts, they, after some years, moved southward and settled the town of Dorchester, South Carolina, where they remained until 1752, when they moved to Liberty County, Georgia. With them came some French Huguenot families from South Carolina.

The history of that community, as written by Dr. Stacy, is one of the most remarkable in the annals of men. Though laboring under the sickness of a malarial locality, those people, by the end of the nineteenth century, with a maximum white population of three hundred and fifty souls, had produced eighty ministers of the gospel, several foreign missionaries, two of the signers of the Declaration of Independence and several Governors and United States Senators. Dr. Abiel Holmes, the father of Dr. Oliver Wendell Holmes, preached at the Midway Church some time before he went to Cambridge, Massachusetts.

Early in 1630 a group of Puritans from the counties of Devon, Dorset and Somersetshire met in the new hospital at Plymouth, England, and after a day of fasting and prayer elected as their pastors Rev. John Warham, of Exeter, and Rev. John Maverick, and decided to settle in New England. They sailed from England on March 30, 1630, in the ship *Mary and John,* of four hundred tons, commanded by Captain Squeb, and reached America in two months. Instead of taking them to Charles River as agreed the ship captain put them and their goods ashore on Nantucket Point and left them there.

They selected a place called by the Indians Matapan, but they named it Dorchester because some of their number came from that town in England. Dr. Stevens, who is authority for this statement, declared that Dorchester so settled was the oldest town in New England. They suffered great hardship and at first lived on clams, mussels and fish, said Captain Clap, who added:

"We did quietly build boats, and some went fishing; but bread was with many a scarce thing, and flesh of all kinds as scarce. And in those days, though I cannot say God sent a raven to feed us as he did the prophet Elijah, yet this I can say to the praise of God's glory, that he sent not only poor ravenous Indians, which came with baskets of corn on their backs to trade with us, which was a good supply unto many, but also sent ships from Holland and from Ireland with provisions, and Indian corn from Virginia, to supply the wants of his dear servants in this wilderness, both for food and raiment.

"Thus God was pleased to care for his people in time of straits, and to fill his servants with food and gladness. Then did all the servants of God bless His holy name, and love one another with pure hearts fervently."

After some years the people of Dorchester turned their eyes southward. There was then a lack of ministers in South Carolina and Joseph Lord, who had graduated at Harvard College and was teaching school at Dorchester, Massachusetts, and studying theology with its pastor, offered to go to South Carolina. On October 22, 1695, those wishing to emigrate with him to South Carolina were organized in a church over which he was made pastor. At that meeting the churches of Boston, Milton, Newton, Charlestown, and Roxbury were represented by delegates or their pastors. This gathering, which met to encourage the settlement of churches and the promotion of religion "in the southern plantations," was an important event in the religious history of New England. In little more than a month they were ready to embark. They gathered for the last time in New England in a church and their former pastor, Mr. Danforth, preached an affectionate farewell sermon. On the fifth of December, 1695, they sailed as the first missionaries who ever left New England. Dr. Stevens speaks of their departure as follows:

"There was something sublime in the spectacle they presented. It was not the departure of one minister or one family but of a whole church. There were there women in their feebleness and children in their helplessness; there were young in their buoyancy and aged in their gravity; all relations of life were there and all had been consecrated to God."

The first part of their voyage was stormy and disagreeable and on the eighth day they fasted because of the perils to which they were exposed, but on the twentieth day they landed in Carolina. On the Ashley River on its northeastern bank, twenty miles from Charleston, they found a rich piece of land with stately woodlands, interlacing vines and drapery of moss. This place they selected for their future home and in memory of their native place they called it Dorchester. Here on the second of February, 1695, they celebrated their arrival in Carolina by the observance of the Lord's Supper.

Reverend Joseph Lord was pastor of the church at Dorchester, South Carolina, for twenty years before he returned to Massachusetts. He was succeeded at Dorchester by Reverend Hugh Fisher, who served that church until he died, October 6, 1734, and was succeeded by John Osgood, a graduate of Cambridge and a native of Dorchester, South Carolina, where he was ordained a minister March 24, 1734. In spite of the disturbance caused by the War with Spain the church prospered under Mr. Osgood's ministry and the number of communicants increased from thirty in 1734 to more than seventy in 1746.

As the location proved to be unhealthy and with increased population the younger members were disposed to move to more profitable settlements, the people of Dorchester looked about for a new location with land enough for their extensive plantations. They had heard of good lands in Georgia and on May 11, 1752, three persons left Beech Hill to view and report upon the land between the Ogeechee and the Altamaha. Within five days they reached a point half way between these rivers which was called Midway and selected that for the location of their community. From the President and his Assistants of Georgia they received a grant of 31,950 acres. At first the proposed removal to the selected land in Georgia was opposed by some, but those disposed to move were in the majority. Early in August six persons went by land and seven by water to survey the new land and make settlement. The schooner which those on land expected to convey them and their provisions did not come and they had to return to their homes. Those on board the schooner were delayed by contrary winds and consumed most of their provisions before they reached Georgia. On their return, August 15, as the schooner lay in the harbor near St. Catherine's Island, a terrible hurricane arose. On the sixteenth, not being able to get out to sea, they went to Tybee, whence they sailed up to Savannah. Leaving their vessel there they went home by land. Some remained in the vessel and encountered a second hurricane on the way to Charleston, but finally reached that port. On their way to Georgia by the schooner one negro fell overboard and was drowned and two horses with the party that went by land were drowned.

Two families attempted to make a settlement in Georgia on the sixth of December, but the day after their arrival one of the party died.

In spite of those discouragements most of the people of Dorchester left Carolina and by March, 1754, the pastor and the whole church had settled in Georgia. Their first care was to provide for religious services and a log house on Midway Neck was used as a church. The first sermon was preached there on June 7, 1754.

In August, 1754, the people of this settlement assembled at the log meetinghouse and entered into an agreement for the civil and religious government of their community. According to the articles of incorporation they agreed to build a meetinghouse, to support a ministry, to settle all disputes by arbitration, to commit public business to three men chosen each year, to have an annual meeting or parish assembly to consult for the good of the society; to be governed in secular matters by the majority, and in ecclesiastical affairs to allow church members a double vote. They agreed that no member of the corporation should sell his settlement or tract of land or any part of it to a stranger or a person out of the society without first giving the refusal of its purchase to the society.

**The First Settlers of Midway**—The list of seventy men and women who received grants of land and became the first settlers of Midway is an honor roll from which many of the great names in the *History of Georgia* are traced. Their names follow, with the number of acres of the land granted to them:

FIRST GRANT, JULY 11, 1752.

| Name | Acres. | Name | Acres. |
|---|---|---|---|
| John Stevens, Sr. | 500 | Daniel Slade | 500 |
| Benjamin Baker | 500 | John Winn | 500 |
| Parmenas Way | 500 | Samuel Bacon | 500 |
| John Lupton | 500 | Edward Sumner | 500 |
| Rev. John Osgood | 500 | Andrew Way | 500 |
| Samuel Stevens | 500 | Joseph Way | 500 |
| Richard Spencer | 500 | Williams Graves | 500 |
| William Baker | 500 | Joseph Norman | 500 |
| Sarah Osgood | 500 | John Stewart | 500 |
| Richard Girardeau | 500 | Robert Echols | 500 |
| Samuel Burnley | 500 | John Quarterman | 500 |
| James Way | 500 | Robert Glass | 500 |
| Edward Way | 500 | Samuel James | 500 |
| Joseph Bacon | 500 | David Russ | 500 |
| Jonathan Bacon | 500 | William Lupton | 500 |
| John Norman | 500 | Richard Baker | 500 |
| Nathaniel Way | 500 | John Stevens, Jr. | 500 |
| Richard Woodcraft | 500 | Joseph Oswald | 500 |
| John Mitchell | 500 | Jacob Weston | 500 |
| Sarah Mitchell | 500 | Joshua Clark | 500 |
| John Edwards | 500 | For a Glebe | 500 |
| John Elliott | 500 | | |
| Barock Norman | 500 | Total | 22,000 |

SECOND GRANT, AUGUST 6, 1752.

| Name | Acres. | Name | Acres. |
|---|---|---|---|
| Daniel Dunnon | 500 | Rebecca Quarterman | 300 |
| Isaac Dunnon | 500 | Joseph Stevens | 250 |
| John Graves | 500 | Thomas Stevens | 250 |
| Palmer Goulding | 500 | Joseph Bacon, Jr. | 250 |
| Joseph Massey | 500 | John Wheeler | 200 |
| Thomas Stevens, Jr. | 500 | Joseph Bacon, Sr. | 200 |
| Isaac Bradwell | 500 | Thomas Way, Jr. | 200 |
| N. Bradwell | 500 | John Shave | 200 |
| James Christie | 500 | John Churchell | 200 |
| Hugh Dowse | 500 | Moses Way | 200 |
| Elizabeth Simmons | 500 | Joseph Winn | 200 |
| Peter Goulding | 500 | John Gorton | 100 |
| William Chapman | 300 | | |
| James Baker | 300 | Total | 9,650 |

In 1755 six more families and two single men arrived at Midway, including Gortons, Winns, Luptons and Bacons.

In 1756 came the Graves, Stewarts and Dunnons, in 1758 the Jeans, Andrews and Saunders. In 1771 more Bacons, Andrews and William Norman.

Years before that Salzburgers settled at Ebenezer, the Moravians near Savannah and the Scotch Highlanders at Darien. With these Scots came John McIntosh, the Dunbars, Bailies, Cuthberts and others. Then after eighteen years came the Midway Colony. All of them had important parts in the development of Georgia.

According to Colonel Charles C. Jones the Dorchester Society began in 1752 to move into what is now the swamp region of Liberty County. On the sixth of December of that year Benjamin Baker and family and Samuel Bacon and family came as pioneers to the new settlement. They were soon followed by Parmenas Way, William Baker, John Elliott, John Winn, Edward Sumner and John Quarterman. Others followed and Reverend Mr. Osgood came with his flock in 1754.

These emigrants settled on land between Mount Hope Swamp, the head of Midway River, on the north, and Bull Town Swamp on the South. The emigration continued for some years and finally ceased in 1771. There were forty-four family removals in all, of which one family came from Charleston, four from Pon-Pon and thirty-nine from Dorchester and Beech Hill. Most of them came in the years 1754, 1755 and 1756. They brought their negroes with them and it appears from the best information available that when the Colony was completely established it had three hundred and fifty white people and fifteen hundred negro slaves. This community settlement was known as the Midway District and in the Colonial Assembly held in Savannah in 1751 Audley Maxwell represented it as a delegate.

There were some people in the Midway District before the emigrants came from South Carolina and many of their families united with the society when it came and joined in supporting religious services.

The residents of Dorchester and Beech Hill, South Carolina, did not all come to Georgia. Some families remained there and their descendants live in the neighborhood. Others went elsewhere.

The plan of operation in the removal was as follows: After laying by crops in Carolina in the fall of the year planters came with their able-bodied hands and during the winter cleared land and built houses. In a few seasons having thus prepared the way they brought their families and servants in the early spring and began to cultivate the soil. This method made the removal as safe and comfortable as possible.

It is strange that people as intelligent as they were located their dwellings and plantation quarters on the edges of swamps and lived under those malarial conditions. The houses were first built of wood, one story high with dormer windows in the roof, without lights, with no inside linings and with chimneys of clay. The negro houses were made of clay or poles. For market rice was the great crop. Corn was planted on uplands and much attention was given to clearing, ditching and draining swamps. Under these conditions with the heat of the sun on the upturned soil malarial conditions prevailed and there was much sickness and mortality. There was so much sickness and deaths were so frequent among children that few reached the age of puberty. Those who reached the age of manhood and womanhood had feeble constitutions according to Colonel Jones, but this seems strange in the face of a record of so many public servants in civic and religious life who went out from there. Colonel Jones says that according to a register kept by the society during the twenty years from 1752 to 1772 there were 193 births and 134 deaths. This for a total population of 1,850 would be a very low death rate. He probably means that many deaths among 350 white people, which would be an average mortality of about twenty per thousand and an average birth rate of about twenty-eight per thousand, which is not far from the present rate in American cities,

Colonel Jones says:

"The mortality was greatest in September, October and November. April, May, June and August appear to have been the healthiest months. Bilious fevers in the fall and pleurisies in the winter and spring were the diseases which proved most fatal. It used to be said that those who survived a severe attack of bilious fever in the fall would certainly die of pleurisy in the winter or spring."

Grain was threshed and beaten by hand and the crops so prepared were sold in Savannah. A trip to that place was the event of the year. Horses were specially fed and attended for the trip a week in advance. Ordinary journeys to church and to visit neighbors were made on horseback. When a young man went courting he went on his finest horse in his best clothes, followed by a servant on another horse, carrying his valise.

This community took an early and active part in the fight for independence and when the people of Boston were suffering for food because of restrictions put upon them by the British Government a shipment of rice to Boston from the Midway District was a welcome contribution.

**Active in the Revolution**—Midway, which with Sunbury became St. John's Parish, was active in events that led to the Declaration of Independence, and its sons fought in the Revolution, with two volunteer companies, the St. John's Rangers and the St. John's Riflemen. James Screven, of Midway, became a brigadier-general. He was killed in action at Spencer Hill in 1778 and was buried in the Midway graveyard. Midway also furnished General Daniel Stewart, Colonel John Baker, Major John Jones, the father of Colonel C. C. Jones, and a number of captains and lieutenants. Two Revolutionary Governors of Georgia, Richard Howley and Nathaniel Brownson, went from Midway.

Like Savannah, Midway suffered during the Revolution. It was severely punished because of its Revolutionary spirit and the settlers were dispersed, their homes were burned, their crops destroyed, their negroes and cattle driven away and they were left in homeless poverty.

In 1782 the survivors returned to Midway and began to build again. The first structure was a temporary church building. They called Reverend Abiel Holmes, of Connecticut, who had graduated from Yale College not long before and he preached for them six years. He was the father of Dr. Oliver Wendell Holmes, who was born some years after the elder Holmes had left Georgia and become the pastor of a church in Cambridge, Massachusetts.

Dr. Abiel Holmes was succeeded by ministers whose names and influence are well known in Georgia. They were:

| | |
|---|---|
| Rev. Cyrus Gildersleve | Rev. T. S. Winn |
| Rev. Murdoch Murphy | Rev. D. L. Buttolph |
| Rev. Robert Quarterman | Rev. John Baker |
| Rev. I. S. K. Axson | Rev. Francis Bowman |

Dr. Stacy says that at the close of the War Between the States Kilpatrick's division of Federal soldiers made Liberty County a camping ground for two months. Houses were entered, silverware taken, homes burned, stock driven away, and fine carriages converted into wagons to haul slaughtered meat. A monument erected to the early settlers was defaced, railroad lines were cut and people were left isolated without supplies. Such was the destitution that the people picked up scattered corn left by horses at the abandoned Federal camps. The negroes in that emergency aided their former masters to find food for their families.

There had been close and cordial relations in the old days between the white people and their black slaves. They worshipped in the same church, the whites on the main floor and the negroes in the gallery. The negroes were publicly received into the church as members and had part with their white masters in the communion service.

Dr. Mallard, in his book *Plantation Life,* gives a beautiful picture of the Midway people, white and black, on Communion Sunday at Midway Church. The whole day was one of devotion from early morning until afternoon and all, old and young, were present at the solemn communion service. They started to church at nine o'clock in carriages and on horseback and the negroes in Jersey wagons, all in their best clothes, all happy and devout and remained at the church after the sermon, the communion service, and the midday recess with cold lunch until afternoon, when they returned to their homes, tired but happy, and after a night's rest, well prepared for the duties of the ensuing week.

In 1781 a second church was organized by the Midway people, who called it Dorchester, after their former homes in South Carolina, Massachusetts and England. The division of the congregation had a depressing effect and the community ceased to grow. By the end of the War Between the States it was almost extinct. The church building was turned over to the negroes, who organized in it a Presbyterian Church of six hundred members. The baptismal font was given to the Dorchester Church and the old bell to the church at Flemington. The silver communion set was divided between those two churches. The negroes did not keep up the church or attend to the graveyard and the property reverted to the Midway Society, which was organized to preserve the old church and the monuments of the Midway community. The old Midway Church, rebuilt after the war, still stands and every year in April there is a reunion of the Midway Society.

**A Great Group of Midway Men**—In a fine paper on Midway, read before a club of leading men, Mr. Samuel N. Evins, an accomplished Atlanta lawyer, made an impressive summary of the achievements of the Midway people, in which he quoted from Dr. Mallard and Dr. Stacy, who have written much on the subject. From his summary the following is quoted:

"To enumerate the achievements of these people is no small task. They had a most decided effect on Georgia, and on their time. Seven counties in this State have gotten their names from this settlement, *viz.,* Liberty, Gwinnett, Hall, Baker, Bacon, Screven and Stewart. Attention has already been called to the officers and soldiers contributed by them to the Revolutionary cause, and to the four Colonial governors who sprang from their midst. Now we note three United States Senators who were among the sons of old Midway. John Elliott, 1819-25; Alfred Iverson, who served from 1842 to the outbreak of the Civil War; and Augustus O. Bacon, a member of the Senate from 1894 to 1922. Senator Iverson afterwards became a brigadier-general in the Confederate Army, which rank was also attained by his son, Alfred Iverson, Jr. The four Colonial governors, Hall, Gwinnett, Brownson and Howley, were also members of the Continental Congress. Three other residents of the district were afterwards sent to Congress, *viz.,* Benjamin Andrew, John A. Cuthbert and William B. Fleming. Joseph E. Ward, who was the first United States minister to China, was a resident of this district, as was also William E. Law, a distinguished lawyer in Savannah. The great scientists, John and Joseph LeConte, were both directly from the Midway settlement. Their people had been identified with the church from the beginning. There were two persons who grew up in that settlement who obtained recognition as writers of fiction. One, the Reverend Francis R. Goulding, author of *The Young Marooners,* and the other, Maria J. McIntosh, a writer of stories for children. Colonel Charles C. Jones, the Georgia historian, was also born and bred in Midway, as were his people before him.

"In other wars than the Revolution the sons of Midway were outstanding. Colonel James S. McIntosh lost his life in the Mexican War. Captain John Kell achieved world-wide fame as executive officer of the Confederate cruiser *Alabama,* under Admiral Simmes. Besides the two Iversons already mentioned, Midway furnished another brigadier-general to the Confederate Army in General Claudius C. Wilson. Commodore James McIntosh of the United States Navy was identified in many ways with Midway and his body lies buried in the old cemetery there.

"The connection of President Theodore Roosevelt and President Wilson with Midway is interesting. The former's mother was Martha Bulloch, granddaughter of General Daniel Stewart, who lies buried in the old churchyard, and President Wilson married Ellen Louisa Axson, a granddaughter of Rev. I. S. K. Axson, who was for many years pastor of the Midway Church.

"The contribution which Midway made to literature, science, politics and war, was small when compared to its gifts to the Church; Bishop Elliott, who was the first Episcopal Bishop in Georgia; Rhett Barnwell, afterwards president of the South Carolina College; and Dr. Richard Fuller, who became a Baptist minister in the south, were all converted under the preaching of Reverend Daniel Baker, one of the great preachers of the Midway settlement. From the loins of John Quarterman, another pastor of the Midway Church, there sprang directly twenty-three ministers, and seven foreign missionaries, a veritable Father Abraham. Although these people were Congregationalists they never once produced a Congregational minister. However, they made up for it by giving to the world fifty Presbyterian ministers, nineteen Baptist preachers, thirteen Methodist parsons, and two Episcopal priests.

"In the field of education they did not lag behind, besides the two LeContes, Dr. Patrick H. Mell, who was for many years Chancellor of the University of Georgia, came from Midway, as did Reverend Dr. Daniel Baker, president of a Presbyterian college in Austin, Texas; Professor Milton E. Bacon, the founder of the LaGrange Female College; Dr. John W. Baker, professor in Old Oglethorpe University; and Captain S. D. Bradwell, State School Commissioner and President of the State Normal College at Athens. To this group should be added Dr. J. M. S. Hardin, Dr. William Lewis Jones, Professor Samuel M. Varnedo and Professor John B. Mallard, who were at different times connected with Georgia schools and colleges.

"Dr. Stacy goes on to recapitulate: 'Four governors, two signers of the Declaration of Independence, six Congressmen, two of whom were Senators, seven counties named after her illustrious sons and the eighth after herself, eighty-two ministers of the gospel, six college professors, three professors in theological seminaries, two university chancellors, six foreign missionaries, two judges of the Superior Courts, three solicitors-general, three presidents of female colleges, one United States minister, four authors, one historian, one professor in a medical college, six editors, one State superintendent of public schools, besides a host of teachers, lawyers, doctors, mayors and what-nots.' "

Dr. Stacy says this wonderful record is due to the scrupulous meeting of pecuniary obligations, reading sermons by deacons, when the pastor was absent, general observance of family worship, hearty endorsement of the Abrahamic covenant, infant baptism, thorough religious training of children, strict observance of the Sabbath and the absence of religious excitement, periodical protracted services and revival machinery. To these Mr. Evins adds, peculiar environment, isolated from the world, absence of the saloon and from the temptations and frivolities of modern life.

Mr. Evins does not agree with Dr. Stacy about the causes of the unusual result. He says that while practicing the common virtues and attending to religious duties do much to develop sturdy character, some of the simplest and most uninteresting people in the world have done these things since the world began. He says:

"The Midway people were crusaders, struggling for the truth as they saw it and willing to undergo any hardship or privation to serve that truth. It was a far cry from Midway back to that day in the new hospital at Plymouth, England, but in all those joyless years they kept their faith, laid great burdens on their souls and developed a conscience that was a priceless heritage and in the end they begat a great race, although the towns they founded crumbled into dust."

**Sunbury**—Sunbury, a town founded in 1758 by Mark Carr, who had been for years a leading man in the Colony, flourished so greatly that it seemed destined to be a rival of Savannah. It was located on a high bluff overlooking the Midway River and from it Bermuda Island, the southern part of Ossabaw and in the distance St. Catherine's Island could be seen.

As no English settlement on the mainland had been made south of the Great Ogeechee River this beautiful site was unoccupied by white men. The settlement of the Midway District made it available. Its attractions are thus described by Colonel Jones:

"To the quiet woods and waters of this semi-tropical region the English were strangers. The Bermuda grass which, at a later period, so completely covered Sunbury Bluff, did not then appear, but magnificent live-oaks, in full-grown stature and solemn mien, crowned the high-ground even to the very verge where the tide kissed the shore. Cedars, festooned with vines, overhung the waters. The magnolia grandiflora, queen of the forest, excited on every hand the admiration of the early visitor. The sweet-scented myrtle, the tall pine, the odoriferous bay, and other indigenous trees lent their charms to a spot whose primal beauty had encountered no change at the hand of man. The woods were resonant with the songs of birds whose bright plumage vied in coloring with the native flowers which gladdened the eye and gave gentle odors to the ambient air. Fishes abounded in the waters and game on the land. Cool sea-breezes tempered the heat of the summer, and severe cold was unknown in the depth of winter. It was a gentle, attractive place, this bold bluff, as it came green and beautiful from the hand of Nature. For twenty years and more it retained its virgin attractions, and now the woodman's axe was heard in its groves, and the keel of the enterprising colonists was parting its tranquil waters."

On October 4, 1757, Mark Carr received a grant of five hundred acres in the Midway District, bounded on the east by the Midway River, on the west by the land of Thomas Carr, on the south by vacant land and on other sides by the river marshes.

To prepare for the building of a town on that site Mark Carr, on June 20, 1758, conveyed three hundred acres of that tract bordering on Midway River to James Maxwell, Kenneth Baillie, John Elliott, Grey Elliott, and John Stevens, of Midway, in trust, providing that the land so conveyed should be laid out as a town by the name of Sunbury, of which one hundred acres were dedicated as a common for the use of the inhabitants. The deed provided that the Trustees named and their successors should dispose of the lots in the town for the benefit of Mark Carr.

Two of the Trustees, John Stevens and John Elliott, were leading members of the Midway congregation and James Maxwell was a resident of the district.

James Maxwell and John Stevens were members of the Provincial Congress which met at Tondees' Tavern in Savannah on July 4, 1775. Kenneth Baillie and Grey Elliott were active and influential citizens and Elliott was selected by the General Assembly of Georgia to aid Benjamin Franklin when he was sent to England by several of the American Colonies to represent their wants and grievances, to protest against oppressive acts of the Crown and to oppose taxation without representation. All the Trustees of Sunbury were men of position and character.

It has been suggested that the place was named for a beautiful town called Sunbury in Middlesex County, England, on the bank of the Thames a little above Hampton Court and eighteen miles from London.

James Maxwell, Kenneth Baillie, John Elliott, Grey Elliott and John Stevens began at once to lay out the town on the west bank of the Midway River. The plan included three public squares, Kings, Church and Meeting, and four hundred and ninety-six lots.

The lots were seventy feet wide and one hundred and thirty feet deep. Forty of them fronted the river and were called Bay Lots. They included the ownership of the shore to low water mark. The lots were grouped in blocks of four, with streets on three sides and a lane or alley on the fourth side. The streets were seventy-five feet wide and the lanes twenty feet. The streets crossed at right angles, some running at right angles from the river and the cross streets and lanes intersecting. Thus laid out the length of Sunbury from north to south was 3,430 feet and the width 2,230 feet at the south and 1,880 feet at the north.

Substantial wharves were built and the most important were owned and used by Kellsell and Spalding, Fisher, Jones and Hughes, Darling and Company and Lamott.

The population and importance of Sunbury increased rapidly and in 1761 the Governor, with the approval of Council, made it a port of entry and appointed Thomas Carr collector, John Martin naval officer, and Francis Lee searcher. Their appointment was confirmed by the British Commissioners of Customs.

Governor Wright wrote Lord Halifax in 1773:

"I judged it necessary for his Majesty's service that Sunbury,—a well settled place, having an exceeding good harbour and inlet from the sea,—should be made a Port of Entry; and I have appointed Thomas Carr, Collector, and John Martin, Naval Officer for the same. There are eighty dwelling houses in the place; three considerable merchant stores for supplying the town and planters in the neighborhood with all kinds of necessary goods; and around it for about fifteen miles is one of the best settled parts of the country."

**HENRY GRADY MONUMENT—ATLANTA**

Captain Hugh McCall says of Sunbury in his *History of Georgia:*

"Soon after its settlement and organization as a town, it rose into considerable commercial importance; emigrants came from different quarters to this healthy maritime port, particularly from Bermuda; about seventy came from that island, but unfortunately for them and the reputation of the town, a mortal epidemic broke out and carried off about fifty of their number the first year: it is highly probable they brought the seeds of the disease with them. Of the remainder, as many as were able, returned to their native country. This circumstance, however, did not very much retard the growing state of this eligible spot; a lucrative trade was carried on with various parts of the West Indies in lumber, rice, indigo, corn, etc. Seven square-rigged vessels have been known to enter the port of Sunbury in one day, and about the years 1769 and 1770 it was thought by many, in point of commercial importance, to rival Savannah. In this prosperous state it continued with very little interruption until the war commenced between Great Britain and America."

In September, 1773, Governor Sir James Wright reported Savannah and Sunbury as the only ports in the Province and said that while Midway River was only twenty-two miles long there was fifteen feet of water up to the town, twelve miles from the sea.

Sunbury had distinguished citizens. Dr. Lyman Hall, one of the signers of the Declaration of Independence lived there, and Button Gwinnett, another signer, lived across the Sound at St. Catherine's Island. George Walton, the third member of that group and a Governor of Georgia, after being wounded and captured by the British in Savannah, was sent to Sunbury, where he remained until he was paroled. Richard Howley and Nathaniel Brownson, both residents of Sunbury, were Revolutionary Governors of Georgia, as were John Elliott and Alfred Cuthbert, who became Senators, and John A. Cuthbert, elected to Congress. Major John Jones, who fell in the siege of Savannah, and Major Lachlan McIntosh were natives of Sunbury, as were John E. Ward and William Daw.

Sunbury had a famous school which had a profound effect on the development of the Midway people. It was conducted by Dr. McWhir, a Presbyterian minister, who came from Ireland. He was a profound scholar and had the rare ability of inspiring his pupils with the ambition to do their best.

Sunbury was headquarters for the forces of General Charles Lee in the expedition against Florida in 1776. Here Colonel Elbert embarked his troops that moved against St. Augustine under the order of Button Gwinnett in 1777.

At Sunbury, during the Revolution, Colonel John McIntosh was in command of the fort, defending it bravely, and when the British Colonel Fuser demanded its surrender, he returned the famous reply, "Come and take it."

After the Revolution Sunbury died down and became one of the dead towns of Georgia.

Unlike Midway, Sunbury was a healthy place and a favorite place of residence for the families of planters who were cultivating rice in the neighboring swamps.

## CHAPTER XXXIV.

# *Reynolds Recalled and Ellis Comes*

Governor Reynolds' military training qualified him for the fortification of Georgia and naturally he gave much attention to that subject. The condition of the Colony at that time was so bad with reference to defense it is fortunate that the Colony was not attacked. In 1756 the population of Georgia was 6,400 persons, and of these only 756 could bear arms and were enrolled in the militia with officers. Although organized in eight companies and drilled six times a year they were badly equipped and being widely separated it was difficult to concentrate them quickly in case of emergency. The fortifications which General Oglethorpe had built up with so much care had fallen into decay. The wooden fort one hundred and twenty feet square at Augusta was so decayed that the walls had to be propped up. Its eight small guns were honeycombed with rust, and there was no supply of ordnance stores. The fortification at Frederica which had been so strong at the time of the Spanish invasion was ruined by decay, and twenty old cannon left there were lying on the ground. In Savannah there were eleven old cannon, three of them four pounders without carriages, twenty-seven old swivel guns and sixty-one old muskets, most of them with broken stocks and some without locks. The log forts built formerly at various points were practically gone.

Under these circumstances Governor Reynolds, with the aid of John Gerar William DeBrahm, one of the Royal surveyors and formerly captain of engineers in the Royal army, formulated a plan for the defense of the Colony, which was outlined as follows in a letter written to the Board of Trade in 1756:

"Georgia being a large but weak Province, is unable to raise a number of men to meet an Enemy in the Field or Woods. It requires therefore to be provided in sundry places with forts wherein few men may defend the Province *(i. e.,* the settled part of the Province) against many, and keep the Inhabitants free from invasions.

"To fortify this Province will require to choose such places where the Enemy must take his passage (as well by water from the East as by land from the West), which places likewise are convenient to communicate one with another by Land as well as by Water, to make their correspondence and assistance as easy as possible.

"The places for Forts near the Sea are first COCKSPUR, a small Island in the mouth of Savannah River commanding the North but much better the South Channel. The North Channel is only for small craft, but the South Channel is for large vessels.

"Secondly. SAVANNAH, being the first landing place and likewise the best settled Town in the Province, on Savannah River.

"Thirdly. HARDWICKE, being likewise the first landing place upon Great Ogeechee River, where also is the passage over that river to correspond between Savannah and Frederica.

"Fourthly. FREDERICA, being the Southermost place of the present Settlements, but the Center between Savannah and St. John's Rivers, upon an Island commanding the chief branch of Altamaha River, a convenient Place to harbour Men of War, and, being also protected by them, also the fittest place for a Garrison Town or Place of Arms.

"THE LAND PASSAGES for the Enemy are along the Rivers Savannah, Great Ogeechee, and Altamaha. These Rivers are therefore all to be fortified in such places where they leave off to be navigable, *viz.:*

"At Augusta, and at the fork of Ochonee and Altamaha Rivers, and upon a South and North Course from these two places on a convenient Spot on Great Ogeechee River, to stop the Enemy's passage along the River and to defend likewise the passage for the communication between the Forks and Augusta.

"To protect this communication it is necessary to raise Two Hundred Rangers, commanded by two Captains with the assistance of four Lieutenants and Six Sargents."

With this general description Governor Reynolds gave detailed specifications for the fortifications at the places named in his letter with the number of men to be stationed at each and the number and size of the cannon to be mounted there for defense. Altogether the recommendations provided for thirty-two hundred men in the garrisons, the Rangers, the Militia and the Indians, with a hundred and seventy-two cannon.

The forts were to be built in earth work faced with facines or turf, and as white labor was scarce and very costly he recommended the purchase of a hundred and fifty negroes to do the work under the direction of overseers and engineers. He estimated the cost in the ten years required for the construction at 32,750 pounds, including the purchase of boats, iron, steel and tools and other incidental expenses. From this he deducted 4,000 pounds for the sale of the negroes left when the work was done. With this deduction the net cost he estimated at 28,750 pounds, or about $140,000 in American money.

It is interesting to note that he estimated the cost of negroes bought in Africa at 4,500 pounds or $22,500 for one hundred and fifty, which was $150 each for 150. He estimated that there would be a hundred negroes left at the end of ten years, and they could be sold for 4,000 pounds, or $20,000, equal to $200 each.

Although the fortifications were badly needed Governor Reynolds' plan was not adopted by the British Board of Trade, and Georgia remained almost undefended.

It appears that in addition to the expense of the plan, which doubtless caused the Board of Trade to hesitate, Governor Reynolds was becoming exceedingly unpopular in Georgia, and the same year was recalled by order of the Commissioners of Trade and Plantations.

**Cause of Reynolds' Recall**—In a letter written by Governor Reynolds to the British Board of Trade on March 29, 1756, he charged that members of the Assembly were too greedy for power; that they did not treat his messages with respect, were niggardly and dilatory in providing for the expense of the government and the court; that they were indifferent about the prompt administration of justice and some of them were incompetent and unfaithful.

In reply to that charge of the Governor, in letters to Jonathan Brown, to Lord Halifax on April 6, 1756, and Alexander Kellet, member of Council and Provost General to the Commissioners of Trade and Plantation on July 7th of the same year, it was asserted that Governor Reynolds had been cordially welcomed when he reached the Colony, and a happy and prosperous administration was expected, but that within a few months he entrusted the affairs of the Province to William Little, a surgeon of the British Navy, whom he had brought over as a private secretary; that Little was unaccustomed to business and showed a despotic spirit; was guilty of extortion as clerk of the General Court, of falsifying a minute of the House of Representatives, of which he was clerk, in order to cover his sinking a bill which had passed both Houses, and also was guilty of forging a minute concerning another bill which had received the approval of the General Assembly; that although the Governor was informed of all this he bestowed upon his secretary other employments of value and that the General Assembly had been dissolved, leaving half the taxes of the former year uncollected and no provision for those of the current year, merely to prevent an inquiry into the conduct of Dr. Little. It was further charged that the Governor constantly endeavored to belittle the Council, ignoring them when important questions were to be discussed and convening them on trivial occasions; that he only communicated to the members a part of the King's instructions; that he often acted in opposition to their advice in matters in which they were to coöperate; that he ignored the presence and office of the members of the Council who accompanied him to Augusta, when the Royal presents were distributed to the Indians, and delegated the whole business to Dr. Little, who was unworthy of the trust; that he suspended Clement Martin, a member of the Council because he presented Council's remonstrance against Dr. Little; that without consulting the Council he appointed judicial and ministerial officers and refused to allow the protests of members of Council to be entered on the minutes; that he inserted or omitted what he pleased in making up the journal of

NAVAL STORES WHARF—SAVANNAH HARBOR

Council; that he had established "a new and extraordinary Judicature," where he alone presided, that he interfered in a lawless way in the conduct of causes in the general court; that he failed to countenance officers in the fearless discharge of their duty; that he had been partial in ceding public lands; that he encouraged vexatious prosecution against those who incurred his anger; that he transcended his powers in filling offices which were only within gift of the Crown; that his conduct of affairs had caused so much dissatisfaction that the Colony instead of increasing in population and wealth was daily retrograding; and that his administration of the government was incompetent, partial and tyrannical.

It appears that Governor Reynolds was too much accustomed to absolute authority on the quarter-deck of a man-of-war, and was not fitted for the difficult position of the Governor of a new province under a new plan of government.

The Commissioners of Trade and Plantations could not ignore this unfortunate development, and in response to their memorial a royal order was issued on August 3, 1756, directing the Commissioners of Trade and Plantations to immediately order Governor Reynolds to come to England and answer for his conduct. At the same time the Commissioners' recommendation that Henry Ellis be appointed Lieutenant-Governor of Georgia during the absence of Reynolds was approved.

Within two days the Commissioners of Trade and Plantations sent a copy of the royal order to Governor Reynolds and directed him to return to England promptly and give account of the condition of the Province and the conduct of the Governor.

This communication was received by Governor Reynolds on February 16, 1757, and he resigned, placing the government in the hands of his successor, Lieutenant-Governor Ellis. Governor Reynolds sailed for England in a merchant ship, called *Charming Martha,* and was captured on the way by a French privateer and carried to the port of Bayonne. Because of this delay he did not reach London until the 7th of July. He submitted an elaborate defense, claiming that while he may have made mistakes he had not been guilty of any criminal offense, and had not wilfully disobeyed orders. He asked the Commissioners to remember that he was the first Royal Governor with the difficult task of framing the earliest laws, establishing a police, adapting a constitution and selecting competent persons to fill minor offices of trust. His defense did not satisfy the Board of Trade and he was allowed to resign as Governor and resume his rank in the navy. As Bishop Stevens said, Governor Reynolds was transferred from the quarter-deck of a man-of-war to the head of a Royal Province and required to arrange, digest and carry out the many steps and changes necessary in the first establishment of a new and untried form of government. This required patience, energy, knowledge, and firmness which Governor Reynolds did not possess. His great weakness was allowing his private secretary to exercise power of which he was unworthy and that made both him and the Governor obnoxious.

Once again in the navy, John Reynolds became a trusted officer of the greatest naval power in the world, and died an Admiral.

**The Administration of Governor Ellis**—Governor Henry Ellis, who succeeded to the position of Chief Executive of Georgia in 1757, had precisely those qualities in which Governor Reynolds was lacking. Cordially received he seemed at the outset to have been a peacemaker, and by a conciliatory but impartial and firm course brought the different factions of the people together and promoted peace, good order and prosperity. From the first he had the confidence, the respect and the cordial coöperation of the people.

His previous life and experience were very different from those of Governor Reynolds. Highly educated he was at forty years of age put in charge by Parliament of an important expedition in search of a new passage across America to the Pacific. For a whole year in trying to find such a passage he had endured the hardships and dangers of a bitter climate. Although he did not find the passage where there was none, his observations and discoveries were reported in a publication which attracted attention and received commendation, not only in England, but in France, Germany and Holland. His services were so appreciated by the learned men of England and the government that he was made a Fellow of the Royal Society.

Through the influence of the Earl of Halifax he was selected as a successor of Governor Reynolds, and the London *Gazette* in a notice of his promotion, spoke of him as an active, sensible and honest man.

Lieutenant-Governor Ellis reached Charleston in January, 1757, and was there received with much courtesy by the Carolina authorities. He reached Savannah on the 16th of February, 1757, and as he landed was received by the assembled multitude with shouts of welcome. Immediately on arrival he went to the residence of Governor Reynolds and paid his respects. Having done that he responded gratefully to the welcome of the people which was made impressive by thunders of artillery from the land battery and ships in port.

With Captain Reynolds, Governor Ellis went to the Council Chamber, where the members were assembled and presented his commission as Lieutenant-Governor of Georgia. It was publicly read, he took the oath of office, the Great Seal was delivered to him, and so he was inducted into the office of Governor.

That evening the change of administration was celebrated by the firing of guns, illumination and the cheers of the people. In contrast William Little, the marplot, was burned in effigy. Congratulatory addresses, complimentary to the Lieutenant-Governor and anticipating benefits from his administration poured in from the freeholders of Savannah, Ogeechee and Midway District, from the Masonic fraternity, and from other organized societies. A significant feature was the welcome tendered the new Governor by a band of school boys associated as a military company. Having paraded before the Governor, who commended their soldierly appearance and maneuvers, the boys through their captain addressed the Governor as follows:

"Sir,—The youngest Militia of this Province presume by their Captain to salute your Honour on your arrival. Although we are of too tender years to comprehend the blessing a good Governor is to a province, our parents will doubtless experience it in its utmost extent, and their grateful tale shall fix your name dear in our memories."

Governor Ellis had before leaving England made himself familiar with the condition of the Colony, its pressing needs and the lamentable state of defense. He also knew of the influence which the French sought to exert over the Cherokees and of the jealousy of the Spaniards for the Province of Georgia.

To retain the good will of the Indians he asked before leaving England that the Commissioners of Trade and Plantations forward presents for the Indians and five hundred muskets to arm the militia of the Province. This request was complied with promptly and added to the security of the Colony, the satisfaction of the colonists and their confidence in his purpose to promote the welfare and security of the Colony.

One of Governor Ellis' first acts was to reinstate two members of the Council who had been removed without just cause by Governor Reynolds. This act was so manifestly fair that no offense was taken.

**Georgia As Governor Ellis Found It**—Soon after his arrival Governor Ellis wrote the British Board of Trade as follows:

"I found the people here exceedingly dissatisfied with each other, and an almost universal discontent arising from the late proceedings and persons in power. Few approached me that were not inflamed with resentment and liberal in invectives; urgent that I should take some immediate and very violent steps, such as a total change in public officers, and the dissolution of the Assembly. Sensible of my own inexperience and of the violence of such counsels, fearful of being misled, and aiming rather at healing the wounds and extinguishing the flame of party than stirring it anew, I forebore making any material alteration until I should be qualified to act from observation and experience in order that the changes I shall then make may rather be attributed to my own judgment than to the advice of designing and interested people. This suspense will give time for Men's passions to subside, and for truth to appear through the cloud of party prejudice that at present obscures it."

## CHAPTER XXXV.

# *An Era of Good Will Under Governor Ellis*

In his *History of Georgia,* published in 1811, Captain Hugh McCall thus describes the condition of Georgia when Governor Ellis arrived in February, 1757:

"The rich swamps on the sides of the rivers lay uncultivated, and the planters had not yet found their way into the interior of the country, where the lands not only exceeded those in the maritime parts in fertility for everything else but rice, but where the climate was more healthy and pleasant. But few of the Georgians had any negroes to assist them in the cultivation of the rice swamps, so that in 1756 the whole exports of the country were only two thousand nine hundred and ninety-six barrels of rice, nine thousand three hundred and ninety-five pounds of indigo, and two hundred and sixty-eight pounds of raw silk, which together with skins, furs, lumber and provisions, amounted to only 16,776 pounds sterling. Georgia continued to be an asylum for insolvent and embarrassed debtors for Carolina and the other colonies, which, added to the indolence that had previously prevailed, kept the Colony sunk in insignificance and contempt."

Captain McCall adds that Governor Ellis in a letter written July 7th of that year said the weather was extremely hot in Savannah, with a temperature of 102 in the shade on the piazza where he wrote. The publication of that letter probably prevented Europeans from coming to Georgia. Captain McCall says that according to the oldest inhabitants of Savannah the temperature there seldom rose above 96, and never above 100, and he adds that the trade winds prevail on that coast in summer. With 100 men at St. Marys for eighteen months only three were in bed with fever. The seashore, he said, was healthy except near stagnant fresh water.

The new Governor's calm, conservative and wise course, devoid of any partiality for any faction and seeking only the general good, soon won for him a high place in the respect and affection of the people.

He promptly asked the Board of Trade to give the Colony a Chief Justice so that judicial proceedings would be conducted with fairness, dignity and uniformity. This was appreciated because under the previous administration some did not get justice, and the authority of the court was openly disputed and set at naught. The Governor's request about maintaining friendly relations with the Indians and rebuilding the forts and defending them with troops also commanded respect and gave the colonists encouragement. In order to give the General Assembly a rest and time for reflection before taking up the serious problems ahead of it Governor Ellis adjourned that body from the 17th of February until the 8th of March. Before it assembled on the latter date he continued the recess until the 16th of June.

In April he visited the southern part of the Colony and became acquainted with many of its leading citizens. On that journey he was impressed with the location of Hardwicke on the Great Ogeechee and approved the suggestion of Governor Reynolds that it be made the capital of the Province.

**Governor Ellis to the Assembly**—On June 16, 1757, Governor Ellis delivered his first address to the Assembly as follows:

"*Gentlemen of the Council and of the Commons House of Assembly:*

"The Honour his Majesty has been graciously pleased to confer on me in appointing me to preside in the Government of this Province calls in a particular Manner for the Exertion of my best Abilities to approve myself not unworthy of so distinguishing a Mark of the Royal Favour.

"Persuaded I am that the surest Means of doing this will be to consult your Felicity and the general Welfare of this Infant Colony.

"Directed by these Considerations I shall always be glad of your Advise and Assistance, and shall esteem every Proposal of yours of the same Tendency as the most important Service you can render me.

"I can with unfeigned Sincerity declare that I enter upon this Station with the most disinterested Views, without Prejudice to any Man or Body of Men, or Retrospect to past Transactions or Disputes, but animated with the warmest Zeal for whatever concerns your Happiness or the publick Utility: sincerely inclined to concur with you in every just and necessary Measure, and fully resolved that if unfortunately my wishes and endeavours prove fruitless, to be the first to solicit my Recall.

"From such Dispositions on my Part I would willingly hope that you will not be wanting on yours; I flatter myself that your Zeal for the publick Good is at least equal, and that you come together in the most dispassionate Temper, divested of Prepossession, Animosity and distrust,—Heartily disposed to coöperate with me in promoting the publick Service by establishing Order, mutual Confidence and domestic Tranquillity, as there never was a Conjuncture when these were more immediately necessary.

"However interesting the Objects that used to engage your Thoughts may seem, they certainly bear no Proportion to those that now demand your Attention. Your Religion, your Liberty, your all is at stake. I do therefore earnestly exhort you to study your true Interests only; not to spend your Time, so valuable to yourselves and the Public, in the Pursuit of Things trivial or unreasonable, that may defeat the great Ends of your Meeting. Lay aside your Jealousies of each Other and of Government, and do not forget that you are People who have great and daily Obligations to your Mother Country for Support and protection in this your exposed and hopeless State; that you have a constitutional Dependence upon her, calculated for your Advantage, Security, and the general Good; and that from a suitable and becoming Conduct alone you will be entitled to, and may reasonably expect a Continuation of her Regard and Assistance; and every sort of Encouragement and Indulgence from me that his Majesty's Instructions (framed upon the purest principles of Equity and the strictest Regard to your Happiness) can authorize.

"It is evident how much you have been the object of the royal Attention and Favour by the late Establishment of a regular System of Government among you, wherein your Interest and Convenience were principally consulted.

"It is further manifested by the Readiness with which the later supply of Arms and Ammunition were granted and Presents for securing the Indians in your Alliance and Defence at a Time of great Exigence when the very Existence of the State is threatened by the Efforts of a powerful and implacable Enemy.

"These Considerations ought to inspire you with the deepest Sentiments of Gratitude, and these Sentiments will be best shown in the Discharge of those Duties you owe yourselves and your Country upon this important Occasion.

"As I know how precious your Time now is, I call you together but for a short Sitting, although upon Points of the last Consequence to your present Safety, Credit, and future Prosperity.

"Gentlemen, it would be needless to represent to you the dangerous Situation you are in, and the absolute Necessity there is of exerting Yourselves vigorously, by employing in the most speedy and efficacious Manner every Means in your Power that may tend to avert those affecting Calamities that have already been so severely felt by some and are justly dreaded by all his Majesty's American Subjects, notwithstanding his paternal Endeavours to prevent them.

"The Chief Part of these Misfortunes may not improperly be ascribed to the shameful Neglect, not to say Perverseness of those who suffer, and by whose timely Efforts and Attention they might in a great Measure have been prevented.

"Instructed by so fatal an Example, and urged by so many pressing and alarming Circumstances, I doubt not that you will distinguish yourselves by an uncommon Zeal and Alacrity in concerting and carrying into Execution such Measures as are most suitable to the dangerous Crisis.

"When Alarms are sounding from every Quarter, and when so active and formidable an Enemy is upon your Borders, projecting by every means that inveterate Malice can suggest the Accomplishment of your Ruin, no Time is to be lost.

"I am sensible it is but little you are able to do, yet that Little should be done with Spirit and Cheerfulness becoming Englishmen who know how to prize the peculiar and inestimable Blessings they enjoy.

"The Construction of Log Forts in proper Situations would certainly contribute to your Safety by affording Places of Retreat where, upon any sudden Emergency, a short stand might be made until Succour could arrive; and any Encouragement that can be given toward procuring an Accession of Inhabitants would accelerate your Prosperity, add to your Strength, and be the best Security in Times to Come.

"These weighty Considerations naturally suggest the Expediency and Necessity of framing forthwith such Laws as shall be most conducive to those salutary Ends."

He addressed the separate bodies as follows:

*"Gentlemen of the Commons House of Assembly:*

"I have ordered the State of the publick Debt to be laid before you, and I rely upon your taking the most effectual and least burthensome Method for its Discharge and for preventing the like Incumbrances for the future. As the Maintenance of the publick Faithe and Credit of this Province is at all Times essentially necessary, more especially at the present when your Safety is so closely connected with it, I, therefore hope it will constitute a capital object of your Deliberations."

*"Gentlemen of the Council and of the Commons House of Assembly:*

"I defer matters of a more general Nature to a future Occasion when the Season will admit of a longer Absence from your Private Concerns, and have now only to recommend to you in the strongest Manner Unanimity and Dispatch, and you may depend on my ready Concurrence in everything that can promote your real Happiness."

**Reply of the Assembly**—The reply of the Assembly framed by Messrs. Habersham, Knox, Harris, Clifton and James Mackay was as follows:

"May it please your Honour.

"We, his Majesty's most dutiful and loyal Subjects, the Council of Georgia in General Assembly met, beg Leave to return your Honour our unfeigned Thanks for your affectionate Speech to both Houses at the opening of this Session.

"With Hearts overflowing with Gratitude to the best of Kings for his paternal Goodness in taking the distressed Circumstances of this Province into his royal Consideration and appointing your Honour to preside over us, we take this first Opportunity of congratulating your Honour upon your safe Arrival in this Province, and promise to ourselves from your Honour's distinguished Abilities, acknowledged Probity and unwearied Application, that the Day of your Arrival will prove the Era of the Prosperity of this Colony.

"We beg Leave to assure your Honour that we shall at all times esteem it our indispensable Duty to offer you our best Advise and Assistance, and shall also chearfully coöperate with you in every just and necessary Measure for the general Welfare and Felicity of this infant Colony; not doubting but your Wishes and Endeavours will merit the Divine Favour, and that your Honour will prove a long and lasting Blessing to this Province.

"We are truly sensible of our exposed and helpless State, and the great Necessity there is for Unanimity and mutual Confidence in this Time of publick Danger, and we do with the greatest Sincerity assure your Honour that we will, to the utmost of our Power, studiously avoid every Occasion of Altercation and the Pursuit of Things trivial or unseasonable, and that we shall ever retain the most grateful Remembrance of the great Obligations we have to our Mother Country for Support and Protection, and of her constant Attention to our Safety so recently manifested by the very seasonable Supply of Arms and Ammunition, and Presents for securing the Indians in our Alliance and Defence in this critical Conjuncture; constantly bearing in Mind our Constitutional Dependence on her, and endeavouring to frame our Conduct so that it may intitle us to a continuance of her Regard and Assistance and to the royal Favour and Indulgence.

"The distressed and calamitous Condition of many of his Majesty's Subjects on this Continent deeply affects us, and we shall, with the greatest Readiness, concur in every Measure in our Power to enable your Honour to defeat the Machinations of our Enemies and to avert those Evils their Malice may suggest for the Accomplishment of our Ruin.

"We are sorry to say that little is in our Power, but that Little we shall do with Spirit and Alacrity, accounting the Preservation of those invaluable Blessings, our Religion, Laws, and Liberties, our nearest Concern.

"We shall give immediate Attention to the framing of such Laws as may best tend to the Security of this Province and the Increase of its Inhabitants, and shall readily join in effectually supporting the public Credit, and preventing future Incumbrances."

**An Era of Good Will**—The cordial spirit, confidence and coöperation between the Governor and the Assembly continued throughout Governor Ellis' term of office. At the start an effort was made by William Little, who had been private secretary to Governor Reynolds, to create trouble for Governor Ellis and reinstate Reynolds. For this purpose Little addressed a letter to the Assembly warning them "not to censure their own conduct" by their representation of conditions in the Province. He also warned them to beware of the insinuations of the new Governor and to distrust professions of friendship made by the officers. The letter was intended to make the Assembly the authors of the Colony's troubles and Little's intention was that his letter should be read by one of his friends, a former member of Council whom Ellis had suspended from his seat in Council and his position as judge. That man expected to be elected a member of the Assembly and then Speaker of the House. Little expected that his letter would cause a division in the Assembly and lead to its dissolution by the Governor. As the result of that there would be disorder which would be used as a basis for the claim that Governor Ellis' administration was a failure and would lead to reinstating Governor Reynolds.

The plot failed because the ex-councilor and ex-judge was not elected to the Assembly. The failure of the plot and the wise measures of Governor Ellis won over the friends of the former Governor and peace was restored.

From that time to the end of Governor Ellis' administration the sessions of the Assembly were held regularly with harmony, ability and honesty in the conduct of public business.

**Georgia Divided Into Eight Parishes**—An important act of the Legislature divided the Province into eight parishes and provided for the establishment of religious worship according to the rites and ceremonies of the Church of England. The Church wardens and vestrymen of the different parishes were authorized to assess rates or taxes for the repair of the churches, the relief of the poor and other parochial services. This act was approved on March 17, 1758, and by it eight parishes were constituted as follows:

CHRIST CHURCH: Including Savannah and land along the Savannah River as far as Goshen, thence in a southwest line to the Great Ogeechee River; and from the town of Savannah eastward to the mouth of the Savannah River, including Sea Islands to the mouth of the Great Ogeechee, and all settlements on the north side of the Ogeechee to the western boundary of the Province.

SAINT MATTHEW: Including the districts of Abercorn and Goshen and the district of Ebenezer from the northwest boundary of Christ Church Parish up the Savannah River to Beaver Dam, and southwest to the mouth of Horse Creek on the Great Ogeechee River.

SAINT GEORGE: Including the district of Halifax from the northwest boundary of St. Matthew Parish up the Savannah River, from the mouth of Mackbeen's Swamp to the head of it and thence to the head of Lambol's Creek and to the Great Ogeechee River.

SAINT PAUL: Including the district of Augusta from the northwest boundary of St. George Parish, southwest as far as the Ogeechee River and northwest up the Savannah River as far as Broad River.

SAINT PHILIP: Including the town of Hardwicke and district of Ogeechee on the south side of the Great Ogeechee, extending northwest up that river as far as the Lower Indian Trading Path leading from Mount Pleasant and southward from the town of Hardwicke as far as the swamp of James Dunham, including the settlements on the north side of the north branches of the River Midway, with the island of Ossabaw; and from the head of Dunham's Swamp in a northwest line.

SAINT JOHN: Including Sunbury in the district of Midway and Newport; and all the territory from the southern bounds of St. Philip Parish southward as far as the north line of Samuel Hastings, and thence southeast to the south branch of Newport, including the islands of Saint Catherine and Bermuda; and from the north line of Samuel Hastings northwest.

SAINT ANDREW: Including the district of Darien from the south boundary of Saint John Parish to the River Altamaha, including the islands of Sapelo and Eastwood and the sea islands north of Egg Island; and northwest up the River Altamaha to its forks.

SAINT JAMES: Including the town and district of Frederica with the great and little St. Simon's Islands and the adjacent islands.

The church already built at Savannah with the adjacent ground used as a burial place was designated as the Parish Church and cemetery of Christ Church Parish.

By a curious provision of the act Bartholomew Zouberbuhler, then minister at Savannah, was made rector of Christ Church and incorporated as a body politic under the name of the Rector and Christ Church in Savannah, with authority to sue and be sued in all the courts of the Province. The act said that he should be in actual possession of the church, cemetery and appurtenances with the glebe land already granted to him and the tenement near the church with its other buildings. He was by law given "the cure of souls within said Parish."

Similar provisions were made for the building and incorporation of parish churches at Augusta and the other parishes. For this purpose Governor Ellis, James Habersham, Francis Harris, James Mackay, James Edward Powell, William Clifton, William Knox, David Montaigut, James Deveaux, Noble Wimberly Jones, Thomas Rasberry, William Russel, William Spencer, and Charles Watson were appointed commissioners as soon as funds were provided by Parliament, by charitable donations or by the General Assembly of Georgia to build churches in each of the other six parishes, Saint Matthew, Saint George, Saint Philip, Saint John, Saint Andrew, and Saint James. With the churches they were to build in each of those parishes a parsonage with outbuildings for the rector and to lay out and enclose a cemetery or burial place for each of those churches. When these churches were built and rectors appointed they were to be incorporated as in the case of Christ Church in Savannah and Saint Paul at Augusta. Vestrymen and church wardens were to be selected and take oath for the faithful performance of their duties.

For the expense of keeping the church buildings in repair, caring for the cemeteries, providing utensils, bread and wine for the sacrament, pay for the clerk and sexton and provision for the poor of each parish, the rector, church wardens and vestrymen were authorized to levy a tax on the real and personal property of the inhabitants sufficient to yield in the parishes of Christ Church and Saint Paul (Savannah and Augusta) 30 pounds ($150) and in parishes where churches had not yet been erected 10 pounds ($50). The act specified the method of collecting that tax.

The rector, church wardens and vestrymen were authorized to appoint sextons and fix their salaries and fees. The rector was a member of the vestry and the church wardens were directed to secure at the expense of the parish a well bound paper or parchment book in which the vestry clerk of the parish was to register the births, christenings, marriages and burials of all persons who were born, christened, married or buried within the parish, and for failure to make such a record there was a penalty of five pounds. For each entry the vestry clerk was given a fee of one shilling. The registers were to be accepted by the court as sufficient proof of births, marriages, christenings and burials, and if any party was convicted of making a false entry or maliciously erasing, altering or defacing an entry or of embezzling an entry or book of record he was guilty of a felony and to be punished with death without benefit of clergy.

Each vestry was instructed to nominate a suitable person to keep a record of its proceedings and act as custodian of its books and papers. Notwithstanding the other power given them rectors were not authorized to exercise any ecclesiastical jurisdiction, or to administer ecclesiastical law.

This act clearly establishing a union of church and state in Georgia seems strange to those who have lived under the present Constitution of Georgia, but it must be remembered that all the American colonies were then under the Government of England, and the Church of England, established several centuries before, was still the State Church, and even in our time the proposal for its disestablishment as a State Church has been vigorously opposed, although in England as in this country, all men are free to worship God, each according to the dictates of his own conscience.

When this act was passed there were a good many dissenters in Georgia, including many of the best citizens, who were Presbyterians, Lutherans, Congregationalists, Methodists, Baptists, and Hebrews. The only exception was in the case of Catholics, who were called Papists, and in spite of that 400 Catholics, Acadians expelled from their own country by the English Government, had found refuge in Georgia and were given food and clothing at the public expense.

One provision of a law throws light on the general apprehension of the people of sudden danger from insurrection or invasion. Every male inhabitant, 16 years of age or more, was by the act of July 28, 1757, to go armed on Sabbath days, fasts and festivals to the place of public worship in the town or district where he lived, carrying "one good gun or pair of pistols with at least six charges of gunpowder and ball."

**Other Laws Enacted**—To encourage skilled labor and attract white men from other colonies to settle in Georgia and work as carpenters, masons, bricklayers, plasterers, and joiners, the General Assembly on March 15, 1758, passed an act forbidding the employment of negro slaves in such work unless white artisans refused to work at fair and reasonable prices, which were to be ascertained by commissioners appointed for the purpose.

To prevent disputes and disagreements between colonists and the Indians, traffic with the natives was forbidden except by special license, and the same was true of acquiring land from the natives.

The law provided for quarantine regulations and commissioners were appointed to superintend the labor of the inhabitants in building log forts at convenient points to protect the Colony.

An act passed on July 19, 1757, provided severe penalties for the transportation of cattle, horses, sheep, hogs, corn, rice, flour and bread, beyond the southern limit of the Province. This was to prevent evil-minded persons from securing provisions and selling them to the enemy.

A system of patrols was created with power to preserve order on plantations throughout the Colony.

In order to quiet the title of lands a law was passed confirming the title of land conveyed by the Trustees or by grants from the Crown since the Trustees surrendered their charter, and this held good against anyone claiming an ownership or interest in property under the Lords proprietors of Carolina, or under any former grant obtained before the charter of Georgia was granted by the Crown to the Trustees. This act received the approval of the home government and gave great relief because a number of old grants affecting land in the southern part of the Province had originated in what appears to be carelessness of the Lords proprietors in Carolina, although they had never been confirmed by actual possession.

All persons who had received grants under the Trustees were required within three years from March 20, 1758, to appear before the Governor and Council, make good their claims and receive the King's grants for the property.

Other acts of the Legislature reduced the rate of interest to eight per cent., prescribed qualifications for jurors, provided more speedy recovery of debts in justices' courts, fixed legal fees of magistrates and constables, prescribed the methods by which women could unite with their husbands in conveying land, created extraordinary courts to try cases arising between merchants and mariners, provided penalties for stealing horses and cattle and punishment for those who changed the mark or brand of another or killed his stock. Fences were regulated and the law concerning militia was carefully revised. Special laws were enacted concerning Savannah. One established a watch, two regulated taverns, punch houses and sale of spiritous liquors, two provided for the conduct of a market, one forbade the erection of wooden chimneys and another authorized Trustees to buy residences for the present and future governors. A curious act regulated the size of bread. Other acts provided for the construction of a magazine, for the repair of Christ Church, for the general regulation of the town, for Tybee Lighthouse, for the support of criminal courts and for the expenses of government. Masters of vessels were prohibited from conveying debtors out from the province. Frauds in lumber were pointed out.

Altogether nearly fifty acts were passed by the General Assembly during the administration of Governor Ellis and received the sanction of the British Government. The Legislature was free from dissensions and with honesty of purpose and unanimity worked together for the best interest of the Province. Their relations with the Governor continued cordial to the end. Under these happy conditions of government, prosperity returned to the Colony and it entered upon an era of development which increased under the administration of Governor Wright.

**Condition of Georgia's Fortifications**—In a letter written to the British Board of Trade on May 30, 1758, Governor Ellis gave this statement concerning the military defenses of the Colony and other important matters:

"Immediately after our Assembly rose I took a Journey to the south in order to examine into the state of things in that Quarter. On my way I touch'd at the river Ogeeche and saw the Fort that had lately been raised there in consequence of the Resolutions of the Assembly last year. It is of a Quadrangular Figure, each side measuring 100 yards, constructed with thick logs set upright, fourteen feet long, five whereof are sunk in the Earth, and has four little Bastions, pierced for small and great guns that would render it very defenceable. From thence I proceeded to Medway where I found the Inhabitants had inclosed their Church in the same manner, and erected a Battery of eight guns at Sunbury in a very proper situation for defending the River.

"I reached Frederica two days after, the ruinous condition of which I could not view without concern. A dreadful Fire, that lately happened there, has destroyed the greatest part of the town. Time has done almost as much for the Fortifications. Never was there a spot better calculated for a place of arms or more capable of being fortified to advantage. It lies on the west side of the Island St. Simon's, opposite the chief and most southern branch of the great river Altamaha. The military works were never very large, but compact and extremely defenceable.

"The Sound will conveniently admit of 40 Gun Ships, and those of 500 Tons burthen may come abreast of the Town; but for three Miles below it the River winds in such a manner that an Enemy must in that space be exposed to our Fire without being able to return it. In short it is of the last importance that that place should be kept in constant repair and properly Garrisoned, as it is apparently and really the Key of this and the rest of the King's Provinces to the South, but the wretched condition in which it now is makes it easy to conjecture what would be its fate should Spanish War suddenly break out.

"From hence I went to the Island of Cumberland on the south point whereof stands Fort William, a Post of no less consequence, as is evident from the Defence it made against Twenty Eight Spanish Vessels and a considerable Land Force that attack'd it unsuccessfully in the year 1742. General Oglethorpe has in my humble opinion displayed a great deal of skill in his choice of such Situations. This Fort commands a noble Inlet from the Sea, —the entrance of the River St. Mary,—which runs deep into the Country,— and the Inland Passage thro' which the runaway Negroes and other Deserters are obliged to go on their way to St. Augustine.

"The works are of no great extent, but admirably contrived to be maintained by a small Garrison, and might be repaired without any great expence;

3000 pounds Sterling would be sufficient, and Frederica might be rebuilt with solid and lasting materials as well as be rendered very strong for about 10,000 pounds, and until these things are done I apprehend this Province, and I may add the next, will be very insecure.

"While I was at Cumberland I saw and had much discourse with Mr. Grey. He is a very unintelligible character, shrewd, sagacious, and capable of affording the best advice to others, but ridiculously absurd in every part of his own conduct.

"He is now settled upon that Island with his family, and engaged in a small Traffick with the Spaniards and Creek Indians. With him I found a person lately come from St. Augustine who informed me that a new Governor and 200 fresh troops from the *Havana* were just arrived there, and that the Spaniards persisted in their design of settling a New Colony in the environs of that Castle; and that they were preparing to build two or three other Forts on the River of St. Juan.

"This information has a little alarmed our people, which is not much to be wondered at considering their defenceless condition. Another circumstance which augments their fears is an account we have received that three French Privateers are now cruising upon our Coast, whilst we have no vessel of War stationed here to molest them, and but a very incompetent force to prevent their Crews doing much mischief should they attempt a descent.

"It is more than a year and a half since a Troop of Rangers were begun to be raised here. The late Governor drew Bills upon the Earl of Loudoun for their Subsistence, which were protested.

"Upon the most urgent and repeated remonstrances his Lordship, ten months ago, furnished me with a Credit upon the Pay Master at New York for 850 pounds Sterling to maintain then 'till further orders.' That sum is expended, but those orders are not yet arrived, notwithstanding his Lordship has embarked for England.

"I am now supporting them upon my own Credit which, that I may be the longer able to do, I have been compell'd to disband half their number, and if General Abercrombie, to whom I have repeatedly and pressingly written upon this subject, does not speedily authorize me to keep them on foot and appropriate a proper Fund for that purpose, I shall be constrained to dismiss the rest."

It appears that Governor Ellis had not received aid from the home government for some months after the foregoing letter was written and he again wrote to the Commissioners of Trade and Plantations on the 25th of October, 1758, calling attention to the need of support for the troop or rangers which, as he said before, had been maintained at his personal expense and on his own credit. He said:

"The want of means to inforce the Laws necessarily brings the Government into contempt, and constrains me to wink at many enormities committed by our own People and the Savages. It is not uncommon for the former to set the Civil Power at defiance, and gangs of the latter have more than once lived at discretion upon the outsettlers and drove away numbers of their cattle. A few months ago some straggling Indians from the Northward, who are now settled in the Creek Country, robbed and murdered a whole family not forty miles from this town. I immediately insisted upon satisfaction from the Creeks who, with some difficulty and reluctance, in part gave it me: for one of the murderers they put publickly to death. The others made their escape but parties are sent in quest of them, and I have strong assurances that they shall suffer the same fate when they can be taken. It is very happy this affair ended thus; for had those savages been more averse to do Justice we could not have compelled them. Our weakness then must have been most apparent, and Crimes of this nature would probably have been perpetrated daily."

**French Privateers Driven Off**—Considerable alarm was caused by the report that French privateers were on the coast of Georgia, ready to prey upon the shipping, and Governor Ellis met the emergency with remarkable resourcefulness. Although the British men-of-war, with headquarters at Charleston, had orders to guard the coast of Georgia against privateers, they failed to perform that duty regularly and seemed to prefer rest in the harbor to active work at sea. Governor Ellis tried to secure greater activity on their part, but finding his request ineffectual, fitted out a ship with a battery of fourteen carriage guns and fourteen swivel guns, put her in command of experienced officers and kept her cruising up and down the coast of Georgia for six weeks. This had a wholesome effect upon the enemy and resulted in more activity by the ships of war at Charleston.

**Relations With the Spaniards**—On May 17, 1758, Governor Ellis, whose official title had been Lieutenant-Governor up to that time, was made Governor-in-Chief of the Province.

Having been relieved of attention to legislation by the enactment of necessary laws Governor Ellis turned his attention to establishing cordial relations with the Spaniards and securing the friendship of the Indians.

At this time Fernez de Herridir was Governor at St. Augustine and Governor Ellis wrote him a letter in complimentary terms, expressing his regret that the Spanish Governor would soon leave and informed him that the Indians had in mind an attack upon Florida. To prevent this Governor Ellis pledged his best efforts. The Spanish Governor sent a courteous reply, but intimated that the disturbances given the Spaniards by the Indians were designed by the English, or Indians in the British interest. Governor Ellis denied that and also denied insinuations of the Spanish Governor that English subjects had illegally settled upon land in Spanish territory.

**Indian War Threatened**—A more serious problem for Governor Ellis was the threat of a terrible Indian war. There was then war between France and England and the defeat of the English forces under Braddock on the

Monongahela River, Mercer at Oswego, and Monroe at Fort William Henry, brought a crisis in affairs and roused the American colonists. A change of the British ministry put William Pitt in charge of the conduct of war and he with characteristic energy and promptness wrote all the provincial governors that the King was determined to prosecute the war vigorously and urged them to raise, officer, and clothe regiments for the defense of their provinces.

On receipt of that letter Governor Ellis laid it before the Assembly. That body in its reply showed the impossibility of furnishing aid to the British Army because of the poverty of the inhabitants of Georgia, the sparseness of population and the necessity for defending themselves. With a larger frontier exposed to the enemy than any other Colony, with fewer people, weaker in resources and protected with only one troop of twenty rangers, unpaid and undisciplined, and without any ship of war to guard the coast, the Assembly could not furnish the supplies desired, but on the contrary, petitioned in vain for the help they sorely needed.

The intrigues of the French with the Indians made it all important that the friendship of the natives be secured and a conference was proposed between Governor Ellis of Georgia, Governor Lyttleton of South Carolina, and Colonel Bouquet, commander of the British forces in the southern provinces, to agree on some plan of operations with the Indians. It was agreed that the Creek Indians should visit Charleston and then Savannah and should be impressed with the power and resources of the English by the kind treatment they received and the evidence of strength which they saw there.

The interview between the two governors took place at Beaufort, South Carolina, and Colonel Bouquet ordered one hundred men of the Virginia troops to Savannah. He also put the Georgia rangers on the King's establishment and payroll.

**Conference With the Creek Indians**—The conference between the Governor of Georgia and the chiefs and head men of the Upper and Lower Creeks occurred at Savannah on October 25, 1757. In order to impress the Indians with the military strength of the Colony, Governor Ellis ordered that they be received by the first regiment of militia commanded by Colonel Noble Jones, that sixteen cannon be mounted in batteries around Savannah and that seven field pieces be placed in position in front of the Governor's residence.

As the Indians approached, escorted by Captain Milledge and the rangers, they were met by Captain Bryan and a cavalcade of leading citizens, who welcomed them in the name of the Governor and refreshed them in a tent pitched for that purpose. After this preliminary reception the Indians, preceded by citizens on horseback and followed by the rangers, entered the town gate, where they were saluted by three cannon from the King's battery, three from the Prince's battery, five from Fort Halifax and five from Loudoun's bastions. At the gate the citizens opened their column to the right and left, facing inwards and the Indians marching between them entered the town, where they were received by Colonel Jones at the head of the regiment and conducted with drums beating and colors flying to the council chamber. In passing the Governor's residence the column was saluted by the battery there and the salute was repeated by guns in the water battery and cannon on vessels in the river.

At the council house the regiment filed to right and left and in parallel lines, facing the chiefs and warriors as they advanced, presented arms. At the steps of the council chamber they were saluted by the Virginia Blues and on entering the house were met by the Governor with outstretched arms with these words: "My friends and brothers, behold my hands and my arms! Our common Enemies, the French, have told you they are red to the elbows. View them. Do they speak the truth? Let your own eyes witness. You see they are white, and could you see my heart, you would find it as pure, but very warm and true to you, my friends. The French tell you whoever shakes my hands will immediately be struck with disease and die. If you believe that lying, foolish talk, don't touch me. If you do not, I am ready to embrace you."

This kind of talk pleased the Indians and they shook hands warmly with the Governor. Friendly greetings followed and the day's exercises ended with a dinner at which the head men of twenty-one Indian towns were entertained. During their stay in Savannah the Indians received many presents and were bountifully feasted.

On the following Thursday, after another parade by the military with martial salutes, they met in the council chamber, which was crowded with citizens. There Governor Ellis again spoke to them in these cordial words:

"Observe, my friends, how serene and cloudless this day appears! I cannot but consider it as a good omen of the success of this interview; and I hope that you are all come with hearts resembling it, unclouded by jealousies, and with dispositions suitable to the good work of tightening the chain and making the path straight forever between us." He then read in their hearing, with great solemnity, a communication which he had prepared, entitled "A Letter from the Great King to His Beloved Children of the Creek Nation."

The Indians were greatly pleased with the Governor's words and a treaty of peace and friendship between Georgia and the Creek Confederacy was signed on November 3, 1757.

The seriousness of the situation in the South was increased when General Abercrombie drove the French out of their strongholds on the Ohio River. The Cherokees joined the English in the capture of Fort Duquesne and the French retreating, burned the houses, abandoned the place and went down the river to establish themselves west of the Cherokee Mountains. This move of the French to the South meant danger for Georgia and the Carolinas and the influence of the French upon the Upper tribes of the Cherokees was soon seen. There was an unfortunate quarrel between the Indians and Virginians, which helped the French and gave them access to the Indian towns. In those days horses ran wild in the woods and both the Indians and the white people on the frontiers would catch horses and use them for their own purposes. While the Indians were returning home from the war with the French through western Virginia, some of them, having lost their horses, caught animals they found, not knowing that they belonged to any person in Virginia. The Virginians resented this and killed twelve or fourteen Indians, taking several prisoners. As the Cherokees had helped the white men to hold their frontiers they bitterly resented the killing of their kindred and returning home told the nation. The flame of indignation spread through the Cherokee towns and those who had lost friends or relatives were furious and threatened vengeance against the white people.

Their chiefs were unable to restrain them and the emissaries of France added fuel to the flame, telling the Indians that the English intended to kill all their men and make slaves of their wives and children. The young Indians fell with fury upon outlying settlements and at Fort Loudoun on the Tennessee River, where there was a garrison of two hundred men. Soldiers foraging in the woods were attacked and killed by the Indians. Governor Lyttleton, of South Carolina, sent out a body of militia and went to Fort Prince George on the Savannah River near the Cherokee town of Keowee. There he made a treaty with six Indian chiefs on the 26th of December, 1759, and by its provisions thirty Indian warriors were left at the fort as hostages. They were confined in a small place and about the same time smallpox broke out in the Governor's camp. His men became dissatisfied and mutinous and the Governor was obliged to return to Charleston.

The Indian war broke out again and the natives claimed that the treaty was made by a few chiefs without authority. Fourteen men were killed by the Indians within a mile of Fort Prince George.

By a stratagem, Occonostota, an Indian chief, induced Captain Coytmore, who commanded the fort, to come out and confer with him at the river's side. Captain Coytmore went and at a signal from Occonostota he was attacked by Indians in ambush and killed. Lieutenants Bell and Foster were wounded. Because of this outrage orders were given in the fort to put the thirty Indian hostages in irons. The Indians stabbed the first man who laid hold on them and wounded two more. On this the garrison butchered the thirty Indian hostages. This further inflamed the Cherokees, many of whom had friends or relatives among the thirty who were slain. The infuriated savages rushed upon the frontiers, killing men, women and children, and those who escaped perished from hunger in the woods.

An appeal for aid was sent to General Amherst, commander-in-chief in America, and he sent a battalion of Highlanders and four companies of Royal Scots under the command of Colonel Montgomery, who sailed from New York for the relief of Georgia and Carolina. Joined by the militia of South Carolina he quickly invaded the Cherokee country and surprised an Indian town, Estatoe. There, under his orders, every Indian except women and children was put to death except a few who managed to escape. It was a town of two hundred houses, well supplied with corn, hogs and poultry, but it was reduced to ashes. Sugar-town and all settlements east of the Blue Ridge had the same fate. About sixty Indians were killed, forty were taken prisoners and the rest driven into the mountains. Having done this with the loss of only three or four men, Colonel Montgomery marched to the relief of Fort Prince George.

Colonel Montgomery pushed the fight against the Indians and both the Highlanders and the Royal Scots fought hard, but the Indians were driven at a great cost to the white men.

Surrounded by Indians and their provisions gone the men in Fort Loudoun were in a desperate condition. At a council of war Captain Steuart, an officer of great sagacity, who was beloved by the Indians who were loyal to the English, went among the Cherokees and arranged for the surrender of Fort Loudoun on the condition that the garrison was to march out with the arms and drums, each soldier having ammunition and all the baggage he could carry. They were to march to Fort Prince George or Virginia as they preferred, and a number of Indians were to escort them and hunt provisions during the march; lame and sick soldiers who could not march were to be cared for at Indian towns until they recovered and then were to be allowed to go to Fort Prince George. The Indians were to furnish as many horses for the march as they could and be paid for them, and the surplus of arms and ammunition was to be given to the Indians when the garrison marched out.

The surrender was made on August 7, 1760, when the white men marched out accompanied by Occonostota and other Indians. They marched fifteen miles that day in the direction of Fort Prince George. They camped on a plain near an Indian town and that night their Indian attendants left them. The next morning at dawn a large body of Indians attacked the camp and poured a heavy fire on the white men. The soldiers, enfeebled by hardship, were unable to make a strong defense. Captain Demere, three other officers and twenty-six men fell at the first fire. Others fled into the woods and were afterward taken prisoners. Captain Steuart and those who remained were seized, bound and carried back to Fort Loudoun. When Attakullakulla, a noted Indian, heard that his friend, Captain Steuart, had escaped death, he went to the fort and bought him from the Indian who captured him, giving him his rifle, clothes and all he could command as a ransom. He then took possession of Captain Demere's house, where he kept Captain Steuart his prisoner as a member of his family and shared with him such provisions as his table afforded until he could be rescued. The other soldiers were kept in severe captivity some time and then ransomed at heavy expense.

Occonostota then planned to attack Fort Prince George. Captain Steuart was brought to the Indian council of war and there told that he must aid in the capture of Fort Prince George by the Indians or witness the burning alive of other captives. Captain Steuart made known his trouble to Attakullakulla, who aided him to escape. Attakullakulla claimed Steuart as his prisoner and said he intended to go hunting a few days and carry his prisoner with him. At the same time Captain Steuart went among his soldiers and told them they could never expect to be ransomed by their government if they gave the Indians any assistance against Fort Prince George.

Accordingly, the old Indian chief, with Captain Steuart, the chief's wife, his brother and two soldiers began a long march through the woods. For nine days and nights they traveled through a wilderness, shaping their course by the sun and moon toward Virginia. On the tenth day they reached the Holston River, where they met a party of three hundred men sent out by Colonel Bird for the relief of soldiers who might escape from Fort Loudoun.

On the fourteenth day they reached Colonel Bird's camp on the Virginia frontier. There Captain Steuart loaded his Indian friend and his party with presents and provisions and sent him back to protect the other prisoners until they could be ransomed and to exert his influence among the Cherokees to restore peace. Major Thompson, commanding the militia on the Georgia and Carolina frontiers, was ordered to deliver ten weeks' provisions at Fort Loudoun and warn the commanding officer of danger. The settlers near Augusta secured their families in stockade forts. A messenger was sent to Attakullakulla asking him to tell the Cherokees that Fort Prince George was impregnable with vast quantities of powder buried under the ground everywhere around it to blow up enemies who came near it. Valuable presents were sent to ransom the prisoners at Fort Loudoun and those still confined in the Indian town who had survived hardship and hunger, disease and captivity were released and delivered to the commanding officer at Fort Prince George.

Still a majority of the Cherokee nation rejected the offer of peace. Their lower towns had been destroyed by Colonel Montgomery and warriors in other settlements had lost friends and relatives. Several Frenchmen had crept into the upper towns and helped to increase the bad feeling against the English provinces. Among these Lewis Latinac, a French officer, actively instigated mischief, furnished the Indians with arms and ammunition and urged them to war, persuading them that the English intended their extermination, and at a great meeting of the nation he pulled out his hatchet and sticking it into a log, cried: "Who is the man that will take this up for the King of France?" Saloue, a young warrior of Estatoe, caught hold of the hatchet and cried: "I am for war! and the spirits of our brothers who have been slain call upon us to revenge their death. He is no better than a woman who refuses to follow me." Others seized the tomahawk, burning with impatience for war.

General Amherst was again asked for aid and Colonel James Grant in command of the Highlanders was sent to the aid of the southern provinces. He arrived at Charleston, where he remained during the winter. A provincial regiment was raised in South Carolina under the command of Colonel Middleton and presents were given the Chickasaws and Catawbas for their aid against the Cherokees. With the aid of the South Carolina regiment and the

Indian allies Colonel Grant had about two thousand six hundred men. With this force early in the spring he began to march. Having served in America several years and been in several engagements with Indians he knew their methods of war.

On May 27 Colonel Grant arrived at Fort Prince George and Attakullakulla, hearing that he was advancing against the Cherokees with a powerful army hastened to the camp to show his desire for peace and told Colonel Grant that he always had been a firm friend of the English, that the outrages of his countrymen covered him with shame and filled his heart with grief, but he would gladly interpose in their behalf to bring about peace. He said he had been censured by his people for his peaceful disposition and that the young warriors delighted in war and despised his counsels after he had tried to get the war club buried and good relations with the provinces reëstablished. Now he was determined to persuade his people to seek safety and agree on terms of peace. He, therefore, begged the colonel to go no further until he returned.

Colonel Grant replied that he had the highest opinion of his honesty and integrity, that he had always been a friend to the English and that if his wise policy had been observed it would have had happy results.

On June 7 Colonel Grant marched from Prince George with thirty days' provisions, with ninety Indians and thirty woodsmen from the frontiers, painted like Indians. They, under command of Captain Kennedy, were ordered to march in front and scour the woods. After some days they found a body of Indians posted on a hill on the right flank and the savages rushed down, pouring heavy fire on the advance guard. The Indians were soon repulsed, but formed again on the heights and Colonel Grant's command had to march a considerable distance between them and the river, from the opposite side of which a large body of Indians fired on the troops as they advanced. Colonel Grant sent a party up the hill to drive the savages from the heights and then faced about his main force to charge the Indians who fired on them from the river. The fight raged from eight o'clock in the morning until eleven. At length the Cherokees gave way and were pursued. They finally disappeared about two o'clock. The loss of the Indians was not known.

Colonel Grant lost between fifty and sixty killed and wounded. To prevent the killed from being scalped Colonel Grant ordered that they be not buried but sunk in the river. To provide horses for the wounded bags of flour were thrown into the river and the army marched on to Estatoe, which they reached about midnight. The next day they burnt that town and fourteen others, destroying the corn, cattle and other stores of the enemy. As a result the miserable savages with their families had to seek shelter and subsistence in the barren mountains.

For thirty days Colonel Grant continued in the Cherokee territory and on his return to Fort Prince George the feet and legs of many of his men were so wounded and their strength and spirit so much exhausted that they were unable to march further without rest. He, therefore, resolved to camp there, rest his men and wait the disposition of the Cherokees resulting from the chastisement which he had given them.

The suffering of the Indians and their families, homeless in the mountains, was very great and a few days after Colonel Grant's arrival at Fort Prince George, Attakullakulla and several Indian chiefs came to the camp and expressed a desire for peace. They had suffered severely for breaking their alliance with the English and listening to the deceitful promises of the French. Convinced at last of the weakness and perfidy of the French, who could neither help them in time of war nor supply their wants in time of peace, they had decided to sever all connection with them forever. Accordingly, terms of peace were drawn up which were beneficial to the southern provinces. The different articles of the treaty were ready and interpreted and Attakullakulla agreed to all but one, which demanded that four Cherokee Indians should be delivered to Colonel Grant at Fort Prince George to be put to death in front of the camp, or four green scalps be brought to him within twelve days. Attakullakulla said no such authority had been given him by his nation and he thought the condition unreasonable and unjust. He, therefore, could not grant it.

**Governor Bull's Wise Action**—Attakullakulla then went with the Indian chiefs to Charleston and asked Governor Bull to remove the objectionable demand from the proposed treaty.

According to Colonel Jones' account Governor Bull called a Council at Ashley Ferry and there replied to Attakullakulla in these words:

"Attakullakulla, I am glad to see you, and as I have always heard of your good behaviour, that you have been a good friend to the English, I take you by the hand, and not only you but all those with you also, as a pledge for their security whilst under my protection. Colonel Grant acquaints me that you have applied for peace. Now that you are come, I have met with my beloved men to hear what you have to say, and my ears are open for that purpose."

A fire having been kindled and the pipe of peace lighted, all present smoked for some time solemnly and in silence. At length Attakullakulla arose and thus spake to the Governor and Council:

"It is a great while since I last saw your Honour. Now I am glad to see you and all the beloved men present. I am come to you as a massenger from the whole nation. I have now seen you and smoked with you, and I hope we shall live together as brothers. When I came to Keowee, Colonel Grant sent me to you. You live at the water side and are in light. We are in darkness, but I hope all will yet be clear with us. I have been constantly going about doing good, and though I am tired, yet I am come to see what can be done for my people who are in great distress." Here he produced the strings of wampum he had received from the different towns of the Cherokee nation, all denoting an earnest desire for peace. Continuing, he added: "As to what has happened I believe it has been ordered by our Father above. We are of a different colour from the white people. They are superior to us. But one God is father of all and we hope what is past will be forgotten. God Almighty made all people. There is not a day but some are coming into and others are going out of the world. The Great King told me the path should never be crooked, but open for every one to pass and repass. As we all live in one land, I hope we shall all live as one people." Thereupon a treaty of peace was ratified.

This happily ended a bloody war which was not only a calamity to the Cherokees and cost South Carolina much loss of life and property, but threatened destruction to the Colony of Georgia and kept its people under a cloud of apprehension for some time.

**A Lawless Gang Dispersed**—On the land between the Altamaha and St. John's rivers, which was outside the jurisdiction of Georgia and that of Florida, many outlaws and fugitives from justice had come together at a place called New Hanover on the Satilla River, thirty miles above its mouth. Some of them lived on Cumberland Island. These people were followers of the notorious Edmund Grey, who had sought to make trouble in the Colony of Georgia some years before. They had and claimed no title but that of occupancy and acknowledging no allegiance to Georgia were regarded as a dangerous population. It was feared that they would cause trouble with the Spaniards of Florida and with the Creek Indians. Under these circumstances orders were received from the British Crown to disperse this band of marauders. To carry out this order commissioners with full power were appointed by South Carolina and Georgia. They went to New Hanover and Cumberland Island, disclosed the purpose for which they had been ordered there and succeeded in inducing the disreputable people there to abandon the territory where, without warrant, they had made their homes. This peaceful solution of the difficulty was very gratifying as it had been feared that force would be required to clear the region of those undesirable people.

**Final Settlement With the Bosomworths**—During Governor Ellis' administration and largely by his influence there was a final settlement of the claim of Mary Bosomworth. To make such a settlement possible a cession of the land between Savannah and Pipe Makers' Creek and the islands of Ossabaw, Sapelo and St. Catherine had been secured by the British Crown from the Indians on May 28, 1751, and the validity of this cession was recognized by the Indian treaty of April 22, 1758. The claim of Mrs. Bosomworth was still outstanding, however, and was regarded as a cloud upon the title of those lands. It was finally decided to give Mary Bosomworth the Island of St. Catherine, where she lived, pay her 450 pounds for goods provided by her in the King's service and 1,600 pounds for her services for some years as agent and interpreter. She agreed to waive all claim to the islands of Ossabaw and Sapelo, which she had claimed before. To meet the expense of the settlement those two islands were sold at auction. Ossabaw brought 1,350 pounds and Sapelo 700 pounds and the proceeds were paid to Mrs. Bosomworth. The land lying between Savannah and Pipe Makers' Creek was sold at public outcry for 638 pounds and that sum was paid into the treasury of the Province.

**Retirement of Governor Ellis in 1760**—Governor Ellis complained of the heat of Savannah and in November, 1759, his health was so bad that he asked for a recall, hoping that his successor would be promptly appointed and he would avoid another warm season in Georgia. Although Sir James Wright was commissioned Lieutenant-Governor on the 13th of May, 1760, he did not arrive until October. Then Georgia had a population of 6,000 white people and 3,500 negroes. In ending his official connection with the Colony on October 13, 1760, Governor Ellis addressed the General Assembly as follows:

*"Gentlemen of the Council and of the Commons House of Assembly:*

"His Majesty having been graciously pleased to grant me his Royal Licence for returning to Europe, and appointed the honourable James Wright Esquire Lieutenant Governor of this Province, I have called you together to inform you thereof, and at the same Time to return both Houses of Assembly my very sincere and hearty acknowledgments for the great Assistance they have afforded me in carrying on the King's Service and the Business of the Colony during the whole Course of my Administration.

"Possessed as I am with the most grateful Sense of this and every other Obligation conferred on me by the good People of Georgia, they may be perfectly assured of my best Wishes and most zealous Endeavours upon all Occasions to promote whatever may contribute to their Happiness and the Welfare of the Province."

**The Assembly's Tribute to Governor Ellis**—In reply to Governor Ellis' valedictory the General Assembly in its address thanked him cordially for his friendly words and expressed sorrow at being deprived of his wise and upright administration, "To which under Divine Providence we hold ourselves indebted for that measure of interior quiet and happiness we have hitherto enjoyed." To these words they added:

"The many useful Laws which have received your Excellency's Assent, whereby Proceedings in the Courts of Law have been rendered more easy and expeditious, and the Civil Rights and Properties of the People fenced against the corrupt Practices of wicked and designing men; the Ability which you have exerted in healing those unhappy Divisions with which the Colony was rent at your Arrival; the Credit you have restored to the Government; and the Zeal with which you have promoted and encouraged every measure tending to the public Advantage, entitle your Excellency to our most grateful and hearty acknowledgments: nor do we esteem it less happy for us, nor less honourable for you Sir, that whilst other more opulent and more populous Provinces have been ravaged by a barbarous and cruel Enemy, this infant Colony, surrounded with more numerous Savages, and with an open and defenceless Frontier to our powerful European Enemy, has not been involved in a ruinous and destructive War."

In conclusion they asked his aid on his return to England in securing for the Colony from the Crown the needed protection, placing Georgia in a state of defense which would not only give security to its inhabitants, but render it "an effectual barrier for his Majesty's Southern Provinces."

Having turned over the affairs of the Colony to his successor, Honorable James Wright, Governor Ellis left Georgia on November 2, 1760. The inhabitants of the Province showed great sorrow at the retirement of a Governor whose kind administration, honest purpose and tireless exertion for the advancement and welfare of the Colony, with his high integrity and exalted character had made a lasting impression upon the people. The Georgia Society, the merchants of Savannah, the citizens of Augusta and others presented him complimentary and affectionate addresses, regretting his departure, praising his administration, commending his character and praying for his welfare. As a token of gratitude the Union Society of Savannah presented him with a handsome piece of silver. Governor Ellis not only had the confidence and love of the people he ruled, but was fortunate in dealing with the Indians, successful in the conduct of the Colony's affairs and highly esteemed by the home government.

After his return to England Governor Ellis was commissioned Governor of Nova Scotia and held that position for two and a half years. At the end of that time he retired because of feeble health and found rest in the south of France. There, occupied with some of his favorite scientific researches, he lived to an old age and died at length within sight of Vesuvius on the beautiful Bay of Naples.

## CHAPTER XXXVI.

# *Governor James Wright's Administration*

Sir James Wright, a native of South Carolina, the son of its Chief Justice and for twenty-one years its Attorney-General, was appointed Lieutenant-Governor of Georgia on the 13th of May, 1760, but did not arrive in Georgia until the 11th of October of that year. Two days later, on the 13th of October, he succeeded Governor Ellis.

Governor Wright was descended from the ancient family of Wright of Kilverstone, whose property in Norfolk County, England, dated from the time of Henry VIII. His grandfather, Sir Robert Wright, Knight, was Chief Justice of the Court of King's Bench in the time of James II and presided at the trial of the seven bishops in 1688. His grandmother was the daughter of Bishop Matthew Wren, a nephew of Sir Christopher Wren.

The new Governor was qualified for his task by his long residence in Carolina and his experience in colonial affairs. His business habits and legal knowledge were a great advantage and aided him in the administration of the government.

**Governor Wright's Inaugural**—Governor Wright was cordially received at Savannah and on the 5th of November, 1760, he delivered the following inaugural address to the General Assembly of Georgia:

"His Majesty having been pleased to permit his Excellency Governor Ellis to return to Great Britain and to honour me with the appointment of Lieutenant Governor of this Province, the Administration is now, on his Excellency's departure, devolved upon me. I am not insensible of the Merit and Abilities of that Gentleman, and consequently of the Disadvantages I may be under in succeeding him.

"But let me assure you Gentlemen, that I shall, with the utmost Diligence and Integrity, discharge my Duty to his Majesty and, consistent with that, will at all Times and in every Respect, with very great Sincerity endeavour to promote the true Interest and Prosperity of this Province: in the pursuit of which I am well persuaded I shall always meet with the Approbation and Aid of all worthy Men and true Lovers of their Country, and therefore cannot fail of your candid Assistance.

"The Very short Time that I have been amongst you Gentlemen has not been sufficient for me to acquire that Knowledge of the State and Condition of the Province necessary to enable me to suggest to you every Circumstance that may be proper for your present Consideration, and which might have made a further adjournment convenient.

"But there is one Object which is very striking and which requires our immediate Attention: I mean the Dangers this Province in general is exposed to from the Creek Indians; the yet defenceless Condition of the Town; and the necessity of putting it into some better State of Security by finishing the Works already begun, and erecting such other within the Lines and elsewhere as may appear necessary for that End: for, although a great deal is already done, yet much is still wanting, and a Supply of proper Guns and Ammunition for the Block Houses and small Forts in order to render the Several Works effectual; and therefore I have thought it expedient to continue Sitting at this Time.

"From our Situation and Circumstances our Plan must chiefly be that of Security and Defence, and although the very great Success with which it has pleased God to bless the Arms of our most gracious Sovereign in the North Part of this Continent is a most interesting and important Event in general, and to us in particular as it gives us sanguine Hopes that this Southern Frontier will very speedily be strengthened, yet Gentlemen, let us not be wanting to ourselves, let us act as becomes us, and every Consideration, every View in which we see our present Circumstances must incite us to exert our utmost Efforts at this critical Conjuncture.

"The Success of the Cherokees against our Sister Colony, which the Savages well know to be populous, rich and powerful, has greatly extended their Influence amongst our Neighbours the Creeks and made them most insolent and daring; but I trust those Dangers that we are exposed to from thence will animate us and convince us how necessary it is to be vigilant, to be active.

"Gentlemen, from your usual and well known zeal for his Majesty's Service and Readiness on all Occasions to promote the Welfare of this Province, I doubt not but you will chearfully concur with me and make such Provision as will be sufficient for the immediate Execution of these salutary Measures on which the Safety and Tranquility so much depend. I must likewise recommend to your Consideration the Condition of the Light House on Tybee Island, and also what Laws are near expiring and may require an Immediate Continuance."

**The Assembly's Reply**—To the Governor's inaugural the Upper House of Assembly made this reply:

"May it please your Honour.

"We his Majesty's must dutiful and loyal Subjects, the Council of Georgia in General Assembly met, beg leave to return your Honour our unfeigned Thanks for your Speech to both Houses of Assembly and to present our hearty Congratulations to your Honour on your safe Arrival in this Province.

"However sensibly we regret the Departure of his Excellency Governor Ellis, we do with great Sincerity assure your Honour that it is with the highest Satisfaction we see your Honour appointed to preside over us. The Ability and Integrity with which you have served our gracious Sovereign and his Subjects in the neighbouring Province, though in a less elevated Station, and the unblemished Probity with which you have discharged the Duties of private Life, as they have gained you his Majesty's Approbation and the Esteem of all Worthy Men, so they are to us the surest Presages of Prosperity and Happiness under your diligent and virtuous Administration.

"We do with the utmost Pleasure congratulate your Honour on the very great Success with which it has pleased God to bless his Majesty's Arms in the different Quarters of the World, and particularly on the happy Reduction of all Canada; an Event equally honourable for our glorious Sovereign and important and interesting to his American Subjects. Nor do we on this occasion only participate in the general Joy. We flatter ourselves that as this Province is now the only Frontier to our European Enemy it will speedily be strengthened, and the Insolence of the neighbouring Savages effectually repressed.

"We are thoroughly sensible of the Dangers which this Colony is exposed to from the Creek Indians, the yet defenceless Condition of the Town, and the necessity there is for putting it and the other parts of the Province in a better State of security; and we do assure your Honour that nothing on our Part shall be wanting for enabling you to carry into Effect so salutary a Measure, and on all Occasions consistent with our Duty to the King shall chearfully concur in every thing that shall tend to render your Administration easy and honourable, and the Colony happy and flourishing."

**Fortifying the Colony**—The first important matter which received the attention of the Assembly and the Governor was the fortification of the Colony. At this time Savannah had three or four hundred houses, most of them small wooden structures. The important buildings were Christ Church, the Independent Meeting House, the council house, the courthouse, and a filature. The length of the town from east to west was 2,100 feet and from north to south 1,425 feet. Within that territory there were six squares or market places, each of them three hundred and fifteen by two hundred and seventy feet.

Surveyor-General DeBrahm proposed for the defense of the city an entrenchment and palisade around it to shelter the families of planters and their slaves. Within this entrenchment the families of planters would be secure from attack by Indians and being near South Carolina there could be quick communication in an emergency and supplies of food and ammunition could be brought thence. DeBrahm's advice was received with favor and he laid out two poligons with three bastions to protect the southern exposure, with the same on the east and the west sides of the city. To the north and east the entrenchments reached the river. At the corners of the bastions twelve-pound cannon were installed. To expedite the work the Commons House of Assembly nominated a committee, with the Governor at its head, composed of James DeVeaux, Lewis Johnson, William Francis, Joseph Gibbons, James Read, and Edmund Tannatt. The Upper House appointed James Habersham, Colonel Noble Jones, James Edward Powell and William Knox.

Protection was given by stockades and forts to Augusta, Ebenezer, Sunbury, Midway, Darien, Barrington, and other points. The mouth of the Savannah River was defended by building Fort George on Cockspur Island.

Governor Wright disapproved recommendation of previous governors that the seat of Government be transferred from Savannah to Hardwicke. This decision gave a new impulse to Savannah and increased its prosperity.

The lighthouse on Tybee Island was repaired and wharves along the Savannah River were improved upon a plan furnished by DeBrahm.

For thirty years Savannah was considered a healthy town and rice planters from South Carolina lived there through the summer and early autumn to escape the fevers that arose from swamps. It seems that dense forests on Hutchinson's Island and to the east and west of the town protected Savannah from noxious vapors and malarial influences of the fields beyond in the swampy regions of the rice fields. When those forests were cut away and the land on which they grew became rice fields the miasmatic conditions affected Savannah and it became necessary to guard the city against those unwholesome conditions by enforcing a dry-culture system in the vicinity of the town.

**Death of King George the Second**—King George the Second of England died on October 25, 1760, but because of the delay of ocean travel the news of his death was not received in Savannah until February, 1761. On the death of the King the Georgia Assembly was dissolved and writs were issued for the election of a new Assembly to convene on March 24, 1761.

Funeral honors were rendered to the late King and George the Third was saluted as King with due pomp and ceremony. Then, for the first and only time a King was proclaimed on Georgia soil.

**Governor Wright's Address to the Assembly**—On March 25, 1761, Governor Wright addressed the Georgia Assembly, paying tribute to the memory of George II and congratulating the Colony on the accession of George III. He said:

The great and important Event of the Death of his late Majesty, of ever blessed Memory, having made it necessary to call a new Assembly, gives me this Opportunity of congratulating you on the happy Accession of our present most gracious Sovereign to the Throne of his royal Grandfather.

"This Accession, Gentlemen, is a most inestimable Mark of Divine Providence: for, under the auspicious Government of a Prince who has given such early Proofs of his Royal Abilities, Regard for the British Constitution, and Love and Affection for his Subjects, we may rest assured that we shall not only continue in the perfect Enjoyment of the many Blessings we have already possessed, but that we shall meet with every further Encouragement and Sup port that this Infant Province may require.

"Animated therefore with a true Sense of our Happiness, let us with the utmost Gratitude and Veneration study to promote his Majesty's Service; let us cheerfully obey his royal Commands, and offer up our sincere Prayers for his long and happy Reign over us."

**The Assembly's Reply**—The Assembly replied as follows:

"We his Majesty's most dutiful and loyal Subjects, the Council of Georgia in General Assembly met, beg Leave to return your Honour our unfeigned and hearty Thanks for your affectionate Speech to both Houses of Assembly.

"The great and important Event of the Death of his late Majesty of blessed Memory having made it necessary for your Honour to convene a new Assembly, we therefore avail ourselves of this Opportunity of congratulating you on the happy accession of our present most gracious Sovereign to the Throne of his Royal Ancestors, being truly sensible of this inestimable Mark of Divine Favour in placing us under the auspicious Government of a prince who has given such early and repeated Proofs of his Royal Abilities, Regard for the British Constitution, and Paternal Affection for his Subjects. From the Consideration of these Princely Virtues we assure ourselves a Continuance of those invaluable Privileges and Blessings we have hitherto enjoyed; and that we shall also meet with every further Encouragement that may conduce to the Protection and prosperity of this Infant Province. We therefore shall, with the utmost Gratitude, disinterested Regard, and a Sense of our own Happiness, make it our Study to promote his Majesty's Service and pay all due Obedience to his Royal Commands."

These expressions of loyalty and good will for the King of England by the Governor and the Legislature of Georgia were undoubtedly sincere and at the time appropriate, but they are in sharp contrast with the action of the people of Georgia a few years later when the same Governor, still loyal to his Sovereign, was arrested by some of the men who had joined him in proclaiming George the Third King of Georgia, as well as King of England.

There is that in the best of men which makes them loyal to the powers that be as long as those powers so conduct themselves and so perform the duties of their high office that they are worthy of support, but when misguided by the thirst for power they become tyrannical and oppressive, the most loyal begin with protest, and if the protest is not heeded, exercise the inalienable right of men to be free by declaring their independence and resisting at any cost the effort to coerce them.

**Wright Made Full Governor**—One of the earliest acts of George III was to promote James Wright from the position of Lieutenant-Governor to that of Captain General, Governor, and Commander-in-Chief in and over the Province of Georgia. This appointment was made on March 20, 1761, but the commission did not reach Governor Wright at Savannah until the 28th of January, 1762. It was then read at the head of the regiment of militia, drawn up in Johnson Square by Colonel Noble Jones. Three volleys were fired and were answered by the guns of Fort Halifax and cannon from the ships in the river. In the evening the ladies were entertained at a ball given by the Governor. It was a brilliant assembly, largely attended and up to that time the most notable gathering of the kind held in Savannah. The houses of Savannah were illuminated and the *South Carolina Gazette* said there was never an occasion on which the joy and satisfaction of the people were more apparent.

About this time there began a long controversy with the Governor of South Carolina over grants of land he had issued to certain South Carolinians for large tracts of land between the Altamaha and St. Mary's rivers. As this controversy was affected by the cession of Florida to England which resulted in making the territory between the St. Mary's and Altamaha rivers English territory, it is well to mention that fact here before going into the controversy.

## CHAPTER XXXVII.

# *Georgia's Territory Extended Southward —Indian Treaties*

By Royal proclamation on the 7th of October, 1763, George the Third announced the conclusion of a treaty with Spain concluded at Paris on the 10th of February of that year by which not only was the territory of Florida ceded to Great Britain, but all the land between the Altamaha and St. Mary's rivers became English territory and the southern boundary of Georgia was extended to the St. Mary's River and extended as far west as the Mississippi. The British Government organized Florida in two parts as East Florida and West Florida and the northern boundary of the two Floridas was made the southern boundary of Georgia as far as the Mississippi River.

In this Georgia ceased to be a frontier Colony and was relieved of anxiety because of her nearness to Spanish rule at St. Augustine and Pensacola. The Colony was also relieved of the long contest with French emissaries emanating from Mobile. Thus relieved and with a sense of security the Colony entered upon a new period of prosperity.

As the natives in that territory remained it was necessary to inform the Indians of the change in government in order to continue friendly relations existing between them and the British Crown. For that purpose the Earl of Egremont, Secretary of State for the Southern Department, by direction of the King wrote the Governors of Virginia, North and South Carolina, and Georgia, instructing them in association with Captain Steuart, the Superintendent of Indian Affairs, to call a congress of the Creeks, Cherokees, Catawbas, Chickasaws, and Choctaws, at Augusta or such other central point as they considered most convenient.

**The Indian Convention at Augusta**—At the suggestion of Governor Wright, endorsed by Captain Steuart, the selection of Augusta was approved and the meeting with the Indians took place there. It was opened with due formality at the King's Fort in Augusta on the 5th of November, 1763. For the English there were present Governor James Wright of Georgia, Governor Thomas Boone of South Carolina, Governor Arthur Dobbs of North Carolina, Lieutenant-Governor Francis Fauquier of Virginia, and Captain John Steuart, Superintendent of Indian Affairs in the Southern Department.

Seven hundred Indians were present and James Colbert was interpreter for the Chickasaws and Choctaws; John Butler, James Beamor and John Watts were interpreters for the Cherokees, and Stevens Forest and John

MONUMENT TO A. H. STEPHENS

Proctor for the Creeks. Colonel Ayers, the Catawba Chief, was interpreter for his nation.

**Indian Leaders Present**—The Upper and Lower Chickasaws were represented by the following chiefs: Hopayamatahah, Poucherimatahah,

Houspastubah, Piamatah, Hopayamingo, Houratimatahah, and twenty warriors. The chiefs Red-Shoes and Chappahomah represented the Choctaws.

The Upper and Lower Creeks were present in the persons of their chiefs, Captain Aleck, Sympoyaffee, Bohotcher, Sausechaw, Boysonecka, Hillibeesunaga, Firmicho, Poyhucher, Poyhuchee, and their followers.

Of the Cherokees fifteen chiefs appeared, representing the Settlements over the Hills, the Middle Settlements, and the Lower Towns. The Over Hill chiefs were Attakullakulla, Ousteneka, Prince of Chotish, Willanawah, Onatoi, Skiagusta of Chotih, and Moitoi. Those from the Lower Towns were Tiftowih of Keehowee, the Wolf, Houkonata, Man Killer of Keehowee, Good Warrior of Estatowih, Young Warrior of the same place, and the Warrior of Tuscoweh. Will, the head man of Whatogah, led the delegation from the Middle Settlement. The Catawbas were represented by their chief, Colonel Ayres, and some followers.

As the conference sat in Georgia it was opened by Governor Wright. As the day was fair he hoped that all talk would be equally so and invited the Indians to hear the utterances of Captain Steuart who had been selected by the four Governors to express their sentiment.

Captain Steuart addressed the Indians as friends and brothers, assuring them that he spoke by command of the great King George, who, under God, the Master and Giver of Breath, was the Common Father and protector of both the English and the Red Men. He said that no conference was ever intended to be more general or more friendly and that, provoked by the repeated cruelties, insults, and falsehoods of the French and Spaniards, the King of England had put forth his strength and defeated both of them; that in order to prevent a repetition of former disturbances His Majesty insisted upon the removal of the French and Spaniards beyond the Mississippi; that all cause of trouble was now at an end and he hoped the Indians and the English would dwell together in peace and brotherly friendship; that all past offenses should be buried in oblivion and forgiveness; that the English were prepared to deal fairly and to supply the Indian nation with everything they might require; and that the fort recently surrendered by the French would be used for the assistance and protection of the natives and for the convenience of a trade which it was believed would be mutually beneficial. In conclusion Captain Steuart said: "The white people value themselves on speaking truth; but to give still greater weight to what we say, the great King has thought proper that his four governors and the superintendent from a great distance should speak the same words at the same time; and, to remove every umbrage or jealousy, that you should all hear them in presence of one another, and bear testimony for one another in case we should ever act contrary to our declarations."

The responses of the Chiefs and various rejoinders continued until the 10th of November, 1763, when the following treaty was formally ratified by all present:

TREATY OF INDIANS WITH SOUTHERN COLONIES.

"ARTICLE I. That a perfect and perpetual peace and sincere friendship shall be continued between his Majesty King George the Third and all his subjects, and the several nations and tribes of Indians herein mentioned, that is to say the Chicasahs, Upper and Lower Creeks, Chactahs, Cherokees, and Catawbas: and each nation of Indians hereby respectively engages to give the utmost attention to preserve and maintain peace and friendship between their people and the King of Great Britain and his subjects, and shall not commit or permit any kind of hostilities, injury, or damage whatever against them from henceforth, and for any cause, or under any pretence whatever. And for laying the strongest and purest foundation for a perfect and perpetual peace and friendship, his most sacred Majesty has been graciously pleased to pardon and forgive all past offences and injuries, and hereby declares there shall be a general oblivion of all crimes, offences and injuries that may have been heretofore committed or done by any of the said Indian parties.

"ARTICLE II. The subjects of the great King George and the aforesaid several nations of Indians shall, forever hereafter, be looked upon as one people. And the several Governors and Superintendent engage that they will encourage persons to furnish and supply the several nations and tribes of Indians aforesaid with all sorts of goods, usually, carried amongst them, in the manner which they now are, and which will be sufficient to answer all their wants. In consideration whereof, the Indian parties on their part, severally engage in the most solemn manner that the traders and others who may go amongst them shall be perfectly safe and secure in their several persons and effects, and shall not on any account or pretence whatever be molested or disturbed whilst in any of the Indian towns or nations, or on their journey to or from the nations.

"ARTICLE III. The English Governors and Superintendent engage for themselves and their successors, as far as they can, that they will always give due attention to the interest of the Indians and will be ready on all occasions to do them full and ample justice. And the several Indian Parties do expressly promise and engage for themselves severally, and for their several nations and tribes pursuant to the full right and power which they have so to do, that they will in all cases and upon all occasions do full and ample justice to the English: and will use their utmost endeavours to prevent any of their people from giving any disturbance, or doing any damage to them in the settlements or elsewhere as aforesaid, either by stealing their horses, killing their cattle, or otherwise, or by doing them any personal hurt or injury; and that if any damage be done as aforesaid, satisfaction shall be made to the party injured: and that if any Indian or Indians whatever shall hereafter murder or kill a white man, the offender or offenders shall, without any delay, excuse, or pretence whatever, be immediately put to death in a public manner in the presence of at least two of the English who may be in the neighborhood where the offence is committed.

"And if any white man shall kill or murder an Indian, such white man shall be tried for the offence in the same manner as if he had murdered a white man, and, if found guilty, shall be executed, accordingly in the presence of some of the relations of the Indian who may be murdered, if they choose to be present.

"ARTICLE IV. Whereas doubts and disputes have frequently happened on account of encroachments, or supposed encroachments committed by the English inhabitants of Georgia on the lands or hunting grounds reserved and claimed by the Creek Indians for their own use: Wherefore, to prevent any mistakes, doubts, or disputes for the future, and in consideration of the great marks of clemency and friendship extended to us the said Creek Indians, we, the Kings, Head-men, and Warriors of the several nations and towns of both Upper and Lower Creeks, by virtue and in pursuance of the full right and power which we now have and are possessed of, have consented and agreed that, for the future, the boundary between the English settlements and our lands and hunting grounds shall be known and settled by a line extending up Savannah river to Little river and back to the fork of Little river, and from the fork of Little river to the ends of the south branch of Briar Creek, and down that branch to the lower Creek path, and along the lower Creek path to the main stream of Ogeechie river, and down the main stream of that river just below the path leading from Mount Pleasant, and from thence in a straight line cross to Sancta Sevilla on the Altamaha river, and from thence to the southward as far as Georgia extends, or may be extended, to remain to be regulated agreeable to former treaties and his Majesty's royal instruction a copy of which was lately sent to you.

"And we the Catawba Head-Men and Warriors, in confirmation of an agreement heretofore entered into with the white people, declare that we will remain satisfied with the tract of land of fifteen miles square, a survey of which by our consent, and at our request, has been already begun; and the respective Governors and Superintendent on their parts promise and engage that the aforesaid survey shall be completed, and that the Catawbas shall not, in any respect, be molested by any of the King's subjects, within the said lines, but shall be indulged in the usual manner of hunting elsewhere.

"And we do by these presents give, grant, and confirm unto his most sacred Majesty, King George the Third, all such lands whatsoever as we the said Creek Indians have at any time heretofore been possessed of or claimed as our hunting grounds, which lye between the sea, the river Savannah, and the lines herein before mentioned and described, to hold the same unto the great King George and his successors forever. And we do fully and absolutely agree that from henceforth the above lines and boundary shall be the mark of division of lands between the English and the Creek Indians, nothwithstanding any former agreement or boundary to the contrary; and that we will not disturb the English in their settlements or otherwise within the lines aforesaid.

"In consideration whereof it is agreed on the part of his Majesty, King George, that none of his subjects shall settle upon or disturb the Indians in the grounds or lands to the westward of the lines herein before described: and that if any shall persume to do so, then, on complaint made by the Indians, the party shall be proceeded against for the same, and punished according to the laws of the English."

On the day after the treaty with the Indians was signed Captain Steuart distributed presents among them and the four governors present at the conference united in a letter to the Earl of Egremont informing him of the satisfactory manner in which the King's command for the conference had been carried out and suggesting the establishment of commercial relations with the Indians on a general, safe and equitable basis.

**Great Benefit to the Colony**—In a letter to the Board of Trade on December 23, 1763, Governor Wright soon after the conference wrote the Commissioners that the increase of territory secured from the Indians would encourage many settlers to come in and would promote the prosperity of Georgia. In this forecast he proved to be correct.

The extensions of Georgia territory made a new commission to Governor Wright necessary, and the former letters-patent making him Captain-General and Governor-in-Chief of the Colony of Georgia as then constituted were revoked, and by a commission issued at Westminster on the 20th of January, 1764, he was invested with gubernatorial authority over the enlarged territory of the province.

No longer threatened by the French and the Spaniards, at peace with the neighboring Indians and with its boundaries widened and guarded on the south and west by two new English plantations, Georgia occupied a position it never had before. With increasing population and commerce, and presided over by a Governor intent upon the promotion of its best interests, the Province rose steadily in importance and was fast realizing of the expectation of its founder, General Oglethorpe.

# CHAPTER XXXVIII.

## *South Carolina Grants Georgia Land*

One of the most serious problems with which Governor Wright had to deal was the granting of land in Georgia by Governor Boone, of South Carolina, to citizens of his own State.

These grants were based on authority given to the Lord's Proprietors of Carolina by a charter of King Charles the Second. That charter covers the territory as far south as the twenty-ninth degree of north latitude, which crosses Florida more than a hundred miles below the southern boundary of Georgia.

As much of this territory was occupied by Spain and conceded Spain by Great Britain, the title to that much of the grant could not be called good. The same is true of the territory between the Altamaha and St. Mary's rivers, which was for many years disputed ground claimed by both Spain and England.

South Carolina had made no settlement there although she claimed that a fort in that territory was built by South Carolinians.

When, in 1763, Spain ceded to England all of Florida, the disputed territory as well as that of Florida proper became the territory of England and was organized by Great Britain, that part in Spanish Florida as East and West Florida and the territory between the Floridas and the Altamaha River, extending west as far as Mississippi, was added to Georgia.

It will be recalled that prior to the cession of 1763, when the territory between the Altamaha and the St. Mary's rivers was not under the jurisdiction of Georgia or Spain, the British Government ordered it cleared of outlaws who had settled there under the leadership of Edmund Grey. Then, in 1759, by order of the British King, Governor Ellis, of Georgia, and Governor Lyttleton, of South Carolina, sent Commissioners Powell and Hern to eject the outlaws from that territory. Those settlers agreed to move and made a show of doing so, but after the Commissioners had returned to Georgia and Carolina, Grey and his associates violated their promise and reëstablished themselves in that territory.

It appears from a letter written by Governor Wright to the Commissioners of Trade and Plantations in October, 1761, that although the charter granted by the King to the Trustees did not extend further than the southernmost stream of the Altamaha River, the Georgia authorities had exercised a qualified control over that region. General Oglethorpe, in fortifying against the Spaniards, had established settlements and forts beyond that line towards Florida. Plantations went as far as the Altamaha and land was claimed as far as the St. John's River. A guard was maintained on Cumberland Island at Fort William.

Information that Spain was about to cede Florida to Great Britain was received in Georgia and Carolina early in 1763. While the English Government was considering the best method of apportioning and disposing of this newly acquired territory a scheme was devised in Charleston to secure the land south of the Altamaha River for South Carolinians. In justification of that Governor Boone contended that the second charter granted to the Lord's Proprietors of Carolina by Charles the Second extended the limits of that Province as far south as latitude twenty-nine and that the cession of land to the Georgia Trustees by the British Crown included only the territory between the rivers Savannah and Altamaha.

He also said that the British Crown had never seen fit to restrain the Carolina authorities from exercising jurisdiction beyond the southern boundary of Georgia. In proof of this he said that for many years a military force had been maintained south of the Altamaha River with a garrison consisting of troops drawn from South Carolina.

Hearing that Governor Boone was about to issue grants upon the authority he claimed and believing that to be inconsistent with the intention of the English King and injurious to Georgia, Governor Wright sent Grey Elliott, a member of the Georgia Council, to Charleston with a formal protest addressed to Governor Boone as "Captain-General and Governor-in-Chief in and over the province of South Carolina and to all others to whom these presents shall come or may concern." The document was a protest and caveat against warrants being issued or attempts being made to survey any land south of the River Altamaha by pretense or color of right or authority from Thomas Boone as Governor of South Carolina or the Council in that Province and against any grant of land, passed or signed by Governor Boone for any of that land to any person or persons until the King's pleasure concerning it should be known.

The protest refers to the fact that the King had already ordered out of that territory persons occupying it without authority and had directed the governor of Georgia and South Carolina to execute that order. As the formal notice of the cession of land by Spain to England had not been received it was premature to act on it and as the King of England had for some years been considering the disposition of that territory, any attempt to intermeddle in it before the King's pleasure was known and his command given thereon would be highly improper and contrary to the King's intention.

In view of these facts Governor Wright in this document protested against the survey of land south of the Altamaha or the granting of it by the Governor of South Carolina, declaring that to be contrary to the King's intention and therefore null and void.

That no person might plead ignorance of the protest Governor Wright demanded that it be entered in the book of caveat against grants usually kept in the secretary's office in the Province of South Carolina. To this document Governor Wright attached his signature and the seal of Georgia on March 30, 1763.

Carrying this protest Grey Elliott went to Charleston and on the 5th of April, 1763, showed it to Governor Boone. The Governor refused to receive or read the document. Mr. Elliott then delivered it to the Secretary of the Province with the request that it be recorded. The Secretary promised to record it, but in the afternoon returned it to Mr. Elliott, saying that he had been ordered by the Governor and Council neither to receive it or enter it upon the records.

On the 20th of April, Governor Wright informed the Earl of Egremont of these transactions and earnestly protested against the immense grants of land which were being made to parties in Carolina who proposed simply to speculate in the land and not occupy it. He said: "Possibly by the time this reaches your Lordship a million acres may be granted to persons now settled in Carolina and the greatest part of whom it is expected will continue to live there. Your Lordship will be pleased to consider how greatly this will affect his Majesty's service in the settlement of this frontier province and how much it must be impeded by those vast tracts being held by such a handful of people who live in another province; and this further ill effect it will have, for nobody will think of coming this way when they hear that the Carolinians have engrossed all the lands and how contrary does this step seem to be to his Majesty's Royal intentions! and your Lordship will be pleased to observe that those who have these very great tracts, or any of the persons who are to have these lands, have not one negro or one shilling's property on this side of the Savannah River.

"I have had accounts my Lord of many hundred families, and they say some thousand people, who were ready to come into this Province (chiefly from North Carolina) as soon as it was extended and I should be authorized to grant these very lands, all of which will be prevented if these proceedings are suffered to take effect. . . . . Mr. Elliott informs me that one Mr. Young who has some negroes in Carolina and also some in Georgia petitioned for a tract of land for all his negroes and on his saying that part of the negroes were in Georgia he was refused land for them and told he should only have land for such negroes as he had in Carolina. So that your Lordship sees the inhabitants of this province are totally excluded. This my Lord seems to us very unequitable that the people of this province who had borne the brunt and fatigue of settling a new colony and have struggled with many difficulties and hardships besides dangers from the savages and, during the war, from the neighboring French and Spanish, and who by their great industry and labor have acquired a few negroes and are in a capacity of settling their children or making other settlements for themselves—it seems to them hard and unequitable that they are not to have an inch of these lands but that the whole or most of the best is to be swallowed up by strangers who never contributed one farthing or one hour's fatigue or hardship toward the support of the province; and for these reasons and many others that must occur, your Lordship will see why I call this a death wound or destruction of Georgia."

To this Governor Wright added that he had never granted any land except to people who actually undertook to settle and improve it and then only in moderate quantities, for it was the number of inhabitants that Georgia wanted and if those lands were annexed to Georgia but held by Carolinians in the manner described it would ruin the province. He said that 343,000 acres were granted to less than two hundred persons, although that much land would accommodate a thousand good families or settlers of the kind who would be sinews of strength to the Colony. This proceeding by the Governor of South Carolina, Governor Wright declared, would be a long step towards the ruin of a flourishing province.

This letter of the Governor was followed by another on the 6th of May, saying that he had the names of grantees of land and the amount given to each. "I am informed," said he, "that 27,250 acres were ordered to 11 persons, viz to one Donnone, on account of Col. Bed's Estate, 5000 acres, to Lord William Campbell, 2000, to Henry Middleton, 3000, to one Stephens 3000, to Henry Lawrens 3000, to William Hopton 2000, to William Guering 2000, and to David and John Deas and one Vanderhorst, together, 5250 acres."

He stated further that many more warrants were ordered for land south of the Altamaha, amounting to 160,000 acres. He said those grants would soon reach St. Augustine, some having already gone as far as St. John's River. He disclosed a very serious situation when he said that the Creek Indians were greatly alarmed at seeing a number of armed men surveying those lands and marking trees. On which he commented:

"They have sent runners all over the nation to assemble them together and what the consequence may be I do not yet say, but am apprehensive that it may involve us in difficulty, for there is a great difference between extending our settlements gradually and easily and an appearance as though the whole country was to be swallowed up at once by armed people; and this the Indians say is a confirmation of what the French had told them, that we should take all their land from them and then drive them back and extirpate them in time."

These letters of Governor Wright to the home government brought a strong letter from the Board of Trade to Governor Boone, of South Carolina, in which they said:

"The making grants of any part of this country is certainly contrary to the spirit and intention of his late Majesty's orders for the removal of

Grey and his adherents from the settlement of New-Hanover, and must not only embarrass the execution of what general arrangements may be necessary in consequence of the cession of Florida, but will also interfere with those measures it may be reasonably supposed his Majesty will now pursue to extend the Government of Georgia and thereby remove those obstacles and difficulties which that well regulated colony has so frequently and justly stated to arise out of the narrow limits to which it is confined."

Following this letter, which was written to Governor Boone on May 30, 1763, the Board of Trade declared its disapprobation of such grants of land by Governor Boone and issued instructions that no grant or charter should be issued for any land south of the Altamaha River, surveyed under warrants from South Carolina. They declared the act of Governor Boone unwarrantable.

Before this order of the Board of Trade was received considerable land had been granted. Governor Boone apologized, but his excuses were deemed unsatisfactory by the board.

Meanwhile the grantees having apparently acquired vested rights, the Board of Trade on the 8th of July, 1763, called on the Attorney-General and the Solicitor-General for their opinion as to whether under all the circumstances the grants of land south of the River Altamaha made by the Governor of South Carolina were valid and lawful.

It does not appear that the report of the legal advisers was received, but the Commissioners of Trade and Plantations seemed to have intended to vacate those grants by process of law as they considered them illegal. Governor Wright urged them to do that, calling their attention to the failure of the South Carolina grantees to comply with the royal instructions, obligatory on every grantee, which required that within a specified period he or they bring into the Province either a white person or a negro for every fifty acres of land claimed and enter upon the proper cultivation of it. He also told them that the surveys on which these grants were based were unreliable and the distances largely guess work, which information he had from many persons of reputation, some of whom were present. He also said that some of the land was laid off in plots without ever going over the land or surveying it, so that the Georgia surveyors did not know where to lay out any of the land with certainty in that part of the country, and that they could find no lines to regulate their surveys by.

In the meantime the Georgia Assembly on the 25th of March, 1765, passed an act requiring all persons claiming land in the province under grants from His Majesty witnessed by the Governor of South Carolina to appear before the Governor in Council and make proof that they had within the Province a family of white persons or negroes amounting to one person for every fifty acres of land in their respective grants and also that the negroes brought into the Province should be brought in in good faith to settle and improve the lands claimed and not with any fraudulent or secret purpose of removing them or any of them or carrying them again outside the limits of Georgia.

Claimants were required to produce their original plats and grants and have them regularly recorded and registered in established offices in Georgia. Upon failure within a specified time to comply with this provision the grants were to be regarded as null and void. If the surveys were irregular and defective the grantees were required under penalty of forfeiture to have the land resurveyed within six months by the Surveyor-General of Georgia.

In forwarding this act of the Legislature to the Board of Trade on the 4th of April, 1765, Governor Wright wrote them that he could not learn that any settlement whatever had been made on the granted land. He declared that none of the grantees had peopled their premises with families or negroes and that not one shilling of tax had been paid or offered to be paid in Georgia, notwithstanding the King's royal proclamation of annexation in October, 1763, and that the parties had held those lands for a year and ten months. He concluded by saying "a specimen my Lords of the great advantage this province is like to receive from the owners of 90,000 acres of the best Land in it."

To finally settle the matter the King approved the report of his advisers, Clare, Soame Jenyns, William Fitzherbert, and Robinson, submitted on May 26, 1767, in which after reviewing the whole matter at length they recommended that the Governor of South Carolina be instructed to have his officers prepare transcripts of all patents granted under the seal of the Province for land south of the Altamaha and all orders, warrants and proceedings relating to them and transmit the documents promptly to the Governor of Georgia, and that the Governor of Georgia be instructed to enter such transcripts in the proper offices of the Colony; that if the Governor of Georgia should find evidence of fraud or abuse in the survey of those lands he should have a new survey made in the presence of the grantees or their representatives, and if more land had been taken in than the grant authorized the Governor should forthwith grant the surplus land to such other persons as should apply for it, on terms and conditions prescribed by the King's instructions.

Finally, the report recommended that the Governor of Georgia be instructed to recommend to the Council and Assembly of Georgia to pass an act establishing a method of enforcing the cultivation of land, causing an inquest to be held on the oaths of a jury of twelve men before a commissioner of escheats and forfeitures to be appointed by the Governor for that purpose, and enacting that "all land which upon a return of such inquest into the office of register of the court of chancery shall appear not to have been duly cultivated according to the terms and conditions of the grant be vested in your Majesty, your heirs and successors without any further or other process."

**Georgia as Governor Wright Found It**—In November, 1766, Governor Wright wrote the home authorities:

"My Lords,—Your Lordships' letter of the 1st of August I had the honor to receive on the 12th inst., by which I am required to transmit to your Lordships an exact account of the several Manufactures which have been set up and carried on within this Province from the year 1734, and of the public encouragement which has been given thereto.

"In obedience to which I am to acquaint your Lordships that there have not been any Manufactures of any kind set up or carried on within this Province, but we are supplied with everything from and through Great Britain. Some few of the poorer and more industrious people make a trifling quantity of coarse homespun cloth for their own families, and knit a few cotton and yarn stockings for their own use, and this done but by very few, and I don't know that there is or has been a yard of linen cloth of any kind manufactured in this Province.

"Hitherto, my Lords, and until the Province becomes much more populous than it just now is, the People can employ their time to much better advantage than manufacturing, as they can be a great deal cheaper and better supplied from Great Britain, and from whence my Lords, all our supplies of Silks, linens, and woollens of every kind are brought, and all our tools, nails, locks, hinges, and utensils of every sort, and great quantities of shoes are likewise imported, although we have some Tanners and Shoemakers here, but chiefly employed in making shoes for the Negroes, also Blacksmiths who work up bar iron imported from the Northern Colonies for building and repairs of Vessels and such other work as is not usually or indeed cannot be imported from Great Britain, as no particular orders or directions can well be given to suit occasional necessary demands and uses. We have built one Ship, one Scow, one Brigantine, and five or six schooners, and a number of coasting Vessels since I have presided here.

"Our whole time and strength, my Lords, is applied in planting rice, corn, peas, and a small quantity of wheat and rye, and in making pitch, tar, and turpentine, and in making shingles and staves, and sawing lumber and scantling, and boards of every kind, and in raising stocks of cattle, mules, horses, and hogs, and next year I hope some essays will be made towards planting and making hemp, and that it will, in due time, become a considerable article with us.

"At present, my Lords, the people here have no idea of manufacturing these commodities, but possibly may hereafter, when they become more numerous, and labour cheaper, especially as they have been within the course of the last year so strongly called upon, and exhorted to it by the Northern Colonies.

"I am, &c., JAMES WRIGHT.

"Savannah in Georgia, 18th Nov. 1766."

## CHAPTER XXXIX.

# *New Parishes Created—Chief Justice Removed*

**Captain Hugh McCall's Account**—The increase of prosperity, population, trade and industry in Georgia which followed the end of the war, the extension of territory and the treaty of peace with the Indians was described in an interesting way by Captain Hugh McCall in his *History of Georgia.* He wrote:

"No Province on the Continent felt the happy effects of this public security sooner than Georgia, which had long struggled under many difficulties arising from the want of credit from friends and the frequent molestations of enemies. During the late war the government had been given to a man who wanted neither wisdom to discern nor resolution to pursue the most effectual means for its improvement. While he proved a father to the people and governed the Province with equity and justice, he discovered at the same time the excellence of its lowlands and river swamps, by the proper management and diligent cultivation of which he acquired in a few years a plentiful fortune. His example and success gave vigor to industry and promoted a spirit of emulation among the planters for improvement. The rich lands were sought for with that zeal, and cleared with that ardor, which the prospect of riches naturally inspired. The British merchants, observing the Province safe and advancing to a hopeful and promising state, were no longer backward in extending credit to it, but supplied it with negroes and goods of British manufacture with equal freedom as to other provinces on the Continent. The planters no sooner got the strength of Africa to assist them than they labored with success, and the lands every year yielded greater and greater increase. The trade of the Province kept pace with its progress in cultivation. The rich swamps attracted the attention not only of strangers but even of the planters of Carolina who had been accustomed to treat their poor neighbors with the utmost contempt; several of whom sold their estates in that Colony and removed with their families and effects to Georgia. Many settlements were made by the Carolinians about Sunbury and upon the Altamaha. The price of produce at Savannah increased as the quality improved—a circumstance which contributed much to the prosperity of the country. The planters situated on the opposite side of the Savannah River found in the capital of Georgia a convenient and excellent market for their staple commodities. In short, from this period the rice, indigo, and naval stores arrived at the markets in Europe of equal excellence and perfection and, in proportion to its strength, in equal quantities with those of its more powerful and opulent neighbors."

**Utopian Schemes Discouraged**—As often happens in periods of rapid prosperity, the new era in Georgia excited the cupidity and ambition of several groups of prominent Englishmen who sought to secure grants for a large part of the newly acquired territory, which they undertook to develop and settle with a large population in a few years, by which they hoped to enrich themselves. Some of them had the temerity to ask that they be given powers of government over a State to be set up as an independent political body within the State of Georgia.

These schemes, looked at now, remind the reader of the "South Sea Bubble," which deceived many Englishmen, and the "Yazoo Fraud," by which Georgia after the revolution lost a large part of its territory. Fortunately the Colony of Georgia was under the control of able men of affairs on the British Board of Trade and the Board of Commissioners of Trade and Plantations, whose practical wisdom and strong common sense refused the request of prominent Englishmen for grants of immense territory within Georgia, to be used in Utopian schemes evidently intended for the profit of the promoters.

One of the groups applying for a large part of the newly acquired territory in Georgia was composed of Dennis Rolle, a member of Parliament; William Reynolds, a London merchant and an elder brother of the Trinity House; George Buch, colonel of the Devonshire Militia; Captain John Buch, his brother; and Dr. Robert Willan, of London. They asked the Board of Trade to cede to them land extending from the southern boundary of Georgia as originally constituted to a line parallel to the equator, drawn from a point two miles below the forks of the River Apalachicola, and thence to the River Altamaha, to be bounded on the west by the Apalachicola and on the east by the Altamaha. They proposed to lay out and settle a town south of the Altamaha and the capital of the territory was to be on the Apalachicola River. The petitioners declared their objects to be the cultivation of silk, indigo, and cotton, the collection of ship timber and naval stores and the establishment of easy communication with the Creeks and the Gulf of Mexico. Their plan was to populate that region with European immigrants and for the government of the territory they asked for the appointment of a Governor at the expense of the Crown during the infancy of the enterprise, or that the applicants be invested with gubernatorial powers as in the cases of Pennsylvania and Maryland.

The Board of Trade did not approve the erection of such a State within a State, but the applicants then petitioned the Earl of Hillsborough and other

Commissioners of Trade and Plantations to grant them Cumberland Island for the purpose of raising cotton, silk, oil, wine and other commodities suited to the climate. The Commissioners of Trade and Plantations declined that application.

A few months later another Utopian scheme was presented to the Board of Trade by Alexander Montgomerie, the tenth Earl of Eglintoun, and his associates, who submitted a proposition to the King and Council by which they undertook to bring into Georgia a hundred thousand colonists, of whom ten thousand were to be sent to Georgia during the first five years and eighteen thousand more within every five years thereafter until the whole number had been sent over and settled. In return for the labor and expense of doing that the Crown was asked to invest in the applicants and their associates the ownership of the region to be thus settled with immigrants. The King was to retain general jurisdiction over the territory and the proprietors in making grants of land to immigrants were to conform to the instructions of the Secretary of State or the Commissioners of Trade and Plantations.

The request of these applicants that a member of the Royal family be placed at the head of the undertaking reminds us of the illusive idea of catching a bird by putting salt on his tail. However, the petitioners agreed to observe the terms of the King's proclamation encouraging settlement of the territory and give security for the payment of a shilling a year for each hundred acres granted, beginning fifteen years from the date of the grant.

The newly acquired territory, having already been assigned to the provinces of Georgia and east and west Florida, the King refused to approve this application of the Earl of Eglintoun and his associates, which appeared to promise more for private profit than for general advantage to the King's possessions in America.

**Wise Action of Governor Wright**—To make sure that the promises made to the Southern Indians in the treaty between them and the English Government negotiated by the Governors of Georgia and North and South Carolina, Governor Wright made wise and strict regulations concerning the intercourse of traders with the natives. Among the conditions were these: Every trader was to so conduct himself that no offense would be given to the Christian religion. Horses, hogs and cattle accompanying the trader must be so controlled that they would do no damage to the crops of the Indians. Traders could not compel an Indian to perform any labor, carry any burden, or buy or sell against his will. Traders were not allowed to receive presents or fees from the Indians or give any of them credit for more than one pound of powder and four pounds of bullets. Indians were to be relieved of all debts previously contracted. No arms, ammunition or goods could be sold to Indians owing allegiance to France or Spain. Traffic in Swan shot was not allowed. Any information received by the traders about the movements of the French and Spaniards must be promptly reported. A trader could not, without special permission from the Governor, bring an Indian within the white settlements. Anyone found trading with the Indians without license must be immediately reported. Servants of traders could not traffic with the Indians and no servant could remain in the Indian territory. Any person in the employment of a trader who committed a capital offense must be taken before a magistrate for trial and punishment. Traders could not talk with the Indians about the affairs and government of the Province. On renewing his license each trader had to submit a statement of skins and effects bought from Indians and all goods sold or left at his trading post. The trader was required to submit a journal of all proceedings during his sojourn in the Indian country. No free Indian, negro or slave could, without special leave, be employed to aid the trader in his business or in rowing boats from any garrison into the Indian territory. Rawhides could not be accepted in exchange for goods. THE SALE OF RUM, SPIRITUOUS LIQUORS, AND RIFLED-BARRELED GUNS WAS ABSOLUTELY PROHIBITED.

Under these regulations and the wise administration of Governor Wright the intercourse between the Colonists and the Indians was for many years friendly and satisfactory. This was largely due to the Governor's watchfulness, wisdom and liberality, his holding traders to strict accountability for their conduct and his frequent interviews with influential chiefs of the Creeks and Cherokees, accompanied by generous presents to the Indians.

**Four New Parishes Created**—In addition to the eight parishes created in 1761 four more were created in 1765 in the new territory between the Altamaha and St. Mary's rivers and were named St. David, St. Patrick, St. Thomas and St. Marys. As a reward for the services of his soldiers in the recent war, King George granted to each field officer who had served in America, 5,000 acres of land; to every captain, 3,000; to a subaltern officer, 2,000; to every non-commissioned officer, 200, and to each private soldier, 50 acres. These grants were free of tax for ten years but subject to the same conditions as to cultivation and occupancy which were attached to other Royal grants in the same territory. These liberal grants by the Crown to veterans of the American War with France and the wise administration of the government of Georgia had much to do with the prosperity of the Colony as described by Captain McCall.

Much attention was given to public roads and the maintenance of ferries at important points to furnish easy communication by direct lines between the principal towns of the province. This was done under the direction of Captain DeBrahm, the able Surveyor-General of the Province. As late as 1764 the road from Charleston to Savannah ended at Purrysburg, from which point the traveler had to come down the river by boat. Soon afterward a new highway was opened so as to terminate at the Savannah River less than two miles below Savannah and the ferry established there greatly facilitated travel and the transmission of mail.

**Chief Justice Removed from Office**—The firmness of the Governor and Council in dealing with evil conduct in high places was tested by the extraordinary behavior of the Chief Justice, William Grover. His office gave him large power which could have been used with great effect in the maintenance of law and order, the punishment of crime and shaping the moral tone of the community. Instead of that, according to the statement of the Council and the Governor, he failed to meet his responsibilities and proved recreant to the trust imposed to him. His conduct attracted general comment and condemnation and an examination of his official course made by the order of Common Council resulted in the unanimous verdict that his behavior was "partial, illegal, indecent, and not consistent with the character, duty and dignity of his office." It was resolved that he was unworthy of holding his position as Chief Justice of the Colony and that the honor of the service demanded his suspension until the pleasure of the King could be ascertained. Governor Wright suspended him from office and in a communication addressed to the Earl of Egremont on January 3, 1763, gave these reasons for the suspension of the judge:

1. Although a member of Council, Chief Justice Grover absented himself from its called meetings and failed to discharge his duty as one of that body.

2. Although a Crown servant with a salary of 500 pounds, instead of assisting in the conduct of public affairs his disposition was to oppose measures for the general good.

3. In a manner unjustifiable he sought to influence the action of the General Assembly.

4. He used his power to discourage military discipline.

5. He was arbitrary and oppressive in enforcing legal process and careless of the rights of personal liberty.

6. He neglected reporting to the Governor judgments and sentences of the court of sessions.

7. He refused to attend a special court of oyer and terminer ordered for the trial of vagabond Spaniards who had murdered McKay, his wife, and two negroes near Darien.

8. His behavior toward the Governor was insubordinate and contumacious.

9. In the discharge of official duty he was partial and not above suspicion.

After full investigation the Board of Trade held that the charges were fully proven and the King removed Grover from office in 1763.

Following the suspension of the Chief Judge a libelous statement was found written upon the wall of a building near the State House in Savannah in which a scurrilous attack was made upon the Governor and Council. The General Assembly on December 10, 1762, addressed a communication to the Governor, denouncing the libel, declaring that the Governor was without fault and asking him to offer a reward of 105 pounds to any person or persons who would discover the author or authors of the libel so they might be convicted. The Governor responded, thanking the two houses of the Assembly for their good opinion of him and declaring that all good men would think it their duty to bring the author of such a base libel to punishment. He also offered the reward.

Although no positive proof was found which would justify punishment of the author of the libel, it was generally believed that it originated with the deposed Chief Justice of the Colony, and the attempt to discredit the Governor and the Council failed utterly.

## CHAPTER XL.

# *The Stamp Act Starts the Movement for Independence*

**The Stamp Act of 1765**—At the end of the French and Indian War, when an era of peace and prosperity appeared to be dawning for the American Colonies, an act of the British Government started a chain of events which led to revolution and war. Instead of peace there was alarm, uprising and armed resistance. Instead of prosperity, commerce was throttled and property was endangered or destroyed. Armed men openly defied the Royal officials and secret organizations were formed to prevent the enforcement of the act of Parliament. In all this the people and Province of Georgia were involved with the other Colonies.

Confronted by a difficult financial problem when their country emerged from war which cost over $300,000,000, English statesmen conceived the idea of meeting the emergency by levying on the American Colonies a stamp tax which they expected to yield $2,500,000 a year, and other taxes which would further increase the burden. Parliament sought to justify that policy by the argument of Charles Townshend, who said, "And now will these American children, planted by our care, nourished up by our indulgence to a degree of strength and opulence, and protected by our arms, grudge to contribute their mite to relieve us from the heavy burden under which we lie?" It was also said that the war had been undertaken for the defense of the American Colonies, and largely at their request.

In answer to the question of Townshend the eloquent Isaac Barre said in the British Parliament of the American Colonists:

"They planted by your care! No: your oppressions planted them in America. They fled from your tyranny to a then uncultivated, inhospitable country where they exposed themselves to almost all the hardships to which human nature is liable, and among others to the cruelties of a savage foe the most subtle, and I will take it upon me to say the most formidable, of any people upon the face of God's earth; and yet, actuated by principles of true English liberty, they met all hardships with pleasure. . . . . They nourished up by your indulgence! They grew by your neglect of them. As soon as you began to care about them, that care was exercised in sending persons to rule them in one department and another who were, perhaps, the deputies of deputies to some members of this house, sent to spy out their liberties, to misrepresent their actions, and to prey upon them: men whose behavior on many occasions has caused the blood of those SONS OF LIBERTY to recoil within them; men promoted to the highest seats of justice, some who, to my knowledge, were glad, by going to a foreign country, to escape being brought to the bar of a Court of Justice in their own. They protected by your arms! They have nobly taken up arms in your defence; they exerted a valor, amidst their constant and laborious industry, for the defence of a country whose frontier was drenched in blood, while its interior parts yielded all its little savings to your emolument. And believe me, remember I this day told you so, the same spirit of freedom which actuated that people at first, will accompany them still. But prudence forbids me to explain myself further. God knows I do not at this time speak from motives of party heat; what I deliver are the genuine sentiments of my heart. However superior to me in general knowledge and experience the respectable body of this house may be, yet I claim to know more of America than most of you, having seen and been conversant in that country. The people, I believe, are as truly loyal as any subjects the King has; but a people jealous of their liberties, and who will vindicate them if ever they should be violated. But the subject is too delicate; I will say no more."

The passage of the stamp act caused angry tumult in the American Colonies, and the delivery of stamps by ships sent for the purpose was resisted with threats of violence to the officials in charge and even to some of the Royal Governors, who sought to enforce the act of Parliament. So great was the tumult that the wiser English statesmen, led by the great Commoner, William Pitt, Edmund Burke and the eloquent Barre, induced Parliament to repeal the offensive act. That wise action was received with joy by the Colonies, who sent thanks to the King and Parliament with renewed expressions of loyalty. The Colonists gloried in the fact that they were Englishmen, with the rights of Englishmen, to which they held firmly and without regard to the cost in life or property, but to the last of hope they were loyal to the mother country.

But the tide of events was too strong to turn back. Under the evil counsel of Charles Townshend, George the Third and his Minister, Lord North, the attempt to tax the Colonists was renewed a little later and the revolution was on.

Before going into details of the turbulent scenes caused by the stamp act it is well here to take a retrospective view of the far-reaching causes of the revolution.

**The Seeds of Liberty**—The American Revolution was not a sudden development caused by the stamp tax and other oppressive measures in 1765 and later. Those measures precipitated the conflict, but the spirit that animated the Americans was inherited from their fathers who brought it from England. The principles of freedom date back to Magna Charta, when the English Barons, backed by the peasants and the people of the towns and cities, wrung from King John the Charter of liberty.

In refusing to submit to taxation without representation, the Colonists reasserted the right which Englishmen had held for five hundred and fifty years under Magna Charta, which also guaranteed trial by jury and freedom from imprisonment and punishment without lawful trial. English statesmen who voted the stamp act seemed to forget that the Colonists were Englishmen, with all the rights of Englishmen, and with the same dauntless spirit which always animated Englishmen in resisting oppression.

**Far-Reaching Effect of French and Indian War**—Events seemed to conspire to bring on the revolution and to fortify the Colonists for the contest. The ultimate effect of the French and Indian War was greater than most men foresaw, but there was one great exception. The French Ambassador at Constantinople, Vergennes, made this remarkable statement:

"England will ere long repent of having removed the only check that could keep her Colonies in awe. They no longer stand in need of her protection. She will call on them to contribute toward supporting the burdens they have helped to bring upon her, and they will answer by striking off all dependence."

Not only did the war bring about the attempt of the British Parliament to tax the American Colonies; it developed a citizen soldiery which proved to be more than a match for those of the British Army under American conditions. This was shown when Washington saved the wreck of Braddock's force, and in many engagements with British armies when the American soldiers were led by Washington, Montgomery, Stark, Schuyler, Wayne, Greene, Morgan, Marion, Sumter and Elijah Clarke.

The French and Indian War prepared the Colonists for the revolution by showing them their own rare fighting qualities, and also by showing that the formidable British regulars were not invincible. As Benjamin Andrews said: "No foe would, at Saratoga or Monmouth see the backs of the men who covered the redcoats' retreat from the field of Braddock's death, scaled the abatis of Louisburg, or brained Dieskau's regulars on the parapet of Fort William Henry."

Another thing of great importance brought home to the Americans by the French and Indian War was the necessity for concerted action and that only in the strength of unity could they hope for successful existence against the power of England. At first the suggestion for an American Federation of Colonists, made years before by Benjamin Franklin, did not receive the support of all the Colonists, but in the presence of a common danger they were brought together. A feeling of good will was fostered by the Southern Colonies when they sent money and troops to their sister states on the more exposed frontier. An example of this was the gift of rice and money sent from the Midway settlement of Georgia to Boston when the oppressive action of the British Government had reduced the people of that city to distressing conditions.

The obstacles overcome in the coöperation of Colonists can only be realized when we recall that without telegraphs, railroads or good roads, communication was slow and difficult. It took seven days to go by stage from Philadelphia to Pittsburgh and four days from Boston to New York. More time was required to go from Georgia to Philadelphia, New York, or Boston, and the mail service was equally slow. In winter it took five weeks for a letter to go from Philadelphia to Virginia. There were few newspapers, only forty-three in the Colonies at the close of the Revolution, and the spread of information was slow. Under these circumstances unity and concert of action between the Colonies had to be created in the face of danger, actually present and backed by armed forces from England.

In 1754 the prospect of war with France led several Colonial Governors to call a Congress of all the Colonies to meet at Albany. It was to secure the friendship of the Indian Six Nations and organize concert of operations against the French. Another object was to prepare a plan of federation, which all the Colonies might adopt. Seven Colonies, New Hampshire, Massachusetts, Rhode Island, Connecticut, New York, Pennsylvania and Maryland sent Commissioners. There was little popular interest then and the only important newspaper that approved the plan was Benjamin Franklin's Pennsylvania *Gazette,* which offered a union device under the motto "Unite or Die."

The plan of federation proposed by the Albany Congress is said to have been framed largely by Benjamin Franklin. It provided a Grand Council composed of representatives elected every three years by the Legislature of each Colony, who were to meet annually at Philadelphia. The Council was to elect its own speaker and was to regulate trade with Indians, make treaties with them and legislate on matters concerning the Colonies as a whole. For that purpose it could levy taxes, enlist soldiers, build forts and nominate civil officers. Its laws were to be submitted to the King for approval. Representation of the Colonies in the Grand Council was to be in proportion to the contribution of each to the continental military service, not less than two or more than seven each. Except in matters of general concern, each Colony was to retain all its power. The executive function and authority of the federation was to be vested in a Governor-General, appointed and paid by the Crown. He was to nominate military officers subject to the approval of the Grand Council and to have a veto on its acts.

This plan, though favored by many of the wisest Americans, was not adopted then, because the time was not ripe for it. There had been some difference between Colonies about boundaries, and trade with the Indians. There were local differences and Colonies were jealous of their separate powers. It took the pressure of danger and the white heat of revolution to weld them together. That came first in committees of correspondence for concerted action after the passage of the Stamp Act. It was not until war had actually begun that a confederacy of the Colonies was created by the Continental Congress and then it took four years for the Colonies to ratify it.

**The Fatal Action of Parliament**—The first action of the English Parliament looking toward the taxation of the Colonies was a resolution of the House of Commons in March, 1764, by which the members voted almost unanimously that England had the right to tax America. That was soon followed by a vote to the effect that taxation of the Colonies was expedient, and a few days later Parliament passed the "sugar and molasses act."

This action of Parliament brought spirited remonstrances from the Colonists, but in spite of that protest Parliament, in March, 1765, passed George Greenville's bill entitled "An Act for Granting and Applying Stamp duties and other duties in the British colonies and plantations in America."

That act, favored by the Ministry and including fifty-five resolutions, was approved by King George the Third on March 22, 1765.

**Oppressive Features of the Stamp Act**—By the act business documents were made illegal and void unless written on stamped paper. The lowest price for it was a shilling and the price increased with the importance of the document. The Stamp paper had to be paid in specie which was very scarce. Most of the medium of exchange was paper currency and all the coin in the Colonies was not sufficient to pay for the stamps required by the act in one year.

A particularly offensive feature of the act provided that those who violated it should be tried without a jury by a judge whose living depended on the sentences he imposed. This was in flagrant disregard of the time-honored right of trial by jury.

The report of the passage of the Stamp Act was like an alarm bell when it reached the Colonies. The Americans were profoundly stirred by it, and their indignation found expression in violent scenes. In Portsmouth an effigy of the Goddess of Liberty was carried to a grave.

The Connecticut Legislature ordered a day of fasting and prayer, and that an inventory be taken of powder and ball. In New York a bonfire was made of stamps in the public square. In Charleston bells were tolled and flags on ships in the harbor were at half-mast.

Colonists agreed to buy nothing from England until the Stamp Act was repealed, and England's trade with the Colonies fell off so that the merchants of Manchester petitioned Parliament for its repeal, saying that nine-tenths of their workmen were idle.

The billeting act, which required the Colonies to feed the British troops quartered among them, caused consternation and indignation. In 1768 the New York Legislature refused to comply with the act and was suspended by Parliament. Four regiments of British soldiers were stationed in Boston that year, and there were heated altercations between citizens and soldiers. A squad of soldiers fired on men and boys attacking them, killing three and wounding eight.

The Virginia Assembly was in session when news of the passage of the Stamp Act came, and it at once adopted resolutions by Patrick Henry denying the right of Parliament to tax the Colonies. In presenting the resolutions Henry made the speech which electrified America and made him a world-wide reputation. Before the vote was taken on all the resolutions, Governor Fauquier dissolved the Assembly, but the resolutions were printed in the newspapers, were generally approved, and most of the Colonies took similar action.

In the meantime the people were not silent or inactive. Secret societies called "Sons of Liberty" sprang up all over the country. They were pledged to resist the enforcement of the Stamp Act and in Georgia became an important factor a few months later.

At Boston on August 14, at daybreak, the effigy of the stamp officer, Oliver, was seen hanging from an elm tree. Near by was a boot which was supposed to represent Lord Bute, the former Prime Minister who is said to have planned the Stamp Act. From the top of the boot projected a head with horns to represent the devil.

That evening the Sons of Liberty cut down those figures and placed them on a bier, which they carried through the streets to King Street, where they destroyed a frame house intended for the stamp office. Carrying lumber of that house to Fort Hill, where Oliver lived, they made a bonfire and burned the effigies in front of the stamp agent's house. A few days later a mob sacked the residence of the Chief Justice, threw his plate into the street and destroyed his fine library. The mob's action there was unjust, for Judge Hutchinson had done all he could to prevent the passage of the Stamp Act.

In most of the Colonies stamp officers were compelled to resign, and boxes of stamp papers that arrived were burned or thrown into the sea. Merchants agreed to import no goods from England, and wealthy men set the example of dressing in homespun clothes, lawyers agreed to overlook the absence of stamps on legal documents and newspapers printed deaths-heads in the place where stamps were required. In New York the Lieutenant-Governor tried to uphold the law and threatened to fire on the people, but was warned that if he did he would be hanged to a lamp post. A torchlight procession carrying images of Colden and the devil broke into the Governor's coach house, took out his best coach, paraded it about town with images on it and finally burned it and the images on Bowling Green in sight of Colden and the garrison. General Gage did not use his troops, for fear of bringing on a civil war. The next day Colden surrendered all the stamps to the Common Council of New York and they were locked up in the City Hall.

In Georgia there were turbulent scenes; even the conservative James Habersham, President of the Council, said:

"The annual tax raised here for the support of our internal policy is full as much as the inhabitants can bear, and suppose the stamps produce only one-eighth of what they would in South Carolina, it would amount to as much in one year as our tax laws will raise in three; and perhaps we have not five thousand pounds in gold and silver come into the province in five years, though the act requires it in one. If this is really the case, as I believe it is, how must every inhabitant shudder at the thought of the act taking place, which, according to my present apprehension, must inevitably ruin them."

**Georgia on the Verge of Civil War**—The excitement in Georgia caused by the Stamp Act was not confined to Savannah. The whole Colony was aroused and bodies of armed men met in different places. "Society was Convulsed," said Dr. Stevens, "And its tumultuous heavings threatened general desolation."

Governor Wright's position as the representative of the British Government was difficult and dangerous. He met the emergency bravely. Stevens shows as follows his courage and firmness and the dangers that confronted him:

"Then was exhibited in an eminent degree the zeal and energy of the Governor; and such was his resolution and weight of character, that for a time all rebellious proceedings ceased; so much so, that he wrote, on the 15th of January, 1766, 'Everything, at present, is easy and quiet, and I hope peace and confidence will be restored in general.' A few days served to dissipate this hope.

"About the 20th, menacing letters were sent to Governor Wright. President Habersham was waylaid at night, his new and well-stored house was threatened with destruction, and he was obliged to take refuge in the garrisoned mansion of the Governor. Towards the close of January, a body of six hundred men assembled within a few miles of the town, and intimated to the Governor that, unless the papers were removed, they would march to Savannah, attack his house and fort, and destroy the stamps. Immediately he sent the papers down to Fort George, at Cockspur Island, and placed them in charge of the rangers. But even this was not deemed sufficient security, and on the 3d of February, they were once more removed, and deposited on board the man-of-war *Speedwell,* which had brought them to the Colony.

"The next day the town was again alarmed by the appearance on the Common of between two and three hundred men, with arms and colors, clamorous for the redress of their grievances. The company of rangers was ordered up from Cockspur, and all the regulars and volunteers, together with a party of marines and seamen from the *Speedwell,* were marshalled for the defence of the town. For several hours the state of affairs was critical, and suspense added its harrowing influence to the trepidation of alarm. By evening, however, nearly all the provincials had dispersed, though a few at night burned an effigy of the Governor, holding in his hand the offensive circular of Secretary Conway, of the 24th October, 1765."

The situation of Governor Wright was one of singular trial and difficulty. The Province was on the verge of civil war, and one act of indiscretion would have plunged it into its ensanguined horrors.

**Results of the Stamp Act**—After a Congress of the American Colonies had on the suggestion of James Otis of Boston been called by the General Assembly of Massachusetts to meet in New York in October, 1765, to consider the act of the English Parliament in imposing a stamp tax on the American Colonists, Speaker Wylly of the Georgia Commons House of Assembly issued a call to the members, asking that they meet in Savannah at an early date. Sixteen members responded, coming together at Savannah on the 2d of September, 1765. Through the influence of Governor Wright they were induced not to send delegates to the Congress of Colonies at New York, but they did prepare and transmit to the Massachusetts Assembly a reply expressing their readiness to coöperate in every measure for the support and protection of the common rights of the Colonists.

Governor Wright evidently at that time underestimated the strength of the movement against the stamp tax, for he wrote the Earl of Halifax, a member of the British Cabinet, on the 20th of September, 1765, that everything was well and doing well. The rapid progress of events was such that he soon changed his mind and on January 31, 1766, wrote Secretary Conway as follows:

**Governor Wright Reports Developments**—"Sir: Yesterday I had the honour to receive the duplicates of your Excellency's letter of the 24th of October, and it is with the utmost concern that I am to acquaint your Excellency that the same spirit of sedition, or rather rebellion, which first appeared at Boston has reached this Province, and I have for three months past been continually reasoning and talking with the most dispassionate and sensible people in order to convince them of the propriety of an acquiescence and submission to the King's authority and that of the British Parliament, until they could point out their grievances, if any, and apply for redress in a constitutional way. I have also Sir, pointed out the dangerous consequences, distresses, and misery they must inevitably bring upon themselves by following the example of the Northern Colonies. This I have done in the strongest and most striking point of view I could place it in, and exactly agreeable to the sense and spirit of your Excellency's letter I had the honor to receive yesterday. At other times I have had recourse to such little force as is in my power, and have in some measure preserved and supported His Majesty's authority and prevented the Stamp papers from being destroyed, but Sir, I must at the same time declare that I have had the great mortification to see the reins of government nearly wrested out of my hands, His Majesty's authority insulted, and the civil power obstructed. But that your Excellency may be more clearly enabled to judge of the true state of affairs in this Province, and to lay the same before His Majesty, I humbly beg leave to state a brief narrative of some transactions here, and which I from time to time have acquainted the Lords of Trade with.

"On the 26th of October, the day of His Majesty's accession, I had ordered a general Muster and in the evening, a little after night, there was a very great tumult in the streets, and some effigies burnt, and a day or two after several incendiary threatening letters were wrote on which I issued a proclamation as your Excellency will see by the enclosed newspaper. I also issued another proclamation against riots and tumultuous and unlawful assemblies, and from that time the spirit of faction and sedition took place and increased, and those persons who falsely call themselves the Sons of Liberty began to have private cabals and meetings, and I was informed that many had signed an Association to oppose and prevent the distribution of Stamped papers, and the act from taking effect. But it was impossible to come at such proof as would enable me to support any legal proceedings against them, and I found they had determined on attacking the distributor as soon as he arrived, and compelling him to resign or promise not to act, as had been done in the Northern Colonies. I had also been informed that they intended to seize upon and destroy the papers whenever they should come. In the meantime Sir, every Argument I could suggest was used to convince them of the rashness of such attempts and the dangerous consequences that must attend them, and every method, both public and private, was pursued by me to bring them to a right way of thinking, and which I frequently thought I had effected, and am sure I should have done but for the inflammatory papers, letters, and messages continually sent to the people here from the Liberty Boys, as they call themselves, in Charlestown, South Carolina, and by whom I am very clear all our disturbances and difficulties have been occasioned.

"And thus matters rested Sir, till the 5th of December when His Majesty's ship *Speedwell* arrived here with the stamped papers on board. I had used every precaution necessary to prevent either papers or officer from falling into the hands of those people, which they were not ignorant of. And when it was known that the *Speedwell* was in the river with the papers, several of the principal inhabitants came to me and gave me the strongest assurances possible that there was then no intention to seize upon or destroy the papers. And they were landed without any appearance of tumult and lodged in the King's store or warehouse under the care of the Commissary. But notwithstanding these assurances with respect to the papers, I still found there was a design against the Officer.

"From the 5th of November everything remained pretty quiet, but I found cabals were frequently held and inflammatory letters sent from Charlestown, and on the 2d of January, about 3 in the afternoon, I was informed that the Liberty Boys in town had assembled together to the number of about 200 and were gathering fast, and that some of them had declared they were determined to go to the Fort and break open the Store and take out the stamped papers and destroy them; on which I immediately ordered the officers to get their men together, but appearances and threats were such that in three days I had not less than 40 men on duty every night to protect the papers, or I am confident they would have been destroyed.

"On the 3d of January Mr. Angus, the distributor for this Province, arrived, of which I had the earliest notice in consequence of measures concerted for that purpose, and immediately sent the scout boat with an officer and a party of men to protect him and suffer nobody to speak to him, but conduct him safely to my house, which was done the next day at noon when he took the State oaths and oath of office, and I had the papers distributed and lodged in all the different offices relative to the shipping and opening our ports, which had been shut for some time. But here the people in general have agreed not to apply for any other papers till His Majesty's pleasure be known on the petitions sent from the Colonies. I kept the Officer in my house for a fortnight, after which he went into the Country, to avoid the resentment of the people, for awhile. No pains have been spared in the Northern Colonies to spirit up and inflame the people, and a spirit of faction and sedition was stirred up throughout the Province, and parties of armed men actually assembled themselves together and were preparing to do so in different parts, but by sending expresses with letters to many of the most prudent I had the satisfaction to find that my weight and credit was sufficient to check all commotions and disturbances in the country at that time, and everything was quiet again and remained so till a few days ago when some incendiaries from Charlestown came full fraught with sedition and rebellion, and have been about the country and inflamed the people to such a degree that they were again assembling together in all parts of the Province and, to the number of about 600, were to have come here on yesterday, all armed, and these people as I have been informed, were to have surrounded my house and endeavoured to extort a promise from me that no papers should be issued till His Majesty's pleasure be known on the petitions sent home, and if I did not immediately comply, they were to seize upon and destroy the papers and commit many acts of violence against the persons and property of those gentlemen that have declared themselves friends of Government. On this last alarm I thought it advisable to remove the papers to a place of greater security, and accordingly ordered them to be carried to Fort George on Cockspur Island where they are protected by a Captain, two subalterns, and fifty private men of the Rangers.

"But I have the satisfaction to inform your Excellency that I have, with the assistance of some well disposed Gentlemen, taken off and got a great many dispersed who were actually on their way down here, but many are still under arms and I can't yet say how the affair will end.

"This Sir, is a wretched situation to be in, and it's clear that further force is necessary to support His Majesty's authority from insults and reduce the people to obedience to the civil power. My task is rendered much more difficult by the people in the next Province going the lengths they have done, and to this day do, and it's said, and I believe it may be true (although Sir, I will not aver to it for a fact), that the Carolinians have offered to assist the people here with 500 men to prosecute their vile attempts.

"Upon the whole Sir, there is still a possibility of bringing the people to reason and restoring the peace and tranquillity of the Province, on which, your Excellency so justly observes, their welfare and happiness depend. A few days will determine this point, and if not, then agreeable to your Excellency's letter, I shall write to General Gage and Lord Colvile for assistance, . . . .

"The whole military force in this Province, Sir, is two troops of Rangers, consisting in the whole of 120 effective men, which occupy 5 forts or posts in different parts of the Province, and 30 of the Royal Americans,—20 of them at Fort Augusta 150 miles from hence, and 10 at Frederica about the same distance. And on the first appearance of faction and sedition I ordered in some of the Rangers from each post and made up the number here at Savannah 56 privates and 8 officers, with which, and the assistance of such gentlemen as were of a right way of thinking, I have been able in some measure to support His Majesty's authority, but I have been obliged to send two officers and 35 of those men with the papers to Fort George."

On the 7th of February Governor Wright acquainted Secretary Conway with what had further transpired in the Colony in relation to the enforcement of the Stamp Act:

"On the 2d inst I had the pleasure to hear the arrival of His Majesty's ship *Speedwell,* Captain Fanshawe, who had promised me when he went from hence, after bringing the papers, that he would return again soon. I assure your Excellency he came at a very reasonable time, as by his taking the papers on board the King's ship I was enabled to order up the Officers and Rangers to town, and then mustered 70 officers and men. Captain Fanshawe brought his ship up, and several gentlemen and others also promised to join me if the Villains should come into town. For notwithstanding I had been able to dispose of a great number, yet two hundred and forty of them were within 3 miles, and, being much exasperated against me for sending the papers away, agreed to come to me and demand that I would order the papers to be delivered up to them, and if I did not, they were to shoot me. This Sir, was avowedly declared by some of them; and on Thursday, the 4th instant, they actually had the insolence to appear at the Town Common with their arms and colours, but finding I had near 100 men I could command and depend upon, and being told that many of them would join me as volunteers, after staying about 3 hours I was informed they differed among themselves and began to disperse, and I have now the great satisfaction to acquaint your Excellency that they were all dispersed; but Sir, some of them declared they were offered the assistance of from 4 to 500 men from Carolina, and if they came, would be ready to return again. If none come from thence I hope to remain quiet. I shall see some of the most dispassionate people and of the most considerable property amongst them, and endeavour to restore the peace of the Province, but even if I succeed in this so far as to obtain promises of submission, yet Sir, some troops will nevertheless be absolutely necessary, for I fear I cannot have entire confidence in the people for some time, and your Excellency sees the insults His Majesty's authority has received, and which I am still liable to. Possibly your Excellency may be surprised that I have not mentioned calling out the militia, but I have too much reason to think I should have armed more against me than for me, and that volunteers were the only people I could have any confidence in or dependence upon."

The only stamps issued in Georgia were used to clear sixty or seventy vessels in the Savannah Harbor whose masters were afraid to sail without stamps. In that one emergency citizens consented to make an exception to the rule enforced against the issue of stamp papers and the payment of stamp duties. For making that exception the Georgia Colonists were condemned in South Carolina. At Charleston, Georgia was denounced as "An infamous colony" and it was resolved that "every vessel trading there should be burnt" and "all persons trafficking with Georgians should be put to death." Two vessels sailing for Savannah were captured before they crossed the Charleston bar, were brought back to the city, and their cargoes were condemned and destroyed.

Commenting on that action, Colonel Charles C. Jones says in his *History of Georgia*:

"Sincerely, however, did the Carolinians repent of this behavior which was unneighborly, lawless, and wholly unjustified by the circumstances of the case. True to the common cause of the colonies, Georgia, in this emergency, was not unmindful of the equities of the moment, and did not, in a whirlwind of passion, lose sight of her better judgment. Overawed by the popular uprising, Governor Bull did not pretend to stem the current, and Carolina achieved a comparatively easy victory. Georgia, on the contrary, prevailed in defiance of an executive who pertinaciously brought every influence and power to bear in behalf of the enactments of Parliament and in direct opposition to the will of the province. Perilous and perplexing was his situation. He acquitted himself like a brave man and a faithful servant of his royal master."

## CHAPTER XLI.

# *Repeal of Stamp Act—Governor Wright's Clash With Assembly*

**Repeal of the Stamp Act**—Seeing America's action on the Stamp Act the great Pitt declared:

"I rejoice that America has resisted . . . . The Gentleman asks when were the Colonies emancipated? I desire to know when they were made slaves? . . . . In a good cause, on a sound bottom, the force of this country can crush America to atoms. If any idea of renouncing allegiance has existed, it was but a momentary frenzy; and if the case was either probable or possible, I should think of the Atlantic sea as less than a line dividing one country from another. The will of Parliament, properly signified, must forever keep the colonies dependent upon the Sovereign kingdom of Great Britain. But on this ground of the Stamp Act, when so many here will think it a crying injustice, I am one who will lift up my hands against it. In such a cause your success would be hazardous. America, if she fell, would fall like the strong man; she would embrace the pillars of the state and pull down the constitution along with her.

"Is this your boasted peace? Not to sheathe the sword in its scabbard but to sheathe it in the bowels of your brothers, the Americans? Will you quarrel with yourselves now the whole house of Bourbon is united against you? The Americans have not acted in all things with prudence and temper. They have been driven to madness by injustice. Will you punish them for the madness you have occasioned? Rather let prudence and temper come first from this side. I will undertake for America that she will follow the example.

Be to her faults a little blind;<br>
Be to her virtues very kind.

"Upon the whole I will beg leave to tell the house what is really my opinion. It is that the Stamp Act be repealed, absolutely, totally, and immediately; that the reason for the repeal be assigned, because it was founded on an erroneous principle. At the same time let the sovereign authority of this country over the Colonies be asserted in as strong terms as can be devised, and be made to extend to every point of legislation that we may bind their trade, confine their manufactures, and exercise every power whatsoever except that of taking their money out of their pockets without their consent."

The battle waged fiercely in Parliament, and terminated at first unfavorably to the American Colonies. Again was it renewed. Grenville moved the enforcement of the Stamp Act. "I shudder at the motion," cried the aged General Howard. "I hope it will not succeed, lest I should be ordered to execute it. Before I would imbrue my hands in the blood of my countrymen who are contending for English liberty, I would, if ordered, draw my sword, but sooner sheathe it in my own body." Benjamin Franklin, summoned to the bar of the House of Commons, declared that America could not pay the stamp tax for want of gold and silver, and for lack of post roads and the means of sending stamps back into the country. "Do you think the people of America would submit to pay the Stamp Duty if it was moderated?" inquired Grenville. "No, never," responded Franklin. "They will never submit to it."

In the heat of the debate in Parliament on the repeal of the Stamp Act, Pitt, who had been painfully ill, hobbled into the House of Commons on crutches, swathed in flannels, and urged members to repeal the act. The vote was 275 for repeal and 167 to soften the act and enforce it.

To the venerable statesman, the American Colonists sent this grateful message:

"To you grateful America attributes that she is reinstated in her former liberties . . . . America calls you over and over again her father. Live long in health, happiness, and honor. Be it late when you must cease to plead the cause of liberty on earth."

**Governor Wright Announces Repeal**—When official information of repeal reached Savannah, Governor Wright convened the Georgia Assembly and when it met on July 16, 1768, he addressed both houses in these words:

"I think myself happy that I have it in my power to congratulate you on this Province having no injuries or damages, either of a public or private nature, with respect to property to compensate, and that you, Gentlemen of the Assembly, have no votes or resolutions injurious to the honor of His Majesty's government, or tending to destroy the legal or constitutional dependency of the Colonies on the Imperial Crown and Parliament of Great Britain to reconsider.

"When you consider the papers I shall now lay before you, I am persuaded your hearts must be filled with the highest veneration and filial gratitude, with a most ardent zeal to declare and express your grateful feelings and acknowledgments, and to make a dutiful and proper return, and show a cheerful obedience to the laws and legislative authority of Great Britain."

**The Assembly's Reply**—To the Governor's address the Assembly replied as follows:

"We, His Majesty's most dutiful and loyal subjects, beg leave to return your Excellency our sincere thanks for your affectionate speech. Hopeful as we were that no occasion would have offered of calling us together till the usual season of our meeting, yet it is with the highest pleasure and satisfaction, and with hearts overflowing with filial affection and gratitude to our most gracious Sovereign, that we embrace the opportunity now presented to us of expressing our most dutiful acknowledgments to the best of Kings for his paternal and princely attention and regard manifested to his faithful subjects in these remote parts of his dominions in graciously condescending to lend his royal ear to their supplications and removing from them those evils they lamented. Nor can we sufficiently venerate and admire the magnanimity and justice of the British Parliament in so speedily redressing the grievances by them complained of.

"We cannot indeed but felicitate ourselves in that we have no injuries or damages either of a public or a private nature, nor any votes or resolutions derogatory to the honor of His Majesty's government or tending to destroy the true constitutional dependency of the Colonies on the Imperial Crown and Parliament of Great Britain to reconsider.

"We will immediately proceed to take into our most serious consideration the papers laid before us by your Excellency, and we shall upon all occasions be ready to testify our loyalty to our King and firm attachment to our Mother Country."

**The Assembly to the King**—On July 22, 1766, the houses of the Georgia Assembly united in this message to King George the Third:

"Most Gracious Sovereign.

"We your Majesty's loyal subjects, the Council and Commons of your Majesty's Province of Georgia in General Assembly met, beg leave to approach your Royal person with hearts full of the most dutiful affection and gratitude. Influenced by principle, and animated by your Majesty's exemplary justice and paternal care in redressing the grievances of your faithful subjects in these remote parts of your wide extended Empire, with the deepest sense of your Majesty's royal clemency and goodness, we humbly offer to your most sacred Majesty our sincere thanks for the repeal of the late Act of the British Parliament commonly called the American Stamp Act. Nor can we Sufficiently admire the magnanimity and justice displayed by the British Parliament on this occasion. Permit us, dread Sire, while we endeavor to express our gratitude to the best of Kings for affording us so speedy and necessary relief, to assure your Majesty that we shall, upon all occasions, strive to evince our loyalty and firm attachment to your Majesty's sacred person and government, being truly sensible of the advantages derived to us from the protection of our Mother Country; and that it is and ever will be our honor, happiness, and true interest to remain connected with and dependent on the Imperial Crown and Parliament of Great Britain upon the solid basis of the British Constitution.

AERIAL VIEW—MACON

That your Majesty's illustrious House may continue to reign over a free, loyal, and grateful people to the latest posterity is, most gracious Sovereign, our constant prayer, unfeigned, wish, and our most sanguine hope.

"By order of the Upper House, JAMES HABERSHAM, PRESIDENT.

"By order of the Commons House of Assembly, A. WYLLY, SPEAKER."

In spite of the friendly tone of the Assembly's message to the King, Governor Wright was wise and discerning enough to see and understand the real situation. In sending the Assembly's message to Secretary Conway he wrote that while many Georgians seemed to be grateful for the "Special grace and favor received" "and appeared to show dutiful obedience to the legislative authority of Great Britain, there were not a few who still retained "the late avowed sentiments and strange ideas of liberty."

**England Insists on Taxing the Colonies**—Although the British Parliament had repealed the act imposing a stamp tax on American Colonies, it did not recede from its claim of the right to tax America. The sugar and the "quartering" acts remained in force and Townshend added a bill which proposed duties on paint, paper, glass and lead, all of British manufacture. The exportation of tea to America was encouraged by a law which for five years gave a drawback of the duty on tea imported into America. These acts showed the Colonists that the British Government was determined to raise revenue in America by taxation, and against that policy the Colonies were united in opinion, holding that taxes on trade, if designed to raise a revenue, were just as much a violation of their rights as any other taxes.

About this time John Dickinson wrote under the heading, "Letters from a Pennsylvania farmer to the inhabitants of the British Colonies," a pamphlet pointing out the danger of allowing any precedent of Parliamentary taxation to be established, on any grounds or to any extent. These letters were widely circulated in America and were reprinted in London by Benjamin Franklin, who represented the Colonists there.

These letters and the declaration of the Colonists against taxation of them by the British Parliament brought matters to a head and Charles Townshend, to meet the situation, announced a policy of coercion, saying, "Let us deliberate no longer; let us act with vigor now while we can call the Colonies ours. If you do not, they will very soon be lost forever."

To this policy of coercion the greatest men in Parliament were opposed. Fox declared "If you persist in your right to tax the Americans you will force them into open rebellion." Burke reminded the House of Commons that the Americans were the children of England and when they asked for bread they should not be given a stone.

In the meantime the Americans were not inactive. Virginia and Massachusetts prepared resolutions of non-importation which were also adopted by Georgia. South Carolina openly advocated resistance to taxation without representation. New York was equally strong in the same way. Agents of the Colonies in England were busy with protest and Colonial legislatures sent memorials to the King, asking repeal of the obnoxious acts, Georgia approved the doctrine advanced by the "Pennsylvania Farmer" and although some wealthy citizens of the Province sided with the Crown, most of the people were for the right of Colonists to tax themselves. In this emergency Governor Wright justified and supported all the acts of Parliament and this soon brought him into conflict with the General Assembly.

Other incidents served to hasten the crisis. On January 16, 1767, the Governor received a communication from Captain Phillips who then commanded detachments of the King's American regiment stationed in South Carolina and Georgia, inquiring where he should apply for supplies for his troops authorized by the terms of the Mutiny Act. The Governor sent this letter with a special message about it to the General Assembly, with a copy of the Mutiny Act. The Council replied that it would concur with the Commons House in adopting any measure thought expedient to comply with the request of Captain Phillips. The Lower House of Assembly made no answer and irritated at the delay the Governor sent for two members of that body and told them that if an answer was not returned at once he would be obliged to issue a second message, in which he would mention some things not pleasant.

**The Lower House Declines**—On the 18th of February the Lower House submitted an address, in which, after professing "Loyalty, duty and affection for their most gracious sovereign, and their respect for the British Parliament," they conceived that a compliance with the requisition contained in the Governor's message "would be a violation of the trust reposed in them by their constituents," and would establish a precedent which they were not justified in introducing.

Thus the Lower House boldly joined issue and as representatives of the people refused to obey the act of Parliament and declined the request and the authority of the Royal Governor.

This put the Governor in a difficult position. Though incensed at their conduct, he did not argue the matter with them, but transmitted an account of the proceedings to the British Ministers. In writing the Earl of Shelburne on April 6, 1767, he gave as a reason for not dissolving the Assembly immediately the fact that there were several members in it who were disposed to support the government, but if a new Assembly were convened he thought it would be composed wholly of men calling themselves "Sons of Liberty," adding the words, "that is in fact, my Lord, Sons of Licentiousness, and such as are disposed to strike at the Sovereignty of Great Britain."

The Lower House confirmed its position in opposing the acts of Parliament in other ways. Two bills had passed the General Assembly for establishment of ferries, but they did not provide for transporting postmen without detention and free of charge as directed by a statute of the 9th of Queen Anne. Seeing the omission the Governor asked the Council to prepare an amendment which would meet the requirement of the act, and that was done, but the Lower House refused to approve the amendment and the measure was lost. The Assembly placed its dissent on the ground that it would not submit to an enforcement of the act of Parliament referred to.

Under these circumstances Governor Wright wrote to the Earl of Shelburne that the Sovereignity of Great Britain in America had received a wound from which it could scarcely recover, and that in his opinion the acts of Parliament would thereafter have little weight in American Provinces.

To this Shelburne replied, expressing astonishment that a Province which had been so highly favored and signally protected by the Mother Country should be guilty of such conduct, adding, "I have it in command from His Majesty to inform you that he expects and requires the Commons House of Assembly in Georgia to render an exact and complete obedience in all respects whatever to the terms of the Mutiny Act."

To punish the Colony for the refusal of its Legislature to furnish supplies for troops under command of Captain Phillips, General Gage ordered all the King's forces withdrawn from the Province. Alarmed at the abandonment of the forts and the defenseless condition of Georgia, the Commons House of Assembly at its next session reversed the action of its predecessor and voted such pay and supplies as were sufficient to maintain a small force to man the principal fortifications and give protection against a servile insurrection or an invasion by Indians.

Another dispute between the Governor and the Council on one side and the Lower House on the other arose in the appointment of Samuel Grath as Agent of the Province in England. The former Agent, Mr. Knox, had been displaced and the Governor wished a Mr. Cumberland appointed. Disregarding this the Commons House of Assembly gave the appointment to Mr. Grath, who was already Agent for the Province of South Carolina. Thinking it would be difficult or impossible for Grath to represent two Colonies whose interest was not always the same the Governor and Council refused to approve his appointment, and used their influence to his discredit as Agent for Georgia by the Official Boards in London.

The Governor and the Assembly also differed about the increase of currency. The merchants of Georgia submitted to the General Assembly a petition in which they said that because of the rapid increase of population, the expansion of commerce and the settlement of East Florida, which drew its supplies largely from Georgia, the province suffered from the lack of sufficient currency, as there was little coin in the country and the amount of currency approved by the Crown and issued by the Georgia Government was inadequate for the purposes of trade. They therefore asked the General Assembly to increase the supply.

The Legislature agreed upon a petition to the King and Parliament, asking for the repeal of the Act forbidding the issuance of currency in America, and asking that Governor Wright be instructed to give his assent to a bill calling in the outstanding issue of 7,410 pounds and authorizing a new issue of 22,000 pounds to meet the needs of the Province.

Believing that relief was needed, but thinking the sum suggested too large, Governor Wright refused to approve an issue greater than 12,000 pounds. In giving his reason for the difference, he said the large skin trade of the Province was carried on without money, as skins were bartered for goods, and the principal articles for which money was paid were rice and lumber. Even these, he said, were largely used in exchange with merchants from abroad, who furnished negroes, dry goods, groceries, etc. Under these circumstances he feared that if the currency were inflated as proposed, instead of remaining at par it would be seriously affected.

In spite of these objections the General Assembly allowed the petition and forwarded it, not through the Governor, but directly to the Colonial Agent in London for presentation to the King.

The Governor was incensed at this discourtesy and, writing to the Secretary of State, he said such a thing had never before been attempted in any American Province. Under these circumstances the petition was denied because of the irregularity in its presentation.

The refusal of the King to approve two acts, passed by the General Assembly and approved by the Governor, providing for more efficient control of the slave population and the encouragement of settlers to come into the Province, greatly disturbed the people of Georgia and tended to further alienate them from the Mother Country.

The dependence on the will of the Home Government and the long delay in securing its approval of needed laws became more and more onerous, as increase in population and wealth made such legislation necessary; and as Georgia became more conscious of ability to sustain herself she, like the other Colonies, longed for independence and wished for liberation from Parliamentary rule.

There was serious inconvenience in the requirement that Georgia legislation be approved by a government 3,000 miles away, when it took two months for the matter to be carried to England and two more months for a reply to come back, with time added for the consideration of it by the home government. Acts of the General Assembly had first to be approved by the Governor. If vetoed by him, an act was dead. If assented to, it was sent to London, where it was referred to the King's Counsel for report. When returned by him without objection it was scrutinized by the Commissioners of Trade and Plantations. If approved by them, the act was sent to the King's Council. If that august body approved it the act received the sign Manual of the King and became a law. It was then placed in the hands of the Board of Trade and by them turned over to the Crown Agent who sent it to the Colonial Governor. Sometimes there would be a delay of two years between the passage of the act by the Colonial General Assembly and the receipt of formal notice that it had received the approval of the Crown.

Under these difficult conditions Georgia was fortunate in April, 1768, in securing the services of Dr. Benjamin Franklin as its agent in Great Britain and his appointment was approved by Governor Wright. A committee instructed to correspond with him and give him such orders and instructions as they thought best for the good of the Province was composed of Councillors, James Habersham, Noble Jones, James Edward Powell, Lewis Johnson and Clement Martin, acting with John Mullryne, John Smith, Noble Wimberly Jones, John Milledge, John Simpson, Archibald Bullock, William Ewen and Joseph Gibbons of the Commons House of Assembly. Dr. Franklin's salary was fixed at a hundred pounds over and above expenses and disbursements.

This appointment of Dr. Franklin, though only made for a year, was extended and he continued to represent the Colony until the outbreak of the Revolution.

**The Governor Breaks with the Assembly**—On the 11th of February, 1768, the Massachusetts House of Representatives, through its speaker, sent a letter to the provincial assemblies, stating the grievances of the American Colonies and asking for a union of petitions to the Parliament and the King for redress, also proposing a confederation of the provinces in opposition to the oppressive acts of the British Government.

When that letter reached Georgia the General Assembly was not in session, but the late Speaker, Alexander Wylly, replied as follows to the Massachusetts Speaker:

SPEAKER WYLLY'S LETTER.

"Province of Georgia, 16 June, 1768.

"SIR—Your respected favor of the 11th of February came to hand only a few days since. I am sorry it is not in my power to give you so full and satisfactory an answer thereto as the importance of the subject requires. The members of the present Assembly of this Province have but lately been elected; and though the writs were returnable and the House was required to meet the first of this month, yet our Governor thought proper, prior thereto, to prorogue the Assembly until November.

"For this reason, Sir, I can only reply to your favor as a private person, or late Speaker, and inform you that before the dissolution of the last Assembly the House took under consideration the several late Acts of Parliament for imposing taxes and duties on the American Colonies, and being sensibly affected thereby, ordered the committee of correspondence to instruct our Provincial Agent, Mr. Benjamin Franklin, to join earnestly with the other Colonies' Agents in soliciting a repeal of those acts, and in remonstrating against any acts of the like nature for the future. These instructions have been transmitted to Mr. Franklin and I have no doubt he will punctually observe them. When the Assembly meets I will lay your favor before the House, and I am sure that such measures will be pursued, in consequence thereof, as will manifest their regard for constitutional liberty and their respect for the House of Representatives of the Province of Massachusetts Bay whose wise and spirited conduct is so justly admired."

**Governor Wright Warns England**—In advising the Earl of Hillsborough of the effect produced by the circular letter from Massachusetts, Governor Wright wrote:

"My Lord, Virginia has entirely concurred, in the strongest manner asserts what she calls her rights, and denies the Parliamentary authority of Great Britain, as your Lordship will see by Mr. Randolph's letter of the 9th of May. The people of Maryland have also expressly approved of that letter and say that when they apprehend their rights to be affected they will not fail boldly to assert and steadily to endeavour to maintain and support them . . . . The people of New Jersey, Connecticut, and Rhode Island have also approved and answered that letter, and this, my Lord, I know is the sense and language of every Colony on the Continent, so that your Lordship sees it has had its effect already. However, your Lordship may be assured that every means in my power shall be exerted to prevent that flagitious attempt to disturb the public peace from any further weight or success. But, my Lord, I fear it will be impossible to counteract or defeat the effect of the Pennsylvania Farmer's poison . . . . They now to the Northward not only deny the power of the British Parliament to tax them, but that they are subject to, or may be governed by any other laws whatever to which they have not given their consent, and it is those things my Lord that cherish the spirit of Independency, and keep up the flame in the Southern Colonies.

"Much, with respect to the conduct of the people here, my Lord, I conceive, will depend on the notice taken of this by Government or Parliament, as the controverted matters between Great Britain and America seem now to be at or near the crisis. And, my Lord, it is not to be expected that a reform is to be effected in America 'till it is at least begun in the Mother Country. The King, my Lord, has not a servant better disposed or more zealously devoted to the support of His Majesty's just authority and the true sovereignty of Great Britain, or who will go greater lengths to do it than myself, but my Lord, what can a Governor do at present in America, where the voice of the people is so general and strong against the measures pursued in the Mother Country, and when some of the Colonies expressly deny the power and authority of Great Britain over them? I am destitute of the means of support and protection either for myself or for those who are friends to government against any insults &c. that may be offered by mobs, &c., &c. And my Lord, I fear it is vain for a Governor to expect to set the people right by reasoning. A Demosthenes or a Cicero would spend his breath in vain, and it gives me the greatest concern to find that the sentiments and opinion I at first conceived and very early intimated, have been so strongly and fully supported by diverse events. But I then clearly saw that certain declarations, followed by the repeal of the Stamp Act and other indulgencies, instead of having the salutary and wished for effect, would only serve to encourage and convince the Americans of the rectitude of their claims and measures, and that they were legal and constitutional—at least such is their apprehension—and I must crave your Lordship's pardon for saying that the disease, as I have observed, having been in some measure promoted and encouraged by the Mother Country, I conceive the remedy and reform must come from thence likewise."

When the Assembly re-convened Noble Wimberly Jones was elected Speaker and Ex-Speaker Wylly laid before the House the communication from Massachusetts and a similar one from Peyton Randolph, Speaker of the Commons House of Assembly of Virginia.

**Resolution of the Georgia House of Assembly**—The Georgia House ordered both communications entered on the *Journal* and adopted the following resolution:

"Resolved, That from the inherent right of the subject to petition the Throne for redress of grievances, a right allowed and confirmed by the Act of William and Mary, the said letters do not appear to the House to be of a dangerous or factious tendency, but on the contrary, in the opinion of this House, only tend to a justifiable union of subjects aggrieved in lawful and laudable endeavors to obtain redress by an application founded upon and expressive of duty and loyalty to the best of Kings, a becoming respect for the Parliament of Great Britain, and an equitable and natural affection for our Mother Country, and arises from the tender and commendable attention of those Colonies to the natural rights and liberties of the British subjects in America, and to which they are undeniably entitled upon the happy principles of our constitution.

"Resolved, That copies of this resolution be, by the Speaker of the House, transmitted to the Speaker of the House of Representatives of the Province of Massachusetts Bay, and to the Speaker of the House of Burgesses in Virginia, and that they be acquainted by him that this House approves of the measures by them pursued to obtain redress of our common grievances, also of the method by them taken of communicating these measures to the other Provinces of the Continent.

"Ordered that the several proceedings and resolutions respecting the said letters be published in the *Gazette* of this Province, and that the Clerk do furnish the printer with a copy of the same."

# CHAPTER XLII.

# *Governor Wright Dissolves the Assembly —He Leaves Georgia*

**The Governor Dissolves the Assembly**—Learning of the adoption of the foregoing resolution by the Assembly, Governor Wright addressed them the following message:

"Mr. Speaker and Gentlemen of the Assembly:

"From the disposition that appeared amongst you at the opening of the Session I flattered myself that it would have been brought to a happy conclusion. It gives me great concern to find it now otherwise, and that you have disregarded the principal matter I had in charge from the King, and thereby missed a fair opportunity of cherishing the confidence His Majesty has in your affections. But by receiving and countenacing the Boston letter in the manner you have done, you have laid me under the necessity of dissolving you. You well know that more than ordinary pains have been taken to prevent this event. If any disagreeable consequences should attend it, you will have brought them upon the Province by a deliberate act, and it is you, and you only who will have to answer to your constituents.

"However you may have been influenced by the conduct of the other Provinces, be assured that your true Liberty and prosperity must depend upon the free and uninterrupted course of Law and Government under the support and protection of the Mother Country, and that you cannot possibly enjoy these invaluable blessings without that protection and support. And how can you expect this or with what right can you pretend to it if you declare yourselves an independent people? To me it appears a flat contradiction to acknowledge the British Parliament to be the supreme Legislative power over the whole British Empire (of which we are a part), and in the same breath to deny the power of that very Parliament over us. Nor can I see or admit the propriety of the Americans declaring that they 'cheerfully acquiesce in the authority of the British Parliament to make laws for a necessary dependence and regulating the trade of the Colonies,' and at the same time denying its authority to make other laws, which I conceive to be a very loose and improper jumble or system of Government without any criterion but the mere caprice of the populace. I presume the authority of the Parliament must be full and complete, or it does not operate at all.

"The distinction between internal and external taxes I conceived, and said to be, a distinction without a difference. I said also that if it was granted to the Americans that they were not subject to be constitutionally taxed by Parliament, not being represented there, then I apprehended the same reasons would hold in every case, and the same objection lie against every law made by Parliament to affect the Colonies. It seems absurd to say that the Colonies are not bound by Acts of Parliament imposing what are called internal taxes because they have not assented to such laws, not being represented in that Parliament, and at the same time to admit that they are bound by and subject to the laws made by the same Parliament. . . . .

"I have declared that if America was to become independent of the Mother Country, from that day you may date the foundation of your ruin and misery.

"These were the sentiments I declared three years ago, and which I still retain, and I most ardently wish I had been able to prevail upon you to be so far of my opinion as to have paid due regard to His Majesty's expectations from you, and to have observed a more prudent conduct in that particular until the matters of difference between great Britain and the Colonies were clearly settled. But as things are circumstanced, here, there is only one thing for me to do, which is, by virtue of His Majesty's authority and in his name, to dissolve this Assembly, and I do accordingly dissolve the same."

**The Assembly to the King**—On the same day when the Commons House of Assembly adopted the resolution for which the Governor dissolved that body, it prepared the following address to the King:

"To the King's most excellent Majesty:

"The humble address of the Commons House of Assembly of the Province of Georgia, 24th December, 1768.

"Most Gracious Sovereign:

"Your dutiful and loyal subjects, the Commons House of Assembly of Georgia, with the greatest humility beg leave to represent to your sacred person the grievances this Province labors under by the late Acts of the Parliament of Great Britain for raising a revenue in America. Equally attached by interest, principle, and affection for our Mother Country, we readily acknowledge a constitutional subordination to its supreme Legislature. At the same time, with inexpressible concern, we much lament that by their imposition of internal taxes we are deprived of the privilege which, with humble deference, we apprehend to be our indubitable right, that of granting away our own property, and are thereby prevented from a ready compliance with any requisition your Majesty may please to make, and which to the utmost extent of our small abilities we have hitherto always most cheerfully obeyed.

"From your Majesty's equity, wisdom, and truly paternal regard for the rights and liberties of your subjects, however remote, we flatter ourselves with, and firmly rely upon, redress in this our unhappy situation; and we are impressed with the deepest sense of gratitude, so we most earnestly hope we shall also experience, in general with our sister Colonies on this occasion, fresh marks of your Majesty's royal Justice and attention to the supplications of your distressed subjects.

"We beg leave to assure your Majesty that none of your numerous subjects can or do more ardently wish and pray for a continuance of your most auspicious reign, and that your latest posterity may happily rule over a free, grateful, and loyal people, than your faithful Commons of Georgia.

"By order of the House. N. W. JONES, Speaker."

This memorial was not sent through the Governor as had been customary, but was forwarded by the Speaker directly to Dr. Franklin, Georgia's Agent in London, with instructions to present it to the King and unite with the Agents of other American Colonies in an earnest effort to bring repeal of oppressive acts of Parliament which disturbed the harmony between England and her American Colonists.

The Earl of Hillsborough wrote to Governor Wright that Dr. Franklin had delivered the address to him and he presented it to the King. Though His Majesty considered the transmission of the address through any channel but the Governor as irregular and disrespectful, he had weighed the contents and found them in letter and spirit to deny and draw into question the authority of Parliament to enact laws binding the Colonists, and the King directed him to say that he disapproves the address, being firmly resolved to support the Constitution as by law established and not to countenance any claims inconsistent with its true principles. The Governor's action dissolving the Assembly was approved.

**Cost of Georgia's Government in 1769**—The cost of maintaining the civil government of Georgia reported by Governor Wright in 1769 was as follows:

| | |
|---|---|
| The Salary of the Governor | 1,000 pounds |
| " " " " Chief Justice | 500 |
| " " " " Secretary of the Province | 100 |
| " " " " Clerk of the Assembly | 20 |
| " " " " Surveyor General | 150 |
| " " " " Receiver General of Quit Rents | 100 |
| " " " " Attorney General | 150 |
| " " " " Provost Marshal | 100 |
| Allowance for 2 Ministers of the Church of England and 2 Schoolmasters | 116 |
| Salary of the Agent for the Affairs of the Colony | 200 |
| Salary of the Pilot, with Expenses of the Boat, etc. | 500 |
| Allowance for the Encouragement of Silk Culture | 100 |
| | 3,036 pounds |

**Trouble with the Indians**—The rules adopted at the Augusta conference with the Indians concerning the conduct of Indian traders had worked well and as long as the traders were required to observe the regulations agreed on there was quiet and good order in the Indian trading territory, but that satisfactory condition ended when the King in 1763 removed those restrictions on traffic with natives. A number of irresponsible parties went into the Indian territory, the region was overstocked with goods, credit was over extended, the Indians were deeply in debt to unscrupulous merchants and dissension resulted.

Governor Wright protested against the royal proclamation which caused so much trouble but the trouble continued and in 1767 Creek Indians on the Oconee River and Little River captured some horses. They were pursued by five of the white settlers, but being reënforced turned on their pursuers and drove them back. Governor Wright in August, 1767, demanded the return of the stolen horses, the recall of the marauding bands of Indians and the observance of the boundary line agreed on at the Augusta conference. Augusta then had 80 houses, a church and two wooden forts and plantations were increasing as far as Little River.

The same year at Jere Wilder's settlement, twenty miles above the ferry on St. Mary's River, thirteen Indians killed Baker and Cummins, wounded Wilder, set fire to the premises, and retreated into East Florida. This was done in revenge for the beating of Indians who had stolen several horses some time before.

Other acts of violence occurred and Governor Wright did his best to restore peace and deal justly with both Indians and white men. To that end he had talks with leading Indians, the Wolf-King, the head men of Coweta, Captain Aleck, Emisteseegoe the head men of the Lower Creeks, Attakulla-kulla, the Chiefs of the Cherokees and other noted Indians.

The importance of those conferences is shown by the strength of the Indian tribes holding commerce with Georgia, estimated as follows by Governor Wright in a letter to the Earl of Hillsborough on October 5, 1768:

| | | |
|---|---|---|
| Upper and Lower Creeks | 3,400 | gun men |
| Choctaws | 2,200 | " " |
| Chickasaws | 400 | " " |
| Cherokees | 2,000 | " " |
| Catawbas | 40 | " " |
| Total | 8,040 | " " |

Carrying out this policy of the Governor, a conference was held in the Council Chamber at Savannah on September 3, 1768. The English were represented by Governor Wright, and Councilmen James Habersham, Noble Jones, James Mackay, Grey Elliott, and James Read. Lachlan McGillivray acted as interpreter. The Indians were headed by Emisteseegoe, the most influential head man of the Creek Confederacy.

Emisteseegoe told the complaints of the Indians and Governor Wright responding pledged every effort to do them justice and to "keep the path clean and white" between the cabin of the Colonist and the wigwam of the Indian.

At the end of the conference Governor Wright presented Emisteseegoe with a commission under the seal of the Province.

**Governor Wright Warns England**—The letter from the Earl of Hillsborough telling Governor Wright of the King's approval of his dissolution of the Georgia Assembly was written at London on the 23d of March, 1769, and after the usual two months voyage across the Atlantic Ocean must have been received at Savannah the last of May.

By the middle of August, 1769, after the rapid progress of events in America during three months that intervened, the Governor of Georgia had seen enough to realize the hopelessness of England's policy in its attempt to force the collection of taxes on America by offensive measures that infuriated the Colonists. On August 15 Governor Wright wrote the Earl of Hillsborough a remarkable letter which must have shocked the complacency of British statesmen by its frank statement of conditions in America which made the success of their policy appear impossible.

After renewed expression of his loyalty to the Crown and even justifying the position of Parliament, he made it clear that the time to curb the spirit of independence in America had passed and it was time to consider a different course. These extracts from his letter make it clear that he saw the inevitable result of the policy of the English King and Cabinet:

"But my Lord, the Americans are so clearly convinced that they are not represented in the British Parliament, and also are so enthusiastically possessed with an opinion that they cannot be constitutionally taxed by a Parliament in which they are not represented, or be subject to be taxed by laws to which they have not consented, I say my Lord, the many printed publications and speeches in Parliament, together with the repeal of the Stamp Duty Law, &c, have so firmly fixed them in their opinion on this point, and of the rectitude of their measures since these unhappy disputes first took place, that I am fully persuaded they never will be brought to change their sentiments or to acquiesce quietly under any tax or duty law. And my Lord, the partial relief proposed to be given in the next session of Parliament by the repeal or taking off the duties upon glass, paper and colours, I humbly conceive will not answer any effectual purpose, and that the spirit of discontent and dissatisfaction will nevertheless continue and be as violent as ever, for the grievance complained of, whether real or imaginary, will still remain unredressed, and no new line drawn or established, settling the power or right of Parliament to tax America, till which I fear there will be continual associations &c injurious to Great Britain as well as the Colonies, and which your Lordship has seen or will see has become almost universal, and the Americans will certainly be drove to observe strict economy and to manufacture everything they possibly can amongst themselves in prejudice to Great Britain. A mere declaration of the right of Parliament to tax America will not now have any weight. There was a time my Lord, when that, and enforcing a particular law (if it had been only for six months), would have most effectually settled and established the point; but believe me, my Lord, the time and the only time has been missed, and those things are considered not as the real and true sense of either Parliament or People, but as the effect of Ministerial influence, and some other mode will now be necessary for settling and bringing this matter to a point; not force or troops which I conceive are of no use further than a few just to prevent riots, and support the Governors &c from public affronts and insults. I don't mention this as with respect to this Province, for I have received none since the Winter and Spring of 1765 and 1766, when I had my full share; tho' I thank God we are now very easy, quiet, and happy; and I believe the People are convinced that my vigilance, activity, and firmness in opposing their measures at that time, and enforcing the Stamp Act, proceeded from an honest principle and resolution to discharge my duty to His Majesty to the utmost of my power and to support the Sovereignty and Honor of Great Britain.

"My Lord, my opinion has ever been, and is well known in this part of the World to be, that according to the present constitution the Parliament has an absolute right to bind the Colonies. . . . .

"But my Lord when people first emigrated to America I conceive it was not thought or could be supposed that America would so soon, if ever, become that vast, populous, and opulent Empire or Dominion that it now is. May it not therefore my Lord, in point of true policy, as well as from motives and principles of equity and justice, now, from the present circumstances and situation of affairs, become expedient to make some alteration in the present Constitution relative to America? But lest what I have already suggested may be considered as too presumptive in me, I shall forbear saying anything further, altho' my Zeal for His Majesty's service and the real happiness of both Great Britain and the Colonies strongly prompt me to proceed."

Had the King and Cabinet of England been big enough and wise enough to heed the warning so tactfully given by an able and loyal servant of England, the then Royal Governor of Georgia, the blood and desolation of a seven years' war with the Colonies might have been saved. In comparison with the superb statesmanship of England in dealing with her over-sea dominions in Canada, Australia, South Africa and Ireland during the last thirty years, the course of George the Third and his Cabinet was weak and deplorable.

**Georgians Refuse English Goods**—As the King and Parliament turned deaf ears to petitions for redress of grievances sent them by the American Colonies, the appeals to sentiment and right were abandoned and the Americans decided upon a policy of non-importation of English goods. It was suggested by Boston merchants and the Assembly of Virginia gave official sanction to the movement by adopting non-importation resolutions. Other Colonies followed and the sentiment in the Colonies was nearly unanimous.

A meeting of merchants at the house of Alexander Creighton in Savannah on September 16, 1769, agreed that acts of Parliament protested by the Colonists were unconstitutional and in violation of the rights of the American Colonies. The meeting approved the non-importation policy and declared that in refusing to accept in payment of duties the current money of the Province which Parliament had declared a legal tender, the British Government had reduced the value of Georgia's currency, and as Georgia was excluded from the benefits of the Spanish trade by which coin could only be secured, the Colonists were put in position where it was impossible to meet the payments demanded by Parliament.

The meeting further resolved that anyone importing articles subject to the objectionable duties when it could be prevented ought to be treated with contempt as an enemy of the country.

**The Non-Importation Resolutions**—Soon after the merchants met there was a public meeting at which Jonathan Bryan, a member of Council and an influential man presided. The non-importation resolutions which follow were reported by a committee and adopted by the meeting:

"We, inhabitants of Georgia, finding ourselves reduced to the greatest distress and most abject condition by the operation of several acts of the British Legislature by means whereof our property is arbitrarily wrested from us contrary to the true spirit of our Constitution and the repeatedly confirmed birthright of every Briton, under all these oppressions finding that the most dutiful and loyal petitions from the Colonies for redress of these grievances have not answered the salutary purpose we intended, and being destitute of all hope of relief from our multiplied and increasing distresses but by our industry, frugality, and economy, are firmly resolved never to be in the least accessory to the loss of any privilege we are entitled to:

"Therefore, we, whose names are hereunto subscribed, do solemnly agree and promise to and with each other that until the said acts are repealed, we will most faithfully abide by, adhere to, and fulfill the following resolutions:

"I. That we will encourage and promote American manufactures, and of this Province in particular.

"II. That as the raising of Sheep for the benefit of wool will be of the utmost utility, we do therefore engage not to kill or sell any lambs that shall be yeaned, before the 1st of May in every year, to any butcher or other person who, we may have reason to think, intends to kill the same.

"III. That we will promote the raising of cotton and flax, and encourage spinning and weaving.

"IV. That we will upon no pretense, either upon our own account or on commission, import into this Province any of the manufactures of Great Britain, or European or East India goods, other than may be shipped in consequence of former orders, except only cloth, not exceeding 1s 4d pr yard, osnabrigs, canvass, cordage, drugs, and hardware of all sorts, paper not exceeding 10s pr ream, fire arms, gunpowder, shot, lead, flints, salt, saltpetre, coals, printed books and pamphlets, white and striped flannels, not above 9s pr yard, white linen not above 1s 8d pr yard, woollen and thread hose not exceeding 24s pr doz: striped cotton not exceeding 1s 4d pr Yard, checks not above 1s 3d per yard, felt hats not above 48s pr doz: bolting cloths, mill and grind stones, cotton and wool cards, and wire, thread not above 8s pr lb., shoes not above 48s pr doz: as also the following goods necessary for the Indian Trade, *viz.* strouds, vermilion, beads, looking glasses, and paint. And exclusive of these articles we do solemnly promise and declare that we will immediately countermand all orders to our correspondents in Great Britain for shipping any goods, wares, and merchandise other than hereinbefore excepted, and will sell and dispose of the goods we now or hereafter may have at the same rates and prices as before.

"V. That we will neither purchase nor give mourning at funerals.

"VI. That from and after the 1st June, 1770, we will not import, buy, or sell, any negroes that shall be brought into this Province from Africa, nor after the 1st of January next any negroes from the West Indies or any other place excepting from Africa aforesaid. And if any goods or negroes be sent to us contrary to our agreement in this subscription, such goods shall be reshipped or stored, and such negroes reshipped from this Province and not by any means offered for sale therein.

"VII. That we will not import on our own account or on commission, or purchase from any masters of vessels, transient persons, or non-subscribers, any wines after the 1st March next.

"VIII. That we will not purchase any negroes imported, or any goods, wares, or merchandise, from any resident of this Province, or transient person, that shall refuse or neglect to sign this agreement within 5 weeks from the date thereof, except it appear he shall have been unavoidably prevented from so doing. And every person signing and not strictly adhering to the same according to the true intent and meaning thereof, and also every non subscriber, shall be looked upon as no friend to his country."

**The King Suspends Bryan**—When King George learned the action of the meeting which adopted these resolutions he was angry and on December 9th instructed the Earl of Hillsborough to order Jonathan Bryan suspended from his seat in Council and removed from any office in Georgia.

The King's reason given was that he was determined to "discountenance every measure that tended to violate the Constitution and excite opposition to the laws."

Governor Wright reported Mr. Bryan's removal from Council in a letter to the Earl of Hillsborough on March 1, 1770.

This act of the British King did not discourage the Colonists and the number of Liberty Boys increased.

**Representation of New Parishes**—The Commons House of Assembly asked the Governor to issue writs of election for representatives of the four new parishes of St. David, St. Patrick, St. Thomas, and St. Mary which had been created in the new territory of Georgia between the Altamaha and St. Mary's rivers. The Assembly urged that the people of those provinces were deprived of representation in making laws.

The Governor thought that it was just that the parishes be represented in the Commons House of Assembly, but doubted whether he had the authority to issue writs of election under the conditions prevailing then. He agreed to consider the request and if it appeared that he had authority to act he would submit the matter to the home government and ask its permission to order the elections. He was advised by Council that he had not the authority and the matter should be referred to the Home Government.

The Commons House of Assembly renewed its request on March 20, 1770, urging that taxation without representation was intolerable and unjust and unless the Governor should act as requested they dared not impose a general tax, as every member abhorred partial representation.

The Governor again conferred with Council and that body gave the same reply as before. He submitted the matter to the Home Government. Writs of election were at first refused by the King and nothing was done until December 11, 1770, when the King agreed that the new parishes should be represented in the Commons House of Assembly and authorized the Governor to approve a bill to that effect, giving the vote to owners of town lots paying the same tax as that on 50 acres of land, the vote to be by ballot instead of *viva voce,* and persons owning houses, lots and land worth 300 pounds to be eligible to serve as representatives, theretofore limited to the owners of 500 acres of land.

There were frequent disagreements of the Governor and Council with the Commons House of Assembly because the Lower House represented the masses, with their revolutionary sentiments. As a result the Commons House of Assembly was several times dissolved for assuming the prerogatives of Parliament and defying the laws of England, but that did not check the spirit of independence which grew with opposition and each new House of Assembly was more independent than the one dissolved.

A case of that kind which angered the people occurred when Noble Wimberly Jones, a son of Noble Jones who had been a leader in the Colony from the first, was elected speaker of the Commons House of Assembly, and because the new Speaker had been influential in opposing the oppressive acts of Parliament, Governor Wright refused to approve his selection for presiding officer and ordered the House to elect another Speaker.

Incensed at this affront to a man who has been called "one of the morning stars of liberty in Georgia" and resenting the interference with their election of their own presiding officer, the House adopted resolutions commending Dr. Jones and declared that their high opinion of him was not affected by the Governor's action.

The House declared that the rejection by the Governor of the Speaker they had unanimously elected was a breach of the privileges of the House and tended to subvert the most valuable rights and liberties of the people and their representatives. The Council denounced that as "an indecent and insolent denial of His Majesty's authority." The Governor retaliated by dissolving the House of Assembly.

**Governor Wright Asks Leave of Absence**—Governor Wright had bought valuable land in Georgia, had put upon it a large number of negro slaves and had settled several plantations. In order to give attention to his own affairs and make a trip to England, he on July 3, 1769, asked leave of absence for a year to begin in the spring of 1770. On November 2nd that year he received a reply granting the leave and James Habersham, President of the Council, whom Wright had suggested, was appointed Governor for the interim. Governor Wright did not begin his leave of absence until July 10, 1771. On July 13 James Habersham took the oaths of office and began to discharge the duties of Governor under the title of "President and Commander-in-Chief of His Majesty's Province of Georgia, Chancellor, Vice Admiral and Ordinary of the same for the time being."

## CHAPTER XLIII.

# *Habersham Dissolves the House—Indians Cede Two Million Acres—Settlement Checked by Indian Outbreaks*

**Irish Colonists Come to Georgia**—In March, 1768, the General Assembly of Georgia passed an act to encourage settlers to come to the Province, and £1,815 were appropriated to aid those who came. That act was disapproved by the King, who had been expected to approve it. Before that reversal of the legislators' action was known, 107 Irish protestants came to Georgia in December of that year. The faith of the Colony had been pledged for their assistance by act of the General Assembly and it was necessary to care for them. The Governor and Council, during the recess of the Legislature, gave the immigrants homes in the fork of Lambert Creek and Great Ogeechee River, relying on the General Assembly to reimburse them for the expense incurred.

The Irishmen built a town which they called Queensbury, where two hundred families found homes in the town and surrounding country.

At this time the Colony prospered under good civic officers. James Hume was Attorney-General, Alexander Wylly was clerk of the Council, and Anthony Stokes, an able and upright lawyer, was Chief Justice. The laws were well and impartially administered, property was secure and in spite of deep-seated dissatisfaction with the government there was outward prosperity. The territory of Georgia then, according to Governor Wright's report to the Earl of Dartmouth, included 6,695,429 acres, about one-fifth of its present area. Of this 120,000 acres were cultivated in 1,400 plantations.

As the results of action by the Governor of South Carolina before the Home Government stopped him, 93,000 acres were held under his grants. Twelve thousand acres were claimed under a patent from the Lord Proprietors of South Carolina. All the rest was held under grants by the Kings of England.

The twelve thousand acres mentioned constituted a barony claimed by Sir William Baker, whose title was disputed by soldiers of General Oglethorpe's regiment, who claimed that those lands were set apart for them by the Trustees when the regiments was disbanded in 1748 and 1749, and that they and their descendants had owned and occupied them ever since.

**Georgia's Trade with Great Britain**—Under the wise administration of Governor Wright Georgia had prospered up to the time when he returned from England in 1772. Governor Wright reported the imports of Georgia from Great Britain in 1772 to be 76,322 pounds and exports to that country 68,688 pounds. The negroes imported the same year were valued at 20,000 pounds, which went to England. Total exports of the Province were 101,240 pounds. The imports from Great Britain consisted of linens, woolens, iron ware, hats, shoes, stockings, clothing, tea, paper, paint and other articles. The exports to Great Britain were mainly deer skins, rice, indigo and naval stores. Georgia received rum and sugar from the West Indies and rum, flour and other provisions from the Northern Colonies. To the West Indies the Province sent rice, corn, peas, lumber, shingles, cattle, horses, live stock and barreled beef and pork. Trade with the Northern Colonies was unsatisfactory, as they took little from Georgia, and in payment for their goods drained Georgia of gold and silver.

The Georgia Colony owned wholly or in part five ships, seven brigantines, thirteen sloops and schooners and ten coasting vessels, all of which had a capacity of 1,990 tons. To operate these there were 212 seamen. At the port of Savannah 161 vessels were entered in 1772 and 56 at Sunbury, altogether 212 with a capacity of 12,124 tons. In 1761 only 45 vessels with 1604 tons entered the Province, showing an increase of 650 per cent. in the trade of Georgia in eleven years. The later effect of the non-importation policy of the Colonists is clear in view of the Governor's report that Georgia bought goods worth 76,000 pounds or $380,000 a year from the Mother Country.

As Georgia, the youngest Colony, imported $380,000 of English products in 1772 the twelve other Colonies must have paid the Mother Country several million dollars a year for goods bought there. From this it is clear that the non-importation policy of the Colonies hit the Mother Country a staggering blow.

Before the movement had become as general as it did later, the merchants of Manchester told Parliament that seven-eighths of their men were idle.

The influence which a man of Governor Wright's ability could wield in the face of popular pressure may be understood from the number of leading men receiving public money.

Some of the salaries paid influential men were:

| | |
|---|---|
| The Governor, 1000 pounds | $5,000 |
| and perquisites, 319 pounds | 1,595 |
| James Habersham, Secretary, salary and perquisites, 572 pounds | 2,860 |

| | |
|---|---|
| Anthony Stokes, Chief Justice, salary and perquisites, 1,020 pounds | 5,100 |
| Henry Yonge, Surveyor-General, 523 pounds | 2,615 |
| Charles Pryce, Attorney-General, 365 pounds | 1,825 |
| Alexander Thompson, Collector of Customs, 358 pounds | 1,790 |

**Governor Habersham Dissolves the Assembly**—The Eighth General Assembly met at Savannah on April 21, 1772, and the House elected Dr. Noble Wimberly Jones Speaker. When informed of that action, Governor Habersham replied, "I have His Majesty's commands to put a negative on the Speaker now elected by the Commons House, which I accordingly do, and I desire that you inform the House that I direct them to proceed to a new choice of Speaker."

A message brought to the Governor by Messrs. Bulloch and Farley informed him that the House had proceeded to a second choice and had reëlected Noble Wimberly Jones. The Governor again disapproved the choice and directed the House to proceed to the selection of some other person for Speaker.

The next afternoon a committee of the House composed of Messrs. LeConte and Farley waited on the Governor and informed him that Archibald Bulloch had been elected Speaker of the House. This choice was approved and Governor Habersham delivered this address:

"His Majesty having been pleased to grant his Excellency Governor Wright leave of absence to go to Great Britain, the government of this Province, on his Excellency's departure, devolved upon me. I am very sensible of the high and important trust committed to me, which calls for the utmost exertion of my best abilities to discharge so as to approve myself to our most gracious Sovereign by promoting the true interest and prosperity of his good subjects in this Province, to effect which you may depend on my most sincere and unwearied endeavours. My long residence in this Province, and the strong attachment I must have for its welfare from motives obvious to you, must make it extremely grateful to me to be in the least instrumental in furthering its growing prosperity, in which I am persuaded I shall have the candid advice and assistance of you Gentlemen, and of every Friend of this Country."

He then told the Assembly of the King's disapproval of the conduct of the last Assembly in denying the right of the Governor to negative the choice of a Speaker. After mention of needed legislation he told the House that the Creek Indians had executed the Indian who murdered John Carey of Queensbury. After inviting the members by suitable legislation to maintain the public faith and credit of the Province, the Governor concluded as follows:

"Suffer me, Gentlemen, to persuade you to pursue peace and harmony, and carefully to avoid all unnecessary altercations which can only tend to delay business and destroy that candour, unanimity, and confidence so necessary to promote the general good for which end you meet in General Assembly; and you may depend upon my hearty concurrence in every measure that may conduce to the service of His Majesty and the welfare of the Province, which are inseparable."

The Assembly, after thanking the Governor for his courteous words, expressed great satisfaction that the government of the Province had, "in the absence of Governor Wright, devolved upon a Gentleman of your Honour's well known character and attachment to the real welfare of Georgia, from whence we entertain the firmest confidence that to promote its growing prosperity will be the favorite object of your administration; and you may be assured that we shall most readily and cheerfully concur with your Honour in every measure that may contribute to so desirable an end."

These agreeable relations were soon disturbed. In looking over the *Journal* of the House Governor Habersham saw that in the face of his second disapproval the House had elected Dr. Jones Speaker a third time and it was because Dr. Jones declined to accept the position that Archibald Bulloch was elected. On seeing that the Governor, on April 25, sent this message to the House:

**The Governor Rebukes the House—**
"Mr. Speaker, and Gentlemen of the Assembly.

"I am extremely sorry to find by your *Journals* that some very exceptionable minutes are entered. I particularly mean your third choice of Noble Wimberly Jones Esqr. as your Speaker, upon whom I had, agreeable to His Majesty's express instructions, twice put a negative, and that your choice of your present Speaker was only in consequence of his declining the chair. If this minute is to stand upon your *Journals* I have no choice left but to proceed to an immediate dissolution. I desire therefore that you will come to a present and speedy determination to recede from it. If you do, I shall, with the most unfeigned satisfaction, proceed to business which you cannot but be sensible will be of the highest advantage to the Province. I shall expect your immediate answer to this message that my conduct may be regulated by it: and shall for that purpose remain in the council chamber."

**Reply of the House**—To that message the House replied:
"May it please your Honour.

"We His Majesty's most dutiful and loyal subjects, the Commons of Georgia in General Assembly met, are very unhappy to find by your message to us of this day that any Minutes entered upon our *Journals* should be construed by your Honour in a manner so very different from the true intent and design of this House. Conscious we are, Sir, that our third choice of Noble Wimberly Jones Esqr as our Speaker was not in the least meant as disrespectful to His Majesty, or to you his representative, nor thereby did we mean to infringe on the prerogative of the Crown. We have seriously reconsidered that particular minute which seems to have given your Honour so much offence, and cannot perceive wherein it is contrary to the strict mode of

Parliamentary proceeding, or repugnant to anything communicated to us by your Honour. We were hopeful that no further impediment would have arisen to retard the urgent business of the public, and still flatter ourselves that we may be permitted to do that justice to our constituents which they have a right to expect from us: and we sincerely assure your Honour that it is our hearty wish and desire to finish the business, by you recommended to us, with all harmony and dispatch.

ARCHIBALD BULLOCH, Speaker."

On receipt of this reply Governor Habersham called the House before him in the Council Chamber, reviewed the whole matter and dissolved the Assembly.

**Members of That Historic House**—The members of that Commons House of Assembly were:

Jonathan Bryan, Noble Wimberly Jones, Archibald Bulloch, and William Young for the town and district of Savannah; Nathaniel Hall for the parish of St. George; David Zubly for the village of Acton; Benjamin Andrews, John Stevens, and Audley Maxwell for Midway and the parish of St. John; Peter Sallins for the parish of St. Patrick; Edward Barnard, Alexander Inglis, and Thomas Shruder for Augusta and the parish of St. Paul; Thomas Carter for the parish of St. David; Henry Bourquin for the district of Little Ogeechee in the parish of Christ Church; William Ewen, Stephen Millen, and John Stirk for the town and district of Ebenezer in the parish of St. Matthew; Samuel Farley for the islands of Wilmington, Tybee, Skidoway, and Green Island in the parish of Christ Church; James Spalding for the parish of St. James; and William LeConte and Jonathan Cockran for the parish of St. Philip. George McIntosh, elected for the parish of St. Andrew, took his seat on the 24th of April; and George Baillie for the parish of St. Thomas, and John Thomas for the parish of St. George, declined to serve as representatives.

In a letter to the Earl of Hillsborough on April 30, 1772, Governor Habersham showed the injurious effect of this dissolution of the Assembly, but insisted that it was necessary to carry out the instructions of the King. Unable to see affairs from Dr. Jones' viewpoint, he criticized him as ungrateful because his family "had reaped more advantages from government than any in the Province." Dr. Jones' father was then Treasurer of the Colony.

**Bad Effect of Dissolution of the House**—The effect of dissolving the House of Assembly was very bad, as pointed out by Dr. William B. Stevens in his history. He said of it:

"These repeated interruptions in Colonial legislation produced serious and alarming consequences. The treasury was overdrawn, and no provision was made to replenish it; statutes of importance had expired, and no new enactment supplied their places; the judiciary was deranged, and no means were

AERIAL VIEW OF ATLANTA

adopted to rectify it; and new necessities, civil and legal, had arisen, requiring legislative action, but the meetings of the Assembly had been rudely dissolved and the political existence of the Colony was vitally endangered. These oppressions increased the adherents of the Colonial cause. The flattering promises of the Ministry to redress their grievances, had not been fulfilled; but new sources of distress had augumented those already existing, and cloud upon cloud, each darker and more foreboding than the former, was casting its gloom over their firmament. The passage of the Boston Port Bill, March 31, 1774, by which Parliament precluded all commerce with that city; followed by another which deprived Massachusetts of its chartered privileges; together with a law for sending State criminals to England 'to be butchered in the King's Bench,' hurried on the catastrophe of war."

**Governor Wright Made a Baronet**—While things were not going well in the Government of Georgia, Governor Wright was well received in England. He had a favorable audience with the King and his zeal in the King's service and his able administration were rewarded by royal action. On December 8, 1772, he was made a baronet. Sailing from England the same month he reached Savannah the middle of February, 1773, and was cordially received by the people.

**Indians Cede Two Million Acres**—For some years the Cherokee Indians in Georgia had been largely indebted to traders, and in June, 1773, their debt was estimated at 40,000 to 50,000 pounds, equal to $200,000 to $250,000. The traders were clamoring for their money, and as the Indians were not able to pay in skins because the hunting was bad they, after some negotiation, ceded to the King of England two million acres of well-watered and productive land in eastern Georgia, from which the counties of Georgia, Wilkes, Lincoln, Taliferro, Greene, Oglethorpe, Elbert and others were created. The deed conveying these lands to the Crown provided that they be sold and the proceeds used as far as necessary to pay the debts which the Indians owed the traders.

When the cession was made by the Indians, the Indian traders to whom the debts were due signed releases, which relieved the Indians of their obligations. The leaders of the traders signing the releases were George Galphin, James Jackson & Co., Martin Campbell & Son, Woodgion, Rae, Whitfield & Co., Edward Barnard, Waters, James Grierson, James Spalding & Co., and Edward Keating.

To realize on the land for the purpose of paying the Indian debts to the traders, which, by the terms of the cession, the government agreed to pay with the proceeds of the sale of the land, that rich territory was offered for sale to settlers in tracts of 100 to 1,000 acres and Governor Wright, in a memorial to the King, made an optimistic estimate of the benefit that would come to the Province by the settlement of those lands.

Dr. Stevens says that the Governor expected great benefit to the Colony from this cession of land by the Indians, and wrote the British Ministry that he thought it would add 10,000 families to the population, give an increase of 15,000 effective men to the militia muster roll, bring $500,000 worth of produce into market and add greater security to the settlements against the hostility of Indians, who, in spite of their promises of peace, were still troublesome and dangerous.

**A New Impulse to Settlement**—To draw the attention of the public to the opportunity offered to secure valuable lands, and thus to attract settlers to Georgia, Governor Wright on June 11, 1773, issued a proclamation in which he described the cession and stated that surveyors were dividing the tract into lots of 100 to 1,000 acres and running the boundary lines. His proclamation is thus summarized:

"He stated that the territory would 'be parceled out in tracts varying from 100 to 1,000 acres the better to accommodate the buyers'; that in conformity to His Majesty's instructions 'one hundred acres would be sold to the master or head of a family, fifty acres additional for the wife and each child, and the same number of acres for each slave owned and brought in by the purchaser'; that in 'further encouragement of the settling of the said lands the masters or heads of families will be allowed to purchase 50 acres for each able bodied white servant man they shall bring in to settle thereon,' and also '25 acres for every woman servant from the age of 15 years to 40 years'; that all persons were at liberty to come into the Province and view these lands, and, as soon as they were surveyed, to make choice of such of them as they desired to purchase and settle upon; that grants would be executed on the most moderate terms, and that for a period of ten years the parcels purchased would be exempt from the payment of quit rents; that the lands offered were 'in general of the most fertile quality and fit for the production of wheat, indico, Indian corn, tobacco, hemp, flax, &c. &c. &c.'; that they comprised 'a pleasant and very healthy part of the Province'; that they were 'extremely well watered by Savannah River, Ogeechee River, Little River, and Broad River, and by a great number of creeks and branches which ran throughout the whole country and emptied themselves into the aforesaid rivers'; that there was an abundance of springs, and that the water was very fine; that Little River, where the ceded lands began, was but twenty-two miles above the town of Augusta; that at this place a ready market would always be found for all produce and stock; that if Savannah was preferred as a point for trade there was easy transportation down the Savannah River, while a good wagon road led from Little River to that commercial metropolis of the Province; that a fort would speedily be built and garrisoned within the ceded lands for the protection of the immigrants, and that all vagrants and disorderly persons would be promptly and severely dealt with; and finally, that these lands adjoined a well-settled part of the Province, where law, justice, and good government obtained."

**Sold for $1.25 Per Acre**—A place of settlement for the tract was made and Colonel Bartlett and Messrs. Young, Holland and Maddox were appointed Commissioners with power to negotiate sales of the land. Not over five shillings an acre was to be charged for it and an entrance fee of five pounds was to be paid for every 100 acres. To facilitate settlement of the tract, land courts were opened at Savannah, and Augusta, and at the confluence of the Broad and Savannah rivers.

At the junction of those rivers, Captain Waters was stationed with a company of soldiers, and Fort James was built there on an eminence between the streams.

It had a stockade enclosing an acre of ground, and within that enclosure were officers' quarters and barracks for a garrison of fifty rangers, who were well mounted, each armed with a rifle, two dragoon pistols, a hanger, a powder horn, a shot pouch and a tomahawk. The stockade ground was square and at each angle there was a blockhouse protected by swivel guns. The blockhouses were a story higher than the stockade which had openings for small arms.

The town of Dartmouth, located above the Fort, was named for the Earl of Dartmouth who had induced the King to favor this cession of Indian lands. Later this town was succeeded by Petersburg, which became a place of some business importance.

The ceded lands were eagerly sought for and settlements on the tract were rapidly made. Some Quakers, who had settled in what is now Columbia County, left that neighborhood because they feared the Indians, came to this tract and went to work at farming. The prospect for the rapid settlement of the ceded land was bright when a new outbreak of Indian hostility discouraged the incoming of settlers.

**Settlement Checked by Indian Outbreaks**—In January, 1774, some Creek Indians attacked Sherrall's fortified settlement where there were five white men, three negro men and twelve women and children. The Indians fired on the men at work on the fort and Sherrall and two others fell. The others went into the houses and one of the negro men, rushing out at an Indian shot him through the head.

There was a strong defense. The Indians set fire to the houses three times and each time the fire was put out. Two neighbors heard the firing and came near, but were run off by the Indians. They escaped and notified Captain Barnard, who got 40 men together, attacked the Indians in the rear and drove them into swamps. In that attack seven persons had been killed and five wounded in the fort. Five Indians killed were carried off by their companions.

A few days later there was a fight between 25 white settlers and 150 Indians. Four white men were killed and a fifth died of wounds. Several dwellings were burned by the Indians. Captain Few and Lieutenants Williams and Bishop got some men together and buried those killed. Lieutenant Samuel Alexander, with a few soldiers, attacked a party of Indians and two of the Creeks were killed.

These outrages by Indians alarmed the new settlers and many sought safety in retreat to safe places. Forts were built on the Savannah and Little rivers and women, children and personal property were taken there for safety.

George Galphin, an Indian trader who had the confidence of both white men and Indians, sent a message to learn from the Chiefs whether they intended peace or war and to demand an explanation of the outrages. The Chiefs replied that the bloody incursion was unauthorized and the Creeks' disposition toward the white inhabitants was friendly.

Big Elk, who led the attack on Sherrall's fort, invited the Cherokees to join him in an invasion of Georgia, but the Cherokees declined. On his way home Big Elk and his party killed and scalped three white men.

The last of March, Head Turkey, a leading Chief of the Upper Creeks, with two chiefs and an Indian trader, went to the Lower Creek town to induce them to make peace with the Georgians. It was agreed that he should wait on Governor Wright and make overtures. On his way to Savannah, Head Turkey was murdered at Augusta by Thomas Fee, in revenge for the butchery of his kinsmen on the frontier by Indians. That act enraged the Indians and Fee fled to South Carolina. Governor Wright offered a reward of 100 pounds for his arrest. He was arrested and put in jail at Ninety-Six, South Carolina. While he was there an armed party came at night, forced the jail and freed Fee. That incensed the Indians, but when they learned that Governor Wright's offer of a reward for Fee's arrest was still good and that the Governor of South Carolina had offered a reward of $200 for him they were satisfied.

Governor Wright told the Creek Chiefs who had come to Savannah that fifteen of his people had been slain within four months by Creeks without provocation and eleven South Carolinians had been killed in the same way. He demanded the blood of the Indians who had murdered innocent Colonists and denied their right to ask justice which they failed to give. He added that if he asked the King of England to do so that he would send him a military force which would exterminate the whole Creek Nation. Under those circumstances his actions showed that he did not desire war. He insisted that no more innocent blood should be shed and said that hereafter if Indians murdered or robbed his people he would exact atonement for every offense.

The Indian Chiefs promised that their nation would in future keep peace with the English. When they left Savannah the Governor ordered Captain Samuel Elbert with a company of grenadiers to escort them through the White settlements, so that they would not be harmed by the people.

While these Chiefs were absent from their nation, several Indian parties crossed the Georgia frontier and committed theft and murder. Later Commissioners from the Upper and Lower Creek towns called on the Governor and told him that their warriors had killed the leader and two of the men who had been guilty of the outrages.

So the difficulties ended and a general treaty of peace was made at a Congress held in Savannah on October 20, 1774. The contracting parties who made that treaty were:

On behalf of Georgia, were his Excellency Sir James Wright, Governor, the Honorable John Stuart, Superintendent of Indian Affairs in the Southern District and one of His Majesty's Councilors, and the Honorable Noble Jones, James Edward Powell, Lewis Johnston, John Graham, James Read, Clement Martin, Anthony Stokes, and James Hume, members of Council. On the part of the Indians, the treaty of amity was signed by seven kings and head warriors of the Lower Creeks, and by thirteen headmen of the Upper Creek Nation.

Immigration into the fine lands ceded by the Indians had been discouraged by the Indian outrages, but with the reëstablishment of peaceful relations by the treaty of October, 1774, confidence was renewed and those who had left their homes returned and new applicants for purchase came in considerable number.

**Payment of Traders' Claims**—As money came in from the sale of land the time had come to pay the valid claims of the traders to whom the Indians had been indebted. Governor Wright undertook to pay those of the traders who were loyal to the English Crown in full but withheld payment from those he considered sympathizers with the revolutionists. He also showed the same partiality in the sale of lands.

George Galphin the leading trader, a man of character, ability and influence with both Indians and white men had been of great service to the Colony in its dealings with the Indians, but because he and some others opposed the oppressive measures of the British Government Governor Wright discriminated against them unjustly. Although their claims were large and undoubtedly just the Governor refused to pay them. While that was approved by the Ministry it cannot be justified as a matter of right and propriety. On June 6, 1775, the demand of George Galphin was audited before the Governor and Council and approved for 9,791 pounds, 15 shillings and 5 pence and made payable from moneys which should be realized from the sale of lands lately ceded to His Majesty by the Cherokee and Creek Indians. As the result of war, the land ceded by the Indians became the property of the State of Georgia, and in 1780 the claims of traders who proved themselves friends of Georgia were admitted by the State. Galphin's claim was of that class, for the Royal Assembly which met in Savannah not long before his death charged him with treason and denounced him as the "rebel superintendent of Indian

Affairs." His great service to Georgia during the Revolution was well known and fully established by leading Georgians.

Galphin's trading place at Silver Bluff on the Savannah River was a great center of commerce with the Indians, and Royal presents for the Indians were frequently distributed there. In Colonial days George Galphin was one of the influential and enterprising citizens of Georgia. His business extended to Charleston, Savannah, St. Augustine, Pensacola and Mobile. Repeatedly he advanced supplies to the Colony which were needed at remote points for parties in the public service. In the Revolution his influence was exerted with the Creek Indians to keep them neutral.

**Bryan's Attempt to Secure Immense Territory**—It was in the period of prosperity not long before the Revolution that Jonathan Bryan and leading men of East Florida conceived a plan to lease from the Indians for ninety-nine years five million acres of land known as the Appalachee Old Fields, bounded on the west by the Gulf of Mexico and the Appalachicola River, on the north, by a line drawn from the junction of the Flint and Chattahoochee rivers to the head of the St. Mary's, and on the southwest by a line running thence to the Gulf of Mexico. The rent agreed on was a hundred bushels of corn a year. The object stated was to cultivate the land and open a trading post with the Indians.

A ninety-nine-year lease of this vast tract was secured from the Chiefs and headmen of the Creek Nation, and the deed of conveyance was signed with their marks by fifteen of the Chiefs and headmen.

Governor Wright, at the conference with Indians at Savannah in 1774, exhibited the deed and informed the Indians through an interpreter of the character and extent of the conveyance. Telache, one of the Indians whose marks were on the deed said he was told that Mr. Bryan only wanted enough land for a cowpen, a field to cultivate corn and a place to build a residence for himself. The other Indians seemed enraged and one of them said he would not leave the house until the deed was burned. Others demanded that it be torn up. Others said that if the paper was not destroyed the Creek Nation would give no credit to the action of the convention. It also appeared that the deed had to be confirmed by the Creek Nation and that had not been done.

It appeared that the Indians did not understand what they were conveying by the deed, and when it was made clear to them they violently repudiated it and threatened war if an attempt was made to enforce it.

At the Governor's suggestion the paper was not destroyed, but the Indians were allowed to tear from it their seals and marks.

Finding that the Creek Nation was opposed to the lease, Mr. Bryan dropped the matter, and so ended an affair which promised grave trouble.

## CHAPTER XLIV.

# *British Tyranny Rouses Resistance of Colonies—The Provincial Congress*

**Americans Infuriated by Tyrannical Acts**—The resistance of the Colonies had the effect of increasing the severity of Great Britain's measures, which were intended to subdue them by suffering.

The trade of Boston was important to England as well as to Massachusetts, but the British Ministry closed the port and for the time destroyed its commerce. The Ministry demanded absolute submission to the acts of Parliament. The Chancellor of the Exchequer said:

"Obedience, not indemnification, will be the test of the Bostonians."

Another exclaimed, "The Town of Boston ought to be knocked about the ears and destroyed. 'Delenda est Carthago.' You will never meet with proper obedience to the laws of this country until you have destroyed that nest of locusts."

The Boston Port Bill was followed in April, 1774, by an act which provided that the Provincial Council of Massachusetts should be appointed by the Crown, that the Governor should have power to appoint and remove judges, sheriffs, and important executive officers. Jurymen were to be nominated by sheriffs, town meetings should not be called without permission in writing from the Governor and their discussions were limited to matters approved by the Governor. Another act authorized the Governor to send to England or another Colony for trial persons charged with murder or other capital offenses.

The tyranny of these acts further inflamed the Americans, in Georgia and South Carolina as well as in Colonies to the north of them.

**The Meeting at Tondee's Tavern**—On July 20, 1774, this call was issued by leading Georgians for a meeting at Tondee's Tavern. Those who signed it were: Noble W. Jones, Archibald Bulloch, John Houstoun, and John Walton.

"The critical situation to which the British Colonies in America are likely to be reduced from the arbitrary and alarming imposition of the late acts of the British Parliament respecting the town of Boston, as well as the acts that at present exist tending to the raising of a perpetual revenue without the consent of the people or their representatives, is considered an object extremely important at this juncture, and particularly calculated to deprive the American subjects of their constitutional rights and liberties as a part of the English Empire. It is therefore requested that all persons within the limits of this Province do attend at the Liberty Pole, at Tondee's Tavern in Savannah, on Wednesday the 27th instant, in order that the said matters may be taken under consideration and such other constitutional measures pursued as may then appear to be most eligible."

The meeting was held on July 27 with John Glen presiding as chairman, and resolutions and letters from committees of correspondence at Boston, Philadelphia, Annapolis, Williamsburg, and Charleston were read and the following committee was appointed to prepare resolutions of similar character: John Glen, John Smith, Joseph Clay, John Houstoun, Noble Wimberly Jones, Lyman Hall, William Young, Edward Telfair, Samuel Farley, George Walton, Joseph Habersham, Jonathan Bryan, Jonathan Cockran, George McIntosh, Sutton Bankes, William Gibbons, Benjamin Andrew, John Winn, John Stirk, Archibald Bulloch, James Screven, David Zubly, Henry Davis Bourquin, Elisha Butler, William Baker, Parmenus Way, John Baker, John Mann, John Benefield, John Stacy, and John Morel.

Acting on the wish of the Committee, Chairman Glen sent letters to the different parishes asking them to elect delegates and send them to Savannah to take part in the meeting to which the Committee on Resolutions was to report.

**Governor Wright's Proclamation**—Learning the action of the Committee and the action of the meeting at Tondee's Tavern calling a second meeting, Governor Wright tried to prevent the parishes from sending delegates by issuing the following proclamation:

"Georgia. By his Excellency Sir James Wright, Bart, Captain General of His Majesty's Province of Georgia, Chancellor, Vice Admiral and Ordinary of the same.

"Whereas I have received information that on Wednesday, the 27th of July last past, a number of persons, in consequence of a printed Bill or Summons issued and dispersed throughout the Province by certain Persons unknown, did unlawfully assemble together at the Watch House in the Town of Savannah under colour or pretence of consulting together for the Redress of Grievances or imaginary Grievances, and that the Persons so assembled for the purposes aforesaid, or some of them are, from and by their own authority, by a certain other Hand Bill issued and dispersed throughout the Province, and by other methods, endeavouring to prevail on His Majesty's liege subjects to have another meeting on Wednesday the 10th instant, similar to the former and for the purposes aforesaid, which summonses and meetings must tend to raise fears and jealousies with His Majesty's subjects under pretence of consulting together for redress of Public Grievances, and are unconstitutional, illegal, and punishable by law.

"And I do hereby require all His Majesty's subjects within this Province to pay due regard to this my Proclamation as they will answer the contrary.

"Given under my hand and the Great Seal of His Majesty's said Province, in the Council Chamber at Savannah, the 5th day of August in the 14th year of the Reign of our Sovereign Lord George III. in the year of our Lord, 1774.

JAMES WRIGHT.

By his Excellency's command.

THO. MOODIE, Dep: Sec:

"God save the King"

**Declaration of the People of Georgia**—In spite of the Governor's proclamation, there was, on August 10, 1774, a meeting of the people of the Province at Tondee's Tavern in Savannah and the Committee appointed at the meeting of July 27th reported the following resolutions which were adopted as an expression of the sentiments of Georgia:

"Resolved, nemine contradicente, That His Majesty's subjects in America owe the same allegiance, and are entitled to the same rights, privileges, and immunities with their fellow subjects in Great Britain.

"Resolved, nemine contradicente, That as protection and allegiance are reciprocal, and under the British Constitution correlative terms, His Majesty's subjects in America have a clear and indisputable right, as well from the general laws of mankind, as from the ancient and established customs of the land so often recognized, to petition the Throne upon every emergency.

"Resolved, nemine contradicente, That an Act of Parliament lately passed for blockading the port and harbour of Boston is contrary to our idea of the British Constitution: First, for that it in effect deprives good and lawful men of the use of their property without judgment of their peers; and secondly, for that it is in the nature of an ex post facto law, and indiscriminately blends as objects of punishment the innocent with the guilty; neither do we conceive the same justified upon a principle of necessity, for that numerous instances evince that the laws and executive power of Boston have made sufficient provision for the punishment of all offenders against persons and property.

"Resolved, nemine contradicente, That the Act for abolishing the Charter of Massachusetts Bay tends to the subversion of American rights; for besides those general liberties, the original settlers brought over with them as their birthright particular immunities granted by such Charter, as an inducement and means of settling the Province; and we apprehend the said Charter cannot be dissolved but by a voluntary surrender of the people, representatively declared.

"Resolved, nemine contradicente, That we apprehend the Parliament of Great Britain hath not, nor ever had, any right to tax His Majesty's American subjects; for it is evident, beyond contradiction, the constitution admits of no taxation without representation; that they are coeval and inseparable; and every demand for the support of government should be by requisition made to the several houses of representatives.

"Resolved, nemine contradicente, That it is contrary to natural justice and the established law of the land, to transport any person to Great Britain, or elsewhere to be tried under indictment for a crime committed in any of the Colonies, as the party prosecuted would thereby be deprived of the privilege of trial by his peers from the vicinage, the injured perhaps prevented from legal reparation, and both lose the full benefit of their witnesses.

"Resolved, nemine contradicente, That we concur with our sister colonies in every constitutional measure to obtain redress of American grievances, and will, by every lawful means in our power, maintain those inestimable blessings for which we are indebted to God and the Constitution of our country—a Constitution founded upon reason and justice and the indelible rights of mankind.

"Resolved, nemine contradicente, That the Committees appointed by the meeting of the inhabitants of this Province on Wednesday, the 27th of July last, together with the deputies who have appeared here on this day from the different parishes, be a general committee to act, and that any eleven or more of them shall have full power to correspond with the committees of the several Provinces upon the Continent; and that copies of these resolutions as well as of all other proceedings, be transmitted without delay to the Committees of Correspondence in the respective Provinces."

**Rice Sent to Boston**—A committee was appointed to solicit subscriptions of money and provisions for the suffering poor of Boston and 579 barrels of rice were contributed and shipped to Boston. The Committee that did that was composed of William Ewen, William Young, Joseph Clay, John Houstoun, Noble Wimberly Jones, Edward Telfair, John Smith, Samuel Farley and Andrew Wells.

There was still a strong sentiment in the Province favorable to the British Government, and the lines drawn between the party for independence and the Royalists in some cases separated families. James Habersham, President of the Council and Acting Governor for a time, was a staunch supporter of the Crown, and his son, Joseph Habersham, was active in the party for independence. The same was true of Noble Jones, one of the first settlers, supporting the Crown, and his son, Noble Wimberly Jones, whom the independent party elected speaker and two Governors rejected because of his activity in the independent group.

The sentiments of the Royalists party were expressed in a communication published by the Georgia *Gazette,* the organ of Governor Wright, over the signatures of James Habersham, Lachlan McGillivray, Josiah Tattnall, James Hume, Anthony Stokes, Edward Langworthy, Henry Yonge, Robert Bolton, Noble Jones, David Montaigut and 93 others, mostly from Savannah.

**Voice of the Royalists**—The communication follows:

"The important meeting of the 10th of August in defence of the Constitutional rights and liberties of the American Subjects," these gentlemen affirmed, "was held at a tavern, with the doors shut for a considerable time: and it is said 26 persons answered for the whole Province and undertook to bind them by resolutions; and when several Gentlemen attempted to go in, the Tavern-keeper, who stood at the door with a list in his hand, refused them admittance, because their names were not mentioned in that list. Such was the conduct of these pretended advocates for the Liberties of America. Several of the inhabitants of St. Paul and St. George—two of the most populous parishes in the Province—had transmitted their written dissents to any Resolutions, and there were Gentlemen ready to present these dissents had not the door been shut for a considerable time and admittance refused. And it is conceived the shutting of the door and refusing admittance to any but resolutioners was calculated to prevent the rest of the Inhabitants from giving their dissent to measures that were intended to operate as the unanimous sense of the Province. Upon the whole, the world will judge whether the meeting of the 10th of August, held by a few persons in a Tavern, with doors shut, can, with any appearance of truth or decency, be called a General Meeting of the Inhabitants of Georgia."

The meeting of August 10, 1774, considered the matter of sending six delegates to the proposed General Congress of the American Colonies, but decided not to do that. The parish of St. John was prepared to act and so dissatisfied with the failure of the meeting to send delegates to the American Congress that its leaders called a convention of their own on August 30, 1774. Delegates from the parishes of St. George and St. David were present by invitation and acted with those of St. John Parish. They adopted a resolution to the effect that "if a majority of the parishes would unite with them they would send deputies to join the general congress and faithfully abide by and conform to such determination as should be there entered into and come from thence recommended."

Georgia was not represented in the first General Congress of the Colonies, and on the return from that congress of the deputies from South Carolina strong efforts were made to induce greater activity by Georgians in the cause of the united Colonies and to secure from Georgia an approval of the resolution adopted by the Congress at Philadelphia. That resolution was a declaration of Colonial rights which many Georgians approved and urged its approval as an expression of the sentiment of Georgians.

The efforts of the South Carolinians to enlist Georgia in the movement for independence was thus reported by Governor Wright in a letter he wrote the Earl of Dartmouth on December 13, 1774:

"I think it my duty to acquaint your Lordship that since the Carolina Deputies have returned from the Continental Congress as they call it, every means possible have been used to raise a flame again in this Province. Those People, it is said, solemnly undertook that this Province should accede to the Resolutions of that Congress, and we have been in hot water ever since, and I suppose the Sons of Liberty here, stimulated by the Carolinians, will take upon them to pass resolves in the name of the whole Province. I shall endeavour as much as possible to prevent it, but the sanction given to Rebellion by the Resolves and Proceedings of that Congress has greatly encouraged the spirit of political enthusiasm which many were possessed of before, and raised it to such a height of Frenzy that God knows what the consequences may be or what man or whose property may escape their resentment."

Twelve Provinces were represented in the Continental Congress. Georgia was the only absentee. The influence of Governor Wright and leading Royalists was then strong enough to prevent Georgia from sending delegates. Their absence was severely criticised and the delegates spared no efforts to induce this Colony to cast its lot with the other twelve.

**The Colonial Rights**—The Colonial rights declared by the Congress of Colonies were epitomized as follows by Colonel C. C. Jones:

"The enjoyment of life, liberty, and property was absolutely claimed. The privilege of being bound by no law to which they had not consented through their representatives was demanded as inherent in the Colonists by virtue of their character as British subjects. The exclusive power of taxation, internal and external, and the right of legislation for the Colonies were declared to reside in their respective assemblies; Parliament possessing the authority to enact only such laws as were requisite for the bona fide regulation of trade. The common law of England was insisted upon as the birthright of the Colonists. 'The right of trial by a jury of the vicinage, the right of public meetings, and the right of petition for the redress of grievances' were pronounced 'inalienable.' Against standing armies maintained in the Colonies without their consent, and against legislation by councils dependent on the Crown, solemn protests were entered. All immunities hitherto enjoyed by the Colonies, whether authorized by charter or by custom, were asserted to be vested rights which could not be abrogated by any exercise of power on the part of the Mother Country. Eleven acts of Parliament passed since the accession of George III—the Sugar act, the Stamp act, the two Quartering acts, the Tea act, the act suspending the New York Legislature, the two acts for the trial in Great Britain of offenses committed in America, the Boston Port Bill, the act for regulating the government of Massachusetts, and the Quebec act—were denounced as having been passed in derogation of the rights of the Colonies."

**The American Association**—To enforce its declaration of rights, the Congress of Colonies agreed on these fourteen points:

The associators were pledged to commercial non-intercourse with Great Britain, Ireland, and the West Indies, and to a non-consumption of tea and British goods. This non-intercourse was to extend to such of the North American Provinces as should decline to unite in the association, and was to continue until the obnoxious acts of Parliament were repealed. The non-importation clauses were to become operative in December, but the non-exportation clauses were postponed for nine months longer. The slave-trade was especially denounced, and entire abstinence from it and from those engaged in it was enjoined. The associators stood pledged to encourage the breeding of sheep. Mourning goods were to be discarded. There was to be no enhancement of the price of goods on hand in consequence of this agreement. Committees were to be raised everywhere, whose duty it should be to publish the names of all who violated the provisions of this compact. All dealings with such "enemies of American liberty" were strictly prohibited.

When the other twelve Colonies were so vigorous in asserting their rights by joint action and had taken steps to form an "American Association" for their mutual interest and protection in the common cause of liberty, the people of Georgia who sympathized with them were embarrassed by the failure of their Colony to act in the same way and to join the other Colonies.

To get out of that predicament a provincial congress was hit upon as the surest method and the 18th of January, 1775, was fixed as the date for the gathering. On December 8, 1774, leading men of Christ Church Parish met at the market place and, with John Glen presiding, elected as delegates to the Provincial Congress Joseph Clay, George Houstoun, Ambrose Wright, Thomas Lee, Joseph Habersham, Edward Telfair, John Houstoun, Peter Tondee, Samuel Farley, William Young, John Smith, Archibald Bulloch, John McCluer, Noble Wimberly Jones, and John Morel.

The result of the call was a failure. Only five of the twelve parishes sent delegates. Governor Wright and the Royalists worked hard to discourage meetings in the parishes to elect delegates, the admiralty directed Admiral Graves to station a small cruiser in the Savannah River, and General Gage was ordered to send Governor Wright a hundred men from the garrison at St. Augustine. On December 20, 1774, Governor Wright wrote the Earl of Dartmouth that the "Liberty folk were very active" but he would use all the means in his power to counteract and oppose them. To which he added:

"If they do accede to the resolutions of the Continental Congress, yet had I but 200 soldiers and a Sloop of War I think I should be able to keep everything quiet and orderly and might be very easy as to their threats about non-importation and non-exportation, and of shutting up the Ports, &c., &c., &c., but your Lordship knows I have not the least support, altho' I have the great satisfaction to acquaint your Lordship that the King's Officers and a great number of Gentlemen are against all the Liberty Measures, as your Lordship would see by the Dissents."

In spite of the efforts of the Governor and the Royalists the spirit of independence grew steadily, not deterred by the threat of force made by sending a cruiser and a company of soldiers to Savannah.

**St. Andrew's District Congress**—A District Congress of St. Andrew's Parish was held the second week of January, 1775, and adopted a series of resolutions commending the course of the brave people of Boston to preserve their liberty, approving the resolution of the Congress of Colonies, condemning the closing of land offices which stopped Colonial growth, calling for encouragement of the poor, and condemning the action of the British Government in passing laws oppressive and injurious to the Colonies. A resolution condemned slavery and demanded emancipation of the slaves. The last resolution called for the election of delegates to represent the district in the Provincial Congress and the election by the Provincial Congress of two delegates to represent Georgia in the Continental Congress to be held at Philadelphia in May, 1775.

The following articles of Association were agreed on by the District Congress:

"Being persuaded that the salvation of the rights and liberties of America depend, under God, on the firm union of the inhabitants in its vigorous prosecution of the measures necessary for its safety, and convinced of the necessity of preventing the anarchy and confusion which attend the dissolution of the powers of government, we, the freemen, freeholders, and inhabitants of the province of Georgia, being greatly alarmed at the avowed design of the Ministry to raise a revenue in America, and shocked by the bloody scene now acting in the Massachusetts Bay, do, in the most solemn manner, resolve never to become slaves; and do associate, under all the ties of religion, honor, and love of country, to adopt the endeavor to carry into execution, whatever may be recommended by the Continental Congress, or resolved upon by our Provincial Convention that shall be appointed, for the purpose of preserving our Constitution, and opposing the execution of the several arbitrary and oppressive acts of the British Parliament, until a reconciliation between Great Britain and America, on constitutional principles, which we most ardently desire, can be obtained; and that we will in all things follow the advice of our general committee, to be appointed, respecting the purposes aforesaid, the preservation of peace and good order, and the safety of individuals and private property.

(Signed)

Lachn, McIntosh,
Geo. Threadcraft,
Charles McDonald,
John McIntosh,
Rayd. Demere,
Jiles Moore,
Samuel McCleland,
Peter Sallens, Jun.,
James Clark,
John Witherspoon, Jun.,
John Witherspoon,
John Fulton,
Samuel Fulton,
Isaac Cuthbert,
Isaac Hall,
Jones Newsom.

A. Daniel Cuthbert,
John Hall,
Jno. McCollough, Sen.,
Jno. McCollough, Jun.,
William McCollough,
Reu. Shuttleworth,
John McCleland,
Richard Cooper,
Seth McCullough,
Thomas King,
Paul Judton,
John Roland,
Pr. Shuttleworth,
Joseph Stobe,
To. Bierry."

**The Provincial Congress of January 18, 1775**—The Provincial Congress proposed by the District Congress of St. Andrew's Parish met in Savannah on January 18, 1775. Governor Wright convened the General Assembly there on the same day, hoping by that either to prevent a session of the Provincial Congress or to modify its action. In that he was disappointed, as the Commons House of Assembly did not agree with the Governor or the Council and was clearly in sympathy with the Provincial Congress.

**Governor Wright to the Assembly**—In his address to the General Assembly Governor Wright said:

"The alarming situation of American affairs at this juncture makes it highly necessary for me to say something to you on that subject: and it is with the utmost concern that I see, by every account, all the Colonies to the northward of us, as far as Nova Scotia, in a general ferment, and some of them in such a state as makes me shudder when I think of the consequences which it is most probable will soon befall them.

"The unhappy disputes with the Mother Country are now become of the most serious nature, and I am much afraid the very extraordinary and violent measures adopted and pursued will not only prevent a reconciliation, but may involve all America in the most dreadful calamities.

"Gentlemen, I think myself very happy in having it in my power to say that this Province is hitherto clear, and I much hope by your prudent conduct it will remain so.

"Be not led away by the voices and opinions of men's overheated ideas. Consider coolly and sensibly of the terrible consequences which may attend adopting resolutions and measures expressly contrary to law, and hostile to the Mother Country, especially at so late a season, when we may almost daily expect to hear the determination of Great Britain on the matters in dispute, and therefore, I conceive can answer no purpose but that of throwing the Province into confusion: and I tremble at the apprehension of what may be the resolution and declaration of the new Parliament relative to the conduct of the People in some parts of America.

"You may be advocates for liberty: so am I, but in a constitutional and legal way. You, Gentlemen, are legislators, and let me entreat you to take heed how you give a sanction to trample upon law and government, and be assured it is an indisputable truth that where there is no law there can be no liberty. It is the due course of law and support of government which only can insure to you the enjoyment of your lives, your liberties, and your estates, and don't catch at the shadow and lose the substance.

"I exhort you not to suffer yourselves to be drawn in to involve this Province in the distresses of those who may have offended. We are in a very different situation and on a very different footing from the other Colonies. Don't consider me as speaking to you merely as the King's Governor of this Province. As such, Gentlemen, it is certainly my duty to support His

Majesty's just rights and authority and to preserve peace and good order within my Government, and to contribute as much as possible towards the prosperity and happiness of the Province and people. Believe me when I tell you I am at this time actuated by further motives than those only of discharging my duty as the King's Governor. I have lived amongst and presided over you upwards of fourteen years and have other feelings. I have a real and affectionate regard for the people, and it grieves me to think that a Province which I have been so long in, and which I have seen nurtured by the Crown at a vast expense to the Mother Country, and grow up from mere infancy, from next to nothing, to a considerable degree of maturity and opulence, should by the imprudence and rashness of some inconsiderate People be plunged into a state of distress and ruin. We have been most happy in (I hope) avoiding Scylla, and let me in the strongest terms conjure you to steer clear of Charybdis."

# CHAPTER XLV.

## *Houses of Legislature Differ—South Carolina's Attitude to Georgia*

**The Two Houses Differ**—The Council or Upper House which remained loyal to the Crown agreed with the Governor in its reply, but the Commons House of Assembly referred to the numerous grievances of the Colonies and their desire for redress, saying: "We cannot be less affected by and concerned for the present alarming situation of affairs between Great Britain and America than your Excellency. We must be equally insensible not to feel our numerous grievances and not to wish them redressed. It is that alone which every good American contends for.

"It is the enjoyment of constitutional rights and liberty that softens every care of life and renders existence itself supportable."

The Council proposed a conference of the two houses on the subject of American grievances and they met in the Council Chamber but could not agree, and the Commons House of Assembly declined to approve the measures proposed by the Council.

The Commons House then went into consideration of the communications from other Colonies, and adopted a series of resolutions submitted to them by the Provincial Congress. These resolutions were similar to those adopted by the meeting of October 14, 1774, and the House added three resolutions, one giving "their grateful acknowledgments to those truly noble, honorable and patriotic advocates of civil and religious liberty who have so generously and powerfully though unsuccessfully espoused and defended the cause of America, both in and out of Parliament."

A second of the additional resolutions thanked "Members of the late Continental Congress for their wise and able exertions in the cause of American liberty."

The final resolution provided that certain persons not named "Be deputies to represent this province in the intended American Continental Congress proposed to be held at the city of Philadelphia on the 10th of next May."

The Commons House set a day to act on the last resolution, but the Governor adjourned the Assembly from February 10 to May 9, which was one day before the Philadelphia Congress was to meet. That prevented the contemplated action by the Commons House of Assembly.

The Provincial Congress, which met at the same time with the General Assembly, included representatives of only five of the twelve parishes. This was the result of Governor Wright's efforts, backed by the Royalist element,

Under these circumstances the Provincial Congress adopted articles of association somewhat different from the form proposed by the Continental Congress, which had been approved by St. John's parish. The St. John's parish committee sent a message to the Provincial Congress, stating what it had done and hoping the Provincial Congress would take the same action. As that was not answered, a second request was sent by the St. John's parish committee and the reply made by the Provincial Congress was not satisfactory. Under those circumstances the St. John's deputies adopted resolutions declaring that "the committees from the several parishes now sitting are not and cannot be called a Provincial Congress" and that they were not and would not be bound by their proceedings. The delegates from St. John's parish reaffirmed their support of the Continental Association.

It appears that the influence and exertions of the Governor and his party had the effect of causing a division among the friends of liberty, which was an impediment to their progress.

The Provincial Congress elected Noble Wimberly Jones, Archibald Bulloch and John Houstoun to represent Georgia in the Continental Congress to be held in May. Having done that it adjourned on January 23, 1775.

The split between two sections of the Independents of Georgia also caused a difference between Georgia and South Carolina. As the Provincial Congress of Georgia did not comply with all the requirements of the General Association proposed by the Continental Congress, the Carolinians decided to hold no intercourse with Georgians and "to consider them as unworthy of the rights of freemen and inimical to the liberties of their country."

The Parish of St. John asked to be exempted from that action of the South Carolinians and sent Joseph Wood, Daniel Roberts and Samuel Stevens to propose alliance with the South Carolinians on the ground that St. John's Parish was a distinct community. Those overtures were declined by the South Carolinians on the ground that St. John's Parish was a part of Georgia.

On March 21, 1775, St. John's Parish elected Dr. Lyman Hall to represent it in the Continental Congress. Dr. Hall was a leader in St. John's Parish, a native of Connecticut and a member of the Midway Congregation. He owned and cultivated a rice plantation on the Savannah and Darien Road a few miles from the Midway Church, lived at Sunbury and was its leading physician. He had been instrumental in the action of the Parish upon its independent course and when he left Georgia on his way to the Continental Congress he carried with him, as a present from his people to the suffering Republicans of Massachusetts, 160 barrels of rice and fifty pounds sterling. On the 13th of

May he presented his credentials to the Continental Congress at Philadelphia and was unanimously admitted to a seat in that body, "as a delegate from the Parish of St. John in the Colony of Georgia, subject to such regulations as the Congress should determine relative to his voting." Until Georgia was fully represented, Dr. Hall refrained from voting on questions which were to be decided by a vote of Colonies, but he took part in the debates and expressed his opinion in cases where an expression of sentiment by Colonies was not required. He declared his earnest conviction that the example shown by his parish would be soon followed and the representation of Georgia would be complete.

The patriotic spirit of St. John's Parish was afterwards recognized when all the parishes had taken part in the revolutionary movement and as a token of praise and general admiration, by a special act of the Legislature, the name LIBERTY COUNTY was given to the consolidated parishes of St. John, St. Andrew, and St. James. Naturally Dr. Lyman Hall became, in 1776, one of the signers of the Declaration of Independence from Georgia.

In this connection Colonel C. C. Jones remarked: "Sir James Wright was not far from the mark when he located the head of the rebellion in St. John's Parish, and advised the Earl of Dartmouth that the rebel measures there inaugurated were to be mainly referred to the influence of the 'descendants of New England people of the Puritan Independent sect who, retaining a strong tincture of Republican or Oliverian principles, have entered into an agreement amongst themselves to adopt both the resolutions and association of the Continental Congress.'

"On the altars erected within the Midway District were the fires of resistance to the dominion of England earliest kindled and Lyman Hall, of all the dwellers there, by his counsel, exhortations, and determined spirit, added stoutest fuel to the flames. Between the immigrants from Dorchester and the distressed Bostonians existed not only the ties of a common parentage, but also sympathies born of the same religious, moral, social, and political education."

**Why Georgia Hesitated**—The reluctance of other Georgia parishes to commit themselves wholly to the movement for independence when the parishes of St. John and St. Andrew were urging them to do so will be understood if we realize the condition of Georgia at that time and the preferential treatment of this Colony by England as thus stated by Bishop Stevens in his *History of Georgia*:

"The hesitation on the part of the other parishes to adopt all the measures of Congress, was the theme of violent and justifiable denunciation; but a momentary glance at the condition of Georgia will remove these aspersions. According to the returns of the Governor to the Lords of Trade, the population in 1774 was but 17,000 whites and 15,000 blacks; and the militia between the ages of sixteen and sixty, only numbered 2828 scattered from Augusta to St. Marys. Within its borders, and along its frontiers, were the Creeks with 4000 gun-men; the Chickasaws with 450 gun-men; the Cherokees with 3000 gunmen; and the Choctaws with 2500 gun-men; comprising all together over 40,000 Indians, 10,000 of whom were warriors, and all, by means of presents, and the influence of Captain Stuart and Mr. Cameron, were firm in their alliance with the royal party, and could be brought in any numbers against the Colony. On the South, lay the garrisoned Province of Florida, with a large military force under Governor Tonyn, and numerous tory bandits, waiting for the signal of the spoiler. On the east was a long line of sea board, with many fine harbors, sheltered bays, large rivers, and well-stocked islands, inviting naval depredations.

"Besides these motives which addressed themselves to the fears of the Colonists, there were others of a moral character. Since its settlement, Georgia had received by grant of Parliament nearly a million of dollars in addition to the bounties which had been lavished on the silk culture, indigo, and other agricultural products. This consideration weighed with much force on many minds; and on such, the Governor took every occasion to impress the baseness of ingratitude towards a Sovereign, whose paternal care had been so peculiarly exerted in their behalf.

"Each of the other Colonies, also, had a charter, upon which to base some right or claim to redress; but Georgia had none. When the Trustees' patent expired, in 1752, all its chartered privileges became extinct; and on its erection into a royal province, the commission of the Governor was its only constitution—living upon the will of the monarch, the mere creature of royal volition. At the head of the government was Sir James Wright, Bart., who, during fourteen years, had presided over it with ability and acceptance. When he arrived, in 1760, the Colony was languishing under the accumulated mismanagement of the former Trustees, and the more recent Governors; but his zeal and efforts soon changed its aspect to health and vigor. He guided it into the avenues of wealth, sought out the means of its advancement, prudently secured the amity of the Indians, and by his negotiations added millions of acres to its territory. Diligent in his official duties, firm in his resolves, loyal in his opinions, courteous in his manners, and possessed of a vigorous and well-balanced mind, he was respected and loved by his people; and, though he differed from the majority of them as to the cause of their distresses, and the means of their removal, he never allowed himself to be betrayed into one act of violence, or into any course of outrage and revenge. The few years of his administration were the only happy ones Georgia had enjoyed, and to his energy and devotedness may be attributed its civil and commercial prosperity.

"With these obstacles within and around her, is it a matter of wonder that Georgia hesitated and wavered? that she feared to assume a course of action which threatened inevitable destruction? Her little phalanx of patriots, scarcely outnumbering the band of Leonidas, were men indeed of Spartan hearts; but Spartan hearts, even at Thermopylae, could not resist the hosts of the despot. And what had they to hope in their feeble state—the parishes divided, the metropolis filled with placemen and officers, the sea-coast guarded by a fleet, and the frontier of two hundred and fifty miles gleaming with the tomahawks of the scalper and the fires of the Indian wigwam? Georgia did falter, but only for a moment; for, soon summoning her energies, she cast aside all fear, and commending her cause to the God of battles, joined in the sacred league which now united thirteen Colonies."

The determination of Georgians to resist the oppression of American Colonies by Great Britain and the waning influence of Governor Wright and the Royalists are shown by the refusal of members to meet again as a Commons House of Assembly. On the 9th of May, 1775, to which date the Governor had adjourned the Assembly, there were not enough members present to organize the House. No more came on the 10th or 11th of May. The House adjourned to the 15th to give time for members from a distance to come in, but the Governor, seeing the unwillingness of members to act as a House, with the advice of the Council, prorogued the Assembly to November 7. Then a quorum was not present and the Assembly was again prorogued. By the time of the last date fixed by the Governor for meeting of the Assembly, Georgia was in the hands of the Republicans, and Royal Government for a time ceased to exist.

**Georgia's Real Position Stated**—As they were elected by a Provincial Congress in which only four of the twelve parishes of Georgia were represented, Noble Wimberly Jones, Archibald Bulloch and John Houstoun did not take their seats in the Continental Congress which met at Philadelphia on May 10, 1775. Realizing that with credentials from only four parishes they would not be accepted as the authorized representatives of Georgia, they felt that this fact did not give a true idea of the sentiments of the people of their Province. Therefore, in order to set Georgia before the Continental Congress in its true relation to the struggle for American liberty they, on April 6, 1775, sent this communication to the President of the Continental Congress:

"Sir" "The unworthy part which the Province of Georgia has acted in the great and general contest leaves room to expect little less than the censure, or even indignation, of every virtuous man in America. Although, on the one hand, we feel the justice of such a consequence, with respect to the Province in general, yet, on the other, we claim an exemption from it, in favor of some individuals, who wished a better conduct. Permit us, therefore, in behalf of ourselves, and many others, our fellow-citizens, warmly attached to the cause, to lay before the respectable body over which you preside, a few facts, which, we trust, will not only acquit us of supineness, but also render our conduct to be approved by all candid and dispassionate men." After recapitulating the proceedings already detailed, they ask:

"What, then, could the congress do? On the one hand, truth forbad them to call their proceedings the voice of the province, there being but five out of twelve parishes concerned; and, on the other, they wanted strength sufficient to enforce them, on the principle of necessity, to which all ought for a time to submit. They found the inhabitants of Savannah not likely soon to give matters a favorable turn. The importers were mostly against any interruption, and the consumers very much divided. There were some of the latter virtuously for the measures; others strenuously against them; but more who called themselves neutrals than either.

"Thus situated, there appeared nothing before us but the alternative, of either immediately commencing a civil war among ourselves, or else of patiently waiting the measures to be recommended by the General Congress. Among a powerful people, provided with men, money, and conveniences, and by whose conduct others were to be regulated, the former would certainly be the resolution that would suggest itself to every man removed from the condition of a coward; but in a small community like that of Savannah (whose members are mostly in their first advance towards wealth and independence, destitute of even the necessaries of life within themselves, and from whose junction or silence so little would be added or lost to the general cause), the latter presented itself as the most eligible plan, and was adopted by the people. Party disputes and animosities have occasionally prevailed, which show that the spirit of freedom is not extinguished, but only restrained for a time, till an opportunity should offer for calling it forth.

"The Congress convened at Savannah did us the honor of choosing us delegates to meet your respectable body at Philadelphia, on the tenth of next month. We were sensible of the honor and weight of the appointment, and would gladly have rendered our country any services our poor abilities would have admitted of; but, alas! with what face could we have appeared for a Province, whose inhabitants had refused to sacrifice the most trifling advantages to the public cause, and in whose behalf we did not think we could safely pledge ourselves for the execution of any one measure whatsoever.

"We do not mean to insinuate that those who appointed us would prove apostates, or desert their opinion; but that the tide of opposition was great—that all the strength and virtue of these our friends might be insufficient for the purpose. We very early saw the difficulties that would occur, and therefore repeatedly and constantly requested the people to proceed to the choice of other delegates in our stead; but this they refused to do. We beg, sir, you will view our reasons for not attending in a liberal point of light. Be pleased to make the most favorable representation of them to the honorable the members of the Congress. We believe we may take upon us to say, notwithstanding all that is past, there are still men in Georgia who, when an occasion shall require, will be ready to evince a steady, religious, and manly attachment to the liberties of America. To the consolation of these, they find themselves in the neighborhood of a Province, whose virtue and magnanimity must, and will, do lasting honor to the cause, and in whose fate they seemed disposed freely to involve their own.

"Noble Wimberly Jones, Archibald Bulloch, John Houstoun."

**South Carolina's Attitude to Georgia**—Governor Wright in a letter to the Earl of Dartmouth, written on April 24, 1775, claimed credit for preventing Georgia from sending delegates to the Continental Congress, saying that he "had given them every kind of opposition he could" and "believed he had succeeded in his efforts." But he showed much uneasiness concerning the hostile attitude of South Carolina toward Georgia. Because this province had failed to become a member of the American Association and did not take part in the action of the Continental Congress the Carolinians resolved to hold no intercourse with the Province.

It appears that the South Carolinians were living in a glass house and in no position to throw stones at Georgians. There was so much difference of opinion in the South Carolina Provincial Congress in June, 1775, concerning the non-exportation resolutions of the Continental Congress that a hot debate between John Rutledge, defending the exception in favor of the export of South Carolina rice, and Gadsden and others attacking it that, in the language quoted by Dr. Duncan Wallace, "great heats prevailed and the members were on the point of falling into downright uproar and confusion." That was prevented by a compromise adopted by a vote of 87 to 75. In 1776 South Carolina's attitude changed. Her Congress praised Georgia's heroism and sent troops to her aid.

## CHAPTER XLVI.

# *Lexington and Concord Battles Unite the Colonies—Seizure of Powder Magazine—Powder Ship Captured*

**Lexington and Concord Battles Unite the Colonies**—In the meantime events were moving swiftly toward revolution. While Governor Wright thought he was successfully resisting the independent movement in Georgia, and several of the colonies hesitated to declare their independence of Great Britain the battles of Lexington and Concord occurred. General Gage, at Boston, had received orders to arrest Samuel Adams and John Hancock and send them to England for trial. Those great leaders of independence in Massachusetts attended the Provincial Conference of that colony at Concord and after its adjournment on the 15th of April, 1775, they remained a few days at Lexington in the house of their friend, Rev. Jonas Clark. Thinking it would be easier to arrest them there than in Boston General Gage, on April 18th sent a force of 800 men under Lieutenant-Colonel Smith, with orders to march to Lexington, seize Adams and Hancock and go on to Concord, where they were to capture or destroy military stores which the colonists had collected there. Colonel Smith's force left Boston at night by an unused route through East Cambridge and struck the high road for Lexington four miles out. Great secrecy was maintained and orders had been issued that nobody should leave Boston at night, but Joseph Warren saw the purpose of the movement and sent out Paul Revere, by way of Charlestown, and William Dawes, of Roxbury, to give the alarm. There was no bridge over Charles River where Revere crossed, but he got over in a little boat and on the farther bank was informed by a signal from a lantern in the belfry of North Church of the direction by which Colonel Smith's force had gone. Then came Revere's historic ride as he galloped over the road to Lexington, shouting the alarm to every house he passed. Reaching Lexington about midnight he told Adams and Hancock the situation. Their first idea was to stay and take command of the militia at Lexington, but it was decided best for them to leave, and before daybreak they left Lexington.

Just at sunrise Major Pitcairn reached Lexington with six companies of British soldiers. There he was confronted by fifty minute-men under Captain

John Parker, a veteran who had served under Wolfe at the Heights of Abraham. To the minute-men Parker said: "Don't fire unless you are fired on, but if they want war it may as well begin here." Then came Pitcairn's command: "Disperse, ye villians! Damn you, why don't you disperse?" As the minute-men stood firm and silent he gave the order to fire, discharging his own pistol with the order. Eight of the minute-men fell dead and ten were wounded at the first volley. The minute-men returned fire, when Colonel Smith came up with reinforcements, and Captain Parker ordered his men to retire.

Before the British reached Concord that evening the stores of munition had been hidden. In the meantime the minute-men had increased to four hundred. They charged the north bridge and drove back 200 British soldiers.

As the Colonists were swarming to the aid of the minute-men, Colonel Smith saw danger and retreated to Boston. The rapid increase of the Americans would probably have overwhelmed him before he got there, but for the fact that Lord Percy came from Boston with 1,200 men and two guns in time to save Smith's exhausted forces, who had been marching eighteen hours almost without food, and when Percy's force surrounded them they fell on the ground, completely overcome by weakness.

The news of the battles of Lexington and Concord electrified America. Carried to every part of the Colonies by fast horses going night and day it reached Savannah on the evening of May 10th and created great excitement and enthusiasm. There was no longer any question of Georgia's attitude, and the leaders of Georgia began at once to act.

**Seizure of a Powder Magazine**—On the east side of Savannah a powder magazine had been built of brick and sunk twelve feet under the ground. It contained a large supply of ammunition and its construction was so substantial that Governor Wright did not think it necessary to post a guard there. There was great need for powder among the revolutionists in all the Colonies, and the Georgia leaders decided to seize this magazine and remove its contents. Acting quietly Doctor Noble Wimberly Jones, Joseph Habersham, Edward Telfair, William Gibbons, Joseph Clay, John Milledge and a few other gentlemen who were members of the council of safety and all active in the cause of American liberty met at the residence of Dr. Jones, decided on a plan and on the night of May 11, 1775, broke open the magazine and removed from it six hundred pounds of gunpowder. Some of this powder was sent to Beaufort, South Carolina, for safekeeping, and the remainder was hidden in the garrets and cellars of the houses belonging to the men who captured it.

Learning of this act Governor Wright immediately issued a proclamation offering a reward of 150 pounds for the arrest of the offenders. Although it is said to have been known who took the powder, the people were profoundly stirred, and the Sons of Liberty were too powerful to permit any action by Royalists or informers.

It is said that some of this powder taken from the magazine at Savannah was sent to Cambridge, Massachusetts, and used by the men of that Colony in the battle of Bunker Hill. It is undoubtedly true that citizens of Savannah three weeks later on the first of June, 1775, sent by the ship *Juliana,* Captain Stringham, by John Eaton LeCone, sixty-three barrels of rice and a hundred and twenty-two pounds of gold and silver for relief of those patriots who had recently left Boston. It is probably true that the powder had been sent to Boston before that.

**Cannon Spiked on the King's Birthday**—It had been customary to celebrate the King's birthday with festivity and military salute at Savannah on the 4th of June. In spite of the rapid progress of independence Governor Wright was not willing to omit the usual celebration, and on the 1st of June issued orders to that effect. On the night of the 2nd of June a number of Savannah citizens came together, spiked all the cannon on the bay, dismounted them and rolled them to the bottom of the bluff. Thus they gave deliberate insult to the King. It was with great difficulty that some of those guns were drilled and restored to their position in the battery in time to be used in the ceremonies of June 4th. As that day was Sunday the celebration took place on Monday following.

**The First Liberty Pole**—On June 5, 1775, the same day on which Governor Wright was celebrating the King's birthday the first liberty pole was erected in Georgia. The Liberty Boys still desiring a reconciliation with the mother country on the basis of a recognition of their constitutional rights had a feast at which they drank two toasts, one to the King and the other to American liberty.

Within a week after the Liberty Pole was raised thirty-four leading men who favored the union of the Colonies met in Savannah and adopted resolutions recommending an early association of Georgia with the other Colonies, and suggesting an equitable adjustment of the unhappy differences between them and Great Britain.

On June 21, 1775, a call was published by Noble W. Jones, Archibald Bulloch, John Houstoun and George Walton, asking the people of the town and district of Savannah to meet at the Liberty Pole the next morning at ten o'clock to select a committee for the purpose of bringing about the union of Georgia with the other Colonies in the cause of freedom. They urged the alarming situation in America and in Georgia as a reason for prompt and general attendance.

In response to this call a large meeting was held at ten o'clock on the 22nd of June, and a Council of Safety was created consisting of William Ewen, president, William LeConte, Joseph Clay, Basil Cooper, Samuel Elbert, William Young, Elisha Butler, Edward Telfair, John Glenn, George Houstoun, George Walton, Joseph Habersham, Francis H. Harris, John Smith, and John Morel, members, and Seth John Cuthbert, secretary. They were instructed to have active correspondence with the Continental Congress, the Councils of Safety in other Provinces, and the committees appointed in other Georgia parishes. Having done this the meeting adjourned, and a number of gentlemen dined at Tondee's Tavern. The Union flag was hoisted on the Liberty Pole, and two field pieces were posted at its foot. Thirteen patriotic toasts to the thirteen Colonies were drunk, and to each there was a response by a salute from a cannon and by martial music.

**Tar and Feathers Applied**—One of the resolutions adopted by that meeting on the 22nd of June provided that Georgia should not protect or become an asylum for any person who because of his conduct might properly be considered unfriendly to the cause of America, or should have drawn upon himself the disapprobation or censure of the other colonists. In defiance of this resolution a young man named Hopkins spoke contemptuously of the objects and actions of the meeting and ridiculed the gentlemen who composed the Committee of Safety. As a result of this he was arrested by a mob, tarred and feathered, hoisted into a cart lighted up for the occasion and paraded through the principal streets of Savannah for four or five hours. At Augusta similar treatment was given to Thomas Brown, who had declared his enmity to the American cause and scoffed at the proceedings of the Continental Congress.

**Separation Deplored**—Strange as it may seem, even at that late hour under the conditions which had caused the men of Massachusetts to shed their blood in defense of American liberty, there was reluctance on the part of many to separate from England. Delegates to the first Continental Congress in September, 1774, did not suggest independence. Several of the colonies urged their representatives in that Congress to seek restoration and harmony with England and that Congress branded as a calumny the charge that it wished independence. Washington then wrote from the Congress that independence was not then desired by any thinking man in America. That feeling continued in the early part of 1775. Pennsylvania instructed her representatives to dissent from any proposition that might lead to separation, and Maryland gave similar instructions to her representatives in January, 1776. In May, 1775, John Adams was cautioned by the Philadelphia Sons of Liberty not to utter the word independence. They said: "It is as unpopular in Pennsylvania and all middle and southern states as the stamp act itself."

But a great change had come about in 1776, and in the spring of that year Washington said: "Reconciliation is impracticable. Nothing but independence will save us."

The American leaders, like Washington had seen the inevitable. Massachusetts, in January, 1776, instructed her delegates in Congress in favor of independence; Georgia did the same in February, South Carolina in March, and North Carolina in April.

**Meeting at Mrs. Cuyler's House**—On June 13, 1775, there was a meeting of citizens of Savannah at the home of Mrs. Cuyler, and resolutions were adopted declaring that those present would do their utmost to preserve peace and good order in the Province, that the acts of raising revenue in America were general grievances, and redress could most likely be secured by joint action rather than by individual measures; that a petition should be addressed to the King of England expressing the apprehension and the feeling of those present and that it was the wish of the meeting that such a petition be adopted by the Provincial Congress on the Fourth of July.

An important section of the resolution was in these words:

"Resolved that the interest of this Province is inseparable from the Mother Country and all the Sister Colonies, and that to separate ourselves from the latter would only be throwing difficulties in the way of its own relief and that of the other colonies, and justly increasing the resentment of all those to whose distress our disunion might be an addition:

"Resolved that this Province ought to, and it is hoped it will forthwith join the other Provinces in every just and legal measure to secure and restore the liberties of all America, and for healing the unhappy divisions now subsisting between Great Britain and her Colonies:

"Resolved That the proceedings of this meeting be laid before the Provincial Congress on Tuesday the 4th of July next, and that Mr. Jamieson and Mr. Simpson do wait upon them with the same as recommended to them by this meeting."

**Governor Wright Asked Leave To Depart**—Thoroughly alarmed by the temper of the Colony and the open avowal of independent opinions, with the growing disposition to place under a ban all who failed to give their voice of sympathy with the complaints and claims of the United Colonies, Governor Wright, on June 9, 1775, wrote the Earl of Dartmouth saying there was no use for Royal Governors to remain under those conditions and asking leave to return home the following spring or sooner.

From his letter the following extract is quoted:

"If these things are done, no man's life or property can be safe, and I look upon mine to be now in danger. There are still many friends to government here, but they begin to think they are left to fall a sacrifice to the resentment of the people for want of proper support and protection; and, for their own safety, and other prudential reasons, they are falling off and lessening every day. Pardon me, my Lord, but a few troops 12 months ago would have kept all the Southern Provinces out of Rebellion, and I much fear many will now be necessary. My Lord, the King has not a servant better disposed to serve his honor and just rights than I am, and I can lay my hand upon my heart and say with an honest and good conscience that I have done everything in my power to support the just sovereignty of Great Britain, law, government, and good order; but I cannot continue in this very uncomfortable situation without the means of protection and support, and therefore I must humbly request that his Majesty will be graciously pleased to give me leave to return home, which I would propose to do next Spring, or sooner as things may be circumstanced, and would therefore hope to have it as soon as may be."

To General Gage he wrote, surprised "that these Southern Provinces should be left in the situation in which they now are: the Governors and King's officers and friends of Government naked and exposed to the resentment of an enraged people. The Governors had much better be in England than remain in America and have the mortification to see their powers executed by committees and mobs."

To Admiral Graves the Governor wrote that Savannah was blocked by four or five boats from South Carolina, and he asked the Admiral's aid to remove that blockade.

**Dartmouth Threatens War**—Replying to Governor Wright, the Earl of Dartmouth wrote on July 5, 1775:

"Advices received from every quarter contain evidences of an intention in almost all the Colonies to the northward to take up arms against the government of this Kingdom. In this situation it is the King's firm resolution that the most vigorous efforts should be made both by sea and land to reduce his rebellious subjects to obedience: and the proper measures are now pursuing not only for augmenting the army under General Gage, but also for making such addition to our naval strength in North America as may enable Admiral Graves to make such a disposition of his fleet as that besides the Squadron necessary for the New England station there may be separate squadrons at New York, within the Bay of Delaware, in Chesapeake Bay, and upon the coast of Carolina."

**Wright's Letters Intercepted**—Governor Wright did not receive the aid he had requested of General Gage and Admiral Graves because they did not receive his letters. As those communications were passing through Charleston the South Carolina Committee of Safety withdrew the letters from the envelopes and put in their places dispatches representing the Province of Georgia as quiet and in no need of troops or war vessels. These dispatches were transmitted in the original envelopes of Governor Wright and completely deceived General Gage and Admiral Graves. The South Carolina Committee of Safety sent the original dispatches to the Continental Congress, and Governor Wright did not know what had occurred until he met General Gage in London and asked why his requisition for troops had not been honored. Then he realized what happened to his communication.

**A Powder Ship Captured**—Governor Wright's statement to Admiral Graves that Carolina ships had blocked the port of Savannah was based on the following incident. The Carolina Committee of Safety received information that a ship had sailed for Georgia with a large supply of powder intended for the use of Indians and for the service of Royalists. The South Carolina committee determined to capture that ship and Captains Barnwell and Joyner, of Beaufort, were ordered to seize the expected ship and take the powder.

With forty well-armed men the two captains went in two barges to the mouth of the Savannah River and camped on Bloody Point in plain view of Tybee Island Lighthouse. The Provincial Congress of Georgia offered aid to these officers in the capture of the British armed schooner which was stationed in the river, and for that purpose there was a junction of the Carolina and Georgia forces. A schooner was commissioned by the Georgia Congress and placed under the command of Captain Bowen and Joseph Habersham. As the Georgia schooner approached the British vessel weighed anchor, put to sea and sailed away. The Georgia schooner took position beyond the bar on the lookout and had been there only a few days when on the 10th of July Captain Maitland's ship, coming from London with powder on board, was seen in the distance. Seeing the schooner and suspecting trouble the ship stopped before entering Tybee Inlet, and in a little while turned and went out to sea. She was quickly pursued by Captain Bowen and the Georgians, and with the Carolina party they boarded her and took possession.

Bishop Stevens in telling of this capture said in his history:

"This was the first provincial vessel commissioned for naval warfare in the Revolution; and the first capture made by order of any congress in America was made by this Georgia schooner in June, 1775. Of the powder taken in this ship nine thousand pounds fell to the share of Georgia, and at the urgent solicitation of the Continental Congress at Philadelphia five thousand pounds were sent thither; and it was by the arrival there of this powder that the American arms were enabled to penetrate into Canada and that Washington drove the British army out of Boston."

Ebenezer Smith Platt, one of the Georgians who made this capture, was at a later period a prisoner of the British, and being identified by two of the crew of Maitland's ship as having had part in the seizure of this powder, he was sent to England under a charge of treason. There he was closely confined for a long time, but finally was recognized as a prisoner of war and was exchanged.

## CHAPTER XLVII.

# *Georgia Joins Other Colonies*

**Georgia No Longer Hesitates**—By this time it was evident from the action of citizens that the period of doubt and hesitation for Georgia had ended, and the Colony was prepared to join the other Colonies and take part in the deliberations and action of the Continental Congress. Meetings were called in every parish of the Province to commission delegates to a Provincial Congress, which was to assemble at Savannah on July 4, 1775. The entire Colony was ready to act and even Governor Wright acknowledged that the Provincial Congress was likely to approve whatever the Continental Congress might do. He wrote the Earl of Dartmouth that even those who opposed such action by the majority were not inclined to expose their lives and property to the resentment of the people, when no support or protection was given them by the home government. He said that five hundred troops would be necessary to protect the Royal Governor of the Province, and suggested the erection of a fort on the common at Savannah with barracks sufficient to accommodate such forces as the King might send. To which he added: "Then the Governor and officers would be in a state of security, whereas now they are and must be exposed to every kind of insult and violence the people may choose to offer them."

**The Provincial Congress of July 4, 1775**—As Colonel Jones says, the Provincial Congress which met at Savannah on the 4th of July, 1775, just one year before the Declaration of Independence, was Georgia's first secession convention. Every parish was represented by leading men who in their character, intelligence and position represented the best interest of the community from which they came. The Congress was in full sympathy with the spirit and the act of the other twelve American Colonies, practically annulled the action of objectionable acts of Parliament within the Province, challenged the supremacy of the realm, and adopted measures looking to the independence and statehood of Georgia.

The meeting was held in Tondee's long room, with the following representatives present, with credentials from their parishes:

"Town and District of Savannah—Archibald Bulloch, Noble Wimberley Jones, Joseph Habersham, Jonathan Bryan, Ambrose Wright, William Young,

John Glen, Samuel Elbert, John Houstoun, Oliver Bowen, John McCluer, Edward Telfair, Thomas Lee, George Houstoun, Joseph Reynolds, John Smith, William Ewen, John Martin, Dr. Zubly, William Bryan, Philip Box, Philip Allman, William O'Bryan, Joseph Clay, John Cuthbert.

District of Vernonburgh—Joseph Butler, Andrew Elton Wells, Matthew Roche, Jr.

District of Acton—David Zubly, Basil Cowper, William Gibbons.

Sea Island District—Col. Deveaux, Col. De Le Gall, James Bulloch, John Morel, John Bohun Girardeau, John Barnard, Robert Gibson.

District of Little Ogeechee—Francis Henry Harris, Joseph Gibbons, James Robertson.

Parish of St. Matthew—John Stirk, John Adam Treutlen, George Walton, Edward Jones, Jacob Wauldhauer, Philip Howell, Isaac Young, Jenkin Davis, John Morel, John Flerl, Charles McCay, Christopher Cramer.

Parish of St. Philip—Col. Butler, William LeConte, Wm. Maxwell, James Maxwell, Stephen Drayton, Adam Fowler Brisbane, Luke Mann, Hugh Bryan.

Parish of St. George—Henry Jones, John Green, Thomas Burton, William Lord, David Lewis, Benjamin Lewis, James Pugh, John Fulton.

Parish of St. Andrew—Jonathan Cochran, William Jones, Peter Tarlin, Lachland McIntosh, William McIntosh, George Threadcraft, John Wereat, Roderick McIntosh, John Witherspoon, George McIntosh, Allan Stuart, John McIntosh, Raymond Demere.

Parish of St. David—Seth John Cuthbert, William Williams, Sen.

Parish of St. Mary—Daniel Ryan.

Parish of St. Thomas—John Roberts.

Parish of St. Paul—John Walton, Joseph Maddock, Andrew Burns, Robert Rae, James Re, Andrew Moore, Andrew Burney, Leonard Marbury.

Parish of St. John—James Screven, Nathan Brownson, Daniel Roberts, John Baker, Sen., John Bacon, Sen., James Maxwell, Edward Ball, William Baker, Sen., William Bacon, Jr., John Stevens, and John Winn, Sen.

*Note*—Only Joseph Butler, James Robertson and Joseph Maddock declined taking their seats.

**The Provincial Congress To Governor Wright**—The following address, signed by the president of the Provincial Congress, was presented to Governor Wright, on July 13, 1775, by a committee composed of Stephen Drayton, Edward Telfair, William LeConte, John Walton, George Houstoun, and Philip Box:

"May it please your Excellency.

"We, his Majesty's dutiful and loyal subjects, the Delegates of this Province in Provincial Congress met, beg leave to address your Excellency.

"In these very critical and alarming times, the good people of this Province found themselves under an absolute necessity to take some measures for the security and preservation of their liberties and everything that is near and dear to them; and they have accordingly chosen a large number of persons to meet together at Savannah to consult on the means to obtain redress under our many and very heavy grievances. These, being accordingly met (to be distinguished from the usual representation), have styled themselves a Provincial Congress, and from the number and character of their names, which your Excellency may see in our last *Gazette,* your Excellency will be convinced the province was never more fully represented in any Assembly; though possibly this measure never would have taken place had we not, from several successive prorogations or adjournments, but too much reason to fear year Excellency had received very strong instructions not to suffer the Assembly to enter into any measures to secure the rights of America, or even to petition for relief, unless in terms which would have been giving up the rights of, and fixing lasting disgrace on, the petitioners.

"Although there is no doubt but a great majority of the inhabitants of this Province always looked upon the claim of Parliament to take away the property of Americans as illegal and oppressive, yet, from a variety of causes not unknown to your Excellency, this Province in the American chain has hitherto been the defaulting link. We have now joined with the other Provinces in the Continental Congress, and have sent a petition to his Majesty, appointed delegates to the American Congress, and entered into such resolutions—which we mean inviolably to adhere to—as will convince the friends and foes of America that we would not live unworthy of the name of Britons, or labour under the suspicion of being unconcerned for the rights and freedom of America.

"Extracts of some letters which are inserted in Parliamentary proceedings widely differ from what must appear to every unprejudiced person to be the real state of the Province.

"We are not acquainted with an individual in Georgia that looks upon the claims of Parliament as just, and all men speak with abhorrence of the measures made use of to enforce them. Our fellow-subjects who formerly entered a dissent which we find was transmitted to the Minister in terms that bespeak the great pleasure it gave the transmitter, now generally say that they never differed from America as to the reality of grievances, but only in the mode of obtaining redress.

"Though candour must allow these mutilated extracts laid before Parliament were probably rather designed by the Minister to screen himself and justify his own measures than to give a just and true account of what information he might have received, yet we cannot help observing the general purport of these letters seems to have a much greater regard to the designs of the Minister than to give an impartial account of the real state of things. Other Provinces, no doubt, if they find themselves mentioned in any part of them, will view them in what light they may think fit; but as to any prejudicial informations they may contain against many persons in this Province, while it is not to be expected that they will give up their feelings as private men, your Excellency may be assured we shall always pay due respect to his

Majesty's representative, and shall with great pleasure acknowledge every service your Excellency may hereafter render to Great Britain and America whose interest we know, and whose connection we wish, to be forever inseparable. Your Excellency may be assured these are objects which we have greatly at heart, and shall ever do what in us lies towards a reconciliation with our Parent State on constitutional principles, as well as endeavour to preserve the peace and good order of the Province."

While Governor Wright said he would not condescend to take any notice of this address he wrote Lord Dartmouth about it on the 18th of July, defending himself against the charges made in the communication. He informed Dartmouth that the Provincial Congress on July 13th sent by two messengers to the Council of Safety in Charleston five thousand pounds of gunpowder and a brass field piece and carriage belonging to the Crown. He admitted that he was powerless to prevent that and again asked permission to return to England and resign the governorship, as the power of the executive had already been wrested from him.

**Georgia Joins the Other Colonies**—The Provincial Congress was organized on July 4, 1775, by the election of Archibald Bulloch as president, and George Walton as secretary, both chosen by unanimous vote.

Immediately after organization the whole body adjourned to the church of Reverend John J. Zubly, who preached a sermon on the alarming state of American affairs from the text: "So speak ye and so do as they that shall be judged by the law of Liberty." On the second day of the session the Congress adopted a resolution requesting Governor Wright to appoint a day of fasting and prayer to be observed throughout the Province in the hope that a "happy reconciliation might soon take place between America and the parent state." Governor Wright accordingly designated the 19th of July, 1775, for fasting and prayer for the purpose stated, which was one day before the date set apart for fasting and prayer for the same purpose by the Continental Congress.

John Jamison and John Simpson having submitted to the Congress the resolutions adopted on the 13th of June by a meeting at Mrs. Cuyler's house, the resolutions were read and on motion it was ordered that they lie upon the table for the perusal of the members.

The Congress adopted a motion "That this congress do put this province upon the same footing with our sister colonies."

In further consideration of this matter as a special order the Congress on the next day, July 6, 1775, adopted sixteen resolutions which are quoted in full. They deal largely with questions of non-exportation and non-importation to and from England and the West Indies.

"1st. Resolved: That this Province will adopt and carry into execution all and singular the measures and recommendations of the late Continental Congress.

"2nd. Resolved: In particular, that we, in behalf of ourselves and our constituents, do adopt and approve of the American Declaration or Bill of Rights published by the late Continental Congress, and also of their several resolves made in consequence of some infractions thereof.

NON-INTERCOURSE WITH ENGLAND.

"3rd. Resolved: That we will not receive into this Province any goods, wares, or merchandise shipped from Great Britain or Ireland, or from any other place, any such goods, wares or merchandise as shall have been exported from Great Britain or Ireland after this day; nor will we import any East India tea from any part of the world; nor any molasses, syrups, paneles, coffee or pimento, from the British Plantations, or from Dominica; nor wines from Madeira or the Western Islands, nor foreign indigo.

"4th. Resolved: That we will neither import nor purchase any slave, imported from Africa or elsewhere, after this day.

"5th. Resolved: As a non-consumption agreement strictly adhered to will be an effectual security for the observation of the non-importation, we, as above, solemnly agree and associate, that from this day, we will not purchase or use any tea imported on account of the East India Company, or any on which a duty hath or shall be paid; and we will not purchase or use any East India tea whatever; nor will we, nor shall any person for or under us, purchase any of those goods, wares, or merchandise we have agreed not to import, which we shall know or have cause to suspect were imported after this day.

"6th. The earnest desire we have not to injure our fellow-subjects in Great Britain and Ireland and the West Indies, induces us to suspend non-exportation until the 10th day of September, 1775, at which time, if the acts and parts of acts of the British Parliament, hereinafter mentioned, are not repealed, we will not, directly or indirectly, export any merchandise or commodity whatsoever to Great Britain, Ireland, or the West Indies, except rice, to Europe.

"7th. Such as are merchants and use the British and Irish trade, will give orders to their factors, agents and correspondents, as soon as possible, in Great Britain and Ireland, not to ship any goods to them, on any pretence whatever, as they cannot be received in this province; and if any merchant, residing in Great Britain or Ireland, shall, directly or indirectly, ship any goods, wares, or merchandise, to America, in order to break the said non-importation agreement, or in any manner contravene the same, on such unworthy conduct being well attested, it ought to be made public; and, on the same being done so, we will not, from thenceforth, have any commercial connections with such merchant.

"8th. That such as are owners of vessels will give positive orders to their captains or masters, not to receive on board their vessels any goods prohibited by the said non-importation agreement, on pain of immediate dismission from their service.

"9th. We will use our utmost endeavors to improve the breed of sheep, and increase their numbers to the greatest extent; and to that end, we will kill them as sparingly as may be, especially those of the most profitable kind; nor will we export any to the West Indies or elsewhere; and those of us who are or may become overstocked with, or can conveniently spare any sheep, will dispose of them to our neighbors, especially to the poorer sort, on moderate terms.

"10th. That we will, in our several stations, encourage frugality, economy, and industry, and promote agriculture, arts, and the manufactures of British America, especially that of wool; and will discountenance and discourage every species of extravagance and dissipation, especially horse-racing, and every kind of gaming, cock-fighting, exhibiting of shows, plays, and other expensive diversions and entertainments; and, on the death of any relation or friend, none of us, or any of our families, will go into any further mourning dress than a black crepe or ribbon on the arm or hat for gentlemen, and a black ribbon and necklace for ladies; and will discontinue the giving of gloves and scarfs at funerals.

"11th. That such as are vendors of goods or merchandise will not take advantage of the scarcity of goods that may be occasioned by this Association, but will sell the same at the rates we have been respectively accustomed to do for twelve months last past; and if any vendor of goods or merchandise shall sell any such goods or merchandise on higher terms, or shall in any manner, or by any device whatsoever, violate or depart from this agreement, no person ought, nor will any of us, deal with any such person, or his or her factor or agent, at any time thereafter, for any commodity whatever.

"12th. In case any merchant, trader, or other persons shall attempt to import any goods or merchandise into this province, after this day, the same shall be forthwith sent back again, without breaking any of the packages thereof.

"13th. That a committee be chosen in every town, district and parish within this province, by those who pay towards the general tax, whose business it shall be attentively to observe the conduct of all persons touching this Association; and when it shall be made to appear, to the satisfaction of a majority of any such committee, that any person, within the limits of their appointment, has violated this Association, that such majority do forthwith cause the truth of the case to be published in the *Gazette,* to the end that all such foes to the rights of British America may be publicly known, and universally contemned as the enemies of American liberty; and thenceforth we will break off all connection with him or her.

"14th. That the Committee of Correspondence in this province do frequently inspect the entries of the custom-house, and inform the committees of other colonies which have acceded to the Continental Association, from time to time, of the true state thereof, and of every other material circumstance that may occur relative to this association.

"15th. That all manufactures of this province be sold at reasonable prices, so that no undue advantage be taken of a future scarcity of goods.

"16th. And we do further agree and resolve, that we will have no trade, commerce, dealings or intercourse whatsoever, with any colony or province in North America, which shall not accede to, or which shall hereafter violate, this Association; but will hold them as unworthy of the rights of freemen, and as inimical to the liberties of their country.

"And we do solemnly bind ourselves and our constituents, under the ties of virtue, honor, and love to our country, to adhere to this Association, until such parts of the several acts of Parliament, passed since the close of the last war, as impose or continue duties upon tea, wines, molasses, syrups, paneles, coffee, sugar, pimento, indigo, foreign paper, glass and painters' colors, imported into America, and extend the powers of the Admiralty Courts beyond their ancient limits; deprive American subjects of trial by jury; authorize to Judges certificate to indemnify the prosecutor from damages, that he might otherwise be liable to from a trial by his peers; require oppressive security from claimants of ships or goods seized, before he is allowed to defend his property, are repealed; and until that part of the act of the 12th George III, ch. 24, entitled 'An Act for the better securing his Majesty's Dock-yards, Magazines, Ships, Ammunition, and Stores,' by which any person charged with committing any of the offences therein described, in America, may be tried within any shire or county within the realm, is repealed; and until the four acts passed in the last session of Parliament, *viz.,* that for stopping the port and blocking up the harbor of Boston; that for altering the charter and government of the Massachusetts Bay; and that which is entitled, 'An act for the better Administration,' etc.; and that for extending the limits of Quebec, etc., are repealed; and until the two acts passed in the present session of Parliament, the one entitled, 'A Bill to restrain the Trade and Commerce of the Colonies of New Jersey, Pennsylvania, Maryland, Virginia, and South Carolina, to Great Britain, Ireland, and the British Islands in the West Indies, under certain Conditions and Limitations'; and the other, an act commonly called the 'Fishery Bill,' are likewise repealed."

**Georgia's Declaration of Rights**—In declaring the constitutional rights of Georgians as citizens and subjects of Great Britain the Provincial Congress on July 10th adopted the following preamble and resolutions:

"Whereas, by the unrelenting fury of a despotic Ministry, with a view to enforce the most oppressive acts of a venal and corrupted Parliament, an army of mercenaries, under an unfeeling commander, have actually begun a civil war in America; and whereas, the apparent iniquity and cruelty of these obstructive measures have, however, had this good effect—to unite men of all ranks in the common cause; and whereas, to consult on means of safety and the method of obtaining redress, the good people of this Province of Georgia have thought proper to appoint a Provincial Congress, the Delegates met at the said Congress, now assembled from every part of the Province, besides adopting the resolutions of the late Continental Congress, find it prudent to enter into such other resolutions as may best express their own sense, and the sense of their constituents on the present unhappy situation of things, and therefore think fit and necessary to resolve as follows, *viz.:*

"Resolved, That we were born free, have all the feelings of men, and are entitled to all the natural rights of mankind.

"Resolved, That by birth or incorporation we are all Britons, and whatever Britons may claim as their birthright is also ours.

"Resolved, That in the British Empire, to which we belong, the Constitution is superior to every man or set of men whatever, and that it is a crime of the deepest dye in any instance to impair, or take it away, or deprive the meanest subject of its benefits.

"Resolved, That that part of the American Continent which we inhabit was originally granted by the Crown, and the charter from Charles the Second expressly makes its constitutional dependence upon the Crown only.

"Resolved, That those who would now subject all America, or this province, to dependency upon the Crown and Parliament, are guilty of a very dangerous innovation which in time will appear as injurious to the Crown as it is inconsistent with the liberty of the American subject.

"Resolved, That by the law of nature and the British Constitution no man can be legally deprived of his property without his consent given by himself or his representatives.

"Resolved, That the acts of the British Parliament for raising a perpetual revenue on the Americans by laying a tax on them without their consent and contrary to their protestations, are diametrically opposite to every idea of property, to the spirit of the Constitution, and at one stroke deprive this vast continent of all liberty and property, and as such must be detested by every well-wisher to Great Britain and America.

"Resolved, That the subsequent laws, made with a view to enforce these acts, *viz.:* the Boston Port Bill, the Alteration of their Charter, the Act to carry beyond sea for Trial, and (what refines upon every species of cruelty) the Fishery Bill, are of such a complexion that we can say nothing about them for want of words to express our abhorrence and detestation.

"Resolved, That the loyalty, patience, and prudence of the inhabitants of New-England under their unparalleled pressures having been construed into timidity and a dread of regular troops, a civil war in support of acts extremely oppressive in themselves hath actually been begun, and there is too much reason to believe that plans have been in agitation big with everything horrible to other Provinces; plans as rash, barbarous and destructive as the cause which they were intended to serve.

"Resolved, That in these times of extreme danger, our Assembly not being permitted to sit, we must either have been a people without all thought or counsel, or have assembled as we now are in Provincial Congress to consult upon measures which, under God, may prove the means of a perpetual union with the Mother Country, and tend to the honour, freedom and safety of both.

"Resolved, That this Province bears all true allegiance to our own rightful Sovereign, King George the Third, and always will and ought to bear it agreeable to the Constitution of Great Britain, by virtue of which only the King is now our Sovereign, and which equally binds Majesty and subjects.

"Resolved, That we are truly sensible how much our safety and happiness depend on a constitutional connection with Great Britain, and that nothing but the being deprived of the privileges and natural rights of Britons could ever make the thought of a separation otherwise than intolerable.

"Resolved, That in case his Majesty or his successors shall at any time hereafter make any requisition on the good people of this Province by his representative, it will be just and right that such sums should be granted as the nature of the service may require, and the ability and situation of this Province will admit of.

"Resolved, That this Province join with all the Provinces in America now met by Delegates in Continental Congress, and that John Houstoun and Archibald Bulloch Esquires, the Rev: Dr. Zubly, Lyman Hall, and Noble Wimberley Jones Esqr. be the delegates from this Province, and that any three constitute a quorum for that purpose.

"Resolved, That a Committee be appointed whose duty it shall be to see that the resolutions of the Continental Congress and Provincial Congress be duly observed, and that every person who shall act in opposition thereto have his name transmitted to the Continental Congress, and that his misdeeds be published in every American paper.

"Resolved, That with all such persons, except the indispensable duties we owe to all mankind (bad men and enemies not excepted) we will have no dealings nor connection: and we extend this our resolution also to all such persons or corporations in Great Britain who have shown themselves enemies to America.

"Resolved, That we will do what in us lies to preserve and promote the peace and good order of this Province; and should any person become an innocent sufferer on account of these grievances, we will do whatever we justly may for his relief and assistance.

"Resolved, That in such calamitous times as the present, every possible indulgence ought to be given to honest debtors; that it would be ungenerous (unless there appear intention of fraud), in any gentleman of the law to sue without previous notice; and any person so sued may apply to the Committee; and should it appear to them that the creditor is in no danger of losing his money, or that he can be properly secured, they shall interpose their friendly offices to persuade him to drop the prosecution; and every prosecutor that shall appear to take advantage of the confusion of the times to distress his debtor, ought to be publicly pointed out and held in abhorrence.

"Resolved, That notwithstanding in a late Bill for restraining the trade of several Provinces in America this Province is excepted, we declare that we look upon this exception rather as an insult than a favor; as being meant to break the union of the Provinces, and as being grounded on the supposition that the inhabitants of such excepted Province can be base enough to turn the oppression of America into a mean advantage."

# CHAPTER XLVIII.

## *Georgia Articles of Association—State's Government Reorganized—Preparing for War—Arrest of Governor Wright*

**Georgia Articles of Association**—On July 13, 1775, the Provincial Congress unanimously adopted this article of Association:

"GEORGIA. Being persuaded that the salvation of the rights and liberties of America depend, under God, on the firm union of the inhabitants in its vigorous prosecution of the measures necessary for its safety, and convinced of the necessity of preventing the anarchy and confusion which attend the dissolution of the powers of government, we, the freemen, freeholders, and inhabitants of the Province of Georgia, being greatly alarmed at the avowed design of the Ministry to raise a revenue in America, and shocked by the bloody scene now acting in the Massachusetts Bay, do, in the most solemn manner, resolve never to become slaves; and do associate under all the ties of religion, and honour, and love to our country, to adopt and endeavour to carry into execution whatever may be recommended by the Continental Congress, or resolved upon by our Provincial Convention appointed for preserving our constitution and opposing the execution of the several arbitrary and oppressive acts of the British Parliament, until a reconciliation between Great Britain and America, on constitutional principles, which we most ardently desire, can be obtained; and that we will in all things follow the advice of our General Committee appointed, respecting the purposes aforesaid, the preservation of peace and good order, and the safety of individuals and private property."

John Smith, Basil Cowper, George Houstoun, Joseph Clay, William Young, Philip Box, Seth John Cuthbert, William O'Bryan, George Walton, William LeConte, William Gibbons, Samuel Elbert, Edward Telfair, and Oliver Bowen were appointed as a committee "to present this Association to all the inhabitants of the Town and District of Savannah to be signed," and these gentlemen were requested to furnish the general committee with the names of all who declined to affix their signatures.

**Representation In Provincial Congress**—The following representation in the Provincial Congress was agreed on by that body on July 14, 1775:

"The Town and District of Savannah shall have seventeen members, District of Little Ogeechee, three; Vernonburgh, two; Acton, two; Sea Islands, three; Goshen and Abercorn, two; Parish of St. Matthew, seven; St. George,

NOBLE WIMBERLY JONES

nine; St. Paul, nine; St. Philip, seven; St. John, twelve; St. Andrew, nine; St. David, three; St. Patrick, two; St. Thomas, two; St. Mary, two; St. James, two; Ceded Lands, three; and that the President and thirty-four members do constitute a Congress to proceed upon business."

By Act of the Provincial Congress on the same day, every man who contributed to the general tax of the Province was made a qualified voter.

**Delegates to the Continental Congress**—The Congress chose as delegates to the Continental Congress John Houstoun, Archibald Bulloch, Rev.

Dr. Zubly, Noble W. Jones, and Dr. Lyman Hall. Dr. Zubly said he could not accept without the approval of his church, and Noble W. Jones and John Houstoun were appointed to confer with the congregation on that subject. Four days later they reported that members of the congregation said they were willing to "spare their minister for a time for the good of the Common Cause," and Dr. Zubly accepted the appointment as a delegate to the Continental Congress.

Dr. Zubly was chosen to prepare a petition to the King "On the present unhappy state of affairs" and did so.

Dr. Zubly, John Smith, William Young, William LeConte, and William Gibbons were instructed to send a letter to the President of the Continental Congress informing him of the action of the Georgia Provincial Congress.

Dr. Zubly, Basil Cowper, John Walton, Joseph Clay and Edward Telfair were appointed a committee to prepare an address of the Provincial Congress to Governor Wright.

A committee of Intelligence consisting of William Young, David Zubly, Stephen Drayton, Daniel Roberts, John Glen, Edward Telfair, William Ewen, Joseph Clay and George Walton was appointed.

On July 12 the Congress took action to meet the necessary expense of Georgia and to qualify suffrage and representation in the Congress.

"Resolved that the Congress being a full representation of the whole Province, the members of the same, their constituents, and all others resident or holding property within the same, are bound to contribute by an equal and general tax towards the sinking of the ten thousand pounds.

"Resolved that this Congress, while sitting, and the Council of Safety in its recess, have power to issue certificates from time to time as occasion shall require, to the amount of ten thousand pounds sterling, and that all such certificates shall be signed by the treasurer and at least three of the members of the Council of Safety.

"Resolved that any person who shall not receive any such certificate in payment, will be guilty of a breach of the public faith, and ought to be considered as an enemy to the Province and treated accordingly.

"Resolved that the said certificates be sunk in three years after a reconciliation shall take place between Great Britain and the Colonies."

**Bills of Credit**—Following is a copy of one of the bills of credit issued by authority of the Provincial Congress of Georgia to be used as a legal tender for the payment of all debts:

"Georgia—1776—No. 5991.

"This certificate entitles the bearer to Four Spanish Milled Dollars, or the Value thereof, according to Resolution of Congress.

JAS. HABERSHAM. WM. EWEN.
E. TELFAIR. WM. OBRYAN. (Seal.)"
GEO. HOUSTOUN.

As Governor Wright in his flight from Savannah had taken with him the great seal of the Province, a new seal was adopted by the Provincial Congress and was used on the bills of credit.

The seal bears the legend LIBERTAS CARIOR AURO, and consists of a pole surmounted with a liberty cap, in association with a winged caduceus and a cornucopia. These devices varied, and the issues were regulated by resolutions of Congress.

**Address To Georgians By Provincial Congress**—A notable deliverance of the Provincial Congress on July 14, 1775, was its address to the people of Georgia, informing them officially of the differences between Great Britain and the American Provinces and the action taken by the Georgia Congress. It was drawn by Rev. Dr. Zubly, Dr. Noble W. Jones, William Young and George Walton and was published as follows:

"To the Inhabitants of the Province of Georgia:

"FELLOW-COUNTRYMEN—We are directed to transmit to you an account of the present state of American affairs, as well as the proceedings of the late Provincial Congress.

"It is with great sorrow we are to acquaint you that what our fears suggested, but our reason thought impossible, is actually come to pass.

"A civil war in America is begun. Several engagements have already happened. The friends and foes of America have been equally disappointed. The friends of America were in hopes British troops could never be induced to slay their brethren. It is, however, done, and the circumstances are such as must be an everlasting blot on their character for humanity and generosity. An unfeeling Commander has found means to inspire his troops with the same evil spirit that possesseth himself. After the starving, helpless, innocent inhabitants of Boston delivered up their arms and received his promise that they might leave that virtuous, devoted town, he is said to have broke his word; and the wretched inhabitants are still kept to fall a prey to disease, famine, and confinement. If there are powers which abhor injustice and oppression, it may be hoped such perfidy cannot go long unpunished.

"But the enemies of America have been no less disappointed. Nothing was so contemptible in their eyes as the rabble of an American militia; nothing more improbable than that they would dare to look regulars in the face, or stand a single fire. By this time they must have felt how much they were mistaken. In every engagement the Americans appeared with a bravery worthy of men that fight for the liberties of their oppressed country. Their success has been remarkable; the number of the slain and wounded on every occasion vastly exceeded theirs, and the advantages they gained are the more honourable, because, with a patience that scarce has an example, they bore every act of injustice and insult till their lives were attacked, and then gave the fullest proof that the man of calmness and moderation in counsel is usually the most intrepid and courageous in battle.

"You will doubtless lament with us the hundreds that died in their country's cause; but does it not call for greater sorrow that thousands of British soldiers sought and found their deaths when they were active to enslave their brethren and their country? However irritating all these proceedings, yet so unnatural is this quarrel, that every good man must wish and pray that it may soon cease; that the injured rights of America may be vindicated by milder means; and that no more blood may be shed, unless it be of those who fomented and mean to make an advantage of these unhappy divisions.

"From the proceedings of the Congress, a copy of which accompanies the present, you will be convinced that a reconciliation on honorable principles is an object which your delegates never lost sight of. We have sent an humble and manly petition to His Majesty; addressed his representative, our Governor; provided, as far as in our power, for internal quiet and safety; and Delegates will soon attend the General Congress to assist and coöperate in any measure that shall be thought necessary for the saving of America.

"His Excellency, at our request, having appointed the 19th inst as a Day of Humiliation, and news being afterwards received that the Continental Congress had recommended the 20th inst to be observed as such, both days have been observed with a becoming solemnity; and we humbly hope many earnest prayers have been presented to the Father of Mercies on that day through this extensive continent, and that He has heard the cries of the destitute and will not despise their prayers.

"You will permit us most earnestly to recommend to you a steady perseverance in the cause of Liberty, and that you will use all possible caution not to say or do anything unworthy of so glorious a cause; to promote frugality, peace, and good order, and, in the practice of every social and religious duty, patiently to wait the return of that happy day when we may quietly sit under our vine and fig tree, and no man make us afraid."

**Georgia to the King**—The following petition was sent to King George Third:

"To the King's most excellent Majesty:

"May it please Your Majesty: Though we bring up the rear of American Petitioners and, from the fate of so many petitions presented to Your Majesty from America, your great city of London, and others of your European subjects, have a most melancholy prospect, we still hope that He by whom Kings rule and to whom monarchs are accountable, will incline you to receive and pay some regard to our most humble and faithful representation.

"In times like these, when the edge of present feelings is blunted by the expectation of calamities still greater, we must take the liberty to speak before we die. We would acquaint our Sovereign with things which greatly affect his interest. We would endeavour to waken the feelings and pity of our common father. Hear us therefore, that God may hear you also.

"Your Majesty is the rightful Sovereign of the most important empire of the universe.

"The blessings of Providence on your arms have put a country in America under you of greater importance and extent than several kingdoms in Europe. In this large extent of territory, by some late acts, Popery is not only tolerated (which we conceive would have been but an act of justice), but an indulgence has been granted, little short of a full establishment, to a religion which is equally injurious to the rights of Sovereign and of mankind. French and arbitrary laws have there by authority taken the place of the just and mild British Constitution, and all this has been done with a professed and avowed design to overawe Your Majesty's ancient Protestant and loyal subjects, some of whom had no small share in the merit of that conquest.

"Acts to raise a perpetual revenue on the Americans without their consent have been enacted, which, at one stroke, turn all your American subjects into slaves, and deprive them of that right which the most oppressive taskmaster does not deny to the servant bought with his own money. Experience must now have shown, as it will clearer should these acts be enforced, that instead of increasing the revenue, or lessening the burdens of your European subjects, they can only serve to increase their taxation.

"Laws which we conceive fraught with so much injustice have been attempted to be enforced by equal cruelty, and whenever we thought ourselves at the height of our troubles, Your Majesty's Ministry have strained their unhappy ingenuity to find out new methods of distress; and, it is believed, methods have been more than thought of too shocking to human nature to be even named in the list of grievances suffered under a British king.

"The goodness of God hath made Your Majesty the father of a very numerous issue, on whom we place the pleasing hopes of a Protestant succession; but Your Majesty's arms in America now every day make mothers childless, and children fatherless. The blood of your subjects has been shed with pleasure rather than with pity, for an action which amounted to no more, even under the worst construction, than an irregular zeal for constitutional liberty; and without any step taken to find out the supposed guilty persons, the capital of your American dominions has been blocked up, deprived of its trade, and its poor of subsistence. Thousands, confessedly innocent, have been starved, ruined, and driven from or kept like prisoners in, their own habitations; their cries and blood innocently shed have undoubtedly reached, and daily do reach, His ears who hateth injustice and oppression.

"Believe us, great Sir, America is not divided; all men (Crown officers not excepted) speak of these acts and measures with disapprobation, and if there has been some difference of opinion as to the mode of relief, the rigorous experiments which your Ministry thought fit to try on the Americans have been the most effectual means to convince these of the iniquitous designs of your Ministry and to unite them all as in a common cause. Your Majesty's Ministers, after thus introducing the demon of discord into your Empire, and driving America to the brink of despair, place all their dignity in measures obstinately pursued because they were once wantonly taken. They hearkened to no information but what represented Americans either as rebels or cowards. Time will every day make it clearer how much they were infatuated and mistaken. Too long, we must lament, have these men imposed on your paternal affection. Deign now, most gracious Prince, in their room, to hearken to the cries of your loyal and affectionate subjects of this extensive Continent; let the goodness of your heart interpose between weak or wicked Ministers, and millions of loyal and affectionate subjects. No longer let the sword be stained with the blood of your children; recall your troops and fleets; and if any misunderstanding remains, let the Americans be heard, and justice and equity take place. Let us be ruled according to the known principles of our excellent Constitution, and command the last shilling of our property and the last drop of our blood in your service.

"Uncertain as to the event of this our humble representation, it affords us a relief that we may, unrestrained, apply to the great and merciful Sovereign of the whole earth, who will not despise the prayer of the oppressed; and to Him we most ardently pray that, the wicked being taken away from before the King, the King's throne may be established in righteousness.

"By order of the Congress, at Savannah, this 14th day of July.

"A. BULLOCH, President."

**Work of the Congress**—The Provincial Congress gave the Council of Safety "full power upon every emergency during the recess of Congress" and urged the friends of America in Georgia to use their utmost efforts to preserve peace and good order and to cultivate harmony with one another. Having done that the body adjourned on July 17, 1775, to August 19 of that year. In that short session the Congress had fully committed Georgia to the measures of the Continental Congress and had joined the other colonies in the struggle for liberty and independence.

On July 20, the Continental Congress was favorably notified that Georgia had acceded to the general association and appointed delegates to attend its session at Philadelphia. On September 13 Zubly, Hall, Bulloch and Houstoun presented their credentials as delegates and took their seats. Noble W. Jones, at the earnest request of his aged father, a Crown officer, did not go.

**Heroic Self-Denial of Georgians**—There was severe self-denial by the people of Georgia in the enforcement of the non-importation resolutions which became effective on September 10, 1775. All trade was cut off with Great Britain, the West Indies and any Colony which did not agree to the rules of the Continental Congress.

Nearly half the population of Georgia were slaves scattered on the plantations and dependent on their masters whose supplies were cut off with no chance for relief. Some vessels came with the needed articles, but the Continental rules were strictly enforced and the ships went away with their cargoes. Georgia as yet had not the resources of other colonies. Their staple products, rice, lumber, indigo, skins, etc., had found a market in the West Indies or Great Britain, where they were exchanged for needed articles, but those markets were now closed. Their gold and silver money had been drained out of the Colony by northern traders who would accept nothing but specie in payment for goods and the Georgia paper currency was depreciating. The Colony as yet had no manufactures to amount to anything and had now to depend for supplies of those needs on a precarious trade that did not meet the needs of the people. Ships were lying in the harbor because they and their cargoes would be seized if they went to sea. As Bishop Stevens says in his history, "the whole industrial machinery of the Province was suddenly arrested and distress was everywhere apparent, but patriotism hushed every murmur and Georgians counted not their own lives dear to them if they might successfully maintain the cause of freedom."

**Militia Reorganized**—On August 8, 1775, the Georgia Council of Safety sent Governor Wright a letter signed by George Walton, William LeConte, Francis H. Harris, William Young, George Houstoun, William Ewen, John Glen, Samuel Elbert, Basil Cowper, and Joseph Clay, asking him to allow the companies of militia to elect their own officers, "as many of the commissioned officers are disagreeable to the people over whom they command." The Governor thought that would have a dangerous tendency and would probably "wrest the control of the militia from the Crown and out of his hand. He submitted the request to the Council, which replied that "for many very substantial reasons the Governor could not comply with their request."

What the Governor and Council refused the people did. When companies were called to the parade ground they displaced officers who had not signed the agreement required by the Provincial Congress and elected in their stead staunch supporters of the American cause.

**Defection of Dr. Zubly**—Dr. Zubly, minister of the Presbyterian Church at Savannah, had by his learning, ability and energetic leadership in the Provincial Congress, won the confidence and affection of the liberty loving people of Georgia and his letter to the Earl of Dartmouth conveying an appeal to the King, written by direction of the Georgia Congress, was full of strength and vigor.

In it he said:

"Proposals publicly made by ministerial writers relative to American domestics, laid the southern provinces under the necessity of arming themselves. A proposal to put it in the power of domestics to cut the throats of their masters can only serve to cover the proposers and abettors with everlasting infamy. The Americans have been called 'a rope of sand,' but blood and sand will make a firm cementation; and enough American blood has been already shed to cement them together into a threefold cord, not easily to be broken."

Naturally he was chosen a delegate to the Continental Congress, presented his credentials and took his seat there, but when that body began to take action looking to separation from Great Britain and creating a republican form of Government, he hesitated to join in what he considered a dangerous course and wrote to Governor Wright from Philadelphia giving him an account of the purpose and plans of the Congress and warning him of the coming event. His conduct was watched and Judge Chase, of Maryland, intimated that his letter to the Governor had been intercepted.

Leaving the Congress suddenly, Dr. Zubly returned to Georgia and openly took sides against the liberty party. That made him obnoxious to the public and in 1777 he was banished from Savannah. He protested in vain against that as unjust and went to South Carolina, where he remained until Savannah was in the hands of the British. He died in 1781, a broken-hearted man.

By the fall of 1775 Georgia was in the hands of the Revolutionists. Governor Wright was powerless. He wrote the home government asking recall, saying "A King's governor has little or no business here." The courts of law were closed, his call for the Assembly was ignored and even the church was closed because the rector, Mr. Smith, was loyal to the Crown.

The executive power of Georgia was in the Council of Safety, and on December 1, 1775, the Provincial Congress took supervision of courts of law and appointed a committee of fifteen to sit quarterly in Savannah as a court of appeals.

The Council of Safety met every Monday morning at ten o'clock at Tondee's tavern with these members:

"George Walton, William Ewen, Stephen Drayton, Noble Wimberly Jones, Basil Cowper, Edward Telfair, John Bohun Girardeau, John Smith, Jonathan Bryan, William Gibbons, John Martin, Oliver Bowen, Ambrose Wright, Samuel Elbert, Joseph Habersham, and Francis Henry Harris."

**Royalist Ministers Silenced**—In silencing all opposition, the men of the liberty party were no respectors of persons. Dr. Traill, of the parish of St. Philip railed at the liberty movement and expressed contempt for the Article of Association. As a result he was ordered to depart from the Province in eight days.

Rev. Haddon Smith, rector of the parish of Christ Church, criticized the course of the Provincial Congress and refused to observe the day of fasting and prayer called for by the Continental Congress. For this conduct he was considered an enemy of the liberty of the Province and the Vigilance Committee ordered him to preach no more in Savannah. He left Georgia and went to South Carolina.

**Chief Justice Reversed**—On August 2, 1775, Ebenezer McCarty was charged with enlisting in Georgia recruits for the South Carolina regiments and Chief Justice Stokes committed him without bail to the common jail of Savannah. A writ of *habeas corpus* was applied for and denied, but citizens got together, forced the jail and set the prisoner free. Following this they marched through the town with drums beating and passed the residences of the Governor and Chief Justice. "Unparalleled insolence, my Lord," said the Governor in a letter to the Earl of Dartmouth, "and this is the situation his Majesty's government is reduced to in the Province of Georgia."

After the Liberty Boys had seized the magazine a captain and twenty men were posted there to guard it as the friends of liberty were not willing to let the powder be taken from them for the Royalists.

The Liberty party took possession of the custom house at Savannah and appointed an officer to prevent vessels from landing cargoes from England; so that the port was practically closed. Governor Wright appealed in vain for a sloop of war to end that situation.

On September 17, 1775, a ship arrived from London with two hundred and fifty barrels of gunpowder on board, sent by the King, consigned to Mr. Stuart, the superintendent, and intended as a Royal present for the Indians. This was too valuable an addition to the supply of ammunition to be overlooked by the Liberty people. They boarded the ship at Tybee, removed the powder, carried it to Savannah and retained possession of it.

A ship came from Senegal with two hundred and four slaves. It was not allowed to land the cargo and, compelled to depart, the captain, in distress, sailed to St. Augustine as the only place where he might save the negroes from starvation.

Deeply humiliated, Governor Wright appealed in vain to the home government for aid, writing to the Earl of Dartmouth: "It is really a wretched state to be left in, and what it is impossible to submit to much longer, government totally annihilated and assumed by congresses, councils, and committees, and the greatest acts of tyranny, oppression, gross insults, etc., committed and not the least means of protection, support or even personal safety, and these almost daily occurrences are too much my Lord."

As Colonel Jones says the Governor's plight was truly pitiable. In October the stockade fort on the land ceded by Indians garrisoned by the King's rangers was surrounded by colonists of the neighborhood and its commanding officer was compelled to surrender. With that act the last shadow of military authority loyal to the Crown passed away. Commenting on this the Governor said, writing to Lord Dartmouth in November, 1775: "The poison has infected the whole Province and neither law, government nor regular authority has any weight or is at all attended to."

When the General Court met on the 10th of October, 1775, ten of the jurors who had been summoned refused to serve and others, as the authority said, "Behaved very insolently." So that the conduct of business was obstructed. The venerable Noble Jones, one of the Associate Justices, was then extremely ill. The Royal cause that fall sustained a serious loss in the

OLD EXECUTIVE MANSION—MILLEDGEVILLE

deaths of Clement Martin, Noble Jones, Associate Justice and Treasurer of the Colony, and James Habersham, President of the Council. All three were members of the Common Council, trusted friends and advisers of the Governor and loyal servants of the King. The vacancies thus created were filled by the appointment of John Hume as Secretary of the Colony in place of Mr. Habersham and Lewis John as Treasurer instead of Colonel Noble Jones. For the vacant chairs in Council, Josiah Tatnall, Sir P. Houstoun, Lachlan McGillivray, and Charles William MacKinen were recommended by the Governor. Before an answer came from the home government concerning these appointments Governor Wright was a prisoner and the King's authority in Georgia was at an end.

The judiciary was the last branch of government taken under control by the Provincial Congress. On December 1, 1775, it began to exercise supervision over all courts in the Colony and a committee of fifteen was appointed to hold quarterly sessions in Savannah as Court of Appeals. The Inferior Courts remained unchanged and to prevent debtors from avoiding payment of their debts persons intending to depart from their parishes or from Georgia were required to give notice of their intended change of residence so their creditors would have opportunity to secure their debts.

John Hume, the King's Attorney-General, declined to obey the order of Congress concerning the conduct of cases in court and denied the authority of Congress. He was ordered to quit the Province within a month. The Chief Justice was warned to observe all congressional instructions which were now the law of the land.

**Georgia's Government Reorganized**—The reorganization of the Georgia Government independent of the Crown was largely accomplished by the end of 1775. The President of the Council of Safety acted as Governor and laws necessary to preserve the peace, maintain order and pay current expenses were published as resolutions of the Provincial Congress by the Council of Safety. Courts competent to deal with cases likely to arise to protect the rights and redress the wrongs of citizens were in operation. Military force had been organized for defense of the Colony and union with the other American colonies had been effected. A Royal Governor still lived in Savannah, but without authority or force to maintain it. The members of the King's Council were there, but they had no voice in the conduct of affairs. Other officers appointed by the Crown were idle and without authority and in all of Georgia there was no power to enforce the will of the King. From this time until Georgia was made a State at the end of the Revolutionary War there was little legislation and little was needed. During the fifteen years of Governor Wright's administration the General Assembly had enacted one hundred and forty-eight acts and resolutions covering a wide range of subjects and providing for the growing needs of the Province, which enjoyed great growth of population and wealth during that period. These laws were allowed to remain in operation where they did not militate against the new government and the changed condition of affairs.

**War Preparations**—In July, 1775, the Provincial Congress appointed an Intelligence Committee of nine members to raise 10,000 pounds for the expense of the Province.

One of the Council's first acts was to reorganize the militia of Georgia by electing officers the friends of liberty could depend on.

At their first meeting they commissioned Andrew Maybank, Joseph Woodruffe, Hezekiah Wade, and John Dooly as captains; James Cochran, John Morrison, Jeremiah Beale, and Thomas Dooly as first lieutenants; James Galoche, Moses Way, Jacob Blunt, Zephaniah Beale, and William Bugg, second lieutenants; and Thomas Dowly, George Philips, and Joshua Smith third lieutenants of the battalion of troops which the Continental Congress, on the 4th of November, had ordered to be raised, at the Continental expense, for the protection of Georgia, and towards which they appropriated five thousand dollars. On the 7th of January following, this battalion was fully organized by the appointment of the following field officers: Lachlan McIntosh, colonel; Samuel Elbert, lieutenant-colonel; and Joseph Habersham, major.

Vigorous measures were taken to enroll, officer, arm and equip the men of Georgia and make them ready for any emergency. Volunteer companies of riflemen, rangers and infantry were organized in the different parishes and reported for service. In the meantime the Council of Safety released vessels importing gunpowder, saltpetre, sulphur, brass field pieces, or muskets, within nine months, from the operation of the non-importation agreement and appointed Samuel Elbert, Edward Telfair and Joseph Habersham a committee to supply the Province with arms and ammunition. They were instructed to contract for 400 stands of arms with bayonets, 20,000 pounds of gunpowder, 60,000 pounds of balls, bullets, bar lead, grape, swan and goose shot, and the Council ordered that the stores at Fort Frederica be immediately secured.

To meet the need for a circulating medium bills of credit in the form of certificates were issued and were to be accepted "upon the faith of the public in this province." It was made a penal offense to refuse to receive them in payment or to depreciate their value.

**Arrest of Governor Wright**—On the 12th of January, 1776, two British men-of-war and a transport from Boston with a detachment of the King's troops under Major Maitland and Major Grant arrived at Tybee and in view of that threat of violence the Georgia Council of Safety, on January 18, ordered:

"That the persons of his Excellency, Sir James Wright, Baronet, and John Mullryne, Josiah Tatnall and Anthony Stokes Esquires be forthwith arrested and secured, and that all non-associates be forthwith disarmed, except those who will give their parole, assuring that they will not aid, assist or comfort any of the persons on board his Majesty's ships of war, or take up arms against America in the present unhappy dispute."

Governor Wright was arrested the same day by Major Joseph Habersham. That incident is thus described by Bishop Stevens:

"Proceeding that very evening to the house of the Governor, who had assembled the Council to consider what was proper to be done, he passed the sentinel at the door, entered the hall, then marched to the head of the table, and laying his hand upon the shoulder of the Governor, said, 'Sir James, you are my prisoner.' The party, astonished at his boldness, and supposing, from his firm manner, that a large force was surrounding them, fled in the utmost precipitation, through doors and windows. This was one of the most signal instances of deliberate and successful daring in the history of the war. For a youth of twenty-four, unarmed and unsupported, to enter the mansion of the chief magistrate, and at his own table, amidst a circle of councillors, place him under arrest, is an act of heroism ranking with the most brilliant exploits in American history. The Governor gave his solemn parole not to go out of town, or hold any correspondence with any officers or others on board the ships at Tybee, and was suffered to remain in his house, under guard. But his confinement proving irksome and painful, as well from the insults to which he was subjected, as from the danger to which he was exposed, from bullets wantonly fired into his house by the guard, he contrived, on the night of the 11th of February to escape, went in haste to Bonaventure, and thence, in an open boat, to his Majesty's ship *Scarborough,* Captain Barclay, on Board of which he was taken at three o'clock in the morning."

# CHAPTER XLIX.

## *Georgia's First Constitution*

**Delegates To Continental Congress Elected**—At its session beginning January 20, 1776, the Georgia Provincial Congress was organized by the election of Archibald Bulloch as President and the proceedings began with a sermon by Rev. Dr. Piercy.

On February 2, 1776, the Congress elected as delegates to represent the Province in the Continental Congress Archibald Bulloch, John Houstoun, Lyman Hall, Button Gwinnett, and George Walton. They were given this letter of instruction:

"GENTLEMEN—Our remote situation from both the seat of power and arms, keeps us so very ignorant of the counsels and ultimate designs of the Congress, and of the transactions in the field, that we shall decline giving any particular instructions, other than strongly to recommend it to you that you never lose sight of the peculiar situation of the province you are appointed to represent: the Indians, both south and northwesterly, upon our backs; the fortified town of St. Augustine made a continual rendezvous for soldiers in our very neighborhood; together with our blacks and tories with us; let these weighty truths be the powerful arguments for support. At the same time we also recommend it to you, always to keep in view the general utility, remembering that the great and righteous cause in which we are engaged is not provincial, but continental. We, therefore, gentlemen, shall rely upon your patriotism, abilities, firmness, and integrity, to propose, join, and concur, in all such measures as you shall think calculated for the common good, and to oppose such as shall appear destructive.

"By order of the Congress. "ARCHIBALD BULLOCH, President.

"Savannah, April 5, 1776."

**Governor Wright's Final Appeal**—From the British man-of-war *Scarborough,* Governor Wright, on February 13, 1776, wrote the Council of Safety, saying that the forces then present would commit no hostilities against the Province and all they wanted was friendly intercourse and fresh provisions. In the King's name he required that the provisions be supplied and calling himself the best friend of the Province advised that they accede to the request. To this he added this exhortation:

"My regard for the province is such that I cannot avoid, and possibly for the last time, exhorting the people to save themselves and their posterity from that total ruin and destruction which, although they may not, yet I most clearly see at the threshold of their doors; and I cannot leave them without again warning them, in the most earnest and friendly manner, to desist from their present plans and resolutions. It is still in their power; and, if they will enable me to do it, I will, as far as I can, engage to give, and endeavor to obtain, for them full pardon and forgiveness for all past crimes and offences; and this I conjure you to consider well and most seriously of, before it's too late. But let things happen as they may, be it remembered, that I this day, in the King's name, offer the people of Georgia the olive branch; that most desirable object and inestimable blessing, the return of peace and happiness to them and their posterity."

The "olive branch" tendered by the Governor was not accepted. His request for provisions for the ships was granted on conditions he refused to accept.

**Relation of Georgia Troops to Continental Army**—To prevent conflict officers of the Georgia battalion signed this agreement:

"IN PROVINCIAL CONGRESS, SAVANNAH,
Feb. 16, 1776.

"PROVINCE OF GEORGIA:—

"Whereas a battalion upon the Continental establishment is now raising in this Province; and whereas doubts may arise how far the same is subject to the control of the Provincial civil power: Now, therefore, be it known, and we, the several subscribers, officers bearing commissions in the same battalion, do hereby declare, that we hold ourselves and the non-commissioned officers and privates, also all others belonging to the said battalion, subject and subservient to such supreme and civil powers of this Province as are or shall be erected for the purpose of defending our rights and liberties.

"And further, we bind ourselves upon the words of soldiers and men of honour, at all times to obey and carry into effect, as far as in us lies, the orders and commands of the present or any future Congress or Council of Safety of this Province as the same shall, from time to time, be issued to us.

"Provided, nevertheless, That the same do not contradict or interfere with the orders or directions of the General Congress, or a Committee thereof, or any general or other officer by them appointed over us.

"In witness whereof, we have hereunto set our names, together with the rank and date of our commissions opposite thereto."

**Those Who Signed the Agreement**—This agreement was signed by the following officers:

Colonel, Lachlan McIntosh.
Lieut. Col., Samuel Elbert.
Major, Joseph Habersham.

FIRST COMPANY.

Captain, Francis Henry Harris. Second Lieut., John Jenkins.
First. Lieut., John Habersham. Ensign, John Rae.

SECOND COMPANY.

Captain, Oliver Bowen. Second Lieut., John Berrien.
First Lieut., George Henley. Ensign, ——— ———.

THIRD COMPANY.

Captain, John McIntosh. Second Lieut., Francis Arthur.
First Lieut., Lachlan McIntosh. Ensign, John Morrison.

FOURTH COMPANY.

Captain, Arthur Carney. Ensign, Delaplaine.
First Lieut., Benjamin Odinsell. John Milton.
Second Lieut., John Eman.

FIFTH COMPANY.

Captain, Thomas Chisholm. Second Lieut., Daniel Cuthbert.
First Lieut., Caleb Howell. Ensign, William McIntosh.

SIXTH COMPANY.

Captain, John Green. Second Lieut., ——— ———.
First Lieut., Ignatius Few.

SEVENTH COMPANY.

Captain, Chesley Bostick. Second Lieut., ——— ———.
First Lieut., John Martin.

EIGHTH OR RIFLE COMPANY.

Captain, Colson. Ensign, ——— ———.
First Lieut., Shadrach Wright. Chaplain, John Holmes.
Second Lieut., George Walton.

**Forwarded To Washington**—The foregoing agreement by officers of the Georgia Battalion was copied and a copy sent to General George Washington, Commander-in-Chief of the American forces, on the 16th of February, 1776, by Colonel Lachlan McIntosh, the battalion commander. In doing so he wrote General Washington, giving an account of the population, resources and dangers of Georgia, mentioning the presence in Tybee Inlet of five British warships, the *Syren,* the *Scarborough,* the *Raven,* the *Tamer* and the *Cherokee,* with several tenders and two large transports on which there were three hundred men, whether intended for Georgia or South Carolina he could not say. He further informed General Washington that Georgia had declared itself in a state of alarm, had determined not to supply the British men-of-war with provisions and had ordered half the militia of the State to Savannah to resist the landing of any British troops. Colonel McIntosh concluded the statement as follows:

"I have received no kind of orders or instructions from the General Congress or your Excellency, nor have I yet been able to obtain even a copy of the American Articles of War, which makes me at a loss how to act in many cases; therefore I shall wish any orders or directions your Excellency will please send me to be as full and frequent and possible; also to be informed how far we are under the control of the Provincial Congress, &c. of this or any other Province where we are upon duty, and what rank we hold when acting with militia or Provincial Troops."

**Georgia's First Constitution**—With the royal governor in flight and five British ships of war in the Savannah River with several hundred soldiers on board, it was necessary to perfect the organization of Georgia's public affairs by the adoption of a Constitution. For this purpose the Provincial Congress on April 15, 1776, adopted the following Preamble and temporary Constitution to serve as the ground work of a more stable Constitution of government which was formed the next year. A copy of the following temporary Constitution, after its adoption, was sent to General Washington by Colonel McIntosh:

"COLONY OF GEORGIA:—

"Whereas, the unwise and iniquitous system of administration obstinately persisted in by the British Parliament and Ministry against the good people of America hath at length driven the latter to take up arms as their last resource for the preservation of their rights and liberties which God and the Constitution gave them;

"And whereas an armed force, with hostile intentions against the people of this Province, having lately arrived at Cockspur, his Excellency Sir James Wright, Baronet, and King's Governor of Georgia, in aid of the views of the administration and with a design to add to those inconveniences which necessarily result from a state of confusion, suddenly and unexpectedly carried off the great seal of the Province with him;

"And whereas, in consequence of this and other events, doubts have arisen with the several magistrates how far they are authorized to act under the former appointments, and the greatest part of them absolutely refused to do so, whereby all judicial powers are become totally suspended to the great danger of persons and property;

"And whereas, before any general system of government can be concluded upon, it is necessary that application be made to the Continental Congress for their advice and directions upon the same; but, nevertheless, in the present state of things, it is indispensably requisite that some temporary expedient be fallen upon to curb the lawless and protect the peaceable;

"This Congress, therefore, as the representatives of the people, with whom all power originates, and for whose benefit all government is intended, deeply impressed with a sense of duty to their constituents, of love to their country, and inviolable attachment to the liberties of America, and seeing how much it will tend to the advantage of each to preserve rules, justice, and order, do take upon them for the present, and until the further order of the Continental Congress, or of this, or any future Provisional Congress, to declare, and they accordingly do declare, order, and direct that the following rules and regulations be adopted in this Province—that is to say—

"1st. There shall be a President and Commander-in-Chief appointed by ballot in this Congress, fcr six months, or during the time specified above.

"2d. There shall be, in like manner, and for the like time, also a Council of Safety, consisting of 13 persons, besides the five delegates to the General Congress, appointed to act in the nature of a Privy Council to the said President or Commander-in-Chief.

"3d. That the President shall be invested with all the executive powers of government not inconsistent with what is hereafter mentioned, but shall be bound to consult and follow the advice of the said Council in all cases whatsoever, and any seven of said Committee shall be a quorum for the purpose of advising.

"4th. That all the laws, whether common or statute, and the acts of Assembly which have formerly been acknowledged to be of force in this Province, and which do not interfere with the proceedings of the Continental or our Provincial Congresses, and also all and singular the resolves and recommendations of the said Continental and Provincial Congress, shall be of full force, validity, and effect until otherwise ordered.

"5th. That there shall be a Chief-Justice, and two assistant judges, an Attorney-General, a Provost-Marshal, and Clerk of the Court of Sessions, appointed by ballot, to serve during the pleasure of the Congress. The Court of Sessions, or Oyer and Terminer, shall be opened and held on the second Tuesday in June and December, and the former rules and methods of proceedings as nearly as may be, shall be observed in regard to summoning of Juries and all other cases whatsoever.

"6th. That the President or Commander-in-Chief, with the advice of the Council as before mentioned, shall appoint magistrates to act during pleasure in the several Parishes throughout this Province, and such magistrates shall conform themselves, as nearly as may be, to the old established forms and methods of proceedings.

"7th. That all legislative powers shall be reserved to the Congress, and no person who holds any place of profit, civil or military, shall be eligible as a member either of the Congress or of the Council of Safety.

"8th. That the following sums shall be allowed as salaries to the respective officers for and during the time they shall serve, over and besides all such perquisites and fees as have been formerly annexed to the said offices respectively:—

| | | |
|---|---|---|
| To the President and Commander-in-Chief after the rate, per annum, of .................................... ..................sterling | 300 | pounds |
| To the Chief Justice .......................... ...................... | 100 | " |
| To the Attorney-General ................................................ | 25 | " |
| To the Provost Marshal ................................................. | 60 | " |
| To the Clerk of Court.................................................. | 50 | " |

Archibald Bulloch was elected President and Commander-in-Chief of Georgia; John Glen, Chief Justice; William Stephens, Attorney-General; and James Jackson, Clerk of Court.

On the 1st of May, 1776, the Council of Safety thus addressed the first Republican President of Georgia:

"May It Please Your Excellency.

"The long session of the late Congress, together with the season of the year, called particularly for a speedy recess; and the House having adjourned while you were out of town it becomes more particularly necessary for us to address your Excellency. All, therefore, with unfeigned confidence and regard, beg leave to congratulate not only your Excellency on your appointment to, but your country on your acceptance of, the supreme command in this Province.

"It would be needless and tedious to recount the various and yet multiplying oppressions which have driven the people of this Province to erect that government which they have called upon you to see executed. Suffice it then to declare that it was only an alternative of anarchy and misery, and, by consequence, the effect of dire necessity. Your Excellency will know that it was the endeavor of the Congress to stop every avenue of vice and oppression, lest the infant virtue of a still more infant Province might in time rankle into corruption: and we doubt not that by your Excellency's exertions all the resolutions made or adopted by Congress will be enforced with firmness without any regard to any individual or any set of men: for no government can be said to be established while any part of the community refuses submission to its authority. In the discharge of this arduous and important task your Excellency may rely on our constant and best endeavors to assist and support you."

To this address President Bulloch replied as follows:

"Honorable Gentlemen,—I am much obliged to you for your kind expressions of congratulation on my appointment to the supreme command of this Colony. When I reflect from whence the appointment is derived, that of the free and uncorrupt suffrages of my fellow citizens, it cannot fail to stimulate me to the most vigorous exertions in the discharge of the important duties to which I am called by our Provincial Congress. While I have the advice and assistance of gentlemen of known integrity and abilities, I doubt not but I shall be enabled to enforce and carry into execution every resolve and law of Congress. And, as far as lies with me, my country may depend I will, with a becoming firmness, and the greatest impartiality, always, endeavor to cause Justice in mercy to be executed."

**President Bulloch's Death**—President Bulloch was the man for the emergency, the soul of honor, an ardent patriot, an able executive, with sturdy manhood, unquestioned courage and large views of public affairs. He was a great source of strength in directing the course of the Colony during its formative period when it was confronted by a powerful enemy whose ships of war threatened Savannah.

According to the custom during the administration of Royal Governors, Colonel McIntosh stationed at the residence of President Bulloch a sentinel. To this the President objected, saying: "I act for a free people in whom I have the most entire confidence, and I wish to avoid on all occasions the appearance of ostentation."

Although Archibald Bulloch was the first man in Georgia to read and publish the Declaration of Independence, he did not live to see the triumph of liberty at the end of the Revolutionary War. He died in 1777 and his death was mourned by the entire Commonwealth.

Georgia was guided by President Bulloch under the temporary Constitution of 1776 until a Constitution of more permanent form was adopted on the 5th of February, 1777, by a convention assembled at Savannah.

## CHAPTER L.

# *Georgia's First Battle With the British Forces—Bombardment of Fort Moultrie*

A severe test of the new organization of Georgia's government and armed forces came in March, 1776. On the first of that month there were lying at the Savannah wharves ready to sail for the sea eleven merchant ships loaded with rice. Some of them were owned by parties not in sympathy with the Americans and they were ready at the first opportunity to sail in disregard of the resolutions of Congress and seek a market for their cargoes.

Knowing that these ships would sail at the first opportunity and recalling the fact that the order of the Continental Congress prohibiting the exportation of rice from the colonies expired by limitation on March 1 and fearing that with the presence of British vessels in Tybee Roads the owners of the vessels would probably try to get them out of the harbor, the Council of Safety met the emergency by the adoption of the following resolutions:

"Resolved that no ships loaded with rice, or any other article of produce, in this Province, shall be permitted to sail without leave of the Council of Safety or next Congress, except such vessels as are or shall be permitted to sail for the purpose of procuring the necessary means of defence.

"Resolved that in case any loss shall be sustained by such detention, the Delegates from this Province shall be instructed to apply to the Continental Congress to make the reimbursement of such loss a general charge.

"Ordered that the rudders be unshipped, and that the rigging and sails be taken away and secured from the several vessels now riding in the port of Savannah."

With the enforcement of these resolutions and of this order Colonel Lachlan McIntosh was charged.

"For the safety of the Province and the good of the United Colonies," it was, on the 2d of March, unanimously resolved by the Council of Safety:

**Property To Be Destroyed**—"That the houses in the town of Savannah and the hamlets thereunto belonging, together with the shipping now in the port of Savannah the property of or appertaining to the friends of America who have associated and appeared or who shall appear in the present alarm to defend the same, and also the houses of widows and orphans, and none others, be forthwith valued and appraised.

"Ordered that Messrs. Joseph Clay, Joseph Reynolds, John McLuer, Joseph Dunlap, and John Glen, or any three of them, be a committee for that purpose, and that they make a return of such value and appraisement to the Council of Safety tomorrow morning at 9 o'clock, or as soon after as possible.

"Resolved That the delegates for this Province shall be instructed to apply to the Continental Congress for an indemnification to such persons as shall suffer in the defence of this town or shipping.

"Resolved That it shall be considered as a defection from the cause of America, and a desertion of property in such persons as have left or who shall leave the town of Savannah or the hamlets thereunto belonging during the present alarm, and such persons shall be precluded from any support or countenance towards obtaining an indemnification.

"Resolved That it be incumbent upon the friends of America in this Province to defend the Metropolis as long as the same shall be tenable.

"Resolved That rather than the same shall be held and occupied by our enemies, or that the shipping now in the port of Savannah should be taken and employed by them, the same shall be burnt and destroyed.

"Resolved That orders shall be issued to the commanding officer directing him to have the foregoing resolutions put into execution."

These resolutions were accompanied by this proclamation:

"In the Council of Safety.
SAVANNAH, March 2nd, 1776.

"Whereas many householders in the town of Savannah, and the hamlets thereunto belonging, have basely deserted their habitations since the commencement of the present alarms:

"And whereas some of them are associates in the great American Union, and, by consequence, their lives and fortunes bound to support it:

"And whereas there is a number of shipping in the port of Savannah belonging and appertaining to persons resident in this Province:

"And whereas we deem it incumbent upon every person, more especially those who have associated, to defend their property with their lives:

"These are therefore to cite and admonish all persons holding any property in the town or hamlets, or shipping aforesaid, forthwith to repair to headquarters in Savannah to defend the same, on pain of suffering all the consequences contained in the foregoing resolutions.

"By Order of the Council of Safety.

WM. EWEN, President."

**A Splendid Sacrifice**—The superb spirit shown by the people of Georgia in their willingness to sacrifice their property and if necessary their lives in defense of liberty excited the admiration of the patriots of South Carolina. When Georgia had gone whole-heartedly into the American liberty movement and cast her fortunes with the other Colonies she was joyously welcomed, and in South Carolina she received enthusiastic praise, and a body of troops under Colonel Bull was sent to her aid. When the Charleston Council of Safety learned of the condition in Georgia and the action taken by the Council of Safety with the support of the people, that South Carolina body, having received copies of the resolutions and orders and the proclamation of March 2nd issued by the Georgia Council of Safety laid before the Provincial Congress of South Carolina, these evidences of Georgia's heroic action and the South Carolina Congress took the action reported by its president, William Henry Drayton, in the following letter to the Georgia authorities:

**South Carolina's Support**—"GENTLEMEN: Your letters of the 1st and 2d inst., and your resolutions, order, and proclamation of these dates, were laid before the Congress, transfusing a general and perfect joy.

"And the Congress, sensible of the vast importance which your exemplary conduct must be to the American cause, unanimously voted their thanks; and I have the honour thus to transmit them to you for your having decisively taken the noble, politic, and vigorous resolution: That the vessels in the port of Savannah, ready to sail, contrary to the interest of America, shall be forthwith unrigged and unruddered, and that rather than the enemy shall possess those vessels and your capital, all shall perish in a noble conflagration lighted by yourselves; an instance of heroic principle not exceeded by any, and equalled but by few, in history.

"Your conduct in citing such of the inhabitants of Savannah as had abandoned their possessions in that town to return to its defence, under penalty of being deemed to have deserted such property and of being excluded from any support towards obtaining an indemnification for any loss they may sustain by a general conflagration, received the highest applause as being worthy of imitation. The policy and justice of the measure are equally conspicuous.

"In short, the Congress feel the greatest satisfaction from their having anticipated your called-for assistance. It is sufficient that we know our friends stand in need of our aid. We hope that our forces under Colonel Bull will fully accommodate your necessity; and you may rest assured that we shall continue to afford the friends of America in Georgia every support in our power."

**The British Attack**—When Captain Barclay saw that his request for the purchase of supplies for the British ships at Savannah was disregarded he decided to capture the vessels loaded with rice which lay at the wharves in Savannah. For this purpose on the last of February with the warship *Scarborough* with twenty guns, the *Tamer* with sixteen guns, the *Cherokee* with ten guns and the *Hinchinbrook* schooner of eight guns, he moved up the Savannah River as far as the Five-Fathom Hole. He was accompanied by Major Grant in command of two or three hundred infantry and marines, who were conveyed in two transport ships, one of which had sixteen guns.

After sounding Back River opposite Hutchinson's Island two of the ships went up. One of them took position in front of Savannah, but the other in attempting to round the upper end of the Island in order to attack the town from above, grounded on a bank opposite Rae's Hall. This vessel, the *Hinchinbrook,* was fired upon by riflemen commanded by Major Joseph Habersham, and their fire soon drove the crew from the deck. Had boats been available they would have boarded and captured the vessel, but lack of boats prevented that, and at high water the *Hinchinbrook* again floated clear of the bank and moved away.

During the night of March 2nd two or three hundred British soldiers commanded by Major Maitland and Major Grant landed from a vessel in Back River and marched across Hutchinson's Island. At four o'clock on the morning of the third they took possession of the rice-laden vessels in the Savannah River near the store on the island opposite Savannah. They did this so quietly that it was nine o'clock in the morning before Savannah authorities knew that British troops were on those merchant ships. It was suspected that they were aided by the captains of the ships, surrendering quietly to the British. News of the capture was carried into Savannah by two sailors who came ashore, pretending to secure some clothing, and gave the information that Captain Rice, who had been selected to execute the order of the Council of Safety directing that all ships in the port be dismantled, having boarded one of those vessels with his boat's crew, was held a prisoner with his party.

The news of their capture by the British created great excitement in Savannah, and Colonel McIntosh with three hundred men went to Yamacraw Bluff, threw up a breastwork there and posted on it three four-pounder guns trained upon the ships. Before opening fire he sent Lieutenant Daniel Roberts of the St. John's Rangers and Captain Raymond Demere of St. Andrew's Parish with a flag of truce to demand the release of Captain Rice and his boat's crew. Rowing across the river these officers boarded the vessel in which Captain Barclay and Major Grant were present. In disregard of the flag of truce Lieutenant Roberts and Captain Demere were arrested by command of the British officers and held as prisoners.

After a half hour, as these commissioners had not returned the ship was hailed through a speaking trumpet and the release of Rice, Roberts and Demere was demanded. As insulting replies were received two four-pounder shots were fired at the vessel. Then the answer came that if the Americans would send on board two men in whom they trusted, the British commander would treat with them. In reply to this Captain Screven of the St. John's Rangers and Captain Baker, of the St. John's Riflemen, were sent. Taking with them twelve men of the St. John's Rangers they rowed immediately under the stern of the vessel, where they demanded the return of Rice and the other officers. Angered by an insulting reply Captain Baker fired at some one on board. This was answered by a discharge of swivel guns and small arms from the vessel, almost sinking the boat and wounding one of the men in it. Screven and Baker retired and the fire on them from the ship continued as long as their boat was within range. The battery at Yamacraw Bluff now began to fire on the ship and for four hours firing continued between the battery and the British troops on the merchant vessel.

The Council of Safety convened and decided to set fire to the shipping. Among the volunteers for this service were Captain Bowen, John Morel, Lieutenant James Jackson, Thomas Hamilton and James Bryan. The ship *Inverness,* of Captain McGillivray, loaded with rice and deerskins, was set on fire and turned adrift in the river. What ensued was thus described by President Ewen, of the Georgia Council, writing to the Council of Safety in South Carolina:

"The soldiers in the most laughable confusion got ashore in the marsh, while our riflemen, and field-pieces with grape-shot, were incessantly galling them. The shipping was now also in confusion. Some got up the river under cover of the armed schooner, while others caught the flame and, as night approached, exhibited a scene as they passed and repassed with the tide, which at any but the present time would be truly horrible, but now a subject only of gratitude and applause. The ships of Captains Inglis and Wardell neither got up the river nor on fire. They were ordered on shore and now are prisoners of Captain Screven in the country, and their vessels brought down close into a wharf. They were permitted to write to Captain Barclay in the evening to inform him of their situation and to request an exchange of prisoners, which the latter peremptorily refused."

**Aid From South Carolina**—Making good its promise of aid to Georgia the South Carolina Council of Safety sent 150 volunteers from Charleston, and 350 of the country militia under command of Colonel Bull, who arrived in time to aid the Georgians in dislodging the enemy. Three of the merchant vessels, loaded with rice, were burnt, six were dismantled, and two escaped to sea.

Before returning to Tybee Roads the British sent a detachment of marines ashore on Skidoway Island to get provisions. It was driven off by a company of militia commanded by Lieutenant Hext. In a skirmish at Cockspur the same day Lieutenant Oates and Lieutenant LaRoach were killed.

As the result of their efforts the British forces failed of their purpose to get supplies, although Governor Wright gave a different report in his letter to Lord Dartmouth on the tenth of March, in which he claimed that the expedition returned to Tybee Roads with fourteen or fifteen merchant ships and vessels of different kinds with about sixteen hundred barrels of rice. This seems impossible in view of the capture or destruction of all but two of the merchant ships.

As Lieutenant Roberts and Captains Demere and Rice were still held as prisoners by the British the Georgians retaliated by arresting James Edward Powell, Anthony Stokes, Josiah Tatnall, John Mullryne and other members of the King's Council remaining in Savannah. Several merchants and other parties who had made themselves obnoxious to the Georgians were forced to leave town and sought refuge in the fleet. Finally on March 20th, Roberts, Demere and Rice were released and members of the Council who had been arrested were released and allowed to remain in Savannah on parole or go on board the ships at Cockspur and take their effects with them.

**Houses Burned On Tybee Island**—As Governor Wright, officers of the fleet and the soldiers of the British were in the habit of going ashore on Tybee Island and making themselves comfortable in the houses there the Council of Safety decided to stop that by destroying the houses. Accordingly on March 25th a detachment of riflemen, light infantry, volunteers and a few Creek Indians, led by President Archibald Bulloch went to the island and burned all the houses but one, in which a sick woman and several children were lying. Two marines from the fleet and a Tory were killed and one marine and several Tories were captured. The warship *Cherokee* and an armed sloop fired upon Bulloch's party incessantly, but without effect.

Expecting a return of the British forces with a new attack on Savannah, the Council of Safety energetically fortified the town and concentrated troops for its protection.

This first battle of the Revolution in Georgia sealed the fate of the Colony. The English attack had been met bravely. Blood had been shed by the Colonists in defense of home and liberty and reconciliation with England was now out of the question. The courage and heroic exploits of the Georgians thrilled their neighboring Colonies, as well as their own people. Concerning the action of the Council of Safety in proposing the destruction if necessary of the homes of the Georgians to prevent their falling into the hands of the British, Captain Hugh McCall says in his *History of Georgia:*

"There are many instances of conflagration by order of a monarch, 'who can do no wrong,' but there are few instances upon record where the patriotism of the citizen, has urged him on to the destruction of his own property to prevent its becoming an asylum to the enemies of his country."

**South Carolinians Engaged**—Of the South Carolina forces which came to the aid of Georgia in the conflict with the British in March, 1776, there were 450 men including officers and privates, commanded by Colonel Stephen Bull, aided by Major Bourquin. Forty of them were posted at Ebenezer to protect the public records and powder which had been sent there for safe-keeping. The detachments included in Colonel Bull's force, as reported by him on March 15th, and sent to Colonel Henry Laurens, president of the South Carolina Council of Safety, were these:

The Charlestown Volunteers, the Charlestown Rangers, the Charlestown Light Infantry, the Charlestown Fuzileers, the Beaufort Light Infantry, the St. Helena Volunteers, the Euhaw Volunteers, the Huspa Volunteers, the Light Horse or Pocotaligo Hunters, detachments from Oakety Creek, St.

Peter's, Black Swamp, Pipe Creek, Boggy-Gut, New Windsor, and Upper Three Runs, and the Beaufort Artillery.

After the 2nd of March there remained near the wharves of Savannah the following vessels, which had escaped destruction by fire and capture by the enemy: the ship *Unity,* Captain Wardell, with 700 barrels of rice on board; the ship *Georgia Packet,* Captain Inglis, with 500 barrels of rice; the brigs *Amity,* freighted with ash and live-oak; the *Rebecca,* Captain Rutherford, with a cargo of lumber; the *Sorick,* Captain Steel; in ballast; the *Beaufort,* Captain Wood, also in ballast; the *Fair Lady,* Captain Robertson, with 30 hogsheads of tobacco; and the schooner *Race Horse,* Captain Burch, in ballast. To prevent all possibility of their departure to sea the Council of Safety ordered their rigging to be brought ashore, and that their rudders should be "unhung."

Colonel Bull was requested to direct the execution of this order of the Council of Safety, but as it was said by evil-minded persons that the Carolinians had taken possession of Savannah Colonel Bull suggested that the matter would better be attended to by Georgia troops, but he would be near with his command to give aid if resistance was offered by the captains and crews of the vessels. Accordingly Lieutenant-Colonel Stirk with forty of the Georgia militia was detailed for this service of dismantling those vessels. He did that in a satisfactory manner.

As the immediate danger of renewed attack by the British was now considered as past and there appeared to be no longer any need for the aid of South Carolina troops Colonel Bull and his command returned home. He disbanded his forces in the southern part of that Colony and went to Charleston, where he gave the Council of Safety an account of the affairs which had been entrusted to him.

Appreciating the valuable aid of the South Carolinians under Colonel Bull at a trying time the Provincial Congress of Georgia, on March 24, 1776, adopted this resolution:

"That the thanks of the Congress be returned to Stephen Bull Esqr. of Sheldon, Colonel of the Granville County regiment of militia, for his important services in command of the Colony forces in Savannah; and that he be desired to signify their thanks to the officers and men then under his command."

Colonel Charles C. Jones quotes from Drayton's *Memoirs,* published at Charleston, in 1821, the statement that the expedition under Colonel Bull for the relief of Georgia cost the Province of South Carolina 6,213 pounds, 7 shillings and 6 pence.

The high courage of the Georgians in their spirited resistance of the British attack on Savannah is realized when we note that besides the forces brought from South Carolina, Georgia had for its defense under command of Colonel McIntosh only 236 men. Of these only one hundred were present for duty. Sixty men were stationed on the Florida line to prevent cattle stealing, a body of cavalry guarded the western frontier against Indian invasion and for the protection of the seacoast there was not a single ship. In the face of these serious conditions the Georgians did not for a moment lose courage. With remarkable calmness they went on, organizing their government, accumulating war-like stores and strengthening the militia. In all of this Archibald Bulloch, the president and commander-in-chief, proved himself a great leader, fully equal to the high duties and the needs of the time.

**Effect of the Prohibitory Bill**—Lord North's prohibitory bill, which was passed by the House of Commons in December, 1775, was the most tyrannical and offensive measure adopted by the British Government to subdue the American Colonies, and the effect of it was to silence all objectors to independence, unite the Americans, intensify their patriotic spirit and hasten preparations for the war which was now inevitable. The measure cut off all trade with the thirteen Colonies, mentioning them by name, forfeited their ships and cargoes and authorized the seizure and condemnation of their vessels at the pleasure and profit of the captors. A letter addressed to Governor Wright instructed him to confiscate the property of all Georgians who refused immediate obedience to the laws of the Crown and professed sympathy with the resolutions of the Continental Congress. The bill was not passed without opposition, and in the debate which lasted six days or more, Edmund Burke asked that the King lay before the House information as to the condition of Georgia, which would enable the House to judge its attitude. On the next Monday morning Johnstone moved "that no evidence has been produced to this House to show that many persons in his Majesty's colony of Georgia have set themselves in open rebellion and defiance to the just and legal authority of the King and Parliament of Great Britain, or have assembled together an armed force, or engaged his Majesty's troops, or attacked his forts, or prohibited all trade and commerce with this Kingdom and the other parts of his Majesty's Dominion."

This motion led to a warm debate between Lord North, Johnstone and Burke, concerning the position of Georgia at that time. Johnstone protested against entering Georgia in a black catalogue and marking it out for destruction, "as well as Massachusetts; the latter for defending their liberties, which were immediately invaded, the former because they disapproved of the inhuman measure of condemning people unheard and untried." It was insisted in that debate that it had not been urged or proven that Georgians had committed a single act which could be called a misdemeanor and the certain consequences of the Prohibitory bill would be "that a whole Province was to be proscribed, its trade ruined, and its inhabitants declared rebels, and compelled to submit to tyranny, or consent to be starved."

Lord North insisted that while Georgia was not acting in arms or in open rebellion it was well known that Georgians had acted in conjunction with the other Colonies and there could be no more decisive proof of their disposition and the part they meant to take than their sending delegates to the Continental Congress.

Mr. Dempster severely criticized Lord North's presumption that Georgia was guilty and his including her in the Prohibitory bill. "That," he declared, was "more horrible in its consequences and more repugnant to the generally established ideas of justice than anything yet imputed to that bloody tribunal, the Inquisition; that it was the very language of Charles the First to his Parliament, and of every other tyrant, from William the Conqueror to that day."

Edmund Burke denounced the bill as "diabolically constructed; for it inflicted punishment for acts thought innocent at the time they were committed, and legalized others, which were acts of atrocious plunder and robbery."

In spite of able and eloquent opposition the bill was passed by the Commons and House of Lords, and approved by the King on December 22, 1775.

The Prohibitory Bill reached Georgia a few days after the attacks on Savannah by the warships. There was thereafter no voice for reconciliation. Remonstrance and petitions were useless. The time had come for resistance, and people were united for independence, and preparation for war began in earnest.

As soon as a copy of the bill was received in Savannah it was sent with a copy of the letter to Governor Wright by a fast express to Charleston, where the Provincial Congress of South Carolina was discussing independence. Within an hour after the bill and the letter to Governor Wright had been read in the South Carolina Congress an order was issued to seize in the name and for the Province of South Carolina the vessel *Fort Henderson,* from Jamaica, loaded with sugar, which had put into Charleston on her way to London. Carolina proceeded at once to adopt an independent constitution.

**Privateers on the Coast**—A cruel feature of the prohibitory bill was the authority it gave for privateering. Governor Tonyn, of East Florida, commissioned privateers which cruised along the coast of the Southern Colonies, plundering the inhabitants and robbing merchants of their cargoes.

**East Florida Outlaws**—The province of East Florida, where a royal Governor held sway, was a retreat for Loyalists from Georgia and Carolina. Organizing themselves in bands known as Florida Rangers and calling Indians to their aid, they made predatory incursions into Southern Georgia and kept the people there in a state of alarm. In the language of Colonel Jones, "Pillage, conflagration and murder marked their footsteps. Restrained by no law, these freebooters feared neither King nor Congress and were wholly addicted to the occupations of plunderers and outlaws." Germyn Wright, a brother of the Governor, had constructed a fort on St. Mary's River, which was a point of rendezvous for the bandits and a place of deposit for their spoils. Its destruction was greatly desired by the Georgians living in that region.

With the hope of surprising and demolishing that fort, Captain John Baker, of St. John's Parish, collected seventy mounted volunteers and marched rapidly toward it. Moving with great secrecy the party reached the neighborhood of the fort without being discovered and believing that the capture could be made best at night Captain Baker held his command in a dense wood and awaited darkness. Learning that a considerable body of Indians was camped in the neighborhood and those savages with the garrison of the fort largely outnumbered his force, he saw that success depended upon surprising the fort, and he could find safety only in rapid retreat after its destruction. Unfortunately a negro discovered his presence and gave the alarm. Three cannon were fired from the fort and answered from the Schooner *St. John,* which lay in St. Mary's River two miles below.

Captain Baker attacked the fort with musketry without success. Expecting that reënforcements for the fort would be sent from the schooner, he sent part of his command to a landing below. Three armed boats came up the river and as they neared the shore Captain Baker's men opened fire on them, killing and wounding several. Those in boats called for quarter, came on shore and surrendered. Among the prisoners were Captain Barkup of the navy, and Lieutenant Bucher of the army. The other boats escaped in the night and information was received through one of the captives that a large body of Indians was encamped on the other side of the river not far away. Seeing there was no hope of capturing the fort and expecting an attack from the Indians, Captain Baker retreated eight or nine miles and encamped.

During the night Daniel and James McGirth, who were on guard, stole most of the horses belonging to Baker's command and deserted with them to the enemy. For this act of treachery the enemy made Daniel McGirth a lieutenant-colonel of the Florida Rangers, commanded by Colonel Thomas Brown, and he entered upon the career of rapine and murder in which he became notorious. James McGirth was made a captain in this same body. Baker returned to Georgia, mortified by failure and the treachery of his own men.

**Bombardment of Fort Moultrie**—The first severe attack on American Colonies by the forces of Great Britain was the bombardment of Fort Moultrie by British ships in June, 1776. King George was determined to regain possession of South Carolina, and sent a strong force to attack Charleston. On the first of June, 1776, a fleet of more than fifty ships of war under Sir Peter Parker, anchored near Charleston. President Rutledge, of South Carolina, and General Armstrong personally inspected the harbor fortifications, called in every available force and disposed of men and material with the best advantage for the protection of the city and its approaches, requiring every possible preparation to resist the invasion, which was made inevitable by the presence of so many ships. A general alarm was sounded, the militia from the interior was called to the coast and aid was asked from sister colonies. The aid came promptly and in such force that by the eleventh of June, 6,522 men of all arms were there to defend Charleston.

The stores and warehouses on the wharves were leveled so as to make clear a defensive line along the East Bay, which was armed with cannon and musketry. The people gave the lead weights of their windows to be melted into musket balls and both masters and servants worked together energetically in building fortifications. All available cannon were mounted at commanding points so that their fire would converge upon the advance of the enemies. South Carolina acted as one man, and a strong man, to meet the invader.

Major-General Charles Lee who had been assigned to the command of the Southern Compartment, came to Savannah with Brigadier-General Howe on the 4th of June, and made a careful inspection of fortifications at Haddrell's Point and on Sullivan's Island.

At this time the fort on Sullivan's Island was only finished in front and on one side. Its rear was open and the troops were camped in huts and booths covered with palmetto leaves. There were on the island 1,200 soldiers and ten thousand pounds of powder had been placed there for small arms and heavy guns.

General Lee thought the place insecure and declared that Fort Sullivan could not hold out half an hour. He said its platform was only a slaughtering stage, and suggested to President Rutledge that both the fort and the island be evacuated. This was indignantly rejected by President Rutledge. General Lee then reduced the forces and withdrew some of the ammunition.

Haddrell's Point was strongly reënforced by Continental and Colonial troops under General Armstrong, and a bridge was thrown across the cove to Sullivan's Island. A heavy traverse was ordered to protect the rear of Fort Sullivan. Anticipating the speedy reduction of Fort Sullivan by the enemy General Lee gave his attention mainly to securing avenues of retreat for the forces on that side of the harbor. His expression was pessimistic and depressing, but had no effect on Colonel Moultrie, who said in his *Memoirs:* "General Lee, one day on a visit to the Fort took me one side and said: 'Colonel Moultrie, you think you can maintain this post?' I answered him: 'Yes, I think I can!' That was all that passed on the subject between us. Another time, Captain Lamperer, a brave and experienced seaman, who had been master of a man-of-war, visited me at the fort after the British ships came over the bar. While we were walking on the platform looking at the fleet, he said to me: 'Well, Colonel, what do you think of it now?' I replied 'that we should beat them.' 'Sir,' said he, 'when those ships come to lay alongside your fort, they will knock it down in half an hour.' 'Then,' I said, 'we will lay behind the ruins and prevent their men from landing.'"

In spite of these warnings Colonel Moultrie remained calm, inspiring his men by his confidence, and giving them a strong impression of victory. When the bombardment began on June 28th Fort Sullivan had thirty-one cannon, of which twenty-five could be brought to bear upon the enemy in front of the fort. A narrow platform was built along the walls for men to stand upon and fire through the loopholes. The garrison included a second South Carolina regiment with 413 men, and the 4th South Carolina artillery detachment of twenty-two men, making 435 in all, commanded by Colonel William Moultrie of the 2nd Regiment.

Between the fourth and eighth of June thirty-six British vessels crossed the bar and anchored in Five Fathom Hole. At the same time Major-General Clinton landed on Long Island with 3,000 infantry, and under a flag of truce sent a proclamation in which he urged an immediate return of duty and in the name of the King offered pardon to all who would lay down their arms and submit to the laws. This document made no impression on the brave men defending the fort.

On June 28th the British Squadron approached Fort Sullivan, and between ten and eleven o'clock the bombardment began from the *Thunder-Bomb* ship, covered by the *Friendship* of twenty-six guns. That was followed by the *Active* of twenty-eight guns and the *Bristol* and the *Experiment* of fifty guns each, and the *Solebay* of twenty-eight guns. The *Syren* and the *Acteon,* each carrying twenty-eight guns, and the *Sphinx* of twenty guns, formed a line in rear of the first, opposite the intervals in ships and united in the cannonade.

This powerful battery of warships with two hundred and fifty-eight guns united in a terrific cannonade against the fort on Sullivan's Island, composed of palmetto logs.

The cannon from the fort returned a deliberate and destructive fire.

After bombardment of more than an hour which failed to silence the fort the British commander ordered the *Syren* and *Acteon* and *Sphinx* to pass the fort and take position toward the cove of Sullivan's Island, from which they could enfilade the fort. Had this movement succeeded it would have been destructive and the men would have been driven from their guns on Sullivan's Island, but the ships assigned to that duty became entangled on a shoal and the *Sphinx* lost her bowsprit. Getting free from that dangerous position the *Syren* and *Sphinx* retired beyond the battle line, beyond the range of the guns of the fort.

In the meantime the ship *Thunder-Bomb* became useless by the recoil of heavily charged mortars.

The engagement was kept up at short range by the *Active,* the *Bristol,* the *Experiment* and the *Solebay* and in the afternoon they were reënforced by the *Syren* and the *Friendship.*

The cannonade ceased at half-past nine o'clock, and at eleven o'clock the British ships, their decks wet with blood and their hulls battered by well directed shots from the fort, silently retired to their former station.

The fire from the fort was mainly directed to the two fifty-gun ships, the *Bristol* and *Experiment,* which encountered a loss of 164 killed and wounded. Among the latter was Sir Peter Parker, whose flagship was the *Bristol.* But for the scarcity of powder within the fort the damage to the enemy would have been far greater.

During this engagement came the thrilling rescue of the Carolina flag by Sergeant Jasper. The flagpole was shot away and fell outside the fort with

BOYHOOD HOME OF WOODROW WILSON, AUGUSTA

the flag. Sergeant Jasper sprang through one of the embrasures, walked in front of the fort its entire length, cut the fallen colors from the broken mast, lashed them to another staff and amid a shower of balls planted the staff bearing the flag on the summit. Having done this, waving his hat, he gave three cheers and shouted "God save liberty and my country forever." Retiring unhurt to his gun he continued to fight through the engagement. For this heroic act, Sergeant Jasper received the thanks of his commander and was offered a commission, but modestly declined it, saying that he preferred to serve as a sergeant.

On the second day's bombardment, when shells were bursting above Fort Pulaski the flag was carried away by shot and fell. Lieutenant Hussey, of the Montgomery Guards, and Private Latham, of the Washington Volunteers, advanced along the parapet while it was swept by deadly missiles, rescued the fallen flag and carried it to a northeastern angle of the fort where it again floated.

Although the fort was struck by many cannon shot from the ships of war the spongy palmetto logs received them without splintering and the injury was less than would have been expected. Only twelve of the garrison were killed and twenty-five wounded.

Of this brilliant victory in defense of South Carolina under conditions which made success appear impossible Dr. Drayton says in his *Memoirs of the American Revolution:*

"The morning of the 29th of June presented a humiliating prospect to British pride. To the southwest of the fort, at the distance of near a mile, lay the *Acteon* frigate fast ashore on the Lower-Middle-Ground. Below the fort, about two miles and a half, the men-of-war and transports were riding at anchor opposite Morris Island, while Sir Peter Parker's broad pennant was hardly to be seen on a jury maintop mast considerably lower than the foremast of his ship. And on the left General Clinton was kept in check by the troops under Colonels Thomson and Muhlenburg. On the contrary, how glorious were the other points of view! The azure colors of the fort, fixed on a sponge-staff, waved gently in the winds. Boats were passing and repassing in safety from and to the fort and Charlestown, and the hearts of the people were throbbing with gratitude and the most exhilarating transports."

Congratulations on this important victory poured in from every quarter. On June 30th General Charles Lee reviewed the garrison and thanked the officers and men for their gallant defense of the fort. Mrs. Barnard Elliott, wife of Major Elliott, presented the 2nd Regiment with embroidered colors, which were received by Colonel William Moultrie and Lieutenant-Colonel Isaac Motte. Colonel Moultrie promised that the colors would be supported honorably by the 2nd Regiment; then he handed the flag to Sergeant Jasper who, as he received the precious emblem, declared that he would never give it up but with his life, and the sequel showed how nobly he kept his word.

On July 4th Governor Rutledge visited the fort, and in the name of South Carolina tendered its brave defenders thanks and congratulations, publicly commending the heroic conduct of Sergeant Jasper. Taking his own sword from his side the Governor presented it to Sergeant Jasper as a reward for his bravery and an incitement for further deeds of valor.

This magnificent victory in defense of South Carolina was of great importance to all the American Colonies and especially to Georgia, South Carolina, North Carolina and Virginia, as they were threatened with a cruel Indian war by the Cherokee Indians, who had already perpetrated horrible outrages. Freed from the danger from without, South Carolina joined with Georgia, North Carolina and Virginia in meeting the Indians. Within three months they were subdued, sued for peace and the danger of further Indian outrages passed away for the time.

## CHAPTER LI.

# *Declaration of Independence—Georgia As A State*

On July 4, 1776, the Continental Congress published the Declaration of Independence which had been agreed upon on July 2, but the Document was perfected and published on July 4. The proceedings which led to the action on that historic document began on June 7 when Richard Henry Lee of Virginia introduced the following resolution which was seconded by John Adams of Massachusetts:

"Resolved, that these United Colonies are, and of right ought to be, free and independent States, that they are absolved from all allegiance to the British Crown, and that all political connection between them and the State of Great Britain is, and ought to be, totally dissolved.

"That it is expedient forthwith to take the most effectual measures for forming foreign alliances.

"That a plan of confederation be prepared and transmitted to the respective Colonies for their consideration and approbation."

These resolutions were considered by the House of Congress as a committee of the whole and in a vote by Colonies it was agreed, seven to five, to postpone final action on the matter of Independence until July 1. To prepare a form of confederation for the Colonies, one committee was appointed on June 12, and another was to consider treaties of alliance with foreign powers. Of the committee to prepare articles of confederation, consisting of one member from each Colony, Button Gwinnett was appointed as a representative from Georgia.

That committee worked steadily for a month and produced articles of confederation which were submitted to Congress and read. The debate on the subject continued some time and the articles with many changes were not acted upon until more than a year later, when Gwinnett had passed from life. Their final ratification by the Colonies was not completed for several years.

On June 15, at the request of Georgia delegates in the Continental Congress, a committee of three, Stephen Hopkins, Benjamin Harrison, and

Samuel Adams, was appointed to consider the State of Georgia. This committee on July 5 recommended that two additional Continental Battalions be raised for the defense of Georgia and blank commissions for the officers be sent to the Georgia Convention to be filled with the names of officers that body should select. North and South Carolina were asked to permit the raising of troops for those Georgia Battalions within their borders. Four galleys were to be built at the expense of the United States by the Georgia Congress and forts were to be built at Savannah and Sunbury. Two companies of artillery were to be raised for these forts. A few days later Congress appropriated $60,000 in favor of the delegates from Georgia, to be used for the Continental Battalions.

It took Congress nearly a month to agree on the great question of Independence raised by Richard Henry Lee in his resolutions of June 7, 1776. The task of preparing the Declaration was assigned to a committee composed of Thomas Jefferson, John Adams, Benjamin Franklin, Roger Sherman and Robert Livingston. When that Committee began its work the Colonies were not all ready to declare their independence. John Adams said that the middle Colonies, which had not been invaded, were not so hot for independence as those which had suffered. There were in Congress many opposed to any declaration and others had been instructed by their assemblies to avert an open rupture with the Mother Country. At the same time the New Hampshire and Delaware Houses had instructed their representatives to declare for independence. Five delegates from New Jersey who were lukewarm were authorized to concur with the other Colonies for independence. Pennsylvania and New York were still uncertain. By degrees the sentiment for independence grew and William Whipple of New Hampshire said in a letter to a friend:

"The middle Colonies are getting in a good way. Next Monday being the 1st of July the grand question is to be debated and I believe determined unanimously. May God unite our hearts in all things that tend to the welfare of the rising empire."

Jefferson's committee submitted its draft of the Declaration to Congress on June 28. It lay upon the table until July 1 when it was taken up by the House in committee of the whole, debated and carried by nine Colonies. Pennsylvania and South Carolina opposed it and Delaware was divided. At the request of Edward Rutledge, the formal vote of Congress was postponed until July 2. Caesar Rodney came from Dover and broke the tie of the Delaware vote in favor of the Declaration. South Carolina then voted for the Declaration and so did Pennsylvania. New York did not vote though her members appeared favorable. Thus, on July 2, twelve Colonies voted for the Declaration of Independence.

The measure was perfected by further consideration on the 3d and 4th of July. Harsh censures on the people of England were struck out and the clause condemning the continued importation of slaves was eliminated. It is said that was done in deference to Georgia and South Carolina.

On July 4 final action was taken by Congress as a committee of the whole House, when the perfected form of the Declaration was submitted, again read and agreed to. The committee was directed to prepare it for the press and copies were ordered sent to the assemblies, conventions and committees or councils of safety of the Colonies and to the commanders of the Continental Troops who were to proclaim it in each of the United States at the head of the army. This action was taken on the evening of July 4, and Jefferson said that every member present came forward and signed a copy of the Declaration. For Georgia it was signed by Button Gwinnett, Dr. Lyman Hall and George Walton.

**The Celebration In Georgia**—The first news of the Declaration of Independence did not reach Georgia until the 10th of August when a messenger delivered to President Bulloch a copy of the document with a letter from John Hancock, President of the Continental Congress. The Provincial Council at once assembled and President Bulloch read aloud to it the historic utterance of the delegates from thirteen Colonies.

The reading of the document made a profound impression and the Council joyously hailed the elevation of Georgia to the dignity of a free and independent State.

The President and Council then went to the public square and in front of the building used by the Provincial Assembly the Declaration of Independence was read again and enthusiastically acclaimed by the citizens of Savannah. Salutes were fired by the Grenadiers and the Light Infantry and a procession in honor of the occasion was formed as follows:

The Grenadiers in front;
The Provost Marshal on horseback, with his sword drawn;
The Secretary, bearing the Declaration;
His Excellency the President;
The honorable the Council, and gentlemen attending;
The Light Infantry;
The Militia of the town and district of Savannah;
and lastly, the citizens.

The procession marched to the Liberty Pole, where they were met by the Georgia Battalion and the Declaration was read a third time. At the command of Colonel McIntosh, thirteen volleys were fired from small arms and field pieces. The entire gathering went from there to the battery, where the Declaration was read publicly for the fourth time and a salute was fired from the siege guns.

The Governor, members of Council, Colonel McIntosh, the Militia and a number of gentlemen dined under the cedar trees and drank a toast to the "prosperity and perpetuity of the United free, and Independent States of America."

That did not end the celebration. The people appeared to be intoxicated with joy and the citizens in larger numbers than ever assembled before in

Savannah, with the Grenadier and Light Infantry Companies, the Georgia Battalion and the Militia, with muffled drums, marched to the front of the courthouse, where His Majesty, George the Third was buried in effigy and the following burial service, prepared for the occasion, was read with due solemnity:

"For as much as George the Third, of Great Britain, hath most flagrantly violated his Coronation Oath, and trampled upon the Constitution of our Country and the sacred rights of mankind: we, therefore, commit his political existence to the ground—corruption to corruption—tyranny to the grave—and oppression to eternal infamy; in sure and certain hope that he will never obtain a resurrection to rule again over these United States of America. But, friends and fellow-citizens, let us not be sorry, as men without hope, for Tyrants that thus depart; rather let us remember America is free and independent; that she is, and will be, with the blessing of the Almighty, Great among the nations of the earth. Let this encourage us in well doing, to fight for our rights and privileges, for our wives and children, and for all that is near and dear unto us. May God give us his blessing, and let all the people say AMEN."

In the same spirit of enthusiasm the adoption of the Declaration of Independence was celebrated in other parts of Georgia. St. John's Parish, the home of Dr. Lyman Hall and Button Gwinnett, two of the signers of the Declaration, was especially strong in its demonstration of approval.

**Georgia as a State**—As the Colonial Congress had recommended that each of the several states forming the American Union should adopt a form of government suited to the new order of affairs and conducive to the happiness and safety of their people and the United States, President Bulloch issued a proclamation, ordering a general election to be held between the first and 10th of September, 1776, for the election of representatives to meet in Savannah in convention on the first Tuesday in October.

The President directed that a circular letter be addressed to the people of the parishes and districts of Georgia, congratulating them on the happy political outlook, reminding them of the important business to be acted upon by the convention and impressing upon them the necessity for selecting delegates of known patriotism and highest character, whose friendship to the cause of freedom had been thoroughly proven and whose political wisdom qualified them to frame the best possible Constitution for the government of the Commonwealth.

Another proclamation was issued for the encouragement of the recruiting service within the State. It was based on a resolution of the Provincial Congress which provided that everyone entering the army who should serve faithfully for three years, or until peace was concluded with Great Britain, should be entitled to a bounty of one hundred acres of land. It was stipulated that if he died in defense of his State his wife or family should receive the land.

**The Indian War**—When it appeared that war was likely between Great Britain and the American Colonies the Georgia Leaders were careful to explain the nature of the dispute to the neighboring Indians and advise them to maintain their friendship for the State. The South Carolina authorities also tried to induce the Indians to take no part in the contest with Great Britain.

These efforts failed because the Royal Superintendent of Indian Affairs and the Florida authorities sought to enlist the red men in behalf of England. The poverty of the Colonies prevented them from giving the Indians the generous supply of presents they had received. Because of the unsettled condition of affairs and influenced by the bribes and advice of English Agents the Cherokees, in violation of their treaties, began outrages on the frontiers of Georgia and the Carolinas. These lawless acts were largely incited by Captain Stuart, British Superintendent of Indian Affairs in the Southern Colonies, and his assistant, Cameron.

While the British forces were threatening Savannah and Charleston troops could not be withdrawn from the coast in sufficient number to make a formidable expedition against the Cherokees. Under these circumstances the frontier settlements suffered severely from atrocious massacres and inhuman cruelty.

When the British fleet left Charleston after its failure in the attack on Fort Moultrie, it was possible to send a strong force against the Indians and for this purpose there was concerted action by Georgia, the Carolinas and Virginia. The South Carolina troops, including the 6th Regiment, a part of the 3d and a body of the Militia, moved under command of Colonel Williamson of District Ninety-Six. General Rutherford, with nineteen hundred North Carolinians, entered the Cherokee country where he was attacked vigorously several times, but succeeded in defeating the Indians. At the same time the Virginia Militia, under Colonel Christie, invaded the Indian country, and Colonel Jack led five companies of Georgians, commanded by Captains John Twiggs, John Jones, Leonard Marbury, Samuel Alexander, and Thomas Harris, altogether about two hundred men, against the Cherokee towns on the head waters of the Tugalo and the Chattahoochee.

Within a few months the Cherokees were conquered and sued for peace. Their towns were burned, their cornfields laid waste, their cattle and horses taken and many were slain. About five hundred of these Indians, driven by hunger, sought refuge with Stuart, the Indian superintendent, in West Florida where they were fed for a while at the expense of the British Government. Many Cherokees were driven into the mountains and lived as they could on roots and native fruits.

Within less than three months the war had ended. The Cherokee Nation was so badly crippled that for some time it was unable to annoy the frontiers. The total American loss did not exceed fifty men. Articles of a Treaty of Peace were concluded on May 20, 1777, and signed at DeWitt's Corner, between the States of South Carolina and Georgia on the one part and the Cherokee Nation on the other.

By this treaty Carolina acquired considerable territory and established a garrison with two independent companies at Seneca. Friendly intercourse with the Indians was resumed and for several years was uninterrupted.

**The Invasion of Florida**—When the British ships retired from the South Carolina coast at the end of June, 1776, General Charles Lee, then commanding the southern department, considered measures to protect South Carolina and Georgia. President Rutledge of South Carolina had asked the Council of Safety at Savannah to send two of its members to Charleston to confer with him on the condition of Georgia and the plan for putting it in the best condition for defense against all enemies "external and internal."

In response to this request Jonathan Bryan, John Houstoun and Colonel Lachlan McIntosh were directed to answer the summons. They arrived in Charleston soon after the victory of Fort Moultrie and were cordially received. Jonathan Bryan spoke for his committee and the people of Georgia, telling of many depredations on the southern and southwestern frontiers committed by lawless bands from Florida and of the desolation inflicted on the coast by privateers, commissioned by Governor Tonyn of East Florida. He suggested a plan of operations by which the bandits might be slain or driven away and St. Augustine might be captured. He strongly urged upon General Lee the defenseless condition of Georgia and the urgent need of assistance for it. In substance he said:

"Not one of the thirteen United Colonies is so weak within or so exposed from without. To the east the inhabitants suffer the ravages of British cruisers. Their negroes are daily inveigled and carried away from their plantations. British fleets may be supplied with beef from several large islands, well stocked with cattle, which line their coasts, and round which large ships may sail. To the south they have the Province of East Florida, the inhabitants and soldiery of which must of necessity make inroads upon Georgia for the articles of provision with which they have been heretofore chiefly supplied. Georgia here stands as a barrier to South Carolina and effectually secures that Province against the like depredations."

With British Troops at St. Augustine and nearby Indian nations able to place fifteen thousand gunmen in the field supplied with ammunition from Florida, and a large slave population likely to be incited to deeds of violence, it is clear that Mr. Bryan did not exaggerate conditions in his statement to General Lee, and the general at once decided upon an expedition against St. Augustine. Assembling the troops from North Carolina and Virginia who were still in Charleston, he informed them that he had planned a secret expedition which involved little danger and promised large success and booty. Responding favorably to this appeal the troops volunteered for that service. By the 6th of August, 1776, four hundred and sixty men from the 1st, 2d, 3d, and 4th regiments of infantry, the rangers and the artillery were contributed by South Carolina authorities.

The unfortunate conditions attending the expedition and its failure are thus described by Dr. Drayton in his *Memoirs of the American Revolution*:

"From the 8th to the 15th of August, in the most unhealthy season of the year, when the constitution is severely tried with heat and moisture and the effluvia of the flowed rice fields is scattering sickness through the land, did General Lee march off on this expedition with the Virginia and North Carolina troops and some of the Colony troops, without necessaries being provided, without even a field-piece or a medicine chest. The rest of the Colony troops, with artillery and such necessaries as could be obtained on the emergency, were sent on by water on the 8th of August, and going through the inland navigation by the way of Beaufort, they arrived at Savannah on the 17th of that month. General Howe and Colonel Moultrie followed soon after, and General James Moore of North Carolina was left in command at Charlestown.

"On the 18th of August General Lee reviewed on the green at Yamacraw every corps, as well as the Georgia Battalions and the troops which had arrived from South Carolina; and about the 22d of August a part of the South Carolina troops and Colonel Muhlenburg's regiment marched for Sunbury. After this troops were detached from Savannah and stationed at Skidoway Island, Ogeechee, Ausabaw Island and other places betwixt Savannah and Sunbury; while the remainder were quartered in Savannah and its vicinity. The hopes which General Lee had encouraged in consequence of his conversation with Mr. Bryan had not been realized, as neither boats, provisions, nor stores were to be procured sufficient for the exigencies of the expedition. There was scarce an officer of the South Carolina troops who had not a violent fit of illness; and those of the other corps suffered in an equal degree, while fourteen or fifteen men were buried each day at Sunbury; unfortunate sacrifices to so inclement a season.

"During all this time the expedition had not proceeded farther than Sunbury, as, from a want of stores, General Lee had sent to Augusta to have a list of articles procured which Colonel Moultrie had given in as necessary. At this time General Lee may be fairly said to have been in check, not by the enemy but by his own hasty and improvident movements, and the force which he had with him was every day becoming less able to carry on the expedition against Florida or to cope with the enemy. From all this, however, he was fortunately relieved by a recall to the northward where General Howe, having taken New York was becoming very formidable. General Lee accordingly left Savannah early in September, ordering the Virginia and North Carolina troops to follow him, and leaving the troops much greater sufferers by his conduct than by the arms of the enemy. And in this manner ended the East Florida expedition."

Colonel Moultrie, to whom the command of the expedition was tendered, declined to go forward with it until he had been furnished at least eight hundred men and supplies which he enumerated. General Lee undoubtedly had been affected by the earnest appeal of the Georgians who were suffering from the inroads of Florida bandits and earnestly desired the destruction of the foul nest of outlaws at St. Augustine. Jonathan Bryan and Nathan Brownson expressed the feeling of the community when they said to General Lee: "That an eruption into the Province of East Florida will be attended with the most salutory consequences to this Province, and will render service to the whole Continent."

But without sufficient force or sufficient supplies, in the worst season of the year, and suffering frightfully from disease, the men were unable to go on and the expedition was given up. Naturally its abandonment gave confidence to the enemy and, as McCall says, induced many who had not been active to join the British in Florida. General Lee had made a woeful mistake and the men of the Southern Colonies paid the deadly cost of his error.

In the meantime Georgia was busy with measures for her own protection. Captain Bowen was sent with credentials to the Governor of Cape Francois to purchase armed vessels, war-like stores, and medicines necessary for the troops in the field. Captain Pray was, on October 18, 1776, ordered by the Council of Safety to go to St. Thomas and secure seamen, small arms, ammunition, and swivel guns. He was authorized to mount on the vessel which was engaged to bring his cargo to Georgia as many carriage guns as it could bear. To defend the southern frontier all available troops were stationed at Darien, Fort Howe, Beard's Bluff and Fort McIntosh.

Lieutenant Bugg, marching with a detachment toward Beard's Bluff, was surprised by Indians concealed in the swamps of Beard's Creek. Three of his men were killed and the detachment put to flight. Captain Chesley Bostwick was ordered to Beard's Bluff with his company and built a stockade fort there.

**The Constitution of 1777**—Responding to the proclamation of President Bulloch the Parishes of Georgia elected delegates to the Constitutional Convention which assembled in Savannah on the first Tuesday in October, 1776. The delegates were men of reputation and experience, were known friends of liberty, had been carefully chosen and realized the important duties before them. It was a time of crisis when the fate of a Nation as well as the fate of Georgia was to be decided and this body was so careful and thorough in its deliberation on the problems before it that it did not adjourn until the 5th of February, 1777, but when it did separate it had made a constitution which lasted through the Revolutionary War as the organic document of Georgia for twelve years as an independent State.

The preamble of that Constitution was as follows:

"WHEREAS the conduct of the Legislature of Great Britain for many years has been so oppressive to the people of America that of late years they have plainly declared and asserted a right to raise taxes upon the people of America and to make laws to bind them in all cases whatsoever without their consent; which conduct being repugnant to the common rights of mankind hath obliged the Americans, as freemen, to oppose such oppressive measures, and to assert the rights and privileges they are entitled to by the laws of nature and reason; and accordingly it hath been done by the general consent of all the people of the States of New Hampshire, Massachusetts-Bay, Rhode-Island, Connecticut, New York, New Jersey, Pennsylvania, the counties of New Castle, Kent, and Sussex in Delaware, Maryland, Virginia, North Carolina, South Carolina, and Georgia, given by their representatives met together in General Congress in the City of Philadelphia:

"And whereas it hath been recommended by the said Congress on the fifteenth of May last to the respective Assemblies and Conventions of the United States where no government sufficient to the exigencies of their affairs hath been hitherto established, to adopt such government as may, in the opinion of the representatives of the people, best conduce to the happiness and safety of their constituents in particular and America in general:

"And whereas the independence of the United States of America has been also declared on the fourth of July one thousand seven hundred and seventy six by the said honorable Congress, and all political connection between them and the Crown of Great Britain is in consequence thereof dissolved:

"We therefore, the Representatives of the people, from whom all power originates and for whose benefit all government is intended, by virtue of the power delegated to us, do ordain and declare, and it is hereby ordained and declared that the following rules and regulations be adopted for the future government of this State."

Then follow sixty-three articles creating the executive, legislative and judicial departments of the State Government, defining their respective powers, the manner in which they were to be chosen and providing the machinery of government for the State.

This Constitution was excellent in many ways and served the people of Georgia in times that tried men's souls. It was noteworthy for the fact that it established religious liberty, made the first provision for public schools to be supported by taxation and penalized failure to vote. The bar against Papists was discarded and the only remnant of that peculiar exception to religious liberty was the provision that members of the Legislature, in addition to the usual qualifications, must be of the Protestant religion.

Briefly summarized the constitution, after providing for the three departments of government, covered almost every contingency likely to arise during the Revolution.

The legislature was composed of members elected annually on the first Tuesday in December by voters of the respective counties and the members must have resided a year in Georgia and three months in the county they represented. They must be of protestant religion, twenty-one years old and owners of 250 acres of land or property worth 250 pounds. As the counties of Glynn and Camden, near to Florida, were in a state of alarm they could each elect a representative from some other county until better conditions prevailed. The Legislature was to meet the first Tuesday in January every year at Savannah or such other place as the Assembly should direct.

On the first day of their session the representatives were to elect a Governor and an executive council selected from their own number. These elections were to be by ballot. The executive council was composed of two members from each county which had ten representatives. This executive council having been selected the remaining representatives constituted the House of Assembly and a majority of the House members could transact business.

At least one member of the Executive Council from each county must be in constant attendance at the residence of the Governor. All members could be present if they wished and in this duty and service they could rotate with each other for longer or shorter periods as they might agree among themselves. Each house of Assembly expired annually on the first Monday in December.

**Counties Created**—The old system of parishes was abolished and counties were created in their stead. The ceded land from the Indians north of the Ogeechee River became the county of Wilkes. The Parish of St. Paul which included Augusta, became Richmond County. The Parish of St. George was made a county and named Burke from Edmund Burke, the great Irishman who spoke in Georgia's behalf against the oppressive measures passed by the English Parliament. The Parish of St. Matthew and that part of St. Phillip above the Cannouchee River were consolidated as the county of Effingham. Christ Church Parish which included Savannah and that part of St. Phillip below the Cannouchee River were consolidated as a county and named Chatham for William Pitt, the Great Commoner who was another friend of the Colony. The Parish of St. John which included the Midway settlement and Sunbury, the Parish of St. Andrew which included the Scotch Highlanders of Darien and the Parish of St. James were united as one county and honored by the name of Liberty, as they had led in the fight for independence. The parishes of St. David and St. Patrick made the seventh county, which was called Glynn, and the eighth county, called Camden, was composed of the parishes of St. Thomas and St. Mary.

The representation of the counties was as follows:

Glynn and Camden, with few inhabitants, had only one representative each. Liberty County, made up of three of the most popular and wealthy parishes, was given fourteen members in the House of Assembly. Each of the other counties had ten representatives. Savannah, because of its importance as a port and a town, was given four members to represent trade, and for the same reason two members were given to the port and town of Sunbury, which was then a prosperous rival of Savannah.

Provision was made for the creation of additional counties if ordered by the House of Assembly, on the condition that when so instituted each new county should have one member, provided the inhabitants had ten electors; if thirty electors, two representatives; if forty, three representatives; if sixty electors, four representatives; if eighty electors, six representatives; if one hundred and upward, ten representatives and at the same time two executive councillors were to be chosen from them as directed for the other counties.

The House of Assembly had the power to frame laws and regulations for the good order and well-being of the State, repeal bad laws, choose its own speaker and officers, make its own rules of procedure, issue writs of election to supply vacancies and authorize adjournments within the year as it saw proper.

Except in cases of great necessity or danger, each law or ordinance was to be read three times on three separate days, and after the second reading was to be sent to the Executive Council for reading and advice.

The qualifications of voters were as follows:

All male white inhabitants twenty-one years old owning property worth ten pounds and liable to tax in Georgia, or being a mechanic in trade, and they must have been residing in the State six months. They could vote for representatives or other officers to be chosen by the people and their vote was by ballot personally cast. They had freedom from arrest while going to or from the polls or attending them. No officer or soldier could appear at the polls in a military capacity. All elections were free and open. The voters must cast their ballots in the counties of their residence and no one holding any title of nobility was permitted to vote for representatives or hold any office of honor, profit or trust in Georgia until he had renounced such distinction in a manner prescribed by the Legislature. Every person absenting himself from an election and neglecting to cast his ballot except for just cause was liable to pay a fine not over five pounds.

The ballots for representatives were to be received by two or more justices of the peace in each county who were to provide a ballot box for the purpose. When the polls closed ballots were publicly compared with the list of voters which had been kept and the result of the election was immediately declared. Certificates were then given to those elected and like certificates were returned to the House of Representatives.

Continental delegates were chosen annually by ballot and had the right to sit, debate and vote in the House of Assembly, of which they were members.

No person holding a position of profit in Georgia or any military commission other than in the State's militia could be a representative. Any representative who accepted such a place of profit or military commission forfeited his seat in the House of Assembly. The justice of the peace was not considered a post of profit. No one could hold more than one office of profit within the gift of the State. The executive power was in the Governor, who exercised it with the advice of the Executive Council. He could reprieve a criminal or suspend the collection of a fine, but pardons must be submitted to the House of Assembly. With the advice of the Executive Council he could convoke the House of Assembly in emergency and fill vacancies which occurred prior to a general election. He issued all commissions, civil and military, under his hand and the great seal of the State. Except when the Council was considering laws and ordinances submitted by the House of Assembly the Governor was to preside at all Council meetings. The Governor was elected annually by ballot and not eligible for office more than one year of three. During his term of office he could hold no military position and had to reside at such place as the House of Assembly should elect. No one could be Governor who had not been a resident of the State for three years.

The Executive Council had to meet the day after election and select a president from its own membership. It had power to appoint its own officers and make its own rules of procedure. In all deliberations of Council the vote was taken by counties and not by individuals.

Each member of Council within three days after a measure was discussed and decided could have his protest formally entered.

During sessions of the Assembly it was the duty of all members of the Council to be present in order to examine laws and ordinances submitted by the House of Assembly. Laws and ordinances so submitted must be returned to the House of Assembly within five days with any remarks the Council saw fit to make concerning them. Committees from Council sent to the House with proposed amendments to any law or ordinance were required to deliver their reasons for such amendments, "sitting and covered," the house at the time, with the exception of the Speaker being uncovered.

In the absence of the Governor, or during his illness, his power was exercised by the President of the Executive Council. Communications from the House to the Governor or to the Executive Council were delivered by committees. Messages from the Governor to the House were delivered by the Secretary of Council and those from the Council by a committee of that body.

The Governor, during his term, was Captain-General and Commander-in-Chief of the militia and of the military and naval forces of the State.

All commissions given to militia officers were valid only during good behavior of those commissioned.

The militia, in counties with a population of two hundred and fifty men or upward capable of bearing arms, was to be organized in one or more battalions. Where the number of people liable to military duty in a county was less than 250, independent companies were to be formed.

A Superior Court of general jurisdiction was established in each county with two sessions a year, and all causes between parties in the same county must be tried in that county. Matters in dispute between parties living in different counties must be tried in the county where the defendant lived, except in cases involving the title to real estate, in which a judicature must be sought in the county where the land was situated. Breaches of the peace, felonies, and treason were tried in the county where the crime was committed. Where the population of a county was not enough to form a court for the trial of causes arising within the county those causes could be tried in the county next adjoining in which a competent court could be found. The bench of the Superior Court was composed of a Chief Justice and any three or more justices living in the county. In the absence of the Chief Justice the senior local justice on the bench acted in his place.

A remarkable provision was made for appeals to a special jury. In that case the jury was to judge of the law as well as the facts.

Captures by sea or land and maritime cases were to be tried by a special court convened by the Chief Justice in the county where the captures were made or the cause of action arose. Quick determination was provided for and the procedure conformed to that of the Superior Court. Grand Juries consisted of eighteen members, any twelve of whom could find a bill.

Courts of conscience were continued with a jurisdiction of ten pounds.

Executions exceeding five pounds, except in the case of a court merchant, could be stayed until the first Monday in March, provided security was given for payment of the judgment.

Costs of action in the Superior Court were limited to three pounds and no case could remain pending longer than two terms. Every State officer could be called to account by the House of Assembly and each county was required to keep public records.

Entails were forbidden. The estate of a person dying intestate was equally divided among the children, the widow taking a child's share or dower at her option.

In each county there was a register of probates appointed by the Legislature to prove wills and grant letters of administration.

All civil officers in the counties were chosen annually on the day of the general election, except justices of the peace and registers of probates, who were appointed by the House of Assembly.

Schools were to be established in each county and supported at the expense of State.

Courthouses and jails were to be built in each county at the expense of the State

Free toleration of all religions was guaranteed, provided they were not repugnant to the peace and safety of the State. The support of religious teachers was entirely optional.

Permission to plead and practice in the courts of Georgia was to be obtained from the House of Assembly and that body could suspend for malpractice. Every freeman could appear in court and conduct his own case.

Excessive fines and inordinate bail were forbidden and the principles of *habeas corpus* were made a part of the Constitution.

The freedom of the press and the right of trial by jury were to remain forever inviolate.

No clergyman was allowed a seat in Legislature.

Amendments to this Constitution could be made only upon petition from a majority of the counties and those petitions in each case had to be signed by a majority of the voters in the counties from which they came. When such petitions were submitted it was the duty of the House of Assembly to call a convention of the people to pass upon the amendments proposed.

The minutes show that on January 24, 1777, a committee of seven was appointed to reconsider and revise the Temporary Constitution of 1776. This committee was chosen by ballot and Button Gwinnett, William Belcher, Joseph Wood, Josiah Lewis, John Adam Treutlen, Henry Jones and George Wells were elected.

Button Gwinnett was chairman of the committee and it is said that he did most of the work in drafting the Constitution, which reflected his political philosophy and that of the liberal wing of the Whig party of Georgia, of which he was then the leader.

The committee evidently lost no time in its work, for on January 29, only five days after its election, Mr. Gwinnett brought in their report and it was read the first time. It was read the second time on January 30, the third time on January 31, and on February 1 was considered by the convention paragraph by paragraph. This consideration continued on February 3 and 4 and on February 5 the Constitution was read the last time, unanimously adopted and five hundred copies were ordered printed. The act of distribution for estates made in the reign of Charles the Second and the *habeas corpus* act were printed and distributed with the Constitution.

**The Great Seal**—The fifty-seventh section of the Constitution of 1777 created a great seal as follows:

"The great seal of this State shall have the following device; on one side a scroll, whereon shall be engraved, 'The Constitution of the State of Georgia'; and motto, *'Pro bono publico'*; on the other side an elegant house, and other buildings; fields of corn, and meadows covered with sheep and cattle; a river running through the same, with a ship under full sail; and the motto, *Deus nobis haec otia fecit.*"

This seal is said to have been designed by Button Gwinnett.

**Fort McIntosh Captured**—For the protection of the Southern frontier, Fort McIntosh had been built on the north side of Satilla River on high ground about eighty yards from the water's edge. There a stockade was built one hundred feet square with a bastion at each corner and in the center a block-house which served both as a magazine and a shelter for the garrison and with it there was a tower for defense. Naturally, a fort so far south in an exposed position would be hard to hold against a strong enemy, but it was built there at the request of the owners of large herds of cattle, which ranged between the Satilla and Altamaha rivers. This fort was for the protection of their property.

Captain Richard Winn, a young officer distinguished under Colonel Moultrie at the bombardment of Fort Moultrie, commanded the garrison consisting of forty men from the 3d South Carolina Regiment and twenty of the Continental troops belonging to the Georgia Brigade.

Lieutenant-Colonel Elbert received information that a strong force of five hundred men from Florida commanded by Colonel Fuser, assisted by the notorious Tory officers Brown, McGirth, and Cunningham, with Loyalists, British regulars and Indians, was marching from St. Augustine toward Georgia. At dawn on February 17, 1777, Colonels Brown, Cunningham and McGirth, with seventy Florida rangers and eighty Indians, attempted to surprise the garrison at Fort McIntosh. They made a hard fight for five hours and were gallantly repulsed by Captain Winn and his small force. At the end of that time the Florida officers demanded unconditional surrender of the fort, threatening death to the whole garrison if it was refused. Captain Winn proposed a suspension of hostilities for an hour, that he might consider the matter. At the end of that time he replied "I have considered your proposition and am bound in honor not to comply. Should we fall into your hands we shall expect to be treated as prisoners of war." This was delivered to Colonel Brown by Sergeant Hollis. In reply Colonel Brown handed him a copy of Lord Howe's proclamation, asking him to present it to Captain Winn.

Hostilities began again and continued until late in the afternoon. Brown then posted guards around the fort and under cover of night withdrew his command a short distance. In the fort one man had been killed and three wounded.

When dark came Captain Winn sent Sergeant Owens to Colonel Francis Harris, commanding at Fort Howe, telling his critical situation and asking that reënforcements be sent at once and saying that the fort would hold out as long as possible and when assistance came the garrison would attack the enemy. Sergeant Owens reached Fort Howe at daylight on the eighteenth, but Colonel Harris had only forty men fit for duty and was unable to go to the relief of Fort McIntosh.

In the meantime Colonel Brown was reënforced by two hundred men coming under Colonel Fuser, and at nine o'clock on the eighteenth the attack on the fort was renewed, and the Indians, hiding behind logs and stumps, got near the fort and by accurate fire upon the loop-holes greatly annoyed the defenders.

Captain Winn's men withstood the attack until three o'clock, when he received a second demand for surrender. To gain time he spent two hours in consultation. At length, receiving no aid from Fort Howe, with ammunition nearly exhausted and only one day's provisions, he proposed a personal conference with Colonel Fuser midway between the fort and its besiegers. Articles of surrender were drawn up and agreed to except one proposed by Captain Winn, which provided that for the safety of the prisoners against Indian treachery, a full company of British regulars should escort them to the Altamaha River opposite Fort Howe and the British Commander should be responsible for the conduct of the Indians and the Florida Rangers toward the prisoners. Colonel Fuser rejected that, saying that he would not be responsible except for the behavior of the British regulars. Captain Winn then declined to surrender and said he did not doubt that he was able to defend the fort until he was reënforced. He reminded Colonel Fuser that the garrison of a fort on the border of Canada which surrendered under similar circumstances was murdered by Indians and called his attention to the known cruelty of Brown, Cunningham and McGirth and the savage disposition of Cussuppa, the chief who commanded the Creek Indians.

When Captain Winn returned to the stockade and told his men what had occurred they strongly endorsed his action and united in the determination to die honorably in defense of the fort. As hostilities were about to be renewed, Colonel Fuser reopened the negotiations and finally consented to include Captain Winn's article in the terms of surrender. The garrison agreed not to take up arms until regularly exchanged and for the faithful observance of the agreement Lieutenant John Milton and Lieutenant William Caldwell were surrendered as hostages. It was understood that all privileges due to their rank as commissioned officers in the Continental Army should be accorded. Taken to St. Augustine these gentlemen were confined in the castle for nine months.

About sunset of February 18 the fort was evacuated and surrendered by Captain Winn and Lieutenant Toles. Their side arms were returned to them.

Marching under escort as agreed, Captain Winn went about two miles in the direction of Fort Howe and encamped. Early in the evening the British officers and soldiers of the guard began returning to their camp near Fort McIntosh. Remonstrance against this strange action was treated with contempt. By ten o'clock all the escort had gone and the Americans were left alone. Suspecting treachery, Captain Winn roused his men and passing through forests and swamps they reached Fort Howe the next morning at ten o'clock, after a forced march of thirty-five miles.

The news of this disaster spread rapidly through Georgia and men able to bear arms rallied to the support of Colonel McIntosh, who was in the field and advancing towards the Altamaha River. General Robert Howe, who had succeeded General Charles Lee in command of the southern department, being notified of the pending invasion, went to Savannah and left instructions with Colonel Moultrie to send a strong detachment to Georgia. Lieutenant-Colonel Marion with six hundred men, four field pieces, an ample supply of ammunition and provisions, reached Savannah on February 28, but in the meantime Colonel McIntosh with the 1st Battalion of his brigade and other troops hastily collected had met the enemy who were surprised at this unexpected strong attack and abandoned the expedition, retreating into Florida.

There was general alarm in Georgia and renewed hostilities were expected. A large part of the militia of the State was ordered into service and the rest instructed to hold itself in readiness to assemble at a moment's warning. In the meantime a camp was established at the Midway meetinghouse in Liberty County.

As the planting season was coming on and country members of the Assembly had to return to their plantations and some of the Council of Safety had left Savannah, it was difficult to get a quorum for action. Under these circumstances six members of the Council, Button Gwinnett, Jonathan Bryan, Benjamin Andrews, John B. Girardeau, Adam Brisbane and William Bryan signed the following paper, giving unusual power to Archibald Bulloch, President of the Senate:

"His Excellency the President is hereby desired to take upon himself the whole Executive Powers of Government, calling to his assistance, not less than five persons of his own choosing, to consult and advise with, on every urgent occasion, when a sufficient Number of Councillors cannot be convened to make a Board. This Power to continue for the space of one month from the date hereof Feby. 22, 1777."

This unusual action met neither objection nor criticism. The times were unusual. There was great danger, and there was hazard in delay when prompt action was necessary to the public safety. The prudence, wisdom, courage and patriotism of President Bulloch were conspicuous and the people trusted him with absolute confidence.

Then a great tragedy intervened. President Bulloch died within a week unexpectedly. The exact date is not known, but it was between the 22d of February and the 1st of March. He was an unusual man. Of commanding presence, great firmness and force of character, he was loved and respected by men of all political parties as no other leader in Georgia was at that time and his death removed a strong influence which had kept down dissension and united all factions in support of the cause of liberty and independence. As the grant of supreme power to him was made by the Council on February 22, 1777, he must have been alive then, but as two military commissions issued on February 24 were signed by Button Gwinnett as President of the Council of

Safety it is probable that Bulloch's death occurred suddenly between those dates.

Archibald Bulloch was a great figure in times that tried men's souls and he left a great name which has been further distinguished by his descendant, Theodore Roosevelt, President of the United States, the son of Martha Bulloch, who was married to Theodore Roosevelt, Sr., at Roswell, Georgia. Archibald Bulloch was buried in the old Colonial Cemetery at Savannah in the family vault.

A few days after President Bulloch's death the Executive Council met and on March 4, 1777, commissioned Button Gwinnett, one of its members, President of Georgia and Commander-in-Chief.

# CHAPTER LII.

## *Gwinnett's Rise to Power—His Fatal Duel With McIntosh*

Button Gwinnett had now reached the highest office in Georgia which came to him unexpectedly through the sudden death of President Bulloch. His career was a remarkable one. Born in England of Welsh parentage in 1732, the son of a minister, he was a man of fine physique, well educated and of good address. Beginning life as a merchant at Bristol, England, he came to America and settled at Charleston, where he began business as a merchant. Attracted by the growing importance of Georgia, he moved to Savannah and established a mercantile business there. Some quaint advertisements, which he published then, show that he dealt in general merchandise, and it appears that he was prosperous as a merchant. In 1768 he made a venture of great risk by the purchase of a large part of St. Catherine's Island and stocking it with cattle. This involved him deeply in debt, which was a heavy burden to him for some years. As Sunbury, in the Midway District, was near Gwinnett's home on St. Catherine's Island, he was there often on business and made the acquaintance of Dr. Lyman Hall, a leader in the movement for independence, and no doubt it was due to Dr. Hall's influence that Button Gwinnett became active in the cause of liberty. They served together as delegates in the Continental Congress and those two with George Walton were the signers of the Declaration of Independence for Georgia.

Gwinnett's first public service of any importance was as a delegate from the Parish of St. John to the Provincial Congress, which met in Savannah in January, 1776. By that body he was elected a delegate to the Continental Congress with Archibald Bulloch, John Houstoun, Lyman Hall and George Walton. In that Congress in addition to his part in the Declaration of Independence, Button Gwinnett was active in framing the articles of confederation for the Colonies and in securing the resolutions of the Continental Congress authorizing the enlistment in Georgia of a regiment of rangers, two battalions of infantry and two companies of artillery to garrison forts at Savannah and Sunbury, and the construction of four galleys, the forts and galleys to be built at the expense and under the direction of the Governor of Georgia.

In October, 1776, while retaining his position as a delegate to the Continental Congress he became a member of the Georgia Council of Safety and was active in framing the Georgia Constitution of 1777. At the time of President Bulloch's death Button Gwinnett was President of the Council of Safety.

**Antagonism Between Gwinnett and McIntosh**—By this time sharp antagonism had developed between Button Gwinnett and Lachlan McIntosh. As the result of resolutions adopted by the Continental Congress and the action of the Georgia Assembly three battalions of infantry and a squadron of dragoons were added to the Georgia troops, serving in the Continental Army and were formed into a brigade. For the command of this brigade with the rank of brigadier-general, Lachlan McIntosh and Button Gwinnett were candidates and McIntosh secured the appointment. His commission as brigadier-general was dated September 16, 1776.

The historians, Hugh McCall and Colonel Charles C. Jones, severely criticize Button Gwinnett for his attitude toward General McIntosh as the result of his failure to secure the brigadier-generalship. There were two sides to the matter with substantial evidence going to show that Button Gwinnett had good reasons for his unwillingness to trust General McIntosh with the troops which invaded Florida soon after Gwinnett became President of Georgia. First we will give the other side.

Hugh McCall, whose *History of Georgia* was published in 1811, had this to say on the subject:

"Jealousies arose between those who were placed at the heads of the different departments; particularly between the civil and military. President Gwinnett and General McIntosh had been candidates for the appointment of brigadier-general, to command the four continental battalions or regiments, raised and to be raised in Georgia. The friends of these gentlemen had warmly interested themselves for their favourite candidate, and some ill-natured comments had escaped from them, respecting the political and military talents of each other. McIntosh was finally the successful candidate. Gwinnett had the address to gain over to his interest, a large majority of the executive council; and in order to mortify the military pride of his adversary, endeavoured to impress the public mind with the dangerous consequences of vesting military commanders and courts-martial with the exercise of any power which could be withheld from them and exercised by the civil authority.

"This ill-judged system was often complained of by General Washington, who frequently felt the baleful effects of its influence. The exercise of the powers assumed by Gwinnett over the army produced the contempt and disrespect of some of the inferior officers toward the general and destroyed the basis of military discipline. . . . . Gwinnett projected an expedition against East-Florida, which he contemplated carrying on with the militia and continental troops, and without consulting General McIntosh upon the subject, or giving him the command of his own brigade."

**President Hancock Charges George McIntosh With Treason**—Now let us examine the evidence before Button Gwinnett as President of Georgia, which caused him to withhold from General McIntosh the command of the expedition against Florida. That expedition began early in May. Nearly two months before it started, President Gwinnett received, on March 16, the following letter from John Hancock, President of the Continental Congress, written early in January, but apparently two months in transition:

"BALTIMORE, January 8, 1777.

"SIR,

I have the honour to inclose you a copy of an intercepted letter from the Governor of East-Florida to Lord George Germaine, containing, among other things, the most convincing proof of the treasonable conduct of Mr. George McIntosh of your State. This Gentleman it seems, is a Member of the Congress in Georgia, and under that character is secretly supporting, by every act in his power, the designs of the British King and Parliament against us.

"The United States of America have hitherto suffered extremely from the misrepresentation of their enemies, but much more from the baseness and perfidy of their pretended friends. I have it therefore in command from Congress to request that you will cause the said George McIntosh to be immediately apprehended, and take every other step in this matter which shall appear to you to be necessary for the safety of the United States of America. I have the honour to be, with great respect, Sir, your most humble servant.

"To the Honourable the President
and Council of the State of Georgia. JOHN HANCOCK, President."

**Resolution of Congress Concerning McIntosh**—The action of Congress on which President Hancock acted was the following resolution adopted on January 1, 1777:

"An intercepted letter from Patrick Tonyn, Esqr., Governor of East Florida, to the right honorable Lord George Germaine, dated St. Augustine, 19th July, 1776, being laid before Congress,

"Resolved, That a letter be written by the President to the president and council of the state of Georgia, enclosing a copy of the said intercepted letter, recommending to the said president and council, that they proceed immediately to apprehend and secure George McIntosh and take such effectual measures therein, as they shall judge necessary, for the safety of the United States of America."

**The Intercepted Letter**—The following extract from the intercepted letter of Governor Tonyn of East Florida to Lord George Germaine gives the basis of the Action of Congress and President Hancock:

"I had also the honour to write your Lordship that I expected from sundry places supplies of provisions, but have not so effectually succeeded in any of them as I have in those taken up by Mr. Panton. He has now brought four hundred barrels of rice into St. John's River, a thousand more are shipped, and expected to arrive every hour. Mr. Panton executed this business with great hazard to life and fortune. He has been greatly assisted by Mr. George McIntosh, who is compelled to a tacit acquiescence with the distempered times, and is one of the Rebel Congress of Georgia, intentionally to mollify and temporize, and to be of all the service in his power. I am informed his principles are a loyal attachment to the King and Constitution. He would, my Lord, be in a dangerous situation was this known."

With these actions by the Congress and the President before him as official communications, President Gwinnett had good reason to be careful about entrusting the command of an expedition against East Florida to the brother of a member of the Georgia Provincial Congress who was charged with treason by the President of the Continental Congress upon a statement by the Governor of Florida.

Light is shed upon Governor Tonyn's statement about McIntosh by this remark of Hugh McCall in his history:

"The loyalists, who had fled from the Carolinas and Georgia, found a secure retreat in East-Florida and the southern settlers in Georgia had been frequently disturbed by the predatory incursions by these banditti who bore the name of "the appalachian rangers." In another page McCall makes this statement:

"The strength of East Florida consisted of loyal refugees from the two Carolinas and Georgia."

Concerning the charge against George McIntosh, McCall says:

"A brother of General McIntosh who had embarked with great zeal in the American cause, had engaged in a speculation with a British merchant, and dispatched some vessels laden with rice and flour to Surinam, for which he had a license from the committee of safety. The British merchant (Panton) had procured other clearances from St. Augustine, for the same vessels, to proceed to British ports. If this circumstance was known to Mr. George McIntosh, Mr. Houstoun, and Mr. Bailie, who were concerned in the speculation, it was a direct violation of the resolution of Congress, which prohibited all intercourse with the enemy. In order to mortify General McIntosh, and destroy his influence and military pride, his brother became an object of Gwinnett's particular resentment and persecution. His utmost exertions were used to make unfavourable impressions on the public mind, against the political principles of the general; asserting that it was dangerous to entrust him with a military commission of such high grade."

It appears that the accounts of both McCall and Colonel Charles C. Jones in which they severely criticize Button Gwinnett, were not justified by the facts, for with the communication from the President and the action of Congress itself before him charging George McIntosh with treason and demanding that the President of Georgia have him arrested, President Gwinnett could hardly fail to comply with such a demand coming from so high a source.

The McIntoshes were men of means and connected by marriage with some of the most influential leaders in Georgia, including members of the Executive Council which elected Gwinnett President. George McIntosh owned a plantation on the Sapella River, married a daughter of Sir Patrick Houstoun, a neighboring planter, and thus became the brother-in-law to John Houstoun, one of the delegates to the Continental Congress. George McIntosh had acquired considerable property and was backed by strong influence. Lachlan McIntosh in early life went to Charleston and entered the service of Henry Laurens who afterwards became President of the Continental Congress. He was taken into the family of Laurens and given opportunity for development. Some years afterward he returned to the Altamaha region where he married and became a land surveyor. In that pursuit he had the opportunity to acquire valuable tracts of land which gave him wealth. Both he and George were active in the early part of the revolution, had been members of the first Provincial Congress and of conventions in which they represented the parish of St. Andrew. George McIntosh had been a member of the Council of Safety, sitting there at times with Button Gwinnett. They were neighbors, as St. Andrew's Parish adjoined that of St. John's where Gwinnett lived. McIntosh was allied through family relationships and military connections with the conservative section of the Whig party, while Gwinnett was the leader of the Radical Whigs. George McIntosh was present in the Council of Safety on March 4 when Gwinnett was elected President but refused to sign his commission. It was only twelve days later that President Gwinnett received President Hancock's letter, charging George McIntosh with treason.

President Gwinnett directed Colonel Hovenden to arrest George McIntosh and the prisoner was brought to Savannah and delivered to the Provost Marshal who was directed to put him in irons and imprison him in the common jail. Gwinnett held that as McIntosh was charged with treason against the United States he should be put in irons.

Putting in irons a leading man and a member of the Council of Safety related to three members of the board and the friend of others, threw the city into an uproar, as the reason for the arrest was not then fully known.

Friends of McIntosh offered bail of 50,000 pounds, which was refused by Gwinnett. They then got together the out-of-town members of Council. Gwinnett laid before them the communication he had received from President Hancock and the action of Congress on the subject. After these documents were read and considered, Council directed that the irons should be removed from McIntosh. John Houstoun, his brother-in-law, stated that he was in a dangerous state of health and would die if he remained in the common jail before he could be brought to trial. On this statement by a member of Council that body ordered McIntosh released. The next day when President Gwinnett was absent in Sunbury on business connected with the expedition against Florida, the Council met, called McIntosh before it and after hearing his side of the story released him on bail of 20,000 pounds, signed by four members of the Council, Adam Fowler Brisbane, Jonathan Bryan, John Houstoun, and William LeConte, besides other citizens.

The offense charged against George McIntosh was that he knowingly shipped rice from his plantation to a British Colony in a vessel which had been cleared for Surinam in Dutch Guiana. There were three partners in the venture, Sir Patrick Houstoun, Robert Baillie and William Panton. Of these Robert Baillie and William Panton were tories and Sir Patrick Houstoun's attitude toward the Colonial cause was a matter of doubt.

According to Colonel Charles C. Jones the matter came up in this way. In May, 1776, William Panton who had been a merchant in Savannah, but was then engaged at an Indian trading post on St. John's River in East Florida, brought into Sunbury a quantity of goods, such as cloths, osnaburg, salt, sugar and other things. As there was a great demand for these commodities, he asked permission from the committee of safety to sell them and buy rice on condition that he would give bond and security according to the resolution of the Continental Congress that the rice and other produce would not be landed at any port subject to the Dominion of England. George McIntosh, Sir Patrick Houstoun and George Baillie had bought goods of considerable amount from Panton. Having received from the Committee of Safety licenses to ship rice which they owned to Surinam with the understanding that the provisions of the intercourse acts should not be violated, they gave to Panton in payment for the goods bought of him bills of exchange on their consignee in Surinam. Panton also became interested in some of the rice. Regular clearances were obtained for the vessels containing the rice from the customs officer at Sunbury and they set out for Surinam. At the mouth of Sapella River they were boarded by William Panton who claimed that the cargoes belonged to him and ordered that the destination of the vessels be changed. A brig was directed to proceed to the West Indies and the schooner to St. Augustine. The sloop was sent to St. John's River.

Colonel Jones says the masters of those vessels subsequently testified that although these orders were against the instructions of the shipper, when informed that Panton held bills of exchange drawn against the proceeds of the cargoes, they consented to obey his directions.

Colonel Jones shows his bias in the following statement:

"On the 8th of January, 1777, McIntosh was seized by order of the President and Council and lodged in the common prison. Gwinnett was then President and gladly availed himself of the opportunity thus afforded to mortify General Lachlan McIntosh and vent his wrath against him upon his brother."

Colonel Jones makes an error of two months in that statement. George McIntosh was not arrested until after President Gwinnett had received from John Hancock, President of the Continental Congress, a letter charging McIntosh with treason. That letter reached Gwinnett on March 16, 1777.

Concerning the further proceedings, Colonel Jones says:

"When interrogated by the friends of McIntosh, Panton confessed that George McIntosh was a man of honor, that he believed him to be 'sincerely attached to the rights and liberties of America,' and that he was not chargeable with the deviation in the voyages of the vessels. Many depositions were taken before Judge Glen, in behalf of McIntosh, to invalidate the suggestions contained in Governor Tonyn's letter to Lord George Germaine. Baillie and Houstoun were both 'placed upon the bill of confiscation and banishment,' and McIntosh was 'rigorously prosecuted.' While he was in confinement awaiting a trial, his property was dissipated. When admitted to bail he set out to lay his case before the Continental Congress. In passing through North Carolina he was pursued and arrested by a party under the command of Captain Nash, who had been directed to overtake and conduct him as a prisoner to the Continental Congress. He did not arrive at the seat of government until the 9th of October. Upon submitting his memorial, fortified by many affidavits and commendatory letters from Jonathan Bryan, John Wereat, Henry Laurens, and other prominent individuals who believed in his innocence and regarded his prosecution as inspired and urged by the enemies of his brother, General Lachlan McIntosh, congress appointed Messrs. Adams, Duane, and Williams to examine into the matter and report their conclusions. In the execution of the duty thus devolved upon them the committee, on the ensuing day, reported that after investigation they were satisfied no sufficient cause had been shown to warrant the detention of Mr. McIntosh."

**A Second Invasion of Florida Fails**—Within two months after Button Gwinnett became President of Georgia a second invasion of Florida was projected. Colonel Charles C. Jones, who was a severe critic of Gwinnett, and evidently friendly to McIntosh, had this to say about the origin of that ill-fated expedition:

"Anxious to signalize his administration by a feat of arms, he planned an expedition against Florida. The prospect of retaliation was pleasing to the public, and in the breast of the President there lurked an ambitious hope that he would be able to overrun and subdue that sparsely populated Province and annex it to Georgia. Instead of intrusting the command of the expedition to General McIntosh, who, as the ranking military officer of the State, was entitled in all fairness and in accordance with custom to expect and to claim it, Gwinnett, heaping affront upon affront, set him aside and determined in person to lead the expedition. His purpose was to form an invading army with the militia and continental troops without consulting General McIntosh on the subject or even allowing him to accompany his brigade."

This is in strong contrast with the account given by Charles Francis Jenkins in his *Life of Button Gwinnett.*

Mr. Jenkins says of Gwinnett's course:

"From undoubted intelligence, he believed that the garrison at St. Augustine would long before now have been evacuated and East Florida joined to Georgia, if it had not been clandestinely supplied by its friends in Georgia with rice, corn, and cattle. It was this growing scarcity of supplies which had caused the various incursions into Georgia, to punish and prevent which the present expedition had been undertaken by the state."

The correctness of President Gwinnett's views was made clear within a year by the desertion of 500 Loyalists from South Carolina and Georgia, who marched through the State, plundering as they went, and joined the British in East Florida. The Loyalists remaining in Georgia were a great source of danger, concealed enemies who saw what the patriots were doing and informed the enemy of it.

Gwinnett's idea was that the expedition against East Florida should be led by General Howe, the commanding general of the Southern Department of the Continental Army, and he gave substantial reasons for not wishing General Lachlan McIntosh to command that movement.

On this subject Mr. Jenkins says:

"When the accusations against George McIntosh were made public property, on March 18th, the general sought a private interview with the President to ask whether there were any charges against General Lachlan McIntosh, to which the president replied in the negative, but pointed out the nearness of his connection with the prisoner, the danger from the warmth of private resentment, the uneasiness of the people and the lack of confidence they would have in the commanding general. Gwinnett requested, on these accounts, that General McIntosh might be removed from his command and sent to another state, but General Howe took no action. At the meeting of the Council held at this time, General Howe informed them that he had no intention of an expedition against East Florida, that the troops were needed in South Carolina, that he intended returning to Charleston, but that he would leave Colonel Sumter's battalion, which, the next day, he ordered to proceed to Sunbury. As he sailed away with the troops which had accompanied him, reports were received of two men having been killed on the Altamaha, and that the enemy were driving off cattle from Beards Bluff."

The Georgians were surprised and sadly disappointed at the unexpected departure of Howe. "He came, he saw and left us in our low estate," says Gwinnett. The old question of the subservience of the military to the civil authority no doubt influenced Howe. Gwinnett says, in a letter which he wrote John Hancock, president of Congress on March 28, 1777:

"In the Declaration of Independence, it was alleged against the British tyrant, 'That he had affected to render the military independent and superior to the civil power.' I am very sorry to observe that something like this has appeared in General Howe's conduct, for tho' he found the situation of this State rendered an expedition to East Florida absolutely necessary and was also particularly informed of the distress of the Floridians, yet, finding the Council had deputed the President of this State, after they thought they could obtain no assistance, to proceed on this expedition, he appeared no way willing to concur and assist in the measure, but raised several chimerical difficulties and rather seemed to obstruct the attempt. However, the true friends of this state are fully convinced that their safety and political happiness depend entirely on our present exertion and that if we succeed in this affair, it will be doing a great service to the American cause in general. St. Augustine has been as it were the key to the Continent, whither the Tories have fled from all parts of the Continent and by that place they have maintained a correspondence with Great Britain to the great prejudice of the United States."

Commenting on this letter Mr. Jenkins says:

"Gwinnett's reasoning would seem to be correct. He was proceeding under the direct orders of the Convention and of the Council. He had importuned General Howe to come and command the expedition and on the eve of its departure had placed in his hands incriminating documents relating to the brother of the general who would succeed General Howe should the latter leave the state. These accusations were clear and emphatic, and from no less an authority than the Continental Congress. Is it any wonder that he and the majority of his associates in the Council of Safety lacked confidence in General McIntosh, and that they were unwilling the expedition should proceed under his command, experienced and brave officer that he was?

"But that it was personal ambition on the part of President Gwinnett that originated the expedition, that in the beginning he had expected any closer connection with it than the presidents of councils of safety and conventions were accustomed to take in the military operations in their respective states, is certainly not demonstrated by the facts, too long slumbering in the musty archives and sadly overlooked by the early historians. Notwithstanding the fact the Council of Safety was filled not entirely by his friends and partisans, and they were willing to place the direction of the expedition in his hands, and through the unusual combination of circumstances he became, in fact, what he was in name, 'Commander in Chief of the military and naval forces' of the state of Georgia."

As to the prospect of success for that expedition Mr. Jenkins says: "If ever a military expedition was foreordained to failure, it was that planned by the Council of Safety of Georgia for the reduction of East Florida in the spring of 1777. The hasty return of General Howe to Charleston, withdrawing his troops, set the seal of inexpediency on the undertaking. The dissensions among the leading men of the colony over the George McIntosh affair, the taking of control of the expedition by President Gwinnett at the direction of the Council, with its retinue of jealousy and distrust, the season of the year with high waters, heat, and general unhealthfulness, were all elements which augured ill for a successful issue.

"The military authorities, the conservatives generally, and those not blinded by the desirability of reducing East Florida, were greatly concerned. There were not enough troops in the state for its defense, and to risk their battalions on a foray that showed more zeal than prudence was to them the height of folly. General Robert Howe in a letter to Washington gives the reasons why he would not or could not undertake the Florida expedition of 1777. He estimated that at least four thousand continental soldiers would be needed for the reduction of St. Augustine."

May was a bad time for the expedition. For success it should have been in winter when the climate was favorable. The experience of the previous year showed that, for at one post where there were five hundred men only seventy were fit for duty. More of the militia would be available in the winter when there was little work on the farm, but in the spring and summer the presence of the men on the farm was necessary for making crops.

In spite of these difficulties the expedition was thought necessary for the protection of Georgia, and President Gwinnett did his best to organize and equip it. He assembled at Sunbury one fourteen-gun sloop, two smaller sloops of eight and ten guns each, and three galleys each mounting a gun and swivels. He sent a messenger to Charleston asking for the frigate *Randolph* and the sloop *Hornet,* but they were not given him.

The expedition consisted of two divisions, the mounted militia under Colonel Baker, going by land, and the Continental troops to embark at Sunbury on the vessels Gwinnett had gathered there. The two divisions were to meet on May 12, 1777, at Sawpit Bluff, at the mouth of Sawpit Creek, seven miles north of the St. John's River, and from there were to advance together for the capture of St. Augustine.

On April 10th the first battalion under Colonel Joseph Habersham and the second under Colonel Samuel Elbert marched out of Savannah and stopped at Sunbury, where General McIntosh established his headquarters. There on the 16th of April he directed all the troops to take the oath of fidelity to the United States before a civil magistrate. The next day he ordered the troops to embark, but for some reason they did not sail for two weeks.

The Council of Safety endeavored to promote harmony and united action by a Council of War, consisting of the Continental and Militia officers. President Gwinnett as Commander-in-Chief called such a council, but General McIntosh did not attend. A second call resulted the same way, and in view of that members of the Council of Safety who were at Sunbury and the field officers of the expedition advised both Gwinnett and McIntosh to return to Savannah and give the command to Colonel Samuel Elbert, the senior colonel of the Continental troops. This was done.

Colonel Elbert was much concerned because his orders to proceed at once with the expedition came from the commander-in-chief and not from General McIntosh, who was his superior officer in the Continental army. He declined to proceed without specific orders from General McIntosh, who then issued the orders. Colonel Elbert had notified both General McIntosh and President Gwinnett as well as the Council of Safety that their orders must come through his superior officer.

On April 27th Colonel Elbert received the orders to move from General McIntosh, and he furnished copies to Colonel Baker, who commanded the militia, and Colonel Sumter of the South Carolina troops, who were stationed at Fort Howe on the Altamaha River. Unfortunately for the expedition Colonel Sumter had been ordered back to Charleston with his men and that weakened the expedition seriously.

Colonel Elbert embarked his regiment on April 30th and sailed the next morning from Sunbury. He anchored that afternoon eight miles from Sunbury opposite St. Catherine's Island.

Colonel Baker had only succeeded in securing 109 men, said to have been mostly from his own county of Liberty. With these he marched to Fort Howe on the Altamaha and found that Colonel Sumter and his battalion had been ordered back to South Carolina. The river was so swollen with spring rains that it took two days to get Colonel Baker's force across. At dawn on May 4th he was attacked by Indians, but drove them off, crossed the Satilla and St. Mary's rivers on rafts, swimming his horses, and reached Sawpit Bluff on May 12th on time.

But Colonel Elbert had not arrived. On May 17th Colonel Baker was attacked by a strong force which compelled him to retreat. Only fifty of his men were in the fight. The rest had fled at the first attack. Colonel Baker barely escaped capture, as one of his men had taken his horse. Eight of the force were killed, nine wounded and thirty-one captured. Two of his captains were taken prisoners and two lieutenants were killed. The whole force was scattered and the few survivors got back through the swamps to Georgia settlements. A few succeeded in joining Colonel Elbert.

In the meantime Colonel Elbert's progress was very slow. By the 12th of May when he was due at Sawpit Bluff he had only reached the mouth of the Altamaha. On the 15th of May Colonel Baker's survivors joined Elbert with news of the defeat of the militia. Elbert's galleys had run aground and he heard the guns of the enemy. His provisions ran low, his scouting parties were attacked and some of them were killed on Amelia Island. Some of his men deserted and he was unable to get the smallest of his vessels through the Amelia narrows. In a council with Commodore Oliver Bowen and officers of the vessels it was agreed that it was impossible to get through the narrows, the flotilla turned northward and Colonel Elbert returned to the Satilla River and stopped there.

Thus the second expedition for the reduction of Florida ended in complete failure.

A year later John Houstoun, who was then Governor of Georgia, undertook another expedition against Florida. It was commanded by General Howe, a Continental officer with a much stronger force, but Houstoun insisted on commanding as the Governor of Georgia. There was mismanagement, disputes over authority, loss of life and failure.

Commenting on this Mr. Jenkins says:

"The story that Button Gwinnett led the ill-fated expedition in 1777 must now forever be at rest. Nor was the setting aside of General McIntosh due to jealousy or the desire for expected glory. Such action was upon the advice if not the direction of members of the Council of Safety and of the field officers of the expedition. A large part of the people of Georgia had lost confidence in General McIntosh's loyalty and integrity. On March 14th President Gwinnett had written General Howe urging that McIntosh be sent out of the state for the safety of Georgia and of the United States, but Howe had taken no notice of this letter except to ask if the general were involved in the George McIntosh affair. The President and his Council of Safety, in their desire to direct the expedition, were doing exactly what the Continental Congress and numerous State Councils of Safety were doing every day. This interference with and direction of military movements and policies by the civil authorities was one of the weaknesses of government of the early days of the Revolution."

**The Duel**—General Lachlan McIntosh had returned from Sunbury to Savannah, and the Assembly which was the first under the new Constitution met about the first Tuesday in May, 1777. Dr. Noble W. Jones was elected Speaker and Samuel Stirk Secretary. The Executive Council, which took the place of the Council of Safety, was selected from members of the Assembly, and consisted of two members from each of the six counties which had ten representatives. Benjamin Andrews was made chairman of the Council.

The most important duty of the Assembly was to elect a Governor, and for that office Button Gwinnett and John Adam Treutlen were candidates. Treutlen was a planter, one of the German immigrants from Saltzburg, Germany, who came to Georgia soon after Oglethorpe first arrived and settled at Ebenezer in what is now Effingham County. He had served with Gwinnett in various public work, the last as a member of the committee which framed the new Constitution. They were friends and members of the same political faction.

Treutlen not only divided the vote of the Liberal Party with Gwinnett, but received votes from conservative Whigs who desired to beat Gwinnett. It is not certain that Gwinnett was an active candidate for the position of Governor, as he was still a member of the Continental Congress, and as such also had a seat in the Georgia Assembly.

There was considerable bitterness between McIntosh and his friends against Gwinnett, and military authorities complained that the civic power meddled too much in military matters, which they claimed destroyed discipline. There was also much antagonism against General McIntosh, and it was claimed by some that he was back of his brother in the shipments of rice to the British garrisons at St. Augustine.

Gwinnett and McIntosh appeared before the Assembly and after hearing them state their cases the Assembly adopted resolutions that "they approved the conduct of Mr. Gwinnett and his Council, so far as these matters had been laid before them."

This action vindicating Gwinnett greatly enraged McIntosh, and in the presence of the Assembly he denounced Gwinnett as a scoundrel. This occurred on May 15, 1777.

Gwinnett consulted his friends and according to the custom of those times he challenged McIntosh to mortal combat. His second was George Wells, a member of the Assembly from Richmond County, and late in the evening Wells delivered to McIntosh a letter from Gwinnett conveying the challenge to a duel to be fought before sunrise the next morning. McIntosh answered that the hour was earlier than he was accustomed to rise, but he would meet when Mr. Gwinnett proposed. Major Joseph Habersham was McIntosh's second, and by an agreement between him and Wells the duel was fought with pistols which McIntosh supplied. The place for the duel was in Sir James Wright's meadow on the outskirts of Savannah.

Early on the morning of Friday, May 16th, Mr. Gwinnett and Mr. Wells found General McIntosh and Major Habersham awaiting them at the appointed place. After politely saluting each other, the General produced his pistols and the charge was drawn to by the seconds to make sure that each weapon was loaded with only a single bullet. A number of curious spectators had gathered on the hillside to view the affair, and the duelists and seconds moved farther away where they were out of sight. When the ground had been selected the seconds asked what should be the distance. Gwinnett replied: "Whatever distance the General pleases." McIntosh suggested "that eight or ten feet would be sufficient." Three paces were stepped off, and Major Habersham requested that another step be added, and that was done making the distance twelve feet. It was then proposed by the seconds that the principals turn back to back and at the signal wheel and fire, but the General answered: "By no means. Let us see what we are about." The principals then took their stand and agreed to fire when the word was given. Both pistols were fired at about the same time. Gwinnett was shot in the leg immediately above the knee. The bone was broken and he fell to the ground saying: "My thigh is broken." McIntosh was shot through the thick of the leg, and not thinking that Gwinnett was worse wounded, asked if his opponent had enough or was for another shot, to which Gwinnett replied, yes, if they would help him up. To this the seconds objected, declaring that both had behaved like gentlemen and men of honor. The General was led up to his fallen foe and both shook hands.

The wounded men were removed to their homes. The weather was hot, and possibly through lack of skill in Gwinnett's physician, gangrene set in, and he died early the following Monday morning, May 19, 1777. McIntosh was confined to his bed for some time, but finally recovered.

It is not known where Gwinnett was buried, but Rev. James Foley is supposed to have been the officiating clergyman. It is said that his grave was in the old Colonial Cemetery, now called Colonial Park in Savannah. His executor provided a gravestone, but that disappeared. In 1848, when a monument to the signers of the Declaration of Independence for Georgia was erected at Augusta efforts were made to find Gwinnett's remains in order that they might rest under that monument with those of his associates, Lyman Hall and George Walton, but without success.

The death of Gwinnett made a great sensation in Georgia and greatly embittered the feeling between the two branches of the Whig party. Those with Loyalist leanings rejoiced over the difficulty of the civil government. Dr. Lyman Hall denounced the authorities for not punishing McIntosh, and urged his arrest and trial for murder. When McIntosh recovered he surrendered to Chief Justice Glen, gave bond, and was afterwards tried and acquitted.

The feeling against the McIntoshes was very bitter. Governor Treutlen wrote President John Hancock, of Congress, telling him the deplorable conditions of affairs in Georgia, and had issued orders to Colonel James Screven, Captain Thomas Scott and Lieutenants Hancock and Cole to conduct George McIntosh to Philadelphia. Mr. Jenkins says that several days were allowed the prisoner to prepare for the journey, but that on the day of their departure General McIntosh through Colonel Joseph Habersham ordered those officers under arrest. Governor Treutlen then chose Lieutenant Ferrell to deliver the prisoner to Congress, but George McIntosh had fled and remained in hiding for some time, but finally made his way to Philadelphia, where a committee of Congress, after reading letters of commendation from his friends recommended his discharge.

In his letter to John Hancock Governor Treutlen said:

"We are surrounded with enemies on every side, and our small friends the Tories, within our bowels, are so very numerous and have such ties of consanguinity that all our efforts against these enemies of American freedom have hitherto been languid and ineffectual. While the command of our Continental troops remains in the hands of the McIntoshes, our people will never think themselves safe, and even the inhabitants of East Florida will have nothing to fear from us."

Governor Treutlen's letter reflected a difficult situation. The State was torn by dissension. There was intense feeling against General McIntosh, and a numerously signed petition addressed to Congress repeated the charges against George McIntosh, deplored the death of Gwinnett, urged that General McIntosh be sent out of the State, and said they had never thought him capable of discharging so important a trust nor had he been remarkable for his zeal in the American cause. William McIntosh, who commanded the cavalry, had been obliged to resign because of the clamor of the people and the unwillingness of men to serve under him. Alexander Baillie, a relative, was caught carrying information to East Florida. Another relative named McIntosh was active among the Indians in stirring them up against the Colonists. General

McIntosh had shielded his brother, it was said, and had tried to prevent his being sent as a prisoner to Philadelphia. The signers of the petitions said their motive was not malice, but solely self-preservation and the good of the American cause. They, therefore, asked that General McIntosh be removed from the State on the ground that nothing could be done that would do more to discourage the enemy or be a more deadly stroke to the Georgia Tories. These petitions were signed by many. There were seventy-seven names from Savannah and one hundred and nine from Liberty County, including Lyman Hall, James Dunwoody, later a delegate to the Continental Congress, William Baker, Sr., and William Baker, Jr., and other members of the Council and the Assembly. There were petitions signed from Effingham, Richmond, and Wilkes Counties. In all five hundred and five Georgians signed the petition, which was made more impressive as it was endorsed by the Governor and members of the Executive Council.

It was claimed by General McIntosh that Mrs. Gwinnett had said he was innocent and blameless, but this does not agree with a letter she wrote to John Hancock, President, and other members of the Congress. In that letter she urged that General McIntosh and Colonel Joseph Habersham be cashiered from the army for participating with a duel and violating the rules of war.

The paper sent on by Governor Treutlen and letters from Mrs. Gwinnett were read to Congress on October 1, 1777, and referred to a special committee of three, composed of Henry Laurens, of South Carolina, Dr. Nathan Brownson, of Georgia, and Cornelius Harnett, of North Carolina.

Congress considered the matter on October 4th, and the friends of McIntosh, led by George Walton, then a member of Congress from Georgia, tried to have copies of the charges and evidence furnished to George McIntosh that he might defend himself.

Instead it was moved that the committee of three, to whom letters from the Governor and Mrs. Gwinnett had been referred should be discharged, which would throw the matter again into Congress, and this motion was carried. On October 8th, Congress granted $20,000 of Continental currency asked for by Governor Treutlen and $500 for the expense of his messenger from and to Georgia.

On the next day, October 9th, Congress voted by states, 8 to 2 with two divided, that it had power to try McIntosh. Maryland and Virginia only voted that Congress had no authority to try him, and Georgia only had jurisdiction in the matter.

Another committee was then appointed, consisting of John Adams, of Massachusetts, James Duane, of New York, and William Williams, of Connecticut, who reported the next day that there was not sufficient cause to detain the prisoner, and he was discharged.

General Lachlan McIntosh had asked that his letter of May 30th, telling of the duel and his troubles might be shown to George Walton, when Mr.

Laurens reached Philadelphia. While petitions were being circulated in Georgia asking for McIntosh's removal and before news of them had reached Philadelphia, George Walton introduced in Congress a resolution to the effect that General McIntosh be directed to join the army under General Washington. This was amended and General Robert Howe, at Charleston was directed to order another brigadier to relieve General McIntosh and assign McIntosh to some other command. On August 5th Walton wrote General Washington, asking that he use McIntosh with the army. He told Washington that McIntosh was a man of sense and judgment with great experience and courage, fit to fight under the General. The next day, August 6th, Congress directed General Howe to order General McIntosh to proceed with all possible expedition to headquarters, where his service was necessary. McIntosh served with the army and was on active duty at Valley Forge during the ice and snow of the winter of 1777. The next summer he was given command of the Virginia and Pennsylvania frontiers, where it was thought his knowledge of Indian warfare would be useful.

It appears that McIntosh was not popular in that part of the army, and Colonel Daniel Brodhead wrote Washington that General McIntosh had the ill will of every man in the department. Washington, it is said, made a patient kindly reply, urging that a good understanding be maintained, and saying that while General McIntosh was immediately under him, "his conduct gave me the most favorable impression in every respect."

In 1779 General McIntosh joined the southern army under General Lincoln, and again the Executive Council of Georgia petitioned Congress to send him elsewhere, saying, "the people at large in the state had such a repugnance to him that the militia would not turn out under his command." The General was not removed, however, and took part in the siege of Savannah. He was captured at the fall of Charleston, exchanged for General O'Hart of the British army, and was stationed in Virginia until the close of the war. He returned to Georgia in 1782 and lived there with his family until his death on February 20, 1806. He was elected to Congress in 1784, and served on the commission to settle the boundary between Georgia and South Carolina. He was buried in the Colonial Cemetery at Savannah.

**Gwinnett's Successor In Congress**—On June 7, 1777, the Georgia Assembly filled the vacancy caused by the death of Button Gwinnett, and elected Joseph Wood, of Liberty County, a delegate to the Continental Congress. The delegates then were Dr. Nathan Brownson, Edward Langworthy, Joseph Wood, Dr. Lyman Hall, and George Walton. Of these five, three, Brownson, Wood and Hall were from Liberty County.

## CHAPTER LIII.

# *McIntosh Leaves Georgia—John Houstoun Governor*

**Colonel Samuel Elbert Succeeds General McIntosh**—On the departure of General McIntosh from Georgia Colonel Samuel Elbert, the senior colonel succeeded to the command of the Continental troops in Georgia. Little progress was made by recruiting officers in filling up the ranks of companies in the battalions authorized by Congress. The bounty and pay allowed by the general government for a whole year's service were not equal to the amount offered by militia men for substitutes to take their places for three months. Those willing to enter the army preferred enlisting for a short time with the militia, where they would be near their homes, to being in the regular service for three years, subjected to strict rules of discipline and liable for duty in distant fields.

Another difficulty arose from the depreciation of the paper currency. For a while it was accepted at par in payment of expenses connected with the war, but had rapidly depreciated in value. Although Congress and State Legislatures prescribed penalties for those who refused to receive the paper currency at par with gold and silver when offered in payment for commodities, and denounced as enemies to the cause of freedom all who tried to lessen its value, the large volume of paper money put out in the country, the slender public revenue, the inability of the general government and the States to redeem it in coin, and the impossibility of providing by taxation for the sure payment of so much paper money caused a feeling of distrust in the public mind, and soon showed the visionary basis on which the circulating medium was founded. Privations in the cause of right and honor and country are for a while endured by citizens, but there is a limit to voluntary devotion and self-sacrifice. "History teaches," says Colonel Jones, "that armies, the most enlightened and patriotic, must be properly fed, clothed, and paid, to insure contentment within and satisfaction at home." In the soldier's estimation duty to country is supplemented by no less binding obligations to family. While surrendering his occupation and personal liberty in fulfillment of the one, he may justly expect to be at least measurably assisted in discharging the other. Hence in a general appeal to the arms bearing population of any community for enlistment the recruiting officer must be prepared to tender substantial inducements in addition to a mere invocation to a display of manhood and an exhibition of love of country."

As the war progressed the scarcity of provisions and the knowledge that pay was to be had only in paper currency which was rapidly depreciating, deterred many from enlisting in the Continental battalions.

The commanding officer directed that all the troops as fast as they were enlisted be forwarded to posts on the Altamaha River. Twenty of these on the way to Fort Howe, while only two miles from that place, were attacked by one hundred and fifty Loyalists and Indians as they were crossing a swamp. Only six of the men and Lieutenants Brown and Anderson escaped. Fourteen were killed. Hearing of this disaster Colonel Screven collected the southern militia, called Lieutenant-Colonel John McIntosh and his regulars from Darien, and went to the scene of action. The dead lay unburied, scalped, their bodies ripped open, their intestines scattered about on the ground, and their faces so mangled that few of them could be recognized.

On the night of July 31st a party of Indians crossed the Ogeechee River, near Morgan's Fort, rushed into the house of Samuel Delk, who was not at home, killed and scalped his wife and four children, and led his eldest daughter, a girl of fourteen, into miserable captivity. She was never heard from afterwards.

On August 10, 1777, boats from a British armed vessel in St. Andrew's Sound, landed on St. Simon's Island. Their crews captured and carried away Captain Arthur Carney, five citizens, several negroes, and as much household furniture as they could carry in barges. Carney, a captain in the 4th Company of the 1st Continental Battalion of Georgia troops, after his capture joined the enemy, and proved not only an active Tory, but a great cattle thief.

These instances show the bloody and cruel nature of the warfare against Georgia, and the character of the enemy which desolated the southern border.

**An Attempt To Unite Georgia With South Carolina**—The General Assembly at South Carolina late in the year 1776 adopted a resolution which stated that a union between South Carolina and Georgia would promote their strength, wealth, and dignity, and insure liberty, independence, and safety. Commissioners were sent to Savannah to treat with Georgia, and of this commission William Henry Drayton is said to have been the chairman and spokesman. Reaching Savannah in January, 1777, he presented his argument for the union of the two States to leading men. The result he stated as follows in a letter written to Humphrey Wells, of Augusta, from Snow Hill, South Carolina, on June 8, 1777:

"Every gentleman in public office with whom I conversed was strongly against the union. However, I had the pleasure to find some gentlemen of fortune, though not in office or convention, who heartily approved the measure." While he was in Savannah the convention met and he was given an audience at his earnest request. For an hour he addressed the body, arguing that although Carolina and Georgia, originally one, were now under separate government, nature, climate, soil, productions, and kindred interests, all demanded that the union should be restored; that if they remained apart jealousies and rivalries would spring up to the prejudice of internal improvements, common productions, and foreign commerce; dangerous disputes would arise respecting boundaries, and the navigation of the Savannah River; and that the value and security of property would be seriously imperiled. A union established, all rivalries and dangers would cease, agriculture, internal trade, and foreign commerce would rapidly increase; the expenses of government would be lessened, and the stability of the consolidated commonwealths be confirmed. To Georgia especially would the suggested union prove most beneficial. Carolina planters would be encouraged to cross the river and fill the land with substantial improvements. Georgia currency, hitherto inferior in value, would be put on a par with that of Carolina. The Savannah River would be cleared of all obstructions, and the commerce of the town of Savannah be rapidly and vastly enhanced. While Georgia would lose the seat of government, prosperity would be so essentially promoted that this trifling circumstance would be speedily forgotten. Should Georgia decline to accede to the proposition the Carolinians, who possessed both intelligence and wealth, would speedily build a city opposite Savannah which, attracting to itself the commerce, both internal and foreign, of the region, would quickly work the ruin of that town. With such arguments Mr. Drayton tried to persuade the convention to sympathize with the views of the South Carolina Legislature. The members heard him patiently and respectfully, but rejected the proposition for union. President Gwinnett, Dr. Noble W. Jones, and all the leading spirits were radically opposed to the scheme on both material and constitutional grounds, and the effort of South Carolina to swallow Georgia signally failed.

Up to this point Mr. Drayton had proceeded in order, but mortified at their failure, the Carolinians sought to accomplish their object by propaganda. Petitions prepared in Carolina and freely distributed in Georgia heaped odium on Governor Treutlen and his Council, magnifying existing grievances, attempting to create dissatisfaction in the masses, and urging the people to take action that would result in the union of the two States as the surest means of self-preservation.

Seeing the malign influence exerted by the South Carolinians and the unrest caused by these inflammatory documents, whose circulation was prejudicial to the peace and welfare of the State, the Executive Council on the 14th of July, 1777, requested Governor Treutlen to issue a proclamation offering a reward for the arrest of Mr. Drayton and those associated with him in that unlawful conduct. Accordingly the Governor on the next day issued this proclamation on July 15, 1777:

"GEORGIA.

By his Honour John Adam Treutlen, Esquire, Captain-General, Governour, and Commander-in-Chief in and over the said State.

A PROCLAMATION.

Whereas it hath been represented unto me, that WILLIAM HENRY DRAYTON, of the State of South Carolina, Esq., and divers other persons, whose names are yet unknown, are UNLAWFULLY endeavouring to POISON the minds of the good people of this State against the Government thereof, and for that purpose are, by letters, petitions, and otherwise, daily exciting animosities among the inhabitants, under the pretence of redressing imaginary grievances, which by the said WILLIAM HENRY DRAYTON it is said this State labours under, the better to effect, under such specious pretences, an union between the States of Georgia and South Carolina, all which are contrary to the Articles of Confederation, entered into, ratified, and confirmed by this State as a cement of union between the same and the other United and Independent States of America, and also against the resolution of the convention of this State in that case made and entered into: THEREFORE, that such pernicious practices may be put an end to, and which, if not in due time prevented, may be of the most dangerous consequences, I HAVE, by and with the advice and consent of the Executive Council of this State, thought fit to issue this Proclamation, hereby offering a reward of ONE HUNDRED POUNDS, lawful money of the said State, to be paid to any person or persons who shall apprehend the said WILLIAM HENRY DRAYTON, or any other person or persons aiding and abetting him in such unlawful practices, upon his or their conviction: And I DO hereby strictly charge and require all magistrates and other persons to be vigilant and active in SUPPRESSING THE SAME, and to take all lawful ways and means for the discovering and apprehending of such offender or offenders, so that he or they may be brought to condign punishment.

Given under my Hand and Seal in the Council Chamber at Savannah, this fifteenth day of July, one thousand seven hundred and seventy-seven.

JOHN ADAM TREUTLEN.

By his Honour's Command,
JAMES WHITEFIELD, Secretary.
*God Save the Congress.*"

To this proclamation Mr. Drayton, on August 1, 1777, wrote a defiant and discourteous reply, in which he charged the Governor with injustice to George McIntosh, and a disregard of the rights of the people of Georgia. He also criticized the Executive Council as well as the Governor for the administration of public affairs and intimated that they were Tories in disguise.

But this foolish rejoinder had no effect. Drayton's scheme had been exposed, and the motives and measures of its supporters had been laid bare. All hope of uniting Georgia with Carolina ended.

**Scarcity of Breadstuffs**—The constant employment of militia and their absence from the farms resulted in a scarcity of provisions, especially breadstuffs, in Georgia, and the condition was so serious that it was necessary for Governor Treutlen to issue a proclamation forbidding the exportation of corn, rice, flour, and other commodities requisite for the subsistence of the people and the support of the troops in the field.

The State currency in the form of Bills of Credit depreciated so rapidly as to cause serious trouble and the Governor found it necessary to issue another proclamation threatening penalties to all who discounted the paper currency. As no provision had been made to redeem those promises to pay, they continued to go down.

**Other Acts of the Legislature**—In order to facilitate the work of the courts and stabilize the situation the Legislature passed an act giving binding force to such statutes passed by the Royal legislatures as were not in conflict with the provisions of the Georgia Constitution or with subsequent State legislation.

A land office was opened and inducements were offered to all who would come in and settle upon the vacant territory.

It was determined to raise two battalions of minute-men to defend the frontiers. The term of enlistment was fixed at two years and large bounties were offered by the State to officers and men. Before these battalions were in the field the protection of the western part of the State was intrusted to Colonel Marbury, who commanded a regiment of dragoons. Later this force was moved south of the Altamaha to guard the cattle there and repel the frequent incursions of the Tory Colonel McGirth.

For the protection of Sunbury a fort was built south of the town on a high point where the high ground ended and wide marshes between the mainland and Bermuda Islands began.

On the 11th of July, when an attack by a French privateer was expected, the Midway people met at Sunbury and raised money for a couple of batteries, and carriages for eight small cannon, which were there. There had been small field works on the bluff which were mentioned by Governor Ellis when he inspected the Province. In 1777 when the meeting was held at Sunbury the planters of Bermuda Island and the Midway District and the citizens of Sunbury contributed to the expense of building and arming the fort at that place. The work was done mainly by slave labor, and the armament was the best that could be secured. Some of the guns probably came from Frederica. The guns were small, 4-, 6-, 9-, 12-, and 18-pounders, with one or two 24-pounders. The fortification was called Fort Morris, but when captured by the British the name was changed to Fort George.

At the beginning of the Revolutionary War the coast defenses of Georgia were in bad condition. Most of the forts were in ruins. In 1773 Governor Wright reported that Fort George on Cockspur Island was built of mud walls faced with palmetto logs, almost in ruins and garrisoned only by an officer and

**Bulloch Hall, with Mittie Bulloch as a bride, mother of Theodore Roosevelt. and her husband. Theodore Roosevelt, Sr.**

thirteen men. Fort Halifax, at Savannah, was built in 1759 and 1760, made of plank filled in with earth and unfit for use. Fort Frederick, built by General Oglethorpe, at Frederica, when his regiment was there, had no garrison for eight years when the Revolutionary War came on, and although some of its tabby walls remained, the structure was passing into decay. Fort Augusta, at the town of that name, was made of three-inch plank. It had been neglected since 1767, and the planks were rotten. Fort Barrington, on the Altamaha River, was in the same condition. Hardly anything remained of the fort at Ebenezer, Fort William on the southern end of Cumberland Island, Fort Argyle and other defenses built in the early days of the Colony.

Fort Morris, built three hundred and fifty yards south of Sunbury, on a bluff overlooking the Midway River, was intended to protect not only the water approach to Sunbury, but also the back river by which that place might be taken in the rear. Its position was well chosen for defense. To the south was an extensive marsh through which Pole-Haul and Dickerson creeks, tributaries of Midway River, were commanded by guns of the fort. This marsh extended in front of the fort, giving substantial protection against landing parties. This fort, south of Sunbury, was an enclosed earthwork. Its walls embraced the parade ground of an acre and its eastern face fronting the river was 275 feet long. The northern and southern faces were 191 feet and 140 feet long, while the curtain looking to the west was 241 feet long.

Some of the cannon of this fort were still in condition during the War Between the States. Two of them were used as signal guns. Found to be in excellent condition, they were cleaned, mounted on siege carriages, and assigned to Fort Bartow, where they remained as a part of its armament until the evacuation of Savannah by the Confederate forces in December, 1864.

Sunbury was used by Revolutionists as a military post with a garrison in the early part of the struggle for independence. Fort Morris was the most important built by Georgians during the Revolution.

**John Houstoun Elected Governor**—The Assembly met in Savannah in January, 1778, and on the tenth of that month elected John Houstoun Governor. He was the son of Sir Patrick Houstoun, a man of liberal education, strong character, and one of the first in the Colony to urge resistance to British aggression. He had twice represented Georgia in the Continental Congress, and was a member when the Declaration of Independence was adopted. But for the defection of Mr. Zubly, which made his presence in Georgia necessary, he would have been one of the signers of the Declaration of Independence. When elected Governor he was a member of the Executive Council.

At the same session the Legislature elected the following officers: John Glen, Chief Justice; William Stephens, Attorney-General; William O'Bryan and Nehemiah Wade, joint Treasurers; James Maxwell, Secretary; and

Thomas Chisholm, Surveyor-General. James Jones was appointed Collector of Customs for the Port of Savannah, and David Reece for Sunbury. Ambrose Wright was made Commissary-General of the State and Superintendent of Public Buildings in Chatham County.

At the meeting of the Executive Council on April 16, 1778, extraordinary action was taken investing the Governor with almost supreme power. In its preamble and resolutions the Council declared the situation in Georgia so alarming that only the most vigorous efforts could defeat the machinations of the enemy, and in such times of danger everything might depend on instant action which could not be taken if the Governor had to wait to call a council. The action taken by the Council was as follows:

"The Council, therefore, impressed with a sense of the calamitous situation of this State, and apprehending it as an unavoidable expedient, do request that his honor, the Governor, will be pleased to take upon himself to act in such manner as to him shall seem most eligible; and to exercise all the executive powers of government appertaining to the militia or the defence of the State against the present danger which threatens it, or in annoyance of the enemy, independent of the Executive Council and without calling, consulting, or advising with them unless when and where he shall find it convenient, and shall choose to do so. And they pledge themselves to support and uphold him in so doing, and to adopt as their own the measures which he shall embrace; and that this shall continue during the present emergency, or until the honorable House of Assembly shall make an order or give their opinion to the contrary."

Governor Houstoun replied to this remarkable action by Council, saying that he was unwilling to do anything without the approval of Council, but as experience shows it was impossible at all times to get them together, when quick action was needed and as Council had expressed the opinion that its action was justifiable under the Constitution and the meeting of the Assembly was near at hand, and as alarms and dangers appeared to thicken on all sides, he agreed to act as Council requested during the present emergency or until the House of Assembly should make an order or give its opinion to the contrary.

It was indeed a serious situation that confronted Georgia when the Council took this unusual action. The State was threatened by danger from without and within. Not only was there a serious threat of invasion on the southern frontier, but general alarm throughout the State, and this was increased by the desertion of a large body of Loyalists from South Carolina and Georgia. Early in April, 1778, a band of Loyalists from the interior of South Carolina, led by Colonel Scophol, who was described by General Moultrie as an illiterate, stupid, noisy blockhead, assembled near Ninety-six, South Carolina, and crossed the Savannah River forty miles south of Augusta. Here they were joined by a party of Loyalists from Georgia, commanded by Colonel Thomas. Seizing some boats conveying corn and flour from Augusta to Savannah they took all the provisions they needed, burnt the rest and sank the boat.

There were between five and six hundred of these outlaws. They marched rapidly to Florida, plundering and destroying everything in their way as they went through Georgia. The thinly populated districts through which they went could offer no resistance to their movement or their depredations, and they reached Florida in safety. There they joined the enemy and strengthened their determination for a formidable invasion of Georgia.

## CHAPTER LIV.

# *Expedition to Florida Fails*

**Governor Houstoun and General Howe Plan an Expedition into Florida**—East Florida, with strong British forces and hundreds of deserters from Georgia and South Carolina who were exceedingly bitter against their native states constituted a serious danger and a constant annoyance to Georgia. The renegade Loyalists from Georgia and South Carolina who marched through Georgia in April, 1778, added largely to the lawless forces at St. Augustine and they and the Indians subsidized by the British frequently plundered the southern part of the State, driving off cattle to feed the people of East Florida. That Province was strong in military forces but weak in food because it did not produce enough to supply the inhabitants, and as a result predatory bands from East Florida made frequent raids into the country of Georgia which lay between the Altamaha and St. Mary's rivers. St. Augustine was the headquarters of these bands as well as the British forces, and the destruction of that nest of robbers was earnestly desired by the Georgia authorities for the protection of their people. Although the expeditions planned by General Lee and Governor Gwinnett had failed, Governor Houstoun decided to make another trial. Having been invested by the Executive Council with great power it was his idea to plan and conduct an expedition which would put an end to the danger from the south and make Georgia secure so far as that source of trouble was concerned.

The army at St. Augustine had been greatly strengthened by the Tories who went there from South Carolina and Georgia, and with more strength and Georgia apparently weak, the authorities at St. Augustine were encouraged to plan a formidable attack on Georgia.

Definite information of such an invasion was brought to Georgia by James Mercer who sailed from St. Augustine on April 17, 1778, and reached Savannah on April 21. To Attorney-General William Stephens he stated that General Prevost had started with forces for the Altamaha River, that a body of Creek Indians was marching to join him there, and three hundred Loyalists had reached St. Mary's River under command of Colonel Brown, who expected 700 more Loyalists to join him, and the object of combining these forces was the conquest of Georgia.

In a conference with General Robert Howe, then commanding the Southern Department of the Continental Army, he and Governor Houstoun decided to concentrate the military strength of Georgia and resist the threatened attack from Florida. Governor Houstoun proposed that he would personally command the Georgia militia numbering about 350 men, but many of them were poorly armed and lacked discipline. The Continental Forces then in Georgia were about 550 and to these were added 250 Continental Infantry and 30 artillerists with two field pieces from South Carolina, commanded by Colonel Charles Coatesworth Pinckney. The Carolina militia under Colonel Bull and Colonel Williamson were ordered to Purrysburg on Savannah River. For all these forces the point of concentration was Fort Howe on the Altamaha River.

On April 6 Colonel Samuel Elbert, with the 3d and 4th battalions of Continental Infantry, or so much of them as were fit for duty, began to march from Savannah to Fort Howe. Thirty-six rounds of ammunition, three spare flints and two days rations of cooked provisions were carried for each soldier. In addition there was a reserve supply of ammunition carried by the battalions, including one hundred rounds of powder and balls for each man.

At Midway meetinghouse in Liberty County on April 9, Captain Melvin, with twenty-four men, was ordered to proceed to Sunbury, embark there on galleys and go to the Altamaha River where he was to take charge of a large flat and boat, filled with army stores, and conduct them to Fort Howe. On April 14 he reached that post with his command.

On April 10, learning the enemy's vessels were at Frederica, he sent three hundred men, with fifty rounds of ammunition, six days provisions and no baggage but blankets, to Darien with orders to board the galleys there and attempt their capture. At the same time Colonel Elbert led the forces under his command to Pike's Bluff, a mile and a half from Frederica.

**Colonel Elbert Captures the Hinchinbrooke**—In a letter to General Howe, written from Frederica on April 19, 1778, Colonel Elbert reported the capture of three British vessels, describing their action as follows:

"Dear General—I have the happiness to inform you that about 10 o'clock this forenoon, the brigantine *Hinchinbrooke,* the sloop *Rebecca,* and a prize brig, all struck the British tyrant's colors and surrendered to the American arms.

"Having received intelligence that the above vessels were at this place, I put about three hundred men, by detachment from the troops under my command at Fort Howe, on board the three galleys, the *Washington,* Captain Hardy, the *Lee,* Captain Braddock, and the *Bulloch,* Captain Hutcher; and a detachment of artillery with two field pieces, under Captain Young, I put on board a boat. With this little army we embarked at Darien, and last evening effected a landing at a bluff about a mile below the town, leaving Colonel

White on board the *Lee,* Captain Melvin on board the *Washington,* and Lieutenant Petty on board the *Bulloch,* each with a sufficient party of troops. Immediately on landing I dispatched Lieutenant-Colonel Ray and Major Roberts, with about one hundred men, who marched directly up to the town and made prisoners three marines and two sailors belonging to the *Hinchinbrooke.*

"It being late, the galleys did not engage until this morning. You must imagine what my feelings were to see our three little men-of-war going on to the attack of these three vessels, who have spread terror on our coast, and who were drawn up in order of battle; but the weight of our metal soon damped the courage of these heroes, who soon took to their boats; and as many as could, abandoned the vessel with everything on board, of which we immediately took possession. What is extraordinary, we have not one man hurt. Captain Ellis, of the *Hinchinbrooke,* is drowned, and Captain Mowbray, of the *Rebecca,* made his escape. As soon as I see Colonel White, who has not yet come to us with his prizes, I shall consult with him, the three other officers, and the commanding officers of the galleys, on the expediency of attacking the *Galatea* now lying at Jekyll."

Colonel Elbert's success in capturing the *Hinchinbrooke* and two other vessels encouraged him to attempt the capture of the *Galatea,* which was anchored at the north end of Jekyll Island. For this purpose he put men on board the *Hinchinbrooke,* the sloop and the galley, but while he was getting ready for action the *Galatea* sailed off, evidently fearing capture.

The capture of British vessels which had threatened the coast had a good effect upon the militia, and General Howe thought it a good time to make the attack on Florida.

On board the *Hinchinbrooke* three hundred suits of uniform clothing belonging to Colonel Pinckney's regiment which had been shipped south and captured by British privateers were found.

Prisoners taken by Colonel Elbert informed him that General Prevost was marching to attack Georgia and the vessels captured by Colonel Elbert were intended to go to Sunbury and join General Prevost there, the General expecting to capture the garrison at Sunbury. Clothing on board the *Hinchinbrooke* which had been captured from a Continental ship was to be distributed among the Loyalists, some of whom were marching from St. Augustine and others were expected to arrive at Sunbury. With those uniforms and additional forces expected to join Colonel Brown there, his regiment of rangers was to be completed and put into uniform.

General Howe ordered Colonel Pinckney to join him as soon as possible and march his forces to Fort Howe. Before he reached there, Colonel McGirth, with some refugees from Georgia, had reached the Midway settlement. There he was met by a superior force of the Americans and had to retreat to St. Marys. When General Prevost learned of General Howe's movement, he turned his attention to repairing defenses on the St. Mary's and St. John's rivers, preparatory to defending the Province of East Florida. Cannon were mounted at Fort Tonyn which was put in condition for defense. This fort was on the St. Mary's River some distance in advance of his other defenses and the ground was not well chosen either for defense or retreat in case of a siege.

On May 10, 1778, the 1st, 3d, and 6th Continental battalions from South Carolina on duty at Fort Howe were organized as a brigade and placed under command of Colonel Charles C. Pinckney. The artillery from Carolina and Georgia were joined under Major Roman. Colonel Elbert acted as Brigadier-General and appointed John Jones his aide-de-camp with the rank of major. John Hamilton was appointed Brigadier-Major to Colonel Pinckney.

General Howe did not reach Fort Howe until the 20th of May. The condition there was described by Colonel Pinckney in a letter to General Moultrie in which he complained that the South Carolina galley with provisions and a schooner were delayed and many sorely needed articles were missing. In the meantime Georgians were criticizing the General and the army for not marching to attack the enemy and storm his lines without provisions or ammunition. In spite of those difficulties the army intended to march to Reid's Bluff the next day, when the Colonel hoped the provisions and ammunition would arrive and they would proceed to St. Mary's River and attack Fort Tonyn. He said that not withstanding criticisms of the expedition at that time of year the capture of the *Hinchinbrooke* and other vessels and the projected expedition were the salvation of Georgia.

Complaining of lack of supplies, he said:

"I cannot help lamenting that you have been too parsimonious in fitting us out for this expedition. What can be more cruel than crowding eight, ten and twelve men into one tent, or obliging those who cannot get in to sleep in the heavy dews? What is more inconvenient than to have only one camp kettle to tend twelve or fifteen men? And in this hot climate to have one small canteen to six or eight men?"

Colonel Pinckney conveyed the request of General Howe that General Moultrie send by boat or schooner five hundred canteens, one hundred camp kettles and thirty-five or forty tents. He reported a number of desertions from White's battalion of British deserters and enclosed a plan of Fort Howe which he said was badly planned and constructed. He further reported information from St. Augustine that the enemy's force included three hundred regulars at Fort Tonyn, sixty at the St. John's fort, 320 at St. Augustine and 80 south of St. Augustine, with Florida rangers, a few Indians and some Carolina Tories. On this he commented: "Nothing could be more fortunate than such a division in their force."

Then he criticized Governor Houstoun, saying that he had ordered from the battalion two hundred barrels of rice for the militia and ordered the galleys to a point thirty miles higher up the river than Fort Howe, although because of shallow water they could not come within ten miles of Fort Howe. Consequently he asked that if a boat was sent from Charleston with provisions it should come to Sunbury. In conclusion he said that the soldiers were badly in need of medicine, and if it was not sent there would be much sickness and the forces would be reduced. In spite of that they would go on.

In a letter to Henry Laurens, President of Congress, General Moultrie wrote from Charleston on July 5, 1778, saying that he had a letter from General Howe dated Fort Howe on May 23 but it did not give the number of men he had there to which Colonel Moultrie adds "we have sent him six hundred Continentals from this state and Colonel Williamson is gone from Ninety-Six with 800 militia and there are between 600 and 700 Continental troops belonging to Georgia and some militia. With these he intends to proceed to St. Marys to dislodge the enemy from a strong post they have established there. He says that it is absolutely necessary or Georgia may as well be given up."

The army moved from Fort Howe on May 27 and camped at Reid's Bluff. From there on June 12, 1778, General Howe wrote General Moultrie that he was setting off at once on the march to St. Marys. He said that he had been waiting several weeks for the militia but only four hundred had arrived and were encamped four miles in the rear, waiting for a large force led by the Governor. He had heard nothing from the Governor, although he had written him several times on important matters. He thought the Governor was trying to encourage the people and was no doubt greatly perplexed. He wished to see the Governor before moving but could not wait longer. His plan was that the brigade under General Elbert should advance to the Satilla River, take possession of it and throw up works on both sides to protect the advance or cover the retreat of the army. General Howe expected to join General Elbert the second day after he wrote and go to St. Marys where they would be joined by Commodore Bowen with his fleet and attack the enemy.

On June 22 a messenger from General Moultrie informed General Howe that Captain Bachop and Captain Osborne of the British Army who had sailed from St. Augustine on June 12 were captured with their sloops by a Connecticut vessel with 18 guns and brought to Charleston. From them he learned that the enemy 1200 strong had marched out of St. Augustine to meet the Americans and were accompanied by Creek Indians. Two galleys with twenty-four-pounder guns and other heavy cannon had been sent to protect the entrance of the St. John's River. John Glass, a deserter from the 1st Regiment, gave the additional information that the enemy's force consisted of 800 British regulars, one hundred men under Colonel Brown, 150 militia, 300 Schoolites and Indians estimated at from 95 to 200.

After giving this information General Moultrie suggested to General Howe that as a strong enemy force with two field pieces was to meet him at the St. John's River or sooner it would be wise to keep his little army together and not move them by brigades or divisions as that might be dangerous in marching through such a country as they were in. To which he added "I was told yesterday that Williamson with his militia was not above five miles from Savannah and that the Governor with his Georgians was near Sunbury. If this be the case, for God's sake, when will you all join? If you still continue moving from each other, nothing but Augustine castle can bring you up. Would it not be best to halt the front, and let them secure themselves and wait till they all come up, then you may go on slow and sure."

General Moultrie then notified General Howe that the people of St. Augustine were greatly alarmed at the prospect of an attack and were transferring their valuables on ship board; that the outlying defense for protection of the town was entirely out of repair, and the interior line quite feeble; that only a few pieces of cannon were mounted at the gate; that negroes were being pressed to work upon the fortifications; that all detachments had been called in from the St. Mary's River; that the castle was defended by walls 25 feet high upon which were mounted 110 guns and two mortars; that although the garrison of the castle was well supplied with provisions, the population of the town was in want; that there was no war vessel in the harbor of St. Augustine; and that the best method of approach was by the Mosquito Road, thus taking the town in reverse.

General Howe met no resistance from the enemy at St. Marys or Fort Tonyn. They had withdrawn their forces into Florida and covered the approaches to St. Augustine.

In the meantime General Howe's army seems to have been in a bad way, demoralized by delays, disagreements, disappointments and illness.

On July 5 General Howe wrote to General Moultrie telling his troubles. He had waited a long time for the galley and a long time for the Georgia militia and Colonel Williamson with his regiment.

"In short," said he, "if I am ever again to depend upon operations I have no right to guide, and men I have no right to command, I shall deem it then as now I do, one of the most unfortunate accidents of my life. Had we been able to move on at once, and those I expected would have been foremost had only been as ready as we were, a blow might have been given our enemies which would have put it out of their power to have disturbed us, at least not hastily, and have been attended with consequences more important than the most sanguine could have expected. But delayed beyond all possible suppositions, and embarrassed, disappointed, perplexed and distressed beyond expression, the utmost we can now achieve will be but a poor compensation for the trouble and fatigue we have undergone, excepting we may be allowed to suppose (what I truly think has been effected) that the movements we have made have drove back the enemy and prevented an impending invasion of the state of Georgia which would otherwise inevitably have overwhelmed it, and also a dangerous defection of the people of both states. This good, I am persuaded, has resulted from it and this is our consolation."

The enemy at the time General Howe wrote were at Alligator Creek, about fourteen miles from the Americans. The Governor's forces and General Howe's forces were on opposite sides of the river about eight miles apart, but he hoped that they might come together.

General Howe sent mounted men under Colonel Elijah Clarke to attack the enemy after his position had been reconnoitered by a strong force. Colonel Clarke was to attack the weakest point and throw the camp into confusion. Then the main body of the army was to advance rapidly in front and storm the works. Colonel Clarke attacked vigorously but the difficulty was too great. Entangled among logs and brushes it was hard for his horses to get through. When they reached the protecting ditch around the fort it was too wide for the horses to jump over and so deep that they could not go through it. Here men and horses were met with a fierce fire from the enemy and had to retire. In this attack Clarke was wounded, three of his men were killed and nine were wounded. The advance attack having failed the main attack from the front was not attempted and as the British received reënforcements the Americans retreated to Fort Tonyn.

Governor Houstoun with the Georgia militia did not reach St. Marys until the 4th of July and Colonel Williamson and his troops did not come until the 11th.

Here the situation was made worse by conflict of authority. Colonel Pinckney, writing to General Moultrie of the delay of the troops in getting together, said:

**Conflict of Authority**—"After we have waited so long for the junction of the militia we now find that we are to have as many independent commanders as corps; Governor Houstoun declaring that he would not be commanded; Colonel Williamson hinting that his men would not be satisfied to be under Continental Command or any other command but his own; and Commodore Bowen insisting that in the naval department he is supreme. With this divided, heterogeneous command, what can be done? Even if the season and every other military requisite were favorable the Continental troops have been so violently attacked by sickness, and the desolation made by it is so rapidly increasing, that if we do not retreat soon, we shall not be able to retreat at all, and may crown this expedition with another Saratoga affair in the reverse."

He added that they had the strongest ground for thinking that the enemy did not mean to fight Howe's forces seriously north of the St. John's River. That he said would be the most imprudent thing they could do and all their movements showed no such intentions.

In a malarial region, with intense heat, bad water, insufficient shelter and salt meat the health of the command was so injured that half of the men were on the sick list. Many had left Fort Howe because of disease. Thirty-five horses had died for lack of food and those remaining were so feeble that they could not drag the cannon, ammunition, provisions and baggage of the army. The soldiers were dispirited and the command was rent by factions. There was no dominant spirit to unite the discordant elements in a harmonious whole. The army was large enough properly handled and wisely led to have overrun Florida and taken St. Augustine, but Governor Houstoun, with the power conferred on him by his Executive Council, refused to take orders from General Howe; Colonel Williamson's troops refused obedience to Continental officers and Commodore Bowen held his naval forces distinct from and independent of the land service. There was no voice strong enough to command the whole army and enforce discipline under one command.

Under these circumstances a council of war was held at Fort Tonyn on the 11th of July to decide whether the expedition should be abandoned. That council was composed of General Howe, Colonel Elbert, Colonel White, Colonel Tarling, Colonel Rae, Lieutenant-Colonel Roberts, Lieutenant-Colonel Scott, Major Wise, Major Habersham, Major Pinckney, Major Grimkie, Colonel Pinckney, Colonel Eveligh, Colonel Kirk, Lieutenant-Colonel Henderson, Lieutenant-Colonel McIntosh, Major Brown, Major Roman, Major Lane, and Major Low. General Howe opened the Council, frankly stating the situation, going over it in detail and after doing so proposed a number of points to be decided by the Council. The questions and answers were as follows:

1. Had the enemy been forced out of Georgia and Fort Tonyn destroyed?
A. Unanimously decided in the affirmative.

2. As the enemy do not mean to oppose us north of the St. John's River, are there any other objects important enough to warrant our advancing?
Unanimously decided in the negative.

3. Is the army aided by the Governor's militia and Colonel Williamson's force in position to cross St. John's River, attack the enemy and secure retreat in case of action?
Resolved unanimously in the negative.

4. Does the serious sickness of the army render retreat necessary?
Decided unanimously in the affirmative.

The General informed the Council that Governor Houstoun denied him the right to command the militia not withstanding the resolution of Congress that in distant expeditions or other military operations and the mode of conducting them the General or other commanding officer must finally judge and determine at his peril. In view of that he asked these questions, concerning his position as commander:

1. Can he with propriety, honor, in safety to himself, or consistent with the service, relinquish the command to the Governor?
Decided unanimously in the negative.

2. Can the army, while the command is divided, act with security, vigor, decision or benefit to the common cause?
Decided unanimously in the negative.

With these unanimous conclusions by the Council of War, General Howe accepted them and decided to withdraw the Continental Troops from the army.

To that effect he issued the following order:

"Camp at Fort Tonyn, 14th July, 1778.

"Parole, Savannah.

"The General leaves the army today. He parts with it with reluctance, and from no other motive than to make those provisions at proper places necessary to its accommodation. He embraces this opportunity to testify how highly he approves the conduct both of officers and men whom he had the honor to command.

"The readiness with which the officers received orders and the punctuality with which they executed them gave pleasure to the General and did honor to themselves. The cheerfulness with which the men supported a long and fatiguing march under a variety of unavoidable, yet distressing, circumstances gives them an undoubted claim to the character of good soldiers, and is a happy presage of the service they will in future render to the glorious cause in which they are engaged. Commanders of brigades will take care that this order be made known both to officers and men."

With the well men of the Continental forces under Colonel Elbert, numbering about 350, General Howe returned to Savannah. The sick and convalescent were put on galleys and other vessels under Colonel Pinckney and carried to Sunbury. The sea air made a great improvement in them and they speedily recovered. Those able to march were sent to Carolina that way and others were sent by sea. The Georgia militia under Governor Houstoun and the South Carolina militia under Colonel Williamson went home by land.

In spite of the mistakes made and the division of command which prevented complete success the expedition prevented an advance by the enemy from Florida in the near future, but biding their time they prepared for another invasion. In the meantime marauding parties desolated plantations in southern Georgia and the Creek Indians committed robbery and murder on the frontier. Commenting on the result Captain McCall remarked that though the expedition caused the states of South Carolina and Georgia much blood and much treasure, the dearly bought experience had some advantage in the final success of the American cause, because it taught the government and the commanders of armies that it was impossible for an army under many commanders to move with effectiveness. Under the circumstances he thought it was remarkable that they were able to retreat without being cut off.

In spite of the unfortunate end of this expedition the conquest of East Florida was regarded as necessary to the peace and safety of Georgia and it was not given up. Plans were being made for a stronger and better movement in the fall but events of the war of the Revolution took such shape that for the time Georgians and Carolinians were unable to attack St. Augustine.

## CHAPTER LV.

# *War Centers in the South—Savannah Captured*

**Peace Overtures Came Too Late**—England undertook too late to make peace with the American Colonies. The Earl of Carlisle, Sir Henry Clinton and Mr. William Eden, were appointed Commissioners "to treat, consult, and agree upon the means of quieting the disorders now subsisting in certain of the Colonies, Plantations, and Provinces in North America," having failed in their efforts to bring about a pacification, resolved to conclude their sitting and to return to England.

The main reason for their failure was the disasters met by English armies in America. The defeat and surrender of Burgoyne following the brilliant victories of Ticonderoga and Crown Point, Washington's defeat and capture of the Hessians at Trenton, the mismanagement of the war by the home government, its enormous cost, $300,000,000 by 1779, the disastrous effect upon English trade and agriculture resulting from the American boycott, the enmity between Clinton and Cornwallis, the capture of British merchant ships by American privateers and the growing opposition of the English people to the use of Indians and mercenaries in barbarous warfare combined to make the war against America unpopular, and English lawyers were taking the American view against taxation without representation.

In the meantime the growing hostility of France and Spain to England resulted in the formal recognition of the United States by France on February 6, 1778, and was followed by war between England and France, later joined by Spain in favor of the Colonies.

Soon after the Declaration of Independence the American statesmen had wisely begun negotiations for the friendship and alliance of European nations. Congress appointed Benjamin Franklin, Silas Deane, and Arthur Lee Commissioners plenipotentiary to negotiate with the French Court for the purpose of inducing the King of France to join with the United States in a treaty of friendship and alliance.

The Commissioners were politely received at first by the French Premier De Vergennes and secret aid was given the Americans, but for some time a public declaration of friendship for the Colonies was discouraged.

Benjamin Franklin, who was a genius at negotiation and knew best how to win the favor of the French Court, made his address to the Queen and soon became a favorite with her party. As a result the policy of the Ministers changed and the Independence of the United States was acknowledged by the treaty of February, 1778.

Lord North who had supported King George the Third in his bitter antagonism of the American Colonies began to take the view that the war with America was a mistake.

Under these circumstances the English Parliament in February, 1778, took steps to restore the condition of the American Colonies and their relations to Great Britain which had existed before the war and declared its intention not to tax the Colonies. The concession had come too late. Washington expressed the feeling of America when he said, "Nothing but independence will now do." Congress and the American States rejected the overtures of Great Britain. The English Commissioners had on the 3d of October, 1778, addressed to the Continental Congress and the Assemblies of the American states a proclamation for the restoration of ante-bellum conditions. The Continental Congress on the 30th of the same month replied with a manifesto in which they declared "the essential rights of man," "with full confidence in the favorable intervention of Providence in human events which were to be decided by the appeal to arms."

**War Centers in the South**—Overtures for peace having failed and the war having gone badly in the north the British Government decided to transfer active operations to the southern provinces. Lord George Germaine hoped to conquer Georgia and South Carolina and to that end the plan was that General Augustine Prevost should invade Georgia from East Florida and a heavy force commanded by Colonel Archibald Campbell, sailing from New York, was to attack Savannah. Thus it was believed that Georgia would be caught between the upper and nether millstones and would soon be ground down into submission.

In pursuance to this plan General Prevost started two expeditions against Georgia from St. Augustine, one by sea towards Sunbury and the other by land, to march through lower Georgia, laying the country waste and joining the other expedition at Sunbury. Lieutenant-Colonel Fuser commanded the expedition by sea and Lieutenant-Colonel Mark Prevost had charge of the one by land.

Colonel Prevost started with 100 British regulars, was joined at Fort Howe by McGirth with 300 Loyalists, refugees and Indians. On November 19, 1778, this force entered Georgia, making prisoners of all men found on plantations and plundering the people of everything of value which could be moved. Colonel John Baker, who had collected some mounted militia, met Prevost and McGirth at the point where the Savannah and Darien Road crosses Bull Town swamp and after a short skirmish the Americans retreated. Colonel

Baker, Captain Cooper and William Goulding were wounded. At the Riceborough Bridge the invaders were again met but the force was not strong enough to resist them.

In the meantime Colonel John White, who had been stationed at Sunbury in command of Continental troops, with about a hundred Continentals and militia and two pieces of light artillery, built a breastwork across the road at Midway Meeting House at the head of a causeway over which the enemy had to advance. He hoped to hold Prevost in check until reënforcements came from Savannah. A messenger was sent to Colonel Elbert, telling him of the invasion and Major William Baker, with a party of mounted militia, was sent to skirmish with the enemy and impede his progress.

On the 24th of November Colonel White was joined by General Screven with 20 militiamen and they moved their position to a point a mile and half south of the Midway Meeting House, where the road ran through a thick woods and an ambuscade might be stationed. McGirth knew the country and suggested to Prevost placing an ambush at the same point which the Americans had selected for the same purpose. The British and Americans arrived on the ground at the same time and fighting began at once. Early in the action General Screven received a severe wound and fell into the hands of the enemy, by whom he was killed while a prisoner and suffering from a mortal wound.

In that action a shot from one of the field pieces passed through the neck of Prevost's horse and both the horse and rider fell. Major Roman DeLisle in command of the artillery thought the British Commander had been killed and advanced his two cannon to take advantage of the confusion. Prevost soon appeared remounted and advanced with full force. Colonel White, being overcome by numbers, retreated to Midway Meeting House, breaking down the bridges across the swamp as he retired and keeping out small parties to annoy the enemy's flanks. Compelled to withdraw still farther he restored to a stratagem to stop the enemy. He prepared a letter as though it had been written to himself by Colonel Elbert, directing him to retreat in order to draw the British as far as possible, and informed him that a large body of cavalry had crossed over the Ogeechee River with orders to attack the enemy from the rear by which their whole force would be captured. This letter was dropped where it would find its way to Colonel Prevost. He received it and evidently thought it genuine, for it had much influence in retarding his advance, which did not go more than six or seven miles towards Savannah beyond the Midway Meeting House. In the meantime McGirth, with a strong party reconnoitering in the direction of Sunbury, learned that the expedition of Colonel Fuser by sea had not arrived. This fact in connection with the concentration of forces by Colonel Elbert and Colonel White at Ogeechee ferry, where a breastwork was thrown up and preparations were made for vigorous resistance to the invaders, decided Prevost to abandon his invasion and return to St. Augustine.

Prevost treated the people of the country between Sunbury and St. John's River as rebels against their Sovereign, refused any agreement for security of the country, burnt Midway Meeting House and all dwellings, negro quarters, rice barns and improvements within reach on his retreat to St. Augustine. The region was ruthlessly plundered and the path of his retreating army was marked by smoking ruins. His soldiers, being unrestrained, pillaged the country and took plate, bedding, wearing apparel and every valuable thing they could carry, subjecting the inhabitants to insults.

Hugh McCall states in his history that Major John Habersham was sent by Colonel Elbert to propose to Colonel Prevost an arrangement by which the region would be protected from pillage and conflagration, but Prevost declined to agree to security for the country, saying that the people had brought their fate upon them by rebellion against their lawful Sovereign.

Colonel Fuser, coming by sea, had been delayed by head winds and did not reach Sunbury until Prevost had retreated so far that he could not be reached. Late in November, 1778, Prevost's vessels with 500 men, battering cannon, light artillery, and mortars anchored off Colonel's Island, formerly known as Bermuda Island. The land forces and field pieces marched towards Sunbury by the main road and the armed vessels sailed up Midway River and took position in front of the fort and in the back river opposite the town, while the land forces invested it on the land side with the infantry and artillery.

Colonel John McIntosh with a hundred and twenty-seven Continental troops and some militia and citizens of Sunbury, less than two hundred in all, held Fort Morris.

Colonel Fuser sent a letter to Colonel McIntosh informing him that four armies were in motion to reduce the Province of Georgia and resistance would only bring destruction upon the country. On delivery of the fort to him with surrender of arms and an agreement to remain neutral until the fate of America was determined he and the inhabitants of the parish would be allowed to remain in peaceable possession of their property. In a postscript Colonel Fuser said that some of the Americans had been firing on the troops and if a stop was not at once put to that he would burn a house for every shot fired.

**Heroic Reply of McIntosh**—To this insolent demand, Colonel McIntosh made this heroic reply:

"Fort Morris, Nov. 25, 1778.

"Sir,—We acknowledge we are not ignorant that your army is in motion to endeavour to reduce this State. We believe it entirely chimerical that Colonel Prevost is at the Meeting House; but should it be so, we are in no degree apprehensive of danger from a junction of his army with yours. We have no property compared with the object we contend for that we value a rush: and would rather perish in a vigorous defence than accept of your proposals. We, Sir, are fighting the battles of America, and therefore disdain to remain neutral till its fate is determined. As to surrendering the fort, receive this laconic reply: COME AND TAKE IT. Major Lane, whom I send with this letter, is directed to satisfy you with respect to the irregular, loose firing mentioned on the back of your letter.

"I have the honor to be, Sir,

"Your most obedient Servant,

JOHN MCINTOSH,

Colonel of Continental Troops."

In delivering this reply Major Lane told Colonel Fuser that the irregular firing he complained of was kept up to prevent the British troops from entering and plundering Sunbury. In regard to Fuser's threat that he would burn a house for every shot fired Major Lane told him that if he approved a course so inhuman and so at variance with the rules of civilized warfare Colonel McIntosh would apply the torch at his end of the town when Fuser fired it from the other side and let the flames meet in mutual conflagration.

The Legislature of Georgia, honoring the gallantry of Colonel McIntosh on this occasion, voted him a sword with the words, "Come and take it," engraved upon it.

**Fuser Retreats**—Evidently Colonel McIntosh's reply had its effect. Colonel Fuser instead of carrying out his threat waited for a report from the Scouts he had sent out to learn the movements of Colonel Prevost and when they might be joined. Learning that Prevost had retreated and was beyond reach, with surprise and chagrin Fuser raised the siege, reëmbarked his troops and returned to the St. John's River, where he met the retreating forces of Prevost, and it is said that these officers charged each other with responsibility for the failure of that expedition.

On his retreat from Sunbury Colonel Fuser landed his British regulars at Frederica to repair the place and put in good condition the fortifications General Oglethorpe had planned there years before.

General Howe collected his forces and marched to Sunbury where he remained a short time. He pointed out the defenseless condition of the place, informed Congress of the danger which threatened the Georgia coast, the lack of men and munitions of war and the disorganization of the scattered army.

The enemy had left St. John's Parish in desolation. The crops had been burned and many people were left without means of subsistence.

In addition to this the people of Sunbury were greatly annoyed by the bad conduct of troops quartered there and General Howe mentioned this in a general order of January 16th, 1778.

On December 8th, 1778, General Howe wrote General Moultrie from Sunbury a discouraging account of the conditions in Georgia. He said Sunbury could not be defended for half an hour from a strong attack. The enemy was at St. Simon's repairing the fort and the scovilites (renegade Royalists) had been detached to carry their booty into Florida from which place they were to return. He said that unless fortifications were improved

Georgia would be lost but he would do his best to protect it. He asked that Colonel Henderson's regiment be held in readiness to move at first notice and the wagons and other things necessary for the march of troops be immediately gotten ready so that the men needed might move promptly.

The regiments of Colonel Huger and Colonel Thompson already had marching orders and there was to be a concentration of forces at Purrysburg from which point they could advance for relief of any point threatened by the enemies. Colonel Owen Roberts was ordered to hasten forward with his artillery to defend Savannah.

That place had poor defenses. A battery had been thrown up on the east side and a few guns were mounted there but they only commanded the river. From the land side the approach was open and the fortifications built years before by Captain DeBrahm had decayed.

**Campbell's Approach with a Strong Force**—The approach of Colonel Campbell with a strong force to attack Savannah was made known by a deserter from the British ship *Neptune* who was examined by Governor Houstoun on December 6, 1778, and a copy of his statement was sent by fast messenger to General Howe at Sunbury. At the same time General Howe received another message from the south, stating that General Augustine Prevost was about to start from St. Augustine with all his forces in a movement against Georgia.

Under these conditions the militia was called to the field and the Governor directed Captain John Milton, the Secretary of State, to pack at once and remove to a place of safety all the public records of his office. They were conveyed in boats to Purrysburg and from there to the residence of Mr. Bryan. Early in December the first vessel of Colonel Campbell's expedition appeared at Tybee. Because of bad weather they withdrew to sea and at first it was believed that the report of their presence at Tybee was a false alarm. With that idea the Governor ordered the public records returned to Savannah, but before that was done the British vessels returned and Captain Milton took the State's papers to Charleston for safe keeping.

Colonel Archibald Campbell's report to Lord George Germaine written at Savannah on January 16, 1779, stated that on Sir Henry Clinton's orders he had sailed from Sandy Hook on November 27, 1778, with the 71st Regiment of Infantry, two battalions of Hessians, four battalions of provincials, and a detachment of the Royal artillery, en route for Georgia. He was escorted by a squadron of warships under Commodore Parker and the entire fleet with the exception of two sloops reached Tybee Island on the 23d of December. By the 27th of December the fleet had crossed the bar and were anchored in the Savannah River.

Two corps of light infantry were formed from the provincial battalion, one attached to Sir James Baird's company of the 71st Highlanders and the other to Captain Cameron's Company of the same regiment.

Baird's Highland company of light infantry, and Lieutenant Clark of the navy were sent in flat boats on the night of December 27th to seize any persons they might find on the banks of the Wilmington River. They captured two men who informed them of conditions and Colonel Campbell and Commodore Parker landed troops the next day at Girardeau's plantation something less than two miles below Savannah. This was the first bluff near the Savannah River as the region between it and Tybee Island was a continuous marsh.

At noon the man-of-war *Vigilant* with a galley, an armed brig and an armed sloop, followed by the transports from three divisions, went up the river on the noon tide. About four o'clock in the afternoon the *Vigilant* approaching Girardeau's plantation was fired on by the guns of two American galleys, but one shot from the *Vigilant* made them retreat. As evening was coming on and some of the transports were grounded several miles below Girardeau's plantation the debarkation of forces was delayed until the next morning. Then at daybreak the first division of the troops, including all the light infantry, the New York volunteers and the first battalion of the 71st Regiment under Lieutenant-Colonel Maitland landed on the river dam in front of Girardeau's plantation. From there a narrow causeway about eight hundred yards long, with a ditch on each side, led through a swamp towards Girardeau's residence, which stood on a bluff thirty feet above the level of the river. The light infantry under Captain Cameron reached the shore first, were formed and led to the bluff where Captain John C. Smith of South Carolina with forty men were posted. They received the British with a fire of musketry, which killed Captain Cameron and two Highlanders, wounding five others. Rushing forward the superior force of the British drove Captain Smith from his position and he fell back to the main army. The bluff was then occupied by the first division of the King's troops, one company of the 2d Battalion of the 71st Regiment, the 1st Battalion of DeLancey, the Wellworth Battalion, and a portion of Wissenbach's Regiment of Hessians.

A company of the 2d Battalion of the 71st Regiment and the 1st Battalion of DeLancey were left to cover the landing place and Colonel Campbell moved on to Savannah in the following order:

The light infantry, throwing off their packs, in advance. Then the New York Volunteers, the 1st Battalion of the 71st Regiment, with two six-pounder guns, and the Wellworth Battalion of Hessians with two three-pounders. A part of Wissenbach's Hessian Battalion closed the rear. Entering the great road to Savannah Wissenbach's Battalion was posted there to secure the rear of the army. A thick wooded swamp covered the left of the line of march, while the cultivated plantation on the right was scoured by the light infantry.

The open country near Tatnall's plantation was reached about three o'clock in the afternoon and the forces were halted in the highway about two hundred steps from the gate which opened into Governor Wright's plantation. The light infantry formed on the right along the rail fence.

**General Howe's Position**—General Howe had formed his forces southeast of Savannah, awaiting reënforcements of militia and Continental troops from South Carolina. His soldiers had not yet recovered from the effect of the Florida Campaign. A fourth of the Georgia Continentals were prostrated by disease and many of the convalescents were too weak to go into battle. It was impracticable to concentrate the militia.

On the eve of battle the relative strength of the opposing armies was as follows:

General Howe's forces, exclusive of militia, 672 rank and file; the British forces more than 2,000.

On December 28th orders were issued to prepare for action and on the 29th General orders were that the first brigade be tolled off into sixteen platoons of the same number of files. The odd files in one platoon on the right wing of the brigade to act as light infantry.

Two field officers appointed to the command of the right wing of both brigades.

The second brigade to be tolled off into eight platoons of the same number of files to be formed on the left of the first brigade to act as light infantry.

Colonel Isaac Huger was to command the right wing of the army, composed of the first brigade and light troops belonging to it.

The artillery of both brigades was to be posted before and during the action as directed and defend their ground until further orders. When ordered or forced to retreat the artillery was to file into the road leading to the western defile where Colonel Roberts was to take the best possible position to protect the retreat of the line.

Savannah was approached by three main roads, one leading from the high ground of the Brewton Hill plantation and Thunderbolt, forming a causeway where it crossed a morass adjacent to the town, with rice fields to the north and wooded swamps on the south; a second road made by the union of the White Bluff and Ogeechee Ferry highways, coming from the south; and a third road leading westward across the deep swamp of Musgrove Creek, with rice fields on the north and an extensive morass towards the south.

On the morning of the 29th when Colonel Elbert saw the enemy landing he urged General Howe to defend Brewton Hill, then known as Girardeau's plantation, and offered with his regiment to prevent the British from getting possession of it. The strategic value of the bluff was clear and Colonel Elbert's knowledge of the locality would probably have enabled him to defeat the enemy in his attempt at lodgement there. Colonel Jones says that "With surprising stupidity General Howe committed the fatal blunder of rejecting this offer, and formed his army for battle southeast of Savannah along the crest of high ground near the town as it then stood. No position more apt for defense could have been selected in the entire neighborhood than the bluff at Girardeau's plantation. A regiment there posted with a few pieces of field artillery, advantageously distributed along the brow, would have utterly shattered the advancing column of the enemy moving along a narrow rice dam a half a mile long with marsh and impracticable grounds on either hand. Persisting in such a movement, the enemy could have been torn to pieces by the plunging and infilading fire. We marvel at the lack of observation and generalship which permitted such an opportunity to pass unimproved. The disparity of forces rendered it all the more obligatory that every advantage should have been taken of this position. It was the key to Savannah. Once in the keeping of Colonel Campbell, the subsequent reduction of the place by means of the preponderating forces under his command became a matter of only a short time and energetic action. Repulsed from this landing place, and defeated in the effort to obtain a base of operations here, the acquisition of Savannah would have proved to the enemy a far more difficult problem."

General Moultrie condemned General Howe for attempting the defense of Savannah under the circumstances but omitted the special censure which Colonel Jones has above made. General Moultrie said in his *Memoirs of the American Revolution*:

"When General Howe perceived that the British by their movements intended a descent upon Savannah he called a council of war of his field-officers to advise with them whether he should retreat from Savannah or stay and defend the town with his troops. The majority of the Council were of opinion that he should remain in Savannah and defend it to the last. This was the most ill-advised, rash opinion that could possibly be given. It was absurd to suppose that 6 or 700 men, and some of them very raw troops, could stand against 2 or 3000 as good troops as any the British had, and headed by Colonel Campbell, an active, brave, and experienced officer.

"From every information which General Howe received he was well assured that the British troops were at least that number. General Howe should have retreated with his 6 or 700 men up the country, especially as he had certain information that General Lincoln was marching with a body of men to join him, and did actually arrive at Purrysburg on the 3d of January, only four days after his defeat."

**The Battle**—General Howe formed a line of battle across the road which led from Brewton Hill and Thunderbolt to Savannah about eight hundred yards from the gate which led to Governor Wright's plantation. On the right was a brigade composed of regiments of Colonel Huger and Colonel Thompson and commanded by Colonel Huger, its left resting obliquely on the road and its right on a wooded swamp covered by houses of the Tatnall plantation in which riflemen were placed. The other brigade, including parts of the 1st, 2d, 3d and 4th battalions of Georgia Continentals, commanded by Colonel Elbert, was posted on the left, its right resting on the road and its left extending to the rice fields of Governor Wright's plantation. Behind the left wing of this brigade was the fort on the Savannah River bluff. The town of

Savannah with the remains of an old line of entrenchments around it was in the rear of the army. One piece of field artillery was stationed on the right of the line and the other on the left. Where the line crossed the Thunderbolt Road a traverse was thrown up and two cannon were planted behind it. A hundred steps in front of this traverse at a critical point between two swamps a trench was cut across the road to impede the progress of the enemy and about the same distance beyond the trench toward the enemy a marshy screen ran parallel to the American line of battle. Where it crossed the road the bridge had been burned. In this situation General Howe awaited the approach of the enemy. Colonel George Walton informed General Howe that there was a private way through the swamp by which the enemy could move from the high ground of Brewton Hill plantation and reach the rear of the American right, and although Walton urged Howe to have that opening guarded, General Howe gave no attention to the matter and as Colonel Jones says, "thus committing another fatal error."

Learning from an old negro man of the private path leading through the woods and swamp to the rear of the American right, Colonel Campbell at once took the negro, Quamino Dolly by name, as a guide, and the first battalion of the 71st British Regiment was ordered to form on the English right of the road and move up in rear of the light infantry which was extended to the right as though threatening the American left. Taking advantage of a hollow which concealed the movement Sir James Baird was ordered to lead the light infantry to the rear and passing to the left enter the path which led to the rear of the American right. In this he had the support of the New York Volunteers under Colonel Trumbull.

While this was in progress the British artillery, massed in a field fronting the American right and shielded from sight by rising ground, was held ready to fire on the American line of battle or upon any force which might enter the wood to stop the light infantry, and Wellworth's Hessian battalion was stationed on the left of this artillery.

The Americans opened fire with cannon to which there was no reply, but Sir James Baird, with the light infantry, having gained the rear of the right of General Howe's army, moved out of the swamp and attacked a body of militia stationed there to guard the road leading to the great Ogeechee Ferry. This militia was quickly put to flight and at the sound of the guns Colonel Campbell ran his field pieces to the front and opened a heavy cannonade. At the same time he ordered a charge all along his lines. Attacked in front and rear the Americans soon gave way, a retreat was sounded, a panic ensued and the Americans made their way as they could in confusion through Savannah. Before they reached the head of the causeway over Musgrove's Swamp west of Savannah, the only way of retreat, the enemy was in position to interrupt the crossing. By extraordinary effort Colonel Roberts held back the British until the center of the army made its escape but the right flank, between two fires suffered severely. The left, under command of Colonel Elbert, continued to fight so bravely that a retreat by the causeway became impossible. He therefore tried to lead his troops between the Springfield causeway and the river. In doing so he was under a heavy fire from the enemy who held the causeway and the adjacent high ground. Reaching Musgrove Creek, Colonel Elbert found it filled with water by the incoming tide and only those who could swim got across, but they did that with loss of their arms and equipment. The others were either drowned or captured. The Georgia militia, about one hundred strong stationed in rear of the right of the American line on the south common under command of Colonel George Walton, received the attack of the columns led by Sir James Baird. The fight was hot but short. Colonel Walton was wounded, fell from his horse and was captured. Pressed by Sir James Baird from the southeast, this command retreating into Savannah was met by the enemy pursuing General Howe and was killed, wounded or captured. Some of its members were bayoneted in the street.

Seeing Colonel Campbell's success Sir Hyde Parker moved his armed vessels up to Savannah, captured all the shipping at the wharves and cut off Savannah from communication with South Carolina. His squadron captured 126 prisoners, three ships, three brigs and eight smaller vessels. He only lost one seaman killed and five sailors wounded.

Failing to rally his routed army on the high ground west of Musgrove's Swamp, General Howe retreated to Cherokee Hill eight miles from Savannah, where he waited for stragglers to come up. From this point he sent Lieutenant Tennill with orders to Lieutenant Aaron Smith of 3d South Carolina Regiment commanding at Ogeechee Ferry, and to Major Lane commanding at Sunbury, to leave their posts and join the army at Sister's and Zubly's ferries. After a march of thirty-six hours through a swampy region, Lieutenant Smith with twenty men joined the rear guard of the army at Ebenezer.

Persuaded by Captain Dollar, commanding a corps of artillery, and many of the leading citizens of Sunbury who feared the result of withdrawing his troops, Major Lane deliberately disobeyed orders to leave that place. He was captured by General Prevost and on his release and return to the army was tried by Court Martial and dismissed from service for disobeying orders.

From Cherokee Hill General Howe marched up the Savannah River to Sister's and Zubly's ferries where he crossed over into South Carolina and abandoned Georgia to her fate. In this disastrous engagement the Americans lost 83, killed and drowned; 38 officers and four hundred and fifteen non-commissioned officers and privates were captured. Among the prisoners were many sick men who were not in the battle. Forty-eight pieces of cannon, twenty-three mortars, ninety-four barrels of powder, a fort, the shipping in port and the capital of Georgia were taken by the enemy. The British loss was only one captain and two privates killed, one sergeant and nine privates wounded. Colonel Campbell reported that every possible care was taken of the houses and town and few or no depredations occurred and led George Germaine to believe that many of the respectable inhabitants of Savannah flocked to the King's standard, but it appears that the houses of all rebels were given up to plunder and brutal outrages were committed by officers and men. Prisoners were both threatened and persuaded and those who refused to enlist in the British Army were put in prison, where they suffered hardship and torture. Among the victims of such treatment was Rev. Moses Allen, chaplain of the Georgia Brigade, who lost his life trying to regain his liberty by swimming to land, and the aged Jonathan Bryan bent with age and infirmity but resolutely standing by the principles of American liberty.

The weakness and the errors of General Howe were severely criticized and subjected to inquiry by the General Assembly of Georgia. On January 17, 1780, its committee made the following report:

"The committee appointed to take into consideration the situation of the State since the 29th of December, 1778, report that the Capital and troops in this State were sacrificed on the said 29th of December, which was the first cause of the distresses and consequences which ensued. Your Committee are of opinion that the delegates of this State were still further discouraged by the said Major-General Howe crossing Savannah River the next day with the troops that escaped from Savannah, and ordering those at Sunbury and Augusta to do the same; leaving the State at the mercy of the enemy without any Continental troops; instead of retreating to the back country and gathering the inhabitants. The country, thus abandoned, became an easy prey to the British troops, they marching up and taking post at Augusta and sending detachments to every part of the State."

A court of inquiry was held and General Howe was acquitted, but his reputation never recovered from the shadow cast upon it by the loss of the capital of Georgia.

**The Howe-Gadsden Duel**—General Gadsden, of South Carolina, was one of General Howe's severest critics. He published a letter condemning General Howe's conduct with extreme severity and General Howe demanded an explanation. When General Gadsden refused to retract or to apologize a duel followed and General Howe's ball grazed General Gadsden's ear. This circumstance was published in New York, which was then the headquarters of the Royal Army, and Major Andre, afterward executed for his trade with Benedict Arnold, wrote a parody on the duel in eighteen stanzes of satire, one of which was as follows:

Such honor did they both display,
They highly were commended,
And thus, in short, this gallant fray
Without mischance was ended.

# CHAPTER LVI.

## *The Fight to Recover Georgia—Brilliant Victory at Kettle Creek—Campbell Evacuates Augusta*

**General Benjamin Lincoln Commands the Southern Department**—On the 26th of September, 1778, Major-General Benjamin Lincoln was, by resolution of Congress, appointed to command of the army in the Southern Department, and ordered to South Carolina. He arrived at Charleston, and on November 24th was joined by new levies from North Carolina, which added to those remaining in South Carolina, gave him a force of 1,200 men. It was composed of a few regular troops, militia and the North Carolina levies, and he advanced to the relief of Georgia. On January 3, 1779, General Lincoln arrived at Purrysburg on the Savannah River on the Carolina side a few miles above Savannah, where he was joined by General Howe and his suite, who informed him of the defeat at Savannah. On the next day, January 4th, the remnant of General Howe's army joined General Lincoln's force, but that officer was in no condition to advance on the British in Georgia, and established headquarters at Purrysburg on the South Carolina side and awaited reënforcements there.

**Effect of the Defeat at Savannah**—With the British victory at Savannah the eastern part of Georgia fell into the hands of the victors, who soon extended their domination as far as Augusta. Their policy was to force the people to submit and take oaths of allegiance to the British Crown. For those who remained faithful to the cause of liberty and independence the attitude of the victors was cruel in the extreme. Captain Hugh McCall, who was in Georgia during the Revolution, says of the situation there after the fall of Savannah:

"By the defeat of the American Troops at Savannah and the capture of the town by the enemy the future services of a considerable portion of the militia in the eastern part of the state were lost to their country; the distress of their families and the ruin of their fortunes was the lot of those who were brave enough to make further resistance; many of them bowed the neck and received the yoke of the British government.

"When General Prevost had united the troops from Florida with those under command of Lieutenant Colonel Campbell his force consisted of 3,000 regular troops and nearly 1,000 loyal militia. He determined to complete the subjugation of Georgia and establish military posts as far as the populous settlements in the back country extended. He confided the garrison of Savannah and the police of the neighboring country to Lieutenant-Colonel Alexander Innes; he established a post at Ebenezer, twenty-five miles above Savannah, under the orders of Lieutenant-Colonel J. M. Prevost; and advanced Lieutenant-Colonel Archibald Campbell to Augusta at the head of 800 infantry and a party of militia to establish a post at that place and take advantage of circumstances in completing the conquest of the state. With the main body he watched the movements of the American general.

"The families of those who adhered to the cause of their country, either in the camp or on board of prison-ships, were stripped by the British of every article of property, or things necessary for subsistence that could be found; they were obliged to sustain life and cover their bodies with such articles as were providently secreted, or were received from the cold-handed charity of a lukewarm neighbour; and however humble or scanty their morsel, gladly would they have shared it with a father, a brother, or a husband, who was offering his blood for his country, or suffering in a loathsome prison on a small allowance of unwholesome food."

Learning of the suffering of the Americans in captivity General Lincoln, at Purrysburg, wrote Lieutenant-Colonel Campbell, who was then marching toward Augusta and proposed a conference with him at Zubly's Ferry for exchange of prisoners and parole of officers until they were exchanged. Negotiations were agreed to and Lieutenant-Colonel James M. Prevost was chosen to confer with Major Thomas Pinckney on this subject. They had an interview on January 31, 1779, and Prevost proposed that regular troops taken in Georgia, the militia taken in arms and men taken on their farms without regard to age should be considered in the exchange of prisoners, and he submitted a list to show the number. This list contained the names of many who had taken protection and those who had taken the oath of allegiance and joined the King's standard. In exchange it was required that the Highlanders at Fredericksburg be included and that the remainder be completed from the prisoners taken with General Burgoyne.

Major Pinckney proposed that continental officers and soldiers should be exchanged for British officers and soldiers of the same rank and that the militia who were willing to take up arms again should be exchanged in the same way and the aged and those who chose to retire and live peaceably on their farms under the British government should be paroled.

The unfairness and absurdity of Colonel Prevost's proposition was in strange contrast with the just and fair proposition made by Major Pinckney. The negotiations continued five days, but Prevost was inflexible and asked a speedy answer, saying that transports were ready to sail with the prisoners to

New York or the West Indies. Much as Major Pinckney disliked to leave the prisoners under continued suffering he found it impossible to agree to the terms proposed.

Sir Hyde Parker showed his bitterness against the Americans by sending to New York all those prisoners who refused to enlist in the British service. Nine of those prisoners died in one day, and the average deaths for a week were seven a day. Because they refused to enlist with the enemy and fight their countrymen a third of these prisoners lost their lives under the cruel and even brutal treatment to which they were subjected.

They were fed on diseased food, and death must have been a relief to them.

**The British At Ebenezer**—The whole coast of Georgia, with the exception of Sunbury, which soon fell, was overrun by the enemy, whose officers exacted a severe tribute. Writing from Purrysburg, on January 10, 1779, to Colonel C. C. Pinckney, General Moultrie said that thousands of poor women, children and negroes were fleeing from Georgia, they knew not whither, a sad spectacle that moved the hearts of his soldiers.

On occupying Ebenezer twenty-five miles above Savannah the British put up a redoubt within a few hundred yards of Jerusalem Church and fortified it. Mr. Triebner, who had always been loyal to the Crown went to Colonel Innes, told his loyalty and took the oath of allegiance. By his influence other Salzburgers took the oath of allegiance and received certificates guaranteeing protection for their persons and property, but there were some notable exceptions who remained true to the cause of liberty. Among them were Governor John Adam Treutlen, William Holsendorf, Colonel John Stirk, Secretary Samuel Stirk, John Schnider, Rudolph Strohaker, Jonathan Schnider, J. Gotlieb Schnider, Jonathan Rahn, Ernest Zittrauer, and Joshua and Jacob Helfenstein.

Strobel, in his book *Salzburgers and Their Descendants,* says:

"The citizens at Ebenezer and the surrounding country were made to feel very severely the effects of the war. The property of those who did not take the oath of allegiance was confiscated and they were constantly exposed to every species of insult and wrong from a hired and profligate soldiery. Besides this, some of the Salzburgers who espoused the cause of the Crown became very inveterate in their hostility to the Whigs in the settlement, and pillaged and then burnt their dwellings. The residence on the farm of the pious Rabenhorst was among the first given to the flames. Among those who distinguished themselves for their cruelty were one Eichel, who has been properly termed an 'inhuman miscreant,' whose residence was at Goshen, and Martin Dasher, who kept a public house five miles below Ebenezer. These men placed themselves at the head of marauding parties, composed of British and Tories, and laid waste every plantation or farm whose occupant was even suspected of favoring the Republican cause. In these predatory excursions the most revolting cruelty and unbridled licentiousness were indulged, and the whole country was overrun and devastated."

As British posts had been established on the western bank of the Savannah River to prevent American forces from coming over from Carolina Ebenezer was on a military thoroughfare for British troops between Augusta and Savannah, and this was a great annoyance to people of that town. British troops were quartered among them and to avoid the rudeness of soldiers and other impositions some residents left their homes at Ebenezer and settled in the country. As Ebenezer was a point to which prisoners were taken from the surrounding country and sent to Savannah the citizens had to witness a great many acts of cruelty by British and Tories upon the Americans who happened to fall into the hands of the British as prisoners of war. The crowning indignity by the British was in using as a hospital the fine brick church built by the Salzburgers. Later it was used as a stable for horses until the close of the war and the departure of British troops. The church records were nearly all destroyed and soldiers shot at objects in the church. One object, the metal swan (Luther's coat-of-arms), which was on the spire of the church received a musket ball.

**The Fall of Sunbury**—When Colonel Campbell had established posts on the Savannah River for fifty miles above Savannah and had overrun the adjacent territory and reduced it to submission he received news of the surrender of Sunbury to General Augustine Prevost. General Prevost had left St. Augustine with an expeditionary force of more than two thousand men and came by boat to Colonel's Island a few miles below Sunbury, where he arrived on January 6th. On the 7th he enveloped the town with light infantry and his main force came up the next day. Two American galleys and an armed sloop on Midway River cannonaded the invaders without effect. On the night of January 8th the main force came up and batteries were placed to command the town. On the 9th General Prevost called for an unconditional surrender. Major Lane commanding the fort declined and General Prevost began a cannonade. Major Lane responded until he saw that the fort would soon be untenable. After a parley to obtain better terms of surrender but without success hostilities were resumed and finally, another parley being refused, Major Lane surrendered the fort and garrison unconditionally, including seventeen commissioned officers and one hundred and ninety-five non-commissioned officers and privates. With them he surrendered 24 brass cannon, a brass mortar, 20 iron cannon, 824 round shot, 100 stands of case and grapeshot, 30 shells, 50 hand grenades, 180 muskets with bayonets, 12 rifles, 40 fusees and carbines, 4 wall-pieces, and a quantity of powder and ammunition.

Among the Americans one captain and two privates were killed and six wounded. The enemy lost one private killed and three wounded.

The American galleys *Washington* and *Bulloch* were run down to Ossabaw Island, stranded there and burned. Their crews took passage on Captain Salter's sloop which sailed for Charleston, but were captured by a British tender and carried to Savannah. Captain John Lawson, with his sloop *Rebecca,* with sixteen guns, reached Charleston safely.

General Prevost changed the name of Fort Morris at Sunbury to Fort George, and after ordering necessary repairs went to Savannah and took command of all the British forces in Georgia. The Continental officers captured at Savannah, with the exception of those confined on prisoner ships were sent to Sunbury for safekeeping.

The wretched condition of South Georgia at that time is thus described by Colonel Charles C. Jones:

"Southern Georgia was now in a wretched condition. Unable to support themselves amid the destitution, demoralization, and restrictions to which the region was subjected, many of the inhabitants set out for Carolina where, aided by the charity of strangers, they hoped to subsist until the coming season afforded an opportunity for planting and harvesting crops in their new homes. Others, possessing the means of subsistence, were so hampered by royal proclamations and were so preyed upon by foreign and domestic foes that they abandoned the country in quest of peace and security."

Sunbury, which had been the rival of Savannah in commerce, a seat of culture, refinement and wealth, never recovered after its capture by the British. It was a center of extensive trade, a health resort for the Midway people, and its elegant homes were noted for their hospitality. It was the home of two of the signers of the Declaration of Independence, and was a center of the movement for American liberty in Georgia.

**Fighting To Recover Georgia**—General Lincoln had a strong position at Purrysburg, where he could observe the movement of General Prevost, while he awaited reënforcements. At that season of the year freshets in the Savannah River overflowed the swamps and were two to four miles wide for a distance of one hundred miles from the sea. This kept the two armies apart. General Lincoln's strength, according to the reports on the first of February, 1779, was 3,639 men, including 600 Continental troops, 500 new levies and 1,300 effective militia. The remainder were invalids without arms. If all the American troops had been effective veterans General Lincoln's force would have been equal to that of the British, but McCall says that most of his men were militia on whom no dependence could be placed when opposed to a veteran army. "From the equality of the militia with the officers and their independence at home," says he, "they were unwilling to submit to the requisite discipline of a camp; they must know where they were to go, what they were going to do, and how long they were to be absent before they would move, and if not satisfied on these points and permitted to do as they pleased, they would be off, knowing that their punishment for desertion would be but a trifling pecuniary mulct."

These conditions were very embarrassing to General Lincoln and added greatly to the difficulty in meeting a well equipped and disciplined force of the enemy under able officers. Commenting on this McCall says:

"If it should be inquired how such a state of things originated it might be answered that it had its source in the unreasonable jealousy that a majority of the members of Congress entertained of a regular army, which could have been easily enlisted for and during the war. If the army had been engaged for the war at an early period the wisdom of the measure would have been apparent, the economy great, the duration short, and the issue certain; but by the mistaken policy of short enlistments and reliance on militia thousands of lives were sacrificed, millions of dollars worth of property destroyed and expended, the war prolonged, and the liberties of America jeopardized."

These conditions were not confined to Georgia or South Carolina. Washington had to contend with them in the northern part of the Colonies and Congress made his task more difficult by promoting inferior men over officers who had distinguished themselves by great gallantry and ability. Benjamin Andrews, in his *History of the United States,* says that Washington fought England with his hands tied, adding "Congress, too afraid of a standing army, would authorize only a short enlistment, so that Washington had frequently to discharge one army and form another in the face of the enemy. His troops were ill disciplined and scantily supplied with clothing, tents, weapons and ammunition. Skilled officers were few, and these rarely free from local and personal jealousies impairing their efficiency."

With such conditions in the Colonies and notably in Georgia, it seems almost miraculous that the American Colonists won their freedom, and the victories they won in the face of such obstacles and difficulties are a wonderful tribute to the undying courage and extraordinary ability of officers and soldiers.

The action of the British officers indicates the terrible trials and extreme suffering to which Georgians true to the cause of liberty were subjected.

On January 4, 1779, Sir Hyde Parker and Lieutenant-Colonel Campbell, commanding in the navy and army of Great Britain in North Carolina, South Carolina and Georgia, issued a proclamation offering peace, freedom and protection to the King's subjects in America, calling on them to unite their forces under the Royal standard without loss of time, condemning a league with France as a measure that would prolong the calamities of war, promising freedom from taxes by the British Parliament, and offering security in the enjoyment of every privilege consistent with the union of interest "on which their mutual advantage, religion and liberties depended." They promised protection to the persons, families, and property of those who would immediately return, acknowledge allegiance to the Crown and support it with their arms, and the proclamation lamented the necessity of enforcing war measures against those who refused to accept the terms of peace and happiness offered them. Deserters were invited to return within three months from the date of the proclamation, and those of the people who wished to enjoy the benefits of the proclamation were asked to come to headquarters at Savannah and take the oath of allegiance.

On January 11th a second proclamation was issued offering a reward of two guineas for every citizen faithful to the American cause, and ten guineas for every Committeeman or Assemblyman who should be taken and delivered to the commanding officer of any of the King's garrisons.

Prices were fixed for all articles of merchandise, farm products and market vegetables, with punishment for violation of the rules by confiscation of the articles offered for sale. Licenses to trade were given only to those who had taken the oath of allegiance, and a penalty of one hundred pounds was announced for those who dealt with any others but the King's subjects. All exports of produce were prohibited unless accompanied by a certificate from the superintendent of port that such articles were not wanted for the use of the King's troops.

Under these circumstances Georgians true to the cause of liberty were fighting a desperate battle against great odds for the protection of their homes, their families, their property and themselves. Bare existence was a problem and victory under conditions then prevailing was almost a miracle, but in the face of defeat, poor equipment and lack of strong organization they fought on and eventually won. Victories by such leaders as Elijah Clarke, Colonel Elbert and others renewed their courage and inspired them with hope. Hardships almost unbearable were cheerfully borne and difficulties that might have appalled brave men were met with undying courage and overcome by feats of valor, the bare recital of which stirs the blood.

The British officers sent emissaries into the back settlement of South Carolina and Georgia to win over the people to the British standard. In South Carolina they had a man named Boyd, who eventually lost his life in battle against his countrymen, and others of less rank. In Georgia they had a man named Thomas, leader of the renegade Loyalists. Boyd was an Irishman by birth, but had been in South Carolina for some years. He was said to have been bold, enterprising and unscrupulous, and had been in New York, where he had an interview with Sir Henry Clinton. In that interview a scheme of insurrection in the back country of South Carolina was planned, and to be carried out as soon as the British troops got possession of Savannah. When that occurred Boyd was to get his troops together and join the Royal standard in Georgia. Informed of the British success at Savannah by Colonel Campbell he began to put the plan into execution.

Up to this time the Savannah River was the limit of British power. Early in February, 1779, a party of the British under Major Gardiner took boats at Savannah and went by inland water passage to take possession of Beaufort at Port Royal, and establish a post there. They effected a landing, but were attacked and defeated by General Moultrie, with a force of the same size, but nearly all militia of Charleston. In one hour forty of the British were killed and wounded, and more would have suffered but for the scarcity of ammunition which prevented more deadly work by the South Carolinians. The British fled to their boats and returned to Savannah.

**The Burke County Affair**—General Prevost had sent Colonel Campbell to Augusta to establish a post there, and on his way Colonel Campbell detached the notorious colonels Brown and McGirth with 400 mounted militia to make a forced march to the jail in Burke County, and ordered Colonel Thomas to meet them there with a party of Loyalists.

They were met by Colonel Benjamin Few and Colonel William Few commanding militia, who were joined by Colonel John Twiggs with a small force, altogether 250 men. Colonel Brown attacked them and was defeated, losing five killed, several wounded and nine made prisoners by the Americans. Twiggs and Few retreated the next day, expecting that Brown would be reënforced by Campbell. Brown's men were reënforced by two majors with refugees from South Carolina and a detachment under Major Sharp. With this reënforcement he renewed the fight. Twiggs met him and defeated him with greater loss than before and Brown was among the wounded. The dashing gallantry of American leaders was brilliantly exemplified there by Captain Joshua Inman, commanding an American troop of horse. So fierce was their onset that he killed three of the enemy with his own hand.

Colonel Elbert, who had been ordered by General Lincoln to the upper part of South Carolina, crossed the Savannah River and joined Colonels Twiggs and Few. Advancing to Brier Creek they skirmished with Campbell's front and continued harassing him in his progress towards Augusta, expecting that they would be reënforced by Colonel Andrew Williamson from South Carolina and Colonel Elijah Clarke from Wilkes County, Georgia. As Williamson and Clarke were engaged elsewhere and could not come to their relief Elbert and Twiggs retired and Campbell took possession of Augusta the last of January, 1779, established a post there and placed it under command of Colonel Brown.

**Colonel Brown's Revenge**—Colonel Brown had become notorious for his cruelty. Colonel Charles C. Jones says of him: "Before the war he was a resident of Augusta and his conduct and language had been so offensive and insulting to the friends of liberty that he was arrested by the parish committee, tried, tarred and feathered and exposed to ridicule in a cart drawn through the town by three mules. After this disgrace he escaped to the British, swearing vengeance against the patriots. Now in command of the town where he had suffered such indignity he was resolved to gratify his revenge sternly cherished and to repay with interest to the citizens of Augusta the ill usage he had suffered at their hands.

"His first measure was the sequestration of the property of the republican inhabitants. This was speedily followed by an order banishing beyond the limits of Georgia all Whig families. Stripped of their possessions and driven from their homes, exposed to insult and enduring numberless privations, these proscribed Georgians were compelled to journey even to the borders of North Carolina where they arrived half famished, broken down by the fatigue and hardships of travel, and some of them with constitutions so badly shattered that all hope of health and life had fled."

**The Attack On Carr's Fort**—At this time General Lincoln was at Purrysburg on the north side of the Savannah River with 500 Continentals and 2,000 provincials. The main body of the British was at Abercorn. In Savannah they had 1,000 Hessians. At the Two Sisters on the river there were 600 men and 200 guarded Zubly's Ferry. At Ebenezer they had a considerable force. The two opposing armies on the north and south side of the Savannah River were so near that General Moultrie said: "We could hear their drums beat every morn from our outposts, nay, hear their sentinels cough."

Although anxious to relieve Georgia, General Lincoln was too weak to cross the river and attack the British. Many of his troops were undisciplined and without arms. "The North Carolina levies, under command of General Richardson," said McCall in his *History of Georgia,* "were discontented and on the eve of returning home." "From Georgia came no recruit," General Moultrie said, "Most of the inhabitants of that State have submitted quietly to the British Government and I believe they will remain neutral unless we go in with a considerable body so as to insure success."

Under these circumstances General Lincoln remained on the defensive, sought reënforcements and prevented the enemy from crossing the river and invading South Carolina.

A few days after leaving Colonel Brown in command of Augusta, Colonel Campbell early in February, 1779, marched thirty miles toward Wilkes County and ordered Lieutenant-Colonel Hamilton with 200 mounted infantry to go to the frontiers of Georgia and there encourage the loyal inhabitants and disarm the disaffected.

At this time Georgia was completely in possession of the British. Open opposition ceased and Colonel Campbell thought the population would permanently yield to the British Government. Severe penalties were given to those who refused to take the oath of allegiance, and for the property of those who were absent under arms in American forces plunder and burning were the rule.

When the people in Wilkes County learned that the British had possession of Augusta those who were able to move collected their household effects and with their cattle fled to South Carolina. Those who remained got together in forts in small bands for mutual protection. A number who had left their wives and children and servants in safe places gathered under Colonel John Dooly on the Carolina shore of the Savannah River thirty miles from Augusta.

McGirth with 300 Loyalists held a position on Kiokee Creek on the Georgia side and both parties watched the ferries and collected boats found on the Savannah River. Returning to Georgia with a part of his command, Dooly was pursued by Lieutenant-Colonel Hamilton, who pressed him so hard that he fired on his rear as he recrossed the Savannah River below the mouth of Broad River.

Hamilton then encamped with a hundred men on Waters' Plantation three miles below Petersburg. Dooly with an equal force was opposite in South Carolina and there he was joined by Colonel Andrew Pickens, with 250 men of his regiment. As the latter had brought most of the men Colonel Dooly yielded the command to him.

On the night of February 10 Pickens and Dooly crossed the Savannah River at Cowen's Ferry three miles above Hamilton's camp and got ready to charge the enemy the next morning. They were surprised to find that Hamilton, in ignorance of their presence, had left his camp and gone through the country to visit its forts and administer oaths of allegiance to the people he met. Supposing that Carr's Fort would be the first point Hamilton would visit Pickens and Dooly sent Captain A. Hamilton of their force with a guide to move rapidly to Carr's Fort and arrange for its defense with such men as he found there. Pickens and Dooly advanced with their force intending to attack the rear of Colonel Hamilton's party while he was attempting to capture the fort.

Captain Hamilton reached the fort in time to execute his order, but found there only seven or eight old men who were not willing to undertake the defense of the fort.

In the meantime Pickens and Dooly with their force were close behind the British when they entered and took possession of the fort and the British were so closely pursued by the Americans as they went in that they had to leave their horses and baggage outside the stockade.

A brisk fire began from both sides but without effect and the Americans decided on a siege. In order to cut off the water supply from the fort, Captain William Freeman with forty Americans of his company dashed through an open space exposed to fire from the fort and took possession of a log house which commanded the only source from which the British could obtain water. Early in the evening the horses and baggage of the British were taken by the Americans and every avenue of escape from the fort was closed. That afternoon the Americans demanded a surrender of the fort from Colonel Hamilton. He refused to surrender but asked that the women and children within the stockade might be allowed to depart. The Americans denied that as they believed that without food and water the enemy could not hold the fort more than twenty-four hours. Possession of the log house near the water supply gave the Americans command of the tops of the huts inside the fort from which the British fire was most injurious. Everything indicated a speedy surrender of the fort when news was received at ten o'clock that night from Captain Joseph Pickens informing his brother that Colonel Boyd with 800 Loyalists from South Carolina was moving through the Ninety-Six district toward Georgia and destroying by fire and sword everything in his path.

Under these circumstances Colonel Pickens and Colonel Dooly raised the siege and moved against Boyd. Some volunteers offered to set fire to the fort at several points and so compel a quick surrender, but in consideration of the women and children within the stockade that idea was abandoned. Carrying off their wounded the Americans departed, leaving Lieutenant-Colonel Hamilton in the fort without horses and baggage. As soon as Pickens and Dooly were out of hearing Colonel Hamilton left Carr's Fort and retreated to Wrightsborough where he remained a few days and then joined Colonel Campbell at Augusta. In the fight at Carr's Fort the British lost 9 killed and 3 wounded; the Americans 5 killed and seven wounded.

**Colonel Boyd Defeated**—Colonel Pickens and Colonel Dooly recrossed the Savannah River and advanced toward the Long Cane settlement to meet Colonel Boyd. Captain Robert Anderson of Colonel Pickens' regiment, with the aid of Captain Joseph Pickens, Captain William Baskin and Captain John Miller, crossed the Savannah River to prevent Boyd from crossing. They were joined by Georgians under Captain James Little. This party then numbered nearly 100 men fit for duty.

To avoid Pickens and Dooly, Colonel Boyd changed his course and reached the river at Cherokee ford. There on a commanding elevation was a blockhouse with two swivel guns defended by a lieutenant and eight men. Boyd demanded a quiet passage which was refused. He then went up the river five miles and by putting his men and baggage on rafts and swimming the horses got across. His men were instructed to land at different points on the Georgia side. The division of the invaders and the number of tall canes growing on the bank of the river made it difficult for Captain Anderson and his men to make effectual opposition, but they contested the landing of Boyd's forces sharply and about sixteen men were killed and wounded and as many more made prisoners. Among the prisoners were Captain Baskin and Captain Miller. Colonel Boyd's loss was a hundred killed, wounded and missing.

Captain Anderson fell back and joined the forces of Colonel Pickens and Colonel Dooly in pursuit of the enemy. On February 12 the Americans passed the Savannah River at Cedar Shoals and advanced to Fish Dam Ford on Broad River. Their forces had been increased by Colonel Clarke with 100 dragoons and Captain Neal was sent with a party to follow the enemy's rear and by frequent couriers keep the American command posted concerning Boyd's movement.

Moving westward, intending to join McGirth on Little River, Boyd crossed Broad River on February 13, 1779, at Webb's Ferry. Learning this the Americans crossed Broad River and camped for a night on Clarke's Creek within four miles of the Loyalists.

Early on the morning of the 14th the Americans advanced rapidly, moving in line of battle where the ground permitted. A strong advance guard was 150 paces in front. The right and left wings of 100 men each were commanded by Colonel Dooly and Colonel Clarke. The center, 200 strong, was led by Colonel Pickens. Officers and men were confident of victory and eager for action. They soon reached the place where the enemy had camped during the night. Unconscious of danger Colonel Boyd had halted at a farm on the north side of Kettle Creek and turned out his horses to graze among the reeds which lined the swamp. His hungry men were slaughtering bullocks and parching corn. Colonel Boyd's second officer was Lieutenant-Colonel Moore of North Carolina and his third was Major Spurgen. The latter was brave and competent.

Captain McCall was sent to reconnoiter the enemy's position and report full information. Having done so he reported the enemy's encampment at the edge of a farm near the creek on an open piece of ground with a cane swamp on two sides and the enemy was apparently ignorant of the approach by Americans.

The Americans then advanced to the attack and as they got near the camp the pickets fired and retreated.

Colonel Boyd hastily formed his line in rear of the camp behind a fence and some fallen timber. Colonel Pickens, leading the center of the Americans, obliqued to the right to more commanding ground. With some difficulty the right and left divisions forced their way through the cane and came into position. Colonel Boyd defended the fence with great bravery, but was overpowered and driven back upon his main force. In retreating he fell mortally wounded, pierced by three balls through his body and thigh.

The fight was now close, hot and general. Some of the Loyalists, hard-pressed, fled into the swamps and crossed the creek, leaving their horses, baggage, and arms behind them.

After an hour's fight the Tories retreated through the swamp. Seeing on the other side of the Creek rising ground in the rear of the enemy's right on which he thought the Loyalists would try to form, Colonel Clarke ordered his left wing to follow him across the stream. His horse was killed under him, but mounting another he followed a path which led to a fort and reached the side of the hill in time to attack Major Spurgen, who was trying to form his command there. Colonel Clarke then had only a fourth of his division, but the firing attracted the rest of his men who rushed to his support. Colonel Pickens and Colonel Dooly pushed through the swamp and the battle was renewed on the other side of the creek. It was a bloody and obstinate conflict and for a while the result seemed in doubt, but the Americans got possession of the hill and the enemy, routed at all points, fled from the scene, leaving seventy of their men dead upon the field and seventy-five wounded and captured. The Americans lost nine killed and twenty-three wounded.

Victory was largely the result of Colonel Clarke's foresight and activity in checking the attempt to reform on the other side of the creek. If the Loyalists had secured a strong position there the result would have been different. It was a hot battle for an hour and forty-five minutes.

As the guard in charge of the prisoners who had been captured when Boyd crossed the Savannah River heard of the disaster to their main body they surrendered their force of thirty-three to the men they held in captivity, promising that if allowed to return in peace to their homes they would take the oath of allegiance to the government of the Confederated States.

When the battle ended Colonel Pickens called on Colonel Boyd, who lay mortally wounded, and offered him every relief in his power. Thanking him for this kindness Colonel Boyd, though mortally wounded, was still brave and asked the result of the battle. When told that the Americans were victorious he said that the result would have been different if he had not fallen. He said that he had started on this march with 800 men. In crossing the Savannah River he had lost 100 in killed, wounded and missing. In the present action he had 700 men and expected that McGirth with 500 men would join him on Little River either that afternoon or the next morning. The point agreed on for their junction of forces was only six miles from the place where the battle was fought. Speaking of his own condition he said that he had only a few hours to live and asked Colonel Pickens to furnish two men to supply him with water and bury his body after death. Delivering to Colonel Pickens valuable articles which he had on his person he asked that they be forwarded to his wife, with a letter telling her the circumstances of his death and burial. These dying requests were carefully complied with and Colonel Boyd died before morning.

Disheartened by the death of their leader and stunned by the heavy blow which fell upon them unexpectedly, Colonel Boyd's followers scattered in different directions. Some fled to Florida, others went to the Creek Nation, others sought refuge with the Cherokees, others went home and asked mercy of the patriots. A remnant of the two hundred under Colonel Moore retreated to Augusta.

Discouraged by the defeat of Colonel Boyd, McGirth fled to Augusta and joined the forces of Colonel Campbell. The prisoners captured at Kettle Creek were taken to South Carolina, tried, found guilty of treason, and sentenced to death. Only five of the worst offenders were executed; the others were pardoned.

Leaving the field of action, the Americans camped near the present site of Washington in Wilkes County and on the 15th of February, 1779, recrossed the Savannah River. In the affair at Carr's Fort and the battle of Kettle Creek the Americans secured six hundred horses and a large quantity of arms, equipment and clothing.

The effect of this brilliant victory is thus described by Colonel Charles C. Jones:

"This accession to the scanty stores of the patriots was most opportune and valuable. In the general gloom which was encompassing all this victory shone like a star of substantial hope, dissipating despair and enkindling confidence in the hearts of the Revolutionists. From the banks of this insignificant stream, rendered historic by the prowess of Pickens, Dooly, Clarke, and their valiant followers, there arose a martial shout which proclaimed the restoration of Whig ascendancy in Upper Georgia and the discomfiture of the Royalist cohorts. With no uncertain sound did the bugle-blasts then blown summon to further feats of patriotic emprise and admonish the King's officers that Georgia was not wholly within their grasp."

**Colonel Campbell Evacuates Augusta**—The brilliant victory at Kettle Creek was soon followed by aggressive movements threatening Augusta so effectively as to cause Colonel Campbell to evacuate that stronghold. General Andrew Williamson of South Carolina advanced with a part of his brigade and some Georgia militia to a point near Augusta on the Carolina side of the Savannah River and camped there. Colonel Leonard Marbury with fifteen dragoons and a body of militia took position near Brownsborough. Colonel John Twiggs got the militia of Richmond County together, passed in rear of the British forces occupying Augusta and surprised one of their outposts at Herbert's where seventy men were stationed. In his attack on them several were killed and wounded and the rest surrendered.

A reconnoitering party of twenty British rangers under command of Captain Whitley and Lieutenants McKenzie and Hall went to Brownsborough. Learning Whitley's position through Scouts, Colonel Marbury sent Captain Cooper with twelve dragoons to attack the enemy's rear while he advanced in front. Captain Cooper advanced so rapidly that he surprised Captain Whitley at his party at dinner and captured all of them before Colonel Marbury came up. Lieutenant Hall of Whitley's party was a native of South Carolina and formerly in the American service. While in command of a small fort on the frontier of Carolina he surrendered it to the Cherokee Indians and without remonstrance permitted every man, woman and child in the fort to be butchered by the savages. Now he was sent to the jail at Ninety-Six for safe keeping and in due time was tried, found guilty and condemned to be hanged. He was executed on the 17th of April.

Remarkable instances of personal daring and hair-breadth escapes were frequent. To obtain a definite knowledge of the number and position of the enemy at Augusta General Elbert sent Lieutenant Hawkins to secure the information. Nearing an outpost he was overtaken at Bear Swamp by three Tories. It was impossible to avoid them. Advancing resolutely he inquired who they were and where they were going. They answered that they were on their way to join Colonel Daniel McGirth. Hawkins, who was wearing an old British uniform, said he was McGirth and believed they were rebels, and he would proceed to hand them over to his party near at hand. They protested that they were not rebels and to prove the truth of that statement, at Hawkins' suggestion, laid their rifles on the ground and held up their right hands. As they did this Lieutenant Hawkins advanced on them with pistols cocked and presented. Taking up their rifles he ordered them to march in front of him, threatening to shoot the first who attempted to turn. In this manner he marched them to the American camp.

The Tories in north Georgia had been routed and the Americans were increasing in number, more formidable in their action, and Colonel Campbell decided to evacuate his position at Augusta. Late in February, 1779, he began his retreat which did not end until he reached Hudson's Ferry on the Savannah River where Lieutenant-Colonel Prevost had built fortifications for his camp and mounted field artillery. Colonel Campbell left Augusta so suddenly that he did not stop to destroy a large quantity of provisions which he had accumulated there. On the way to Hudson's Ferry he was followed and harassed by small bodies of Americans.

## CHAPTER LVII.

# *Georgia Plundered by British—Heroic Resistance—Two Governors Elected*

**Defeat of General Ash**—While Colonel Campbell was operating in north Georgia, General Prevost thought the time opportune to attack South Carolina and sent Major Gardiner with 200 men to take possession of Port Royal Island. He did not remain there long. Early in February Major Gardiner was attacked by General Moultrie and forced to retire.

When Colonel Campbell retreated from Augusta, General Ash with 2,300 men crossed the Savannah River and pursued Campbell as far as Brier Creek, where he stopped and camped between the Creek and the Savannah River.

At that time General Lincoln was still at Purrysburg with between three and four thousands troops. General Rutherford with 700 or 800 men was at Williamson's house on Black Swamp. General Williamson with twelve hundred men was at Augusta. Having an army of about 8,000 men under his command General Lincoln decided to enter Georgia and expel the British from the State or confine them to a narrow space along the coast. To consider this matter a council of war was held at General Rutherford's quarters on March 1, 1779. Those present were General Lincoln, General Moultrie, General Ash and General Rutherford. It was decided that with the exception of a guard left at Purrysburg all available troops of the army should be concentrated at the point occupied by General Ash from which to begin a march for the recovery of Georgia. At the Council General Ash said he was entirely safe, that his camp on Brier Creek was secure and the enemy appeared to be afraid of him, thinking that his numbers were greater than they were, and all he required was a detachment of artillery with one or two field pieces. To furnish the artillery called for General Lincoln ordered Major Grimkie with two light guns and cannoneers to join General Ash.

Colonel Campbell saw what was intended by General Lincoln and undertook by a rapid blow to prevent the concentration of American forces and defeat the plan to circumscribe the King's troops. He therefore undertook to dislodge General Ash at once.

To this end Colonel Campbell sent Major McPherson with the 1st Battalion of the 71st Regiment, some irregulars and two field pieces toward

Brier Creek Bridge as a feint to attract the attention of the Americans and conceal his main movement which Lieutenant-Colonel Prevost was to lead. Taking the 2d Battalion of the 71st Regiment, Sir James Baird's corps of Light Infantry, three Grenadier companies, Captain Tawe's light dragoons and 150 Florida Rangers and militia, about nine hundred men in all, Colonel Prevost made a detour of forty or fifty miles, crossing Brier Creek above General Ash, to fall upon his rear. Early on the morning of March 2, 1779, Colonel Prevost having moved up the south side of Brier Creek reached the point where he was to cross that stream. As the bridge there had been destroyed he had to build another, and that delayed the passage of the Light Infantry and Cavalry until night, when they crossed the creek and were ordered to cut off all communications with the American camp. By daylight next morning the rest of Prevost's troops with the artillery crossed the creek and moved toward General Ash's army.

Unaware of Prevost's approach, General Ash sent Major Ross of South Carolina with three hundred horsemen to cross the creek and reconnoiter the position of the enemy at Hudson's Ferry thirteen miles away. He expected to be reënforced by General Rutherford and it was his plan to attack the enemy if Major Ross reported that feasible. Ross came in sight of McPherson's command but did not realize the necessity of reporting it to General Ash.

Colonel Leonard Marbury who was guarding the upper path of Brier Creek with his dragoons exchanged shots with the enemy as they passed Paris' Mill. A courier was sent to inform General Ash of this but was captured on the way and the first news of Marbury's encounter with the enemy came through General Elbert. The first positive information Ash received of Prevost's demonstration in his rear came by courier from the advance of Williamson's command. It was quickly confirmed by a messenger from Colonel Smith who had charge of the baggage guard.

General Ash had unfortunately weakened his command by detailing part of it to duty at other points and when the battle began he had only eight hundred men. He had a guard of one hundred men a mile in advance of his camp where the road crossed Brier Creek and it was supported by the light infantry and a four-pounder gun a short distance in its rear.

When he knew of the approach of the British, General Ash ordered the long roll to be beaten and as the men fell in line it was found that they had not been supplied with ammunition. They were poorly equipped, some with rifles, others with shot guns, a few with muskets and some without arms. Line of battle was formed in three divisions, the right under Colonel Young, the center under General Bryant and the left consisting of sixty Continental troops, 150 Georgia militia and a field piece under General Elbert aided by Lieutenant-Colonel John McIntosh.

The advance of the enemy drove in the American picket at three o'clock in the afternoon and Colonel Prevost was ready for action. His Light Infantry with two field pieces formed on the right to follow a road leading to the American camp. His center was composed of the 2d Battalion of the 71st Regiment and some Florida Rangers and Carolina Loyalists preceded by light artillery. His left including 150 dragoons was ordered to turn the American right. Three companies of Grenadiers and fifty dragoons were held in reserve four hundred yards in the rear. Fifty riflemen were posted in ambush at a pass by which the Americans it was thought might attempt to turn the British left and gain their rear.

General Ash advanced to a position a quarter of a mile in front of his camp and there awaited the enemy's attack, with his left on Brier Creek and his right extending to a point within eight hundred yards of the Savannah River Swamp. At four o'clock Colonel Prevost began the fight with artillery 150 yards from the Americans and pressed forward. Ash's center did not stand the shock but broke and fled in confusion. The right soon followed in flight. The left under General Elbert remained and fought so hard that Prevost had to order up his reserve to support his right against Elbert. In spite of the greater number of the enemy confronting him, General Elbert kept up the fight until most of the men in his command were killed, wounded, or captured.

The men of the American center and right sought refuge in a deep swamp near the Savannah River. Those who could swim reached the Carolina shore, but many were drowned in the attempt to cross.

Captain McCall estimated the American loss at 150 killed and drowned, 27 officers and 162 non-commissioned officers and privates captured. General Prevost in returns furnished to General Lincoln on the 10th of March gave the names of 24 officers and 162 non-commissioned officers and privates captured at Brier Creek by the British. General Elbert was one of those captured. These figures do not include officers and men who were drowned while attempting to swim across the river. The British lost only five privates killed and one officer and ten privates wounded. Seven pieces of artillery, a quantity of ammunition, baggage and small arms were captured by the British. Colonel Prevost said that 150 Americans were killed on the field and in the swamps and Captain McCall estimated the same number. The large number killed in that action seemed to verify the report that Sir James Baird during the pursuit of Americans cried aloud to his light infantry, "Every man of you that takes a prisoner shall lose his ration of rum." It is said that a number of the militia who sought refuge in the swamp were bayoncted by the British soldiers. Failing to rally the fugitives, General Ash reported that he had made his escape into the river swamp.

Writing of this disaster in his *Memoirs of the American Revolution,* General Moultrie said:

"General Ash's affair at Brier Creek was nothing less than a total rout. Never was an army more completely surprised, and never were men more panic-struck as General Ash's letter and the evidences at the Court show. The poor fellows! Most of them threw down their arms and ran through a deep swamp two or three miles to gain the banks of a wide and rapid river, and plunged themselves in to escape the bayonet. Many of them endeavoring to reach the opposite shore sunk down and were buried in a watery grave, while those who had more strength and skill in swimming gained the other side, but were still so terrified that they straggled through the woods in every direction. A large body of them were stopped early the next morning at Bee's Creek Bridge, about 20 miles, by a detachment of the 2d Regiment under Captain Peter Horry, marching to camp, who told me he had just heard of the affair at Brier Creek and saw a large body (200 or 300) of the fugitives coming in a hasty and confused manner, most of them without their arms, and Gen. Ash and Bryant with them. He drew up his men at the bridge. General Ash rode up to him and requested that he would stop those men, that they were running away. General Bryant said they were not running away. General Ash insisted they were. Captain Horry then asked of the two generals who was the commanding officer? It was answered General Ash. Then, sir, I will obey your orders, and presented fixed bayonets and threatened to fire upon the fugitives if they attempted to come forward, which stopped them. Afterwards Captain Horry proceeded to camp with his detachment, and Generals Ash and Bryant brought back the fugitives.

"We never could ascertain the number of men that were lost in this unfortunate affair, as many of them made no stay anywhere until they got to their own homes in North Carolina. The loss of arms was almost total, and it was a very serious consideration with us at that time as we could not replace them. Colonel Elbert, with a few Continentals and a field-piece or two, fought some little time, but they were soon surrounded and made prisoners.

"This unlucky affair at Brier Creek disconcerted all our plans, and through the misfortunes of General Howe and General Ash the war was protracted at least one year longer, for it is not to be doubted that had we crossed the river with our army and joined General Ash, which we were preparing to do, we should have had a body of 7,000 men; besides that strong reinforcements were marching to us from every quarter sufficient to drive the enemy out of Georgia; and all the wavering and all the disaffected would have immediately joined us; and it is more than probable that Carolina would not have been invaded had this event not taken place."

A court of inquiry held on the 13th of March including General Moultrie, General Rutherford, Colonel Armstrong, Colonel Pinckney, Colonel Locke and Edmund Hyrne after hearing from General Ash and a number of witnesses held that General Ash did not take the precautions that he should have taken to secure his camp and get prompt information of the enemy's movements, but they acquitted him of the imputation that he lacked courage when he escaped in the swamp.

The complete rout of General Ash's army had a very disheartening effect upon the militia of Georgia and South Carolina. Many who had intended to join the Americans, on receipt of this news returned home. Others who had been undecided which side to take no longer hesitated and sought the protection of the British.

The condition of Georgia at that time was deplorable. British troops within the State numbered four thousand including the 71st Regiment, Baird's Light Infantry, DeLancey's New York Corps, volunteers from New York and New Jersey, Carolina Royalists, parts of the 16th and 60th regiments, two battalions of Hessians, Brown's Rangers, and militia composed of Florida and Georgia Loyalists. At Paris' Mill they established a strong camp defended by guns captured at Brier Creek and two others. A fort was built at Sister's Ferry with two six-pounder guns, two Howitzers and other field pieces. The hill commanding the Savannah River was fortified and guarded by artillery and infantry. Three miles south of Ebenezer there was a battery and a picket and the town of Ebenezer was strongly fortified. Savannah was protected by fortifications with eighteen-pounder guns with an abattis in front. The British were resolved to hold Georgia at all hazards and for the time General Lincoln was staggered by the blow at Brier Creek which crushed General Ash's army.

Following up the victory of Brier Creek Colonel Campbell appointed three commissioners of claims to open an office in Savannah and take possession of all land and negroes belonging to men who were active in opposing the King's Government. Provision was made to use the negroes in cultivating the land, with the idea that the net proceeds of the crops would be used to pay the expenses of the King's troops. Some of those who had submitted to the rule of the Crown hoped that by this means they would be relieved of taxation, but that proved to be an illusion.

**An Indian Uprising**—After the defeat of Colonel Boyd at Kettle Creek a number of Georgians who had left Wilkes County and sought security in South Carolina returned to their homes, but they had not been there long before they were alarmed by the approach of a large body of Creek Indians under the command of the British Indian agents Tate and McGillivray. This danger was promptly met. Colonel Pickens with 200 men of his regiment came to the help of Georgia. Colonel Dooly was already in the field with 100 mounted men and Colonel Elijah Clarke with his command was on the frontier. Every male of 16 years and over came with arms and at Wrightsborough Colonel Pickens and Colonel Dooly were reënforced by detachments from the regiments of Colonel Few, Colonel Roy and Colonel Hammond and two troops of horse under Major Ross. The Indians had camped near Fulson's Fort. Lieutenants Alexander and Williamson by reconnoitering at night found the enemy to be eight hundred strong. With this information Colonel

Pickens in command of the forces marched forward hoping to reach the Indian camp before daylight and take it by surprise. Some traitor had warned the Indians, who broke up into small parties and fled in different directions. In the pursuit which followed some were overtaken and killed. Major Ross, Captain Newsom and Lieutenant Bently were killed. The Indians were expelled from the territory and quiet was restored.

**Capture of Two American Galleys**—After General Ash's defeat, General Lincoln's force remained at Purrysburg where he kept watch of the enemy on the Georgia side of the Savannah River. An attempt was made to capture the two British galleys, *Comet* and *Hornet,* which lay in the river below Purrysburg. On the night of March 20 two American galleys, the *Congress* and the *Lee,* commanded by Captains Campbell and Milligan, attempted to surprise and capture the British galleys and forty militia were sent by land to seize a house opposite the point where the British galleys lay. The American galleys coming down the river ran aground and that delayed them until nine o'clock before they were in position to use their guns on the enemy. In the meantime the British galley *Thunderer* came to the assistance of the *Comet* and the *Hornet* and quickly dislodged the militia by fire from its battery. After an hour's fight the British got into boats to board the American galleys whose crews, seeing that they were not strong enough to resist, took their boats and escaped, leaving the galleys and some of their companions to the enemy. Of the Americans Captain Campbell and three men were killed, six wounded and ten captured. The British lost 1 killed and 1 wounded. The capture of these American galleys left the Savannah River in control of the enemy's vessels.

**A Conflict of Authority**—General Lincoln's army was losing strength by the desertion of militia. The enemy under General Prevost, on the contrary, was reënforced by additions from New York and Florida to such an extent that he had five thousand men.

Under these circumstances with no immediate prospect of an advance by General Lincoln a number of militia men who had lost their cattle by raids of the enemy and were almost starving asked General Lincoln for leave to return home and look after their families until he was strong enough to cross the Savannah River and redeem Georgia from the rule of the enemy. General Lincoln granted the request and many went away. It was understood that if hard pressed by the enemy they might in order to secure a peaceful residence on their own farms take the oath of allegiance to the Crown.

Governor Rutledge of South Carolina, displeased at the inactivity of the army, on April 5 ordered General Williamson in command of South Carolina forces to invade Georgia, harass the enemy and destroy all cattle, horses, provisions, and carriages they should find on the line of march. These instructions displeased General Lincoln, first, because they were not addressed to him as the commanding officer of the army of which General Williamson's force was a part, and second, because the execution of the order would seriously interfere with the understanding between General Lincoln and the militia whom he had allowed to return to their homes. An unpleasant condition was threatened by this conflict of authority when General Moultrie, wisely and with good judgment took up the matter and by showing the facts to Governor Rutledge induced him to rescind the order.

**Horrible Treatment of Prisoners**—There was an exchange of prisoners in March and those who returned to Georgia were in wretched condition. Captain McCall says:

"They were so much emaciated when they arrived in camp that they were obliged to be carried from the boats in which they were brought from the prison-ships. They complained highly of the ill treatment which they had experienced on board these filthy, floating dungeons, of which their countenances and emaciated bodies exhibited condemning testimony. They asserted that they had been subsisted on condemned pork which nauseated the stomach, and oat meal so rotten that swine would not have fed on it; that the staff-officers and members of Council from Savannah shared in common with the soldiery. Even the venerable Bryan was obliged to partake of such repasts or die of hunger. The Jews of Savannah were generally favourable to the American cause, and among this persuasion was Mordecai Sheftall, commissary general, and his son, who was his deputy. They were confined in common with the other prisoners, and, by way of contempt to their offices and religion, condemned pork was given them for the animal part of their subsistence. In consequence of such food, and other new devices of mal-treatment, five or six died daily, whose bodies were conveyed from the prison ships to the nearest marsh and trodden in the mud from whence they were soon exposed by the washing of the tides, and at low water the prisoners beheld the carrion crows picking the bones of their departed companions." Well might General Moultrie exclaim at sight of such misery: "Does not this demand retaliation and a prison ship?" Colonel Charles C. Jones says of this: "Earnestly did General Lincoln protest against these inhumanities, but both General Prevost and Sir Hyde Parker were deaf to the voice of justice and mercy. Savage in the main was the temper of the King's servants toward the revolutionists."

**General Prevost Invades South Carolina**—On April 19, 1779, General Lincoln called a council of General officers at his headquarters at Black Swamp. Those present were General Lincoln, General William Moultrie, General Isaac Huger and General Jethro Sumner. Captain Morgan had come with a fresh supply of arms and ammunition and General Lincoln informed the council that the men in camp, including those under General Williamson, 500 promised from Orangeburg, and 700 from North Carolina, already in South Carolina, amounted to 5,000 and he asked the opinion of officers present whether after leaving a thousand men at Black Swamp and Purrysburg it would not be advisable with the others to cross the Savannah River near Augusta and take a strong position in Georgia to prevent the enemy from receiving supplies from the back country, to circumscribe his limits and to prevent his junction with the Indians. The officers present approved the measure and advised that it be carried into effect. Accordingly General Moultrie and 1,200 men were left at Purrysburg and Black Swamp to guard the crossings of the Savannah River and stop any invasion of Carolina by the enemy.

On April 20th General Lincoln with 2,000 Light Infantry and Cavalry started for Augusta and his baggage and artillery were ordered to follow. From Silver Bluff which he reached on the 22d he directed General Moultrie to send the Continental Troops to that place with the exception of the 2d and 5th South Carolina regiments and all the artillery but one small gun. If the enemy showed a disposition to advance on Charleston General Moultrie was instructed to seize the important passes in front of the enemy and obstruct his progress so that General Lincoln would have time to come up.

On the 23d of April a party of thirty white men disguised as Indians crossed the Savannah River at Yemassee four miles below Purrysburg and surprised the American guards. When pursued by Colonel Henderson they escaped through a swamp.

On the 25th of April General Prevost started for South Carolina with his troops. Most of them crossed at Purrysburg and some at other points. The intention was to surprise General Moultrie, but he with less than 1,000 men retired toward Charleston obstructing the advance of Prevost as much as possible. With 2,000 regulars and 700 Loyalists Prevost pressed on.

Seeing that this movement of the British was a serious attempt to take Charleston General Lincoln abandoned the plan for the relief of Georgia and moved rapidly to protect Charleston.

General Prevost advanced toward Charleston forcing General Moultrie before him and succeeded in investing the city so completely that surrender was considered.

At the suggestion of Laurens, a South Carolina leader who had been a presiding officer of the American Congress, it was proposed that relief for South Carolina against the invasion of Prevost be secured by arming 3,000 negroes, with the suggestion that if they fought well they should be emancipated.

This idea was approved by General Lincoln and by Congress when a son of Laurens presented the matter there, but it was disapproved by Washington, as he saw that arming the negroes was a game in which the British could beat the Americans. In South Carolina the suggestion was received with alarm. For a hundred years the negroes on plantations had been disarmed to prevent the repetition of servile insurrections which had occurred in the early history of the Colony. Now to put guns in the hands of 3,000 negroes they considered a dangerous experiment.

The Executive Council of South Carolina sent General Prevost a proposition, amounting to surrender of the city of Charleston, on the condition that Carolina should remain neutral until the end of the war and then return to the British government or become independent as the treaty of peace should provide.

General Prevost refused to negotiate with the civil authorities and insisted on dealing with General Moultrie. "Well then," said General Moultrie, "we will fight it out." Relief came unexpectedly through the arrival of Count Pulaski with his legion and the approach of General Lincoln with his forces. Seeing the American Army was too strong for him General Prevost retired, but left a garrison at Port Royal with 800 men under Colonel Maitland.

**Carolina Plundered by the British**—Although Prevost's invasion of Carolina was a failure from a military standpoint it was a sore affliction to the people of that State. Dr. Ramsey in his *History of South Carolina* says:

"This incursion into South Carolina and subsequent retreat contributed very little to the advancement of the Royal cause, but it added much to the wealth of the officers, soldiers, and followers of the British Army, and still more to the distresses of the inhabitants. The forces under the command of General Prevost marched through the richest settlements of the State, where there are the fewest white inhabitants in proportion to the number of slaves. The hapless Africans, allured with hopes of freedom, forsook their owners and repaired in great numbers to the Royal Army. They endeavored to recommend themselves to their new masters by discovering where their owners had concealed their property, and were assisting in carrying it off. All subordination being destroyed, they became insolent and rapacious, and in some instances exceeded the British in their plunderings and devastations. Collected in great crowds near the Royal Army, they were seized with the camp-fever in such numbers that they could not be accommodated either with proper lodgings or attendance.

"The British carried out of the State, it is supposed, about three thousand slaves, many of whom were shipped from Georgia and East Florida and sold in the West Indies: but the inhabitants lost upwards of four thousand, each of whom was worth, on an average, about two hundred and fifty Spanish dollars."

The same authority says that when the British retreated they had more plunder than they could carry off. As the American Army kept them off the mainland they had to go from one island to another and a number of the horses they had taken from the people were lost. They did not have enough boats to carry all the negroes. Making desperate efforts to get on the boat negroes clung to the sides, and to get rid of them, soldiers chopped off some of their fingers. Many of the negroes prostrated by disease were afraid to return home, and forsaken by their new masters, were left destitute and died in the woods. Those carried off by the army were collected on Otter Island where camp fever raged. Without medicine or proper attendance hundreds of them died and their bodies lay in the woods, where they were devoured by beasts and birds, and for nearly one hundred years their bones lay scattered on that island.

The vandalism of the British soldiers was extreme. Even graves were broken open and searched for treasure. Windows, chinaware, looking glasses and pictures were dashed to pieces. Domestic animals were shot down and left dead on the ground. Beautiful gardens were laid waste.

There was less wealth in Georgia than in Carolina, but in proportion to what the people had their losses were as great. The greed of the victors took from those opposed to the royal cause not only luxuries but bare necessaries of life and caused poverty and suffering.

**Brilliant Feats of Arms**—While General Lincoln was defending South Carolina against the invasion of the British, Georgia was not entirely unprotected. Colonel Dooly and Colonel Clarke were tireless in protecting the Georgia frontiers from Indians and treacherous Loyalists. Colonel Twiggs, Colonel Few and Colonel Jones cut off supplies from the enemy and attacked them at every opportunity. Armed privateers, flying the American flag, cruised along the coast, guarding exposed plantations, capturing marauding parties and sometimes catching merchantmen in the British service.

Captain Spencer, learning that a party of British officers were to dine with Thomas Young of Belfast on June 4, 1779, surprised and captured the party. Moving up Midway River in the evening with his privateer ship he landed between eight and nine o'clock at night and entering Young's house with twelve men captured Colonel Cruger and the English officers at the table. Holding them under guard until morning, he took their paroles and let them return to Sunbury. Colonel Cruger was soon afterward exchanged for Colonel McIntosh who had been captured at Brier Creek.

Colonel Twiggs, marching down the south side of the Great Ogeechee River with seventy men, stopped at the plantation of James Butler called Hickory Hill. There on June 28, 1779, he learned that Captain Muller and forty mounted grenadiers, led by three militia guides, were coming to attack him. Major Cooper of Marbury's dragoons and Captain Inman with thirty men were thrust forward to meet the enemy. Forming across a rice dam on which Captain Muller approached they fired so accurately that several British saddles were emptied. The British commanding officer, although shot through the thigh, supported himself with a sword and encouraged his men. Soon he was struck by a second ball which passed through his arm and lodged in his body. A few minutes later Lieutenant Swanson, second in command, fell wounded. Seeing the confusion thus caused the enemy Colonel Twiggs sent ten men to their rear and cut off their retreat. The whole detachment except three militia guides who fled at the first fire were captured. Seven of the British were killed and ten wounded. Of the Americans Colonel Maybank and Captain Whitaker were wounded.

As the wounded needed attention and Savannah was the nearest point where a surgeon could be secured, William Middleton was sent there with a flag. While in General Prevost's headquarters a British officer asked him to tell about the skirmish. When he had done so the officer said "If an angel was to tell me that Captain Muller, who has served twenty-one years in the King's Guard, had been defeated by an equal number of rebels, I would disbelieve him."

Middleton asked the officer's address and said that though they were not then on equal terms he hoped to be able at some future time to call him to account for his rudeness. Colonel Prevost rebuked the officer for using improper language to the bearer of a flag and the officer retired. Captain Muller died of his wounds before the surgeon arrived to attend him.

About the same time Major Baker with thirty men attacked and defeated near Sunbury a party of Georgia Royalists commanded by Captain Goldsmith, killing and wounding several of them. Among those killed was Lieutenant Gray whose head was almost severed from his body by a saber in the hands of Robert Sallette.

**The Cost of Sallette's Head**—Robert Sallette was one of those rare characters who sometimes come to the front in war. The following account of one of his dashing exploits is taken from *White's Historical Collections of Georgia,* page 537:

"He appears to have been a sort of roving character, doing things in his own way. The Tories stood very much in dread of him; and well they might, for never had they a more formidable foe. On one occasion, a Tory, who possessed considerable property offered a reward of one hundred guineas to any person who would bring him Sallette's head. This was made known to our hero, who provided himself with a bag, in which he placed a pumpkin, and proceeded to the house of the Tory and told him that having understood he had offered one hundred guineas for Sallette's head, he had it with him in the bag (at the same time pointing to the bag), and that he was ready to deliver it, provided the money was first counted out for him. The Tory, believing that the bag contained Sallette's head, laid down the money, upon which Sallette pulled off his hat and placing his hand upon his head, said, 'Here is Sallette's head.' This answer so frightened the Tory that he immediately took to his heels, but a well directed shot from Sallette brought him to the ground."

On August 3, 1779, Captain Samuel Spencer sailed into Sapelo Sound and was attacked by a British vessel armed with six guns. After a fight for fifteen minutes he boarded and captured her.

McGirth and his followers began pillaging the Western settlements with a hundred and fifty men, Colonel Twiggs pursued him, overtook the party on Buckhead Creek, charged them, and within a quarter of an hour put them to flight with nine killed, nine wounded and four captured. McGirth was shot through the thigh but escaped into a neighboring swamp on his horse.

By such brilliant exploits the English troops and the Tories were held in check and the drooping spirits of Georgians were revived.

**Georgia's War Government**—On the capture of Savannah, in December, 1778, by the British the Executive Council of Georgia made Augusta the seat of government, but that arrangement lasted only a short time, for Colonel Campbell soon occupied Augusta with the British troops. Until Augusta was evacuated by the British in February, 1779, the government of Georgia hardly existed. What there was left of it moved from place to place with the fortunes of war. The public records had been sent to Charleston for safe keeping and the proceedings of the Executive Council were meager, with very scant records. The treasury was empty and no attempt was made to levy and collect taxes. The paper bills of credit which had been issued by the State depreciated so much that they hardly had any purchasing power. There was little money to pay the troops, especially the militia, and the currency used to pay soldiers in the Continental service was almost invalid.

Under these conditions the confiscated property of Royalists was used to pay obligations made in buying necessary supplies for soldiers in the field.

The Legislature was not in session and the courts were closed. In the ever-present danger from the enemy and the impoverished condition of people the Council of Safety did the best they could, hoping for a time when better conditions would prevail.

When the Georgians recovered possession of Augusta, members of the Council met there at the residence of Matthew Hobson to select a President and attend to such business as they could. They were the only power representing the State at that time and exercised both legislative and executive functions. Affairs continued in that condition until the time came for the General Assembly to meet. So much of Georgia was occupied by the British and the people were so disturbed that only twenty-five members of the Assembly met in Augusta in July, 1779. Realizing that they were too few to organize and administer government according to the provisions of the Constitution, but seeing the need for providing some kind of machinery to preserve the State Government and attend to its business, members of the Assembly present on July 24, 1779, agreed upon and published a document which inaugurated an oligarchical form of government.

These representatives of the people of the counties of Wilkes, Richmond, Burke, Effingham, Chatham, Liberty, Glynn, Camden, and other freemen having met in Charleston, created as an Executive Council or Supreme Council of the State from the 27th of July, 1779, to the first Tuesday in January, 1780, the following men:

**The Supreme Council**—John Wereat, Joseph Clay, Joseph Habersham, Humphrey Wells, William Few, John Dooly, Seth John Cuthbert, William Gibbons, senior, and Myrick Davies.

The proclamation of creating the Supreme Council made this delegation of authority to those men:

"You hereby have full power and authority, and are authorized, empowered, and required to elect fit and discrete persons to represent this State in Congress, and to instruct the delegates so chosen in such matters and things as will tend to the interest of this State in particular, and the United States of America in general, the said delegates taking care, from time to time, to transmit to you, the said Council, or other authority of the State for the time being, an account of their proceedings in Congress aforesaid; to regulate the public treasury of the said State, to borrow or otherwise negotiate loans for the public safety; to regulate the militia, and appoint an officer, if necessary, to command; to appoint, suspend, and discharge all civil officers if it shall be found expedient; to demand an account of all expenditures of public money, and to regulate the same, and where necessary, order payments of money; to adopt some mode respecting the current money of this State, and for sinking the same; to elect and commission the Chief Justice of the State, or assistant Justices, or other Justices of the Peace, and other officers of each County; to convene courts for the trial of offences cognizable by the laws of the land in such place or places as you shall think fit; always taking care that trial by Jury be preserved inviolate, and that the proceedings had before such courts be in a summary way so that offenders be brought to a speedy trial and justice be amply done as well to the State as to the individuals.

"You, or a majority of you, the said Council, have full power and hereby are requested, on conviction of offenders, to order punishment to be inflicted extending to death; and when objects deserving mercy shall be made known to you, to extend that mercy and pardon the offence, remit all fines, mitigate corporal punishments, as the case may be, and as to you or a majority of you shall seem fit and necessary. And you, the said Council or a majority of you, at all times and places when and where you shall think fit, have hereby full power and competent authority to meet, appoint your own President, settle your own rules, sit, consult, deliberate, advise, direct, and carry in execution all and every act, special and general, hereby delegated to you, and all and every such other acts, measures, and things as you or a majority of you shall find expedient and necessary for the welfare, safety, and happiness of the freemen of this State.

"And in case any of the persons herein appointed to exercise the supreme authority as aforesaid shall refuse to act, die, or depart this State, or shall by any other means be prevented from exercising the same, then, and in such case, you the said Council hereby chosen, or a majority of you, shall, and you are hereby authorized, empowered, and required to fill up such vacancies by choosing fit and discrete persons or person to act in their or his room and stead, which person or persons so chosen is or are hereby invested with every power and authority in as full and ample a manner as if they had been appointed by this present instrument of writing.

"And we do hereby declare all officers, civil and military, and all persons, inhabitants of this State, subject to and answerable to your authority, and will ratify and confirm whatever you may do for or concerning the public weal, according to the best of your judgment, knowledge, and ability. And further, we do hereby promise you our support, protection, and countenance.

"In witness whereof we have hereunto set our hands this twenty-fourth day of July in the year of our Lord 1779."

As a justification for this unusual delegation of supreme power to a few men, the members of Legislature referred to the invasion of the State by British forces, the great evils which had arisen to disturb civil government and prevent the Constitution of the State from being carried into effect. Under these circumstances they said it was necessary to adopt such temporary form of government as would be most conducive to the welfare and happiness of the people, the security of their rights and the maintenance of legal authority as far as conditions made possible, until the time when quiet should be restored and the constitution could take its regular course. In taking this action the Legislature required members of the Supreme Executive Council to take a solemn oath that they would use their best skill and judgment to perform the duties of their position faithfully, conscientiously, without favor, affection or partiality and would do their utmost to maintain and defend the State of Georgia, secure the rights of the people and execute justice and mercy.

**John Wereat Elected President**—The Supreme Council organized on July 24th by electing John Cuthbert President *Pro Tem* and on the sixth of August, 1779, perfected permanent organization by unanimously electing John Wereat President. The members then took the oath of office and began the discharge of their duties. As only a part of the State was in possession of the Georgians regular meetings of the Legislature were impossible. The people were divided. Some had taken the oath of allegiance to the British Crown after the fall of Savannah. Other Loyalists had gone to Florida and joined the forces of the enemy. Others in the militia or in the Continental forces were fighting for freedom but it was hard to keep the militia in line of duty, as they were not enlisted for long periods and they acknowledged allegiance only to the State of Georgia. There was blood, turmoil and antagonism in most of the State. Under these conditions unusual action was necessary to hold the Republicans together and support their armed forces in the field. It appears that although the action taken was extraordinary and without constitutional warrant, it had the approval of those people of Georgia who remained true to the cause of liberty. This oligarchical government continued for some months and there was no suggestion of misconduct, injustice or despotic action by any of them.

**Return of General McIntosh**—Brigadier-General McIntosh, with the approval of General Washington, returned to Georgia in the summer of 1779. This was approved by Congress on receipt of the following letter from General Washington written to that body on May 11, 1779:

"Brigadier-General McIntosh will have the honor of delivering you this. The war in Georgia—being the State to which he belongs—makes him desirous of serving in the Southern army. I know not whether the arrangements Congress have in contemplation may make it convenient to employ him there, but I take the liberty to recommend him as a gentleman whose knowledge of service and of the country promises to make him useful. I beg leave to add that General McIntosh's conduct, while he acted immediately under my observation, was such as to acquire my esteem and confidence, and I have had no reason since to alter my good opinion of him."

General McIntosh was second in command to General Lincoln, conferred frequently with the Supreme Council and was active in strengthening the military conditions of the State and restraining the British forces.

In a letter to General Lincoln on the 18th of August, 1779, the Supreme Council referred to the fact that while a large part of Georgia was in the hands of the enemy and those counties still holding out against them were subject to invasion, with only a few militia to defend them, they had not been disheartened but kept a brave spirit, hoping for support from the Continent and Carolina. But for that the State would have been left by them and the wavering ones would have joined the enemy and aided it in operations against Carolina. The arrival of General Scott's army at this critical time, they said, had a salutary effect and greatly heartened the militia who were now cheerfully under arms to oppose invasion by the enemy's irregulars and Indians. General McIntosh had sent some Continental troops to support the militia and it was hoped that the enemy would be kept back. In spite of this there was not strength enough even with the help of General McIntosh to meet a serious attempt of the British to capture the upper part of the State. Such an invasion was expected in the fall, as the enemy's troops needed food and there were large supplies of grain in the territory held by the Americans. If they succeeded in gaining the upper part of Georgia, the Council said, Carolina would be in danger, because the enemy was aware of a great defection in the upper part of the back country, and there was reason to believe that they received encouragement from the people in that section. Added to this danger was that from the Indians whom the British sought to array against the Americans by sending them presents, and there was little doubt that they would bring the Indians to South Carolina when they could. The Council feared that if the British troops came into north Georgia many of the inhabitants, worn out with failing opposition and fearing the loss of all they had, would make terms with the enemy, and some might join the enemy against their countrymen. In the meantime there was danger that many suffering families would leave the State, going far north, for which they were already preparing, and nothing but support could prevent that dangerous migration.

Under these circumstances they urged General Lincoln to order General Scott with his troops into Georgia.

The Governor of South Carolina was also asked to help with men and money in the retention of north Georgia by the patriots and prevent the English from subjugating the whole State. These appeals were not in vain and had much to do with the combined efforts of General Lincoln and his army, supported by the French Army under Count d'Estaing, to recover Savannah in the fall of 1779.